Lecture Notes in Computer Science 1559

Edited by G. Goos, J. Hartmanis and J. van Leeuwen

Springer

Berlin
Heidelberg
New York
Barcelona
Hong Kong
London
Milan
Paris
Singapore
Tokyo

Pierre Flener (Ed.)

Logic-Based Program Synthesis and Transformation

8th International Workshop, LOPSTR'98
Manchester, UK, June 15-19, 1998
Selected Papers

Springer

Series Editors

Gerhard Goos, Karlsruhe University, Germany
Juris Hartmanis, Cornell University, NY, USA
Jan van Leeuwen, Utrecht University, The Netherlands

Volume Editor

Pierre Flener
Department of Information Science, Uppsala University
Box 311, S-751 05 Uppsala, Sweden
E-mail: pierref@csd.uu.se

Cataloging-in-Publication data applied for

Die Deutsche Bibliothek - CIP-Einheitsaufnahme

Logic based program synthesis and transformation : 8th international workshop ; selected papers / LOPSTR '98, Manchester, UK, June 15 - 19, 1998. Pierre Flener (ed.). - Berlin ; Heidelberg ; New York ; Barcelona ; Hong Kong ; London ; Milan ; Paris ; Singapore ; Tokyo : Springer, 1998
(Lecture notes in computer science ; Vol. 1559)
ISBN 3-540-65765-7

CR Subject Classification (1998): F.3.1, D.1.1, D.1.6, I.2.2, F.4.1

ISSN 0302-9743
ISBN 3-540-65765-7 Springer-Verlag Berlin Heidelberg New York

Typesetting: Camera-ready by author
SPIN 10702874 06/3142 – 5 4 3 2 1 0 Printed on acid-free paper

Preface

LOPSTR'98 (see http://www.csd.uu.se/~pierref/lopstr98/) was the 8th edition of the LOPSTR workshop series (see http://www.cs.man.ac.uk/~kungkiu/lopstr/). In order to reflect the current emphasis on computational logic, the series was renamed *Logic-based Program Synthesis and Transformation*, as opposed to the former Logic Program Synthesis and Transformation. This means that papers on *any* computational-logic-based techniques, languages, and tools for the interactive or automated development of *any* kinds of programs were now solicited. There was also strong encouragement to submit papers discussing programming-in-the-large issues or practical applications.

The selection process ran in three phases. First, based on the submitted 36 extended abstracts, the programme committee invited 27 author teams to present their research at the workshop; pre-workshop proceedings with the accepted abstracts were available as a technical report (see ftp://ftp.cs.man.ac.uk/pub/TR/UMCS-98-6-1.html). The revised and extended scope triggered abstracts from all continents, including 50% from outside the "usual geographic sphere of influence" of LOPSTR. Also, 66% of these abstracts were written by first-time LOPSTR author teams. These figures seem to prove the effectiveness of the changes operated by the 1998 programme committee. Secondly, shortly after the workshop, the programme committee invited the authors of the 24 most promising abstracts and presentations to submit full papers. Thirdly, after a round of conference-level refereeing, the 16 best full papers were included in this volume, which constitutes thus the post-workshop proceedings. Another 8 short papers appear in this volume, written by the invited speaker (see below), by authors who voluntarily refrained from writing the solicited full paper, and by authors whose full papers were not accepted (they appear in no particular order).

As a workshop, LOPSTR'98 continued the tradition of being a lively and friendly forum for presenting recent and current research, as well as discussing future trends in the synthesis and transformation of programs. There were nine sessions, called Specification, Synthesis, Transformation, Analysis, Synthesis & Schemas, Verification, Specialisation, Composition & Reuse, and Industrial Applications, hence covering larger ground than usual, with the first (massive) appearance of papers exploiting constraint technology, discussing pragmatics and real-life applications, addressing specification language issues, or covering component-based software development.

The invited speaker was Pierre Wolper, of the Université de Liège in Belgium. He discussed his perspective on algorithms for synthesising reactive systems, by first reviewing the main results from that area and then, provocatively, but in a down-to-earth manner, trying to identify the main reasons for their non-exploitation.

Steve Roach (NASA Ames) went through many iterations of a very impressive demonstration of the AMPHION program synthesiser (see http://ic-www.arc.nasa.gov/ic/projects/amphion/), showing how it is, for instance, in day-to-day use at NASA for generating, through much reuse, programs from graphical specifications provided by space scientists who have no background in computational logic or software engineering.

LOPSTR'98 was organised by the Department of Computer Science of the University of Manchester, and took place in parallel to JICSLP'98 (the *Joint International Conference and Symposium on Logic Programming*), from 15 to 19 June 1998. Delegates to one event could freely attend all sessions of the other event. Many of the JICSLP'98 participants were frequently observed to prefer the LOPSTR'98 sessions.

LOPSTR'98 also coincided with the celebrations of the 50th anniversary of the world's first stored-program computer, the *Baby*, built at Manchester in 1948 (see http://www.computer50.org/). The delegates had the opportunity to attend a promenade concert given by the Halle Orchestra, as well as the magnificent *Golden Anniversary Celebration* at the Bridgewater Hall. The latter featured a dramatic reconstruction of the invention of the Baby, the switching-on of a replica of the Baby by its original co-builder Prof. Tom Kilburn, lively presentations by UK industry leaders about the role of computers in the future, and the conferral of several honorary degrees.

The future of LOPSTR and its possible rapprochement with the IEEE international conferences on *Automated Software Engineering* (ASE, formerly KBSE: *Knowledge-Based Software Engineering*, see http://www.sigart.acm.org/ Conferences/ase/past/) were discussed in the JICSLP'98 post-conference workshop on *Automated Software Engineering and Logic Programming*. See http://www.cs.man.ac.uk/~kung-kiu/ase-lp/ for the record of this meeting.

LOPSTR'98 was sponsored by the Association for Logic Programming, the ESPRIT Network of Excellence in Computational Logic, and the Prolog Development Center, whose contributions are here gratefully acknowledged.

I also want to take this opportunity to formally thank the workshop chair, Kung-Kiu Lau, and his team, Ian Pratt and Lynn Howarth, for a fabulously smooth event. My thanks also go to Francesca Toni and David Pearce for their help, to the programme committee for invaluable assistance with the academic aspects of the workshop, including three rounds of refereeing, and to Norbert E. Fuchs, the chairman of LOPSTR'97, for his helpful advice.

December 1998

Pierre Flener
Programme Chair
LOPSTR'98

Programme Committee

Nicoletta Cocco	University of Venice, Italy
Pierre Flener (programme chair)	Uppsala University, Sweden
Andreas Hamfelt	Uppsala University, Sweden
Kung-Kiu Lau (workshop chair)	University of Manchester, UK
Baudouin Le Charlier	University of Namur, Belgium
Michael Leuschel	University of Southampton, UK
Michael Lowry	NASA Ames, USA
Ali Mili	Institute for Software Research, USA
Lee Naish	Melbourne University, Australia
Mario Ornaghi	University of Milan, Italy
Alberto Pettorossi	University of Rome II, Italy
Dave Robertson	University of Edinburgh, UK
Richard Waldinger	SRI International, USA

Reviewers

The following people helped the Programme Committee to review the papers: Richard Banach, Marco Benini, Annalisa Bossi, Agostino Cortesi, Stefania Costantini, Danny De Schreye, Yves Deville, Mauro Ferrari, Nevin Heintze, Gaetano Aurelio Lanzarone, Bern Martens, Ulrich Nitsche, Maurizio Proietti, Sophie Renault, Sabina Rossi, Matteo Vaccari, Sofie Verbaeten, Michael Winikoff, Hamza Zidoum.

Sponsors

Association for Logic Programming
ESPRIT Network of Excellence in Computational Logic
Prolog Development Center A/S, Brøndby-Copenhagen, Denmark

Table of Contents

Attempto Controlled English — Not Just Another Logic Specification Language

Norbert E. Fuchs, Uta Schwertel, and Rolf Schwitter

Department of Computer Science, University of Zurich
{fuchs, uschwert, schwitter}@ifi.unizh.ch
http://www.ifi.unizh.ch

Abstract. The specification language Attempto Controlled English (ACE) is a controlled natural language, i.e. a subset of standard English with a domain-specific vocabulary and a restricted grammar. The restriction of full natural language to a controlled subset is essential for ACE to be suitable for specification purposes. The main goals of this restriction are to reduce ambiguity and vagueness inherent in full natural language and to make ACE computer processable. ACE specifications can be unambiguously translated into logic specification languages, and can be queried and executed. In brief, ACE allows domain specialists to express specifications in familiar natural language and combine this with the rigour of formal specification languages.

1 Introduction

Specifications state properties or constraints that a software system must satisfy to solve a problem [IEEE 91], describe the interface between the problem domain and the software system [Jackson 95], and define the purpose of the software system and its correct use [Le Charlier & Flener 98]. In which language should we express specifications to accommodate these demands?

The answer to this question depends on many factors, particularly on the specifiers and their background. Though many programs are specified by software engineers, often domain specialists — electrical engineers, physicists, economists and other professionals — perform this task. There are even situations where software engineers and knowledge engineers are deliberately replaced by domain specialists since they are the ultimate source of domain knowledge [Businger 94]. One major goal of our research is to make formal specification methods accessible to domain specialists in notations that are familiar to them and that are close to the concepts and terms of their respective application domain.

Traditionally, specifications have been expressed in natural language. Natural language as the fundamental means of human communication needs no extra learning effort, and is easy to use and to understand. Though for particular domains there are more concise notations, natural language can be used to express any problem. However, experience has shown that uncontrolled use of natural language can lead to ambiguous, imprecise and unclear specifications with possibly disastrous consequences for the subsequent software development process [Meyer 85].

P. Flener (Ed.): LOPSTR'98, LNCS 1559, pp. 1–20, 1999.

Formal specification languages — often based on logic — have been advocated because they have an unambiguous syntax and a clean semantics, and promise substantial improvements of the software development process [cf. www.comlab.ox.ac.uk/archive/formal-methods]. In particular, formal specification languages offer support for the automatic analysis of specifications such as consistency verification, and the option to validate specifications through execution [Fuchs 92]. Nevertheless, formal specification languages suffer from major shortcomings — they are hard to understand and difficult to relate to the application domain, and need to be accompanied by a description in natural language that "explains what the specification means in real-world terms and why the specification says what it does" [Hall 90]. Similar observations were made earlier by [Balzer 85] and by [Deville 90].

It seems that we are stuck between the over-flexibility of natural language and the potential incomprehensibility of formal languages. While some authors claim that specifications need to be expressed in natural language and that formal specifications are a contradiction in terms [Le Charlier & Flener 98], other authors just as vigorously defend the appropriateness of formal specification methods [Bowen & Hinchey 95a; Bowen & Hinchey 95b]. We, however, are convinced that the advantages of natural and formal specification languages should be and can be combined, specifically to accommodate the needs of domain specialists.

Our starting point lies in the observation that natural language can be used very precisely. Examples are legal language and the so-called controlled languages used for technical documentation and machine translation [cf. www-uilots.let.ruu.nl/~Controlled-languages]. These languages are usually ad hoc defined and rely on rather liberal rules of style and on conventions to be enforced by humans. Taking these languages as a lead we have defined the specification language Attempto Controlled English (ACE) — a subset of standard English with a domain-specific vocabulary and a restricted grammar in the form of a small set of construction and interpretation rules [Fuchs et al. 98; Schwitter 98]. ACE allows users to express specifications precisely, and in the terms of the application domain. ACE specifications are computer-processable and can be unambiguously translated into a logic language. Though ACE may seem informal, it is a formal language with the semantics of the underlying logic language. This also means that ACE has to be learned like other formal languages.

There have been several projects with similar aims, but in most cases the subsets of English were not systematically and clearly defined. For example, [Macias & Pulman 95] developed a system which resembles ours with the important difference that their system restricts only the form of composite sentences, but leaves the form of the constituent sentences completely free. As a consequence, the thorny problem of ambiguity remains and has to be resolved by the users after the system has translated the specification into a formal representation.

The rest of the paper is organised as follows. In section 2 we motivate the transition from full English to Attempto Controlled English and present a glimpse of ACE. Section 3 describes the translation of ACE specifications into discourse representation structures and into other logic languages. In section 4 we outline the semantics of ACE specifications. Section 5 overviews querying and executing specifications. Finally, in section 6 we conclude and address further points of research. The appendix contains a complete example of an ACE specification together with its translation into the logic language of discourse representation structures.

2 From English to Attempto Controlled English

First, we will introduce Attempto Controlled English (ACE) by an example and then summarise its main characteristics. More information can be found in [Fuchs et al. 98; Schwitter 98].

2.1 An Example

Specifications, and other technical texts, written in full natural language tend to be vague, ambiguous, incomplete, or even inconsistent. Take for example the notice posted in London underground trains [Kowalski 90]:

> Press the alarm signal button to alert the driver.
>
> The driver will stop immediately if any part of the train is in a station.
>
> If not, the train will continue to the next station where help can be more easily given.
>
> There is a £50 penalty for improper use.

The notice leaves many assumptions and conclusions implicit. Kowalski shows that clarity can be improved, ambiguity reduced, and assumptions and conclusions made explicit when one follows guidelines for good language use. To do so, Kowalski reformulates the notice in the declarative form of logic programs. Take for instance the first part of the third sentence. Filling in the missing condition referred to by not, Kowalski rewrites it as

> The driver stops the train at the next station if the driver is alerted and not any part of the train is in a station.

Though much improved even this sentence is incomplete since the agent who alerts the driver is still implicit.

To eliminate this and other deficiencies of full natural language we have proposed the specification language Attempto Controlled English (ACE) as a well-defined subset of English. Since ACE is computer-processable we go beyond what [Kowalski 90] achieved — ACE specifications are not only clearer and more complete, but can also be automatically translated into a logic language, be queried and executed.

Here is a version of the complete London underground notice in ACE. The third sentence is the one discussed above. Note that the agent who alerts the driver is now made explicit.

If a passenger presses an alarm signal button then the passenger alerts the driver.

If a passenger alerts the driver of a train and a part of the train is in a station then the driver stops the train immediately.

If a passenger alerts the driver of a train and no part of the train is in a station then the driver stops the train at the next station.

If the driver stops a train in a station then help is available.

If a passenger misuses an alarm signal button then the passenger pays a £50 penalty.

In the appendix you can find this ACE text together with its translation into the logic language of discourse representation structures.

2.2 ACE in a Nutshell

In this section we briefly present the components of ACE, viz. the vocabulary and the construction and interpretation rules.

Vocabulary. The vocabulary of ACE comprises

- predefined function words (e.g. determiners, conjunctions, prepositions),
- user-defined, domain-specific content words (nouns, verbs, adjectives, adverbs).

Users can define content words with the help of a lexical editor that presupposes only basic grammatical knowledge. Alternatively, users can import existing lexica.

Construction Rules. The construction rules define the form of ACE sentences and texts, and state restrictions on the lexical and phrasal level. The construction rules are designed to avoid typical sources of imprecision in full natural language.

ACE Specifications. An ACE specification is a sequence of sentences. There are

- simple sentences,
- composite sentences,
- query sentences.

Simple Sentences. Simple sentences have the form

subject + verb + complements + adjuncts

where complements are necessary for transitive or ditransitive verbs and adjuncts are optional. Here is an example for this sentence form:

The driver stops the train at the station.

Composite Sentences. Composite sentences are built from simpler sentences with the help of predefined constructors:

- coordination (and, or),
- subordination by conditional sentences (if ... then ...),
- subordination by subject and object modifying relative sentences (who, which, that),
- verb phrase negation (does not, is not),
- noun phrase negation (no),
- quantification (a, there is a, every, for every).

Query Sentences. There are

- *yes/no*-queries,
- *wh*-queries.

Yes/no-queries are derived from simple sentences by inverting the subject and the verb be (Is the train in the station?), or by inserting do or does if the verb is not be (Does the driver stop the train?). *Wh*-queries begin with a so-called *wh*-word (who, what, when, where, how, etc.) and contain do or does (Where does the driver stop the train?), unless the query asks for the subject of the sentence (Who stops the train?).

Anaphora. ACE sentences and phrases can be interrelated by anaphora, i.e. by references to previously occurring noun phrases. Anaphora can be personal pronouns or definite noun phrases. In

A passenger of a train alerts a driver. He stops the train.

the personal pronoun he refers to the noun phrase a driver and the definite noun phrase the train refers to the indefinite noun phrase a train.

Coordination. Coordination is possible between sentences and between phrases of the same syntactic type, e.g.

A passenger presses an alarm signal button and the driver stops the train.

A passenger presses an alarm signal button and alerts the driver.

A driver stops a train immediately or at the next station.

Coordination of verbal phrases can be simplified. Instead of

A passenger presses a red button or presses a green button.

we can write

A passenger presses a red button or a green button.

Lexical Restrictions. Examples for lexical restrictions and typographical conventions are:

- verbs are used in the simple present tense, the active voice, the indicative mood, the third person singular (presses),
- no modal verbs (may, can, must etc.) or intensional verbs (hope, know, believe etc.),
- no modal adverbs (possibly, probably etc.),
- ACE allows the user to define synonyms (alarm signal button, alarm button) and abbreviations (ASB standing for alarm signal button),
- content words can be simple (train) or compound (alarm signal button, alarm-signal-button).

Phrasal Restrictions. Examples for phrasal restrictions are:

- complements of full verbs can only be noun phrases (press a button) or prepositional phrases (send the ambulance to the station),
- adjuncts can only be realised as prepositional phrases (in a station) or adverbs (immediately),
- *of*-constructions (the part of the train) are the only allowed postnominal prepositional modifiers.

Interpretation Rules. Interpretation rules control the semantic analysis of grammatically correct ACE sentences. They, for example, resolve ambiguities that cannot be removed by the construction rules. The result of this analysis is reflected in a paraphrase. Important rules are:

- verbs denote events (press) or states (be),
- the textual order of verbs determines the default temporal order of the associated events and states,
- prepositional phrases in adjunct position always modify the verb, e.g. give additional information about the location of an event (The driver {stops the train in a station}.),
- anaphoric reference is possible via pronouns or definite noun phrases; the antecedent is the most recent suitable noun phrase that agrees in number and gender,
- noun phrase coordination within a verb phrase is interpreted as coordination reduction; the elided verb is distributed to each conjunct (The driver presses a red button and [presses] a green button.),
- the textual occurrence of a quantifier (a, there is a, every, for every) opens its scope that extends to the end of the sentence; thus any following quantifier is automatically within the scope of the preceding one.

Learning ACE. In contrast to rules of formal languages the construction and interpretation rules of ACE are easy to use and to remember since they are similar to English grammar rules and only presuppose basic grammatical knowledge. One should bear in mind, however, that in spite of its appearance ACE is a formal language that — like other formal languages — must be learned. Companies like Boeing and Caterpillar have been using controlled languages for technical documentation for many years. They report that these languages can be taught in a few days, and that users get competent in a few weeks [CLAW 98]. Thus we claim that domain specialists need less effort to learn and to apply the rules of ACE than to cope with an unfamiliar formal language.

3 From ACE to Discourse Representation Structures

ACE sentences are translated into discourse representation structures — a syntactical variant of full first-order predicate logic. We will first discuss the translation process, and then the handling of ambiguity.

3.1 Translation

ACE specifications are analysed and processed deterministically by a unification-based phrase structure grammar enhanced by linearised feature structures written in GULP, a preprocessor for Prolog [Covington 94]. Unification-based grammars are declarative statements of well-formedness conditions and can be combined with any parsing strategy. Prolog's built in top-down recursive-descent parser uses strict chronological back-tracking to parse an ACE sentence. Top-down parsing is very fast for short sentences but for longer composite sentences the exponential costs of backtracking can slow down the parsing. It turns out that we can do better using a hybrid top-down chart parser that remembers analysed phrases of an ACE sentence. Actually, the chart is only used if it is complete for a particular phrase type in a specific position of an ACE sentence — otherwise the Attempto system parses the sentence conventionally.

Correct understanding of an ACE specification requires not only processing of individual sentences and their constituents, but also taking into account the way sentences are interrelated to express complex propositional structures. It is well-known that aspects such as anaphoric reference, ellipsis and tense cannot be successfully handled without taking the preceding discourse into consideration. Take for example the discourse

A passenger enters a train. The train leaves a station.

In classical predicate logic these two sentences would be represented as two separate formulas

$$\exists X \exists Y (passenger(X) \land train(Y) \land enter(X, Y))$$
$$\exists U \exists W (train(U) \land station(W) \land leave(U, W))$$

This representation fails to relate the anaphoric reference of the definite noun phrase the train in the second sentence to the indefinite noun phrase a train in the first sentence. We solve this problem by employing discourse representation theory that resolves anaphoric references in a systematic way combining the two propositions into one [Kamp & Reyle 93].

In our case, ACE sentences are translated into discourse representation theory extended by events and states (DRT-E) [cf. Kamp & Reyle 93, Parsons 94]. DRT-E is a variant of predicate logic that represents a multisentential text as a single logical unit called a discourse representation structure (DRS). Each part of an ACE sentence contributes some logical conditions to the DRS using the preceding sentences as context to resolve anaphoric references. A DRS is represented by a term `drs(U,Con)` where `U` is a list of discourse referents and `Con` is a list of conditions for the discourse referents. The discourse referents are quantified variables that stand for objects in the specified domain, while the conditions constitute constraints that the discourse referents must fulfill to make the DRS true. Simple DRS conditions are logical atoms, while complex DRS conditions are built up recursively from other DRSs and have the following forms *ifthen(DRS1,DRS2)*, *or(DRS1,DRS2, ...)*, *not(DRS)*, *ynq(DRS)* and *whq(DRS)* representing conditional sentences, disjunctive phrases, negated phrases, *yes/no*-queries, and *wh*-queries.

The translation of the two ACE sentences

A passenger enters a train. The train leaves a station.

generates the DRS

```
[A,B,C,D,E]
passenger(A)
train(B)
event(C,enter(A,B))
station(D)
event(E,leave(B,D))
```

The first ACE sentence leads to three existentially quantified discourse referents (`[A,B,C]`) and the first three conditions of the DRS. The second ACE sentence is analysed in the context of the first sentence. It contributes two further discourse referents (`[D,E]`) and the fourth and the fifth condition of the DRS. The two event conditions have been derived from lexical information that classifies the verbs enter and leave as being associated with events.

Analysing the second sentence in the context of the first one allows the Attempto system to resolve the train as anaphoric reference to a train. The search space for antecedents of anaphora is defined by an accessibility relation among nested DRSs. A discourse referent is accessible from a DRS *D* if the discourse referent is in *D*, in a DRS enclosing *D*, in a disjunct that precedes *D* in an *or*-DRS, or in the antecedent of an *ifthen*-DRS with *D* as consequent. The resolution algorithm always picks the closest accessible referent that agrees in gender and number with the anaphor.

Here is a more complex example from the ACE version of the underground notice. The sentence

If a passenger alerts a driver of a train then the driver stops the train in a station.

is translated into the DRS

```
[]
IF
     [A,B,C,D]
     passenger(A)
     driver(B)
     train(C)
     of(B,C)
     event(D,alert(A,B))
THEN
     [E,F]
     station(E)
     event(F,stop(B,C))
     location(F,in(E))
```

The outermost DRS has an empty list of discourse referents and an *ifthen*-DRS as condition. Both the *if*-part and the *then*-part are DRSs. The discourse referents (`[A,B,C,D]`) occurring in the *if*-part of the DRS are universally quantified, while the discourse referents (`[E,F]`) in the *then*-part of the DRS are existentially quantified. The prepositional phrase in a station leads to the condition `station(E)` and to the predefined condition `location(F,in(E))` that indicates the location of the event `F`. The Attempto system resolves the driver and the train as anaphoric references to a driver and to a train, respectively.

A DRS can be automatically translated into the standard form of first-order predicate logic and into clausal form. ACE sentences without disjunctive consequences lead to Prolog programs.

3.2 Constraining Ambiguity

Ambiguity is the most prevalent problem when natural language is processed by a computer. Though ambiguity occurs on all levels of natural language, here we will only discuss a case of syntactical ambiguity. Take the three sentences

The driver stops the train with the smashed head-light.

The driver stops the train with great effort.

The driver stops the train with the defect brake.

Note that all three sentences have the same grammatical structure, and that all three sentences are syntactically ambiguous since the prepositional phrase with... can be attached to the verb stops or to the noun train. A human reader will perceive the first and the second sentence as unambiguous since each sentence has only one plausible interpretation according to common sense, while the third sentence allows two plausible interpretations since with the defect brake can refer to stops or to train. For this sentence additional contextual knowledge is necessary to select the intended interpretation. Altogether, we find that humans can disambiguate the three sentences with the help of contextual, i.e. non-syntactical, knowledge.

Standard approaches to handle ambiguity by a computer rely on *Generate and Test* or on *Underspecified Representations.*

Generate and Test. The traditional account is first to generate all possible interpretations, and then to eliminate those which are not plausible. The elimination of implausible interpretations can be done by presenting all interpretations to the user who selects the intended one [e.g. Macias & Pulman 95], or by formalising relevant contextual knowledge and automatically selecting the most fitting interpretation on the basis of this knowledge [e.g. Hindle & Rooth 93]. *Generate and Test* suffers from several shortcomings: it is inefficient and can lead to the combinatorial explosion of interpretations; manually selecting one of many interpretations is a burden on the user; formalising relevant contextual knowledge for the automatic disambiguation is difficult.

Underspecified Representations. A sentence gets just one semantic representation based on its syntactic form leaving certain aspects of the meaning unspecified [Alshawi 92; Reyle 93]. Fully specified interpretations are obtained by filling in material from formalised contextual knowledge. This approach has a drawback that we encountered already: it is difficult to formalise rules that lead to more specific interpretations because complex contextual effects — world knowledge, linguistic context, lexical semantics of words etc. — play a crucial role in the human disambiguation process.

In approaches based on *Generate and Test* or on *Underspecified Representations* disambiguation depends in one way or other on context. Thus the same syntactic construct could get different interpretations in different contexts which are perhaps only vaguely defined [Hirst 97]. This may be desirable for the processing of unrestricted natural language but is highly problematic for specifications. Writing specifications is already very hard. If on top of this the specification language allowed context-dependent interpretations then writing, and particularly reading, specifications would indeed be very difficult, if not entirely impossible.

To avoid this problem, ACE resolves ambiguity by a completely syntactical approach without any recourse to the context.

More concretely, ACE employs three simple means to resolve ambiguity:

- some ambiguous constructs are not part of the language; unambiguous alternatives are available in their place,
- all remaining ambiguous constructs are interpreted deterministically on the basis of a small number of interpretation rules that use syntactic information only; the interpretations are reflected in a paraphrase,
- users can either accept the assigned interpretation, or they must rephrase the input to obtain another one.

For the third example sentence

The driver stops the train with the defect brake.

the Attempto system would generate the paraphrase

The driver {stops the train with the defect brake}.

that reflects ACE's interpretation rule that a prepositional phrase always modifies the verb. This interpretation is probably not the one intended by the user. To obtain the other interpretation the user can reformulate the sentence employing the interpretation rule that a relative sentence always modifies the immediately preceding noun phrase, e.g.

The driver stops the train that has a defect brake.

yielding the paraphrase

The driver stops {the train that has a defect brake}.

Altogether, ACE has just over a dozen interpretation rules to handle ambiguity.

4 Semantics of ACE Specifications

In this chapter we introduce the model-theoretic interpretation of ACE, and explain ACE's model of time, events and states.

4.1 Model-Theoretic Interpretation

A discourse representation structure is a syntactic variant of full first-order predicate logic and thus allows for the usual model-theoretic interpretation. According to [Kamp & Reyle 93] any interpretation of a DRS is also an interpretation of the text from which the DRS was derived. Concretely, we have the following definition:

Let D be the DRS derived from the set S of ACE sentences with the vocabulary V, and M be a model of V. Then S is true in M iff D is true in M.

Thus we can associate meaning to ACE specifications in a way that is completely analogous to the model-theoretic interpretation of logic formulas. We can give each ACE sentence a truth value, i.e. we call a sentence true if we can interpret it as describing an actual state of affairs in the specified domain, or we label the sentence false if we cannot establish such an interpretation.

We can interpret simple sentences as descriptions of distinct events or states. The sentence

A driver stops a train.

is true if the word driver can be interpreted as a relation *driver* that holds for an object A of the specified domain, the word train as a relation *train* that holds for an object B of the specified domain, and the word stop as a relation *stopping event* that holds between A and B. Otherwise, the sentence is false.

Once we have assigned meaning to simple sentences we can give meaning to composite sentences. Again, this is completely analogous to classical model theory. A conjunction of sentences is true if all conjoined sentences are true. A disjunction of sentences is true if at least one of the sentences of the disjunction is true. A sentence with a negation is true if the sentence without the negation is false. An *ifthen*-sentence is only false if the *if*-part is true and the *then*-part is false; otherwise, the *ifthen*-sentence is true. A sentence with a universal quantifier is true if the sentence without the universal quantifier is true for all objects denoted by the quantified phrase.

4.2 Events and States

Attempto Controlled English has a model of time, events and states that closely resembles that one of the event calculus [Sadri & Kowalski 95].

Each verb in a sentence denotes an event or a state. Events occur instantaneously, while states — i.e. relations that hold or do not hold — last over a time period until they are explicitly terminated.

Each occurrence of a verb is implicitly associated with a time. If the verb denotes an event this is the time point at which the event occurs; if the verb denotes a state this is the time point from which on the state holds.

Per default the textual order of verbs establishes the relative temporal order of their associated events or states. E.g. in

A passenger alerts a driver. The driver stops a train. The train is in a station.

the event alert is temporally followed by the event stop which is temporally followed by the onset of the state be in a station. Our default assumption "textual order = temporal order" is supported by psychological and physiological evidence [Münte et al. 98].

Users can override the default temporal order by explicitly specifying times through prepositional phrases like at 9 o'clock, and by adding prepositional phrases like at the same time, or in any temporal order. A future version of ACE will allow users to combine sentences with the help of temporal prepositions like before, after and while.

5 Deductions from Discourse Representation Structures

We describe how deduction from discourse representation structures can be used to answer queries, to perform hypothetical and abductive reasoning, and to execute a specification. Furthermore, we briefly indicate how users can define domain theories and ontologies.

5.1 Theorem Prover for Discourse Representation Structures

On the basis of a proposal by [Reyle & Gabbay 94] we have developed a correct and complete theorem prover for discourse representation structures. To prove that a discourse representation structure *DRS2* can be derived from a discourse representation structure *DRS1*

$$DRS1 \vdash DRS2$$

the theorem prover proceeds in a goal-directed way without any human intervention. In the simplest case an atomic condition of *DRS2* is a member of the list of conditions of *DRS1* — after suitable substitutions. In other cases, the left or the right side of the turn-stile are reformulated and simplified, e.g. we replace

$$L \vdash (R1 \vee R2) \quad \text{by} \quad L \vdash R1 \text{ and } L \vdash R2$$

or

$$L \vdash (R1 \Rightarrow R2) \quad \text{by} \quad (L \cup R1) \vdash R2$$

This theorem prover will form the kernel of a general deduction system for DRSs. The deduction system will answer queries, perform hypothetical reasoning ('What happens if ... ?'), do abductive reasoning ('Under which conditions does ... occur?'), and execute specifications. All interactions with the deduction system will be in ACE.

5.2 Query Answering

A specification in a logic language describes a particular state of affairs within a problem domain. We can examine this state of affairs and its logical consequences by querying the specification in ACE. ACE allows two forms of queries

- *yes/no*-queries asking for the existence or non-existence of the state of affairs defined by the ACE specification,
- *wh*-queries (who, what, when, where, how, etc.) asking for specific details of the state of affairs described by the ACE specification.

Here is an example of a *wh*-query. Once we have translated the ACE sentence

A passenger enters a train.

into the DRS *S*

```
[A,B,C]
passenger(A)
train(B)
event(C,enter(A,B))
```

we can ask

Who enters a train?

The query sentence is translated into the DRS Q

```
[]
WHQ
    [A,B,C]
    who(A)
    train(B)
    event(C,enter(A,B))
```

and answered by deduction

$$S \vdash Q$$

Query words — like who — are replaced during the proof and answers are returned to the user in ACE, i.e.

[A passenger] enters a train.

5.3 Hypothetical Reasoning

When a logic specification partially describes a state of affairs there can be various possibilities to extend the specification. These extensions can lead to diverse logical consequences, some of which are desirable, while others are not. That is, we may want to ask the question 'What happens if ...?'.

'What happens if ...?' questions mean that we test a particular hypothesis H by examining its implied consequence C in the context of a given logic specification S.

$$S \vdash (H \Rightarrow C)$$

With the help of the deduction theorem this can be restated as

$$(S \cup H) \vdash C$$

i.e. we derive the logical consequence C of the union of S and H.

Here is a simple example shown on the level of ACE. If we extend the specification

If a passenger alerts a driver then the driver stops a train.

by the sentence

A passenger alerts a driver.

then we can deduce the ACE sentence

A driver stops a train.

as the logical consequence of the specification and its extension.

5.4 Abductive Reasoning

Once we have devised a logic specification we may want to investigate under which conditions a certain state of affairs occurs. If the conditions are already described by the logic specification we have the situation of a simple query. However, if the specification does not yet contain the pre-conditions of the state of affairs we are interested in then the question 'Under which conditions does ... occur?' can lead to abductive extensions of the specification.

Abduction investigates under which conditions A we can derive a particular consequence C from the logic specification S.

$$(S \cup A) \vdash C$$

Again a simple example. Given the specification

If a passenger alerts a driver then the driver stops a train.

If a train arrives at a station then a driver stops the train.

we want to know under which conditions the state of affairs occurs that is described by the sentence

A driver stops a train.

Abduction will give us first the ACE sentence

A passenger alerts a driver.

and then the ACE sentence

A train arrives at a station.

as two possible conditions.

5.5 Executing an ACE Specification

Model-oriented logic specifications build a behavioural model of the program to be developed [Wing 90], and one might be interested in executing this model to demonstrate its behaviour, be it for validation, or for prototyping. Formally, this form of execution is based on the reflexivity of the deduction relation.

$$S \vdash S$$

The derivation succeeds trivially. However, it can be conducted in a way that the logical and the temporal structure of the specification are traced, and that users can convince themselves that the specification has the expected behaviour. Furthermore, if predicates have side-effects — i.e. operations that modify the state of the system such as input and output — these side-effects can be made visible during the derivation. The concrete side-effects are realised by the execution environment.

Executing the ACE specification

A passenger alerts the driver. The driver stops the train. The train is in the station.

leads to the execution trace:

```
event:  A alerts B
    A:  passenger
    B:  driver

event:  B stops D
    D:  train

state:  D is in F
    F:  station
```

Validating a specification can be difficult since users may find it hard to relate its logical consequences to the — possibly implicit or incomplete — requirements. The Attempto system eases this task by expressing the execution trace in the terms of the problem domain. This not only reduces the semantic distance between the concepts of the application domain and the specification but also increases the efficiency of the validation process.

5.6 Domain Knowledge

The Attempto system is not associated with any specific application domain, nor with any particular software engineering method. By itself it does not contain any knowledge or ontology of application domains, of software engineering methods, or of the world in general. Thus users must explicitly define domain knowledge. Currently, this is possible with the help of ACE sentences like

Waterloo is a station.

Every train has a driver.

Even constraints can be expressed. If a specification states in one place that a train is out of order, and in another place that at the same time the same train is available, the contradiction can be detected if we explicitly define that out of order and available exclude each other, e.g.

No train is out of order and available at the same time.

In the future, ACE will provide meta-statements like

Define a train as a vehicle.

which will allow users to define domain theories and ontologies more concisely. With other meta-statements users will be able to specify constraints, safety properties, and exceptions.

6 Conclusions

We have developed Attempto Controlled English (ACE) as a specification language that combines the familiarity of natural language with the rigour of formal specification languages. Furthermore, we have implemented the Attempto specification system that allows domain specialists with little or no knowledge of formal specification methods to compose, to query and to execute formal specifications using only the concepts and the terms of their respective application domain.

The Attempto system translates ACE specifications into discourse representation structures (DRSs). Being a variant of first-order predicate logic, DRSs can readily be translated into a broad range of other representations. While the Attempto system comprises an automatic translation of DRSs into first-order predicate logic, clausal logic and Prolog, other DRSs were manually translated into the input language of the Finfimo theorem prover [Bry et al. 98]. This means that ACE is not only a specification language but also a convenient means to express theorems, integrity constraints and rules.

Currently, we are extending ACE with plurality and with complementary notations for graphical user interfaces and algorithms. Furthermore, we are investigating ways how to structure large ACE specifications.

Acknowledgements

We would like to thank Pierre Flener, Alberto Pettorossi, Julian Richardson, Dave Robertson and other participants of LOPSTR'98 for fruitful discussions and many constructive remarks. Also, we would like to express our gratitude to the anonymous reviewers for their helpful comments.

References

1. [Alshawi 92] H. Alshawi, The Core Language Engine, MIT Press, 1992
2. [Balzer 85] R. M. Balzer, A 15 Year Perspective on Automatic Programming, IEEE Transactions Software Engineering, vol. 11, no. 11, pp. 1257-1268, 1985
3. [Bowen & Hinchey 95a] J. P. Bowen, M. G. Hinchey, Seven More Myths of Formal Methods, IEEE Software, July 1995, pp. 34-41, 1995
4. [Bowen & Hinchey 95b] J. P. Bowen, M. G. Hinchey, Ten Commandments of Formal Methods, IEEE Computer, vol. 28, no. 4, pp. 56-63, 1995
5. [Bry et al. 98] F. Bry, N. Eisinger, H. Schütz, S. Torge, SIC: Satisfiability Checking for Integrity Constraints, Research Report PMS-FB-1998-3, Institut für Informatik, Universität München, 1998
6. [Businger 94] A. Businger, Expert Systems for the Configuration of Elevators at Schindler AG, Talk at Department of Computer Science, University of Zurich, July 1994
7. [Le Charlier & Flener 98] B. Le Charlier, P. Flener, Specifications Are Necessarily Informal, or: The Ultimate Myths of Formal Methods, Journal of Systems and Software, Special Issue on Formal Methods Technology Transfer, vol. 40, no. 3, pp. 275-296, March 1998

8. [CLAW 98] Second International Workshop on Controlled Language Applications CLAW'98, Carnegie Mellon University, 21-22 May 1998
9. [Covington 94] M. A. Covington, GULP 3.1: An Extension of Prolog for Unification-Based Grammars, Research Report AI-1994-06, Artificial Intelligence Center, University of Georgia, 1994
10. [Deville 90] Y. Deville, Logic Programming, Systematic Program Development, Addison-Wesley, 1990
11. [Fuchs 92] N. E. Fuchs, Specifications Are (Preferably) Executable, Software Engineering Journal, vol. 7, no. 5 (September 1992), pp. 323-334, 1992; reprinted in: J. P. Bowen, M. G. Hinchey, High-Integrity System Specification and Design, Springer-Verlag London Ltd., 1999 (to appear)
12. [Fuchs et al. 98] N. E. Fuchs, U. Schwertel, R. Schwitter, Attempto Controlled English (ACE), Language Manual, Version 2.0, Institut für Informatik, Universität Zürich, 1998
13. [Hall 90] A. Hall, Seven Myths of Formal Methods, IEEE Software, vol. 7, no. 5, pp. 11-19, 1990
14. [Hindle & Rooth 93] D. Hindle, M. Rooth, Structural Ambiguity and Lexical Relations, Computational Linguistics, vol. 19, no. 1, pp. 103-120, 1993
15. [Hirst 97] G. Hirst, Context as a Spurious Concept, AAAI Fall Symposium on Context in Knowledge Representation and Natural Language, Cambridge, Mass., 8 November 1997
16. [IEEE 91] IEEE Standard Glossary of Software Engineering Terminology, Corrected Edition, February 1991 (IEEE Std 610.12-1990)
17. [Jackson 95] M. Jackson, Software Requirements & Specifications: A Lexicon of Practice, Principles and Prejudices, Addison-Wesley, 1995
18. [Kamp & Reyle 93] H. Kamp, U. Reyle, From Discourse to Logic, Introduction to Modeltheoretic Semantics of Natural Language, Formal Logic and Discourse Representation Theory, Studies in Linguistics and Philosophy 42, Kluwer, 1993
19. [Kowalski 90] R. Kowalski, English as a Logic Programming Language, New Generation Computing, no. 8, pp. 91-93, 1990
20. [Macias & Pulman 95] B. Macias, S. G. Pulman, A Method for Controlling the Production of Specifications in Natural Language, The Computer Journal, vol. 38, no. 4, pp. 310-318, 1995
21. [Meyer 85] B. Meyer, On Formalism in Specifications, IEEE Software, vol. 2, no. 1, pp. 6-26, 1985
22. [Münte et al. 98] T. F. Münte, K. Schiltz, M. Kutas, When temporal terms belie conceptual order, Nature, no. 395, p. 71, 1998
23. [Parsons 94] T. Parsons, Events in the Semantics of English: A Study in Subatomic Semantics, Current Studies in Linguistics, MIT Press, 1994
24. [Reyle 93] U. Reyle, Dealing with Ambiguities by Underspecification: Construction, Representation and Deduction, Journal of Semantics, 10, pp. 123-178, 1993
25. [Reyle & Gabbay 94] U. Reyle, D. M. Gabbay, Direct Deductive Computation on Discourse Representation Structures, Linguistics and Philosophy, 17, August 94, pp. 343-390, 1994
26. [Sadri & Kowalski 95] F. Sadri, R. Kowalski, Variants of the Event Calculus, in: L. Sterling (ed.), Proc. ICLP'95, 12th International Conference on Logic Programming, MIT Press, pp. 67-82, 1995
27. [Schwitter 98] R. Schwitter, Kontrolliertes Englisch für Anforderungsspezifikationen, Dissertation, Universität Zürich, 1998
28. [Wing 90] J. M. Wing, A Specifiers's Introduction to Formal Methods, IEEE Computer, vol. 23, no. 9, pp. 8-24, 1990

Appendix

Original Version of the London Underground Notice

Press the alarm signal button to alert the driver.
The driver will stop immediately if any part of the train is in a station.
If not, the train will continue to the next station where help can be more easily given.
There is a £50 penalty for improper use.

ACE Version with Sentence by Sentence Translation into DRSs

If a passenger presses the alarm signal button then the passenger alerts the driver.

```
[]
IF
   [A,B,C]
   passenger(A)
   alarm_signal_button(B)
   event(C,press(A,B))
THEN
   [D,E]
   driver(D)
   event(E,alert(A,D))
```

If a passenger alerts the driver of a train and a part of the train is in a station then the driver stops the train immediately.

```
[]
IF
   [A,B,C,D,E,F,G]
   passenger(A)
   driver(B)
   train(C)
   of(B,C)
   event(D,alert(A,B))
   part(E)
   of(E,C)
   station(F)
   state(G,be(E))
   location(G,in(F))
THEN
   [H]
   event(H,stop(B,C))
   manner(H,immediately)
```

If a passenger alerts the driver of a train and no part of the train is in a station then the driver stops the train at the next station.

```
[]
IF
   [A,B,C]
   passenger(A)
   driver(B)
```

```
    train(C)
    of(B,C)
    event(D,alert(A,B))
    IF
       [E]
       part(E)
       of(E,C)
    THEN
       []
       NOT
          [F,G]
          station(F)
          state(G,be(E))
          location(G,in(F))
THEN
    [H,I]
    next(H)
    station(H)
    event(I,stop(B,C))
    location(I,at(H))
```

If the driver stops the train in a station then help is available.

```
[]
IF
   [A,B,C,D]
   driver(A)
   train(B)
   event(C,stop(A,B))
   station(D)
   location(C,in(D))
THEN
   [E,F]
   help(E)
   state(F,available(E))
```

If a passenger misuses the alarm signal button then the passenger pays a £50 penalty.

```
[]
IF
   [A,B,C]
   passenger(A)
   alarm_signal_button(B)
   event(C,misuse(A,B))
THEN
   [D,E]
   £_50_penalty(D)
   event(E,pay(A,D))
```

A Step Towards a Methodology for Mercury Program Construction: A Declarative Semantics for Mercury

Dante Baldan, Baudouin Le Charlier, Christophe Leclère, and Isabelle Pollet

Institut d'Informatique
Facultés Universitaires Notre-Dame de la Paix
Rue Grandgagnage 21
B-5000 Namur (Belgium)
{dba,ble,clc,ipo}@info.fundp.ac.be

Abstract. Declarative methodologies for logic program construction have been proposed for Prolog. They roughly consist of 1) building a purely logical version of the program based on a clear declarative semantics and 2) performing a number of checks about modes, types, termination and multiplicity. We plan to define a similar methodology for Mercury. This choice is motivated by the fact that type, mode, and multiplicity must be explicitly specified in Mercury, allowing the compiler to perform the second step above. In order to propose a methodology to perform the first step, we need a declarative semantics for Mercury, which has not yet been explicitly defined. The goal of the paper is to propose such a semantics pursuing simplicity and naturalness. We chose to define the semantics with respect to a unique interpretation domain, called the "universe", which is a kind of higher-order version of the Herbrand universe. Based on this simple domain, the denotation of terms and goals is naturally defined as well as the models of programs. Although the declarative semantics is primarily introduced to improve "manual" program construction by programmers, it could be used in a synthesis context.

1 Introduction

The work presented in this paper originates from two assumptions: 1) constructing logic programs requires some form of explicit reasoning (i.e., a logic program is not both a specification and a program, it is just a program); 2) logic programs should be constructed according to a declarative approach that basically amounts to show that the model intended by the user (described through a specification) is a (distinguished) model of the program.

Declarative methodologies for logic program construction have been proposed for Prolog (see e.g., [1, 4, 7, 9]). They roughly consist of 1) building a purely logical version of the program based on a clear declarative semantics and 2) performing a number of checks about modes, types, termination, and multiplicity,

P. Flener (Ed.): LOPSTR'98, LNCS 1559, pp. 21–40, 1999.

as well as some permutations of clauses and literals, to ensure that Prolog actually computes the relation described by the logical version. We plan to define a similar methodology for Mercury [10]. This choice is motivated by the fact that type, mode, and multiplicity information can (and must) be explicitly specified in Mercury, allowing the compiler to automatically perform the second step described above. However, in order to propose a methodology to perform the first step, we need a declarative semantics for Mercury, which has not yet been explicitly defined. The goal of this paper is to propose such a semantics.

When designing our declarative semantics for Mercury, we have pursued two main objectives: simplicity and naturalness. This is because, in our opinion, the declarative semantics should be a straightforward mathematical underpinning of the intuitive meaning of the programs, allowing the programmer to check his/her understanding of programs both easily and explicitly. As a consequence, we chose to define the semantics with respect to a unique interpretation domain, called the "universe", which is a kind of higher-order version of the Herbrand universe used in e.g., [4]. Based on this simple domain, the denotations of terms and goals (formulas) are naturally defined as well as the models of programs. In this paper, we present a declarative semantics for Mercury, $\mathcal{D}_0$, which is not completely satisfactory because it does not handle polymorphism, but is simple enough to illustrate the basic intuition behind our final declarative semantics $\mathcal{D}$.

Notice that, although the declarative semantics is primarily introduced to improve "manual" program construction by programmers, it could also be used in a synthesis context [5, 6] to automatically translate synthesized programs into equivalent Mercury programs (see Section 6).

The rest of this paper is organized as follows. Section 2 introduces the notation used in the paper. Section 3 presents an adaptation of Deville's methodology for Mercury program construction. Section 4 presents the definition of the declarative semantics $\mathcal{D}_0$, whereas the declarative semantics $\mathcal{D}$ is given in Section 5. Finally, Section 6 summarizes how we will use the declarative semantics in the program construction process.

2 Notation

Given two sets A and B, $A \to B$ is the set of total functions from A to B. If $f \in A \to B$ then $dom(f) = A$ is the domain of f. $\wp(A)$ is the set of subsets of A and $\times$ indicates the Cartesian product of sets. A finite sequence $x_1, \ldots, x_n$ of elements (e.g. Cartesian product of sets, tuples of elements) is indicated by x^* or x^n. The length of x^* is denoted by $|x^*|$, whereas n is the length of x^n. $(x\ y)^*$ is an abbreviation for $(x_1, y_1), \ldots, (x_n, y_n)$ where $n = |(x\ y)^*|$. The empty sequence is denoted by Ω. If f is an n-ary function with $n > 1$, then $f(x^*)$ and $f[x^*/d^*]$ denote $f(x_1, \ldots, x_{|x^*|})$ and the function f' that differs from f only on x^* where $f'(x^*) = d^*$, respectively. If f is a 1-ary function then $f(x^*)$ and $f[x^*/d^*]$ denote the sequence $f(x_1), \ldots, f(x_{|x^*|})$ and the function f' that differs from f only for $f'(x_1) = d_1, \ldots, f'(x_{|x^*|}) = d_{|d^*|}$, respectively. In both notations, we assume that $|x^*| = |d^*|$.

When presenting examples, the arity of every constructor, type constructor, and identifier will be specified with an integer: for instance, **strange**/2 means that (constructor, type constructor, or identifier) **strange** has arity 2. *Bool* denotes the set of boolean values $\{TRUE, FALSE\}$, $\neg$, $\wedge$, and $\vee$ denote negation, conjunction, and disjunction, respectively, in first order logic. $\mathbb{N}$ and $\mathbb{Z}$ denote the sets of natural and integer numbers, respectively. $List(\mathbb{Z})$ and for all $n \in \mathbb{N}$, $List_n(\mathbb{Z})$ indicate the set of lists of integers and the set of lists of integers having n elements, respectively.

3 Deville's Methodology for Mercury Program Construction

3.1 Introduction

We present the general guidelines of our proposal of Deville's methodology for Mercury program construction and we compare them with Deville's methodology for Prolog program construction [4]. It is worthwhile to note that Deville's methodology for Mercury program construction has not yet been well established and we will explain only the general points of our proposal. In the following, we will abbreviate Deville's methodology for Prolog (Mercury) program construction into Deville's methodology for Prolog (Mercury). Figure 1 illustrates the main steps of Deville's methodology for Prolog and Mercury. Both methodologies are presented through three steps where the first one is the elaboration of a specification of a predicate. The second step of Deville's methodology for Prolog (Mercury) consists of constructing a logic (declarative) description from which a Prolog (Mercury) program is derived in the last step.

The specification in Deville's methodology is composed of an informal description of a relation and a description of types, directionality, and multiplicity of the predicate (or function) being defined. In Figure 1 informal parts of specification are given in *italic* whereas formal parts are presented in `typewriter`. We observe that Prolog does not provide any language support for types, directionality, or multiplicity information, although that information can be built on top of Prolog, as it was done in Folon [7]. On the contrary, information about types, directionality, and multiplicity is expressible in Mercury and, for the sake of simplicity, we directly copy that information both in the declarative description and in the final Mercury code. This can be done because we restrict types to what can be formally defined in Mercury. A more powerful methodology could arguably be based on types considered as *arbitrary* sets of ground terms as in [4, 9] but, for simplicity, we prefer to use directly Mercury type definitions.

The second step of Deville's methodology for Prolog is the construction of a logic description, which is a first order logic formula formalizing the information contained in the specification. The semantics of logic descriptions is based on Herbrand interpretations and models [8]. The second step of Deville's methodology for Mercury is similar and consists of the construction of a declarative description. However, such declarative descriptions are higher order formulas.

Since there is no previously available semantics for such formulas, we provide a declarative semantics for Mercury, called $\mathcal{D}$, for formalizing the concept of sound and complete declarative description with respect to a specification.

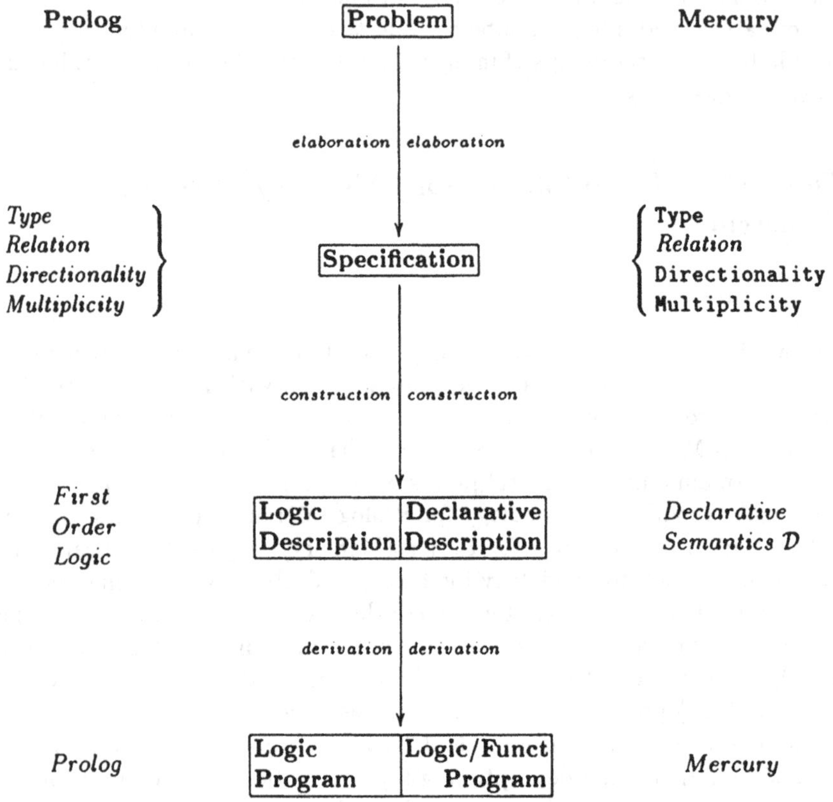

Fig. 1. Deville's Methodology for Prolog and Mercury

The last step of Deville's methodology for Prolog is the derivation of a Prolog program from a logic description. In order to obtain a correct Prolog program, a dataflow analysis (using the type and directionality information of the specification) has to be performed to determine a permutation of the clauses and of the literals such that incompleteness, unfairness, unsoundness, and floundering problems do not occur. In the Mercury case, many transformations needed to obtain an operationally correct Mercury program are already performed by the existing Mercury compiler. In this paper, we focus on the second step of the methodology (declarative description and declarative semantics), disregarding the directionality and multiplicity parts of specification.

We can summarize that Deville's methodology for Mercury is obtained from Deville's methodology for Prolog by replacing "logic description" with "declarative description", "first order logic" with "higher order logic", "Herbrand models" with "models in our declarative semantics". Deville's Methodology for Mercury is illustrated through the development of a Mercury (higher-order) declarative description in Section 3.2.

3.2 Example of Deville's Methodology for Mercury

We illustrate Deville's Methodology for Mercury through the predicate `map/3` taking a function, a list of possible inputs for that function, and a corresponding list of outputs. Since the functional argument of `map/3` is completely arbitrary, `map/3` has a polymorphic type, i.e., its type contains type variables.

predicate `map(F,L1,L2)`

- **Specification**:
  - **Type**:

```
F  : func(T1)=T2
L1 : list(T1)
L2 : list(T2)
list(T) ---> [] ; [T|list(T)]
```

  - *Relation*: `L2 = [F(`X_1`),...,F(`X_n`)]`, where `L1 = [`X_1`,...,`X_n`]`
- **Declarative Description**:

```
F  : func(T1)=T2
L1 : list(T1)
L2 : list(T2)
list(T) ---> [] ; [T|list(T)]
```

```
map(F,L1,L2) ⇔ (L1 = [] ∧ L2 = []) ∨
               (L1 = [X1|L3] ∧ L2 = [X2|L4] ∧ X2 = F(X1) ∧
                map(F,L3,L4))
```

The first part of the declarative description contains information about types and it is exactly the same as the one in the specification. The construction of the second part of the declarative description follows the same guidelines as in Deville's methodology for Prolog [4]. In this particular case, we use `L1` as induction parameter whereas "to be a proper suffix of" is the well-founded relation, needed in Deville's methodology. The base case comes out immediately and notice that we do not check the type of `F` as it would be needed in Deville's methodology for Prolog because we use a typed logic, and thus, the type of every variable (and identifier) is checked by a type system [3]. The inductive case comes directly from the definition of the relation. Notice that `F(X1)` is a higher-order term, because `F` is a variable and not a functor.

Apart from the last remark, we can say that the derivation step of Deville's methodology for Prolog is converted into Deville's methodology for Mercury with little effort. Also, the derivation of the Mercury code for `map/3` is immediate using the declarative description:

```
:- type list(T) ---> [] ; [T|list(T)]

:- pred map(func(T1)=T2,list(T1),list(T2)).
map(F,L1,L2) :- (L1 = [], L2 = []) ;
                (L1 = [X1|L3], L2 = [X2|L4], X2 = F(X1), map(F,L3,L4)).
```

4 First Attempt: The Declarative Semantics $\mathcal{D}_0$

4.1 Introduction

We present the definition of a declarative semantics $\mathcal{D}_0$, which is simple enough to illustrate the basic intuition behind our final declarative semantics $\mathcal{D}$ but which is not completely satisfactory as it does not handle polymorphism (see Section 4.6). The declarative semantics $\mathcal{D}_0$ is defined for abstract programs written according to the abstract syntax *AS*, summarized in Figure 2. Correctly typed Mercury programs can be translated into *AS* as a by-product of the type inference algorithm presented in [3]. Nevertheless, the fact that the program is correctly typed is not essential to the definition of $\mathcal{D}_0$, which is an untyped semantics. Note however, that, we assume, in abstract syntax *AS*, that there is no incomplete (identifier or term) call or application. An identifier call (or application) is incomplete if the arity of that identifier is strictly greater then the number of arguments supplied in that call. Incomplete calls and applications are replaced by explicit predicate and function terms, respectively, by the type inference algorithm given in [3]. Table 1 describes the syntactic domain for *AS*. The arity of every constructor, type constructor, and identifier is given by $a \in (\mathbf{C} \cup \mathbf{Tc} \cup \mathbf{Id}) \to \mathbb{N}$.

Symbols	Descriptions
$v \in \mathbf{V}$	Variables
$c \in \mathbf{C}$	Constructors
$id \in \mathbf{Id}$	Identifiers
$tv \in \mathbf{Tv}$	Type Variables
$tc \in \mathbf{Tc}$	Type Constructors
$pid \in \mathbf{Pid}$	Program Identifiers
$te \in \mathbf{Te}$	Terms
$g \in \mathbf{G}$	Goals
$ty \in \mathbf{Ty}$	Types
$tydef \in \mathbf{Tydef}$	Type Definitions
$fdef \in \mathbf{Fdef}$	Function Definitions
$pdef \in \mathbf{Pdef}$	Predicate Definitions
$prog \in \mathbf{Prog}$	Programs

Table 1. Symbols used in *AS*

$$
\begin{aligned}
te &::= v \mid c\ te^* \mid \mathbf{pred}\ v^*\ g \mid \mathbf{func}\ v^*\ v\ g \mid \\
&\quad\ \mathbf{apply}\ id\ te^* \mid \mathbf{apply}\ te\ te^* \\
g &::= \mathbf{true} \mid \mathbf{fail} \mid \mathbf{unif}\ te\ te \mid \\
&\quad\ \mathbf{call}\ id\ te^* \mid \mathbf{call}\ te\ te^* \mid \\
&\quad\ \mathbf{not}\ g \mid g\ \mathbf{and}\ g \mid g\ \mathbf{or}\ g \mid \\
&\quad\ \mathbf{if}\ g\ \mathbf{then}\ g\ \mathbf{else}\ g \mid \mathbf{exists}\ v^*\ g \\
ty &::= tv \mid tc\ ty^* \mid \mathbf{pred}\ ty^* \mid \mathbf{func}\ ty^*\ ty \\
tydef &::= tc\ tv^*\ (c\ ty^*)^* \\
pdef &::= id\ (\mathbf{pred}\ ty^*)\ v^*\ g \\
fdef &::= id\ (\mathbf{func}\ ty^*\ ty)\ v^*\ v\ g \\
prog &::= pid\ tydef^*\ pdef^*\ fdef^*
\end{aligned}
$$

Fig. 2. Abstract Syntax *AS*.

We assume that `sum/1` is a function taking a list of integers and returning the sum of the integers in that list. The application of Deville's Methodology for Mercury to `sum/1` is straightforward and we do not present it for space reasons.

We will illustrate $\mathcal{D}_0$ through the abstract program P_{AS} corresponding to the Mercury program P composed by the Mercury code for `map/3` given at the end of Section 3.2 and predicate:

```
:- pred goal.
goal :- map(sum,[[1],[1,2],[1,2,3]],[1,3,6]).
```

The abstract program P_{AS} is:

```
list(T) ([],[T|list(T)])
goal pred() :- call(map, (func(A1)=A2 :- unif(A2,apply(sum,(A1))),
                         [[1],[1,2],[1,2,3]], [1,3,6]))

map pred(func(T1)=T2,list(T1),list(T2)) (F,L1,L2) :-
(exists [X1,X2,L3,L4]((unif(L1,[]) and unif(L2,[])) or
                  ((unif(L1,[X1|L3]) and unif(L2,[X2|L4]))
                   and
                  (unif(X2,apply(F,(X1))) and call(map,(F,L3,L4))))))
```

It is worthwhile to note that, in P_{AS}:

1. the type of every predicate (function) is contained in the definition of the predicate (function) itself;
2. every predicate call is explicitly indicated by `call`;
3. every function application is explicitly indicated by `apply`;

4. every occurrence of a function (predicate) identifier as argument is replaced by a function (predicate) term containing an application (call) of that identifier.
5. every variable is either in the head of a predicate (or function) definition or explicitly existentially quantified.

An example of premise 4 is given by the term `func(A1)=A2 :- unif(A2,apply (sum,(A1)))` replacing the occurrence of `sum/1` as argument of `map/3` within predicate `goal/0`. We introduced the transformation indicated at point 4 to avoid having identifiers as terms both to give a simpler declarative semantics and to stress that identifiers are not terms. Abstract programs are admittedly harder to parse than corresponding Mercury codes. Nevertheless, we (classically) use the abstract syntax AS to present the semantics, since AS exhibits the "deep" syntactic structure of the language (e.g., it is explicit and non ambiguous).

The rest of the section is organized as follows. Section 4.2 illustrates the universe of values U. Section 4.3 gives the denotation of terms and goals in $\mathcal{D}_0$, whereas the denotation of types is given in Section 4.4. Section 4.5 presents the semantics $\mathcal{D}_0$ whose limits are given in Section 4.6.

4.2 The Universe of Values U

We propose a unique domain of values U rather than defining a domain based on the syntactical objects of an abstract program. Our choice follows Deville's methodology for Prolog in which the declarative semantics is based on a unique universe of Herbrand obtained from *a priori* fixed sets of constants and functors. The universe of values U is based on an infinite set **C** of constructors, fixed once and for all. We assume that integers (and other basic built-in types of Mercury) are contained in **C** as constructors of arity zero.

Since we want to use the declarative semantics $\mathcal{D}_0$ to support Deville's methodology for Mercury, we think that the universe of values U should contain "true" functions and predicates defined as sets of pairs (in a "naïve" set-theoretic sense) rather than lambda terms. We claim, indeed, that "true" functions and predicates are close to the way a programmer reasons about functions and predicates in writing Mercury programs. Since functions and predicates are higher order objects, we define a hierarchy to represent them. Informally speaking, the universe of values U is the top of a hierarchy whose bottom level contains all ground terms in the logic programming sense, level 1 contains functions and predicates over bottom level, level 2 contains functions and predicates over level 1, and so on. Also, Mercury terms composed of a constructor whose arguments contain function or predicate terms, are mapped to values in U composed by that constructor having "true" functions and predicates as arguments. It is worthwhile to note that our definition of U as a hierarchy forbids the consideration of recursive domains D such as, e.g., $D = A + (D \to D)$. We take the position that such domains D are lacking an intuitive semantics and that they are unpractical for program construction reasoning. Moreover, our declarative semantics is not aimed to model non termination, and, hence, we follow the usual first order logic approach in the definition of interpretations of formulas by including only total functions in our domain of values. We illustrate the elements in U using integers and constructors occurring in P_{AS} ({[]/0, ./2}) and then we give the formal definition of U.

The first level in the hierarchy is indicated by U_0 and it is the usual Herbrand universe of first order logic. More precisely, U_0 is the set of all first order ground terms constructed using the list constructor ./2 and constants $[], 0, \pm1, \pm2, \ldots$. Examples of elements in U_0 are: $[]$, 0, ±1, $\pm2, \ldots$, $[0]$, $[1]$, $[-1]$, $[2]$, $[-2]$, $\ldots$, $[0, 0|0]$, $[0, 1|0]$, $[0, -1|0]$, $[0, 2|0]$, $[0, -2|0]$, ... Notice that no type constraint is imposed on terms, and, thus, in addition to nil-terminated lists, there are also ill-formed lists.

The second level in the hierarchy of sets defining U is occupied by U_1 which is defined as follows. Let U_0' be the union of U_0 and the sets containing:

- all functions whose domain is the Cartesian product of subsets of U_0 and whose codomain is a subset of U_0. For example, U_0' contains $Sum : List(\mathbf{Z}) \rightarrow \mathbf{Z}$, which takes a list of integers and returns the sum of the integers in the list, and $Plus : \mathbf{Z} \times \mathbf{Z} \rightarrow \mathbf{Z}$, which is the usual arithmetic summation;
- all predicates whose domain is the Cartesian product of subsets of U_0. For example, U_0' contains $Collinear_n : List_n(\mathbf{Z}) \times List_n(\mathbf{Z}) \rightarrow Bool$, testing whether for every pair $([x_1, \ldots, x_n], [y_1, \ldots, y_n])$ of lists of integers there exist two integers r and s such that $x_i * r = s * y_i$, for $i = 1, \ldots, n$.

U_1 is the smallest set containing U_0' and all objects composed of a constructor whose arguments are elements of U_1. For example, U_1 contains $[Sum]$ and $[Collinear_n|0]$. It is worthwhile to note that U_1 includes lists containing functions and/or predicates. We think that such values are the natural interpretation of lists containing higher-order terms which represent functions and/or predicates. U_i $(i > 1)$ is defined similarly. The universe of values U is the union of all such sets.

Definition 1. *Let* **C** *be the set of all constructors. The domain of values, called* universe U, *is the union of the sets in the increasing chain* $U_0 \subseteq U_1, \ldots$ *defined as follows.*

U_0 *is the set of the first order ground terms constructed using all constructors in* **C**. *For every* $i \geq 0$, *let:*

1. $Func_i = \{(D_1 \times \ldots \times D_n) \rightarrow D : n \in \mathbb{N}, D_1, \ldots, D_n, D \in \wp(U_i)\}$;
2. $Pred_i = \{(D_1 \times \ldots \times D_n) \rightarrow Bool : n \in \mathbb{N}, D_1, \ldots, D_n \in \wp(U_i)\}$;
3. $U_i' = U_i \cup Func_i \cup Pred_i$.

U_{i+1} *is the smallest set containing* U_i' *and such that:* $\forall c \in C, d_1, \ldots, d_{a(c)} \in U_{i+1}$ *it holds that* $c(d_1, \ldots, d_{a(c)}) \in U_{i+1}$. *The universe of values* U *is:*

$$U = \bigcup_{i=0}^{\infty} U_i$$

We remark that the domains of functions (and predicates) in U are "(hyper)-rectangles", i.e., the Cartesian product of subsets of U. We think that such a choice is consistent with the denotation of the type of a function term in *AS*. For instance, if *te* is a function term in *AS* with two arguments whose types are both `int`, then the denotation of *te* is a function f whose domain is $\mathbb{Z} \times \mathbb{Z}$. Clearly, if we are interested only on the values of f on a subset A of $\mathbb{Z} \times \mathbb{Z}$, then f is not uniquely determined because any other function whose domain is $\mathbb{Z} \times \mathbb{Z}$ and equal to f on A is well-suited to be the denotation of *te*. We will use the axiom of choice to select any of such denotations in the semantics of function terms.

The following functions $\mathcal{F}$ and $\mathcal{P}$ formalizes the notion of function and predicate application in the universe U. When a function or a predicate is applied to a value outside its domain, we report a special value named *error*.

$$\mathcal{F} : U \times U^* \to U \cup \{error\} \qquad \mathcal{P} : U \times U^* \to Bool \cup \{error\}$$

$$\mathcal{F}(f, d^*) = \begin{cases} f(d^*) & \textit{if } f \textit{ is a function and } d^* \in dom(f) \\ error & \textit{otherwise} \end{cases}$$

$$\mathcal{P}(p, d^*) = \begin{cases} p(d^*) & \textit{if } p \textit{ is a predicate and } d^* \in dom(p) \\ error & \textit{otherwise} \end{cases}$$

For the sake of simplicity, in the following we write $f(d^*)$ and $p(d^*)$ in place of $\mathcal{F}(f, d^*)$ and $\mathcal{P}(p, d^*)$, respectively.

4.3 The Denotation of Terms and Goals in $\mathcal{D}_0$

In order to define the denotations of goals and terms $\mathcal{D}_0$, we introduce some preliminary concepts. We define the notion of admissible sets that are subsets of U contained in U_i for some $i \in \mathbb{N}$. We will consider only functions and predicates whose domain and codomain consist of admissible sets. This restriction is necessary to ensure that the denotation of every term belongs to U.

Definition 2. *A subset D of U is* admissible *if and only if there exists $i \in \mathbb{N}$ such that $D \subseteq U_i$, where U_i, $i = 1, \ldots$ is the sequence of sets defining U (see Def. 1). The set of admissible sets is denoted by $\mathcal{A}(U)$.*

The denotation in $\mathcal{D}_0$ of terms and goals is obtained through the values associated with variables and identifiers. More precisely, every variable and identifier is associated with a value in U and with a domain, i.e., an admissible set, representing a set of possible values for that variable or identifier. The denotation of a term *te* (goal g) can be either a value in U (*Bool*) or *error* if the value of a subterm is found incompatible with its domain during the evaluation of *te*. The following definition formalizes the previous intuition.

Definition 3. *An* Identifier Environment *is a function in* **Ienv** $=$ **Id** $\to U$ *and ι indicates an identifier environment. A* Set Environment *is a function in* **Senv** $=$

$(\mathbf{V}\cup\mathbf{Id}\cup\mathbf{C}) \rightarrow \mathcal{A}(U)$ and ϵ indicates a set environment. A Variable Environment *is a function in $\mathbf{Venv} = \mathbf{V} \rightarrow U$ and ν indicates a variable environment.*

Using Definitions 2 and 3, the denotation of a term $\mathcal{V}$ is obtained through a set environment, an identifier environment, and a variable environment. In the definition of $\mathcal{V}$, ϵ and ι are "hidden" arguments, i.e., they are not explicitly indicated in the left hand side of any of the equations for $\mathcal{V}$. Hidden arguments are specified by enclosing their domains into brackets in the signature of the semantic function. We adopted that convention for having a light notation and for concentrating the attention of the reader on the most relevant parts of the definition of $\mathcal{V}$: hidden arguments are never modified in the right hand side of the definitions; so, they can be thought as "global". Any occurrence of ϵ and ι in the right hand side of an equation is to be interpreted as a reference to the corresponding hidden argument of $\mathcal{V}$. We assume that *error* propagates through the evaluation of all rules.

Definition 4 (Denotation of Terms). *The denotation of terms is defined by induction on the definition of terms in AS:*

$$\mathcal{V} : \mathbf{Te} \rightarrow [\mathbf{Senv}] \rightarrow [\mathbf{Ienv}] \rightarrow \mathbf{Venv} \rightarrow U \cup \{error\}$$

$$\mathcal{V}[\![v]\!]\nu = \begin{cases} \nu[\![v]\!] & \textit{if } \nu[\![v]\!] \in \epsilon[\![v]\!] \\ error & \textit{otherwise} \end{cases}$$

$$\mathcal{V}[\![c\ te^*]\!]\nu = c(\mathcal{V}[\![te^*]\!]\nu)$$

$$\mathcal{V}[\![\mathtt{pred}\ v^*\ g]\!]\nu = \begin{cases} \lambda d^* \in \epsilon[\![v^*]\!]\,.\,\mathcal{G}[\![g]\!]\nu[v^*/d^*] & \textit{if } \forall d^* \in \epsilon[\![v^*]\!] : \\ & \mathcal{G}[\![g]\!]\nu[v^*/d^*] \neq error \\ error & \textit{otherwise} \end{cases}$$

$$\mathcal{V}[\![\mathtt{func}\ v^*\ v\ g]\!]\nu = \begin{cases} \mathsf{choice}(S) & \textit{if } S \neq \emptyset \\ error & \textit{otherwise} \end{cases}$$

$$\mathcal{V}[\![\mathtt{apply}\ id\ te^*]\!]\nu = \begin{cases} (\iota[\![id]\!])(\mathcal{V}[\![te^*]\!]\nu) & \textit{if } \iota[\![id]\!] \in \epsilon[\![id]\!] \\ error & \textit{otherwise} \end{cases}$$

$$\mathcal{V}[\![\mathtt{apply}\ te\ te^*]\!]\nu = (\mathcal{V}[\![te]\!]\nu)(\mathcal{V}[\![te^*]\!]\nu)$$

where $S = \{f \in D^* \rightarrow D : \forall d^* \in D^* : \mathcal{G}[\![g]\!]\nu[v^*/d^*, v/f(d^*)] = TRUE\}$, choice *indicates "any function" (axiom of choice), $D^* = \epsilon[\![v^*]\!]$, and $D = \epsilon[\![v]\!]$.*

As for $\mathcal{V}$, ϵ and ι are "hidden" arguments also in the denotation of goals $\mathcal{G}$. We assume that *error* propagates through the evaluation of all rules.

Definition 5 (Denotation of Goals). *The denotation of goals is given by induction on the definition of goals in AS:*

$$\mathcal{G} : \mathbf{G} \rightarrow [\mathbf{Senv}] \rightarrow [\mathbf{Ienv}] \rightarrow \mathbf{Venv} \rightarrow \mathit{Bool} \cup \{\mathit{error}\}$$

$$\mathcal{G}[\![\mathtt{true}]\!]\nu = \mathit{TRUE}$$

$$\mathcal{G}[\![\mathtt{fail}]\!]\nu = \mathit{FALSE}$$

$$\mathcal{G}[\![\mathtt{unif}\ te_1\ te_2]\!]\nu = (\mathcal{V}[\![te_1]\!]\nu = \mathcal{V}[\![te_2]\!]\nu)$$

$$\mathcal{G}[\![\mathtt{call}\ id\ te^*]\!]\nu = \begin{cases} (\iota[\![id]\!])(\mathcal{V}[\![te^*]\!]\nu) & \mathit{if}\ \iota[\![id]\!] \in \epsilon[\![id]\!] \\ \mathit{error} & \mathit{otherwise} \end{cases}$$

$$\mathcal{G}[\![\mathtt{call}\ te\ te^*]\!]\nu = (\mathcal{V}[\![te]\!]\nu)(\mathcal{V}[\![te^*]\!]\nu)$$

$$\mathcal{G}[\![\mathtt{not}\ g]\!]\nu = \neg(\mathcal{G}[\![g]\!]\nu)$$

$$\mathcal{G}[\![g_1\ \mathtt{and}\ g_2]\!]\nu = (\mathcal{G}[\![g_1]\!]\nu \wedge \mathcal{G}[\![g_2]\!]\nu)$$

$$\mathcal{G}[\![g_1\ \mathtt{or}\ g_2]\!]\nu = (\mathcal{G}[\![g_1]\!]\nu \vee \mathcal{G}[\![g_2]\!]\nu)$$

$$\mathcal{G}[\![\mathtt{exists}\ v^*\ g]\!]\nu = \begin{cases} \mathit{error} & \mathit{if}\ \exists d^* \in \epsilon[\![v^*]\!] : \mathcal{G}[\![g]\!]\nu[v^*/d^*] = \mathit{error} \\ \mathit{TRUE} & \mathit{if}\ \forall d^* \in \epsilon[\![v^*]\!] : \mathcal{G}[\![g]\!]\nu[v^*/d^*] \neq \mathit{error} \\ & \mathit{and} \\ & \exists d^* \in \epsilon[\![v^*]\!] : \mathcal{G}[\![g]\!]\nu[v^*/d^*] = \mathit{TRUE} \\ \mathit{FALSE} & \mathit{if}\ \forall d^* \in \epsilon[\![v^*]\!] : \mathcal{G}[\![g]\!]\nu[v^*/d^*] = \mathit{FALSE} \end{cases}$$

$$\mathcal{G}[\![\mathtt{if}\ g_1\ \mathtt{then}\ g_2\ \mathtt{else}\ g_3]\!]\nu = \begin{cases} \mathit{error} & \mathit{if}\ \mathcal{G}[\![g_1]\!]\nu = \mathit{error} \\ \mathcal{G}[\![g_2]\!]\nu & \mathit{if}\ \mathcal{G}[\![g_1]\!]\nu = \mathit{TRUE} \\ \mathcal{G}[\![g_3]\!]\nu & \mathit{if}\ \mathcal{G}[\![g_1]\!]\nu = \mathit{FALSE} \end{cases}$$

4.4 The Denotation of Types

It is worthwhile to note that no reference to types has been taken into account up to now nor in the denotation of terms (Definition 4) nor in the denotation of goals (Definition 5). This allows us to incorporate the denotation of types into the declarative semantics as a distinguished choice of admissible sets, stressing that types are just used for avoiding that *error* be the denotation of terms and goals.

The denotation of a type ty is obtained by associating every type variable in ty with an admissible set and every type constructor tc in ty with an admissible set obtained through the type definition for tc. In order to formalize that intuition, we introduce the following definition.

Definition 6. *A* Domain Environment *is a function in* $\mathbf{Denv} = \mathbf{Tv} \to \mathcal{A}(U)$ *and* δ *indicates a domain environment. A* Type Constructor Environment *is a function in* $\mathbf{Tcenv} = \mathbf{Tc} \to \mathbf{Denv} \to \mathcal{A}(U)$ *and* γ *indicates a type constructor environment. Finally,* $tvarlist \in \mathbf{Tc} \to \mathbf{Tv}^*$ *is a function associating every type constructor* tc *with a list* tv^* *of distinct type variables such that* $a(id) = |tv^*|$.

Every type is evaluated by extending every domain environment, i.e., every denotation of type variables. We remark that γ is a "hidden" argument. For the sake of simplicity, we assume that every Mercury primitive type, such as `int`, are evaluated into their "natural" set of values. For example, `int` is evaluated, by definition, into $\mathbb{Z}$.

Definition 7 (Denotation of Types). *The denotation of types is given by induction on the definition of types in AS.*

$$\mathcal{T} : \mathbf{Ty} \to \mathbf{Denv} \to [\mathbf{Tcenv}] \to \mathcal{A}(U)$$

$$\mathcal{T}[\![tv]\!]\delta = \delta[\![tv]\!] \qquad \mathcal{T}[\![tc\ ty^*]\!]\delta = \gamma[\![tc]\!](\delta[tv^*/D^*])$$

$$\mathcal{T}[\![\texttt{func}\ ty^*\ ty]\!]\delta = (D^* \to D) \qquad \mathcal{T}[\![\texttt{pred}\ ty^*]\!]\delta = (D^* \to Bool)$$

where $tv^* = tvarlist(tc)$, $D^* = \mathcal{T}[\![ty^*]\!]\delta$, *and* $D = \mathcal{T}[\![ty]\!]\delta$.

4.5 Models of Type Correct Programs

In order to take into account Mercury primitive functions (predicates) such as integer addition, we can assume that every $\iota \in \mathbf{Ienv}$ and $\epsilon \in \mathbf{Senv}$ provide the semantics of these operations (predicates) without requiring the existence of a corresponding definition in the program.

A type correct program defines a type constructor environment through a fix-point computation [2]. For example, `list/1` is associated with all nil-terminated lists composed by elements of admissible sets. Also, given a domain environment δ, a type correct program defines a set environment which is obtained through the types of identifiers and the type definitions provided by that program.

$$\mathcal{F}_0 : \mathbf{Prog} \to \mathbf{Denv} \to \mathbf{Senv} \qquad \mathcal{F}_0[\![P]\!]\delta = \epsilon$$

where for all v and id in P:

$$\epsilon[\![v]\!] = \mathcal{T}[\![ty_v]\!]\delta\gamma \qquad \epsilon[\![id]\!] = \mathcal{T}[\![ty_{id}]\!]\delta\gamma$$

where ty_v and ty_{id} are the types of v and id, respectively, and γ is the type constructor environment associated with P. The type of identifiers in a type correct program P is provided directly by P whereas the type of variables in P is provided by the type inference algorithm [3] applied to P. We are now in position to define the models of type correct programs.

Definition 8. *Let P be a type correct program and $\gamma \in$ **Tcenv** be the type constructor environment defined by that program. A model of P in $\mathcal{D}_0$ is $\iota \in$ **Ienv** such that for every $\delta \in$ **Denv** and $\nu \in$ **Venv**:*

1. *For every predicate definition $(id\ (\mathtt{pred}\ ty^*)\ v^*\ g)$ in P:*

$$\iota[\![id]\!] \in \epsilon[\![id]\!] = D^* \to Bool \quad \text{and} \quad \forall d^* \in D^* : \iota[\![id]\!]d^* = \mathcal{G}[\![g]\!]\epsilon\iota\,\nu[v^*/d^*]$$

where $D^* = \mathcal{T}[\![ty^*]\!]\delta\gamma$ and $\epsilon = \mathcal{F}_0[\![P]\!]\delta$;

2. *For every function definition $(id\ (\mathtt{func}\ ty^*\ ty)\ v^*\ v\ g)$ in P:*

$$\iota[\![id]\!] \in \epsilon[\![id]\!] = D^* \to D \text{ and } \forall d^* \in D^* : \mathcal{G}[\![g]\!]\epsilon\iota\,\nu[v^*/d^*, v/f(d^*)] = TRUE$$

where $D^* = \mathcal{T}[\![ty^*]\!]\delta\gamma$, $D = \mathcal{T}[\![ty]\!]\delta\gamma$, $f = \iota[\![id]\!]$, and $\epsilon = \mathcal{F}_0[\![P]\!]\delta$.

We remark that the quantification over ν in Definition 8, is purely technical since v^* and v are the only free variables occurring in g (cf. [3]).

4.6 A Sample Model in $\mathcal{D}_0$ of P_{AS}

Let $\iota \in$ **Ienv** be defined as follows:

- $\iota[\![\mathtt{goal/0}]\!] = TRUE$;
- $\iota[\![\mathtt{map/3}]\!] = map \in ((List(\mathbb{Z}) \to \mathbb{Z}) \times (List(List(\mathbb{Z}))) \times (List(\mathbb{Z}))) \to Bool$, where, $\forall (f, [x_1, \ldots, x_n], [y_1, \ldots, y_m]) \in (List(\mathbb{Z}) \to \mathbb{Z}) \times (List(List(\mathbb{Z}))) \times (List(\mathbb{Z}))$:

$$map(f, [x_1, \ldots, x_n], [y_1, \ldots, y_m]) = \begin{cases} \bigwedge_{k=1}^{n}(y_k = f(x_k)) & \text{if } m = n \\ FALSE & \text{otherwise} \end{cases}$$

- $\iota[\![\mathtt{sum/1}]\!] = sum \in List(\mathbb{Z}) \to \mathbb{Z}$, where, $\forall [y_1, \ldots, y_m] \in List(\mathbb{Z})$:

$$sum([y_1, \ldots, y_m]) = \sum_{i=1}^{m} y_i$$

It is easy to verify [2] that ι is a model in $\mathcal{D}_0$ of P_{AS}. In the definition of ι, we exploit that there is only one call of `map/3` with instantiated arguments. Consider, in fact, the abstract program P'_{AS} obtained from P_{AS} by adding to the body of `goal/0` the predicate call `map(reverse,[[1],[1,2],[1,2,3]],[[1],`

[2,1],[3,2,1]]), where the function **reverse**/1 takes a list and reverses it. P'_{AS} contains two different calls to **map**/3 with two different functions as first argument. Clearly, we cannot define an identifier environment as before, because we have to take into account two possible instances of **map**/3, i.e., we have to handle polymorphism of identifiers. The solution proposed in our declarative semantics $\mathcal{D}$ is that every instance of the type of identifiers is associated with a different predicate (or function) in U. This will be done in Section 5.1 by modifying the definitions of identifier environments and set environments. It would be also possible handling polymorphism by associating every predicate (function) identifier with a unique predicate (function) in U, whose domain is "large" enough to contain all possible instances of the type of that identifier. This would mean handling polymorphism by assuming that every function has only one ("big") type, but we think that this is too far from the intuition of a programmer about types.

5 Declarative Semantics $\mathcal{D}$

We present our declarative semantics $\mathcal{D}$ which is able to express the polymorphism of identifiers. $\mathcal{D}$ has the same universe U of values as $\mathcal{D}_0$ and the evaluation $\mathcal{T}$ of types does not change. There are two differences between $\mathcal{D}$ and $\mathcal{D}_0$: (1) set environments of $\mathcal{D}_0$ are replaced by set environments for identifiers and constructors, and by set environments for variables in $\mathcal{D}$, (2) identifier environments in $\mathcal{D}_0$ are redefined in $\mathcal{D}$ in order to handle the polymorphism of identifiers.

This section is organized as follows. Section 5.1 presents the denotations of terms and goals in $\mathcal{D}$. Section 5.2 defines $\mathcal{D}$ and Section 5.3 illustrates a model in $\mathcal{D}$ of P'_{AS}.

5.1 The Denotation of Terms and Goals

As anticipated at the end of Section 4.6, $\mathcal{D}$ is obtained from $\mathcal{D}_0$ by introducing new definitions of identifier environments and set environments. An identifier environment, in $\mathcal{D}$, expresses the polymorphism of identifiers by associating every identifier with a (partial) function whose domain is the set of all tuples of admissible sets and whose codomain is U. For simplicity, we extend such partial functions to total functions by associating *error* with every value outside their original domain. Using the new definition of identifier environment, we overcome the problem encountered at the end of Section 4.6, because every function (predicate) identifier is associated with a family of functions (predicates) in U and not with a single function (predicate) as in $\mathcal{D}_0$.

Set environments for constructors and identifiers express the polymorphism of constructors and identifiers by associating every constructor and identifier with a (partial) function whose domain is the set of tuples of admissible sets and whose codomain is $\mathcal{A}(U)$. As for identifier environments, we extend such partial functions to total functions by associating *error* with every value outside their original domain. As for $\mathcal{D}_0$, set environments for constructors and identifiers allow us to define $\mathcal{D}$ as an untyped semantics, i.e., a semantics where the denotation of types is not needed in the denotation of terms and goals.

A set environment for variables, in $\mathcal{D}$, is a set environment of $\mathcal{D}_0$ restricted to variables, i.e., it associates every variable with an admissible set. Finally, as in $\mathcal{D}_0$, every variable is associated with a value in U by a variable environment.

Definition 9. *An* Identifier Environment *is a function in* $\mathbf{Ienv} = \mathbf{Id} \to \mathcal{A}(U)^* \to U \cup \{error\}$ *and* ι *indicates an identifier environment. A* Set Environment for Constructors and Identifiers *is a function in* $\mathbf{ISenv} = (\mathbf{C} \cup \mathbf{Id}) \to \mathcal{A}(U)^* \to \mathcal{A}(U) \cup \{error\}$ *and* ϵ_i *indicates a set environment for constructors and identifiers. A* Set Environment for Variables *is a function in* $\mathbf{VSenv} = \mathbf{V} \to \mathcal{A}(U)$ *and* ϵ_v *indicates a set environment for variables. A* Variable Environment *is a function in* $\mathbf{Venv} = \mathbf{V} \to U$ *and* ν *indicates a variable environment.*

We present the denotations of terms and goals in $\mathcal{D}$ and we introduce an auxiliary function Δ that computes the domain of a term. Δ is used to compute the tuples of admissible sets for the second argument of identifier environments and set environments for identifiers, and thus, it was not needed in $\mathcal{D}_0$ because identifier environments and set environments in $\mathcal{D}_0$ do not have such an input argument.

Every term is associated by Δ with an admissible set depending on the admissible sets associated with the variables occurring in that term. The value of Δ is either an admissible set or *error*. We can have *error* in the evaluation of a predicate or function term if the corresponding goal contains a term which is recursively associated with *error*. The bottom case for having *error* is when the domain of a function term is not compatible with the type of its argument. We also assume that *error* propagates through domain evaluation. We remark that, in the definition of Δ, both ϵ_i and ϵ_v are considered "hidden" arguments.

Definition 10 (Domain of Terms). *The domain of terms is defined by induction on the definition of terms in AS.*

$$\Delta : \mathbf{Te} \to [\mathbf{ISenv}] \to [\mathbf{VSenv}] \to \mathcal{A}(U) \cup \{error\}$$

$$\Delta[\![v]\!] = \epsilon_v[\![v]\!]$$

$$\Delta[\![c\, te^*]\!] = (\epsilon_i[\![c]\!])(\Delta[\![te^*]\!])$$

$$\Delta[\![\mathbf{pred}\ v^*\ g]\!] = \begin{cases} (\epsilon_v[\![v^*]\!] \to Bool) & \text{if } \forall te \text{ in } g : \Delta[\![te]\!] \neq error \\ error & \text{otherwise} \end{cases}$$

$$\Delta[\![\mathbf{func}\ v^*\ v\ g]\!] = \begin{cases} (\epsilon_v[\![v^*]\!] \to \epsilon_v[\![v]\!]) & \text{if } \forall te \text{ in } g : \Delta[\![te]\!] \neq error \\ error & \text{otherwise} \end{cases}$$

$$\Delta[\![\texttt{apply}\ id\ te^*]\!] = (\epsilon_i[\![id]\!])(\Delta[\![te^*]\!])$$

$$\Delta[\![\texttt{apply}\ te\ te^*]\!] = \begin{cases} D & \textit{if } \Delta[\![te]\!] = D^* \to D \neq \textit{error and} \\ & \Delta[\![te^*]\!] = D^* \textit{ does not contain error} \\ \textit{error} & \textit{otherwise} \end{cases}$$

The denotation of a term is obtained through a set environment for constructors and identifiers, a set environment for variables, an identifier environment, and a variable environment. We remark that, in Definition 11, ϵ_i, ϵ_v, and ι are "hidden" arguments. With respect to Definition 4, we replaced **Senv** with **ISenv** and **VSenv**. We give in Definition 11 only the case of identifier application because, thanks to "hidden" arguments, all other cases are the same as in Definition 4. We assume that *error* propagates through the evaluation of all rules.

Definition 11 (Denotation of Terms). *The denotation of terms is the following:*

$$\mathcal{V} : \mathbf{Te} \to [\mathbf{ISenv}] \to [\mathbf{VSenv}] \to [\mathbf{Ienv}] \to \mathbf{Venv} \to U \cup \{\textit{error}\}$$

where

$$\mathcal{V}[\![\texttt{apply}\ id\ te^*]\!]\nu = ((\iota[\![id]\!])(\Delta[\![te^*]\!]))(\mathcal{V}[\![te^*]\!]\nu)$$

The denotation of a goal is obtained, as for terms, through a set environment for identifiers, a set environment for variables, an identifier environment and a variable environment. As in Definition 11, ϵ_i, ϵ_v, and ι are "hidden" arguments. With respect to Definition 5, we replaced **Senv** with **ISenv** and **VSenv**. We give in Definition 12 only the case of identifier call because, thanks to "hidden" arguments, all other cases are the same as in Definition 5. We assume *error* propagates through the evaluation of all rules.

Definition 12 (Denotation of Goals). *The denotation of goals is given by induction on the definition of goal in AS.*

$$\mathcal{G} : \mathbf{G} \to [\mathbf{ISenv}] \to [\mathbf{VSenv}] \to [\mathbf{Ienv}] \to \mathbf{Venv} \to \textit{Bool} \cup \{\textit{error}\}$$

$$\mathcal{G}[\![\texttt{call}\ id\ te^*]\!]\nu = ((\iota[\![id]\!])(\Delta[\![te^*]\!]))(\mathcal{V}[\![te^*]\!]\nu)$$

5.2 Models of Type Correct Programs

We recall that a type correct program defines a type constructor environment through a fixpoint computation [2]. A type correct program defines a set environment for constructors and identifiers which is obtained through the types of identifiers and the type definitions provided by that program. Also, every pair composed by a domain environment and a type constructor environment defines a set environment for variables. With respect to $\mathcal{D}_0$, $\mathcal{F}_0$ is split into $\mathcal{F}_1$ and $\mathcal{F}_2$ according to the splitting of **Senv** into **ISenv** and **VSenv**. Let γ be the type constructor environment defined by P. We have:

$$\mathcal{F}_1 : \mathbf{Prog} \to \mathbf{ISenv} \qquad \mathcal{F}_1[\![P]\!] = \epsilon_i$$

where:

- for all function definitions (id (**func** ty^* ty) v^* v g) in P:

$$dom(\epsilon_i[\![id]\!]) = \{\mathcal{T}[\![ty^*]\!]\delta\gamma : \delta \in \mathbf{Denv}\}$$

$$\forall\delta \in \mathbf{Denv} : \epsilon_i[\![id]\!](\mathcal{T}[\![ty^*]\!]\delta\gamma) = (\mathcal{T}[\![ty^*]\!]\delta\gamma) \to (\mathcal{T}[\![ty]\!]\delta\gamma)$$

- for all predicate definitions (id (**pred** ty^*) v^* g) in P:

$$dom(\epsilon_i[\![id]\!]) = \{\mathcal{T}[\![ty^*]\!]\delta\gamma : \delta \in \mathbf{Denv}\}$$

$$\forall D^* \in dom(\epsilon_i[\![id]\!]) : \epsilon_i[\![id]\!]D^* = D^* \to Bool$$

- for all type definitions $tc(tv^*)$ $(\ldots, c(ty^*), \ldots)$ in P:

$$dom(\epsilon_i[\![c]\!]) = \{\mathcal{T}[\![ty^*]\!]\delta\gamma : \delta \in \mathbf{Denv}\}$$

$$\forall\delta \in \mathbf{Denv} : \epsilon_i[\![c]\!](\mathcal{T}[\![ty^*]\!]\delta) = \gamma[\![tc]\!]\delta$$

Also, we have:

$$\mathcal{F}_2 : \mathbf{Prog} \to \mathbf{Denv} \to \mathbf{VSenv} \qquad \mathcal{F}_2[\![P]\!]\delta = \epsilon_v$$

where for all v in P:

$$\epsilon_v[\![v]\!] = \mathcal{T}[\![ty]\!]\delta\gamma$$

where ty is the type of v provided by the type inference algorithm [3] and γ is the type constructor environment defined by P. We introduce the definition of model of a type correct program in $\mathcal{D}$.

Definition 13. *Let P be a type correct program and $\gamma \in$ **Tcenv** be the type constructor environment defined by that program. A model of P is $\iota \in$ **Ienv** such that for every $\delta \in$ **Denv** and $\nu \in$ **Venv**:*

1. *For every predicate definition (id (**pred** ty^*) v^* g) in P:*

$$\forall d^* \in D^* : (\iota[\![id]\!]D^*)d^* = \mathcal{G}[\![g]\!]\epsilon_i\epsilon_v\iota\,\nu[v^*/d^*]$$

where, $D^* = \mathcal{T}[\![ty^*]\!]\delta\gamma$, $\epsilon_i = \mathcal{F}_1[\![P]\!]$, and $\epsilon_v = \mathcal{F}_2[\![P]\!]\delta$;

2. *For every function definition (id (**func** ty^* ty) v^* v g) in P:*

$$\forall d^* \in D^* : \mathcal{G}[\![g]\!]\epsilon_i\epsilon_v\iota\,\nu[v^*/d^*, v/f(d)] = TRUE$$

where, $D^* = \mathcal{T}[\![ty^*]\!]\delta\gamma$, $f = \iota[\![id]\!]D^*$, $\epsilon_i = \mathcal{F}_1[\![P]\!]$, and $\epsilon_v = \mathcal{F}_2[\![P]\!]\delta$.

5.3 A Model of the Program P'_{AS}

We revisit the abstract program P'_{AS}, which is type correct, illustrating how our declarative semantics $\mathcal{D}$ overcomes the limits of $\mathcal{D}_0$. It is easy to prove [2] that the identifier environment ι defined as follows is a model of P'_{AS}:

- $\iota[\![\texttt{goal/0}]\!]\Omega = \mathit{TRUE}$ and $\forall D^* \neq \Omega : \iota[\![\texttt{goal/0}]\!]D^* = \mathit{error}$;
- $\iota[\![\texttt{map/3}]\!]D^* = \mathit{map}_{D^*} \in D^* \rightarrow \mathit{Bool}$, where $D^* = ((D_1 \rightarrow D_2) \times (\mathit{List}(D_1)) \times (\mathit{List}(D_2)))$, with $D_1, D_2 \in \mathcal{A}(U)$, and $\forall (f, [x_1, \ldots, x_n], [y_1, \ldots, y_m]) \in D^*$:

$$\mathit{map}_{D^*}(f, [x_1, \ldots, x_n], [y_1, \ldots, y_m]) = \begin{cases} \bigwedge_{k=1}^{n} (y_k = f(x_k)) & \mathit{if}\ m = n \\ \mathit{FALSE} & \mathit{otherwise} \end{cases}$$

  and $\forall D'^* \neq D^* : \iota[\![\texttt{map/3}]\!]D'^* = \mathit{error}$;
- $\iota[\![\texttt{sum/1}]\!]\mathit{List}(\mathbf{Z}) = \mathit{sum} \in (\mathit{List}\ (\mathbf{Z})) \rightarrow \mathbf{Z}$, where $\forall [y_1, \ldots, y_m] \in \mathit{List}(\mathbf{Z})$:

$$\mathit{sum}([y_1, \ldots, y_m]) = \sum_{i=1}^{m} y_i$$

  and, $\forall D^* \neq \mathit{List}(\mathbf{Z}) : \iota[\![\texttt{sum/1}]\!]D^* = \mathit{error}$;
- $\iota[\![\texttt{reverse/1}]\!]\mathit{List}(\mathbf{Z}) = \mathit{reverse} \in \mathit{List}(\mathbf{Z}) \rightarrow \mathit{List}(\mathbf{Z})$, and $\forall [y_1, \ldots, y_m] \in \mathit{List}(\mathbf{Z})$:

$$\mathit{reverse}([y_1, \ldots, y_m]) = [y_m, \ldots, y_1]$$

  and, $\forall D^* \neq \mathit{List}(\mathbf{Z}) : \iota[\![\texttt{reverse/1}]\!]D^* = \mathit{error}$.

6 Discussion

The declarative semantics, which has just been defined, can be used to build logic descriptions [4] in Deville's style, which is mainly based on structural induction and ensures —roughly speaking— that the user's intended model is the unique model of the program; the novelty is that logical descriptions can now be higher-order. Further works will adapt SLDNF-resolution [8] to the context of Mercury to make it possible to prove that well typed and moded Mercury programs actually compute a set of answers covering the declarative semantics.

In the context of schema guided synthesis of logic programs [5, 6], we conjecture that it is natural to see the isoinitial models of open programs as denotations of polymorphic functions and procedures in Mercury. This would ensure that well-moded Mercury translations of correct open programs [5, 6] are operationally correct.

7 Acknowledgments

We would like to thank Yves Deville and Alberto Pettorossi for their constructive criticisms and useful suggestions. This work is supported by the ESSI Project 25503 ARGO.

References

1. Krzysztof R. Apt. *From Logic Programming to Prolog*. Prentice Hall, 1997.
2. Dante Baldan and Baudouin Le Charlier. Declarative Semantics for Mercury. Technical report, Institute d'Informatique, FUNDP, Namur, Belgique, 1998.
3. Dante Baldan, Baudouin Le Charlier, Chistophe Leclère, and Isabelle Pollet. Abstract Syntax and Typing Rules for Mercury. Technical report, Institute d'Informatique, FUNDP, Namur, Belgique, 1998.
4. Yves Deville. *Logic Programming: Systematic Program Development*. MIT Press, 1990.
5. Pierre Flener, Kung-Kiu Lau, and Mario Ornaghi. Correct-schema-guided synthesis of steadfast programs. In M. Lowry and Y. Ledru, editors, *Proceedings of ASE'97*, Computer Society Press. IEEE, 1997.
6. Pierre Flener, Kung-Kiu Lau, and Mario Ornaghi. On correct program schemas. In N. E. Fuchs, editor, *Proceedings of LOPSTR'97*, LNCS. Springer-Verlag, 1997.
7. Jean Henrard and Baudouin Le Charlier. Folon: An environment for declarative construction of logic programs (extended abstract). In M. Bruynooghe and M. Wirsing, editors, *Proc. of PLILP'92*, volume 631 of *LNCS*, Leuven, Belgium, August 1992. Springer-Verlag.
8. John W. Lloyd. *Foundations of Logic Programming*. Springer Series: Symbolic Computation–Artificial Intelligence. Springer-Verlag, second, extended edition edition, 1987.
9. Lee Naish. Types and Intended Meaning. In F. Pfenning, editor, *Types in Logic Programming*. MIT Press, 1992.
10. Zoltan Somogyi, Fergus Henderson, and Thomas Conway. The execution algorithm of Mercury, an efficient purely declarative logic programming language. *Journal of Logic Programming*, 29(1–3):17–64, October–November 1996.

Pragmatics in the Synthesis of Logic Programs

David Robertson[1] and Jaume Agustí[2]

[1] Division of Informatics, University of Edinburgh, 80 South Bridge, Edinburgh, UK
dr@aisb.ed.ac.uk

[2] IIIA (CSIC), Campus UAB, 08193 Bellaterra, Barcelona, Spain
agusti@iiia.csic.es

Abstract. Many of the systems which we, and those who have worked with us, have built were intended to make it easier for people with particular backgrounds to construct and understand logic programs. A major issue when designing this sort of system is pragmatics: from the many logically equivalent ways of describing a program we must identify styles of description which make particular tasks easier to support. The first half of this paper describes three ways in which we have attempted to understand the pragmatics of particular domains using well known methods from computational logic. These are: design using parameterisable components; synthesis by incremental addition of program slices; and meta-interpretation. These are helpful in structuring designs but do not necessarily provide guidance in design lifecycles - where less detailed designs are used to guide the description of more detailed designs. The second half of this paper summarises an example of this form of guidance.

1 Why Domain Specific Systems are Needed

This paper concerns the use of generic forms of design of logic programs in domain-specific applications. Much of the logic programming literature has a different concern: to construct systems which are as general as possible, and preferably independent of domain. The reason why we are interested in focussed systems is that the problems we tackle normally involve engineers who have neither the time nor inclination to learn deeply about logic (for example some of the systems described in Section 2.1 were used by ecological modellers, while some of the systems described in Section 2.2 were used by novice programmers). They tend to be interested in preserving the styles of description which they already know and trust, so our uses of logic programming must mesh with these. However, we do not want to make our systems so domain-specific that we must invent a new style of design each time we tackle a new problem. This creates a tension between the desire for generic design methods and the need for lifecycles which are tailored to particular domains.

In Section 2 we show how we have used generic methods from logic programming to underpin domain-specific design systems. In each of these sections we begin by summarising the method; then exemplify its use in applied projects; finally explaining those factors which limited the size of our applications. To

P. Flener (Ed.): LOPSTR'98, LNCS 1559, pp. 41–60, 1999.

save space, we have anchored the discussion in simplified formal descriptions of the methods - used as an aid to explanation rather than a description of the full method.

Some general themes recur in the different methods. We often use a high level language targeted at a particular engineering group. This appears as the problem description (Φ) in Section 2.1 and as the parameterisation conditions (Ψ) of Section 2.2. We frequently supply a library of standard design patterns, such as the parameterisable components of Section 2.1 or the program slices of Section 2.2. Sometimes we can split the design lifecycle into different stages which are highly modular but which connect closely for later analysis, as in the meta-interpretation of Section 2.3.

In Section 3 we note a problem with the systems described in the earlier sections. The general themes associated with each method apply in a localised way to a particular stage of design. Although the use of logic as a standard language helps us to share information between the different methods it does not, in itself, describe the process of refinement which often takes place when we use a high-level design to guide the construction of a more detailed design. Our work on this problem is at an early stage so we use a formal example as a means of describing our current view of this problem. We introduce a method of refinement which uses generic set-based notation for high-level designs; refining these to task-specific definitions; then further refining these with domain-specific details.

2 Pragmatics at Individual Stages of Design

The purpose of this section is to summarise, in as succinct a style as possible, the notions of pragmatics which we have found effective in a number of applied projects. In describing how ideas from logic program underpin these applications we have left aside the discussion of the interfaces by which groups of engineers supply the necessary problem descriptions (Φ and Ψ in Sections 2.1 and 2.2) and satisfy selection conditions (*Select*, *Best*, *Choose*, *Instantiated* and *Completed* in Sections 2.1 and 2.2). Inventing these user interfaces has been a major issue in almost every system we have designed but space limitations prohibit a discussion of these issues here. Readers with an interest in the interfaces used should refer to the papers cited for each system. Unlike the underlying formal methods, the interfaces we build normally differ between domains of application because each new domain brings new assumptions about the way in which groups of engineers wish to communicate.

2.1 Parameterisable Components

We have used parameterisable components in situations where it was possible to predict standard patterns of program description on a fairly large scale (*i.e.* where many of the patterns comprise more than one predicate) and where variation in use of these patterns can be controlled via parameters which can be explained to the engineers in our target domain. Although generic notions of parameterisability exist within logic programming (*e.g.* [10]) and functional programming (*e.g.* [4]) we use more specific forms of parameterisation adequate for our applications. Our method of designing such systems is as follows:

- We identify basic features of the domain which engineers use in order to select and instantiate standard patterns. Using an interface tailored to the task, statements in this restricted language are supplied by those engineers. We call this a problem description and represent it below using the symbol, Φ.
- We build a library of parameterisable components, each of the form:

  $$component(N, C, D, P)$$

  where N is the name of the top-level predicate defined by the component and C is a set of conditions which must all be satisfied from the problem description in order to instantiate the component. When instantiated, D is a set of clauses defining the program for N, and P is the set of subsidiary predicates which we require in order to supply us with an executable component. If the component is self-contained then P is empty.
- We construct a system which selects and instantiates components according to the problem description supplied by engineers. We describe this, in its simplest form, using the predicate $parameterise(P, \Phi, D)$ which denotes that a program consisting of the set of clauses D for satisfying the predicates named in P can be constructed through parameterisation using the problem description, Φ. The predicate $Select(P, N, P_r)$ selects from P the predicate named N to construct, leaving remaining names P_r. The predicate $Best(S, K)$ chooses the most appropriate component, K, from the set, S of candidates.

$$\begin{array}{l} parameterise(\{\}, \Phi, \{\}) \\ parameterise(P, \Phi, D \cup D_r) \leftarrow \\ \quad Select(P, N, P_r) \wedge \\ \quad Best(\{(C', D', P') | \left(\begin{array}{c} component(N, C, D, P'') \wedge \\ \forall G. G \in C \rightarrow \Phi \vdash G \end{array} \right) \}, (C, D, P_n)) \wedge \\ \quad parameterise(P_r \cup P_n, \Phi, D_r) \end{array}$$

Our earliest use of this form of design was in constructing animal population models from problem descriptions couched in the terminology used by ecologists (see [9]). An example of a component (simplified from [9]) is determining whether two animals (A and B) are considered to be in proximity to each other at time point T. There are various standard ways of defining this but one way is by assuming that the physical area is divided into grid squares and each animal is assigned a square. By satisfying $grid(G)$ and $locations(L)$ we find out what is the appropriate grid and where the animals are initially located. This information, when added to the definition of proximity, gives us the program for the component. To complete the definition we need to know how the dynamics of change in location works so *located_at* is in the set of new predicates.

$$
component(in\_proximity, \left\{ \begin{array}{l} grid(G), \\ locations(L) \end{array} \right\},
\left\{ \begin{array}{l} in\_proximity(A, B, T) \leftarrow \\ \quad located\_at(A, L_1, T) \wedge \\ \quad adjoining(L_1, L_2) \wedge \\ \quad located\_at(B, L_2, T), \\ in\_proximity(A', B', T') \leftarrow \\ \quad located\_at(A', L', T') \wedge \\ \quad located\_at(B', L', T') \wedge \\ \quad not(A' = B') \end{array} \right\} \cup G \cup L,
\{located\_at\})
$$

Engineers using this sort of system control design only through the problem description - in other words, they have little or no control over the decisions taken by the *Select* and *Best* predicates introduced earlier. Such decisions often involve domain-specific knowledge so the size of problem which we can tackle by this means is limited by the amount of such knowledge which we can supply and maintain. Nevertheless, there exist practical applications which are small enough to be tractable but large enough to be worthwhile. For example:

- The WWW site for our research group (URL `http://www.dai.ed.ac.uk/groups/ssp/index.html`), was built and is maintained by automatic generation from a problem description. It can be explained succinctly in terms of the abstract description above. The problem description, Φ, is given using a simple set of facts describing our research group. Each $component(N, C, D, P)$ specifies part of the site by instantiating D via conditions C derivable from Φ. The conditions in C can all be determined automatically in this very narrow application, and the range of possible components is sufficiently small that *Select* and *Best* can also be determined automatically. In other words, those altering the problem description don't need to know how the specification is synthesised. The specification is converted automatically to HTML via the Pillow translator (currently available from `http://www.clip.dia.fi.upm.es`).
- A prototype system for connecting safety shutdown logic to segments of codes of design practice is described in [5]. In this case, the problem description, Φ, is a set of formal descriptions of parts of the codes of practice. Each $component(N, C, D, P)$ defines a standard segment of the specification of the shutdown logic, where C relates D to Φ. The control over choice of component (via *Select* and *Best*) is under the control of designers. The design support system keeps track of how the codes of practice relate to the designers' choices of components.

2.2 Synthesis by Slices

The idea of constructing predicates via a sequence of "slices" manifests itself in different forms in the logic programming community. We have been most strongly influenced by the style of development called "techniques editing", first explained in [6] and later elaborated by others (for example [3]). Our method of designing these systems is as follows:

- We identify the basic flows of control (often called "skeletons") which our target group of engineers will want to use. Each of these is defined by a set of clauses which define a predicate P of arity, n. A set of parameterisation conditions, Ψ_s, (applied similarly to those described in Section 2.1) are used to instantiate appropriate variables in the clauses.

$$skeleton(\Psi_s, \left\{ \begin{array}{c} P(A_1, \ldots, A_n) \leftarrow C_1 \\ \vdots \\ P(A'_1, \ldots, A'_n) \leftarrow C_m \end{array} \right\})$$

- We define transformations (often called "techniques") as shown below. Each transformation adds an argument, N, to P and may add additional goals to the body of each clause (transforming each C to C'). Each transformation requires the instantiation of a set of parameterisation conditions, Ψ_t.

$$\left\{ \begin{array}{c} P(A_1, \ldots, A_n) \leftarrow C_1 \\ \vdots \\ P(A'_1, \ldots, A'_n) \leftarrow C_m \end{array} \right\} \stackrel{\Psi_t}{\Rrightarrow} \left\{ \begin{array}{c} P(A_1, \ldots, A_n, N_1) \leftarrow C'_1 \\ \vdots \\ P(A'_1, \ldots, A'_n, N_m) \leftarrow C'_m \end{array} \right\}$$

  These transformations normally do not alter the original flow of control of the predicate, thus making it easier subsequently to combine predicates.
- We build an interface with which the target group of engineers can select a flow of control and progressively extend it. We summarise this process using the predicate $techniques(D)$ which succeeds if there is a definition, D, obtainable by techniques editing. The predicate $Choose(S_f, F)$ chooses an appropriate flow of control, F, from the set of skeletons, S_f. $Instantiate(\Psi)$ instantiates the parameters of a skeleton or of a transformation. $Next(S_t, T)$ chooses a transformation step appropriate to the current partial definition. $Completed(D)$ denotes that we have applied sufficiently many transformations to complete our definition.

$$\begin{array}{rl} techniques(D) \leftarrow & Choose(\{(\Psi'_s, D'_s) | skeleton(\Psi'_s, D'_s)\}, (\Psi_s, D_s)) \wedge \\ & Instantiate(\Psi_s) \wedge \\ & extend(D_s, D) \end{array}$$

$$\begin{array}{rl} extend(D_s, D) \leftarrow & Next(\{(\Psi'_t, D'_n) | D_s \stackrel{\Psi'_t}{\Rrightarrow} D'_n\}, (\Psi_t, D_n)) \wedge \\ & Instantiate(\Psi_t) \wedge \\ & extend(D_n, D) \\ extend(D, D) \leftarrow & Completed(D) \end{array}$$

This approach is most often applied to small-scale design of predicates, using a small library of highly adaptable skeletons and techniques. An example of a skeleton in such a library might be a definition of list traversal, where the parameterisation conditions *predicate_name*(P) and *n_cases*(N) supply the predicate name and number of recursive cases. Each T is a test which is later supplied by the user of the program and is used to differentiate the recursive cases of the skeleton.

$$skeleton(\{predicate\_name(P), n\_cases(N)\}, \left\{ \begin{array}{l} P([H_1|T_1]) \leftarrow T_1 \wedge P(T_1) \\ \vdots \\ P([H_N|T_N]) \leftarrow T_N \wedge P(T_N) \\ P([]) \end{array} \right\})$$

A difficulty with using skeletons and techniques at this scale is that the decisions which users must make (both in selecting and parameterising the components) are both numerous and detailed. In the example above we must know we want to base our program on list traversal in order to choose the skeleton and, once chosen, we must be able to say how many recursive cases we need. In some cases it can be desirable to make such decisions explicit. For example:

- In our use of techniques editing in supporting novice Prolog programmers [1] we worked at a fine level of detail but limited the diversity of the library used by novices so that the range of decisions they had to make was still small. The parameterisation conditions for skeletons, Ψ_s, are established via simple questions such as the number of cases in a traversal skeleton. The parameterisation conditions for techniques, Ψ_t, is similarly direct. At any point in design, the choice of *Next* step is from a small repertoire and the decision of when the design is *Completed* can be determined with respect to whatever example the novice programmer chose to tackle.
- A more diverse library is contained in the techniques editing tool of the LSS system. We have used this for more sizeable designs - the largest being a reconstruction of the tool itself [8]. However, this sort of system can only be used by engineers who are trained in the use of logic programming techniques because the questions which one must answer in satisfying Ψ_s and Ψ_t can be sophisticated (such as the precise form of term deconstruction). The choice of *Next* step, although from a fixed set of options each time, also demands Prolog expertise. Only designers can tell when the design is *Completed* because it is always possible to add more slices to a predicate.
- In more recent work, Castro has applied techniques editing to a narrow domain of application (the synthesis of animal population dynamics models). In his system the library of skeletons and techniques is domain-specific and Ψ_s and Ψ_t are complex. To avoid the ecological modellers using his system from having to learn about parameterisation Castro used a problem description (similar in purpose to the one in Section 2.1) to allow description of features in ecological terminology. These are then translated into the language needed for parameterisation.

2.3 Enhancement by Meta-Interpretation

Sometimes when we have built programs we want to construct additional mechanisms which don't change the definitions of the original programs but give us new ways of using them. For example, we might want to relate the execution of a program to some form of commentary on what it is doing. A natural way of doing this in a logic programming style is through meta-interpretation. Different variants of this method of design exist but we have been most influenced by the ideas of layered meta-interpretation given in [14]. This type of meta-interpreter tends to be problem-specific so the method is best explained by a simplified example.

Suppose that we have a collection of equations of the form $equation(V_v, I, P)$, where V_v is a variable-value pair of the form $value(X, V)$ (with X being the name of the output variable and V recording its value); I is the list of inputs needed by the equation; and P is the procedure relating inputs to output. For example:

$$equation(value(x, X), [value(y, Y)], X \textit{ is } Y + 10)$$
$$equation(value(y, Y), [], Y = 5)$$

We might write a simple interpreter for these equation definitions which solves for any variable-value pair by selecting an appropriate equation; solving its inputs recursively and calling the equation's procedure.

$$solve(V_v) \leftarrow equation(V_v, I, P) \wedge solve\_inputs(I) \wedge P$$

$$solve\_inputs([V_v|T]) \leftarrow solve(V_v) \wedge solve\_inputs(T)$$
$$solve\_inputs([])$$

We can use this program to find the values for variables. for example, solving the goal $solve(value(x, X))$ binds X to 15.

We may later find that just solving the equations isn't enough. We also want to retain certain contextual information related to our interpreter's choice of variable-values. We use assertions of the form $context(V_v, E)$ to denote that the variable-value pair V_v is endorsed by the set of contextual information E. For example:

$$context(value(x, V), \{cx\})$$
$$context(value(y, V), \{cy\})$$

We could adapt our original interpreter to propagate this contextual information by adding an extra "slice" to predicates *solve* and *solve_inputs*. For example, the program:

$$e\_solve(V_v, E_i \cup E_v) \leftarrow equation(V_v, I, P) \wedge e\_solve\_inputs(I, E_i) \wedge P \wedge context(V_v, E_v)$$

$$e\_solve\_inputs([V_v|T], E_v \cup E_r) \leftarrow e\_solve(V_v, E_v) \wedge e\_solve\_inputs(T, E_r)$$
$$e\_solve\_inputs([], \{\})$$

will find both variable-values and endorsements by satisfying goals of such as $e\_solve(value(x, X), E)$, binding X to 15 and E to $[cx, cy]$. The problem in doing this is that the means of solving the equations and propagating endorsements ar now closely bound together in the same predicate definitions. An alternative way of achieving the same result without transforming the equation interpreter is to define the endorsement strategy as a meta interpreter which sits "on top of" the original equation interpreter. For example:

$$\begin{aligned}
endorsed(solve(V_v), E_b \cup E_v) \leftarrow\ & clause(solve(V_v), B) \wedge \\
& context(V_v, E_v) \wedge \\
& endorsed(B, Eb) \\
endorsed((A \wedge B), E_a \cup E_b) \leftarrow\ & endorsed(A, E_a) \wedge \\
& endorsed(B, E_b) \\
endorsed(G, \{\}) \leftarrow\ & not(G = (A \wedge B)) \wedge \\
& is_built_in(G) \wedge \\
& G \\
endorsed(G, E) \leftarrow\ & not(G = solve(V_v) \vee is_built_in(G)) \wedge \\
& clause(G, B) \wedge \\
& endorsed(B, E).
\end{aligned}$$

Using this interpreter we can obtain the same endorsements as before by giving goals such as $endorsed(solve(value(x, X)), E)$. However, we have a much looser connection between the equation solving and endorsement strategies, so we could alter either (within limits) without having to change the other. We don't have this flexibility in the *e_solve* definition.

We have applied this sort of design strategy in reconstructing simulation models which were originally implemented in a System Dynamics notation (a standard process engineering paradigm in which state variables are thought of as "tanks" with "flows" of substance between them being controlled by systems of equations). The largest of these is the BIONTE model of key vegetation production processes in the Amazon. Its Carbon and Nitrogen sub-models contain a total of 210 variables, of which 60 are parameters. Each of these parameters (and the equations connecting them to the 14 state variables) were obtained from different combinations of field data, physiological measurement and literature survey. Hence the context of the model is highly heterogeneous. Brilhante [2] reconstructed the BIONTE Carbon and Nitrogen sub-models using meta-interpretation to reproduce the equation solving strategy for simulation and confirmed that it produced results which closely matched the original model[1]. We then extended the meta-interpreter to propagate contextual information, which could then be used to assess the heterogeneity of the data supporting predictions given by the model. The original extensions to the interpreter were by normal extension (like in *e_solve* above) but we later used a layered approach.

The main difficulty in this style of design is its flexibility. The point of meta-interpretation is normally to express some sort of explicit problem solving strategy and these vary depending on the problem in hand. Although it is possible to imagine sets of parameterisable components or techniques (in the style described earlier) for building meta-interpretation strategies, we are not aware of this being done in practice. Until it is, we lack the empirical evidence to determine whether useful notions of standard practice exist at this level of description.

3 The Need for Integration Across Lifecycles

The uses of transformation described in the previous sections are diverse in their application while also being based on comparatively straightforward, abstract principles. However, there remains a major practical obstacle to their use on a larger scale: they are not integrated within any commonly accepted design lifecycle. Each of our synthesis systems is targeted at a particular aspect of design but we have looked less closely at the pragmatics of connecting design stages. However, it is the ability to establish such connections which makes large-scale formal design possible. In the remainder of this paper we describe some of our most recent work which is beginning to address this problem, and is complementary to the methods described earlier.

In this section we introduce a method for describing generic inference strategies at a very high level and refining these to task-specific inference strategies. Central to our method is the idea that any inference strategy can be described as a logic program which takes as arguments sets of Horn clauses. We call each of those sets an axiom set. Inference is described by manipulating axiom sets. To give a flavour of what happens later, consider the definition below, which defines whether some axiom set, A_2, follows from another axiom set, A_1. It does this by progressively expanding A_1, using some deduction mechanism, until it can be demonstrated capable of deducing everything in A_2. Its base case is when all the axioms in A_2 are covered by those in A_1, while its recursive case enlarges A_1 to a bigger axiom set, A_3.

$$follows(A_1, A_2) \leftarrow covered(A_1, A_2)$$
$$follows(A_1, A_2) \leftarrow enlarge(A_1, A_3) \wedge follows(A_3, A_2)$$

Given definitions for *covered* and *enlarge*, this describes a particular inference strategy. However, we can describe it more generally by replacing specific

[1] This surprised us since our interpreter used simple differences between time points when applying equations, rather than the approximations to continuous change normally used in System Dynamics modelling.

conditions by more general constraints between the axiom sets. In our example, the *covered* relation requires that everything which can consistently be deduced from A_2 can also be deduced from A_1; while the *enlarge* relation requires that the new set of axioms, A_3, allows at least as much (and probably more) to be deduced from it than from A_1. In the formal notation which we describe below, this is expressed as:

$$follows(A_1, A_2) \leftarrow i(A_1) \supseteq i(A_2)$$
$$follows(A_1, A_2) \leftarrow i(A_1) \subseteq i(A_3) \wedge follows(A_3, A_2)$$

In the remainder of this section we will describe (in Section 3.1) the language we use to describe generic strategies like the one above; give refinement rules which allow these to be specialised to task-specific but domain-independent strategies (Section 3.2); introduce an example which demonstrates how this sort of refinement might work in practice (Section 3.3); and finally show, for the example, how the addition of domain-specific refinements can produce an executable specification (Section 3.4).

3.1 Language

As the basis for our transformations, we define a language for describing axiom sets, their interpretations, and relations between them. These relations are of two kinds: generic relations which are understood purely in terms of set inequalities, and specialised relations which describe standard ways of satisfying these inequalities. The choice of language for the latter is a pragmatic one, reflective of our understanding of what should be "standard". Therefore we make no claim that our choice is the ideal one.

Definition 1 *A restricted Horn clause is an expression of the form $C \leftarrow P$, where C is a unit goal and P is either a single unit goal or a conjunction of unit goals, and denotes that conclusion, C, is true whenever precondition, P, is true. Negation is not allowed in the conclusion or precondition.*

Definition 2 *The term $a(S)$ denotes an axiom set, where S is either a variable or a set of restricted Horn clauses.*

Definition 3 *The term $i(S)$ denotes the interpretation of an axiom set, S. This is the set of all ground unit goals which can be deduced from S.*

Definition 4 (Extension) $\mathbf{extended(A, E)}$ *denotes that a set of axioms, A can be extended to yield the set of axioms, E. This is true if E contains all the axioms of A plus some subset of all the axioms which can be deduced from the axioms in A.*

Definition 5 (Axiom Constraint) $\mathbf{constrained(A, X_1, X_2)}$ *denotes that additional constraints, consistent with axiom set A, have been added to the body of* *clause* X_1 *to yield clause* X_2. *For example, if* X_1 *is of the form* $C \leftarrow P_1$ *then* X_2 *could be* $C \leftarrow P_1 \wedge P_2$ *where* P_2 *is an additional constraint which does not lead to an inconsistency with the other axioms in* A.

Definition 6 (Axiom Relaxation) relaxed($\mathbf{A}, \mathbf{X_1}, \mathbf{X_2}$) *denotes that constraints have been removed from the body of clause* X_1 *to yield clause* X_2, *in a way which is consistent with axiom set* A. *For example, if* X_1 *is of the form* $C \leftarrow P_1 \wedge P_2$ *then* X_2 *could be* $C \leftarrow P_1$ *where removing* P_2 *does not lead to an inconsistency with the other axioms in* A.

Definition 7 (Specialisation) specialised($\mathbf{A_1}, \mathbf{A_2}$) *denotes that the axiom set* A_1 *can be adapted to form an axiom set,* A_2, *for which all ground goals deducible from* A_2 *are deducible in* A_1 *but some goals deducible from* A_1 *may not be deducible in* A_2.

Definition 8 (Generalisation) generalised($\mathbf{A_1}, \mathbf{A_2}$) *denotes that the axiom set* A_1 *can be adapted to form an axiom set,* A_2, *for which all ground goals deducible from* A_1 *are deducible in* A_2 *but some goals deducible from* A_2 *may not be deducible in* A_1.

Definition 9 (Filtering) filtered($\mathbf{A}, \mathbf{X}$) *denotes that axiom* X *satisfies some test which is determined with respect to axiom set* A.

Definition 10 (Deletions) deletions($\mathbf{A_1}, \mathbf{A_2}$) *denotes that a subset,* A_2, *of axiom set* A_1 *can legitimately be deleted, according to some decision procedure defined with respect to* A_1.

Definition 11 (Addition) additions($\mathbf{A_1}, \mathbf{A_2}$) *denotes that the new axiom set,* A_2, *consistent with axiom set* A_1, *can legitimately be added to* A_1.

Definition 12 (Subset Generation) subseteq($\mathbf{A_2}, \mathbf{A_1}$) *denotes that axiom set* A_2 *is a subset derived from the axioms in* A_1.

3.2 Refinement Operations

We now define a collection of transformation rules which relate generic set inequalities between axiom sets and their interpretations to the specialised relations from Section 3.1. We have divided these into two groups: the first concerned with narrowing a set of axioms or its interpretation; the second widening a set of axioms or its interpretation. Each rule defines a rewrite from the set inequality (on the left of the arrow) to a more specific condition (on the right) which is consistent with the inequality.

Narrowing First we give the transformation rules for reducing the size of interpretations or axiom sets. Rules 1 to 6 relate set inequalities to our specialised relations. Rules 7 and 8 are based on general properties of sets.

Refinement 1 *The interpretation of axiom set A_2 is narrower or equal to that of A_1 if we can deductively extend A_1 to give axiom set I_1 and that set narrows to A_2.*

$$i(A_1) \supseteq i(A_2) \;\Rightarrow\; \mathbf{extended(A_1, I_1)} \wedge a(I_1) \supseteq a(A_2)$$

Refinement 2 *The interpretation of axiom set A_2 is narrower or equal to that of A_1 if A_2 is composed of constrained versions of some of the axioms of A_1. This uses the predicate $map\_some(S_1, E_1, R, E_2, S_2)$ which is true if at least one (and possibly every) element E_1 of set S_1 maps via the relation R to a corresponding element, E_2 of S_2.*

$$i(A_1) \supseteq i(A_2) \;\Rightarrow\; map\_some(A_1, X_1, \mathbf{constrained(A_1, X_1, X_2)}, X_2, A_2)$$

Refinement 3 *The interpretation of axiom set A_2 is narrower or equal to that of A_1 if A_2 is obtained from A_1 by specialisation.*

$$i(A_1) \supseteq i(A_2) \;\Rightarrow\; \mathbf{specialised(A_1, A_2)}$$

Refinement 4 *Axiom set A_2 is contained in A_1 if A_2 is a subset formed from A_1.*

$$a(A_1) \supseteq a(A_2) \;\Rightarrow\; \mathbf{subseteq(A_2, A_1)}$$

Refinement 5 *Axiom set A_2 is contained in A_1 if A_2 contains those axioms from A_1 which pass some filtering test. This uses the predicate $apply\_some(S_1, E_1, T, S_2)$ which is true if at least one (and possibly every) element E_1 of set S_1 satisfies test T, with S_2 being a set of all such elements.*

$$a(A_1) \supseteq a(A_2) \;\Rightarrow\; apply\_some(A_1, X_1, \mathbf{filtered(A_1, X_1)}, A_2)$$

Refinement 6 *Either the axiom set or interpretation of A_2 is narrower than or equal to the corresponding axiom set or interpretation of A_1 (so T below must be i or a) if there are elements which can be deleted from A_1 to form A_2.*

$$T(A_1) \supseteq T(A_2) \;\Rightarrow\; \mathbf{deletions(A_1, A_3)} \wedge remove(A_3, A_1, A_2)$$

Refinement 7 *The narrowing relation is transitive.*

$$S_1 \supseteq S_2 \;\Rightarrow\; S_1 \supseteq S_3 \wedge S_3 \supseteq S_2$$

Refinement 8 *Set S_2 is narrower than or equal to set S_1 if S_2 is the union of sets S_3 and S_4 which are each narrower than S_1.*

$$S_1 \supseteq S_2 \;\Rightarrow\; S_1 \supseteq S_3 \wedge S_1 \supseteq S_4 \wedge union(S_3, S_4, S_2)$$

Widening We now give the transformation rules for increasing the size of interpretations or axiom sets. These are duals of the ones we used for narrowing above, so rule 9 below is a dual of rule 1 above, and so on.

Refinement 9 *The interpretation of axiom set A_2 is wider or equal to that of A_1 if we can deductively extend A_1 to give axiom set I_1 and that set widens to A_2.*

$$i(A_1) \subseteq i(A_2) \;\Rightarrow\; \mathbf{extended(A_1, I_1)} \wedge a(I_1) \subseteq a(A_2)$$

Refinement 10 *The interpretation of axiom set A_2 is wider or equal to that of A_1 if A_2 is composed of relaxed versions of all of the axioms of A_1. This uses the predicate $map\_all(S_1, E_1, R, E_2, S_2)$ which is true if every element E_1 of set S_1 maps via the relation R to a corresponding element, E_2 of S_2.*

$$i(A_1) \subseteq i(A_2) \;\Rightarrow\; map\_all(A_1, X_1, \mathbf{relaxed(A_1, X_1, X_2)}, X_2, A_2)$$

Refinement 11 *The interpretation of axiom set A_2 is wider or equal to that of A_1 if A_2 is obtained from A_1 by generalisation.*

$$i(A_1) \subseteq i(A_2) \;\Rightarrow\; \mathbf{generalised(A_1, A_2)}$$

Refinement 12 *Axiom set A_2 contains A_1 if A_1 is a subset formed from A_2.*

$$a(A_1) \subseteq a(A_2) \;\Rightarrow\; \mathbf{subseteq(A_1, A_2)}$$

Refinement 13 *Axiom set A_2 contains A_1 if all axioms of A_1 pass some filtering test which allows them to belong to A_2. This uses the predicate $apply\_all(S_1, E_1, T, S_2)$ which is true if every element E_1 of set S_1 satisfies test T, with S_2 being a set of all such elements.*

$$a(A_1) \subseteq a(A_2) \;\Rightarrow\; apply\_all(A_1, X_1, \mathbf{filtered(A_1, X_1)}, A_2)$$

Refinement 14 *Either the axiom set or interpretation of A_2 is wider than or equal to the corresponding axiom set or interpretation of A_1 (so T below must be i or a) if there are elements which can be added to A_1 to form A_2.*

$$T(A_1) \subseteq T(A_2) \;\Rightarrow\; \mathbf{additions(A_1, A_3)} \wedge union(A_3, A_1, A_2)$$

Refinement 15 *The widening relation is transitive.*

$$S_1 \subseteq S_2 \;\Rightarrow\; S_1 \subseteq S_3 \wedge S_3 \subseteq S_2$$

Refinement 16 *Set S_2 is wider than or equal to set S_1 if S_2 is the intersection of sets S_3 and S_4 which are each wider than S_1.*

$$S_1 \subseteq S_2 \;\Rightarrow\; S_1 \subseteq S_3 \wedge S_1 \subseteq S_4 \wedge intersection(S_3, S_4, S_2)$$

3.3 Domain-Specific Example

From Section 3.1 we have a language in which to describe generic inference strategies and Section 3.2 gives us transformation rules with which we may refine these to specialised, task-specific definitions. But could this ever be useful in practice? We address this issue by taking an example from what is (arguably) the most commonly used informal design method in the knowledge-based systems community: KADS ([13]). The entire KADS method is complex and still evolving but a key element of it is a library of inference structure diagrams which often form the starting point for system design. We restrict our attention to one diagram from this part of the KADS method.

Numerous KADS inference structures for classification tasks have been described. The diagram gives one form of classification in the KADS style. The boxes in the diagram are (roughly speaking) sources of knowledge on some topic while the ellipses are (roughly speaking) functions which relate knowledge sources. The idea is that we have some observations about the objects we wish to classify and some background theory which relates objects to classes through distinguishing features. Classification takes place by generating possible classes to which an object might belong; based on these classes, specifying attributes which may discriminate them; from these obtaining features for comparison; and matching these against the attributes of the objects which are known from our observations. Once this has been done sufficiently either to provide a close match or signal a mismatch, the inference mechanism produces an answer in the form of a truth value.

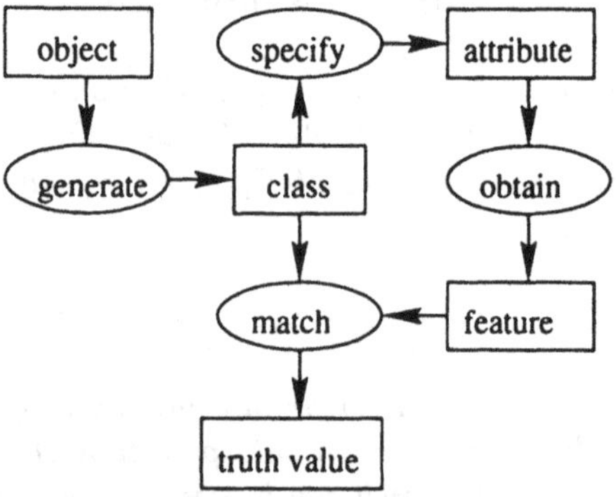

The diagram above is informal because we cannot say precisely what the interpretation of its knowledge sources or functions should be. Two solutions to this problem have already been explored. The most common solution (and the one adopted in "mainstream" KADS) is to add a mixture of formal and informal information to say more about what the inference mechanism should do. This is useful but it doesn't provide a formal route from early models (like the one above) to executable specifications. A second solution, explored by projects like ML^2 ([12], [11]), is to attempt to give a formal semantics for the style of design used in KADS. The difficulty with this route is that the resultant formal system is complex (since the way KADS diagrams are interpreted in practice is complex) and therefore it is difficult to design lightweight systems of refinement for it.

A third solution, explored in this section, is to look within logic for notions of specification and requirement which do a job similar (but not necessarily equivalent) to the KADS inference structures; then relate these to the original KADS methods. We demonstrate this in the remainder of this section.

First we must invent a generic way of describing classification tasks. One way of viewing this sort of task is that classification relates three key elements: the theory used in classification; the observations of a particular situation which are used to support classification; and the classification itself. Taking this view, we can define classification recursively. We have a classification when the theory allows it. If the theory does not allow it then we extend the theory by selecting appropriate observations and enlarging the theory as a consequence of the additional information. This view is expressed formally by the inference strategy below.

We have a classification, C, based on a theory, T, and observations, O, if the interpretation of the theory includes that of the classification or if a subset, A, of the observations, O, when added to the theory gives some enlarged theory T_n from which we can produce a classification. Those observations added to the theory when extending it are removed from the set of observations to be considered.

$$
\begin{aligned}
&classified(T,O,C) \leftarrow i(T) \supseteq i(C) &(1)\\
&classified(T,O,C) \leftarrow a(O) \supseteq a(A)\wedge &(2)\\
&\qquad union(A,T,T_1)\wedge\\
&\qquad i(T_1) \subseteq i(T_n)\wedge\\
&\qquad remove(A,O,O_n)\wedge\\
&\qquad classified(T_n,O_n,C)
\end{aligned}
$$

We can refine this high-level definition of classification by applying the transformation rules from Section 3.2. For example, we can make the following transformations:

- Applying refinement 1 to the first condition of clause 2 gives us the transformation:

$$i(T) \supseteq i(C) \;\Rightarrow\; \mathbf{extended(T, I_1)} \wedge a(I_1) \supseteq a(C)$$

  the result of which we further refine using rule 5 as follows:

$$a(I_1) \supseteq a(C) \;\Rightarrow\; apply\_some(I_1, X_1, \mathbf{filtered(I_1, X_1)}, C)$$

  finally giving the new first condition of clause 1 as:

$$\mathbf{extended(T, I_1)} \wedge apply\_some(I_1, X_1, \mathbf{filtered(I_1, X_1)}, C)$$

- Applying refinement 7 to the first condition of clause 2 gives us the transformation:

$$a(O) \supseteq a(A) \;\Rightarrow\; a(O) \supseteq S_3 \wedge S_3 \supseteq a(A)$$

then we refine the left hand side of the result (instantiating S_3 to $a(A_2)$) with rule 4:

$$a(O) \supseteq a(A_2) \;\Rightarrow\; \mathbf{subseteq(A_2, O)}$$

and we refine the right hand side of the result with rule 5:

$$a(A_2) \supseteq a(A) \;\Rightarrow\; apply\_some(A_2, X_1, \mathbf{filtered(A_2, X_1)}, A)$$

finally giving the new first condition of clause 2 as:

$$\mathbf{subseteq(A_2, O)} \wedge apply\_some(A_2, X_1, \mathbf{filtered(A_2, X_1)}, A)$$

- Applying refinement 14 to the third condition of clause 2 gives us the transformation:

$$i(T_1) \subseteq i(T_n) \;\Rightarrow\; \mathbf{additions(T_1, A_3)} \wedge union(A_3, T_1, T_n)$$

These refinements produce the more specific definition of classification given below:

$$\begin{aligned} classified(T, O, C) \leftarrow\ & \mathbf{extended(T, I_1)} \wedge && (3) \\ & apply\_some(I_1, X_1, \mathbf{filtered(I_1, X_1)}, C) && \\ classified(T, O, C) \leftarrow\ & \mathbf{subseteq(A_2, O)} \wedge && (4) \\ & apply\_some(A_2, X_1, \mathbf{filtered(A_2, X_1)}, A) \wedge && \\ & union(A, T, T_1) \wedge && \\ & \mathbf{additions(T_1, A_3)} \wedge && \\ & union(A_3, T_1, T_n) \wedge && \\ & remove(A, O, O_n) \wedge && \\ & classified(T_n, O_n, C) && \end{aligned}$$

This definition is more specific than the one we started with, since it stipulates particular ways of narrowing or widening the axiom sets and interpretations. However, it makes no commitment to the domain in which we might apply this sort of classification. That is the focus of the next section.

3.4 Domain-Specific Refinements

At this point we have a description of classification which is task-specific (it describes a particular class of classification problems) but it is not domain-specific because we have not committed ourselves to the details necessary to apply it. To do this, we first describe the axioms which we expect to appear in the theory, observation and classification arguments (T, O and C in clauses 3 and 4 above). For our example, suppose that these are as follows:

- The theory axioms are either of the form $classifiable(C(X), [A_1, \ldots, A_n]) \leftarrow A_1(X), \ldots, A_n(X)$ (where C is a classification for object X and each A is an attribute of it) or are of the form $consequence(A(X)) \leftarrow A_1(X), \ldots, A_m(X)$ (where A is an attribute of X considered to follow from knowing the other attributes A_i).

- The observational axioms are attribute definitions of the form $A(X)$, where A is an attribute and X some object.
- The classification will contain axioms of the form $is\_classified(C(X), [A_1, \ldots, A_n])$, where C is a classification for object X and each A is an attribute used to classify it.

A typical goal which we would like to satisfy might be:

$$\begin{array}{l} classified([consequence(fast(X)) \leftarrow red(X), \\ \quad classifiable(sports\_car(C_1), [fast]) \leftarrow fast(C_1), \\ \quad classifiable(sports\_car(C_2), [small, light]) \leftarrow small(C_2) \wedge light(C_2)], \\ \quad\quad [red(car21), small(car21), light(car21)], \\ \quad\quad Classes) \end{array}$$

and we would expect this to instantiate $Classes$ to either $[is\_classified(sports\_car(car21), [fast])]$ or $[is\_classified(sports\_car(car21), [small, light])]$, depending on the choice of observations it includes in the classification.

The task-specific template can be refined to produce this behaviour, provided that designers in the domain have appropriate refinements available from a domain-specific library. To provide variety in design there should be a number of possible refinements available to the designer but, to keep our example short, we supply exactly those needed for this problem. These are refinements 17 to 21 below.

Refinement 17 *A form of extension from axiom set, A, to axiom set, E, is by forming a classification.*

$$\mathbf{extended(A, E)} \Rightarrow form\_classification(A, E)$$

A classification is formed by finding the set of classes, C, which are classifiable based on attribute set, S.

$$\begin{array}{l} form\_classification(A, E) \leftarrow \\ \quad setof(is\_classified(C, S), satisfy(classifiable(C, S), A), E) \end{array}$$

A goal, G, is satisfiable from axiom set A if it appears in A or can be derived from A by satisfying the conditions of a clause; or if it is a conjunction and both parts can be satisfied from A.

$$\begin{array}{rl} satisfy(G, A) & \leftarrow member(G, A) \\ satisfy(G, A) & \leftarrow member((G \leftarrow P), A) \wedge satisfy(P, A) \\ satisfy((G_1, G_2), A) & \leftarrow satisfy(G_1, A) \wedge satisfy(G_2, A) \end{array}$$

Refinement 18 *A form of filtering of axiom X, given axiom set, A, is to show that X is the best classification known from A.*

$$\mathbf{filtered(A, X)} \Rightarrow best\_classification(A, X)$$

We define the best classification to be C_1 with supporting attributes, S, if there is no other classification, C_2, known from axioms A with a larger number of supporting attributes.

$$\begin{aligned}&best\_classification(A, is\_classified(C_1, S_1)) \leftarrow \\ &\quad length(S_1, L_1)\wedge \\ &\quad not\begin{pmatrix} member(is\_classified(C_2, S_2), A)\wedge \\ not(C_2 = C_1)\wedge \\ length(S_2, L_2)\wedge \\ L_2 > L_1 \end{pmatrix}\end{aligned}$$

Refinement 19 *A form of filtering of axiom X is to test whether it is an attribute definition.*

$$\mathbf{filtered(A, X)} \;\Rightarrow\; is\_attribute(X)$$

Any object, X is allowed to have the attributes, red, light or small.

$$\begin{gathered} is\_attribute(red(X)) \\ is\_attribute(light(X)) \\ is\_attribute(small(X)) \end{gathered}$$

Refinement 20 *A way of forming the subset, A_1, from set, A_2, is by choosing any one of the elements of A_2 as a single-element subset.*

$$\mathbf{subseteq(A_1, A_2)} \;\Rightarrow\; choose\_one(A_1, A_2)$$

We have a single element subset of set A for any element of A.

$$choose\_one([X], A) \leftarrow member(X, A)$$

Refinement 21 *Axiom set A_2 is one which may be added to axiom set A_1 if the axioms in A_2 are considered consequences for classification in A_1.*

$$\mathbf{additions(A_1, A_2)} \;\Rightarrow\; consequences(A_1, A_2)$$

Consequences, A_2, are those axioms, C, which satisfy the consequence definitions in A_1.

$$consequences(A_1, A_2) \leftarrow findall(C, \begin{pmatrix} satisfy(consequence(C), A_1)\wedge \\ not(member(C, A_1)) \end{pmatrix}, A_2)$$

By applying the domain-specific transformations above to the appropriate subgoals of clauses 3 and 4 we obtain the final definition given in clauses 5 and 6 below.

$$\begin{aligned} classified(T, O, C) \leftarrow\ & form\_classification(T, I_1)\wedge \\ & apply\_some(I_1, X_1, best\_classification(I_1, X_1), C) \end{aligned} \quad (5)$$

$$
\begin{aligned}
classified(T, O, C) \leftarrow\ & choose\_one(A_2, O) \wedge \\
& apply\_some(A_2, X_1, is\_attribute(X_1), A) \wedge \\
& union(A, T, T_1) \wedge \\
& consequences(T_1, A_3) \wedge \\
& union(A_3, T_1, T_n) \wedge \\
& remove(A, O, O_n) \wedge \\
& classified(T_n, O_n, C)
\end{aligned} \tag{6}
$$

We can execute this in the normal Prolog style and to produce the behaviour required at the beginning of this section.

Our example has shown a notion of refinement which connects different levels of design but we do not claim that the particular refinement system which we have demonstrated is ideal. Much more work remains to be done to make it mathematically and pragmatically stable. For instance, we have not shown formally that our refinement rules are correct - nor have we argued that they give complete coverage of a particular class of logic programs. This is because we do not yet believe that we have the most appropriate set of rules. In this context, appropriateness is not simply a mathematical question because we will require refinements to be chosen by humans. Therefore we expect the details of this method to change as this aspect of our work matures.

4 Conclusions

Strong notions of pragmatics are necessary in the application of formal methods because engineers cannot afford to waste time trying numerous inappropriate (but mathematically correct) styles of description before learning ones which are appropriate to their style of work. Our descriptions of pragmatics are based on patterns of use of logic, tempered with experience in how and where to apply these patterns. In Section 2 we have shown three such patterns; described the problems we have tackled using them; and explained some of the factors which limit the sizes of our systems.

One of the advantages of systems with explicit notions of pragmatics should be that they can be used cooperatively. If we possess additional knowledge about how a specification has been built then perhaps we can use this knowledge in other systems which are used to extend or adapt the existing definition. This issue isn't well explored but it is suggested by the methods we have described. The notions of parameterisation from Section 2.1 can be used to supply components for later extension by the techniques of Section 2.2. The products of either of these two methods could be augmented by meta-interpretation of the sort described in Section 2.3. An example of what we can do with existing tools is given in [7].

However, the fact that we can potentially communicate between different forms of description using a shared formal language doesn't mean that notions of design lifecycle emerge from the blend of methods. Just as was the case for individual methods, we need to study the pragmatics of refinement from high-level to detailed designs. In Section 3 we introduced an example of this sort of system and demonstrate a parallel between it and an existing, informal method.

References

1. A. W. Bowles, D. Robertson, W. W. Vasconcelos, M. Vargas-Vera, and D. Bental. Applying Prolog Programming Techniques. *International Journal of Human-Computer Studies*, 41(3):329–350, September 1994. Also as Research Paper 641, Dept of Artificial Intelligence, University of Edinburgh.
2. V. Brilhante. Inform-logic: A system for representing uncertainty in ecological models. Technical report, Department of Artificial Intelligence, University of Edinburgh, 1996. MSc Thesis.
3. T.S. Gegg-Harrison. Basic Prolog schemata. Technical Report CS-1989-20, Department of Computer Science, Duke University, September 1989.
4. J. Goguen. Principles of parameterised programming. In A. Biggerstaff and A. Perlis, editors, *Software Reusability Volume 1: Concepts and Models*, pages 159–225. Addison Wesley, 1989.
5. J. Hesketh, D. Robertson, N. Fuchs, and A. Bundy. Lightweight formalisation in support of requirements engineering. *Journal of Automated Software Engineering*, 5(2):183–210, 1998.
6. M. Kirschenbaum, A. Lakhotia, and L.S. Sterling. Skeletons and techniques for Prolog programming. Tr 89-170, Case Western Reserve University, 1989.
7. D. Robertson. Distributed specification. In *Proceedings of the 12th European Conference on Artificial Intelligence*, Budapest, Hungary, August 1996.
8. D. Robertson. An empirical study of the LSS specification toolkit in use. In *Proceedings of the 8th International Conference on Software Engineering and Knowledge Engineering, Nevada, USA*. Knowledge Systems Institute, Illinois, 1996. ISBN 0-9641699-3-2.
9. D. Robertson, A. Bundy, R. Muetzelfeldt, M. Haggith, and M Uschold. *Eco-Logic: Logic-Based Approaches to Ecological Modelling.* MIT Press (Logic Programming Series), 1991. ISBN 0-262-18143-6.
10. D.T. Sannella and L.A. Wallen. A calculus for the construction of modular Prolog programs. *Journal of Logic Programming*, 12:147–177, 1992.
11. F. van Harmelen and M. Aben. Structure-preserving specification languages for knowledge-based systems. *International Journal of Human-Computer Studies*, 44:187–212, 1996.
12. F. van Harmelen and J.R. Balder. (ML)2: A formal language for kads models of expertise. *Knowledge Acquisition*, 4(1), 1992.
13. B. J. Wielinga, A. Th. Schreiber, and J. A. Breuker. KADS: A modelling approach to knowledge engineering. *Knowledge Acquistion Journal*, 4(1):5–53, 1992. Special issue 'The KADS approach to knowledge engineering'. Reprinted in: Buchanan, B. and Wilkins, D. editors (1992), *Readings in Knowledge Acquisition and Learning*, San Mateo, California, Morgan Kaufmann, pp. 92-116.
14. L.U. Yalcinalp and L.S. Sterling. Uncertainty reasoning in Prolog with layered meta-interpreters. Technical Report TR 90-110, Center for Automation and Intelligent Systems Research, Case Western Reserve University, Ohio, USA, 1990.

Using Decision Procedures to Accelerate Domain-Specific Deductive Synthesis Systems

Jeffrey Van Baalen and Steven Roach
M.S. 269-2
NASA Ames Research Center
Moffet Field, CA
{jvb, sroach}@ptolemy.arc.nasa.gov

Abstract. This paper describes a class of decision procedures that we have found useful for efficient, domain-specific deductive synthesis, and a method for integrating this type of procedure into a general-purpose refutation-based theorem prover. We suggest that this is a large and interesting class of procedures and show how to integrate these procedures to accelerate a general-purpose theorem prover doing deductive synthesis. While much existing research on decision procedures has been either in isolation or in the context of interfacing procedures to non-refutation-based theorem provers, this appears to be the first reported work on decision procedures in the context of refutation-based deductive synthesis where witnesses must be found.

1 Introduction

This paper describes a class of decision procedures that we have found useful for efficient, domain-specific deductive synthesis, and a method for integrating this type of procedure into a general-purpose refutation-based theorem prover. These procedures are called *closure-based ground literal satisfiability procedures.* We suggest that this is a large and interesting class of procedures and show how to integrate these procedures to accelerate a general-purpose theorem prover doing deductive synthesis. We also describe some results we have observed from our implementation.

Amphion/NAIF[17] is a domain-specific, high-assurance software synthesis system. It takes an abstract specification of a problem in solar system mechanics, such as "when will a signal sent from the Cassini spacecraft to Earth be blocked by the planet Saturn?", and automatically synthesizes a FORTRAN program to solve it. Amphion/NAIF uses deductive synthesis (a.k.a proofs-as-programs [6]) in which programs are synthesized as a byproduct of theorem proving. In this paradigm, problem specifications are of the form $\forall\vec{x}\exists\vec{y}[P(\vec{x}, \vec{y})]$, where $\vec{x}$ and $\vec{y}$ are vectors of variables. We are only interested in constructive proofs in which witnesses have been produced for each of the variables in $\vec{y}$. These witnesses are program fragments.

Deductive synthesis has two potential advantages over competing synthesis technologies. The first is the well-known but unrealized promise that developing a declarative domain theory is more cost-effective than developing a special-purpose synthesis engine. The second advantage is that since synthesized programs are correct relative to a domain theory, verification is confined to domain theories. Because declarative domain theories are simpler than programs, they are presumably easier to verify. This is of particular interest when synthesized code must be high-assurance.

P. Flener (Ed.): LOPSTR'98, LNCS 1559, pp. 61-80, 1999.

The greatest disadvantage that general-purpose deductive synthesis systems have is that systems based on theorem proving[1] are almost always unacceptably inefficient unless the domain theory and theorem prover are carefully tuned. This tuning process consists of iteratively inspecting proof traces, reformulating the domain theory, and/or adjusting parameters of the theorem prover, a process that usually requires a large amount of time and expertise in automated reasoning.

In order to assist in constructing efficient synthesis systems, we are developing a tool, Meta-Amphion [10], the goal of which is: given a domain theory, automatically generate an efficient, specialized deductive synthesis system such as Amphion/NAIF. The key is a technique, that is under development, that generates efficient decision procedures for subtheories of the domain theory and then integrates them with a general-purpose refutation-based theorem prover. Some success has been achieved with this automated technique [14]. However, significantly more research is required to enhance the automated process of designing decision procedures to replace subsets of a theory.

However, we have found that deductive synthesis systems can be manually tuned very effectively by manually performing the process we are trying to automate. Hence, one can accelerate a deductive synthesis system by manually inspecting a domain theory and identifying subtheories for which we already have or can construct replacement decision procedures. This technique has, in our experience, been far easier and has often produced more efficient systems than the traditional technique of inspecting proof traces and tuning parameters. For instance, Figure 1 summarizes our experience with the Amphion/NAIF system. It is a graph of the performance of three different versions of Amphion/NAIF. It shows the number of inference steps required to find proofs as the input problem specification size (number of literals) grows for an un-optimized system, a traditionally hand-tuned system, and a system tuned by replacing subtheories with decision procedures (Tops). Figure 2 compares the traditionally hand-tuned system vs. the system tuned with decision procedures (Tops).

While much existing research on decision procedures has been either in isolation [11][16][5] or in the context of interfacing procedures to non-refutation-based theorem provers [13][2], we are unaware of any work done on decision procedures in the context of refutation-based deductive synthesis where witnesses must be found. This paper presents a decision procedure interface to a theorem prover with several inference rules including binary resolution and paramodulation. These inference rules have been extended to enable the class of ground literal satisfiability procedures to be integrated with the theorem prover in a straightforward and uniform manner. Procedures can be plugged in on a theory-by-theory basis, allowing the theorem prover to be tailored to particular theories. We show that when these procedures have the additional property of being *closure based*, they can be used to produce witnesses for deductive synthesis. The class of ground literal satisfiability procedures is such that the witnesses produced are

1. Amphion/NAIF utilizes a refutation-based theorem prover. We initially considered using Prolog; however, the domain theory required extensive use of equality, making the Prolog implementations available at the time inappropriate.

typically straight-line program fragments that are incorporated into larger programs produced by the general-purpose theorem prover.

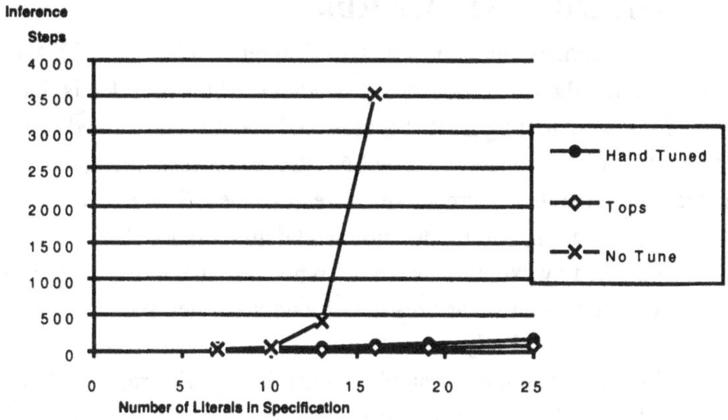

Figure 1: A comparison of the performance of three different versions of Amphion/NAIF.

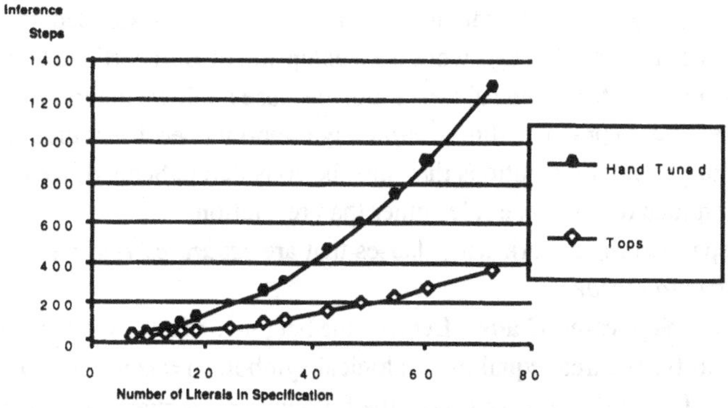

Figure 2: A closer comparison of the two tuned versions of Amphion/NAIF.

Section 2 introduces *separated clause notation*, the notation used by our extended inference rules. The motivation for these rules is that they enable decision procedures to be integrated with the theorem prover and used in place of subsets of a theory. The integration of procedures requires procedures that compute satisfiability and procedures that compute entailment. Section 3 describes procedures for testing satisfiability in a theory. Section 4 describes decision procedures that test entailment in a theory and that compute witnesses for deductive synthesis. The example used in Sections 2-4 is in the domain of LISP list structure and involves a decision procedure originally developed by Nelson and Oppen. This is used for simplicity of presentation. Then in Section 5, a decision procedure from the Amphion/NAIF domain is described. Section 6 describes the implementation of the interface and the results of using procedures like the one described in Section 5 for deductive synthesis in Amphion/NAIF. Finally, Section 7 discusses related work and concludes.

2 Separated Inference Rules

This section describes our extension to the inference rules in the SNARK [17] theorem prover enabling the use of decision procedures. The basic idea is that all clauses are separated into two parts: a part that is reasoned about by integrated decision procedures and a part that is reasoned about by SNARK. First, *separated clause* form is defined, and then the separated inference rules are described. SNARK has inference rules resolution, hyperresolution, paramodulation, and demodulation. The overall extension has been accomplished by extending each inference rule in a uniform manner. This paper only discusses separated binary resolution and separated paramodulation, but the other rules are extended similarly.

Separated binary resolution is similar to resolution with restricted quantifiers or *RQ-resolution* [3]. Recall that, given a first-order theory T and a first-order formula Φ, we prove $T \models \Phi$ by refutation by showing that $T \cup \{\neg\Phi\}$ is unsatisfiable. Assuming that T is satisfiable, this amounts to showing that no model of T is a model of $\neg\Phi$. The general idea of our binary resolution rule (as well as RQ-resolution) is as follows. If there is a method for determining satisfiability of a formula relative to a theory $T_2 \cup \{\neg\Phi\}$, we prove $T \models \Phi$ by showing that no model of T_1 can be extended to a model of $T_2 \cup \{\neg\Phi\}$, where $T_2 = T - T_1$. Our work is an extension of Burckert's in two ways. First, our resolution rule differs from RQ-resolution because it allows function symbols to appear in T_2 and $\neg\Phi$. In practice, this is extremely important because it drastically reduces the number of potential resolutions that must be considered. Second, we have extended the separation idea to inference rules other than resolution.

The separated rules work with clauses that are *separated relative* to a subtheory, called a *restriction theory*.

Definition 2.1 (Separated Clause) Let L be the language of a theory T, a first-order theory with equality. We treat equality as a logical symbol, so = is not in L. Let $L_1 \subseteq L$ be the language of $T_1 \subseteq T$. A clause C with the following properties is said to be *separated relative to* T_1:

1. C is arranged into $C_1 \vee C_2$, where both C_1 and C_2 are disjunctions of literals (i.e., clauses).
2. All the function and relation symbols in C_1 come from L_1 and all the function and relation symbols in C_2 come from $L - L_1$.

Notice that $C_1 \vee C_2$ can be written $\overline{C_1} \Rightarrow C_2$, where $\overline{C_1}$ is the negation of C_1. Since C_1 is a disjunction of literals, $\overline{C_1}$ is a conjunction of the negations of the literals in C_1. If $C = [\overline{C_1} \Rightarrow C_2]$ is a clause separated relative to some theory, $\overline{C_1}$ is called the *restriction* of C and C_2 is called the *matrix* of C. A set of clauses is separated relative to a theory if each of the clauses in the set is separated relative to the theory.

Constant (0-ary function) symbols are not discussed in the definition of separation because they may appear in C_1 or C_2 regardless of which language they are in. As explained below, this is a property of the mechanism for passing information between the matrix and the restriction of clauses as they are manipulated by our extended inference rules.

A clause is separated in two steps. In the first step, literals are placed in the restriction or matrix of a clause based on their predicate symbol. In the second step, each non-constant term t in the restriction whose head symbol is in L-L_1 is replaced by a new variable x, and xt is disjoined to the matrix. Similarly, each non-constant term in the matrix whose head symbol is in L_1 is replaced by a new variable x, and $x=t$ is conjoined to the restriction.

Example 2.1 Suppose we have a theory T_1 of LISP list structure whose non-logical symbols are the function symbols *head, tail, cons,* and *nil.*. Then the separation of the formula *tail(K)nil* relative to T_1 is $(x=tail(K)) \Rightarrow (xnil)$.

Separated binary resolution computes a resolvant of two clauses, C' and C'', each separated relative to a theory T_1. This resolvant is also a clause separated relative to T_1. Informally, a resolvant is computed as follows. First, ordinary resolution is performed on the matrices (right hand sides) of C' and C'' to form the matrix of the resolvant. The resulting substitution σ is used in forming the restriction of the resolvant which is the conjunction of the restrictions of C' and C'' with the substitution σ applied. If the new restriction is unsatisfiable in T_1, the resolvant is *true* and, as a practical matter for resolution refutation, can be discarded.

Definition 2.2 (Separated Binary Resolution) Let C' and C'' be variable disjoint clauses separated relative to a theory T_l. Let $C' = \alpha_1 \wedge \ldots \wedge \alpha_n \Rightarrow l_1 \vee Q$ and $C'' = \beta_1 \wedge \ldots \wedge \beta_p \Rightarrow l_2 \vee R$, where Q and R are (possibly empty) clauses and $n,p0$. If l_l and $\bar{l}_2$ unify with most general unifier σ and $\exists[(\alpha_1 \wedge \ldots \wedge \alpha_n \wedge \beta_1 \wedge \ldots \wedge \beta_p)\sigma]$ is satisfiable in T_l, the *separated resolvant* of C' and C'' is the separation[2] of $(\alpha_1 \wedge \ldots \wedge \alpha_n \wedge \beta_1 \wedge \ldots \wedge \beta_p)\sigma \Rightarrow (Q \vee R)\sigma$.

Example 2.2 The third clause below is a separated resolvant of the first two clauses.

$(x = cons(u, v)) \wedge (K = cons(u, z)) \wedge (w = cons(z_1, nil)) \Rightarrow (z \neq append(v, w))$

$(x_1 = tail(K)) \wedge (y_1 = \mathrm{cons}(u_1, nil)) \Rightarrow ((x_1 = append(front(x_1), y_1)) \vee (u \neq \mathrm{last}(x_1)))$

2. The separation of the resolvant does not have to be a separate step. However, it simplifies the presentation.

$$\left(\begin{array}{l}(x = cons(u, v)) \wedge (K = cons(u, z)) \wedge (w = cons(z_1, nil)) \\ \wedge ((z = tail(K)) \wedge (w = cons(u_1, nil)))\end{array}\right) \Rightarrow (u \neq last(z)) \vee (v \neq front(z))$$

The literal z *append(v,w)*(in the first clause) is unified with $x_1 = append(front(x_1), y_1)$ (in the second clause) producing the unifier $\{x_1 \leftarrow z, v \leftarrow front(z), w \leftarrow y_1\}$. The matrix of the resolvant is obtained as in ordinary binary resolution and the restriction is the result of applying the unifier above to the conjunction of the restrictions of the two parents. The resulting clause is separated, moving *front(z)* to the matrix.

Lemma 2.1 (Soundness of separated binary resolution) Let Ψ be a set of separated clauses, and let ψ be a clause derived from two elements of Ψ by separated binary resolution. If M is a model of Ψ, M is a model of $\Psi \cup \{\psi\}$.

Proof: Soundness follows immediately from the soundness of ordinary binary resolution. The satisfiability check on the restriction of the resolvant is not necessary for soundness of the rule overall. Rather, if the restriction of the resolvant is unsatisfiable, the separated clause is a tautology. []

Definition 2.3 (Separated Paramodulation) Let $l[t]$ be a literal with at least one occurrence of the term t. Let C' and C'' be variable disjoint clauses separated relative to a theory T_1. Let $C' = \alpha_1 \wedge \ldots \wedge \alpha_n \Rightarrow l[t] \vee Q$ and $C'' = \beta_1 \wedge \ldots \wedge \beta_p \Rightarrow (r = s) \vee R$, where Q and R are (possibly empty) clauses and n,p 0 If t and r unify with most general unifier σ and $\exists[(\alpha_1 \wedge \ldots \wedge \alpha_n \wedge \beta_1 \wedge \ldots \wedge \beta_p)\sigma]$ is satisfiable in T_1, a *separated paramodulant* of C' and C'' is the separation of

$$(\alpha_1 \wedge \ldots \wedge \alpha_n \wedge \beta_1 \wedge \ldots \wedge \beta_p)\sigma \Rightarrow l\sigma[s\sigma] \vee Q\sigma \vee R\sigma$$

where $l\sigma[s\sigma]$ represents the result obtained by replacing a single occurrence of $t\sigma$ in $l\sigma$ by $s\sigma$.

As with resolution, soundness of separated paramodulation follows from the soundness of the ordinary paramodulation rule.

An ordinary resolution refutation of a set of clauses C consists of a sequence of clauses where each clause is an element of C or is derived from two preceding clauses in the sequence by binary resolution or paramodulation. An ordinary refutation is *closed* when the empty clause, which we denote [], is derived. A *separated refutation* is a sequence of separated clauses derived using the separated rules. Unlike an ordinary refutation, a separated refutation is not necessarily closed when a clause with an empty matrix is derived. Instead, in general, there is a set of clauses $\{C_1 \Rightarrow [], \ldots, C_n \Rightarrow []\}$ each of which has a separated refutation such that $T \models [\exists C_1 \vee \ldots \vee \exists C_n]$, where $\exists F$ is the existential closure of F. A proof of this fact can be found in [Burckert91] where it is also shown that this disjunction is finite so long as T_1 is first-order (this is a consequence of Compactness). Hence, a *closed separated refutation* is a separated refutation that ends with a collection of separated clauses all of whose matrices are empty such that the existential closure of the disjunction of their restrictions is a theorem of T_1.

Lemma 2.2 (Soundness of separated refutation) If the separation of a set of clauses C has a closed separated refutation, C is unsatisfiable.

Proof: This result follows immediately from soundness of separated binary resolution and separated paramodulation, and the fact that if a set of separated clauses is unsatisfiable, so is the unseparated clause set. []

An inference system with ordinary binary resolution and ordinary paramodulation is complete if reflexivity axioms are included. In order for a system including separated versions of these rules to be complete, separated versions of congruence axioms for some theory predicate and function symbols are added. An example of a predicate congruence axiom is $(x = y) \Rightarrow (P(x) \Leftrightarrow P(y))$. Space does not permit a proof of the completeness of separated resolution and paramodulation here.

[3] points out that for some restriction theories, closed separated refutations can always be obtained by considering the entailment of the restrictions of only individual clauses. For instance, it is proven that if T_I is a definite theory, i.e., a theory that can be written as a set of definite clauses, closed separated refutations are guaranteed for query clauses whose restrictions contain only positive literals. This paper focuses on the case where entailment of only single restrictions needs to be checked. When this is not the case, getting a closed separated refutation requires an additional inference rule (such as consensus [7]) or it requires decision procedures to be used in a more complicated manner than presented here. Thus far, the simpler case has been sufficient in our work on deductive synthesis.

The definition of a separated clause often prevents the derivation of clauses with empty matrices when terms that are not in the restriction language appear. These terms keep getting separated back into the matrix. For instance in example 2.2 above because *front* is in L-L_I, instead of substituting *front(z)* into the restriction of the resolvant, $\vee$ *front(z)*is disjoined in the matrix. In such cases, the matrix of a clause will end up containing only literals of the form t $x$for some variable x and some term t in the language L-L_I not containing x, Such a clause can be viewed as having an empty matrix with the disequalities considered as substitutions for variables in the restriction. Our system completes refutations by applying these substitutions to the restriction (rendering the clause no longer separated) and then checking the entailment of the resultant restriction with symbols in L-L_I uninterpreted. This can be seen in the last step of the following example.

Example 2.3. Let T_{LISP} be a theory of LISP list structure with function symbols *head*, *tail*, *cons*, and *nil*. Given the theory T:

$(x = x) \wedge (K \neq nil) \wedge (tail(K) \neq nil)$

$(K \neq nil) \Rightarrow ((tail(K) \neq nil) \Rightarrow tail(K) = append(front(tail(K)), cons(last(tail(K), nil))))$

$append(cons(u, v), w) = cons(u, append(v, w))$

$(x \neq nil) \Rightarrow (x = cons(head(x), tail(x)))$

$(head(cons(x, y)) = x) \wedge (tail(cons(x, y)) = y) \wedge (cons(x, y) \neq nil)$

we want to show that $\exists y_1, z_1[K = append(y_1, cons(z_1, nil))]$ is a theorem of T. In this theory, the functions *front* (which "computes" all but the last of a list) and *last* (which "computes" the last element of a list) are constrained in terms of the functions *append, cons,* and *tail.* Witnesses found in proving the theorem above can be viewed as synthesized definitions of the functions *front* (a witness for y_1) and *last* (a witness for z_1) under the assumption for an input list *K*, that *K nil*and *tail(K) nil.*Note that we make these assumptions here so as to focus on the witnesses found by a decision procedure. When these assumptions are relaxed, the fragments generated by the decision procedure are incorporated into recursive definitions of *front* and *last.*

A refutation that is separated relative to T_{LISP} is given below. Clauses 1-5 below are the first three axioms above separated relative to T_{LISP}. Note that these are the clauses of $T\text{-}T_{LISP}$. The last two formulas above are axioms of T_{LISP} and are needed only in determining satisfiability and entailment of restrictions. Therefore, they do not appear in the proof. We give as justification for step 10 "substitute." The clause of this step is obtained from step 9 by treating the disequalities in the matrix as a substitution that is applied to the restriction. Since the existential closure of the restriction of 10 is a theorem of T_{LISP} (regardless of the interpretation of *front* and *last*), the proof is finished. As discussed in Section 4, the witnesses for *front* and *last* are obtained from the consequences of the restriction of step 10.

1	Given	$\Rightarrow K \neq nil$
2	Given	$(x = tail(K)) \Rightarrow x \neq nil$
3	Given	$(x = tail(K)) \wedge (y = cons(z, nil)) \wedge (w = tail(K)) \Rightarrow \left(\begin{array}{c} (x = nil) \vee (K = nil) \vee (z \neq last(w)) \vee \\ (x = append(front(x), y)) \end{array} \right)$
4	Given	$(x = cons(u, v)) \wedge (y = cons(u, z)) \Rightarrow ((append(x, w) = y) \vee (z \neq append(v, w)))$
5	Negated conclusion	$(x_1 = cons(z_1, nil)) \Rightarrow (K \neq append(y_1, x_1))$
6	resolve 4 and 5 $\{y_1 \leftarrow x, x_1 \leftarrow w, y \leftarrow K\}$	$(x = cons(u, v)) \wedge (K = cons(u, z)) \wedge (w = cons(z_1, nil)) \Rightarrow (z \neq append(v, w))$
7	resolve 1 and 3	$(x = tail(K)) \wedge (y = cons(u, nil)) \Rightarrow (x = nil) \vee (x = append(front(x), y)) \vee (u \neq last(x))$
8	resolve 2 and 7	$(x_1 = tail(K)) \wedge (y_1 = cons(u_1, nil)) \Rightarrow (x_1 = append(front(x_1), y_1)) \vee (u \neq last(x_1))$
9	resolve 8 and 6 $\left\{ \begin{array}{l} x_1 \leftarrow z, v \leftarrow front(z), \\ w \leftarrow y_1 \end{array} \right\}$	$(x = cons(u, v)) \wedge (K = cons(u, z)) \wedge (w = cons(z_1, nil))$ $(z = tail(K)) \wedge (w = cons(u_1, nil))$ $\Rightarrow (u_1 = last(z))(v \neq front(z))$

10	substitute	$(x = cons(u, front(z))) \wedge (K = cons(u, z)) \wedge$ $(w = cons(z_1, nil)) \wedge (z = tail(K)) \wedge$ $(w = cons(last(z), nil))$ $\Rightarrow [\,]$

3 Procedures for Testing Satisfiability

The separated inference rules presented in the previous section depend on procedures which perform two actions. These are (1) a test for satisfiability of restrictions; and (2) a test for entailment of the restriction of any formula which has an empty matrix. This section describes procedures that test satisfiability of restrictions. We identify a class of procedures that can be used for this purpose.

When we have a procedure for deciding satisfiability of a conjunction of literals in a theory $T_1 \subseteq T$, we use separated inference rules to prove a theorem Φ in a theory T. The clauses of T-T_1 and $\neg\Phi$ are separated relative to T_1, and the procedure is used at each inference step to test the satisfiability of derived restrictions.

The restrictions are conjunctions of literals possibly containing variables. Even though these restrictions may have variables, it is possible to use *ground literal satisfiability procedures (GLSPs)* to determine satisfiability of the conjunctions in restrictions. We do this by replacing the variables in the restrictions by new constant symbols. The fact that we can use GLSPs to determine satisfiability here is established by Theorem 3.1.

Definition 3.1 (Ground Literal Satisfiability Procedure) A *ground literal satisfiability procedure for a theory T* is a procedure that decides whether or not a conjunction of ground literals F is satisfiable in T. The language of F must be the language of T but may be extended by a collection of uninterpreted function symbols (including constants).

Theorem 3.1 (Applicability of GLSPs) If P is a GLSP for a theory T_1, P can be used to decide the satisfiability in T_1 of the restriction of any clause separated relative to T_1.

Proof: Let $C = [\overline{C_1} \Rightarrow C_2]$ be a clause separated relative to T_1. Let $x_1,\ldots,x_n$ be the variables in $\overline{C_1}$. Let σ be the substitution $\{x_1 \leftarrow c_1, \ldots, x_n \leftarrow c_n\}$, where the c_i are new uninterpreted constant symbols. Replace the restriction of C with $(x_1 = c_1) \wedge \ldots \wedge (x_n = c_n) \wedge \overline{C_1}\sigma$.

We show that (a) $(x_1 = c_1) \wedge \ldots \wedge (x_n = c_n) \wedge \overline{C_1}\sigma$ is satisfiable just in case $\overline{C_1}$ is and (b) the satisfiability of C implies the satisfiability of $((x_1 = c_1) \wedge \ldots \wedge (x_n = c_n) \wedge \overline{C_1}\sigma) \Rightarrow C_2$. Note that a conjunction of equalities constructed in this fashion is always satisfiable. Hence, we can replace any separated clause C with the clause $((x_1 = c_1) \wedge \ldots \wedge (x_n = c_n) \wedge \overline{C_1}\sigma) \Rightarrow C_2$ and decide the satisfiability of the restriction of such a clause by deciding the satisfiability of the ground conjunction $\overline{C_1}\sigma$.

(a) Since $\overline{C_1}$ is the generalization of a subconjunction of $(x_1 = c_1) \wedge \ldots \wedge (x_n = c_n) \wedge \overline{C_1}\sigma$, if $(x_1 = c_1) \wedge \ldots \wedge (x_n = c_n) \wedge \overline{C_1}\sigma$ is satisfiable, $\overline{C_1}$

is satisfiable. Now suppose $\overline{C_1}$ is satisfiable in a model M under the variable assignment I. Extend M to M^* which interprets each c_i the same as I assigns x_i. Then $<M^*, I> \models (x_1 = c_1) \wedge \ldots \wedge (x_n = c_n) \wedge \overline{C_1}\sigma$.

(b) If C is satisfiable, either C_2 is satisfiable or $\overline{C_1}$ is unsatisfiable. If C_2 is satisfiable, then $((x_1 = c_1) \wedge \ldots \wedge (x_n = c_n) \wedge \overline{C_1}\sigma) \Rightarrow C_2$ is satisfiable. Otherwise, since $\overline{C_1}$ is satisfiable just in case $(x_1 = c_1) \wedge \ldots \wedge (x_n = c_n) \wedge \overline{C_1}\sigma$ is, $(x_1 = c_1) \wedge \ldots \wedge (x_n = c_n) \wedge \overline{C_1}\sigma$ is also unsatisfiable. []

The fact that any GLSP can be interfaced to the separated inference rules is a fortunate situation because there appear to be a large number of useful GLSPs. The argument supporting this claim has three parts. First, a significant number of GLSPs have been identified and published [11][12][5]. Second, other work reports on techniques for extending some GLSPs that have been identified. Third, there are techniques that enable GLSPs to be combined.

Nelson & Oppen in [12] show how to extend a GLSP for the theory of equality with uninterpreted function symbols to the theory T_{LISP}. Their procedure can be integrated with our theorem prover and used to check satisfiability of restrictions in the running example, e.g., the restriction of the clause derived in step 9 of Example 2.1

$$(x = cons(u, v)) \wedge (K = cons(u, z)) \wedge (w = cons(z_1, nil)) \wedge (z = tail(K)) \wedge$$
$$(w = cons(u_1, nil))$$

can be checked for satisfiability in the theory of LISP list structure using Nelson & Oppen's procedure considering all the variables to be constants.

We have used techniques similar to Nelson & Oppen to construct several new procedures by extending a GLSP for congruence closure (one such procedure is described in Section 5). Also, [8] gives techniques for constructing GLSPs based on congruence closure for conjunctions of ground literals containing predicates. The essential idea is to introduce boolean constants *True* and *False* and to represent $P(t_1, \ldots, t_n)$ as $P(t_1, \ldots, t_n) = True$ and $\neg P(t_1, \ldots, t_n)$ as $\neg P(t_1, \ldots, t_n) = False$. Then, if the congruence closure graph of a conjunction F contains *True*=*False*, F is unsatisfiable.

Finally, both [11] and[16] describe techniques for combining GLSPs with disjoint languages into a GLSP for the union of these languages. Much work has been done recently on the closely related topic of combining decision procedures for equational theories [1].

Hence, we are in the convenient situation of being able to combine GLSPs to create a GLSP for a restriction theory. Given a theory T, we can design from components a decision procedure for a restriction theory. (See [10] or [14] for examples of techniques for automatically designing decision procedures from components.)

4 Deductive Synthesis Decision Procedures

This section shows that if a GLSP has the additional property of being *closure-based* it can be used not only to check satisfiability but also to check for entailment and to produce witnesses for deductive synthesis. All of the procedures mentioned in Section 3 as well as all of the procedures we have used in our work on deductive synthesis are closure based.

As discussed in Section 2, producing a closed separated refutation requires decision procedures for computing both satisfiability and entailment of restrictions. For the entailment problem, we need decision procedures that check the entailment of clauses containing existentially quantified variables and possibly also to produce witnesses for those variables. We call such procedures *literal entailment procedures*.

Definition 4.1 A *literal entailment procedure (LEP)* for a theory T is a procedure that decides for a conjunction of literals F in the language of T (possibly containing free variables) whether or not $T \models \exists F$.

While in general the satisfiability procedure and the entailment procedure for a restriction theory are separate procedures, we have found that closure-based GLSPs can also be used as LEPs.

Definition 4.2 (Closure-based satisfiability procedure) A *closure-based* satisfiability procedure for a theory T computes satisfiability in T of a conjunction of formulas Φ by constructing a finite set Ψ of ground consequences of $T \cup \{\Phi\}$ such that Ψ contains a ground literal and its negation just in case Φ is unsatisfiable in T.

The congruence closure procedure is a closure-based satisfiability procedure for the theory of equality with uninterpreted function symbols. It constructs a congruence closure graph [8] and in so doing computes a finite set of ground consequences of a conjunction of input ground equalities. As new equalities are added to a conjunction, new nodes representing terms are added to the graph and/or congruence classes are merged. Many GLSPs that extend congruence closure are also closure-based satisfiability procedures.

A closure-based GLSP with theory T can be used as a LEP as follows. Given a conjunction of literals $F(x_1,...,x_n)$, where the x_i are the existentially quantified variables in F, the procedure is used to check the satisfiability of $T \cup \{F(c_1,...,c_n)\}$, where the c_i are new constant symbols substituted for the corresponding variables. Since the procedure is closure based, in computing satisfiability, it computes consequences of $T \cup \{F(c_1,...,c_n)\}$. If consequences of the form $c_i = t_i$ are computed for all $i=1,...,n$, the procedure is run again on $\neg F(t_1,...,t_n)$. If this clause is unsatisfiable in T, witnesses have been identified for the original variables x_i. The idea of the first call to the procedure is to determine if in every model of $T \cup \{F(c_1,...,c_n)\}$, $c_i = t_i$, $i=1,...,n$. The idea of the second call is to determine if $F(t_1,...,t_n)$ is true in every model of T, i.e., $T \models \exists F$.

We illustrate how a closure-based satisfiability procedure is used as a LEP with Nelson & Oppen's GLSP for T_{LISP}.

Example 4.1 In step 10 of example 2.3, it must be shown that the existential closure of

$$F(x, u, z, w, z_1) = \begin{bmatrix}(x = cons(u, front(z))) \wedge (K = cons(u, z)) \wedge (w = cons(z_1, nil)) \wedge \\ (z = cons(u, front(z))) \wedge (w = cons(last(z), nil))\end{bmatrix}$$

is a theorem of T_{LISP}. First, the Nelson & Oppen GLSP is used to check the satisfiability of this conjunction (assuming that the variables are uninterpreted constants). In doing so, the procedure computes the following additional equalities. From $K=cons(u,z)$, we get *u=head(K)* and *z=tail(K)*. Hence, *x=cons(head(K),front(tail(K))*. From *w=cons*(z_1,*nil*) and *w=cons(last(z),nil)*, we get

head(cons(z_1,*nil*))=*head(cons(last(z),nil))*.

Hence, z_1=*last*(z) and z_1=*last(tail(K))*.

What the procedure has shown is that if we treat the variables in the above formula as constants, in every model of T that is also a model of this formula, *x=cons(head(K),front(tail(K)))* and z_1=*last(tail(K))*. That is, that $F(c_x, c_u, c_z, c_w, c_{z_1})$ is satisfiable in the theory T_{LISP} and that c_x=*cons(head(K),front(tail(K)))* and $c_{z_1} = last(tail(K))$. Next, to establish that *cons(head(K),front(tail(K))*, is a witness for *x* and that *last(tail(K))* is a witness for z_1, the procedure is used to check the unsatisfiability of $\neg F(t_1, \ldots, t_n)$. Since this is a disjunction that is unsatisfiable just in case all of its disjuncts are, each literal of $\neg F(t_1, \ldots, t_n)$ can be checked separately. If $\neg F(t_1, \ldots, t_n)$ is unsatisfiable, $T \models F(t_1, \ldots, t_n)$ and $T \models \exists F$. We have exploited the following fact in this analysis.

Lemma 4.1 Let $F(c_1,\ldots,c_n)$ be a conjunction of ground literals that is satisfiable in a theory *T*. Further, suppose that the constant symbols $c_1,\ldots,c_n$ do not occur in *T*. If $T \cup F(c_1, \ldots, c_n) \models ((c_1 = t_1) \wedge \ldots \wedge (c_n = t_n))$ where each t_i is a term not containing any of the c_js, $T \models \forall x_1, \ldots, x_n(F(x_1, \ldots, x_n) \Rightarrow ((x_1 = t_1) \wedge \ldots \wedge (x_n = t_n)))$.

Proof: Suppose $T \cup F(c_1, \ldots, c_n) \models ((c_1 = t_1) \wedge \ldots \wedge (c_n = t_n))$. Then, by the deduction theorem, $T \models (F(c_1, \ldots, c_n) \Rightarrow ((c_1 = t_1) \wedge \ldots \wedge (c_n = t_n)))$, Also, since the c_i do not appear in *T*, the first-order law of universal generalization gives us $T \models \forall x_1, \ldots, x_n(F(x_1, \ldots, x_n) \Rightarrow ((x_1 = t_1) \wedge \ldots \wedge (x_n = t_n)))$.[]

Lemma 4.1 gives us license to use a GLSP to find potential witnesses for existentially quantified variables, i.e., terms that make *F* true in every model of $T \cup \{F\}$. The GLSP is then used to check that these potential witnesses are, in fact, witnesses, i.e., that they make *F* true in every model of *T*.

We have used the separated refutation system in the context of deductive synthesis where we are only interested in constructive proofs in which witnesses have been produced for existentially quantified variables in a theorem. In this context, decision procedures may be required to produce witnesses. Closure-based GLSP have an added benefit in deductive synthesis, namely that such a GLSP establishes that the existential closure of a restriction is a theorem by constructing witnesses. These witnesses can be extracted to produce programs in deductive synthesis. For example, in proving the theorem $\exists y_1, z_1[K = append(y_1, cons(z_1, nil))]$ in example 2.3, the Nelson & Oppen GLSP produces witnesses for y_1 and z_1. These are *cons(head(K),front(tail(K))* and *last(tail(K))* respectively, which are the synthesized programs for *front(K)* and *last(K)* under the assumption that *Knil* and *tail(K)nil*.

Thus far in our deductive synthesis work, all the GLSPs we have developed can be used to generate witnesses in this manner.

5 Amphion/NAIF Decision Procedures

This section discusses the implementation of procedures for Amphion/NAIF. Amphion/NAIF is a deductive-synthesis system that facilitates the construction of programs that solve problems in solar system mechanics. Programs generated by Amphion/NAIF consist of straight-line code using assignment statements and calls to elements of the SPICE subroutine library. The SPICE library was constructed to solve problems related to observation planning and interpretation of data received by deep space probes.

An Amphion domain theory has three parts: an abstract theory whose language is suitable for problem specifications, a concrete theory that includes the specification of the target components, and an implementation relation between the abstract and concrete theories. Specifications are given in the abstract language, and programs are generated in the concrete language. Abstract objects are free from implementation details. For example, a point is an abstract concept, while a FORTRAN array of three real numbers is a concrete, implementation level construct.

At the abstract level, the Amphion/NAIF domain theory includes types for objects in Euclidean geometry such as points, rays, planes, and ellipsoids, augmented with astronomical constructs such as planets, spacecraft, and time. The abstract functions and relations include geometric constraints such as whether one geometric object intersects another. The concrete portion of the Amphion/NAIF domain theory defines types used in implementing a program or in defining representations, and it defines the subroutines and functions that are elements of the target subroutine library.

The implementation relations are axiomatized through abstraction maps using a method described by Hoare [9].These are maps from concrete types to abstract types. The function *abs* is used to apply an abstraction map to a concrete object. For example, *abs*(*coordinates-to-time*(*TS*), *tc*) denotes the application of the abstraction map *coordinates-to-time*, parameterized on the time system *TS*, to the time coordinate *tc*, i.e., this term maps a concrete time coordinate *tc* in time system *TS* to an abstract time.

In the NAIF theory, many implementation relations are axiomatized as equalities. For example, an abstract time may be encoded by any of several data representations such as Julian date or Calendar date. An example of an equality axiom relating two concrete objects to a single abstract object is

$$\forall ts_1, ts_2, tc \begin{pmatrix} abs(coordinates\text{-}to\text{-}time(ts_1), tc) = \\ abs(coordinates\text{-}to\text{-}time(ts_2), convert\text{-}time(ts_1, ts_2, tc)) \end{pmatrix}$$

This axiom says that two abstract times are equivalent. The first abstract time is derived from time coordinate *tc* in time system ts_1. The second abstract time is the time conversion function *convert-time* applied to the first time coordinate to convert it from one system to another. This axiom is used to introduce invocations of the *convert-time* function into a synthesized program. These synthesized code fragments convert time data from one representation to another.

The terms in a specification usually do not match perfectly with axioms in the domain theory. Inference steps are required to generate matching terms. When these inference steps include resolution or paramodulation, choice points are introduced into the theorem prover's search space. For example, a specification may state that an input time is in the Julian time system, but it may require that the time be in the Ephemeris time system for the appropriate inferences to carry through. The theorem prover will apply the *convert-time* axiom (using paramodulation) to convert the input time coordinate from Julian to Ephemeris, then apply the appropriate inferences. Each paramodulation represents a multi-branched choice point in the search space. As a practical matter, this branching usually causes a combinatorial explosion in theorem proving. One class of decision procedure interfaced to the theorem prover in Amphion/NAIF performs representation conversions, like the time conversion just described, without search. In Amphion/NAIF, inserting decision procedures to eliminate choicepoints has a dramatic speedup effect.

5.1 A Procedure for Time Conversion

The procedure for time conversion is the simplest example of a representation conversion decision procedure used in Amphion/NAIF. When this procedure is interfaced to the theorem prover, the domain theory is separated relative to the NAIF subtheory of time. For example, an axiom such as

$$\forall t_1, t_2 \left(\begin{array}{l} \mathit{sum\text{-}of\text{-}times}(\mathit{abs}(\mathit{coordinates\text{-}to\text{-}time}(\mathit{EPHEMERIS}), t_1), \\ \qquad\qquad \mathit{abs}(\mathit{coordinates\text{-}to\text{-}time}(\mathit{EPHEMERIS}), t_2)) = \\ \mathit{abs}(\mathit{coordinates\text{-}to\text{-}time}(\mathit{EPHEMERIS}), \mathit{sum\text{-}time\text{-}coords}(t_1, t_2)) \end{array} \right)$$

is separated, yielding

$$\begin{array}{l} (X_1 = \mathit{abs}(\mathit{coordinates\text{-}to\text{-}time}(\mathit{EPHEMERIS}), U_2)) \wedge \\ (X_2 = \mathit{abs}(\mathit{coordinates\text{-}to\text{-}time}(\mathit{EPHEMERIS}), U_3)) \wedge \\ (X_3 = \mathit{abs}(\mathit{coordinates\text{-}to\text{-}time}(\mathit{EPHEMERIS}), \mathit{sum\text{-}time\text{-}coords}(U_2, U_3))) \\ \qquad \Rightarrow (\mathit{sum\text{-}of\text{-}times}(X_1, X_2) \neq X_3) \end{array}$$

The decision procedure implements congruence closure to compute the consequences of a set of equalities some of which are between abstract time terms, i.e., it is used on the restriction of clauses like the one above. The congruence closure algorithm computes the consequences of a conjunction of ground equalities by maintaining equivalence classes of terms in a congruence closure graph [8]. As described in Sections 3 and 4, for this purpose, the variables in the restriction are treated as constants. These constants are specially marked to distinguish them from constants appearing either in the domain theory or an input specification. The equivalence classes of two terms are merged either when an equality between those terms is introduced or when two terms are found, by congruence, to be equal, i.e., if $t_i{=}s_i$, $i{=}1,..,n$, then $f(t_1, ..., t_n) = f(s_1, ..., s_n)$. Hence, the equalities involving *abs* terms appearing in the restriction of a clause and the consequences of those equalities are represented in a congruence closure graph, rather than as literals of a clause.

The time conversion procedure is, in fact, an extension of congruence closure because it also finds witnesses for some of the specially marked constants (those that were substituted for variables) in *abs* terms. When a term in an equivalence class of *abs* terms is ground, witnesses are produced for variables in the other terms in the class when those other terms contain (non variable) time systems. There are two cases. Case 1 is when the time systems in the two *abs* terms are the same. In this case witnesses are generated based on the domain theory axiom

$$\forall ts, tc_1, tc_2(abs(coordinates\text{-}to\text{-}time(ts), tc_1) = abs(coordinates\text{-}to\text{-}time(ts), tc_2)) \Rightarrow (tc_1 = tc_2)$$

Case 2 is when the time systems are different. These witnesses are produced based on the domain theory axiom

$$\forall ts_1, ts_2, tc(abs(coordinates\text{-}to\text{-}time(ts_1), tc) = abs(coordinates\text{-}to\text{-}time(ts_2), convert\text{-}time(ts_1, ts_2, tc)))$$

For example, if there is an equivalence class containing the term *abs(coordinates-to-time(EPHEMERIS),A)* and containing the term *abs(coordinates-to-time(JULIAN),tc)*, the procedure produces the witness *convert-time(EPHEMERIS,JULIAN,A)* for *tc*.

When the *convert-time* procedure is used in Amphion/NAIF, the axioms above are no longer needed. Hence, they are removed from the domain theory.

5.2 A Proof Using the Time Conversion Procedure

The axiom shown below indicates how a sum of two times is computed. In this axiom, the final time is computed as a sum only if both times are in Ephemeris representation

$$\forall t_1, t_2\begin{pmatrix} sum\text{-}of\text{-}times(abs(coordinates\text{-}to\text{-}time(EPHEMERIS), t_1), \\ \qquad abs(coordinates\text{-}to\text{-}time(EPHEMERIS), t_2)) = \\ abs(coordinates\text{-}to\text{-}time(EPHEMERIS), sum\text{-}time\text{-}coords(t_1, t_2)) \end{pmatrix}$$

The operation of the *convert-time* procedure can be demonstrated by supposing SNARK is given the following specification.

$$\forall jt, et, \exists ut\begin{pmatrix} sum\text{-}of\text{-}times(abs(coordinates\text{-}to\text{-}time(JULIAN), jt), \\ \qquad abs(coordinates\text{-}to\text{-}time(EPHEMERIS), et)) = \\ abs(coordinates\text{-}to\text{-}time(UTC), ut) \end{pmatrix}$$

This specification asks: when given two distances, one represented in JULIAN format and one in EPHEMERIS format, find the sum of those distances in UTC format. The first step in the proof of this specification is to negate the conclusion and generate the Skolem form. Then *jt* and *et* become new Skolem constants, and *ut* becomes universally quantified. This formula separated relative to the NAIF theory of time is:

$$\begin{aligned} &(Y_1 = abs(coordinates\text{-}to\text{-}time(JULIAN), jt)) \wedge \\ &(Y_2 = abs(coordinates\text{-}to\text{-}time(EPHEMERIS), et)) \wedge \\ &(Y_3 = abs(coordinates\text{-}to\text{-}time(UTC), ut)) \\ &\quad \Rightarrow (sum\text{-}of\text{-}times(Y_1, Y_2) \neq Y_3) \end{aligned}$$

The conjunction in the antecedent is the restriction which is stored as a congruence closure graph. The disequality is the matrix available to SNARK's extended inference rules. SNARK unifies the matrix of the above formula with the complementary literal in the (now rewritten) *sum-of-times* axiom, shown below.

$$(X_1 = abs(coordinates\text{-}to\text{-}time(EPHEMERIS), U_2)) \wedge$$
$$(X_2 = abs(coordinates\text{-}to\text{-}time(EPHEMERIS), U_3)) \wedge$$
$$(X_3 = abs(coordinates\text{-}to\text{-}time(EPHEMERIS), sum\text{-}time\text{-}coords(U_2, U_3)))$$
$$\Rightarrow (sum\text{-}of\text{-}times(X_1, X_2) \neq X_3)$$

The unifier $\{Y_1 \leftarrow X_1, Y_2 \leftarrow X_2, Y_3 \leftarrow X_3\}$ is obtained. The matrix of the resolvant is the empty clause. The unifier is then passed to the *convert-time* procedure which now attempts to merge the closure graphs of the two restrictions. This generates the following three equalities:

$$abs(coordinates\text{-}to\text{-}time(JULIAN), jt) = abs(coordinates\text{-}to\text{-}time(EPHEMERIS), U_2)$$

$$abs(coordinates\text{-}to\text{-}time(EPHEMERIS), et) = abs(coordinates\text{-}to\text{-}time(EPHEMERIS), U_3)$$

$$abs(coordinates\text{-}to\text{-}time(UTC), ut) = abs(coordinates\text{-}to\text{-}time(EPHEMERIS), sum\text{-}time\text{-}coords(U_2, U_3))$$

Since *jt* and *et* are constants, the procedure determines that a binding can be generated for variables U_2 and U_3. The procedure then generates the witness $U_2 \leftarrow$*convert-time(JULIAN, EPHEMERIS, jt)*. Also the binding $U_3 \leftarrow et$ is generated for the second equality literal.

Finally, the variable *ut* is bound to the term *convert-time(EPHEMERIS, UTC, sum-time-coords(convert-time(JULIAN, EPHEMERIS, jt), et))*. This term is the answer term bound to the existentially quantified variable in the original specification. This term is a program that converts *jt* to ephemeris time, adds this converted time to *et* (already in the EPHEMERIS time system), and converts the resultant time to the UTC time system.

6 Implementation

We have augmented the SNARK resolution theorem prover with the separated inference rules described previously. We have also added a set of decision procedures to SNARK specifically for Amphion/NAIF and used the resulting system to generate programs. This section describes the results of this work. This work has been motivated by research into Meta-Amphion; however, a detailed discussion of Meta-Amphion is outside the scope of this paper. We believe that the work presented here is of general interest in its own right because it shows a new way of accelerating deductive synthesis engines, specifically full first-order refutation-based theorem provers, using decision procedures.

Our experience with Amphion/NAIF has been that the performance of the theorem prover has been an important consideration in the maintenance of the system. As with all general purpose theorem provers, SNARK is subject to combinatorial explosion in the search for a solution to a problem. As shown in Figure 1, the search space for all but the smallest problems is unacceptable when using an untuned system.

A great deal of time and effort has been devoted to tuning Amphion/NAIF. Figure 1 shows that the hand tuning (done over the course of a year and a half by an expert in deductive synthesis) was very effective in reducing the synthesis time, frequently reducing the time from hours or days to minutes. The central problem has not been the lack of success in tuning Amphion/NAIF; it has been the cost in time and effort required to tune the system particularly after the domain theory has been modified. The goal of Meta-Amphion is to assist in the construction and maintenance of deductive synthesis domain theories, and in particular, to assist in tuning declarative domain theories.

In general, a deductive synthesis system is tuned by generating example problems, observing the system as it attempts to solve the problems, then tuning the system to direct it towards solutions for the example problems. There are two primary methods of tuning the system: (1) changing the agenda ordering, and (2) reformulating the domain theory axioms.

SNARK selects an unprocessed formula from the set of supported formulas, then applies every applicable inference rule to the formula, possibly constructing many new (unprocessed) formulas. The agenda-ordering function orders formulas after each inference step, in effect choosing the next supported formula to be processed.

The original, general-purpose agenda-ordering function sorted formulas on the basis of the size (number of sub-terms) and the number of abstract terms in the formula. Thus SNARK favored formulas with fewer abstract terms. It also searched for solutions with a smaller number of terms before looking at larger terms. (SNARK only completes its search when a ground, concrete term is found for each output variable.) Since smaller answer terms represent shorter programs, shorter programs are generated before longer ones.

The hand-tuned agenda-ordering function weighs each formula according to several factors. In addition to the number of abstract terms in a formula, the hand-tuned agenda-ordering function also counts the number of non-ground convert-time terms. Formulas with more non-ground convert-time terms appear lower on the agenda. This prevents SNARK from generating terms such as

convert-time(Ephemeris, Julian, convert-time (Julian, Ephemeris, tc)).

This term results in the conversion of a time coordinate from the Ephemeris time system to the Julian time system and back again.[3] The agenda ordering function has similar weighting schemes for other terms for which tuning has been necessary.

When the decision procedures are used, the procedure for *coordinates-to-time* collects all the abstract time terms. It delays generating a *convert-time* term until a ground *convert-time* can be constructed.

3.In this case, this formula is rewritten by two rules into an identity. However, with paramodulation, new variables are introduced. No rewriting occurs since the new variables do not match. The result is that chains of convert-time terms may be generated. Each of these terms is then a target for resolution or paramodulation to generate more formulas, none of which lead to a solution.

We compared the performance of three Amphion/NAIF systems: an untuned system with a simple agenda-ordering function; an extensively hand-tuned system; and a system which uses several decision procedures. The untuned system describes the state of Amphion/NAIF prior to expert tuning. This is exactly the type of system we expect Meta-Amphion to be given as input. The hand-tuned system was the result of extensive tuning by a theorem proving expert. Not only was a specialized agenda ordering function developed, but several of the axioms were reformulated to force the theorem prover to behave in a particular manner. Such reformulation depends on in-depth knowledge of the workings of the theorem prover. For the decision procedure system, a set of five decision procedures was written and used. Each of these procedures was interfaced to SNARK using the inference rules described previously.

The domain theories for each of these systems consisted of approximately 325 first-order axioms. Many of these axioms are equalities, some of which are oriented and used as rewrite rules. A series of 27 specifications was used to test these synthesis systems. These specifications ranged from trivial with only a few literals to fairly complex with dozens of literals. Thirteen of the specifications were obtained as solutions to problem specifications given by domain experts, thus this set is representative of the problems encountered during real-world use.

As shown in Figure 1, the untuned system showed exponential behavior with respect to the specification size for the number of inference steps (and the CPU time) required to generate a program. The hand-tuned and decision-procedure-tuned (TOPS) systems both grew much less rapidly, with the decision-procedure-tuned system growing at about one third the rate of the hand-tuned system in the number of inference steps required to obtain a proof, as shown in Figure 2.

The performance of the system using the decision procedures was unaffected by changing between the simple and sophisticated agenda-ordering functions. This is not surprising since the decision procedures and the hand tuning both targeted the same inferences, and when using the procedures, the terms counted by the agenda ordering function are hidden inside the data structures of the procedures.

Although the programs generated using the decision procedures were not always identical to programs generated without them, for each case we proved that the programs computed the same input/output pairs.

7 Conclusion

A major hindrance to the construction and use of deductive synthesis systems is the cost associated with constructing and maintaining the domain theories associated with them. A primary cost of maintaining a domain theory is the cost of tuning the deductive synthesis system to the theory. Our work continues on the Meta-Amphion system whose goal is to automatically design specialized deductive synthesis systems from untuned domain theories. Much of our effort is on techniques to automate the process of replacing subtheories with automatically generated decision procedures. The decision procedure design process is one of design from components, where the components are parameterized procedures. The process involves combination and instantiation. The component procedures turn out to be closure-based ground literal satisfiability procedures. As described in this paper, we have also found this class of procedures useful in a new type of hand-tuning of deductive synthesis systems. We have defined the class of closure-based ground literal satisfiability procedures, introduced extensions of a refutation-based general-purpose theorem prover to enable any procedure in this class to be integrated with the theorem prover to accelerate deductive synthesis, and proven that these extensions are correct.

We have shown how we have used the manual decision procedure insertion technique to accelerate Amphion/NAIF, a system that is in regular use by NASA space scientists. Also, we are using the technique in the development of other "real-world" systems such as a system to synthesize three dimensional grid layouts in Computational Fluid Dynamics and a system to automatically generate schedulers for Space Shuttle payloads.

The research methodology we are employing is to manually identify sets of axioms that give rise to combinatorial explosion problems in theorem proving, just as we do when tuning manually. Then we generalize these problems into problem classes and create generalized solutions in the form of parameterized decision procedures. These parameterized procedures are added a library in Meta-Amphion. Meta-Amphion also has an evolving library of techniques that enable it to analyze a domain theory, identify instances of problem classes for which it has a decision procedure, and automatically instantiate the procedure for the problem class. Meta-Amphion also proves that the procedure is a solution to the specific problem, then modifies the domain theory appropriately.

In general, the soundness of solutions found using decision procedures very much depends on the soundness of the procedures themselves. Another ongoing activity in the Meta-Amphion project is to develop methods for proving the correctness of parameterized decision procedures.

ACKNOWLEDGEMENTS

Tom Pressburger read and helped with useful discussions of several drafts of this paper. Mahadevan Subramaniam, Mike Lowry, John Cowles and the anonymous reviewers also provided helpful comments.

REFERENCES

[1] Baader, F. & Tinelli, C., "A New Approach for Combining Decision Procedures for the Word Problem, and its Connection to the Nelson-Oppen Combination Method," CADE14, pp. 19-33, 1997.

[2] R. Boyer and Moore, J, *Integrating Decision Procedures into Heuristic Theorem Provers: A Case Study of Linear Arithmetic*, Institute for Computing Science and Computer Applications, University of Texas as Austin, 1988.

[3] Burckert, H. J., "A Resolution Principle for a Logic With Restricted Quantifiers," *Lecture Notes in Artificial Intelligence*, Vol. 568, Springer-Verlag, 1991.

[4] Chang, C & Lee, R.C., *Symbolic Logic and Mechanical Theorem Proving*, Academic Press, New York, 1973.

[5] Cyrluk, D., Lincoln, P., Shankar, N. "On Shostak's decision procedures for combinations of theories," *Automated Deduction--CADE-13* in *Lecture Notes in AI* 1104, (M. A. McRobbie and J. K. Slaney Eds), Springer, pp. 463-477, 1996.

[6] Deville, Y. and Lau, K., "Logic Program Synthesis," *Journal of Logic Programming*, 19,20: 321-350, 1994.

[7] Dunham, B. and North, J., "Theorem Testing by Computer," *Proceedings of the Symposium on Mathematical Theory of Automata*, Polytechnic Press, Brooklyn, N. Y., pp. 173-177, 1963.

[8] Gallier, J. H., *Logic for Computer Science: Foundations of Automatic Theorem Proving*, Harper and Row, 1986.

[9] C.A.R. Hoare, "Proof of Correctness of Data Representations," *Acta Infomatica*, Vol. 1, pp. 271-281, 1973.

[10] M. Lowry and J. Van Baalen, "META-Amphion: Synthesis of Efficient Domain-Specific Program Synthesis Systems", *Automated Software Engineering*, vol 4, pp. 199-241, 1997.

[11] Nelson, G., and Oppen, D., "Simplification By Cooperating Decision Procedures," *ACM Transactions on Programming Languages and Systems*, No. 1, pp. 245-257, 1979.

[12] Nelson, G., and Oppen, D., "Fast decision procedures based on congruence closure," *Journal of the ACM*, 27, 2, pp. 356-364, 1980.

[13] Owre, S., Rushby, M., and Shankar, N., "PVS: A Prototype Verification System," CADE-11, *LNAI* Vol. 607, pp. 748-752, 1992.

[14] Roach, S., "TOPS: Theory Operationalization for Program Synthesis," Ph.D. Thesis at University of Wyoming, 1997.

[15] Shostak, R., "A practical decision procedure for arithmetic with function symbols," *Journal of the ACM*, Vol. 26, pp. 351-360, 1979.

[16] Shostak, R., "Deciding Combinations of Theories," *Journal of the ACM*, Vol. 31, pp. 1-12, 1984.

[17] M. Stickel, R. Waldinger, M. Lowry, T. Pressburger, and I. Underwood, "Deductive Composition of Astronomical Software from Subroutine Libraries," *CADE-12*, 1994. See http://ic-www.arc.nasa.gov/ic/projects/amphion/docs/amphion.html

Synthesis of Programs in Abstract Data Types

Alessandro Avellone, Mauro Ferrari, and Pierangelo Miglioli

Dipartimento di Scienze dell'Informazione
Università degli Studi di Milano
Via Comelico 39, 20135 Milano–Italy
{avellone,ferram,miglioli}@dsi.unimi.it

Abstract. In this paper we propose a method for program synthesis from constructive proofs based on a particular proof strategy, we call *dischargeable set construction*. This proof-strategy allows to build proofs in which *active patterns* (sequences of application of rules with proper computational content) can be distinguished from *correctness patterns* (concerning correctness properties of the algorithm implicitly contained in the proof). The synthesis method associates with every active pattern of the proof a program schema (in an imperative language) translating only the computational content of the proof. One of the main features of our method is that it can be applied to a variety of theories formalizing ADT's and classes of ADT's. Here we will discuss the method and the computational content of some principles of particular interest in the context of some classes of ADT's.

1 Introduction

The general idea of Constructive Program Synthesis is that a constructive proof of a specification S implicitly contains an algorithm to solve S. A popular approach to Constructive Program Synthesis is known as *proofs-as-programs* (see, e.g., [2, 14]) and is based on the fact that constructive proofs can be (almost) directly interpreted as executable programs using, for example, the Curry-Howard isomorphism, or other kinds of operational interpretations, like the one in [14]. Other approaches, as e.g. [15, 16], apply a similar strategy to classical proofs for which a translation in a constructive system can be given. The essence of these approaches is that a proof (or a translation of a proof into an appropriate functional programming language) can be directly executed by a suitable computational model assigning computational meaning to every rule of the calculus in hand. But, as it is well-known ([8]), the proof of a specification does not only contain the information needed to compute the solution of the specification, the so-called *computational content of the proof*, but it also contains information related to the *correctness proof of the inner algorithm*. The presence of this irrelevant information makes inefficient

P. Flener (Ed.): LOPSTR'98, LNCS 1559, pp. 81–100, 1999.

a "naive" approach to program synthesis and "pruning" operations are needed to obtain more efficient programs [3, 8].

In this paper we follow a different approach, we call *program-extraction*, in which we do not give a computational content to *every* rule of the calculus in hand, but only to some patterns of rules. These patterns, we call *active-patterns*, can be directly translated into program schemata in a target programming language (here we use an imperative language), while *correctness-patterns* are ignored.

The identification of *active* and *correctness* patterns follows from the development of a proof method based on the notion of *dischargeable set* which has been deeply investigated in [1]. In that work it is shown how to build a dischargeable set for a given specification corresponds to build a proof (in a natural deduction calculus) with a *given structure*, and this structure allows to distinguish active patterns from correctness patterns.

In this paper we will not discuss in detail the notion of *dischargeable set*, but we will concentrate our attention on the computational content of some interesting *active-patterns* related to the application of certain rules. In particular we will discuss some "non-standard" induction rules giving rise to interesting program schemata.

Another feature of our method is that it can be applied to first-order theories formalizing *Abstract Data Types* (*ADT's* for short) and *classes of ADT's* according to the characterization based on the notions of *closed* and *open framework* discussed in literature in [9, 10] and, with another terminology in [12]. The synthesis of programs in the context of open frameworks (formalizing classes of ADT's) allows to construct programs parametric in some functions and procedures; in any instantiation of the open framework (that is in any ADT of the corresponding class) the instantiation of the parametric program gives rise to a completely defined program. According to this consideration we can say that our method provides a mechanism of software reusability.

The paper is so organized. In the next section we will discuss the notions of open and closed framework that will constitute the axiomatizations of ADT's and classes of ADT's in which we will write the specifications defined in Section 3. In Section 4 we introduce, by examples, the notion of dischargeable set, which is formally described in Appendix A. In Section 5 we discuss the computational content of some induction principles by showing the related program schemata.

2 ADT specifications

In this paper we will always consider specifications in the context of an axiomatization characterizing ADT's or classes of ADT's. To do so we begin by introducing the fundamental definitions of open and closed framework. Intuitively, a framework is a first-order theory embodying all the relevant knowledge of the problem domain of interest. We endow frameworks with *isoinitial semantics.* For a detailed discussion on frameworks we refer the reader to [9, 10] and to [12], where they have been introduced with a different terminology. We remark that in this work we are interested in program synthesis *from constructive proofs*, but we also want to treat ADT's in the usual context of *classical semantics.* In this sense our choice of isoinitial semantics, instead e.g. of the more usual initial semantics, is motivated; indeed, under some conditions, theories with isoinitial model can be combined with constructive logics giving rise to constructive systems (for a detailed discussion we refer the reader to [5, 12]).

A *(many sorted) signature* Σ is a triple $\langle \mathsf{Sorts}, \mathsf{Fun}, \mathsf{Rel}\rangle$, where Sorts is the set of sort symbols and Fun and Rel are sets of function declarations and relation declarations respectively. The first-order language $\mathcal{L}_\Sigma$ over Σ is defined as usual starting from Σ and the set of logical constants $\wedge$, $\vee$, $\rightarrow$, $\neg$, $\forall$ and $\exists$.

A *closed framework* is a pair $\mathcal{F} = \langle \Sigma, \mathbf{T}\rangle$, where Σ is a many sorted signature and $\mathbf{T}$ is a Σ-theory (that is a theory whose axioms are wff's of $\mathcal{L}_\Sigma$) defining in a unique way (in a sense which will be clear later) all the symbols in Σ.

We will present frameworks according to the following example formalizing the usual Peano Arithmetic:

Framework PA
SORTS : $\mathbb{N}$;
FUNCTIONS : $0 :\rightarrow \mathbb{N}$;
$\mathsf{s} : \mathbb{N} \rightarrow \mathbb{N}$;
$+, \cdot : \mathbb{N}, \mathbb{N} \rightarrow \mathbb{N}$;
AXIOMS : $\forall x\, (\neg 0 = \mathsf{s}(x))$; $\forall x, y(\mathsf{s}(x) = \mathsf{s}(y) \rightarrow x = y)$;
$\forall x(x + 0 = x)$; $\forall x, y(x + \mathsf{s}(y) = \mathsf{s}(x + y))$;
$\forall x(x \cdot 0 = 0)$; $\forall x, y(x \cdot \mathsf{s}(y) = x + x \cdot y))$;
$H^*(0) \wedge \forall x(H^*(x) \rightarrow H^*(sx)) \rightarrow \forall x H^*(x)$

In the induction principle, H^* indicates a schema variable, that is $H^*(0) \wedge \forall x(H^*(x) \rightarrow H^*(\mathsf{s}(x))) \rightarrow \forall x H^*(x)$ is a shorthand for the infinite set of axioms obtained by substituting any wff of the language of **PA** for H^*.

Differently from a closed framework, which completely defines a theory, an open framework depends on some parameters and characterizes a class of theories. To formalize this feature some definitions are in order. A *parametric signature* is a signature $\Sigma(P)$ where some symbols and declarations, the ones occurring in the list of parameters P, are put into evidence as *parameters* (see, e.g., [12]). A *parametric theory* $\mathbf{T}(P)$ over $\Sigma(P)$ is any $\Sigma(P)$-theory. We can write $\mathbf{T}(P) = \mathbf{C}_P \cup \mathbf{Ax}$, where $\mathbf{C}_P$ is the set of *constraints*, that is axioms *only* containing parametric symbols and $\mathbf{Ax}$ is the set of *internal axioms*, axioms containing at least a defined (i.e., non-parametric) symbol. The internal axioms are intended to formalize the defined symbols of $\Sigma(P)$, while the constraints represent requirements to be satisfied by actual parameters. The operation of instantiation is formally modeled by the notion of signature morphism, a map between signatures preserving arities and sorts, see [7,12].

An *open framework* is a pair $\mathcal{F}(P) = \langle \Sigma(P), \mathbf{T}(P) \rangle$ where $\Sigma(P)$ is a parametric signature and $\mathbf{T}(P)$ is a $\Sigma(P)$-theory. An example of an open framework is:

Framework LIST(Elem, $\lhd$, $\doteq$)
SORTS: Elem, List;
FUNCTIONS: $\mathtt{nil} \rightarrow$ List; $\;.\;$: Elem, List $\rightarrow$ List;
$\quad \mathtt{car}$: List $\rightarrow$ Elem; $\mathtt{cdr}$: List $\rightarrow$ List;
RELATIONS: $\preceq$, $=$: List, List, $\lhd$: Elem, Elem, $\doteq$: Elem, Elem;
AXIOMS: $\forall \alpha : \text{List}\ \forall x : \text{Elem}(\neg \mathtt{nil} = x.\alpha)$;
$\quad \forall \alpha, \beta : \text{List}\ \forall x, y : \text{Elem}(x.\alpha = y.\beta \rightarrow x = y \wedge \alpha = \beta)$;
$\quad \forall \alpha : \text{List}(\mathtt{nil} \preceq \alpha)$;
$\quad \forall \alpha, \beta : \text{List}\ \forall x, y : \text{Elem}(x \lhd y \wedge \alpha \preceq \beta \rightarrow x.\alpha \preceq y.\beta)$;
$\quad \forall \alpha, \beta : \text{List}\ \forall x, y : \text{Elem}(\neg x \lhd y \rightarrow \neg x.\alpha \preceq y.\beta)$;
$\quad \mathtt{cdr}(\mathtt{nil}) = \mathtt{nil}$; $\forall \alpha : \text{List}\ \forall x : \text{Elem}(\mathtt{cdr}(x.\alpha) = \alpha)$;
$\quad \forall \alpha : \text{List}\ \forall x : \text{Elem}(\neg \alpha = \mathtt{nil} \rightarrow \mathtt{car}(x.\alpha) = x)$;
$\quad H^*(\mathtt{nil}) \wedge \forall \alpha : \text{List}\ \forall x : \text{Elem}(H^*(\alpha) \rightarrow H^*(x.\alpha)) \rightarrow \forall \alpha : \text{List}\ H^*(\alpha)$;
CONSTRAINTS: $\forall x, y : \text{Elem}(x \lhd y \wedge y \lhd x \leftrightarrow x \doteq y)$;
$\quad \forall x, y, z : \text{Elem}(x \lhd y \wedge y \lhd z \rightarrow x \lhd z)$;
$\quad \forall x, y : \text{Elem}(x \lhd y \vee y \lhd x \vee x \doteq y)$;

Here, the constraints define the parametric relation symbol $\lhd$ as a total order over Elem and the internal axioms on $\preceq$ define it as a total order over List.

We endow closed frameworks with *isoinitial semantics*. Here we only recall that a model $\mathcal{I}$ (in the usual classical sense) of a theory $\mathbf{T}$ is *isoinitial* iff, for any model $\mathcal{M}$ of $\mathbf{T}$, there exists a unique isomorphic embedding $\psi : \mathcal{I} \rightarrow \mathcal{M}$. Moreover, a model of $\mathbf{T}$ is *reachable* if any element of its domain is denoted by a closed term of the language. A detailed discussion about isoinitial semantics, its relation with ADT's specification, and its interaction with constructive proof-theory can be found in [4–6,12]. Here we only remark that isoinitial models meet the usual conditions required for ADT, as e.g. uniqueness up to isomorphisms.

Definition 1 *A closed framework is* adequate *iff it has a reachable isoinitial model $\mathcal{I}$.*

The main property of adequate closed frameworks is that they completely define the intended meaning of the symbols of their signatures. Indeed it is possible to prove that, if $\mathcal{F} = \langle \Sigma, \mathbf{T} \rangle$ is an adequate closed framework, and $\mathcal{I}$ is the related isoinitial model, then, for any ground literal L in the language $\mathcal{L}_\Sigma$, $\mathbf{T} \vdash_{\overline{\mathbf{CL}}} L$ iff $\mathcal{I} \models L$; where $\mathbf{T} \vdash_{\overline{\mathbf{CL}}} L$ means that L is provable from $\mathbf{T}$ using classical logic and $\mathcal{I} \models L$ means that L holds in $\mathcal{I}$ according to the usual classical interpretation.

Adequacy of open frameworks is based on the notion of instantiation. An *instantiation* of an open framework $\mathcal{F}(P)$ with the closed framework $\mathcal{A} = \langle \Sigma', \mathbf{T}' \rangle$ is the closed framework

$$\mathcal{F}(P :: \mathcal{A}) = \langle \Sigma' \cup \mu(\Sigma_D), \mathbf{T}' \cup \mu(\mathbf{Ax}) \rangle$$

where:

1. μ is a signature morphism between the parametric symbols of $\Sigma(P)$ and Σ' such that, for any constraint A of $\mathbf{T}(P)$, $\mathbf{T}' \vdash_{\overline{\mathbf{CL}}} \mu(A)$.
2. The signature is obtained by substituting the parametric symbols of $\mathbf{T}(P)$ with their "implementation" in the framework $\mathcal{A}$ (through the signature morphism μ). Here Σ_D indicates the set of non-parametric symbols of $\Sigma(P)$.
3. The theory is obtained by replacing the constraints of $\mathbf{T}(P)$ with the axioms of $\mathcal{A}$ and translating the internal axioms of $\mathbf{T}(P)$ in the new language.

Definition 2 *An open framework $\mathcal{F}(P)$ is* adequate *iff, for every adequate closed framework $\mathcal{A}$, $\mathcal{F}(P :: \mathcal{A})$ is an adequate closed framework.*

General results about closed and open frameworks and sufficient conditions to guarantee a closed (or open) framework to be adequate are given in [12].

3 Specifications

Adequate open and closed frameworks constitute the contexts in which we write specifications. Hence, let $\mathcal{F}(P) = \langle \Sigma(P), \mathbf{T}(P) \rangle$ be an adequate open (possibly closed) framework, and let $\mathrm{Iso}(\mathcal{F}(P))$ be a class containing, for any closed instantiation $\mathcal{F}(P :: \mathcal{A})$ of $\mathcal{F}(P)$, an isoinitial model of $\mathcal{F}(P :: \mathcal{A})$. Moreover, let $\Delta(\underline{x})$ be a finite (possibly empty) set of wff's over $\mathcal{L}_{\Sigma(P)}$ with free variables in $\underline{x}$, which is intended to represent the set of *preconditions*. The specifications over $\mathcal{F}(P)$ and their meanings are defined as follows:

1. **Assign** $:= \Delta(\underline{x}) \Rightarrow \ll \exists z \psi(\underline{x}, z) \gg$
   For every $\mathcal{I} \in \mathrm{Iso}(\mathcal{F}(P))$, it expresses the task of computing, for every n-tuple $\underline{a}$ of the appropriate sorts in $\mathcal{I}$ such that $\mathcal{I} \models \Delta(\underline{x}/\underline{a})$[1], a value b such that $\mathcal{I} \models \psi(\underline{x}/\underline{a}, z/b)$[2].
2. **Test-Disjunction** $:= \Delta(\underline{x}) \Rightarrow [\psi_1(\underline{x}) \vee \psi_2(\underline{x})]$
   For every $\mathcal{I} \in \mathrm{Iso}(\mathcal{F}(P))$, it expresses the task of deciding, for every n-tuple $\underline{a}$ of the appropriate sorts in $\mathcal{I}$ such that $\mathcal{I} \models \Delta(\underline{x}/\underline{a})$, if either $\mathcal{I} \models \psi_1(\underline{x}/\underline{a})$ or $\mathcal{I} \models \psi_2(\underline{x}/\underline{a})$ holds.
3. **Assign-Disjunction** $:= \Delta(\underline{x}) \Rightarrow [\exists z^* \psi_1(\underline{x}, z^*) \vee \exists z^* \psi_2(\underline{x}, z^*)]$
   For every $\mathcal{I} \in \mathrm{Iso}(\mathcal{F}(P))$, it expresses two distinct tasks:
   (a) Decide, for every n-tuple $\underline{a}$ of the appropriate sorts in $\mathcal{I}$ such that $\mathcal{I} \models \Delta(\underline{x}/\underline{a})$, whether $\mathcal{I} \models \exists z \psi_1(\underline{x}/\underline{a}, z)$ or $\mathcal{I} \models \exists z \psi_2(\underline{x}/\underline{a}, z)$.
   (b) For every n-tuple $\underline{a}$ of the appropriate sorts in $\mathcal{I}$ such that $\mathcal{I} \models \Delta(\underline{x}/\underline{a})$, if $\mathcal{I} \models \exists z \psi_1(\underline{x}/\underline{a}, z)$, compute a value b such that $\mathcal{I} \models \psi_1(\underline{x}/\underline{a}, z/b)$, otherwise, if $\mathcal{I} \models \exists z \psi_2(\underline{x}/\underline{a}, z)$, compute a value b such that $\mathcal{I} \models \psi_2(\underline{x}/\underline{a}, z/b)$.
4. **True-Fun** $:= \Delta(\underline{x}) \Rightarrow [\exists z^* \psi(\underline{x}, z^*)]$
   For every $\mathcal{I} \in \mathrm{Iso}(\mathcal{F}(P))$, it expresses two distinct tasks:
   (a) Decide, for every n-tuple $\underline{a}$ of the appropriate sorts in $\mathcal{I}$ such that $\mathcal{I} \models \Delta(\underline{x}/\underline{a})$, the truth value of the predicate $\exists z \psi(\underline{x}/\underline{a}, z)$;
   (b) For every n-tuple $\underline{a}$ of the appropriate sorts in $\mathcal{I}$ such that $\mathcal{I} \models \Delta(\underline{x}/\underline{a})$ and $\mathcal{I} \models \exists z \psi(\underline{x}/\underline{a}, z)$, compute a value b such that $\mathcal{I} \models \psi(\underline{x}/\underline{a}, z/b)$.

We remark that function and relation symbols occurring in the specifications are interpreted according to the "intended" classical models of the open framework, while the meaning of the logical constants occurring in it *is not the classical one.*

As an example, let us consider the specification $[\exists z^*(z \cdot z = x)]$ in the context of the framework **PA** (the standard model of arithmetic is an isoinitial model of **PA**, and hence this framework is adequate). This

[1] This means that $\mathcal{I} \models A(\underline{x}/\underline{a})$ for any wff $A(\underline{x}) \in \Delta(\underline{x})$.

[2] For the sake of simplicity here we identify an element of the model with the term in *canonical form* denoting it in the language.

specification expresses, according to the above interpretation, the task of deciding whether x is a perfect square or not, and in the former case it also express the task of computing the square root of x. Of course, the only fact that a meaningful specification can be written does not imply that the corresponding task can be performed. But, if we are able to exhibit a proof of a suitable wff associated with the specification in a constructive formal system, then we are guaranteed on the computability of the specification.

To give a complete account, we recall that a formal system $\mathbf{T} + \mathbf{L}$ (where $\mathbf{T}$ is a theory and $\mathbf{L}$ is a deductive apparatus) is *constructive* if the following properties hold:

1. If $\mathbf{T} \vdash_{\mathbf{L}} A \vee B$ with $A \vee B$ a closed wff, then either $\mathbf{T} \vdash_{\mathbf{L}} A$ or $\mathbf{T} \vdash_{\mathbf{L}} B$.
2. If $\mathbf{T} \vdash_{\mathbf{L}} \exists x A(x)$ with $\exists x A(x)$ a closed wff, then there exists a closed term t of the language such that $\mathbf{T} \vdash_{\mathbf{L}} A(t)$.

The wff associated with the specification $[\exists z^*(z \cdot z = x)]$ is $\exists z(z \cdot z = x) \vee \neg\exists z(z \cdot z = x)$, and its classical truth is a trivial matter. On the other hand, if we have a proof of this wff in a constructive formal system, e.g., in intuitionistic arithmetic $\mathbf{PA} + \mathbf{INT}$ (where $\mathbf{INT}$ is any calculus for first-order intuitionistic logic), then we are guaranteed that, for any closed instance of the specification with a closed term t, either $\exists z(z \cdot z = t)$ or $\neg\exists z(z \cdot z = t)$ is provable in $\mathbf{PA} + \mathbf{INT}$. Since $\mathbf{PA} + \mathbf{INT}$ is recursively axiomatizable and constructive, by a well known result (see e.g. [11]), we have, at least in principle, a mechanical way to fulfill the decision task involved in the specification. Similarly, constructivity guarantees that if $\exists z(z \cdot z = t)$ is provable then also $(t' \cdot t' = t)$ is provable in the theory $\mathbf{PA} + \mathbf{INT}$ for some closed term t'.

4 Active Proof Patterns and synthesis rules

In this section we present the method of dischargeable sets. Here we do not discuss in detail the theoretical basis of the method, but we will be concerned on the way resulting proofs can be translated into programs, trying to put into evidence the computational contents of some logical and mathematical principles.

Let us consider an adequate closed framework $\mathcal{F} = \langle \Sigma, \mathbf{T} \rangle$ with isoinitial model $\mathcal{I}$, and a specification of the kind $\Delta(\underline{x}) \Rightarrow [\exists z^* \psi(\underline{x}, z)]$ (an analogous discussion can be made for the other specifications described in Section 3). The first step in finding an algorithm to solve a specification amounts to assume that it can be solved; formally this corresponds to the assumption that the related computability wff

$$\bigwedge \Delta(\underline{x}) \rightarrow (\exists z \psi(\underline{x}, z) \vee \neg \exists z \psi(\underline{x}, z))^3$$

is provable in a constructive formal system **T**+**L** (where **L** is a deductive apparatus including intuitionistic logic with identity **INT**).

The computability of the specification implies that the set of all possible elements $\underline{a}$ satisfying $\Delta(\underline{x})$ in the isoinitial model $\mathcal{I}$ can be divided into two sets; namely:

1. The set D^+ of all $\underline{a}$ satisfying the preconditions $\Delta(\underline{x})$ such that $\mathcal{I} \models \exists z \psi(\underline{x}/\underline{a}, z)$;
2. The set D^- of all $\underline{a}$ satisfying the preconditions $\Delta(\underline{x})$ such that $\mathcal{I} \models \neg \exists z \psi(\underline{x}/\underline{a}, z)$.

Now, let us suppose that D^+ and D^- can be expressed by some appropriate sets of wff's, called *t-wff's*, i.e., let us suppose that there exist $n+m$ sets of wff's $\Gamma_1^+(\underline{x}), \cdots, \Gamma_n^+(\underline{x})$ and $\Gamma_1^-(\underline{x}), \cdots, \Gamma_m^-(\underline{x})$ such that:

(F1) $\underline{a} \in D^+$ iff there exists $\Gamma_i^+(\underline{x})$ $(1 \leq i \leq n)$ such that $\mathcal{I} \models \Gamma_i^+(\underline{x}/\underline{a})$;
(F2) $\underline{a} \in D^-$ iff there exists $\Gamma_j^-(\underline{x})$ $(1 \leq j \leq m)$ such that $\mathcal{I} \models \Gamma_j^-(\underline{x}/\underline{a})$.

Moreover, let us suppose that:

(F3) For $1 \leq i \leq n$, $\Delta(\underline{x}), \Gamma_i^+(\underline{x}) \vdash_{\mathbf{T+L}} \psi(\underline{x}, t(\underline{x}))$ for an appropriate term $t(\underline{x})$;
(F4) For $1 \leq j \leq m$, $\Delta(\underline{x}), \Gamma_j^-(\underline{x}) \vdash_{\mathbf{T+L}} \neg \exists z \psi(\underline{x}, z)$.

If we are able to satisfy conditions (F1)-(F4), then we have "reduced" the problem of solving the specification to the problem of deciding, given a possible input $\underline{a}$ satisfying the preconditions $\Delta(\underline{x})$, which is among $\Gamma_1^+(\underline{x}/\underline{a}), \cdots, \Gamma_n^+(\underline{x}/\underline{a})$ and $\Gamma_1^-(\underline{x}/\underline{a}), \cdots, \Gamma_m^-(\underline{x}/\underline{a})$ the one satisfied in the isoinitial model. Obviously, the problem has been "reduced" if the wff's occurring in these sets are "simpler" than the wff representing the specification. As a matter of fact, in this case the method can be iterated and can be applied to the wff's occurring in such sets. Thus, if the family of sets $\{\Gamma_1^+(\underline{x}), \ldots, \Gamma_n^+(\underline{x}), \Gamma_1^-(\underline{x}), \ldots, \Gamma_m^-(\underline{x})\}$ is *dischargeable* (according to the formal definition given in Appendix A), then we can translate the sequence of facts (F3) and (F4) into a program.

For instance, let us consider the specification $[\exists z^* x{<}z{\leq}y]$ in the framework **PA** expressing the task of deciding whether $x{<}y$ or not and in the former case of finding a z such that $x{<}z{\leq}y$. The set of all input pairs $\langle x, y \rangle$ can be divided into three disjoint sets, identified by the following sets of wff's:

$$\Gamma^+ = \{x{\leq}y,\ \neg x{=}y\} \quad \Gamma_1^- = \{x{=}y\} \quad \Gamma_2^- = \{\neg x{\leq}y\}$$

---

[3] $\bigwedge \Delta(\underline{x})$ represents the conjunction of the wff's belonging to $\Delta(\underline{x})$

Moreover, if **L** is any deductive apparatus including intuitionistic logic with identity, it is possible to prove the following facts:

$$\Gamma^{+} \vdash_{\mathbf{PA}+\mathbf{L}} x{<}\mathtt{s}(x){\leq}y \tag{4.1}$$

$$\Gamma_1^{-} \vdash_{\mathbf{PA}+\mathbf{L}} \neg x{<}y \tag{4.2}$$

$$\Gamma_2^{-} \vdash_{\mathbf{PA}+\mathbf{L}} \neg x{<}y \tag{4.3}$$

Thus, the problem of solving the specification $[\exists z^{*} x{<}z{\leq}y]$ has been transformed into the problem of deciding whether either $x{\leq}y$ and $\neg x{=}y$ (in which case $x{<}y$ holds and $z \equiv x+1$) or $x{=}y$ (in which case $\neg x{<}y$ holds) or $\neg x{\leq}y$ (in which case $\neg x{<}y$ holds).

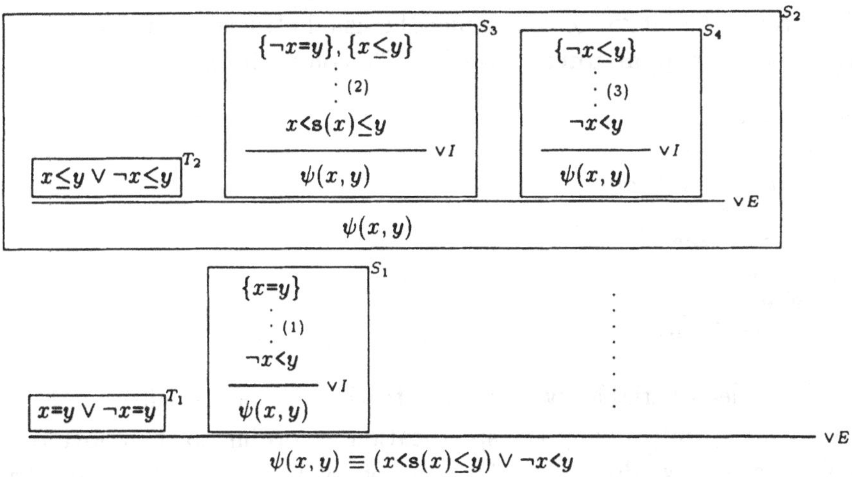

Fig. 1.

The sets of wff's $\Gamma^{+} = \{x{\leq}y, \neg x{=}y\}$, $\Gamma_1^{-} = \{x{=}y\}$, and $\Gamma_2^{-} = \{\neg x{\leq}y\}$ are an example of dischargeable set w.r.t. $\psi(x,y) \equiv (x < \mathtt{s}(x){<}y) \vee \neg x{<}y$. Moreover, according to the theory of dischargeable sets (see Theorem A4), the proofs of Facts (4.1), (4.2), and (4.3) can be arranged (using the natural deduction formalism) in the proof of Figure 1. We remark that this proof only uses the rules for the connective $\vee$ and the quantifier $\exists$. This corresponds to the fact that in our approach the latter are the *logical rules* with a *proper computational content* and that they determine an active pattern (a more detailed discussion can be found in [1]).

Moreover, the proof of Figure 1 makes explicit the relation between Facts (4.1)-(4.3) and the process of computing the specification. If we are able to decide the outermost test T_1, then we can accordingly consider one of the inner subproofs S_1 and S_2. If $x = y$ holds then we consider S_1 and this immediately gives the result $\neg x<y$. On the other hand, if $\neg x = y$ holds then we consider S_2; at this point, if we are able to decide the test T_2, we can continue the computation following either S_3 or S_4. The latter gives the result $\neg x<y$, while the subproof S_3 give the result $x < \mathtt{s}(x) \leq y$ and the relation $z = \mathtt{s}(x)$ between the input and the output variables.

Thus, having found the dischargeable set, we have "reduced" the problem of solving the specification $[\exists z^* x<z\leq y]$ to the problem of solving the specifications $[x=y]$ and $[x\leq y]$. Moreover, the above proof suggests in which way the corresponding sub-programs must be arranged in a program of the original specification. The proof of the above example is translated into the following peace of program, where we use a PASCAL-like programming language containing the usual structures **if-then-else**, **while-do-end**, **repeat-until**, **case** and the composition ";".

```
if x=y then
  tv:= false
else if x≤y then begin
        z:=x+1;
        tv:=true
        end
     else
        tv:= false;
```

Here the boolean variable **tv** stores the truth-value of the wff $x<y$.

We remark that, solving the specification according to the above (informal) strategy, we do not need the proofs of Facts (4.1)-(4.3); indeed these subproofs correspond to *correctness patterns*. According to the previous remark, we could use classical logic instead of a constructive logic to prove Facts (4.1)-(4.3). The interaction between constructive and non-constructive (classical) proofs can be formally justified in the context of a constructive modal logic with a modality representing classical truth (see, e.g. [13]).

Finally, we notice that in more complete examples dischargeable sets may also contain wff's, called *f-wff's*, representing functions to be computed in order to solve the specification; in our top down approach, these wff's are translated into new specifications. For instance, let us consider the specification

$$\Delta(x,v) = \{\exists k(v*v = k \wedge x<k)\}$$
$$\Rightarrow [\exists z^*(\exists k(z^* * z^* = k \wedge x<k \wedge z^*<v)) \vee \exists z^*(z^* = \sqrt{x})]$$

which arises from the top-down analysis of the specification $\ll \exists z(z = \sqrt{x}) \gg$ we will treat in Section 5.2, where $\sqrt{x}$ represents the integer square root of x.

In this case, the set of all input pairs $\langle x, v\rangle$ can be divided into two disjoint sets, identified by the sets of wff's $\Gamma^+ = \{x{<}m{*}m,\ m{=}v\text{-}1\}$ and $\Gamma^- = \{\neg x{<}m{*}m,\ m{=}v\text{-}1\}$, depending on the function $f(v) = v\text{-}1$. Moreover, the following facts hold:

$$\Delta(x,v), \Gamma^+ \vdash_{\text{PA}+\text{L}} \exists k(m{*}m = k \wedge x{<}k \wedge m{<}v)$$
$$\Delta(x,v), \Gamma^- \vdash_{\text{PA}+\text{L}} m = \sqrt{x}$$

Hence, we obtain the following program:

```
m=v-1;
if (x<m*m) then begin
   z := m;
   tv := false
  end
else begin
   z := m;
   tv := true
  end
```

5 Induction Principles

The dischargeable sets we have considered in the previous section coincide with proofs in **T**+**L** in which the active patterns connected with the connective $\vee$ and the quantifier $\exists$ have been separated from the correctness patterns. But, as one should expect, in a general framework a proof of the computability wff related to a specification uses some induction principles. Here we will study the active patterns corresponding to the application of two induction rules we call TAIL RECURSION and DESCENDING CHAIN, which naturally arise in the context of several ADT's.

5.1 The Tail Recursion Principle

Tail Recursion is a particular kind of recursion where the recursive procedure call is the last instruction of the calling program. As it is well known, this kind of recursion can be unfolded into an iterative program. Here we present a (pseudo)-natural deduction rule, we call TR, whcih can be seen as the deductive counterpart of Tail Recursion, and we give the iterative program schema for this rule.

First of all we state the conditions that an open framework must satisfy for the TR principle to be valid in the corresponding theory.

The principle TR is valid in the context of a given framework $\mathcal{F}(P) = \langle \Sigma(P), \mathbf{T}(P) \rangle$ if:

(C1) Let s be the sort on which the induction works. Then, there exist a function $f : s, s_1, \ldots, s_h \rightarrow s$ and a finite set $\{c_1, \ldots, c_m\}$ of constants of sort s in $\mathcal{F}(P)$ such that, for any $t : s$, there exists a *s-f-canonical* term $t' : s$ such that $t = t'$ is provable in $\mathbf{T} + \mathbf{L}$. Where the set of s-f-canonical terms is inductively defined as follows:
- Every constant in $\{c_1, \ldots, c_m\}$ is a s-f-canonical term;
- If t'' is a s-f-canonical term and $t_1 : s_1, \ldots, t_h : s_h$ are closed terms, then $f(t'', t_1, \ldots, t_h)$ is a s-f-canonical term.

(C2) There exist function symbols $g : s \rightarrow s, g_1 : s \rightarrow s_1, \ldots, g_h : s \rightarrow s_h$ in $\mathcal{F}(P)$ which are axiomatized as the inverse functions of f.

In the case of a specification of the kind $\Delta(\underline{x}) \Rightarrow [\psi(x_1, \cdots x_n, z)]$[4] with x_1 the induction variable, the Tail Recursion Principle has the following form:

$$\dfrac{\begin{array}{ccccccc} \Delta(\underline{x}) & & \Delta(\underline{x}) & \Delta(\underline{x}), \Gamma_1 & & \Delta(\underline{x}), \Gamma_k \\ \vdots\,\pi_{c_1} & & \vdots\,\pi_{c_m} & \vdots\,\pi_1 & & \vdots\,\pi_k \\ \widehat{\psi(c_1, \underline{x}_2, z)} & \ldots & \widehat{\psi(c_m, \underline{x}_2, z)} & \psi(f(w, \underline{y}), \underline{x}_2, z)^{\pm} & \ldots & \psi(f(w, \underline{y}), \underline{x}_2, z)^{\pm} \end{array}}{\psi(x_1, \cdots, x_n, z) \vee \neg\psi(x_1, \cdots, x_n, z)}\ \mathrm{TR}$$

where $\underline{x}_2$ is $x_2, \ldots, x_n$ and $\underline{y}$ is $y_1, \ldots, y_h$. Moreover, $\widehat{\psi(\underline{x}, z)}$ denotes the wff $\psi(x_1, \cdots, x_n, z) \vee \neg\psi(x_1, \cdots, x_n, z)$ and $\psi(f(w, \underline{y}), \underline{x}_2, z)^{\pm}$ is either $\psi(f(w, \underline{y}), \underline{x}_2, z)$ or $\neg\psi(f(w, \underline{y}), \underline{x}_2, z)$. Finally, the proofs $\pi_1, \ldots, \pi_k$ must satisfy the following conditions:

(P1) For each $1 \leq i \leq k$, if $\psi(w, \underline{x}_2, z)$ belongs to Γ_i, then π_i is a proof of $\psi(f(w, \underline{y}), \underline{x}_2, z)$, while if $\neg\psi(w, \underline{x}_2, z)$ belongs to Γ_i, then π_i is a proof of $\neg\psi(f(w, \underline{y}), \underline{x}_2, z)$.

(P2) The set $\{\Gamma_1, \ldots, \Gamma_k\}$ is dischargeable w.r.t. $\widehat{\psi(f(w, \underline{y}), \underline{x}_2, z)}$.

The program schema corresponding to the above rule is the iterative version of a recursive call by Tail Recursion given in Figure 2. In this figure, x_1 is the recursion variable, $P_{c_1}, P_{c_2}, \cdots, P_{c_m}$ are the sub-programs corresponding to the base cases and $g, g_1, \ldots, g_h$ are the implementations of the functions of point (C2). Finally, if P is the program obtained by

[4] The TR rule can be reformulated also for the other specifications described in Section 3.

```
ExCond:=false;
repeat
 case x1 in
     c1: begin
           Pc1; ExCond:=true
         end;
     c2: begin
           Pc2; ExCond:=true
         end;
              ⋮
     cm:begin
           Pcm; ExCond:=true
         end;
 otherwise
     begin
         x1:=g(x1);
         y1:=g1(x1);
         ⋮
         yh:=gh(x1);
         P*;
     end
until ExCond;
```

Fig. 2. Program schema for TR

the dischargeable set $\{\Gamma_1, \ldots \Gamma_k\}$, then P^* is obtained by transforming P according to the following rules:

(R1) Every piece of program of P of the form:

if $\psi(w, \underline{x}_2, z)$ **then** ... **else** ... is removed

(R2) Every piece of program of P of the form:

tv:=**true** $w := f(w, \underline{y})$	is replaced by	tv:=**true** Excond:=**true**

(R3) Every piece of program of P of the form:

tv:=**false**	is replaced by	tv:=**false** Excond:=**true**

The previous rule TR and the corresponding program schema can be generalized to the case of simultaneous induction on several variables as shown in the following example. (For a discussion on such kinds of induction rules we refer the reader to [12].) Let us consider the framework **List**(Elem, $\lhd$, $=$); this framework satisfies conditions (C1) and (C2), indeed:

1. Every list α can be constructed using the constant `nil` and the function $.$: Elem, List $\rightarrow$ List;
2. $\mathtt{cdr}(x.\alpha) = \alpha$ and $\mathtt{car}(x.\alpha) = x$.

Now, let us consider the specification $[\alpha \preceq \beta]$ expressing the task of deciding whether the list α is less than or equal to the list β. We can prove the related computability wff using the TR rule as follows:

$$\dfrac{\begin{array}{cccccc} & & x \lhd y & \neg x \lhd y, \neg x{=}y & \neg x \lhd y,\; x{=}y, \neg \alpha \preceq \beta & \neg x \lhd y,\; x{=}y, \alpha \preceq \beta \\ \vdots\,\pi_1 & \vdots\,\pi_2 & \vdots\,\pi_3 & \vdots\,\pi_4 & \vdots\,\pi_5 & \vdots\,\pi_6 \\ \mathtt{nil} \preceq \beta & \widehat{\alpha \preceq \mathtt{nil}} & x.\alpha \preceq y.\beta & \neg(x.\alpha \preceq y.\beta) & \neg(x.\alpha \preceq y.\beta) & x.\alpha \preceq y.\beta \end{array}}{\alpha \preceq \beta \vee \neg \alpha \preceq \beta}\,\mathrm{TR}$$

where proofs π_1-π_6 can be easily constructed. The corresponding program is given in Figure 3.

We notice that the program of Figure 3 depends on the implementation of the procedures for deciding the parametric binary relations $\lhd$ and $=$ defined over the sort Elem. Now, the theory of frameworks guarantees that in every closed instantiation of the adequate open framework **LIST**(Elem, $\lhd$, $=$) these relations are indeed decidable. Therefore, if we instantiate the framework **LIST**(Elem, $\lhd$, $=$) with a closed framework where these procedures have already been implemented, we are assured on the correctness of the resulting instantiated program.

5.2 Descending Chain Principle

The Descending Chain Principle has been studied in the context of ADT's and program synthesis [12, 14]. Here we describe this principle applied to a specification of the kind $\Delta(\underline{x}) \Rightarrow \ll \exists z^* \psi(\underline{x}, z) \gg$. Also in this case, the principle can be applied to the other specifications defined in Section 3. The DCH rule is:

$$\dfrac{\begin{array}{cc} \Delta(\underline{x}) & \Delta(\underline{x}), [A(\underline{x}, y)]_1 \\ \vdots\,\pi_1 & \vdots\,\pi_2 \\ \exists \underline{z} A(z, \underline{x}) & \exists z (A(\underline{x}, z) \wedge z \prec y) \vee \exists z \psi(\underline{x}, z) \end{array}}{\exists z\; \psi(\underline{x}, z)}\,\mathrm{DCH},1$$

```
ExCond:=false;
repeat
 case α in
      nil: begin
             P1;
             ExCond:=true
           end;
      otherwise begin
           case β in
                nil: begin
                       P2;
                       ExCond:=true
                     end;
                otherwise begin
                 α:=cdr(α);
                 β:=cdr(β);
                 x:=car(α);
                 y:=car(β);
                 if x ◁ y then begin
                      tv:=true;
                      ExCond:=true
                    end
                 else if not (x= y) then begin
                           tv:=false;
                           ExCond:=true
                         end;
                end;
      end
until ExCond;
```

Fig. 3.

where y (the *parameter* of the rule) does not occur free in ψ and in the other undischarged assumptions of the proof π_2.

For the principle to be valid, the framework $\mathcal{F}(P)$ must satisfy the following condition:

(C) The relation symbol $\prec$ must be interpreted in any model of $\text{Iso}(\mathcal{F}(P))$ as a well founded order relation.

$A(\underline{x}, y)$ is called the DCH-*wff*. This induction principle corresponds to a **repeat-until** loop where the exit condition is given by the DCH-wff $A(\underline{x}, z)$. The **repeat-until** loop computes a decreasing sequence of values (with respect to $\prec$) approximating the solution; the solution is reached at the end of the cycle. Hence, the program schema corresponding to the DCH rule is:

```
P1;
repeat
  P2;
until (not tv);
```

where P_1 and P_2 are the sub-programs obtained by translating the proofs π_1 and π_2 respectively, and tv is the boolean variable storing the truth value of the DCH-wff.

In many cases, the DCH-wff is closely connected with the computability wff related to the specification and, if the computability wff represents a function, then the DCH-wff represents a function approximating the desired solution.

As an example, let us consider the specification $\ll \exists z(z = \sqrt{x}) \gg$ in the framework **PA** expressing the task of computing, for each natural number x, its integer square root.

A possible approximation of the solution could be the following one: for each $x \in \mathbb{N}$ compute a $z \in \mathbb{N}$ such that $x \prec z{*}z$. Thus, let $A(x, z, i) \equiv z{*}z{=}i \wedge x{<}i$, then, using $\exists k A(x, v, k)$ as the DCH-wff, we get:

$$\dfrac{\begin{array}{c} \\ \vdots\,\pi_1 \\ \exists z \exists y\,(z \cdot z = y \wedge x < y) \end{array} \quad \begin{array}{c} [\exists k\,(v \cdot v = k \wedge x < k)]_1 \\ \vdots\,\pi_2 \\ \exists z(\exists k\,(z \cdot z = k \wedge x < k \wedge z < v)) \vee \exists z(z = \sqrt{x}) \end{array}}{\exists z(z = \sqrt{x})}\ \text{DCH},1$$

Since the proof π_1 simply corresponds to the assignment $z := x{+}1$, and the proof π_2 can be translated into the program at the end of Section 4, the program obtained for the specification $\ll \exists z(z = \sqrt{x}) \gg$ is:

```
z:=x+1;
repeat
 m := z-1;
 if (x<m*m) then begin
    z := m;
    tv := true
   end
 else begin
    z := m;
    tv := false
   end
until not(tv);
```

6 Conclusions and future works

In this paper we have presented a synthesis method based on the notion of discheargeable set allowing to distinguish active patterns from correctness patterns and we have showed how some of these patterns can be translated into an imperative language. Moreover, we have discussed how the method can be used to synthesize programs in ADT's and in classes of ADT's. In the last case we obtain parametric programs which can be reused in any ADT of the class.

Concerning our future work, we aim to implement the proof method of *dischargeable sets construction* and the related synthesis mechanism inside the logical framework ISABELLE. For this purpose we are developing proof schemata for driving the construction of the proof in a top-down way, implementing a given algorithmic strategy (as, e.g., divide-et-impera). This implies a research on the correspondence between logical rules and algorithmic strategies.

From a theoretical point of view we are also investigating some constructive modal logics (with a modal operator representing classical truth) allowing to combine in a single formal framework constructive proofs, required for the construction of active patterns, with classical subproofs, sufficient for the construction of correctness patterns.

References

1. A. Avellone. *The algorithmic content of constructive proofs: translating proofs into programs and interpreting proofs as programs.* PhD thesis, Dipartimento di Scienze dell'Informazione, Università degli Studi di Milano, Italy, 1998.
2. J. Bates and R. Constable. Proof as programs. *ACM Transaction on Programming Languages and Systems*, 7(1):113–136, 1985.
3. U. Berger and H. Schwichtenberg. The greatest common divisor: A case study for program extraction from classical proofs. *Lecture Notes in Computer Science*, 1158:36–46, 1996.
4. A. Bertoni, G. Mauri, and P. Miglioli. On the power of model theory to specify abstract data types and to capture their recursiveness. *Fundamenta Informaticae*, VI(2):127–170, 1983.
5. A. Bertoni, G. Mauri, P. Miglioli, and M. Ornaghi. Abstract data types and their extension within a constructive logic. In G. Kahn, D.B. MacQueen, and G. Plotkin, editors, *Semantics of data types*, LNCS 173, pages 177–195. Springer Verlag, 1984.
6. A. Bertoni, G. Mauri, P. Miglioli, and M. Wirsing. On different approaches to abstract data types and the existence of recursive models. *EATCS bulletin*, 9:47–57, 1979.
7. H. Ehrig and B. Mahr. *Fundamentals of Algebraic Specifications 1*. Berlin:Springer–Verlag, 1985.
8. C.A. Goad. Proofs as description of computation. In *CADE 5*, pages 39–52. Springer–Verlag, LNCS, 1980.
9. K.-K. Lau and M. Ornaghi. On specification frameworks and deductive synthesis of logic programs. In Logic Program Synthesis and Transformation. *Proceedings of LOPSTR'94*, Pisa, Italy, 1994.

10. K.-K. Lau and M. Ornaghi. Towards an object-oriented methodology for deductive synthesis of logic programs. *Lecture Notes in Computer Science*, 1048:152–169, 1996.
11. P. Miglioli, U. Moscato, and M. Ornaghi. Program specification and synthesis in constructive formal systems. In K.-K. Lau and T.P. Clement, editors, *Logic Program Synthesis and Transformation, Manchester 1991*, pages 13–26. Springer-Verlag, 1991. Workshops in Computing.
12. P. Miglioli, U. Moscato, and M. Ornaghi. Abstract parametric classes and abstract data types defined by classical and constructive logical methods. *Journal of Symbolic Computation*, 18:41–81, 1994.
13. P. Miglioli, U. Moscato, M. Ornaghi and G. Usberti. A constructivism based on classical truth. *Notre Dame Journal of Formal Logic*, 30(1): 67–90, 1989.
14. P. Miglioli and M. Ornaghi. A logically justified model of computation. *Fundamenta Informaticae*, IV,1,2:151–172,277–341, 1981.
15. C.R. Murthy. Classical proofs as programs: How, what, and why. *Lecture Notes in Computer Science*, 613:71–88, 1992.
16. H. Schwichtenberg. Proofs as programs. In P. Aczel, H. Simmons, and S. S. Wainer, editors, *Proof Theory. A selection of papers from the Leeds Proof Theory Programme 1990*, pages 81–113. Cambridge University Press, 1993.

A Dischargeable sets

Let Γ and Γ' be two finite and non-empty sets of wff's and let A and B be two wff's; we say that *Γ and Γ' are conjugated w.r.t. A and B* iff either $A \in \Gamma$ and $B \in \Gamma'$ or $B \in \Gamma$ and $A \in \Gamma'$. $[\Gamma, \Gamma']_{A,B}$ will denote the fact that Γ and Γ' are conjugated w.r.t. A and B.

Given $\mathcal{I} = \{\Gamma_1, \dots, \Gamma_n\}$ where any Γ_i is a finite and non-empty set of wff's, and given to wff's A and B, we say that *$\Gamma \in \mathcal{I}$ occurs conjugated in $\mathcal{I}$ w.r.t. A and B* iff there exists $\Gamma' \in \mathcal{I}$ such that $[\Gamma, \Gamma']_{A,B}$.

Definition A1 *Let $\mathcal{I} = \{\Gamma_1, \dots, \Gamma_n\}$ be such that any Γ_i is a finite and not empty set of wff's, let A and B be two wff's, and let $\Gamma \in \mathcal{I}$ be any set occurring conjugated in $\mathcal{I}$ w.r.t. A and B. Then a* discharging set of $\mathcal{I}$ generated by Γ w.r.t. A and B *is any set $\mathcal{I}^{\Gamma}_{A,B}$ defined as follows:*

1. if $A \equiv B$, then
   (a) for every j $(1 \le j \le n)$, if $\Gamma_j \neq \Gamma$, then $\Gamma_j \in \mathcal{I}^{\Gamma}_{A,B}$;
   (b) if $(\Gamma \setminus \{A\}) \neq \emptyset$ then $(\Gamma \setminus \{A\}) \in \mathcal{I}^{\Gamma}_{A,B}$.
2. Otherwise:
   (a) $\Gamma_j \in \mathcal{I}^{\Gamma}_{A,B}$ for every j $(1 \le j \le n)$ such that $\Gamma_j \neq \Gamma$ and $[\Gamma, \Gamma_j]_{A,B}$ is not satisfied;
   (b) Let S be a non-empty subset of all the $\overline{\Gamma}$ such that $[\Gamma, \overline{\Gamma}]_{A,B}$ is satisfied (possibly the set of all such $\overline{\Gamma}$ is selected). For every $\overline{\Gamma} \in S$, if $(\Gamma \cup \overline{\Gamma}) \setminus \{A, B\} \neq \emptyset$, then $(\Gamma \cup \overline{\Gamma}) \setminus \{A, B\}$ belongs to $\mathcal{I}^{\Gamma}_{A,B}$.

Obviously, according to different choices of the set $\mathcal{S}$ in point (2b), we obtain different sets $\mathcal{I}^{\Gamma}_{A,B}$.

Definition A2 *Let $\mathcal{I} = \{\Gamma_1, \dots, \Gamma_n\}$ be such that every Γ_i is a finite and not empty set of wff's. Let Δ be a finite (possibly empty) set of wff's, let ψ and ϕ be two wff's, and let $\mathbf{T}+\mathbf{L}$ be any formal system. We say that $\mathcal{I}$ is a $\Delta\psi\phi$-*dischargeable set *(in $\mathbf{T}+\mathbf{L}$) iff one of the following conditions is satisfied:*

1. *$\mathcal{I}$ is empty;*
2. *There exist $\Gamma_i \in \mathcal{I}$, $\Xi \subseteq (\bigcup_{j=1\dots n} \Gamma_j \setminus \{A, B\})$ and two wff's A and B such that*
   (a) *$\Gamma' = \Gamma_i \cup \Xi$,*
   (b) *$\mathcal{I}' = (\mathcal{I} \setminus \{\Gamma_i\}) \cup \{\Gamma'\}$,*
   (c) *$\Delta, \Xi \vdash_{\mathbf{T+L}} A \vee B$,*
   (d) *Γ' occurs conjugated in $\mathcal{I}'$ w.r.t. A and B,*
   (e) *there is a set $\mathcal{I}'^{\Gamma'}_{A,B}$ which is $\Delta\psi\phi$-dischargeable.*
3. *There are $\Gamma_i \in \mathcal{I}$ $(1 \le i \le n)$, $\Xi \subseteq (\bigcup_{j=1\dots n} \Gamma_j \setminus \{A, B\})$, and a wff $A(x)$ such that*
   (a) *$\Gamma' = \Gamma_i \cup \Xi$,*
   (b) *$\mathcal{I}' = (\mathcal{I} \setminus \{\Gamma_i\}) \cup \{\Gamma'\}$,*
   (c) *Γ' occurs conjugated in $\mathcal{I}'$ w.r.t. $A(x)$ and $A(x)$,*
   (d) *for all $B \in \Gamma'$, if $B \not\equiv A$ then x is not a free variable of B,*
   (e) *x is not a free variable of any wff in Δ, of ψ and of ϕ,*
   (f) *$\Delta, \Xi \vdash_{\mathbf{T+L}} \exists z\, A(z)$, and*
   (g) *the set $\mathcal{I}'^{\Gamma'}_{A(x),A(x)}$ is $\Delta\psi\phi$-dischargeable.*

By the previous definition, if $\mathcal{I}$ is a non empty $\Delta\psi\phi$-dischargeable set, there exist a set Γ, two wff's A and B and a set $\mathcal{I}' = \mathcal{I}^{\Gamma}_{A,B}$ which is $\Delta\psi\phi$-dischargeable; again, if $\mathcal{I}'$ is not empty, there exist a set Γ', two wff's A' and B' and a set $\mathcal{I}'' = \mathcal{I}'^{\Gamma'}_{A',B'}$ which is $\Delta\psi\phi$-dischargeable; and so on. Therefore, associated with a non empty $\Delta\psi\phi$-dischargeable set $\mathcal{I}$, there is a non empty sequence of wff's $\langle\{A_1, B_1\}, \dots, \{A_n, B_n\}\rangle$, we call *discharging sequence of $\mathcal{I}$*.

As an example, let A, B, $C(x)$, ϕ and ψ be wff's such that x does not occur free in ϕ, ψ and B; moreover, let us suppose that $\phi \vdash_{\mathbf{CL}} A \vee \neg A$, $\psi \vdash_{\mathbf{CL}} B \vee \neg B$, and $\phi \vdash_{\mathbf{CL}} \exists z C(z)$. Then, the set

$$\mathcal{I} = \{\{\neg B\}, \{A, B\}, \{A, C(x), B\}, \{\neg A\}\}\ ,$$

is an example of $\phi\psi\neg\psi$-dischargeable set. As a matter of fact, $\mathcal{I}$ generates the discharging set

$$\mathcal{I}' = \mathcal{I}^{\{\neg B\}}_{B,\neg B} = \{\{A\}, \{A, C(x)\}, \{\neg A\}\}\ ,$$

$\mathcal{I}'$ generates

$$\mathcal{I}'' = \mathcal{I}'^{\{A\}}_{A,\neg A} = \{\{C(x)\}\} ,$$

and $\mathcal{I}''$ generates the empty set $\mathcal{I}''^{\{C(x)\}}_{C(x),C(x)}$.

Now, hereafter, we will call *dis-adequate* (shorthand for dischargeable-adequate) any wff $\phi(x, z)$ of the kind $\exists y_1 \ldots \exists y_m \phi'(x, z, y_1, \ldots, y_m)$ with $m \geq 0$ such that ϕ' is not an existential wff. We call ϕ' the *immediate subformula related to* ϕ.

Definition A3 *Let Δ be a finite (possibly empty) set of wff's and let $\phi(x, z)$ and $\psi(x, z)$ be two dis-adequate wff's. A $\Delta\psi\phi$-dischargeable set $\mathcal{I} = \{\Gamma_1, \ldots, \Gamma_n\}$ is said to be* Δ-dischargeable with respect to $\psi \vee \phi$ *(in* $\mathbf{T} + \mathbf{L}$*) iff, for every $\Gamma_i \in \mathcal{I}$, either $\Delta, \Gamma_i \vdash_{\mathbf{T+L}} \psi'$, or $\Delta, \Gamma_i \vdash_{\mathbf{T+L}} \phi'$, where ϕ' and ψ' are the immediate subformulas related to ϕ and ψ respectively.*

The connection between formal systems and Δ-dischargeable sets w.r.t. $\psi \vee \phi$ is stated by the following theorems.

Theorem A4 *Let Δ a finite set of wff's, and let ϕ and ψ be two dis-adequate wff's. Moreover, let $\mathcal{I} = \{\Gamma_1, \ldots, \Gamma_n\}$ be a Δ-dischargeable set w.r.t. $\psi \vee \phi$ (in $\mathbf{L} + \mathbf{T}$). Then $\Delta \vdash_{\mathbf{T+L}} \psi \vee \phi$.* □

We remark that the proof of the above theorem (given in full detail in [1]) implicitly contains an algorithm to construct a proof of $\Delta \vdash_{\mathbf{T+L}} \psi \vee \phi$ given a $\Delta\phi\psi$-dischargeable set.

Obviously, given a solvable specification, the problem of building a dischargeable set for it is not trivial, and is as difficult as to write the desired program.

OOD Frameworks in Component-Based Software – Development in Computational Logic

Kung-Kiu Lau[1] and Mario Ornaghi[2]

[1] Department of Computer Science, University of Manchester
Manchester M13 9PL, United Kingdom
kung-kiu@cs.man.ac.uk
[2] Dipartimento di Scienze dell'Informazione, Universita' degli studi di Milano
Via Comelico 39/41, 20135 Milano, Italy
ornaghi@dsi.unimi.it

Abstract. Current Object-oriented Design (OOD) methodologies tend to focus on objects as the unit of reuse, but it is increasingly recognised that frameworks, or groups of interacting objects, are a better unit of reuse. Thus, in next-generation Component-based Development (CBD) methodologies, we can expect components to be frameworks rather than objects. In this paper, we describe a preliminary attempt at a formal semantics for OOD frameworks in CBD in computational logic.

1 Introduction

Most of the existing (semi-formal) Object-oriented Design (OOD) methods such as Fusion [4,6] and Syntropy [5] use classes or objects as the basic unit of design or reuse. These methods are based on the traditional view of an object, as shown in Figure 1, which regards an object as a closed entity with one fixed role.

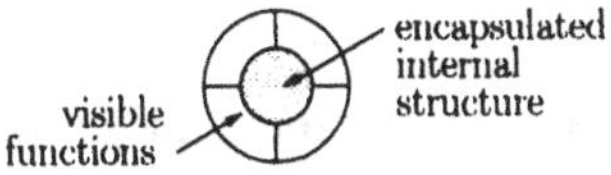

Fig. 1. Traditional view of an object.

This, however, does not reflect the nature of objects (and classes that describe them) in practical systems. In particular, objects tend to have more than one role in more than one context or framework. Consequently, it is increasingly recognised that classes are not the best focus for design (see e.g. [13,25]). Typical design artefacts are rarely just about one object, but about groups of objects and the way they interact.

Therefore in the next generation of component-based development (CBD) methodologies, we can expect components to be not just objects, but groups of (interacting) objects. In the CBD methodology *Catalysis* [7,23,16], for example,

P. Flener (Ed.): LOPSTR'98, LNCS 1559, pp. 101–123, 1999.

objects can have multiple roles in different OOD frameworks, and are formed by composing frameworks, as depicted in Figure 2.

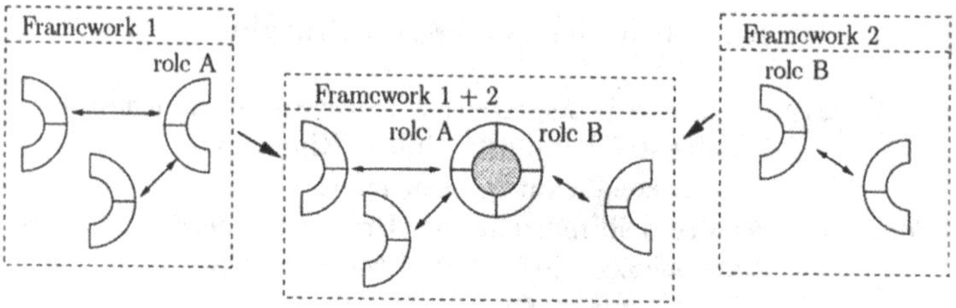

Fig. 2. Objects by composing OOD frameworks.

In computational logic, we have formulated a formal approach to program development [18, 19, 14], in which we use what we call *specification frameworks* to formalise problem domains. These frameworks have purely declarative (model-theoretic) semantics. In this paper we will show (how) we can extend such frameworks to make them correspond to OOD frameworks. The latter are groups of (interacting) objects with local states. Our extension thus has to introduce states and hence objects. However, in the paper we will not address temporal aspects such as state transitions.

2 Overview of Our Approach to Program Development

Our approach to program development in computational logic is based on a three-tier formalism (with model-theoretic semantics) illustrated in Figure 3.

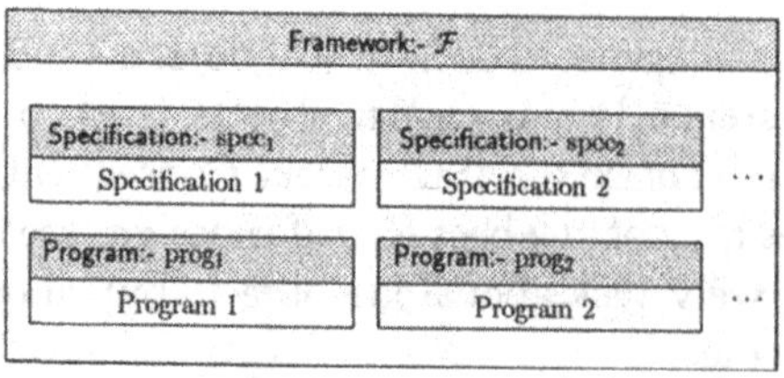

Fig. 3. A three-tier formalism.

At the top level, we have *specification frameworks* (or *frameworks* for short).[1] A framework is a first-order theory that axiomatises a problem domain. Model-theoretic semantics for frameworks is based on *isoinitial models*.

In the middle, we have *specifications*. Specifications are always given in the context of a framework. A specification is a set of formulas that define a new relation or function symbol in terms of the symbols of the framework.

At the bottom level are *(correct) programs*. For every specified relation r, a framework may contain a correct program for computing r. We have a model-theoretic definition of correctness, based on *steadfastness* [22].

Frameworks may be parametric, thus supporting classes, subclasses, inheritance, and framework composition. In particular, a composite framework inherits all the properties, specifications and correct programs of its components; correctness is preserved by framework composition, and the inherited programs can be composed to yield new correct (composed) programs. Thus, frameworks capture the declarative semantics of reusable components needed by CBD methodologies, and of their correctness and their composition [21].

However, so far our frameworks are *static*, i.e. they are immutable theories. In this paper, we will introduce states into our frameworks, and we will show that we thus obtain a formalism suitable for next-generation CBD: in particular, our approach provides a formalisation of OOD frameworks and their composition.

3 Specification Frameworks

Specification frameworks are defined in the context of many sorted first-order logic with identity. In this section we introduce and formalise such frameworks. We will attempt to give a self-contained treatment, because our existing formalisation of frameworks does not contain or emphasise the key aspects that are required for introducing states and objects. So we wish to hereby warn the reader about the somewhat heavy, formal material that lies ahead.

We begin by recalling some relevant terminology and notation.

A many-sorted first-order *signature* Σ consists of a set S of *sort symbols*, a set F of *function declarations* and a set R of *relation declarations*. A function declaration is of the form $f : [a] \to s$, where f is a function symbol, $[a]$ is its arity[2] and s is its sort. Function symbols of empty arity are called constant symbols. A relation declaration is of the form $r : [a]$, where r is a relation symbol and $[a]$ is its arity.

The meaning of the symbols of a signature Σ is given by *Σ-structures* (or *Σ-interpretations*). As usual, the meaning of a sort symbol s in a structure i is a set, called the *domain* of s, while function and relation declarations[3] are interpreted in i as functions and relations. The meaning of a (declaration of a) symbol σ in a structure i will be denoted by σ^{i}.

[1] To avoid confusion, we will always use frameworks to refer to specification frameworks only. OOD frameworks will always be called OOD frameworks.

[2] $[a]$ is a list of sort symbols.

[3] We interpret declarations, in order to allow overloading.

A Σ-structure i is *reachable* if, for every sort symbol s of Σ and every element α of the domain s^{i}, there is a ground term t such that $val_{\mathsf{i}}(t) = \alpha$, where $val_{\mathsf{i}}(t)$ is the value of t in the interpretation i, and is recursively defined in the usual way.

For a set Ax of Σ-sentences, $\mathsf{i} \models Ax$ means that every sentence of Ax is true in i. If $\mathsf{i} \models Ax$, then i is called a *model* of Ax.

In first-order logic with identity, overloaded identity $=: (s, s)$ (for every sort s) is always understood, and $=: (s, s)$ is interpreted, in *every* interpretation i, as the identity over s^{i}. Moreover, the standard identity axioms are always understood.

In this context, a *framework* $\mathcal{F} = \langle \Sigma, Ax \rangle$ is composed of a signature Σ and a finite or recursive set Ax of Σ-axioms.

The purpose of a framework is to axiomatise a problem domain and to reason about it, with the help of an interactive theorem prover. In our approach, a *problem domain* contains the ADT's and classes needed to define the objects of the application at hand.

We distinguish between *closed* and *open* frameworks. The relationship between open and closed frameworks plays a crucial role in our interpretation of objects. Roughly speaking, in object-oriented programming terminology, open frameworks represent classes, and closed frameworks represent their instances, i.e. objects.

3.1 Closed Frameworks

In a closed framework $\mathcal{F} = \langle \Sigma, Ax \rangle$ the purpose of the axioms Ax is to 'completely' characterise the meaning of the symbols in the signature Σ. This can be achieved by singling out an *intended model* i of Ax. We will use reachable isoinitial models as intended models.

Definition 1 (Isoinitial Models). Let Ax be a set of Σ-axioms. A Σ-structure i is an *isoinitial model* of Ax iff, for every other model m of Ax, there is one isomorphic embedding $i : \mathsf{i} \to \mathsf{m}$.

Definition 2 (Closed Frameworks). A framework $\mathcal{F} = \langle \Sigma, Ax \rangle$ is *closed* iff there is a reachable isoinitial model i of Ax, called the *intended model* of Ax.

Thus, our closed frameworks are *isoinitial theories*, namely theories with reachable isoinitial models. They are similar to *initial theories*, which axiomatise reachable initial models. The latter are popular in algebraic abstract data types and specifications [30]. The difference is that initial models use homomorphisms, instead of isomorphic embeddings. We briefly discuss some relevant consequences here (for a more detailed comparison, see [2]).

Let Ax be a set of Σ-axioms with a reachable model i, and consider the following properties:

(i) For every ground atom A, $\mathsf{i} \models A$ iff $Ax \vdash A$.
(ii) For every ground literal L, $\mathsf{i} \models L$ iff $Ax \vdash L$.
(iii) For every ground atom A, $Ax \vdash A$ or $Ax \vdash \neg A$.

i is an initial model of Ax if and only if (i) holds, while i is an isoinitial model of Ax if and only if (ii) holds. Thus, in an initial theory the falsity of a ground atom A corresponds to the non-provability of A, while in isoinitial theories it corresponds to the provability of $\neg A$. That is, isoinitial theories behave more properly, with respect to negation.

Since negation is important for reasoning about specification and correctness, we have chosen isoinitial theories. A second reason for this choice is that condition (ii) can be replaced by condition (iii), called *atomic completeness*. This is a purely proof-theoretical condition, i.e., i $\models \ldots$ disappears. This makes it more manageable. For example, we have used it to link isoinitiality to termination of logic programs [20], and in [26] a constructive proof-theory for isoinitiality has been based on atomic completeness. A third reason lies in our distinction between closed and open frameworks. Closed frameworks are required to be rich enough, to have an intended model. If such a model does not exist, then they are open. If we use initial theories, this distinction becomes very weak, as shown by the following example.

Example 1. Consider a framework for natural numbers, of the form:

Framework $\mathcal{NAT}$;

SORTS: Nat;

DECLS: $0 : [\,] \to Nat$;
$s : [Nat] \to Nat$;

AXIOMS: Ax;

where, as we pointed out before, $=$ and its standard axioms are understood.

$\mathcal{NAT}$ is a closed initial framework, even for an empty set of axioms (i.e., with $Ax = \emptyset$). Indeed, the Herbrand Universe $\mathcal{H}(0, s)$ generated by $\{0, s\}$ is a reachable initial model of $\emptyset$. This shows that very weak frameworks are accepted as being closed. In particular, in such frameworks we cannot prove negated facts, like, in this example, $\neg s(0) = s(s(0))$.

By contrast, to get an isoinitial theory axiomatising $\mathcal{H}(0, s)$, we need the following *freeness axioms* for $\{0, s\}$:

$$Ax = \{\forall x \,.\, \neg 0 = s(x),\ \forall x, y \,.\, s(x) = s(y) \to x = y\}$$

These state that different ground terms represent different numbers, i.e., the framework works properly with respect to negation.

A framework with an isoinitial model can be constructed incrementally, by *adequate expansions*, namely expansions by new symbols δ, that preserve the meaning of the old signature:

Definition 3 (Adequate Expansions of Closed Frameworks). $\mathcal{F}' = \langle \Sigma + \delta, Ax \cup D_\delta \rangle$ is an *adequate expansion* of $\mathcal{F} = \langle \Sigma, Ax \rangle$ if $\mathcal{F}'$ is a closed framework and its isoinitial model is a $(\Sigma + \delta)$-expansion[4] of that of $\mathcal{F}$.

[4] As usual, a $(\Sigma + \delta)$-expansion of a Σ-interpretation i is a $(\Sigma + \delta)$-interpretation i′ that coincides with i over Σ.

In an expansion, the axioms D_δ are called a *definition* of δ. A definition is adequate iff the corresponding expansion is. Adequate definitions are a very useful tool for incremental construction of frameworks, starting from a small kernel. There are various kinds of adequate definitions.

Example 2. We can expand the kernel $\mathcal{NAT}$ of natural numbers by useful functions and/or predicates. For example, the following is an adequate expansion of $\mathcal{NAT}$.

Framework $\mathcal{PA}$;

IMPORT: $\mathcal{NAT}$;

NEW:	$+ : [nats, Nat] \to Nat;$	WHERE $x + 0 = x$
		$x + s(y) = s(x + y)$
	$* : [nats, Nat] \to Nat;$	WHERE $x * 0 = 0$
		$x * s(y) = x * y + x$
	$1 : [\,] \to Nat;$	WHERE $1 = s(0)$
	$\leq : [Nat, Nat];$	WHERE $x \leq y \leftrightarrow \exists z \,.\, x + z = y$

All the new symbols are introduced by adequate definitions: $+$ and $*$ by (adequate) *recursive* definitions, and 1 and $\leq$ by (adequate) *explicit* definitions.

Of course, we need methods for proving the adequacy of a definition. Let us briefly consider this issue for *explicit* definitions, which suffice for our purposes. In a framework $\mathcal{F} = \langle \Sigma, Ax \rangle$, explicit definitions have the following general forms:

- An *explicit definition* of a new relation r is a $(\Sigma + r)$-formula of the form $\forall x \,.\, r(x) \leftrightarrow R(x)$ where the *defining formula* $R(x)$ is a Σ-formula.
- An *explicit definition* of a new function f is a $(\Sigma + f)$-formula of the form $\forall x \,.\, F(x, f(x))$ where the *defining formula* $F(x, y)$ is a Σ-formula such that $Ax \vdash \forall x \exists! y \,.\, F(x, y)$.

In [17] we have shown how adequate explicit definitions can be established by means of programs synthesis. In [26] it is shown that constructive proof-systems can be used to prove adequacy. For this paper, it suffices to know that if the defining formula is quantifier-free, then an explicit definition is *always* adequate.

3.2 Open Frameworks

An open framework does not have an isoinitial model, since its axioms leave open the meaning of some symbols of the signature, that we call *open* symbols. Non-open symbols will be called *defined* symbols.

We denote an open framework by $\mathcal{F}(\Omega) = \langle \Sigma, Ax \rangle$ where Ω are the open symbols. Since Ω may contain open sorts, we consider Ω-reachable models, where Ω-reachability is reachability in an expansion containing a new constant for each element of each open sort.[5] Moreover, we require that the axioms be sufficient

[5] We do not worry about the cardinality of the new constants.

to characterise the meaning of the defined symbols, in terms of the open ones. This corresponds to adequacy, which, for open frameworks, can be introduced as follows.

Definition 4 (Ω-equivalence). Let $\mathcal{F}(\Omega) = \langle \Sigma, Ax \rangle$ be an open framework, and let i and i' be two models of Ax. We say that i and i' are Ω-equivalent if, for every open symbol $\sigma \in \Omega$, $\sigma^{\mathsf{i}} = \sigma^{\mathsf{i}'}$.

Ω-equivalence is an equivalence relation. Therefore it partitions the class of models of $\mathcal{F}(\Omega) = \langle \Sigma, Ax \rangle$ into *Ω-equivalence classes*, or *Ω-classes* for short. In an Ω-class, we will consider Ω-isomorphic embeddings, i.e., isomorphic embeddings that behave as the identity function over the (possible) open sorts. Ω-isoinitial models are defined like isoinitial models, but they use Ω-isomorphic embeddings instead of isomorphic embeddings.

Definition 5 (Adequate Open Frameworks). $\mathcal{F}(\Omega) = \langle \Sigma, Ax \rangle$ is an *adequate open framework* if and only if every Ω-class contains an Ω-reachable Ω-isoinitial model.

Thus an adequate open framework axiomatises a class of intended models, namely the Ω-isoinitial models contained in the Ω-classes. An Ω-isoinitial model j of an Ω-class represents the intended meaning of the defined symbols, when the open symbols are interpreted as in j itself. We say that j is an *intended model* of the open framework. Since the framework is open, we have many non-isomorphic intended models.

Example 3. The following example is trivial, but it serves to explain ideas and problems simply and clearly.

Framework $\mathcal{TRIV}(X, q)$;

SORTS: X, s;

DECLS: $j : [X] \to s$;
$p : [X]$;
$q : [X, X]$;

AXIOMS: $j(x) = j(y) \to x = y$
$p(x) \leftrightarrow \exists y \,.\, q(x, y)$;

Let us interpret, for example, X as the term structure $\{0, s(0), s(s(0)), \ldots\}$ of the natural numbers, and $q(x, y)$ as the predicate $x > y$. We get the interpretation $\{j(0), j(s(0)), j(s(s(0))), \ldots\}$ of s and $x \neq 0$ of $p(x)$. Indeed, this interpretation is an X-reachable isoinitial model in the (X, q)-class interpreting X and q as before, i.e., it is an intended model.

We can prove that, if a framework $\mathcal{F}(\Omega)$ is adequate, then, for every intended model j, there is a suitable closed expansion of $\mathcal{F}(\Omega)$ that axiomatises it. The new axioms of such an expansion essentially coincide with all the Ω-formulas that are true in the interpretation of the parameters. However, since we need axiomatisations that can be managed by a theorem prover, the problem is to state which axioms are needed to get the desired closed instances.

Example 4. Consider the framework $\mathcal{TRIV}(X, q)$ of Example 3. To fix an interpretation of the open symbols X and q, a completion procedure has to add a closed set Ax_{new} of new axioms, whose isoinitial model corresponds to that interpretation. Furthermore, the new axioms must satisfy the following requirement:

$$\text{for every ground } t,\ Ax_{new} \vdash \exists y \,.\, q(t,y) \text{ or } Ax_{new} \vdash \neg\exists y \,.\, q(t,y) \qquad (1)$$

which ensures atomic completeness for the defined symbol p.

In this example, condition (1) guarantees that the new axioms complete the open framework into a closed one. Conditions of this kind will be called *constraints*. We have the following situation:

> An open framework explicitly contains its *constraints* (if any), and a *completion procedure* is a procedure to add axioms that satisfy the constraints. By a completion procedure, we can build many closed expansions, that we call *instances*.

Also, adequate open frameworks can be built incrementally, starting from a small, well understood kernel, and defining new symbols by *adequate definitions*, namely definitions that are inherited in a sound way (for more details, see [17, 14]).

The existence of many instances implies *reusability*: every theorem, expansion, specification or correct program developed in an open framework are inherited, and can be *reused* in all its instances. Reusability was an important motivation behind open frameworks and has been used in [22] to treat parametric frameworks. In this paper, we will also use them to define objects with states. To this end, we introduce a completion procedure based on explicit definitions.

We shall assume that we start with an open framework that already contains a closed subframework $\mathcal{G}$, i.e., is of the form $\mathcal{F}(\Omega) + \mathcal{G}$. This assumption is not restrictive, since it suffices to import $\mathcal{G}$ in $\mathcal{F}(\Omega)$. We can use $\mathcal{G}$ to close the meaning of the open relations and functions, as follows:

- *Sort closure.* The operation:

  $$\text{CLOSE} \quad X \quad \text{BY} \quad s$$

  renames the open sort X by a sort s of the closed subframework $\mathcal{G}$. This operation generates the framework $\mathcal{F}'(\Omega') + \mathcal{G}$, where $\mathcal{F}'(\Omega')$ is obtained by renaming X by s in $\mathcal{F}(\Omega)$.
- *Relation closure.* The operation:

  $$\text{CLOSE} \quad r \quad \text{BY} \quad \forall x \,.\, r(x) \leftrightarrow R(x)$$

  defines the meaning of an open relation $r(x)$ by a formula $R(x)$ of the closed subframework $\mathcal{G}$. We require that the declaration of r contains only sorts of $\mathcal{G}$, and $\forall x \,.\, r(x) \leftrightarrow R(x)$ is an *adequate* explicit definition of r in the closed framework $\mathcal{G}$.

– *Function closure*. The operation:

$$\text{CLOSE} \quad f \quad \text{BY} \quad \forall x \,.\, F(x, f(x))$$

defines the meaning of an open function $f(x)$ by a formula $F(x,y)$ of the closed subframework $\mathcal{G}$. We require that the declaration of f contains only sorts of $\mathcal{G}$, and $\forall x \,.\, F(x, f(x))$ is an *adequate* explicit definition of f in $\mathcal{G}$.

To close all the open symbols of an open framework $\mathcal{F}(\Omega)$ by a closed framework $\mathcal{G}$, we can start from $\mathcal{F}(\Omega) + \mathcal{G}$ and proceed as follows:

(i) Close the open sorts, and obtain a framework $\mathcal{F}'(\Omega') + \mathcal{G}$, where, in the open part $\mathcal{F}'(\Omega')$, all the open sorts of $\mathcal{F}(\Omega)$ have been renamed by closed sorts of $\mathcal{G}$.

(ii) Then close the relation and function symbols, and obtain a framework $\mathcal{F}'(\Omega') + \mathcal{G}'$, where $\mathcal{G}'$ is the (adequate) expansion of $\mathcal{G}$ by the explicit definitions used to close the open relations and functions.

We can prove the following theorem (we omit the proof, for conciseness).

Theorem 1. *Let $\mathcal{F}(\Omega)$ be an adequate open framework and $\mathcal{G}$ be a closed framework. Let $\mathcal{F}'(\Omega') + \mathcal{G}'$ be the final result of steps (i) and (ii) above. If $\mathcal{G}'$ satisfies the (possible) constraints of $\mathcal{F}'(\Omega')$, then $\mathcal{F}'(\Omega') + \mathcal{G}'$ is an adequate expansion of $\mathcal{G}'$ and its isoinitial model is an isoinitial model of the Ω'-class*[6] *that interprets Ω' as the isoinitial model of $\mathcal{G}'$.*

That is, the closed instance of $\mathcal{F}'(\Omega') + \mathcal{G}'$ is an adequate expansion of $\mathcal{G}$, and its intended model is defined according to $\mathcal{F}'(\Omega')$. Indeed, it coincides with the intended model of $\mathcal{F}'(\Omega')$ that interprets the sorts of Ω' according to $\mathcal{G}$, and the functions and relations of Ω' according to the explicit definitions used to close them.

Example 5. We can close $\mathcal{TRIV}(X, q)$ as follows:

IN $\mathcal{TRIV}(X, q)$:
IMPORT $\mathcal{PA}$;
CLOSE: X BY Nat;
$\quad q$ BY $\forall y \,.\, q(x,y) \leftrightarrow y < x$.

The result is the following closed framework:

Framework $\mathcal{TRIV}(Nat, q) + \mathcal{PA}'$
IMPORT $\mathcal{PA}$;
SORTS: s;
DECLS: $j : [Nat] \to s$;
$\quad p : [Nat]$;
$\quad q : [Nat, Nat]$;
AXIOMS: $q(x,y) \leftrightarrow y < x$
$\quad j(x) = j(y) \to x = y$
$\quad p(x) \leftrightarrow \exists y \,.\, q(x,y)$;

[6] $\mathcal{F}'(\Omega')$ is an adequate open framework, since it is a renaming of $\mathcal{F}(\Omega)$.

$\mathcal{PA}'$ is the expansion of $\mathcal{PA}$ by the explicit definition $q(x,y) \leftrightarrow y < x$, used to close q. According to $\mathcal{PA}'$, Nat is interpreted as the set $\{0, s(0), s(s(0)), \ldots\}$ of natural numbers, and $q(x,y)$ as $y < x$. The corresponding intended model of $\mathcal{TRIV}(Nat, q)$ interprets s as $\{j(0), j(s(0)), j(s(s(0))), \ldots\}$ and $p(x)$ as $x \neq 0$ (see Example 3). The same interpretation is given by the isoinitial model of $\mathcal{TRIV}(Nat, q) + \mathcal{PA}'$, i.e., $\mathcal{TRIV}(Nat, q) + \mathcal{PA}'$ is an adequate expansion of $\mathcal{PA}'$, where the interpretation of p and s is that defined by $\mathcal{TRIV}(Nat, q)$, when the parameters are interpreted according to $\mathcal{PA}'$.

To conclude this section, we remark that Example 5 corresponds to parameter passing which replaces X by Nat and q by $<$. The only difference is that both q and $<$ are in the final signature.[7] That is, our closure operations can be used to implement parameter passing. On the other hand, our mechanism is more general, since we could close open relations and functions by any kind of adequate, possibly recursive, definitions.

4 Classes and Objects

In the previous section we have presented the foundations for (specification) frameworks. In this section, we will show that these frameworks can be used to model both classes and objects in the terminology of object-oriented programming.

We shall use only frameworks that are adequate: frameworks that represent ADTs are called *ADT-frameworks*, and those that represent classes and objects are called *OBJ-frameworks*, respectively.

4.1 ADT-frameworks

A *closed ADT-framework* is a closed framework $\mathcal{F}$ that axiomatises an abstract data type (ADT). For example, the closed framework $\mathcal{PA}$ is a closed ADT-framework. It axiomatises the data type of natural numbers.

An *open ADT-framework* is an open framework $\mathcal{F}(\Omega)$, that axiomatises a class of intended ADT's. The intended ADT's are the intended models of $\mathcal{F}(\Omega)$, as defined in the previous section.

The *instances of* an open ADT-framework can be built by closing the open symbols in the way explained in the previous section. Once an instance is obtained, it is and remains static, i.e., ADT's cannot evolve.

Example 6. The following is the kernel of an adequate (open) framework of lists:

[7] However, by eliminability of explicit definitions, we could eliminate q if we wanted.

ADT-Framework $\mathcal{LIST}(X, \lhd)$

IMPORT: $\mathcal{PA}$;

SORTS: $X, List$;

DECLS:
$$\begin{aligned} nil &: [\,] \rightarrow List; \\ \cdot &: [X, List] \rightarrow List; \\ nocc &: [X, List] \rightarrow Nat; \\ elemi &: [List, Nat, X]; \\ \lhd &: (X, X); \end{aligned}$$

AXIOMS:
$$\begin{aligned} & free(nil, .); \\ & nocc(x, nil) = 0; \\ & a = b \rightarrow nocc(a, b.L) = s(nocc(a, L)); \\ & \neg a = b \rightarrow nocc(a, b.L) = nocc(a, L); \\ & elemi(L, i, a) \leftrightarrow \exists x : X \,.\, \exists N : List \,.\, \exists j : Nat \,. \\ & \quad (i = 0 \wedge L = a.N) \vee (i = s(j) \wedge L = x.N \wedge elemi(N, j, a)); \end{aligned}$$

CONSTRS: $TotOrd\lhd$.

where the abbreviations $free(nil, \cdot)$ and $TotOrd\lhd$ stand, respectively, for the freeness axioms of *nil* and $\cdot$, and the total ordering axioms for the *open* symbol $\lhd$.

The axioms characterise the *defined* symbols *List*, *nil*, $\cdot$, *nocc* and *elemi* in terms of the open ones, while the constraints are used to constrain the open symbol $\lhd$ to be a total ordering.

Once we have fixed an interpretation of the open symbol X, we get the structure of finite lists with elements in X. If, in this structure, we interpret $\lhd$ as a total ordering, then we get an X-reachable isoinitial model in the class of models of $\mathcal{LIST}(X, \lhd)$ that have the same interpretation of X and $\lhd$.

4.2 OBJ-frameworks

A OBJ-framework is also an adequate open framework $\mathcal{F}(\Omega)$. Its *closed instances* can be built in the way explained in the previous section. An OBJ-framework $\mathcal{F}(\Omega)$ will also be called a class, and its instances will be called *objects* of that class. The axioms used to close $\mathcal{F}(\Omega)$ into an object represent the *state* of the object, and are called *state axioms*. State axioms can be updated, i.e. an object is a dynamic entity.

When an object is created, the symbols of the signature of the class may be renamed, so that different objects have different signatures. We will use the following convention:

- The signature of an OBJ-framework may contain dotted symbols, namely symbols whose names begin with a dot.
- Each object has a *name*, and different names represent different objects. When creating a new object with name n, dotted symbols are renamed by prefixing their names with n. Therefore, the signatures of two different objects will contain different dotted symbols. Dotted symbols are used for

dynamic symbols, whose axioms and meaning may evolve in different ways for different objects.
- Non-dotted symbols are left unchanged. They are used for the static ADT-parts of the OBJ-framework (typically imported from pre-defined ADT-frameworks) that will be the same in all objects. For example, the ADT of natural numbers is always the same, in any object that uses it.

In an OBJ-framework $\mathcal{F}(\Omega)$, dotted symbols are dynamic. Therefore they must be open, and as such we do not need to list them as open symbols, i.e., we can write $\mathcal{F}$ instead of $\mathcal{F}(\Omega)$. This reflects the different uses ADT and OBJ-frameworks are intended for. In the former, the open symbols act as *parameters*, that can be closed by *external* closed frameworks, giving rise to immutable closed ADT-frameworks. In the latter, dynamic symbols act as a *state*. They can be dynamically closed *within* the framework itself, giving rise to dynamic objects.

Example 7. An *OBJ*-framework for car objects could be:

$$
\begin{array}{ll}
\multicolumn{2}{l}{\textbf{OBJ-Framework } \mathcal{CAR}(.km, .option);} \\
\text{IMPORT:} & \mathcal{INT}, year96; \\
\text{DECLS:} & \quad .km : [\,] \to Int \\
 & .option : [year96.opts] \\
\text{CONSTRS:} & .km \geq 0
\end{array}
$$

where $\mathcal{INT}$ is a predefined ADT of integers, and $year96$ is an object that contains the sort $year96.opts$ of the possible options for a car in the year 96.

An object of class $\mathcal{CAR}$ is created, for example, by:

$$
\begin{array}{llll}
\multicolumn{4}{l}{\text{NEW } spider : \mathcal{CAR};} \\
\text{CLOSE:} & spider.km & \text{BY} & spider.km = 25000; \\
 & spider.option & \text{BY} & spider.option(x) \leftrightarrow x = Airbag \lor x = AirCond.
\end{array}
$$

where $spider.km = 25000$ is the explicit definition that closes the constant $spider.km$, while $spider.option(x) \leftrightarrow x = Airbag \lor x = AirCond$ is the explicit definition that closes the predicate $spider.option(x)$.

The state of a spider object can be updated, by redefining its state axioms:

$$
\begin{array}{l}
\text{UPDATE } spider : \mathcal{CAR}; \\
spider.km = 27000 \\
spider.option(x) \leftrightarrow x = Airbag \lor x = AirCond
\end{array}
$$

As we can see, the constant $spider.km$ has been changed.

When creating and updating objects, we have to guarantee that the explicit definitions used to close the open symbols are adequate, and that the constraints are satisfied. The former condition is automatically satisfied if we use quantifier-free defining formulas. The latter condition, in general, requires a proof. Since proofs are typically time consuming, it is better to design methods for the whole class that guarantee constraint satisfaction.

Example 8. In the previous example, we have used quantifier-free defining formulas. Therefore, adequacy is guaranteed. Methods for the class $\mathcal{CAR}$, that are guaranteed to satisfy the constraints are:

$$create(k, y_1, \ldots, y_k) : -\ k \geq 0, assert(.km = k),$$
$$assert(\forall x(.optio(x) \leftrightarrow x = y_1 \vee \ldots \vee x = y_k).$$

$$kmupdate(x) : -\ x > .km, replace((.km = K), (.km = x)).$$

where $replace(A, B)$ is defined by $retract(A).assert(B)$. In the creation method *create*, the constraint $.km \geq 0$ follows from $k \geq 0$. In the updating method *kmupdate*, the new values for $.km$ are required to be greater that the old ones. Since the latter already satisfy the constraint, we are all right.

Note that here the syntax is not relevant. We have not yet fully formalised the dynamic aspects such as state transition (see the discussion in the conclusion). The above examples give only an idea.

5 OOD Frameworks

Having introduced classes and objects in the previous section, in this section we show how we can define OOD frameworks as frameworks containing composite objects, i.e. as composite OBJ-frameworks. We shall do so by formalising composite objects as systems of objects. We then show that our composite OBJ-frameworks indeed correspond to OOD frameworks as used in CBD methodologies like *Catalysis*.

5.1 Systems of Objects

To introduce systems of objects, we need the notion of multiple instance of a set $\mathcal{O}_1, \ldots, \mathcal{O}_n$ of OBJ-frameworks.

Definition 6 (Multiple Instances). Let $\mathcal{O}_1, \ldots, \mathcal{O}_n$ be a set of OBJ-frameworks, and $a_1, \ldots, a_k$ be instances of them.[8] A *multiple instance* $\{a_1, \ldots, a_k\}$ is defined as the union (of the signatures and of the axioms) of all the single instances $a_i, 1 \leq i \leq k$.

To give a semantics of multiple instances, we need a link between the isoinitial models of the individual instances $a_j, 1 \leq j \leq n$, and the isoinitial model of the multiple instance.

Definition 7 (Additivity and Strong Additivity). A set of adequate OBJ-frameworks is *additive* if its multiple instances $\{a_1, \ldots, a_k\}$ satisfy the following properties:

(i) If each $a_j, 1 \leq j \leq n$ satisfies the constraints, then $\{a_1, \ldots, a_k\}$ is a closed framework.

[8] Each OBJ-framework may have 0, 1 or more instances.

(ii) Let i be the isoinitial model[9] of $\{a_1, \ldots, a_k\}$. For every $j, 1 \le j \le k$, the isoinitial model i_j of a_j is isomorphically embedded into the reduct of i to the signature of a_j.

It is a *strongly additive* set of OBJ-frameworks if, in (ii), the isoinitial model i_j of a_j is isomorphic to the reduct of i to the signature of a_j.

We have the following theorem:

Theorem 2 (Representativity). *Let $\{a_1, \ldots, a_k\}$ be a multiple instance of a set $\mathcal{O}_1, \ldots, \mathcal{O}_n$ of adequate OBJ-frameworks.*

If $\mathcal{O}_1, \ldots, \mathcal{O}_n$ is strongly additive, then every sentence of the language of $a_j, 1 \le j \le k$, is true in its isoinitial model if and only if it is true in the isoinitial model of the multiple instance.

If $\mathcal{O}_1, \ldots, \mathcal{O}_n$ is additive, then every quantifier-free sentence of the language of $a_j, 1 \le j \le k$, is true in its isoinitial model if and only if it is true in the isoinitial model of the multiple instance.

In a multiple instance $\{a_1, \ldots, a_k\}$, the formulas of the language of an individual instance a_j correspond to the properties that are 'locally observable' in a_j, while the formulas of the (larger) language of the multiple instance represent properties that are 'globally observable'.

Strong additivity entails that the truth of any locally observable sentence is preserved in the global multiple instance. Additivity guarantees to preserve only those local properties that can be expressed by quantifier-free sentences.

Additivity is sufficient to prove the following proposition:

Proposition 1. *If a set of OBJ-frameworks is additive, then we can update a multiple instance, by adding, deleting or updating groups of individual instances, without altering the isoinitial models of the other individual instances.*

This guarantees that we can confine our updates to a part of a set of co-operating objects, without undesired side-effects on the other parts. Additivity suffices for our purposes. As we will see, there are cases where strong additivity is too restrictive.

Now, we can introduce the notion of a system of objects. Composite OBJ-frameworks will be based on such systems.

A system of cooperating objects $\mathcal{S}[\mathcal{O}_1, \ldots, \mathcal{O}_n]$, based on an additive set $\mathcal{O}_1, \ldots, \mathcal{O}_n$ of adequate OBJ-frameworks, is an object whose state, at any time t, is characterised by a multiple instance of $\mathcal{O}_1, \ldots, \mathcal{O}_n$, and (possibly) by other dynamic symbols, defined at the system level.

The methods for changing the state of $\mathcal{S}[\mathcal{O}_1, \ldots, \mathcal{O}_n]$ are the methods for creating new instances of a class $\mathcal{O}_j \in \{\mathcal{O}_1, \ldots, \mathcal{O}_n\}$ and deleting or updating an already existing individual object. Since $\mathcal{O}_1, \ldots, \mathcal{O}_n$ is additive, these operations update the global state of the system, without altering the isoinitial models of the untouched individual objects.

[9] i is unique up to isomorphism.

There are various ways of defining system methods. For example, they may be based on messages, as in many object-oriented programming languages. A possibility that we are investigating is introducing a meta-level where time is made explicit, and where system methods become logic programs. This formalisation is in its infancy and will not be presented here. Nevertheless, regardless of how system methods are formalised, it is clear that, at every time t, a system has the following properties:

- $\mathcal{S}[\mathcal{O}_1, \ldots, \mathcal{O}_n]$ has dynamic signatures and axioms. At each time t, it 'contains' a multiple instance of $\mathcal{O}_1, \ldots, \mathcal{O}_n$. It has a *global* signature $\Sigma_{sys}(t)$ and a *global* set of axioms $Ax_{sys}(t)$, and each individual instance a_j has its own signature $\Sigma_j(t)$ and axioms $Ax_j(t)$.
- Since the system is a multiple instance, for each individual instance a_j in it, $\Sigma_j(t)$ is a subsignature of $\Sigma_{sys}(t)$, and $Ax_j(t)$ is the restriction of $Ax_{sys}(t)$ to the signature $\Sigma_j(t)$. Moreover, in $\Sigma_{sys}(t)$, we can distinguish a static and a dynamic part.
- The static part consists of the signature and the axioms of the (closed) ADT's included in the OBJ-frameworks $\mathcal{O}_1, \ldots, \mathcal{O}_n$. This part is, globally, a closed ADT. We will denote it by ADT_{sys}.
- The dynamic part contains the dotted symbols and the axioms that have been used to close them in the various individual objects contained in the system at time t. Beside the dotted symbols, a system may contain non-dotted dynamic symbols, together with the related closing axioms. Non-dotted dynamic symbols are useful for expressing dynamic properties that are common to groups of objects and, hence, are not to be renamed (in contrast to dotted symbols which always are). In particular, there may be non-dotted system symbols, whose axioms are managed at the system level, i.e., outside the constituent OBJ-frameworks.

The presence of non-dotted dynamic symbols may affect additivity, so they must be treated with some care. The following proposition states a sufficient condition for strong additivity:

Proposition 2. *Let $\mathcal{S}[\mathcal{O}_1, \ldots, \mathcal{O}_n]$ be a system of objects. If all the dynamic symbols are dotted, then the system is strongly additive.*

If there are dynamic non-dotted symbols, then strong additivity and additivity may not hold. However, there are interesting cases where at least additivity is guaranteed. For example, if we have a non-dotted dynamic sort s, and s is closed, in each individual instance, by the freeness axioms of a set of constant symbols, then additivity is guaranteed.

We may also organise the objects of a system into sub-groups, so that we isolate properties that are common to a subgroup, but are not visible by the objects of another subgroup. This, of course, requires us to introduce a suitable renaming policy, e.g., by allowing multiple dottings, like path-names of a system with a tree-structure. We do not discuss this issue here, although our theoretical foundations are strong enough to embrace it.

Considering the possibility of non-dotted system symbols, a very useful tool is introducing the names of the individual objects (or of groups of objects, in a more complex renaming structure) in the signature. To this end, we assume that every system $\mathcal{S}[\mathcal{O}_1, \ldots, \mathcal{O}_n]$ has itself a reserved name *sys* and its global signature always contains a system reserved sort symbol *obj* and system reserved predicates $O_1, \ldots, O_n$. We require that the following *system constraint* is preserved by the methods for creating and destroying objects.

At each time t, the isoinitial model $\mathsf{i}(t)$ is such that:

(i) $obj^{\mathsf{i}(t)}$ is the set of names of the objects contained in the system at time t.

(ii) $\mathsf{i}(t) \models O_j(n)$ if and only if n is the name of an individual object of class $\mathcal{O}_j$, contained in the system at time t.

Once we have the names of the objects, we can also introduce expressive axiom schemas,[10] as shown by the following example:

Example 9. Suppose we want to define a predicate $.id : [obj]$, such that, in every object with name n, $n.id(x)$ holds if and only if x is the name of the object itself, i.e., $x = n$. We write down the axiom schema:

$$\#N.id(n) \leftrightarrow n = \#N$$

where the meta-symbol $\#N$ stands for any object name. So, if *ted* is an object-name, we get the instance $ted.id(n) \leftrightarrow n = ted$.

Now, we can introduce composite objects.

5.2 Composite Objects

A composite object is like a system $\mathcal{S}[\mathcal{O}_1, \ldots, \mathcal{O}_n]$, but now the additional global signature does not contain the symbols *sys*, *obj*, ..., that we have introduced in a system framework. It contains other (in general dotted) symbols, that are open symbols of the composite object not already contained in the components. Apart from this, we can reason exactly as we have done for systems of objects.

Example 10. Let us assume that we are working in a system containing at least the following OBJ-frameworks:

OBJ-Framework $\mathcal{CAR}$;

IMPORT: ...;

DECLS: $.weight : \rightarrow int$

$.km : \rightarrow int$

[10] As usual, an axiom schema is a template for a given general form of axioms.

OBJ-Framework $\mathcal{PERSON}$;

IMPORT . . .;

DECLS: $.name : \rightarrow string$;
$.age : \rightarrow int; \ldots$

CONSTRS: $.age \geq 0$

We want to compose them into a driver framework, where a driver is a person allowed to drive a non-empty set of cars. We can set up a composite framework like

OBJ-Framework $\mathcal{DRIVER}[\mathcal{PERSON}, \mathcal{CAR}]$;

DECLS: $.drives : [obj]$;

CONSTRS: $\#X.drives(c) \rightarrow PERSON(\#X) \wedge \#X.age \geq 18 \wedge CAR(c)$;
$(\exists c : obj)(.drives(c))$;

SPEC: $\#X.DriverComponent(n) \leftrightarrow n = \#X \vee \#X.drives(n)$;

PROG: $\#X.Component(N) : - \ N = \#X; \#X.drives(N)$.

Note that we are in the context of a system framework, and the system language, i.e., the sort *obj* and the predicates *PERSON*, *CAR*, *DRIVER*,. . ., can be used in the OBJ-frameworks of the system framework.

In the framework $\mathcal{DRIVER}$, we have also shown an example of a specification and a corresponding correct program[11] (or method). As we said, specifications and correct programs may be part of an open or closed framework, and hence of OBJ-frameworks.

Here the composite object states links on its components, constraining creation and deletion methods. We cannot create an object $n.\mathcal{DRIVER}$, if n is not a person. Furthermore, we need at least one car c. Thus, a method for creating a $\mathcal{DRIVER}$ object will be of the form:

$$\begin{array}{l} \#X.create(\#C_1, \ldots, \#C_k) : - \ not\#X.error(\#C_1, \ldots, \#C_k), \\ \quad add(\#X, state(\#X.drives(c) \leftrightarrow c = \#C_1 \vee \ldots \vee c = \#C_k)). \\ \#X.error(\#C_1, \ldots, \#C_k) : - \\ \qquad \neg(PERSON(\#X), CAR(\#C_1), \ldots, CAR(\#C_k)) \end{array}$$

where *error* displays appropriate error messages, and programs for *add*, *PERSON*, *CAR* are defined at the system level. $PERSON(X)$ fails if X is not a constant of sort *obj*, or if it is not the name of a $\mathcal{PERSON}$-object contained in the system. CAR is similarly defined. *add* updates the state-axiom closing *obj*, includes the signature of the $\#X$-instance of $\mathcal{DRIVER}$, and adds the state-axioms $state(\ldots)$.

Complementary methods for deleting cars and persons will be of the form:

$$\begin{array}{l} \#X.delete : - \ not\#X.error, cancel(\#X). \\ \#X.error : - \ DRIVER(\#N), \#N.Component(\#X). \end{array}$$

[11] In this example we will use a PROLOG-like formalism, but our discussion is independent of the chosen language.

where, similar to *add* and *cancel* can be defined at the system level. Note that the predicate *.Component* is needed in deletion methods of components of composite objects. We can assume that each composite OBJ-frameworks has to specify, at least, its own predicate *.Component*, as well as a correct method for computing it.

As we can see from the example, we can specify methods like $.Component(X)$, and we can reason about their synthesis and correctness in the usual way in our approach to program development. In contrast, in our previous work we have never specified methods for creating, deleting or updating objects. This is because we do not have a language to formally specify them; as a consequence, we can speak about their correctness only informally. A formal system specification language should contain appropriate system symbols, and making time explicit seems to us very useful. We are studying these aspects. A short discussion will be given in the conclusions.

Finally, we briefly show that composite OBJ-frameworks are OOD frameworks as used in CBD methodologies like *Catalysis*. First, the composite OBJ-framework $\mathcal{DRIVER}$ can be represented in *Catalysis* by the simple (closed) OOD framework shown in Figure 4.[12] Here the person object is fixed (and so is

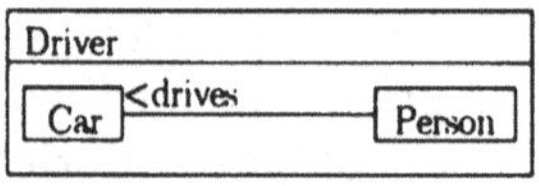

Fig. 4. The Driver OOD framework.

the composite driver object), like the traditional object in Figure 1.

A more interesting example is one where an object is formed by composing OBJ-frameworks in each of which the object plays a different role.

Example 11. In the OBJ-framework $\mathcal{DRIVER}[\mathcal{PERSON}, \mathcal{CAR}]$, the role of a person is to drive a car. So we can rename the Driver OOD framework in Figure 4 as the PersonAsDriver OOD framework.

Equally a person could also be a guest at a motel, i.e., we can build an OBJ-framework $\mathcal{GUEST}[\mathcal{PERSON}, \mathcal{MOTEL}]$. Thus a person can play the roles of driver and guest respectively in the PersonAsDriver and PersonAsGuest OOD frameworks, as shown in Figure 5. Then we can compose the two frameworks into $\mathcal{DRIVER} + \mathcal{GUEST}[\mathcal{PERSON}, \mathcal{CAR}, \mathcal{MOTEL}]$, where a person has two roles. This is depicted by Figure 6. In PersonAsDriverGuest, a person object is a composite object of the kind depicted in Figure 2.

Finally, we briefly discuss *open* OBJ-frameworks. In the previous example, both $\mathcal{DRIVER}$ and $\mathcal{GUEST}$ have the general structure of an user, i.e., they have

[12] We will present a simplified version of the (UML-like) notation used in *Catalysis*. More details can be found in [23, 16].

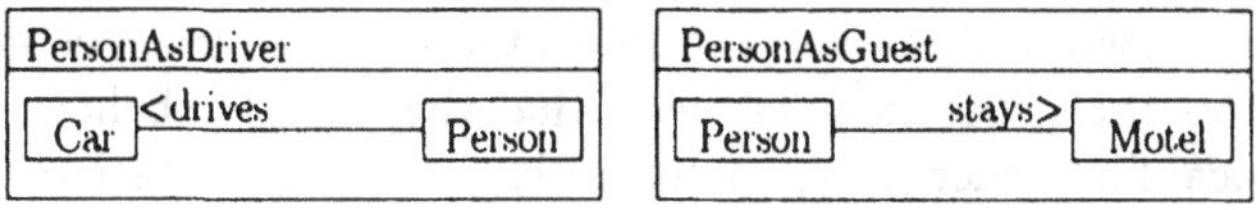

Fig. 5. PersonAsDriver and PersonAsGuest OOD frameworks.

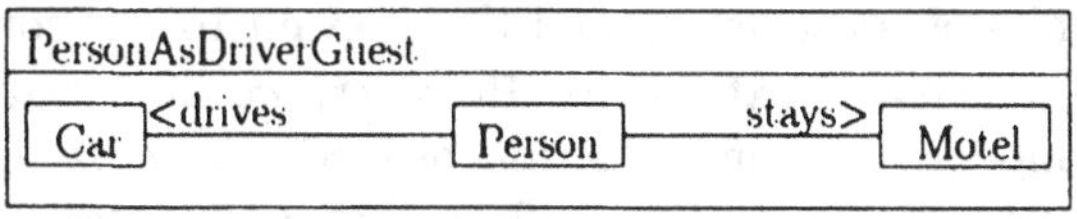

Fig. 6. PersonAsDriverGuest OOD framework.

the form $< \mathcal{USER} >$ $[< \mathcal{USING} >, < \mathcal{USED} >]$. Here we have *open* OBJ-frameworks (indicated by the presence of the parameters $< \mathcal{USING} >$ and $< \mathcal{USED} >$), which cannot close their (possible) dynamic symbols by themselves.

In general, open OBJ-frameworks need to incorporate more knowledge, to become OBJ-frameworks of the kind we have considered here, where dynamic symbols can be closed without any additional knowledge. We have not treated open OBJ-frameworks here for lack of space. They would allow us to model open OOD frameworks as used in *Catalysis*.

6 Conclusion

We have presented semantic foundations for OOD frameworks as used in current CBD methodologies, in particular *Catalysis*. Our three-tier formalism makes explicit the existence of two levels of reuse. The first level of reuse occurs at the (top) level of specification frameworks. Here reuse is based on the classical inheritance mechanisms and is governed by constraints. The second level of reuse occurs at the levels of specifications and programs. Here reuse is governed by specifications, which indicate how to correctly compose open correct programs, to get new correct (composite) programs. The second level of reuse thus pertains to *correct program reuse*, which, we believe, contributes to a better understanding of and support for reusability in OOD and CBD. We have already studied correct program reuse within ADT's, through the notion of steadfastness. The next step is to extend our study to state transitions, by formalising the dynamics of object systems.

We have also a model-theoretic, i.e. declarative, semantics. Our semantics is model-theoretic and hence declarative. Such a semantics is important we believe for defining, and reasoning about, the key elements of next-generation CDB methodologies, and should provide a sound theoretical basis for their implementations. As an example, our use of isoinitial theories (and models) is motivated by our desire for a good declarative semantics; but we do not expect ordinary users to handle such theories, which should be well-hidden in CBD implementations. Rather, users will reason in terms of the intended interpretations of the symbols of the ADT's, classes and objects that they use. We believe that the semantics classical first-order logic, based on classes of interpretations that satisfy common properties, models in a natural and intuitive way the variety of uses and meanings that open ADT's and classes can assume in different contexts.

Our approach is similar to that proposed by Maibaum [24] in the use of theories as the units of construction and the relevant role of conservative (and, in our approach, adequate) extensions. However, we have a different emphasis on intended models. The introduction of errors is most likely during the phase of specification design, and we believe that a clear declarative semantics is very important and helpful to reduce the risks of mistakes at this level. Another difference is that our modularity is ruled by framework constraints, rather than guaranteed by general conditions, like interpolability. Moreover, we want to model correct reusability of open programs, rather than stepwise implementation. Nevertheless, refinement based on mediating theories is interesting, as also shown by SPECWARE [29], and it seems that it could be imported in our approach, as an orthogonal technique.

Our model-theoretic characterisation of states and objects stands in contrast to the type-theoretic approach by Abadi & Cardelli [1], however.

The work that is most closely related to ours is that of Bourdeau & Cheng [3], which formalises a semantics for object model diagrams in OMT [27]. Basically they translate object model diagrams into algebraic specifications (and semantics) expressed in Larch [12]. Thus they use initial theories, as opposed to isoinitial theories that we use. Our preference for isoinitial semantics has already been discussed in Section 3. Another motivation is that, using initial semantics, additivity entails only that *positive* locally observable quantifier-free sentences are preserved at the system-level, i.e., any problems with negation will affect additivity.

Moreover, the formalisation proposed by [3] is not oriented to (open) OOD frameworks, i.e. groups of interacting objects. In other words, they consider objects as the unit of reuse, whereas our formalisation supports OOD frameworks as the unit of reuse. As we pointed out before, industry is increasingly recognising that objects are not the best focus for design, and OOD frameworks are becoming widely used as the basic unit of reuse.

Other approaches to formal semantics for CBD methodologies are mainly so-called integrated methods. For example France *et al* [9] derives Z [28] specifications from Fusion [4,6] diagrams. At present, such methods do not have completely formal semantics.

So far, our semantics provides a sound formalisation of OOD frameworks used in the CBD methodology *Catalysis*. However, in order to implement these frameworks, we need a formalism to describe and specify state transitions. In our semantics, we have only states at particular instants, i.e., each object has an intended model only at a fixed time, and we can treat state transition in a limited way. We can deal with the problem of constraint satisfaction, but not with the global system behaviour. More precisely, we cannot specify temporal properties, like liveness or deadlock freeness.

In order to achieve this capability, we are studying a temporal model for systems of objects. After a first attempt, inspired by evolving algebras [11], we decided to model states by evolving axioms. At each time, an evolving axiom A represents an observable instantaneous property. Evolving axioms are not so far from dynamic attributes (as used in, e.g., [8] and TROLL [10]). For example, a dynamic attribute $a : int$ with (current) value 5 corresponds to the (evolving) axiom $a = 5$, but evolving axioms allow us to describe larger classes of attributes, including data bases. To express dynamic behaviour, we need to model actions and time, taking into account the modularity induced by the presence of composite objects (similar ideas can be found, e.g., in [15]). Our aim is to introduce time in the specification language, and to deal with correctness of state transition methods in this extended context.

Acknowledgments

We wish to thank the referees for their helpful comments and suggestions. We also thank Juliana Küster-Filipe, Braunschweig University, Germany for her detailed feedback on an earlier draft.

References

1. M. Abadi and L. Cardelli. *A Theory of Objects*. Springer-Verlag, 1996.
2. A. Bertoni, G. Mauri, and P. Miglioli. On the power of model theory in specifying abstract data types and in capturing their recursiveness. *Fundamenta Informaticae* **VI**(2):127–170, 1983.
3. R.H. Bourdeau and B.H.C. Cheng. A formal semantics for object model diagrams. *IEEE Trans. Soft. Eng.*, 21(10):799-821, 1995.
4. D. Coleman, P. Arnold, S. Bodoff, C. Dollin, H. Gilchrist, F. Hayes, and P. Jeremaes. *Object-Oriented Development: The Fusion Method*. Prentice-Hall, 1994.
5. S. Cook and J. Daniels. *Designing Object Systems*. Prentice-Hall, 1994.
6. D.F. D'Souza and A.C. Wills. Extending Fusion: practical rigor and refinement. In R. Malan *et al*, editors, *Object-Oriented Development at Work*. Prentice-Hall 1996.
7. D.F. D'Souza and A.C. Wills. *Catalysis: Components, Objects and Frameworks in UML*. Addison-Wesley, October 1998. Draft available at http://www.trireme.com/catalysis/book.
8. J.L. Fiadeiro and T. Maibaum. Categorical semantics of parallel program design. *Science of Computer Programming* 28:111-138, 1997.
9. R.B. France, J.-M. Bruel, M. Larrondo-Petrie, E. Grant, and M. Saksena. Towards a rigorous object-oriented analysis and design method. *Proc. 1st IEEE Int. Conf. on Formal Engineering Methods*, pages 7-16, IEEE Computer Society, 1997.
10. A. Grau, J. Küster Filipe, M. Kowsari, S. Eckstein, R. Pinger and H.-D. Ehrich. The TROLL approach to conceptual modelling: syntax, semantics and tools. In T.W. Ling, S. Ram and M.L. Leebook, editors, *Proc. 17th Int. Conference on Conceptual Modeling*, *LNCS* 1507:277-290, Springer, 1998.

11. Y. Gurevich, Evolving Algebras 1993: Lipari Guide. In E. Börger, editor, *Specification and Validation Methods*, pages 9–36, Oxford University Press, 1995.
12. J.V. Guttag and J.J. Horning. Larch: Languages and Tools for Formal Specification. Springer-Verlag, 1993.
13. R. Helm, I.M. Holland, and D. Gangopadhay. Contracts — Specifying behavioural compositions in OO systems. *Sigplan Notices* 25(10) (*Proc. ECOOP/OOPSLA 90*).
14. C. Kreitz, K.-K. Lau, and M. Ornaghi. Formal reasoning about modules, reuse and their correctness. In D.M. Gabbay and H.J. Ohlbach, editors, *Proc. Int. Conf. on Formal and Applied Practical Reasoning*, *LNAI* 1085:384–399, Springer-Verlag 1996.
15. J. Küster Filipe. Using a modular distributed temporal logic for in-the-large object specification. In A. Brogi and P. Hill, editors, *Proc. 1st Int. Workshop on Component-based Software Development in Computational Logic*, pages 43-57, September 1998, Pisa, Italy.
16. K.-K. Lau, S. Liu, M. Ornaghi, and A. Wills. Interacting Frameworks in *Catalysis*. To appear in *Proc. 2nd IEEE Int. Conf. on Formal Engineering Methods*, 9-11 December 1998, Brisbane, Australia.
17. K.-K. Lau and M. Ornaghi. On specification frameworks and deductive synthesis of logic programs. In L. Fribourg and F. Turini, editors, *Proc. LOPSTR 94 and META 94*, *Lecture Notes in Computer Science* 883, pages 104–121, Springer-Verlag, 1994.
18. K.-K. Lau and M. Ornaghi. Towards an object-oriented methodology for deductive synthesis of logic programs. In M. Proietti, editor, *Proc. LOPSTR 95*, *LNCS* 1048:152–169, Springer-Verlag, 1996.
19. K.-K. Lau and M. Ornaghi. A formal approach to deductive synthesis of constraint logic programs. In J.W. Lloyd, editor, *Proc. 1995 Int. Logic Programming Symp.*, pages 543–557, MIT Press, 1995.
20. K.-K. Lau and M. Ornaghi, Isoinitial Models for Logic Programs: A Preliminary Study, in J.L. Freire-Nistal, M. Falaschi, and M. Vilares-Ferro, editors, *Proceedings of the 1998 Joint Conference on Declarative Programming*, pages 443-455, A Coruña, Spain, July 1998.
21. K.-K. Lau and M. Ornaghi. On specification and correctness of OOD frameworks in computational logic. In A. Brogi and P. Hill, editors, *Proc. 1st Int. Workshop on Component-based Software Development in Computational Logic*, pages 59-75, September 1998, Pisa, Italy.
22. K.-K. Lau, M. Ornaghi, and S.-Å. Tärnlund. Steadfast logic programs. To appear in *J. Logic Programming*.
23. K.-K. Lau, M. Ornaghi, and A. Wills. Frameworks in *Catalysis*: Pictorial Notation and Formal Semantics. *Proc. 1st IEEE Int. Conf. on Formal Engineering Methods*, pages 213-220, IEEE Computer Society, 1997.
24. T. Maibaum. Conservative extensions, interpretations between theories and all that! In *Proc. TAPSOFT 97*, *LNCS* 1214:40-66, Springer Verlag, 1997.
25. R. Mauth. A better foundation: development frameworks let you build an application with reusable objects. *BYTE* 21(9):40IS 10-13, September 1996.
26. P. Miglioli, U. Moscato and M. Ornaghi. Abstract parametric classes and abstract data types defined by classical and constructive logical methods. *J. Symb. Comp.* 18:41-81, 1994.
27. J. Rumbaugh, M. Blaha, W. Premerlani, F. Eddy, and W. Sorenson. *Object-Oriented Modeling and Design*. Prentice-Hall, 1991.
28. J.M. Spivey. *The Z Notation*. Prentice Hall, 2nd edition, 1992.

29. Y.V. Srinvas and R. Jüllig Specware: Formal support for composing software. In *Proc. MCP 95*, *LNCS* 947:399-422, Springer Verlag, 1995.
30. M. Wirsing. Algebraic specification. In J. Van Leeuwen, editor, *Handbook of Theoretical Computer Science*, pages 675–788. Elsevier, 1990.

The Use of Renaming in Composing General Programs

Antonio Brogi, Simone Contiero, and Franco Turini

Dipartimento di Informatica, Università di Pisa
Corso Italia 40, 56125 Pisa, Italy
{brogi,contiero,turini}@di.unipi.it

Abstract. Most modern computing systems consist of large numbers of software components that interact with each other. Correspondingly, the capability of re-using and composing existing software components is of primary importance in this scenario. In this paper we analyse the role of renaming as a key ingredient of component-based programming. More precisely, a meta-level renaming operation is introduced in the context of a logic-based program composition setting which features a number of other composition operations over general logic programs, that is, logic programs possibly containing negative premises. Several examples are presented to illustrate the increased knowledge representation capabilities of logic programming for non-monotonic reasoning. The semantics of programs and program compositions is defined in terms of three-valued logic by extending the three-valued semantics for logic programs proposed by Fitting [10]. A computational interpretation of program compositions is formalised by means of an equivalence preserving transformation of arbitrary program compositions into standard general programs.

1 Introduction and Motivations

Most modern computing systems consist of large numbers of software components that interact with each other. Correspondingly, the process of software development is changing from writing large pieces of software in some programming language to writing small pieces of software in some (meta-)language to suitably "glue" existing components and put them at work together.

Our work aims at contributing to setting firm foundations for developing program composition methodologies. We investigate the issues of program composition in a setting where both the language of components and the meta-language for composing them have a formal mathematical semantics. More precisely, we choose logic-based programming for specifying the components and a set of meta-level composition operations on logic programs as the gluing (part of the) meta-language. In previous work [4,6] we have proposed the use of a basic set of meta-level operations on logic programs for mastering the complexity of designing complex systems. More precisely, we have considered a modular approach to software development, where a complex system is partitioned into a

P. Flener (Ed.): LOPSTR'98, LNCS 1559, pp. 124–142, 1999.

number of small pieces that are designed to be combined together via composition operations.

In this paper, the role of *renaming* as a key ingredient for component-based programming is analysed. The capability of renaming symbols is indeed of primary importance in a program composition setting. On the one hand, independently developed components may employ different vocabularies of symbols. Different components may use different names for the same procedure, or may instead denote different procedures by the same name. These problems typically arise when building complex systems by combining large numbers of pre-existing components. In these situations, the capability of renaming symbols to eliminate vocabulary differences is a powerful support for the reuse of existing software components. On the other hand, renaming can be also employed to implement forms of information hiding and import/export among modules. Intuitively speaking, (part of) the code of a component may be made hidden to other components by renaming its symbols into fresh symbols that do not occur in any other component.

To analyse the importance of renaming for component-based programming, we will consider renaming as a basic meta-level operation on components, and formally define its meaning as a program transformation operation. More precisely, we will introduce a renaming operator in the context of the family of composition operations presented in [4], and we shall focus our discussion on some examples to illustrate the expressive power of renaming.

The computational interpretation of renaming is defined via an equivalence preserving syntactic transformation of general program expressions into standard general programs, which can be then executed by any state-of-the-art interpreter for logic programs.

The paper is structured as follows. Section 2 describes our program composition setting, while Sections 3 and 4 are devoted to discuss programming examples. Section 5 shows how the three-valued semantics characterisation of general programs suitably extends to program compositions, including the renaming operator. Finally, Section 6 contains some concluding remarks.

2 General Program Expressions

Throughout the paper, we shall use the standard terminology and notation of logic programming [1]. A literal is an atom or its negation, and a (general) query is a finite conjunction of literals. A *general clause* is a clause of the form $A \leftarrow \overline{L}$ where A is an atom and $\overline{L}$ is a query. A *general program* is a finite set of general clauses. Following [2], we consider a universal language in which all programs and queries are written, and we denote by $\mathcal{B}$ the Herbrand base of the language and by $ground(P)$ the fully instantiated version of program P.

We also consider four basic meta-level operations for composing general programs: *union* ($\cup$), *intersection* ($\cap$), *restriction* ($\prec$), and *renaming* (RN). Starting from a collection of named general programs, these operations define the following class of *general program expressions*:

$$E ::= P \mid E \cup E \mid E \cap E \mid E \prec E \mid RN(\rho, E)$$

where P is (the name of) a general program. Syntactically, both operands of $\cup$, $\cap$ and $\prec$ are program expressions. In a renamed expression $RN(\rho, E)$ the first operand is instead a *renaming substitution*.

A renaming substitution is defined as a set of pairs $\{p'_1/p_1, ..., p'_h/p_h\}$ where $\{p_1, ..., p_h\}$ and $\{p'_1, ..., p'_h\}$ are disjoint sets of predicate symbols. This first restriction is aimed at avoiding the confusion caused when a symbol plays both the role of the renamed symbol and the role of the renaming one, and allows idempotence to be enjoyed by renaming.

Moreover, $\forall i, j \in [1, h] : (i \neq j \implies p_i \neq p_j)$. This second restriction is obviously required in order to avoid ambiguities. Namely, there should be at most one way of renaming each symbol. It is worth observing that the renaming ρ is not forced to be injective. As will be discussed in the sequel, there are concrete cases in which we can take advantage of non-injectivity.

As a third and last constraint, a renaming substitution $\rho = \{\pi'/\pi\}$ is applicable to a program expression E if the set of predicate symbols π' is disjoint from the set of predicate symbols occurring in E [1].

Informally speaking, the effect of renaming a program expression E via a renaming substitution $\rho = \{p'_1/p_1, ..., p'_h/p_h\}$ is that every occurrence of a predicate symbol p_i in E is replaced by p'_i in the renamed program expression $RN(\rho, E)$. We will denote by $A\rho$ the application of a renaming substitution ρ to an atom A. Similarly, we will denote by $I\rho$ and $P\rho$ the application of ρ to a set of atoms I and to a program P. Moreover, we will sometimes abuse notation and denote a renaming substitution ρ simply by $\{\pi'/\pi\}$, where π' and π are sets of predicate symbols.

Any composition of general programs can be transformed into an equivalent general program. Namely, we define a syntactic transformation τ that maps any general program expression E into a general program $\tau(E)$ which is equivalent to E.

$$\begin{array}{lll}
\tau(P) & = P & \text{if } P \text{ is a general logic program} \\
\tau(E \cup F) & = \{A \leftarrow \overline{L} \mid & A \leftarrow \overline{L} \in \tau(E) \ \vee \ A \leftarrow \overline{L} \in \tau(F)\} \\
\tau(E \cap F) & = \{A \leftarrow \overline{L} \mid & \exists A', A'', \overline{L'}, \overline{L''}, \vartheta : \\
 & & A' \leftarrow \overline{L'} \in \tau(E) \ \wedge \ A'' \leftarrow \overline{L''} \in \tau(F) \ \wedge \\
 & & \vartheta = mgu(A', A'') \ \wedge \ A = A'\vartheta \ \wedge (\overline{L} = \overline{L'}\vartheta \cup \overline{L''}\vartheta)\} \\
\tau(E \prec F) & = \{A \leftarrow \overline{L} \mid & A \leftarrow \overline{L} \in \tau(E) \ \wedge \ name(A) \notin defs(\tau(F))\} \\
\tau(RN(\rho, E)) & = \tau(E)\rho &
\end{array}$$

where $name(A)$ denotes the predicate symbol of atom A, and $defs(P)$ denotes the set of predicate symbols defined in a program P.

[1] The set of predicate symbols occurring in a program expression E is defined as the set of predicate symbols occurring in the program $\tau(E)$, obtained by applying the transformation τ (see later) to E.

The transformation τ merely depends on the syntactic structure of the given expression, namely on the composition operations and on the syntax of the programs forming it. When the program expression is already a general program then τ is just the identity function. The *union* of two programs corresponds to the set-theoretic union of the clauses of the separate programs. The *intersection* operation combines two programs by merging pairs of clauses with unifiable heads into clauses having the (duplicate-free) conjunctions of the bodies of the original clauses as a body. The net effect is that the two programs act as sets of constraints one upon the other. Consider for instance the programs

```
P:                                    Q:
Likes(x,y) <-  ¬ Bitter(y).           Likes(Bob,y) <-  Sour(y).
Hates(x,y) <-  Sour(y).
```

Then the program $\tau(P \cap Q) = \{$ Likes(Bob,y) $\leftarrow \neg$ Bitter(y), Sour(y). $\}$ consists of just one clause obtained by joining the first clause of P with the clause of Q. Notice that $\tau(P \cap Q)$ does not contain a definition for predicate **Hates**, since the latter is not defined in Q.

The *restriction* operation filters the set of clauses of a program by eliminating all the clauses defining predicates which are defined in another program. Namely, $\tau(P \prec Q)$ contains all the clauses of P which define predicates for which no definition is present in Q. For instance, in the previous example we have that $\tau(P \prec Q) = \{$ Hates(x,y) <- Sour(y). $\}$.

Finally, as far as *renaming* is concerned, the transformation of an expression $RN(\rho, E)$ is simply obtained by applying the renaming substitution ρ (applicable to E) to the general program $\tau(E)$. For instance:
$\tau(RN(\{$Loves/Likes$\}, (P \cap Q))) = \{$Loves(Bob,y) <- $\neg$ Bitter(y), Sour(y). $\}$

3 Reusing Components

The ability of renaming symbols is of primary importance when considering the problem of combining independently developed components.

Consider for instance a simple program *Graph* for determining, via standard transitive closure, the existence of a path between two nodes in a directed graph. Namely *Graph* defines a relation Path in terms of an Arc relation over the nodes of a graph. Program *Graph* can be then composed with a program containing the representation of an actual graph. For instance, we may wish to use *Graph* with an existing database *Trains* containing information on train connections between cities:

```
Graph:                                Trains:
Path(x,y) <-  Arc(x,y).               Train_connection(Florence, Milan).
Path(x,z) <-  Arc(x,y), Path(y,z).    Train_connection(Pisa, Florence).
                                      ...
```

The renaming operator can be then exploited for combining *Graph* with *Trains* so to find the existence of train connections between cities. The example — that is over-simplified here because of space limits — is however representative of the general situation of a program defining some property (Path in this case) over some generic relation (Arc). Such a composition can be obtained by renaming predicate Arc into Train_connection by means of the expression:

$$RN(\{\text{Train\_connection}/\text{Arc}\}, Graph) \cup Trains.$$

It is worth observing furthermore, that renaming may also support the merging of different predicates into a single one. Referring to the previous example, let us now imagine to have two separate data bases containing information on train connections and flight connections between cities. Then, by renaming the predicates Train_connection and Flight_connection into Arc and by performing the union of the renamed programs with program *Graph*, it is possible to find out the paths connecting two cities and employing at each step either the train or the plane.

This non-injective use of renaming highlights how, in our framework, renaming is not just a vocabulary switch, but rather a mechanism for changing the cooperation degree among separate modules.

Notice that, in the above examples, the reuse supported by renaming can also be achieved by introducing "bridge clauses" to link separate components. Namely we may simply consider the expressions

$$Graph \cup Trains \cup \{\ \text{Arc(x,y) <- Train\_connection(x,y).}\}$$

and

$$Graph \cup Trains \cup \left\{ \begin{array}{l} \text{Arc(x, y) <- Train\_connection(x, y).} \\ \text{Arc(x, y) <- Flight\_connection(x, y).} \end{array} \right\}$$

It is worth observing however that, besides the extra derivation step introduced by bridge clauses, renaming and bridge clauses are different in essential ways. Intuitively speaking, this is due to the fact that renaming *changes* the meaning of a program, while bridge clauses only *extend* the meaning of a program.

Consequently, the corresponding behaviours are not equivalent, as the following example shows. Consider the programs:

A:
```
Likes(Bob,x)    <- Positive(x).
Likes(Mary, x)  <- SportsPerson(x).
Positive(Tina).
SportsPerson(John).
```

B:
```
Likes(Sue,x).
SportsPerson(Sue).
```

Suppose that, by adopting a hypothetical reasoning viewpoint, we wish to combine *A* with *B* while considering Sue as a positive person rather than a sports person [2].

[2] It is worth pointing out here that the original programs are not affected by the use of renaming (and neither by the use of the other operators), hence the forms of update we realise are to be seen as virtual and hypothetical rather than effective (and destructive).

Let us now compare the programs $P1 = \tau(A \cup RN($[Positive/SportsPerson]$, B))$ and $P2 = \tau(A \cup B \cup \{$ Positive(x) <- SportsPerson(x) $\})$, resulting respectively from the choice of employing renaming and from the choice of employing bridge clauses:

P1:

```
Likes(Bob,x)  <- Positive(x).
Likes(Mary, x)<- SportsPerson(x).
Likes(Sue,x).
SportsPerson(John).
Positive(Sue).
Positive(Tina).
```

P2:

```
Likes(Bob,x)  <- Positive(x).
Likes(Mary, x)<- SportsPerson(x).
Likes(Sue,x).
SportsPerson(John).
SportsPerson(Sue).
Positive(Tina).
Positive(x)    <- SportsPerson(x).
```

It is easy to observe that the resulting programs *P1* and *P2* are not equivalent since Sue is still considered a sports person in *P2* and, for instance, we can deduce — differently from *P1* — that Mary likes Sue.

Finally, renaming can be exploited together with other composition operations to define more structured compositions. For instance, consider a database *Holidays* containing general rules for choosing a country for the next trip. Predicate Good_Place(c,s) is intended to indicate that country c is a good place for a visit during season s.

Holidays:

```
Good_Place(c,s)    <-  ¬ Dangerous(c,s), Attractive(c,s).
Dangerous(c,s)     <-  Rainy_Season(c,s).
Dangerous(c,_)     <-  Civil_War(c).
Attractive(c,s)    <-  Hot_Season(c,s), Nat_Beauty(c).
Attractive(c,_)    <-  Art_Country(c).
Civil_War(Algeria).
Art_Country(Italy).
Nat_Beauty(Brasil).
...
```

Imagine also to have a knowledge base *Prices* containing information on the cost of living in foreign countries, and a set *Prefs* of rules specifying additional information on possible preferences.

Prices:

```
Rich_Country(Sweden).
Med_Country(Spain).
Poor_Country(Brasil).
...
```

```
  Prefs:
Medium(x,s)     <-  ¬ Rich_Country(x), Med_Season(x,s).
Exclusive(x,s)  <-  Rich_Country(x), High_Season(x,s).
Cheap(x,s)      <-  Poor_Country(x), ¬ High_Season(x,s).
...
```

To constrain the search on the basis of a small budget, we may employ the expression:

$$Cheap\_Holiday = (RN(\{\mathsf{Good\_Place/Cheap}\}, Prefs)\ constrains\ Holidays) \cup Prices$$

where $A\ constrains\ DB = (A \cap DB) \cup (DB \prec A)$. Namely the predicates renamed in *Prefs* are used to constrain the general rules in *Holidays* defined by means of predicate Good_Place. The obtained expression also keeps all other rules from *Holidays* as well as the rules in *Prices*. Notice that other choice criteria can be expressed by different compositions of the same programs, for instance by changing the renaming substitution into {Good_Place/Exclusive}.

4 Information Hiding

In the setting described so far, all symbols and predicate definitions of a component are by default visible to other components. There are however situations in which we would like to hide (part of) the code of a component to the other components.

Let us first consider a simple form of hiding that can be directly implemented by means of the *renaming* operator. Consider for instance an over-simplified database of a journal containing information on papers submitted for publication:

```
  Journal_DB:
Status (paper, Accepted)       <-   Accepted(paper).
Status (paper, Rejected)       <-   Rejected(paper).
Status(paper, UnderReview)     <-   ¬ Status(paper, Accepted),
                                    ¬ Status(paper, Rejected),
                                    Reviewers(paper, ref1, ref2),
                                    Missing_Review(paper, ref1, ref2).
Reviewers(P23-97, Brown, Smith).
...
```

In order to allow external users to query the database on the status of a paper, the database manager would reasonably need to hide some of the information present in the database, like for instance the names of the referees that are reviewing a paper. Intuitively speaking, such a simple form of hiding can be implemented by renaming part of the symbols in the database with fresh system symbols that cannot occur in any user program. For instance, the name of the relation Reviewers can be replaced by a fresh system predicate name, thus making Reviewers not visible to other components.

A more general form of information hiding is motivated by the abstract data type view of components. Consider for instance the programs:

Palindrome:

```
Pal(list) <-  Reverse(list,r), list=r.
```

Lists:

```
Reverse([ ],[ ]).
Reverse([x|xs],ys) <-  Reverse(xs,zs), Append(zs,[x],ys).
Append([ ],ys,ys).
Append([x|xs],ys,[x|ws]) <-  Append(xs,ys,ws).
```

where program *Palindrome* defines a predicate `Pal` for determining whether a given sequence is palindrome. The definition of predicate Pal makes use of the Reverse operation on lists, which is defined in *Lists*. Following an abstract data type view, only the names of the operations on lists should be made visible to other modules, while their implementation should be hidden.

We now show how renaming can be exploited in a disciplined way to implement various forms of information hiding. Let us first consider an operation $Export(\pi_n, E)$, whose intended meaning is to leave only the names of predicates in π_n visible to other modules, while hiding to other modules the code of all predicates in E.

Such a form of information hiding can be implemented by means of the *renaming* and *union* operations. Namely, the expression $Export(\pi_n, E)$ can be defined as the *union* of two expressions:

(1) the expression E suitably renamed so as to replace each predicate symbol p in E with a fresh predicate symbol p' (not visible to the other components), and

(2) a set of bridge clauses of the form $p(x) \leftarrow p'(x)$ linking each predicate p in π_n with the corresponding fresh system predicate p'.

Syntactically, if π is the set of predicate symbols occurring [3] in E and π' is a set of *fresh* predicate symbols in a one-to-one correspondence with the set π, then $Export(\pi_n, E)$ can be defined as:

$$Export(\pi_n, E) \;=\; RN(\pi'/\pi, E) \;\cup\; \{p(x) \leftarrow p'(x) \mid p \in \pi_n \wedge (p'/p) \in \pi'/\pi\}.$$

Namely, predicate names in E are renamed with fresh system predicate names, which do not occur in any other user program[4], so that the entire code of E becomes not accessible to other components. Bridge clauses re-introduce a link to the names of predicates in π_n so that these names become again visible to other components.

[3] The predicate symbols occurring in an expression E actually are all predicate symbols occurring in the program $\tau(E)$.

[4] The choice of fresh system predicates must be defined in such a way that once a symbol has been chosen it will never be chosen again. This can be easily implemented by means of a system function able to generate on demand a stream of different predicate names.

For instance, the operation $Export(\pi_n, E)$ can be used to hide the entire code of an expression E while leaving all the names in E visible to other modules. For instance, in the previous example, in the expression:

$$Palindrome \cup Export(\{\mathsf{Reverse}, \mathsf{Append}\}, Lists)$$

only the names of predicates in *Lists* are visible to *Palindrome*, while the entire code of *Lists* is hidden. The operation $Export(\pi_n, E)$ can be also used to hide the code of an expression E while leaving only *some* of the procedure names in E visible to other modules. For instance the expression:

$$Palindrome \cup Export(\{\mathsf{Reverse}\},\ Lists)$$

combines programs *Palindrome* and *Lists* so that the former can only use the name of the operation Reverse defined in the latter. On the other hand, the code of Reverse is hidden to *Palindrome*, while Append is fully hidden (both the name and the code) to *Palindrome*. It is worth noting that this usage of renaming supports the reconstruction of the form of exportation present in conventional modular programming languages, such as Ada and Modula, with a substantial difference. Namely, in our framework, by moving renaming at the meta-level, each original module can be adapted in several ways to different situations, simply by deciding, at the gluing level (viz. at the meta-level), which symbols to hide and which ones to keep visible. This allows a higher degree of both flexibility and generality.

In logic-based programming, procedure (viz. predicate) definitions consist of sets of clauses which may be distributed over different components, in contrast with the monolithical structure of procedure definitions in conventional languages.

Moreover in logic-based programming the knowledge about a procedure is available at two different levels. The *intensional* definition of a procedure is the code of the predicate, i.e. the set of clauses defining it. The *extensional* definition is instead the set of atomic formulae provable for that predicate. Following this observation, the use of renaming in a logic program composition setting may hence support different forms of information hiding.

Let us now consider the more general situation in which we wish: (a) to hide the code and leave visible the name of some predicates, (b) to leave visible both the name and the code of other predicates, and finally (c) to hide both the code and the name of the remaining predicates.

To this end, let us consider a more general definition of the *Export* operation of the form $Export^{+}(\pi_n, \pi_c, E)$, whose intended meaning is to leave the names of predicates in π_n visible while hiding their code, and to leave visible both the name and the code of predicates in π_c. All other predicates in E but not in $(\pi_n \cup \pi_c)$ are fully hidden.

Syntactically, if π is the set of predicate symbols occurring in E and π' is a set of *fresh* predicate symbols in a one-to-one correspondence with the set $(\pi - \pi_c)$, then $Export^{+}(\pi_n, \pi_c, E)$ can be defined as follows:

$$Export^{+}(\pi_n, \pi_c, E) = RN(\pi'/(\pi - \pi_c), E) \cup$$
$$\{p(x) \leftarrow p'(x) \mid p \in \pi_n \wedge (p'/p) \in \pi'/(\pi - \pi_c)\}.$$

Namely the effect of $RN(\pi'/(\pi-\pi_c), E)$ is to make the code and the names of all predicates in E except those in π_c not accessible to other components, while the bridge clauses re-introduce a link to the names of predicates in π_n so that these names become again visible to other components. Notice that $Export^{+}$ properly generalises the definition of $Export$ as $Export(\pi_n, E) = Export^{+}(\pi_n, \{\}, E)$.

We conclude this section by illustrating another example, whose purpose is to further show the benefits of a meta-level renaming operator. Let us reconsider the graph example of Sect. 3. Imagine again to have two separate data bases containing information on train connections and flight connections between cities. We may then need to find out whether from a given city it is possible to reach a destination (i.e., another city) by using either the train only or the plane only.

A proper combination of renaming and bridge clauses assists us to deal with this disjoint union problem. Namely, we can explicitly build the program

```
    B:
Path(x,y) <-  Train_Path(x,y).
Path(x,y) <-  Plane_Path(x,y).
```

and the expression

$B \cup RN(\rho_1, Graph) \cup RN(\rho_2, Graph) \cup Trains \cup Flights$

where

$\rho_1 = \{\text{Train\_Path/Path, Train\_connection/Arc}\}$ and
$\rho_2 = \{\text{Plane\_Path/Path, Flight\_connection/Arc}\}$.

Alternatively, by relying on the derived $Export^{+}$ operator, we may directly take into account the expression

$$Export^{+}(\{\text{Path}\}, S_1, RN(\rho_1, Graph) \cup Trains) \cup$$
$$Export^{+}(\{\text{Path}\}, S_2, RN(\rho_2, Graph) \cup Flights)$$

where $\rho_1 = \{\text{Train\_connection/Arc}\}$, $\rho_2 = \{\text{Flight\_connection/Arc}\}$,
$S_1 = \{\text{Train\_connection}\}$ and $S_2 = \{\text{Flight\_connection}\}$.

5 Semantics

So far we have tried to illustrate some significant possible uses of a renaming operator for component-based programming, in the context of a family of meta-level composition operations over logic programs. The computational interpretation of program expressions has been defined in Sect. 2 by means of the syntactic transformation τ that maps arbitrary program expressions back into general programs, which can be then executed by any state-of-art interpreter for logic programs.

It is however important to define an abstract semantics of program compositions, besides this transformational semantics, so as to characterise the intended meaning of each composition without the need of referring to the corresponding transformed program. Brogi and Turini showed [7] the need of resorting to higher-order semantics in order to define compositional semantics for definite programs with non-trivial sets of composition operations. The same consideration applies to compositions of *general* programs, where in addition the orthogonal aspects of compositionality and non-monotonicity must be reconciled.

A compositional semantics for general program expressions containing $\cup$, $\cap$ and $\prec$ operations has been defined in [4] in terms of three-valued logic. Although, at least at first sight, renaming does not seem to cope with compositionality, it is possible to show that the above semantics extends to deal with the *renaming* operator introduced in this paper.

In order to do this, we first briefly recall from [4] some definitions and results.

Fitting [10] proposed to use a three-valued logic [15] to formalise the meaning of general programs. Three-valued logic models the idea that a query can yield *three* possible outcomes: success, failure, and divergence. Accordingly, a notion of three-valued Herbrand interpretation is introduced. Formally, a *three-valued Herbrand interpretation* is a pair $I = (I^+, I^-)$ of Herbrand interpretations, where I^+ are atoms assumed to be true, and I^- are atoms assumed to be false. All other atoms are assumed to be unknown. Fitting [10] defined a three-valued immediate consequence operator Φ, which given a general program P and a three-valued interpretation I yields a three-valued interpretation. Namely:

$$\Phi(P)(I) = (T, F)$$

where

$$T = \{A \mid \exists\, \overline{L} : (A \leftarrow \overline{L}) \in ground(P) \text{ and } \overline{L} \text{ is true in } I\ \}$$

and

$$F = \{A \mid \forall\, \overline{L} : (A \leftarrow \overline{L}) \in ground(P) \text{ implies } \overline{L} \text{ is false in } I\ \}.$$

For example, if a program P consists of the two clauses $\{a \leftarrow b. \quad c.\}$ and $I = (\emptyset, \{b\})$, then $\Phi(P)(I) = (\{c\}, \{a, b\})$.

A compositional semantics for program expressions has been defined in [4] by inductively extending the definition of Φ so that its first argument is an arbitrary general program expression. In the following, we will use the notations $\Phi^+(E)(I)$ and $\Phi^-(E)(I)$ to denote the positive part and the negative part, respectively, of the three-valued interpretation $\Phi(E)(I)$. Moreover, if J is a (two-valued) Herbrand interpretation, we will denote by $Ext(J)$ the "extension" of J w.r.t. $\mathcal{B}$, that is J extended with all the atoms in $\mathcal{B}$ having the same predicate as some atom in J. Formally, for each $J \subseteq \mathcal{B}$:

$$Ext(J) = \{p(\overline{t}) \mid p(\overline{t}) \in \mathcal{B} \wedge \exists \overline{u} : p(\overline{u}) \in J\}.$$

Then, for any pair E_1, E_2 of program expressions and for any three-valued Herbrand interpretation I, we put:

$$\Phi(E_1 \cup E_2)(I) = (\Phi^+(E_1)(I) \cup \Phi^+(E_2)(I),\ \ \Phi^-(E_1)(I) \cap \Phi^-(E_2)(I))$$

$$\Phi(E_1 \cap E_2)(I) \;=\; (\Phi^+(E_1)(I) \cap \Phi^+(E_2)(I),\;\; \Phi^-(E_1)(I) \cup \Phi^-(E_2)(I))$$

$$\Phi(E_1 \prec E_2)(I) \;=\; (\Phi^+(E_1)(I) - Ext(K),\; \Phi^-(E_1)(I) \cup Ext(K))$$

where $K = \Phi^+(E_2)(\mathcal{B}, \mathcal{B})$.
Namely, the atoms assumed to be true for $E_1 \cup E_2$ and I are the atoms assumed to be true for E_1 and I *or* for E_2 and I. In a dual manner, the atoms assumed to be false for the $E_1 \cup E_2$ and I are the atoms which are assumed to be false for E_1 and I *and* for E_2 and I. The duality of the *union* and *intersection* operations is reflected by the corresponding definition of the Φ operator. Finally, concerning the *restriction* operation $\prec$, the atoms assumed to be true for $E_1 \prec E_2$ and I are all the atoms $p(\bar{t})$ assumed to be true for E_1 and I except those for which predicate p is "defined" in E_2. Namely, the latter set of atoms can be defined as the extension $Ext(K)$ of the set of atoms K which are assumed to be true in E_2 starting from the whole Herbrand base $\mathcal{B}$.

Let us now discuss in detail the case of renaming. To this aim, if $\rho = \{\pi'/\pi\}$ is a renaming substitution and I is a (two-valued) Herbrand interpretation, we use the notation:

$$\mathcal{R}(\rho, I) = \{p(t) \mid p'(t) \in I \;\wedge\; p'/p \in \rho\} \;\cup\; (I - \{p(t) \mid p \in \pi\}).$$

The notation trivially extends to three-valued (Herbrand) interpretations, that is, if $I = (I^+, I^-)$ then $\mathcal{R}(\rho, I) = (\mathcal{R}(\rho, I^+), \mathcal{R}(\rho, I^-))$. The definition of the immediate consequence operator Φ can be then extended to deal with renamed program expressions as follows. For each expression E, three-valued interpretation I, and applicable renaming substitution ρ, we put:

$$\Phi(RN(\rho, E))(I) \;=\; (J^+\rho\,,\; \{p(t) \mid p \in \pi\} \;\cup\; (J^- - \{p'(t) \mid p' \in \pi'\})\rho\;)$$

where $J = \Phi(E)(\mathcal{R}(\rho, I))$.
Namely the immediate consequences of a renamed program expression $RN(\rho, E)$ w.r.t. a three-valued interpretation I are obtained from the set J of the immediate consequences of the original expression E w.r.t. the interpretation $\mathcal{R}(\rho, I)$. The positive consequences simply correspond to the renaming of J^+ via ρ. The negative consequences instead are obtained from the negative consequences J^- (suitably filtered of all the renamed atoms) renamed via ρ and augmented with all the atoms whose predicate symbol belongs to π.

For example, the program $P = \{a \texttt{<-} b,\ \neg c.\ \}$, together with the renaming substitution $\rho = \{a'/a,\ b'/b\}$ and the interpretation $I = (\{b'\}, \{c\})$ give rise to the interpretation $\mathcal{R}(\rho, I) = (\{b\}, \{c\})$ and to the consequences:

$$\begin{aligned}\Phi(RN(\rho, P))(I) &= ((\Phi^+(P)(\mathcal{R}(\rho, I)))\rho\,,\ \{a,b\} \cup (\Phi^-(P)(\mathcal{R}(\rho, I)) - \{a', b'\})\rho) = \\ &(\Phi^+(P)(\{b\}, \{c\})\rho\,,\ \{a,b\} \cup (\Phi^-(P)(\{b\}, \{c\}) - \{a', b'\})\rho) = \\ &(\{a\}\rho\,,\ \{a,b\} \cup (\{a', b', b, c\} - \{a', b'\})\rho) \;=\; (\{a'\}\,,\ \{a, b, b', c\}).\end{aligned}$$

It was noted that the renaming operator alone is independent from the underlying semantics. This is true in a way, since it is straightforward to define a renaming operator coupled with other well-known semantics for general logic programs, like the well-founded or the stable model semantics. However, as we will discuss in Sect. 6, the advantages of combining renaming with the other operators seems to be lost when departing from our chosen semantics.

It is worth observing that the operations *union*, *intersection*, *restriction* and *renaming* enjoy a number of algebraic properties which are listed in Fig. 1. For the sake of simplicity, the laws are stated as equalities between program expressions, although they represent semantics equalities. Namely $E = F$ means $\Phi(E) = \Phi(F)$. The constant 1 denotes the program containing a unit clause $P(\overline{x})$. for each predicate symbol P of the language, while the constant 0 denotes the empty program. The algebraic properties listed in Fig. 1 provide a formal basis for reasoning on (virtual) composition of general program expressions. For instance, syntactically different program expressions may be formally compared and simplified, and equivalent program expressions may be replaced one by another for improving efficiency.

$A \cup 1 = 1$	$A \prec A = 0$
$A \cup 0 = A$	$A \cup B = B \cup A$
$A \cap 1 = A$	$A \cap B = B \cap A$
$A \cap 0 = 0$	$(A \cup B) \cup C = A \cup (B \cup C)$
$A \prec 1 = 0$	$(A \cap B) \cap C = A \cap (B \cap C)$
$A \prec 0 = A$	$A \cup (B \cap C) = (A \cup B) \cap (A \cup C)$
$A \cup A = A$	$A \cap (B \cup C) = (A \cap B) \cup (A \cap C)$
$A \cap A = A$	$A \prec (B \cup C) = (A \prec B) \cap (A \prec C)$
$RN(\rho, RN(\rho, A)) = RN(\rho, A)$	$RN(\rho, A \cup B) = RN(\rho, A) \cup RN(\rho, B)$

Fig. 1. The algebra of general program expressions.

Besides the identities shown in the table, there are other interesting relations that need some additional conditions to hold. For instance, $RN(\rho, A \cap B) = RN(\rho, A) \cap RN(\rho, B)$ holds provided that $\rho = \{\pi'/\pi\}$ is applicable both to A and to B, and furthermore that $defs(A) \cap \pi = defs(B) \cap \pi$. It is worth observing that, when ρ is injective, the latter condition is not necessary for the equivalence to hold. The same conditions are needed in order to satisfy the equation $RN(\rho, A \prec B) = RN(\rho, A) \prec RN(\rho, B)$.

Finally, it is worth observing that the transformation τ introduced in Sect. 2 preserves the three-valued semantics defined by Φ. More precisely, each program expression E is Φ-equivalent to the transformed general program $\tau(E)$, as stated by the following proposition.

Proposition 1. *Let E be a general program expression. Then for any three-valued Herbrand interpretation I:*

$$\Phi(E)(I) = \Phi(\tau(E))(I).$$

We have already proved by structural induction [4] the validity of Proposition 1 for program expressions not including the renaming operator. We now show how the above proposition extends to the case in which general program expressions includes the *renaming* operator.

In order to do this, we need some preliminary results.

Lemma 1. *Let A be a ground atom, let ρ be a renaming substitution and let I be a two-valued Herbrand interpretation. Then the following relation holds:*

$$A \in \mathcal{R}(\rho, I) \Longleftrightarrow A\rho \in I$$

Proof.
Let $\rho = \{\pi'/\pi\}$ and $A = q(t)$. We have to prove the following:
$q(t) \in \ \{p(t) \mid p'(t) \in I \ \wedge \ p'/p \in \rho\} \cup \ (I - \{p(t) \mid p \in \pi\}) \Longleftrightarrow q(t)\{\pi'/\pi\} \in I$

($\Longrightarrow$) Let us reason by cases:
(i) : $q(t) \in \mathcal{R}(\rho, I) \wedge q \in \pi \ \Rightarrow \ \{$ by definition of $\mathcal{R}(\rho, I)$ $\}$
$q(t) \in \{p(t) \mid p'(t) \in I \wedge p'/p \in \rho\} \ \wedge q \in \pi \ \Rightarrow q(t)\{\pi'/\pi\} \in I$
(ii) : $q(t) \in \mathcal{R}(\rho, I) \wedge q \notin \pi \ \Rightarrow \ \{$ by definition of $\mathcal{R}(\rho, I)$ $\}$
$q(t) \in (I - \{p(t) \mid p \in \pi\}) \wedge q \notin \pi \ \Rightarrow q(t) \in I \wedge q \notin \pi \ \Rightarrow q(t)\{\pi'/\pi\} \in I$

($\Longleftarrow$) We must show that: $q(t)\rho \in I \Longrightarrow q(t) \in \mathcal{R}(\rho, I)$. Again, by cases:
(i) : $q(t)\{\pi'/\pi\} \in I \wedge q \in \pi \ \Rightarrow \ \{$ let $q'/q \in \rho$ $\}$ $q'(t) \in I \wedge q'/q \in \rho \ \Rightarrow$
$\{$ by definition of $\mathcal{R}(\rho, I)$ $\}$ $q(t) \in \mathcal{R}(\rho, I)$
(ii) : $q(t)\{\pi'/\pi\} \in I \wedge q \notin \pi \ \Rightarrow \{$ since $q(t)$ is not affected by ρ $\}$
$q(t) \in I \wedge q \notin \pi \ \Rightarrow \{$ by definition of $\mathcal{R}(\rho, I)$ $\}$ $q(t) \in \mathcal{R}(\rho, I)$ □

Observation 1 *Let I be a three-valued Herbrand interpretation, $\overline{B}$ be a conjunction of ground literals and ρ be a renaming substitution. Then:*
(i) $\overline{B}$ is true in $\mathcal{R}(\rho, I) \Longleftrightarrow \overline{B}\rho$ is true in I
(ii) $\overline{B}$ is false in $\mathcal{R}(\rho, I) \Longleftrightarrow \overline{B}\rho$ is false in I

Proof.
Straightforward, being a direct consequence of the above lemma. □

Observation 2 *Let E be a program expression and $\rho = \{\pi'/\pi\}$ be a renaming substitution applicable to E. Then:*
$\forall A, \overline{B}$: $\quad A \leftarrow \overline{B} \in ground(\tau(E)) \Longleftrightarrow (A \leftarrow \overline{B})\rho \in (ground(\tau(E)))\rho$

Proof.
Straightforward. By definition of applicable renaming substitution. □

Now we can address the additional case of Proposition 1 dealing with renaming. That is, we show that, for each program expression E, and each three-valued Herbrand interpretation I, the following relation holds

$$\Phi(RN(\rho, E))(I) = \Phi(\tau(RN(\rho, E)))(I)$$

The case of renaming is handled by analysing, for the positive and negative part respectively, three different (sub-)cases. In fact, each symbol belongs to exactly one of the three disjoint sets π, π' and the complement of $(\pi \cup \pi')$ [5]. Each case is based on a series of equivalence steps. The steps for the positive cases are sketched below.

Proof.
Case (i): $\Phi^+(RN(\rho, E))(I)$
(i.1): $name(A) \in \pi$.
By definition of $\Phi^+(RN(\rho, E))$ and of renaming ρ, we have that $\forall I \ \nexists A : A \in (\Phi^+(E)(\mathcal{R}(\rho, I)))\rho \ \wedge \ name(A) \in \pi$. On the other side, since the program $\tau(RN(\rho, E)) = \tau(E)\rho$ does not contain any definition for symbols occurring in π it turns out that $\forall I \ \nexists A : A \in (\Phi^+(\tau(RN(\rho, E))))(I)$.

(i.2): $name(A) \in \pi'$.
The relation $A \in \Phi^+(RN(\rho, E))(I)$ holds, by definition of $\Phi^+(RN(\rho, E))$ and of renaming ρ, if and only if $\exists A' : A = A'\rho \wedge name(A') \in \pi \wedge A' \in \Phi^+(E)(\mathcal{R}(\rho, I))$. By inductive hypothesis on E and by definition of Φ^+, we get that $\exists A', B : A = A'\rho \ \wedge \ A' \leftarrow B \in ground(\tau(E)) \ \wedge \ B \ is \ true \ in \ \mathcal{R}(\rho, I)$. ¿From Observation 2 we have $\exists A', B : A = A'\rho \ \wedge \ (A' \leftarrow B)\rho \in (ground(\tau(E)))\rho \ \wedge \ B \ is \ true \ in \ \mathcal{R}(\rho, I)$. Now, from Lemma 1, we obtain $\exists A', B : A = A'\rho \ \wedge \ A \leftarrow B\rho \in (ground(\tau(E)))\rho \ \wedge \ B\rho \ is \ true \ in \ I$. Since for each program P and each renaming ρ, the relation $(ground(P))\rho = ground(P\rho)$ holds, then $\exists A', B : A = A'\rho \wedge A \leftarrow B\rho \in ground(\tau(E)\rho) \wedge B\rho \ is \ true \ in \ I$. By definition of Φ^+, this equals $A \in \Phi^+(\tau(E)\rho)(I)$. By definition of $\tau(RN(\rho, E))$ we finally achieve $A \in \Phi^+(\tau(RN(\rho, E)))(I)$.

(i.3): $name(A) \notin (\pi \cup \pi')$.
The relation $A \in \Phi^+(RN(\rho, E))(I)$, by definition of $\Phi^+(RN(\rho, E))$, equals to $A = A\rho \ \wedge \ A \in \Phi^+(E)(\mathcal{R}(\rho, I))$. Now, by inductive hypothesis, we have $A = A\rho \ \wedge \ A \in \Phi^+(\tau(E))(\mathcal{R}(\rho, I))$. This, by definition of Φ^+, holds if and only if $\exists B : A \leftarrow B \in ground(\tau(E)) \wedge B \ is \ true \ in \ \mathcal{R}(\rho, I)$. This, by Lemma 1, means that $\exists B : A \leftarrow B \in ground(\tau(E)) \wedge B\rho \ is \ true \ in \ I \wedge A = A\rho$. Since for each program P and each renaming ρ, the relation $(ground(P))\rho = ground(P\rho)$ holds, then $\exists B : (A \leftarrow B)\rho \in ground((\tau(E))\rho) \wedge B\rho \ is \ true \ in \ I \wedge A = A\rho$. By definition of Φ^+, this equals $A \in \Phi^+(\tau(E)\rho)(I)$, from which we finally obtain, by definition of τ, the relation $A \in \Phi^+(\tau(RN(\rho, E)))(I)$.

Case (ii): $A \in \Phi^-(RN(\rho, E))(I)$
The proof is analogous to *Case* (*i*), and hence omitted. □

By virtue of the above equivalence result, the three-valued semantics of general program expressions can be then related [4] to various operational semantics for general programs proposed in the literature.

[5] Each proof step may implicitly use the set membership hypothesis specified at the beginning of the proof case.

6 Concluding Remarks

The concept of renaming has been widely studied and employed in mathematics and computer science for different purposes, including program composition. For instance, adopting an algebraic approach for defining the semantics of module and module compositions, Bergstra et al. [3] introduced a renaming operator for combining different signatures. However, the kind of renaming they proposed is "permutative", that is, if a is replaced by b, then b is replaced by a. This can be useful for avoiding name clashes, but not for purposes such as increasing or decreasing the cooperation between different parts of code, as we intend to use it. Indeed, our renaming operation is idempotent rather than permutative, and it is not even injective in the general case. This allows a description of several kinds of code integration. In reality, our renaming operator is more similar to the concept of signature morphism [13]. In this respect, the notion expressed by our function $\mathcal{R}(\rho, I)$ can be viewed as an adaptation of the forgetful function to our context.

It is worth outlining that a renaming facility can be easily defined to cope with other semantics for general programs, such as the stable model semantics [11], or the well-founded semantics [19]. This is not surprising, since renaming by itself is just a vocabulary change. Nonetheless, we argue that renaming can become really useful when used in combination with other operators, like the ones we presented in this paper. For instance, given the programs

```
G:                                                    F:
Direct_Conn(x,y)     <-  Arc(x,y).                    Flight(Pisa,Paris).
Undirect_Conn(x,y)   <- ¬ Arc(x,y),                   Flight(Paris,London).
                          Path(x,y).

Path(Pisa,London).
Path(Pisa,Paris).
```

and building the expression $E = G \cup RN(\{\mathsf{Arc/Flight}\}, F)$ we obtain, through the calculus of the powers of $\Phi(E)$ starting from the empty interpretation $(\emptyset, \emptyset)$, the positive conclusions Direct_Conn(Pisa,Paris), Direct_Conn(Paris,London) and Undirect_Conn(Pisa,London).

A similar result could not be obtained by combining the renamed models of the two programs. Indeed, evaluating separately the powers of Φ for the programs G and F and then renaming predicate Flight into Arc leads to derive unwanted conclusions, such as Undirect_Conn(Pisa,Paris) and not to obtain some of the desired information (e.g., Direct_Conn(Pisa,Paris)).

The same problem occurs also with other well-known semantics, such as the well-founded semantics [19], the stable models semantics [11] or perfect models semantics [17].

In our case, we succeed because our compositionality results for three-valued semantics have been established in terms of the three-valued immediate consequence operator associated with programs rather than in terms of the models of programs. In this respect, the other cited semantics for general programs seem to lack an easy compositional, second order characterisation.

The need for resorting to second order semantics for defining compositional semantics of logic programs was already pointed out in the case of definite programs. Brogi and Turini [7] showed that the equivalence relation induced by the immediate consequence operator T is the fully abstract compositional equivalence relation for an algebra of logic programs containing several composition operations over definite programs. In this perspective the compositionality of other models could be studied in terms of second order functions used for computing such models. For instance, one could consider the fixpoint operator used for computing the well-founded models of a program. However, differently from the case of Fitting's Φ operator, it seems that in the case of well-founded semantics there is no simple composition on fixpoint operators which is homomorphic to the operation of union on programs.

Several other efforts have been devoted to investigate the composition of general logic programs. Some compositionality results for extended logic programs, including general programs, were established by Brogi et al. in [5]. The authors showed that many semantics for general programs (such as stable models, well-founded models, stationary expansions [18], complete scenaria [8]) can be defined in terms of the Herbrand models of the positive version of a program. The compositionality of Herbrand models w.r.t. the union of programs then induces general compositionality results for the various semantics considered. While these results can be applied to different semantic frameworks, only the operation of union between programs is considered. Unfortunately, as shown for instance in [7], the Herbrand model semantics is not compositional for other operations, like the *intersection* or *restriction* operations considered in this paper.

Lifschitz and Turner [16] investigated the idea of *splitting* a logic program into parts in the context of the answer set semantics [12]. The basic idea is that, in many cases, a program can be divided into a "bottom" part and a "top" part, such that the latter does not refer to predicates defined in the former. Lifschitz and Turner showed that computing the answer sets for a program can be simplified when the program is split into parts. They also showed that the idea of splitting can be applied for proving properties of simple program compositions, like a conservative extension property for a program P extended by rules whose heads do not occur in P.

Etalle and Teusink [9] and Verbaeten et al. [21] studied the problems of defining compositional semantics for general logic programs. Etalle and Teusink [9] define a compositional semantics for general programs by means of a first-order unfolding operator. Such a semantics is applied for composing "open" general programs by considering the union of programs as the only composition operation.

Verbaeten et al. in [21] present several results on the compositionality of general logic programs by generalising the well-founded semantics of logic programming. More precisely, they identify some conditions under which the class of extended well-founded models of the union of two general programs coincides with the intersection of the classes of extended well-founded models of the two programs.

All these approaches differ from ours since the union of programs is the only composition operation considered, and since a restrictive naming policy is imposed on the predicate names of the programs to be composed. Namely, in contrast with our naming policy, predicate definitions cannot be spread over different programs.

Recently, Verbaeten and Bossi [20] provide an attempt to compose separate programs sharing predicate definitions, according to the generalisation of the well-founded semantics already presented in [21]. As it is argued in [20], this will reflect the quite common situation in which two programs both have an incomplete knowledge over the same predicate. The authors discuss some conditions required in order to enforce the compositionality of the chosen semantics characterisation, when dealing with such situations.

The use of parameterisation proposed by Hill [14] for typed logic-based languages shares some of the objectives of our work. Hill considered two kinds of parameters: "open" parameters to support code linking, and "renaming" parameters to support code reuse.

As we have shown, both these mechanisms can be expressed in our setting, and the main differences between our work vs. [14] are to consider a family of composition operations vs. only one module composition operation, and the use of untyped vs. typed programs.

¿From an implementation viewpoint, the transformation τ for the renaming operation has been developed in `SICStus` Prolog. This actually enriches, in a practical applicability perspective, the toolkit for composing general logic programs described in [4].

Future work will be devoted, on the one side, to tackle real-size problems and applications exploiting the proposed framework. On the other side, also other semantics for general programs with respect to compositionality as well as different kind of programs and program compositions are worth investigating.

References

1. K. R. Apt. Logic programming. In J. van Leeuwen, editor, *Handbook of Theoretical Computer Science*, pages 493–574. Elsevier, 1990. Vol. B.
2. K. R. Apt and R. Bol. Logic Programming and Negation: A Survey. *Journal of Logic Programming*, 19-20:9–71, 1994.
3. J. A. Bergstra, J. Heering, and P. Klint. Module Algebra. *Journal of the ACM*, 37(2):335–372, 1990.
4. A. Brogi, S. Contiero, and F. Turini. Composing General Logic Programs. In J. Dix, U. Furbach, and A. Nerode, editors, *Proc. of LPNMR'97*, number 1265 in LNAI, pages 273–288. Springer Verlag, 1997.
5. A. Brogi, E. Lamma, P. Mancarella, and P. Mello. A Uifying View for Logic Programming with Non-Monotonic Reasoning. *Theoretical Computer Science*, 184(1-2):1–59, 1997.
6. A. Brogi, P. Mancarella, D. Pedreschi, and F. Turini. Modular Logic Programming. *ACM Transactions on Programming Languages and Systems*, 16(4):1361–1398, 1994.

7. A. Brogi and F. Turini. Fully abstract compositional semantics for an algebra of logic programs. *Theoretical Computer Science*, 149(2):201–229, 1995.
8. P.M. Dung. Negation as hypotheses: An abductive foundation for logic programming. In K. Furukawa, editor, *Proc. 8th International Conference on Logic Programming*, pages 3-17. The MIT Press, 1991.
9. S. Etalle and F. Teusink. A Compositional Semantics for Normal Open Programs. In M. Maher, editor, *Proc. of JICSLP 96*, pages 468–482, 1996.
10. M. Fitting. A Kriple-Kleene semantics for general logic programs. *Journal of Logic Programming*, 4:295–312, 1985.
11. M. Gelfond and V. Lifschitz. The stable model semantics for logic programming. In R. A. Kowalski and K. A. Bowen, editors, *Proc of the Fifth International Conference and Symposium on Logic Programming, Seattle, 1988*, pages 1070–1080. The MIT Press, 1988.
12. M. Gelfond and V. Lifschitz. Classical negation in logic programming and disjunctive databases. *New Generation Computing*, 9:365–385, 1991.
13. J. A. Goguen and R.M. Burstall. Institutions: Abstract Model Theory for Specification and Programming. *Journal of the ACM*, 39(1):95–146, 1992.
14. P. Hill. A Module System for Systematic Software Development: Design and Implementation. In A. Brogi and P. Hill, editors, *LOCOS 97 Proc. of the Post Conference Workshop on Logic Based Composition of Software for the ICLP 97*, 1997.
15. S.C. Kleene. *Introduction to Metamathematics*. van Nostrand, New York, 1952.
16. V. Lifschitz and H. Turner. Splitting a logic program. In Pascal Van Entenryck, editor, *Proc. 11th International Conference on Logic Programming*, pages 23–37. The MIT Press, 1994.
17. T. Przymusinski. On the declarative semantics of deductive databases and logic programs. In J. Minker, editor, *Foundations of Deductive Databases and Logic Programming*, pages 193–216. Morgan Kaufmann, Los Alto, CA, 1988.
18. T. Przymusinski. Stationary semantics for normal and disjunctive logic programs. In C. Delobel, M. Kifer, and Y. Masunagar, editors, *Proc. of DOOD'91*. Springer-Verlag, 1991.
19. A. van Gelder, K. Ross, and J. Schlipf. The well-founded semantics for general logic programs. *Journal of the ACM*, 38(3):620–650, 1991.
20. S. Verbaeten and A. Bossi. Composing complete and partial knowledge. In A. Brogi and P. Hill, editors, *Proc. of COCL, First Int. Workshop on Component-based Software Development in Computational Logic*, pages 109–123, 1998.
21. S. Verbaeten, M. Denecker, and D. De Schreye. Compositionality of normal logic programs. In J. Maluszynski, editor, *Logic Programming, Proc. of the 1997 International Symposium*, pages 371–395, 1997.

Inductive Synthesis of Logic Programs by Composition of Combinatory Program Schemes

Andreas Hamfelt[1]* and Jørgen Fischer Nilsson[2]

[1] Computing Science Department, Uppsala University
[2] Department of Computer Science, Technical University of Denmark

Abstract. Based on a variable-free combinatory form of definite clause logic programs we outline a methodology and supporting program environment CombInduce for inducing well-moded logic programs from examples. The combinators comprise *fold* combinators for recursion on lists. The combinator form is distinguished by enabling piecewise composition of semantically meaningful program elements according to the compositional semantics principle. The principle of combining programs from combinators admits induction of programs without appealing to most-specific-generalization and predicate invention in contrast to prevailing ILP approaches. Moreover, the combinator form avoids confusing object and metavariables in the applied metalogic program environment. In addition useful algebraic rewriting rules can be formulated conveniently with the combinators.
Keywords: logic program schemata, logical combinators, synthesis by composition and specialization of schemas, inductive synthesis, metalogic program environment.

1 Introduction

Induction of logic programs (ILP) is traditionally conducted as a generalization process in which program clauses are synthesized based on a number of program input/output examples. In the logic programming context it is natural to appeal to anti-unification of terms and atomic formulae, see e.g. [13]. This prevailing approach conforms with induction of logical rules from mass data as carried out in the machine learning tradition.

The present approach to ILP focuses on pure logic programs for list processing, which call for recursive formulations except for the most trivial cases. However, in the above mentioned bottom-up oriented approaches it has turned out to be difficult to synthesize recursive program structures (i.e., programs applying recursively defined predicates) from sample facts with no *a priori* indication of recursive structure. In MetaInduce in [6] we tried to tackle this problem by suggesting that the program structure to be induced has to comply with given recursion schemes of universal nature. The induction process then essentially reduces to synthesizing of auxiliary predicates applied as parameters or arguments

* Supported by a grant from Volvo Research Foundation, Volvo Educational Foundation and Dr Pehr G. Gyllenhammar's Research Foundation.

P. Flener (Ed.): LOPSTR'98, LNCS 1559, pp. 143–158, 1999.

to the recursion schemes. The auxiliary predicates in simpler cases would be defined by non-recursive clauses formed by a least general generalization procedure from the examples. In more complex cases the whole induction procedure may be invoked recursively to invent a new recursively defined auxiliary predicate.

The approach to be introduced here, COMBINDUCE, also draws on recursion schemes but differs from METAINDUCE by applying a novel combinatory form of logic programs COMBILOG introduced in [9] enabling variable-free formulations of definite clauses. The use of combinatory logic enables us to discard of least general generalization as well as predicate invention. Thus a key issue in the paper is the usefulness of the combinatory form of programs for ILP in which recursion schemes are added as "super"-combinators.

A key feature in our inductive synthesis is insistence on well-moded programs as a constraint which drastically reduces the search space.

Among the various ILP methods discussed in [10–13] DIALOGS [4] is probably the system coming closest to our proposal. However, as mentioned COMBINDUCE does not apply least general generalization and predicate invention.

The paper is outlined as follows: Sect. 2 introduces to the combinator form of clauses applied in COMBILOG. Sect. 3 extends COMBILOG with recursion combinators for list processing. Sect. 4 outlines a methodology and environment for inductive synthesis of logic program using the combinatory form. Finally sect. 5 discusses examples of program induction and outlines the synthesizer as a metalogic program.

2 Compositional Logic Programming

In the structured programming tradition programs are composed from specifications in a top-down problem decomposition manner, according to which a larger program is obtained by putting together smaller programs by means of combining forms. In functional programming functional composition offers itself as one of the forms together with conditionals and certain recursion forms, cf. e.g. [2, 17]. In logic programming it is more difficult to identify combinators since—in contrast to binary predicates—there are no standard combining forms for n-ary predicates.

In functional programming a combining form such as, say, functional composition is naturally understood as a higher order function taking functions as arguments and yielding a function as result. Similarly, in the context of logic and logic programming new predicates (model-theoretically conceived of as truth-valued functions) are to be formed by composition of basic predicates or program defined predicates by means of combining forms functioning as higher-order predicates.

2.1 Combinators for Logic Programs

In a recent paper [9] we pursue the compositional principle in the context of logic programming by proposing a variable-free combinator form of definite clauses termed COMBILOG. We consider here only pure definite clauses

$$p(t_{01},\ldots,t_{0n_0}) \leftarrow q_1(t_{11},\ldots,t_{1n_1}) \wedge \ldots \wedge q_\beta(t_{\beta 1},\ldots,t_{\beta n_\beta})$$

devoid of extra-logical and non-monotonic features. Assume that a collection of defining definite clauses for a predicate p be of the form

$$p(\boldsymbol{X}) \leftarrow \bigvee_i^{\gamma} \bigwedge_j^{\beta_i} q_{ij}(\boldsymbol{t_{ij}})$$

where $\boldsymbol{X}$ are tuples of distinct variables and $\boldsymbol{t_{ij}}$ are tuple terms conforming with the arity of the predicates. The elimination of left hand side non-variable terms proceeds by appealing to a distinguished clause $id(X, X)$ through rewritings (cf. e.g. [15]) which do not affect the declarative semantics. Without essential loss of generality it is assumed that compound terms are list terms, and moreover that goal clauses are of the form $\leftarrow p(\boldsymbol{X})$.

In COMBILOG this is replaced by combinatorial defining clauses

$$p \leftarrow \varphi$$

where φ is a ground combinatory predicate term of the form

$$\langle cterm \rangle ::= \langle pid \rangle \mid \langle comb \rangle(\langle cterm \rangle\{,\langle cterm \rangle\}^*)$$

where $\langle pid \rangle$ is a predicate identifier and $\langle comb \rangle$ is one of the three combinators *and*, *or*, and $make[\mu_1,\ldots,\mu_m]$, where μ_i are index numbers. These three combinators are identified as the least semantically meaningful building blocks being sufficient and necessary in our reconstruction of clauses. The combinators can be defined as follows in the informal use of higher order predicates.

$$\begin{aligned}
&or(P,Q)(X_1,\ldots,X_n) \leftarrow P(X_1,\ldots,X_n)\\
&or(P,Q)(X_1,\ldots,X_n) \leftarrow Q(X_1,\ldots,X_n)\\
&and(P,Q)(X_1,\ldots,X_n) \leftarrow P(X_1,\ldots,X_n) \wedge Q(X_1,\ldots,X_n)\\
&make[\mu_1,\ldots,\mu_m](P)(X_{\mu_1},\ldots,X_{\mu_m}) \leftarrow P(X_1,\ldots,X_n)
\end{aligned}$$

Here P and Q are predicate arguments and the combinators may be conceived of as higher order predicates used similarly to higher order functions in functional programming. These combinators are of generic arity and in addition *make* is indexed with m distinct positive index numbers. It should be observed that the above clauses serve explanatory purposes; they do not belong to the object language.

As an example the combinator inverse for binary predicates comes about as the definition of combinator $make[2,1]$, that is, as an instance of the above generic definition

$$make[2,1](P)(X_2,X_1) \leftarrow P(X_1,X_2)$$

These combinators are inspired by a proposal by Quine [16] for a variable-free form of full first order predicate logic, see [9] for a comparison and discussion.

It should be observed that COMBILOG is not intended as a fully-fledged higher order logic programming language. Although the combinators function as higher-order functions, they serve to form program denotations, and they are not available as data in contrast, say, to λ-Prolog.

The predicate identifiers include, besides user introduced predicate names, the primitive predicates *id*, *cons*, $const_c$, *true*, *false* definable by the following unit clauses (no clauses for *false*)

$id(X, X)$
$cons(U, V, [U|V])$
$const_c(c)$ for all relevant constants c, including []
true

As an example the clause $head([X|\_], X)$, i.e.,

$$head(L, X) \leftarrow cons(X, T, L)$$

in COMBILOG is defined by

$$head \leftarrow make[3,1](cons)$$

As it appears, in COMBILOG all manipulations of non-variable terms are relegated to the primitive predicates *cons* (is 3-ary) and $const_c$ (is 1-ary).

Sect. 3 and following sections provide more complex program examples.

2.2 Semantics for Combinators

In [9] is proven combinatory completeness (relative to the defining definite clauses above) of these combinators in a canonical form with the defining term

$$or_i^\gamma(make[\mu_i](and_j^{\beta_i}(make[\mu_{ij}]q_{ij})))$$

where

$$or_i^n(\phi_i) = \phi_1 \; or \; \phi_2 \; or \; \ldots \; or \; \phi_n$$

and

$$and_i^n(\phi_i) = \phi_1 \; and \; \phi_2 \; and \; \ldots \; and \; \phi_n.$$

The defining term reflects the defining formula $\bigvee_i^\gamma \bigwedge_j^{\beta_i} q_{ij}(t_{ij})$.

The combinatory form of clauses invites formulation of a compositional semantics so that the relational denotation of the term $comb(\varphi_1, \ldots, \varphi_n)$ is determined as a function F_{comb} of the relational denotations $[\![\varphi_i]\!]$ of the subterms φ_i:

$$[\![comb(\varphi_1, \ldots, \varphi_n)]\!] = F_{comb}([\![\varphi_1]\!], \ldots, [\![\varphi_n]\!])$$

The semantical definitions of the combinators are as follows

$$
\begin{aligned}
[\![and(\varphi,\psi)]\!] &= [\![\varphi]\!] \cap [\![\psi]\!] \\
[\![or(\varphi,\psi)]\!] &= [\![\varphi]\!] \cup [\![\psi]\!] \\
[\![make[\mu_1,\ldots,\mu_m](\varphi)]\!] &= \{\langle t_{\mu_1},\ldots,t_{\mu_m}\rangle \in H^m \mid \exists \langle t_1,\ldots,t_n\rangle \in [\![\varphi]\!]\}
\end{aligned}
$$

or more explicitly for *make*

$$
\begin{aligned}
[\![make[\mu_1,\ldots,\mu_m](\varphi)]\!] &= \{\langle t'_1,\ldots,t'_m\rangle \in H^m \mid \exists \langle t_1,\ldots,t_n\rangle \in [\![\varphi]\!] \\
&\qquad \text{s.t. for } i = 1..m \text{ if } \mu_i \le n \text{ then } t'_i = t_{\mu_i}\}
\end{aligned}
$$

where H is the Herbrand universe of the program. Thus $make[1,2,\ldots,n]$ is the identity combinator for n-ary relations, i.e.,

$$[\![make[1,\ldots,n](P)]\!] = [\![P]\!]$$

and the term $make[1,2,\ldots,n](true)$ yields the n-ary universal relation H^n from the 0-ary *true*, i.e.,

$$[\![make[1,2,\ldots,n](true)]\!] = H^n .$$

The denotations of the primitive predicates are as follows

$$
\begin{aligned}
[\![id]\!] &= \{\langle t,t\rangle \in H^2 | t \in H\} \\
[\![cons]\!] &= \{\langle t',t'',[t'|t'']\rangle \in H^3 \mid t',t'' \in H\} \\
[\![const_c]\!] &= \{\langle c\rangle\} \text{ for all relevant constants } c \\
[\![true]\!] &= \{\langle\rangle\} \\
[\![false]\!] &= \{\ \}
\end{aligned}
$$

These definitions are proved in [9] to make the semantics coincide with the usual least model and fix point semantics of corresponding definite clauses for a Combilog program.

Thus, in the construction of the least fixed point for a combinatory form of program the iteration step reduces to set union, intersection and generalized projection.

3 Recursion Combinators

In the combinator language Combilog as summarised above recursion is handled like in ordinary logic programs by introduction of predicates defined in terms of themselves directly or indirectly. One way of eliminating these recursive definitions would be to introduce a general fix point combinator (cf. the Y combinator in combinatory logic). However, we prefer to introduce list-oriented recursion operators analogously to functional programming practice [3,17]. In [7,8] we propose two *fold* combinators for list recursion defined, e.g., as follows.

$$
\begin{aligned}
&foldr(P,Q)(Y,[\,],Z) \leftarrow Q(Y,Z) \\
&foldr(P,Q)(Y,[X|T],W) \leftarrow foldr(P,Q)(Y,T,Z) \land P(X,Z,W) \\
&foldl(P,Q)(Y,[\,],Z) \leftarrow Q(Y,Z) \\
&foldl(P,Q)(Y,[X|T],W) \leftarrow P(X,Y,Z) \land foldl(P,Q)(Z,T,W)
\end{aligned}
$$

which are relational counterparts of the well known functional operators [2, 3, 17]. Similar to the logic combinators we have for the recursion combinator *foldr* (and the logically equivalent operator *foldrrev*, see below) the semantical definition:

$$\begin{array}{ll} [\![foldr(P,Q)]\!] & = \bigcup_{i=0}^{\infty} [\![foldr_i(P,Q)]\!]. \\ [\![foldr_0(P,Q)]\!] & = \{\langle y, [], z\rangle \in H^3 | \langle y, z\rangle \in [\![Q]\!]\} \\ [\![foldr_{i+1}(P,Q)]\!] & = \{\langle y, [t_1|t_2], w\rangle \in H^3 \; | \exists z \in H \text{ s.t.} \\ & \quad \langle y, t_2, z\rangle \in [\![foldr_i(P,Q)]\!] \wedge \langle t_1, z, w\rangle \in [\![P]\!] \} \end{array}$$

Similar recursion operators are proposed in [5] applying λ-Prolog, whereas our combinators are made available in ordinary logic programming as explained in the next section.

For instance the relational *append* predicate definition in the formulation

$$append([], X, X)$$
$$append([X|T], Y, Z) \leftarrow append(T, Y, U) \wedge cons(X, U, Z)$$

in the *fold*-extended COMBILOG becomes

$$append \leftarrow make[2,1,3](foldr(cons, id))$$

where *make*[2, 1, 3] swaps the two first arguments (since *foldr* differs from *append* in that the second argument, not the first, is the induction parameter). The use of append with only third argument being ground calls for a replacement with a logically equivalent variant of *foldr*.

$$foldrrev(P,Q)(Y,[],Z) \leftarrow Q(Y,Z)$$
$$foldrrev(P,Q)(Y,[X|T],W) \leftarrow P(X,Z,W) \wedge foldrrev(P,Q)(Y,T,Z)$$

The short and elegant combinatory formulation of *append* is seductive since combinatory formulations are admittedly sometimes awkward. For instance the unit clause

$$make\_unit\_list(X, [X|[]])$$

via the reformulation

$$make\_unit\_list(X,Y) \leftarrow const_{[]}(Z), cons(X,Z,Y)$$

which serves to remove non-variable terms, yields the combinatory definition

$$make\_unit\_list \leftarrow make[1,3](and(make[2,1,3](const_{[]}), cons))$$

being in the canonical form mentioned in sect. 2.2.

In [8] we prove that logic program recursion with the *fold* schemes suffices for expressing all partial and general recursive functions. However, this is a purely theoretical result; in logic programming practice non-linear recursion forms such as *and-or* problem reduction schemes are convenient, cf. [4]. Still the empirical investigation in [8] tells that most common pure logic programs can be naturally formulated within the *fold* schemes; therefore we confine ourselves to the *fold* schemes in the present context.

Actually in [8] we state and in [7] we prove duality theorems which in the present combinator form looks like

$$[\![foldr(P,Q)]\!] = [\![make[3,2,1](foldl(make[1,3,2](P), make[2,1](Q)))]\!]$$

$$[\![foldl(P,Q)]\!] = [\![make[3,2,1](foldr(make[1,3,2](P), make[2,1](Q)))]\!]$$

connecting the two *fold* operators in the declarative, that is model theoretic or fix point, understanding of logic programs.

For logic program expressible with the *fold* combinators, in the combinator formulation of such programs it is unnecessary to introduce user specific predicate names since a program may take form of ground combinator term comprising only the primitive predicates.

4 Synthesizing Combinatory Logic Programs

In this section we sketch a methodology and programming environment for conducting inductive synthesis of logic programs in the pure combinator form

$$\langle cterm\rangle ::= \langle comb\rangle(\ [\ \langle cterm\rangle\ \{\ ,\ \langle cterm\rangle\ \}^*\ ]\ )$$

where primitive predicates are conceived of as 0-ary primitive combinators and $\langle comb\rangle$ includes, besides *and*, *or* and the indexed *make*, the operators *foldl(rev)* and *foldr(rev)*.

The program synthesis environment is established as a metalogic program in which the combinator terms appear as ordinary terms using a technique originating in [18], pursued in [8,9]. This is exemplified with the generic predicate *apply*, which expresses application of a predicate term to its arguments, hence serving as an abstract machine for logic programs. For *and* and *make* there are the clauses:

$$\begin{array}{l}
apply(and(P,Q),[X_1]) \leftarrow apply(P,[X_1]) \wedge apply(Q,[X_1]) \\
apply(and(P,Q),[X_1,X_2]) \leftarrow apply(P,[X_1,X_2]) \wedge apply(Q,[X_1,X_2]) \\
\quad\vdots \\
apply(and(P,Q),[X_1,\ldots,X_n]) \leftarrow \\
\qquad apply(P,[X_1,\ldots,X_n]) \wedge apply(Q,[X_1,\ldots,X_n]) \\
apply(make([\mu_1,\ldots,\mu_m],P),[X_{\mu_1},\ldots,X_{\mu_m}]) \leftarrow apply(P,[X_1,\ldots,X_n])
\end{array}$$

up to some fixed maximum arity m and n.

For *foldr* there is the clause

$$\begin{array}{l}
apply(foldr(P,Q),[Y,[\,],Z]) \leftarrow apply(Q,[Y,Z]) \\
apply(foldr(P,Q),[Y,[X|T],W]) \leftarrow \\
apply(foldr(P,Q),[Y,T,Z]) \wedge apply(P,[X,Z,W])
\end{array}$$

Similarly for primitive predicates *id*, *cons*, $const_c$ and *true*

$$apply(id, [X, X])$$

$$apply(cons, [X, T, [X|T]])$$

$apply(const_c, [c])$ for each relevant constants c

$$apply(true, [])$$

For instance, for combinator $make[3, 1]$ we have

$$apply(make([3, 1], P), [X_3, X_1]) \leftarrow apply(P, [X_1, X_2, X_3])$$

The *apply* predicates enable execution of combinatory programs in the metalogic programming environment established with ordinary clauses. Thus the query $\leftarrow p$ with p defined by $p \leftarrow \varphi$ is stated as

$$\leftarrow apply(\varphi, [X_1, \ldots, X_m])$$

Consider, for example, the derivation

$$\leftarrow apply(make([3, 1], cons), [X_1, X_2])$$
$$\leftarrow apply(cons, [X_2, \_, X_1])$$

The resulting semantics is proved equivalent in [9] to the semantics defined in sect. 2.2. for the combinators.

During the course of the induction the combinator terms being synthesized may be non-ground, with the variables representing unknown (sub)combinator terms. Thus our induction procedure proceeds by specializing (instantiating) partially specified combinatory program forms guided by a given program result test suite.

An advantage of the combinatory program form in the synthesis processes is that the absence of the object program variables eliminates confusion with the metavariables whose range are combinatory terms, i.e., subprograms. More importantly, the fact that the strict compositional semantics is reflected directly in the syntax ensures that subprograms represented by combinators can be synthesized independently of the embedding program context. This is in contrast to ordinary logic programs where a clause has to be completed before it represents a semantically meaningful entity.

The combinator term to be synthesized fulfills the following grammar

$$
\begin{aligned}
\langle cterm \rangle \quad ::= \; & make[i_1, \ldots, i_n](\langle primpred \rangle) \mid \\
& make[i_1, \ldots, i_n](foldr(\langle cterm \rangle, \langle cterm \rangle)) \mid \\
& make[i_1, \ldots, i_n](foldrrev(\langle cterm \rangle, \langle cterm \rangle)) \mid \\
& make[i_1, \ldots, i_n](and(\langle cterm \rangle, \langle cterm \rangle)) \\
\langle primpred \rangle \quad ::= \; & id \mid cons \mid const \mid true \mid false
\end{aligned}
$$

corresponding to the above canonical form enriched with the *foldr* combinator. The identity combinator $make[1, 2, \ldots, n]$ is left implicit in terms.

The *or* operator is omitted since we have the following equivalences

$$[\![foldr(or(P_1, P_2), Q)]\!] = [\![or(foldr(P_1, Q), foldr(P_2, Q))]\!]$$
$$[\![foldr(P, or(Q_1, Q_2))]\!] = [\![or(foldr(P, Q_1), foldr(P, Q_2))]\!]$$

which entails that a program requiring the *or* combinator can be *a priori* decomposed into *or*-free programs since *or* can distributed over *foldr* in both arguments and hence can be propagated to the top.

We insist on synthesized programs being well-moded, cf. [1] for reasons clarified in the next section. This means that program predicates are assigned mode specifications telling the input arguments (+) and output arguments (−). The well-modedness constraint implies that if the input arguments are ground, ground terms will be produced in the output arguments.

As an initial simple example for illustrating the induction principle is considered the synthesis of the *head* predicate $head([X|\_], X)$ from sect. 2.1.

Assume given the test suite $[\ [[a, b], a],\ [[b], b]\ ]$ together with the mode specification $[+, -]$. Following the above grammar for the combinator program we consider first as candidate a program consisting simply of a primitive predicate. The only primitive predicate which conforms with the arity is *id* which fails on the test samples.

As a next step is considered a combinator program of the form $make[i_1, i_2](P)$ where P is primitive and $i_1, i_2 \in \{1..3\}$, 3 being the maximum arity of the primitives.

The choice $P = false$ is ruled out because the denotation of the program is then the empty set which does not cover the examples. The choice $P = true$ yielding a universal relation is ruled out since the corresponding program does not conform with the mode requirement.

Finally is considered $P = cons$, which yields a correctly moded program with $make[3, 1]$ and $make[3, 2]$. However only the program $make[3, 1](cons)$ covers the test examples, and is therefore considered the result of the inductive synthesis as the smallest well-moded program covering all test examples.

5 Outline of the CombInduce Synthesizer

Having above described the principles for our inductive synthesis approach we now turn to a more systematic account of our synthesis method. The aim of the synthesis process is to provide a syntactically smallest n-ary predicate term φ which covers the suite of test example n-tuples $t_1, t_2, \ldots, t_s$, i.e.

$$\bigcup_{i=1}^{s} \{t_i\} \subseteq [\![\varphi]\!] \subseteq [\![make[1, 2, \ldots, n](true)]\!] = H^n$$

As indicated mode constraints are critical to our induction approach since abandoning of the constraints would admit the universal relation as simplest solution in absence of negative examples. Let us introduce the notion of *valence* for the combined constraints of modes, types and arity, assuming synthesis of well-moded programs [1] only [7]. The intuition is that composition of combinators are subject to constraints like valence constraints on chemical atoms and radicals. For simplicity's sake data type constraints are not taken into account in the below formulation.

In principle the synthesis can be carried out as a search for the smallest predicate term φ fulfilling the above set inclusion. The imposed valence constraints prunes the search tree in the top-down construction of the program term whenever the valence constraint turns out to be violated. It is our contention that the valence constraints drastically reduce the search space as already indicated by the above small example.

5.1 The CombInduce Synthesizer as a Metalogic Program

The heart of the synthesizer are defining clauses for a mutually recursive predicates *syn* and *syn_make* drawing on the above defining clauses for the combinators. This program structure is to ensure that combinators obey the above grammar. We suggest that the search is bounded by the size of the term being synthesized measured in terms of the number of identifiers, similarly to the iterative depth first strategy. Thus termination is not ensured. The bound is set successively at 1, 2, ... For simplicity's sake the search control is abstracted in the below program outline.

The top level is

$$synthesize(\Phi, Valencel, Exl) \leftarrow syn\_make(\Phi, Valencel, Exl)$$

Synthesis of the above example *head_of_list* is initiated with a goal clause

$$\leftarrow synthesize(\Phi, [[+,-]], [\ [[a,b],a],\ [[b],b]\ ])$$

where the synthesized predicate term obtains as binding to Φ.

$$\begin{aligned}&syn\_make(make(Il, P), Valencel, Exl) \leftarrow\\&\quad make\_valence(Il, Valencel, Valencel1),\\&\quad make\_example(Il, Exl, Exl1),\\&\quad syn(P, Valencel1, Exl1)\end{aligned}$$

The auxiliary predicates *make_valence* and *make_example* carry out necessary permutations as specified by the index list *Il*.

For the primitives there are

$$\begin{aligned}&syn(id, Valencel, Exlist) \leftarrow\\&\quad check\_valence(Valencel, [[-,+],[+,-]]),\\&\quad test\_examples(id, Exlist)\\&syn(cons, Valencel, Exlist) \leftarrow\\&\quad check\_valence(Valencel, [[+,+,-],[-,-,+]]),\\&\quad test\_examples(cons, Exlist)\end{aligned}$$

$syn(const_c, Valencel, Exlist) \leftarrow$
$\quad check\_valence(Valencel, [-]), test\_examples(const_c, Exlist)$
$syn(true, [], \_)$
$syn(false, [], [])$

$test\_examples(Pid, [])$
$test\_examples(Pid, [Ex|Exl]) \leftarrow apply(Pid, Ex), test\_examples(Pid, Exl)$

Recall that *apply* is defined in sect. 4.

The mode notation is rather self-explanatory; for instance the modes for *id* require that either the second or first argument (or both) be ground upon invocation of *id*.

More clauses for the predicate *syn* corresponding to the *fold* and *and* combinators are added in the below subsections.

5.2 Synthesis with the *Fold* Combinators

In order to bring *foldr* combinators into play the following clauses are added

$syn(foldr(P, Q), Valencel, Exl) \leftarrow$
$\quad valence(foldr, Valencel, Valencel1, Valencel2),$
$\quad make\_examples\_foldr(Exl, Exl1, Exl2),$
$\quad syn\_make(Q, Valencel1, Exl1),$
$\quad syn\_make(P, Valencel2, Exl2)$

$syn(foldrrev(P, Q), Valencel, Exl) \leftarrow$
$\quad valence(foldrrev, Valencel, Valencel1, Valencel2),$
$\quad make\_examples\_foldrrev(Exl, Exl1, Exl2),$
$\quad syn\_make(Q, Valencel1, Exl1),$
$\quad syn\_make(P, Valencel2, Exl2)$

The predicate *valence* establishes relationship between the valences of the combinator term $foldr(P, Q)$ and valences of its predicate arguments P and Q according to the following mode specifications from [7].

$foldr([+,+,-],[+,-])[+,+,-]$
$foldr([+,+,-],[-,-])[-,+,-]$
$foldrrev([+,-,+],[-,+])[-,+,+]$
$foldrrev([+,-,-],[-,-])[-,+,-]$
$foldrrev([-,-,+],[-,+])[-,-,+]$

The first line tells that if $foldr(P, Q)$ is to be used with the mode $[+,+,-]$ then the mode requirement for P is $[+,+,-]$ and for Q is $[+,-]$, etc.

As an example consider the inductive synthesis of *append*, say, from the test suite *Exl*

$$[\ [[a],[],[a]],\ [[],[],[]],\ [[a,b],[c],[a,b,c]]\ ]$$

and with valence specification *Valencel* equal to the list $[\,[+,+,-]\,]$. When the search process comes across the term

$$make[2,1,3](foldr(P,Q))$$

according to the above mode specification for the unknown subterm Q is obtained from the example $[[],[],[]]$ by use of *foldr* the test suite $[\,[[],[]]\,]$ with valence list $[\,[+,-]\,]$ yielding $Q = id$ as simplest solution. For the unknown subterm P by use of *foldr* on the remainder examples $[\,[[a],[],[a]],\ [[a,b],[c],[a,b,c]]\,]$ is obtained the test suite $[\,[a,[],[a]],\ [b,[c],U],\ [a,U,[a,b,c]]\,]$ with valence list $[\,[+,+,-]\,]$ solved by $P = cons$. The logical variable U linking the test examples stems from the recursive unfolding of *foldr* carried out in *make_examples_foldr*.

Actually the curtailed test suite

$$[\,[[a],[],[a]],\ [[],[],[]]\,]$$

would suffice for synthesizing the same solution for *append*.

The same test suite with the valence specification $[-,-,+]$ in the induction process calls for use of *foldrrev* instead of *foldr* giving

$$make[2,1,3](foldrrev(P,Q))$$

According to the above mode spefication for the unknown subterm Q is obtained the test suite $[\,[[],[]]\,]$ with valence list $[\,[-,+]\,]$ yielding $Q = id$, and for the unknown subterm P is obtained the test suite $[\,[a,[],[a]],\ [a,U,[a,b,c]],\ [b,[c],U]\,]$ with valence list $[\,[-,-,+]\,]$ solved by $P = cons$.

This example illustrates selection of the proper *foldr* variant in order to obtain a correctly-moded program constituting an integral part of our inductive synthesis method.

Extension with the *foldl* variants is straightforward.

5.3 Synthesis Involving the And Combinator

The *and* combinator is the most complex component in the present approach, in part due to the mode patterns, in part due to the possibility of increasing the arity of predicates reflecting use of right hand side variables only in clauses. In order to illustrate these problems we consider the example from above *make_unit_list*

$$make\_unit\_list(X,[X\,|\,[]])$$

becoming in COMBILOG:

$$make\_unit\_list \leftarrow make[1,3](and(make[2,1,3](const_{[]}),cons))$$

We consider induction of *make_unit_list* from the two examples $[a,[a]]$ and $[[a,b],[[a,b]]]$ with the mode specifications $[+,-]$ and $[-,+]$. All of the valence constraints have to be satisfied by a synthesized program.

In bottom up oriented approaches to ILP synthesis of this program is trivially achieved as the least general generalization of the examples. By contrast synthesis of this program in this present approach is more intricate since as already noticed it calls for the compound combinator form

$$make[\mu](and(make[\mu_1](\varphi_1), make[\mu_2](\varphi_2)))$$

This is achieved by the following clause in which the list variable *Il*, *Il*1 and *Il*2 represent, respectively, the index lists μ, μ_1 and μ_2.

$$\begin{aligned}&syn\_make(make(Il, and(make(Il1, P1), make(Il2, P2)), Valencel, Exl) \leftarrow\\&\quad valence(Valencel, Valencel1, Valencel2, Il, Il1, Il2),\\&\quad make\_example(Il, Il1, Il2, Exl, Exl1),\\&\quad syn(P1, Valencel1, Exl1),\\&\quad syn(P2, Valencel2, Exl1)\end{aligned}$$

The auxiliary predicate *valence* is to assign valences to subterms $P1$ and $P2$ observing well-modedness constraints in jointly choosing μ, μ_1 and μ_2.

In the present example we synthesize

$$make[1,3](and(make[2,1,3](P1), make[1,2,3](P2)))$$

which is reducible to

$$make[1,3](and(make[2,1,3](P1), P2))$$

in which the *and* combinator is ternary conforming with the clause

$$(X, Y) \leftarrow P1(Z), P2(X, Z, Y)$$

With these choices of μ, μ_1 and μ_2, $P1$ has the mode specification $[-]$ but no examples provided. The first choice for $P1$ then is constant $const_{[]}$. Actually if type constraint be taken into account the type has to be a list so $const_{[]}$ is the only *const* combinator available. For $P2$ the specificed modes are $[\ [+,+,-],\ [-,+,+]\ ]$ and the examples with the chosen values for $P2$ are $[[a,b],[],[[a,b]]]$ and $[a,[],[a]]$, giving $P2 = cons$, thus

$$(X, Y) \leftarrow const_{[]}(Z), cons(X, Z, Y)$$

Observe that the equivalent and heuristically more appealing solution

$$(X, Y) \leftarrow cons(X, Z, Y), const_{[]}(Z)$$

is not obtainable since it is not a well-moded program. However, this solution is obtainable if the well-modedness requirement is abandoned locally in the above clause for *syn_make*.

Various heuristics may be introduced to the program for instance exploiting $[\![and(P,Q)]\!] \subseteq [\![P]\!]$.

5.4 Synthesis with Would-be Appeal to Predicate Invention

Let us conclude by synthesizing *naive_reverse* from the test suite

$$[\ [[], []],\ [[a], [a]],\ [[a, b], [b, a]]\ ].$$

When the search process comes across the term

$$make[2,3](foldr(P1, Q1))$$

from the example $[[], []]$ may be obtained by use of *foldr* the proposal

$$Q1 = make[1,1](const_{[]})$$

for the unknown subterm $Q1$.

For $P1$ is obtained by use of *foldr* the test suite

$$[\ [a, [], [a]],\ [b, [], Z],\ [a, Z, [b, a]]\ ].$$

Then the search process comes across the proposal

$$P1 = foldr(P2, Q2)$$

giving at present

$$make[2,3](foldr(foldr(P2, Q2), make[1,1](const_{[]}))$$

The two first examples $[a, [], [a]]$ and $[b, [], Z]$ are covered by *make_unit_list*, as synthesised in sect. 5.3. This suggests the bindings $Z = [b]$ and $Q2 =$ *make_unit_list*, thus yielding for $P1$ the specialization

$$[\ [a, [], [a]],\ [b, [], Z],\ [a, Z, [b, a]]\ ]\{Z/[b]\} = [\ [a, [], [a]],\ [b, [], [b]\ ],\ [a, [b], [b, a]]\ ].$$

For $P2$ is in turn obtained example $[b, Z', [b, a]]$ for which *cons* can be synthesized.

The resulting term is

$$make[2,3](foldr(foldr(cons, make\_unit\_list), make[1,1](const_{[]}))$$

It would be natural to include *make_unit_list* in a library as a given predicate.

Observe that without the example $[[a], [a]]$ the synthesis process would not have succeeded since this hardly suffices for inducing appropriate argument predicates $Q2$ and $P2$.

6 Conclusions

We have outlined principles for inductive synthesis of logic programs based on composition of building blocks in the form of logical combinators, including recursion combinators. Our approach carries out the synthesis as a top down composition of the combinators guided by the given test suite, but without generalizing program elements from the test suite.

One advantage of the combinatory approach is that no explicit predicate invention is called for within the range of the considered *fold*-expressible class of well-moded programs. Moreover the combinators avoid technical complications in metaprogramming with object language variables.

Validation of feasibility of the COMBINDUCE method *vis-à-vis* other ILP methods is awaiting experimental studies to be reported in coming papers. The considered examples show that trivial examples may be awkward in our method whereas non-trivial examples from the view of ILP like *append* are easy. Of course many trivial examples could be coped with more easily by inclusion of an appropriate library of non-primitive predicates. However, in this paper we have stressed the principles of our method, leaving heuristic tuning of the system as future work.

We also plan to extend the range of considered programs by including divide-and-conquer combinators cf. [8] as entertained e.g., in DIALOGS [4].

References

1. K. Apt & E. Marchiori: Reasoning About Prolog Programs: From Modes Through Types to Assertions. *J. Formal Aspects of Computing*, (1994) 6A pp. 743–764.
2. J. Backus: Can Programming be Liberated from the von Neumann Style ? A Functional Style and Its Algebra of Programs. *Comm. of the ACM*, 21, 8, 1978. pp. 613–641.
3. R. Bird & O. de Moor: *Algebra of Programming*, Prentice Hall, 1997.
4. P. Flener: Inductive Logic Program Synthesis with DIALOGS. In [12] pp. 175–198.
5. Gegg-Harrison, T. S.: Representing Logic Program Schemata in λ-Prolog. In L. Sterling (ed.) *Procs. Twelfth International Conference on Logic Programming 1995*, MIT Press, London, 1995. pp. 467–481.
6. A. Hamfelt & J. Fischer Nilsson: Inductive Metalogic Programming. In S. Wrobel (ed.) *Procs. Fourth International Workshop on Inductive Logic programming* (ILP-94), Bad Honnef/Bonn, GMD-Studien Nr. 237, 1994. pp. 85–96.
7. A. Hamfelt & J. Fischer Nilsson: Declarative Logic Programming with Primitive Recursive Relations on Lists. In M. Maher (ed.) *Procs. Joint International Conference and Symposium on Logic Programming 1996*, MIT Press, London, 1996, pp. 230–242.
8. A. Hamfelt & J. Fischer Nilsson: Towards a Logic Programming Methodology Based on Higher-order Predicates. *J. New Generation Computing*, vol 15, no 4, 1997. pp. 421–448.
9. A. Hamfelt, J. Fischer Nilsson & A. Vitoria: A Combinatory Form of Pure Logic Programs and its Compositional Semantics. Submitted for publication 1998.
10. N. Lavrac & S. Dzeroski: *Inductive Logic Programming*. Ellis Horwood, New York, 1994.
11. S. Muggleton (ed.): *Inductive Logic Programming*. Academic Press, London, 1992.
12. S. Muggleton (ed.): Inductive Logic Programming, Proceedings of the 6th International Workshop on Inductive Logic Programming, 1996, *Lecture Notes in Artificial Intelligence* 1314, Springer, 1996.

13. S.-H. Nienhuys-Cheng & R. de Wolf: Foundations of Inductive Logic Programming, *Lecture Notes in Artificial Intelligence* 1228, Springer, 1997.
14. J. Fischer Nilsson & A. Hamfelt: Constructing Logic Programs with Higher Order Predicates. In M. Alpuente & M. I. Sessa (eds.) *Procs. Joint Conference on Declarative Programming 1995* (GULP-PRODE'95), Universita' Degli Studi di Salerno, Salerno, 1995. pp. 307–312.
15. A. Petorossi & M. Proietti: Transformation of Logic Programs. In D. M. Gabbay, C. J. Hogger & J. A. Robinson (eds.) *Handbook of Logic in Artificial Intelligence and Logic Programming*, Oxford University Press.
16. W. V. Quine: Predicate-functor Logic. In J. E. Fenstad (ed.) *Procs. Second Scandinavian Logic Symposium*, North-Holland, 1971. pp. 309–315.
17. C. Reade: *Elements of Functional Programming*, Addison-Wesley, 1989.
18. D. H. D. Warren: Higher-order extensions to PROLOG: are they needed ? In D. Michie (ed.) *Machine Intelligence 10*, Ellis Horwood and Edinburgh University Press, 1982. pp. 441–454.

Specialising Logic Programs with Respect to Call/Post Specifications

Annalisa Bossi and Sabina Rossi

Dipartimento di Matematica e Informatica
via Torino 155, 30173 Venezia, Italy
{bossi,srossi}@dsi.unive.it

Abstract. In this paper we present a program specialisation method which, given a call/post specification, transforms a logic program into a *weakly call-correct* one satisfying the post-condition.
The specialisation is applied to *specialised partially correct* programs. This notion is based on the definition of *specialised derivation* which is intended to describe program behaviour whenever some properties on procedure calls are assumed. Top-down and bottom-up semantics of specialised derivations are recalled.

1 Introduction

Specialisation methods allow to restrict a program to a narrower context of application. The aim is that of obtaining a more efficient program which behaves as the original one on the considered subdomain.

In the field of logic programming, the narrowed context is usually described by means of a set of queries of interest. Specialisation methods are based on the idea of partially evaluating program clauses [5, 16, 20, 21] with respect to this set of queries. The goal is to detect clauses which are redundant in the restricted context, or to specialise them preventing costly failing derivations. If the original program is correct with respect to a pre/post specification [4, 9, 10, 2], and the considered queries satisfy the precondition, then the correctness of the specialised program is ensured. Nothing is guaranteed on the queries which are not in the set of interest. They may succeed with "wrong" answers, produce a finite failure or an infinite computation. We simply do not care about them.

The specialisation that we propose in this paper restricts the search space of a program to the set of derivations satisfying the property that, at each step, the selected atom "respects" a given call-condition. The main feature of our specialisation is that if the original program is "correct" (we say, specialised partially correct) with respect to a call/post specification then the specialised program is (partially) correct for all queries. The execution of a query which does not satisfy the specification ends with a finite failure.
As an application, our approach allows us to support types without the need of augmenting programs with any kind of type declaration.

P. Flener (Ed.): LOPSTR'98, LNCS 1559, pp. 159–178, 1999.

To give an intuition, consider the program **SUM** defined by:
sum $(X, 0, X) \leftarrow$.
sum $(X, s(Y), s(Z)) \leftarrow$ **sum** (X, Y, Z).

The intention is that of defining the sum between natural numbers which are represented by the constants 0, $s(0)$, $s(s(0))$ and so on. However, there are queries like **sum** $(a, s(0), s(a))$ which succeed even if some arguments are not numerals. In order to avoid such "wrong" solutions, one can make use of type checking predicates defined by additional Prolog procedures [17–19].
Our specialisation can be used to solve this problem by restricting the program to a suitable context of application that is expressed in the form of a call/post specification. Similarly to classical pre/post specifications, a call/post specification consists of two parts, a call-condition and a post-condition. While the notion of post-condition is the standard one, the notion of call-condition used in this paper is not standard. It represents an invariant property that is required to be satisfied by atomic queries after the unification with the input clause.
Going back to the example above, consider the call-condition characterizing all atoms of **sum** where the last argument is

- either the constant 0,
- or a term of the form $s(\_)$.

Consider also the post-condition denoting all atoms of **sum** whose arguments are natural numbers with the third one being the sum of the first two. Hence,

Call $= \{$**sum** $(u, v, z) \mid u, v$ are terms and z is either 0 or a term of the form $s(\_)\}$
Post $= \{$**sum** $(u, v, z) \mid u, v, z$ are natural numbers and $z = u + v\}$

By applying our specialisation transformation we obtain the specialised program:

sum $(0, 0, 0) \leftarrow$.
sum $(s(X), 0, s(X)) \leftarrow$.
sum $(X, s(Y), s(Z)) \leftarrow$ **sum** (X, Y, Z).

We do not enter into the details of the specialisation here. We just observe that it is applied to the head of clauses. The specialised program called with the query **sum** $(a, s(0), s(a))$ fails. Moreover, it produces correct answers for any non failing input query.

Summarizing, in this paper we present a program specialisation which, given a call/post specification, transforms a logic program into a *weakly call-correct* one satisfying the post-condition. More precisely, the specialised program meets the following requirements: for any execution,

- each selected atom unified with the head of the input clause satisfies the call-condition;
- and each computed instance of a query satisfies the post-condition.

The specialisation is applied to so-called *specialised partially correct* programs. This notion is a generalization of the well-known concept of *partially correct* program [11,4,9,10,2,3]. It is based on the definition of *specialised derivation* which is a derivation where all the selected atoms are instantiated in order to satisfy a given call-condition. Thus, a specialised partially correct program satisfies the property that all its successful specialised derivations produce answers satisfying the post-condition. Specialised derivations has been introduced in [7] where we show that they can be computed both by a top-down and a bottom-up construction, in the style of the *s*-semantics [12,13,6]. We recall here such semantics. The equivalence of these two semantics can be proven by using the standard semantics of specialised programs as a link between them. The specialised semantics is useful to reason on the notion of specialised partial correctness. In particular it allows us to provide a sufficient condition to prove that a program is specialised partially correct with respect to a given call/post specification. It consists in one application of the specialised immediate consequence operator to the post-condition.

The paper is organized as follows. Section 2 recalls some basic notations and concepts. In Section 3 specialised derivations and their semantics are presented. In Section 4 our program specialisation is introduced. Section 5 discusses the equivalence between the top-down and the fixpoint semantics of specialised derivations. In Section 6 we provide a method for verifying specialised partial correctness of programs. Finally, in Section 7 we discuss a meaningful example.

2 Preliminaries

The reader is assumed to be familiar with the terminology of and the basic results in the semantics of logic programs [1,3,15].

Let $\mathcal{T}$ be the set of terms built on a finite set of *data constructors* $\mathcal{C}$ and a denumerable set of *variable symbols* $\mathcal{V}$. Variable-free terms are called *ground*.
A *substitution* is a mapping $\theta : \mathcal{V} \to \mathcal{T}$ such that the set $D(\theta) = \{X \mid \theta(X) \neq X\}$ (*domain* of θ) is finite. For any expression E, we denote by $\theta_{|E}$ the restriction of θ to the variables in $Var(E)$. ϵ denotes the empty substitution.
The *composition* $\theta\sigma$ of the substitutions θ and σ is defined as the functional composition, i.e., $\theta\sigma(X) = \sigma(\theta(X))$. The pre-ordering $\leq$ (more general than) on substitutions is such that $\theta \leq \sigma$ iff there exists θ' such that $\theta\theta' = \sigma$. We say that θ and σ are *not comparable* if neither $\theta \leq \sigma$ nor $\sigma \leq \theta$.
The result of the application of a substitution θ to a term t is an *instance* of t denoted by $t\theta$. We define $t \leq t'$ iff there exists θ such that $t\theta = t'$. We say that t and t' are *not comparable* if neither $t \leq t'$ nor $t' \leq t$. The relation $\leq$ on terms is a preorder. We denote by $\approx$ the associated equivalence relation (*variance*). A substitution θ is a *unifier* of t and t' if $t\theta = t'\theta$. We denote by $mgu(t_1, t_2)$ any idempotent *most general unifier* (*mgu*, in short) of t_1 and t_2. The definitions above are extended to other syntactic objects in the obvious way.

2.1 Programs and Derivations

Atoms, queries, clauses and programs are defined as follows. Let $\mathcal{P}$ be a finite set of *predicate symbols*. An *atom* is an object of the form $p(t_1, \ldots, t_n)$ where

$p \in \mathcal{P}$ is an n-ary predicate symbol and $t_1, \ldots, t_n \in \mathcal{T}$. A *query* is a possibly empty finite sequence of atoms $A_1, \ldots, A_m$. The empty query is denoted by $\Box$. We use the convention adopted by Apt in [3] and use bold characters to denote sequences of atoms. A *clause* is a formula $H \leftarrow \mathbf{B}$ where H is an atom, called *head*, and $\mathbf{B}$ is a query, called *body*. When $\mathbf{B}$ is empty, $H \leftarrow \mathbf{B}$ is written $H \leftarrow$ and is called a *unit clause*. A *program* is a finite set of clauses.

Computations are constructed as sequences of "basic" steps. Consider a non empty query $\mathbf{A}, B, \mathbf{C}$ and a clause c. Let $H \leftarrow \mathbf{B}$ be a variant of c variable disjoint with $\mathbf{A}, B, \mathbf{C}$. Let B and H unify with mgu θ. The query $(\mathbf{A}, \mathbf{B}, \mathbf{C})\theta$ is called an *SLD-resolvent of* $\mathbf{A}, B, \mathbf{C}$ *and* c *w.r.t.* B, *with an mgu* θ. The atoms B and $B\theta$ are called the *selected atom* and the *selected atom instance*, respectively, of $\mathbf{A}, B, \mathbf{C}$. We write then

$$\mathbf{A}, B, \mathbf{C} \stackrel{\theta}{\Longrightarrow}_{P,c} (\mathbf{A}, \mathbf{B}, \mathbf{C})\theta$$

and call it *SLD-derivation step*. $H \leftarrow \mathbf{B}$ is called its *input clause*. If P is clear from the context or c is irrelevant then we drop a reference to them. An SLD-derivation is obtained by iterating SLD-derivation steps. A maximal sequence

$$\delta := Q_0 \stackrel{\theta_1}{\Longrightarrow}_{P,c_1} Q_1 \stackrel{\theta_2}{\Longrightarrow}_{P,c_2} \cdots Q_n \stackrel{\theta_{n+1}}{\Longrightarrow}_{P,c_{n+1}} Q_{n+1} \cdots$$

of SLD-derivation steps is called an *SLD-derivation of* $P \cup \{Q_0\}$ provided that for every step the standardization apart condition holds, i.e., the input clause employed is variable disjoint from the initial query Q_0 and from the substitutions and the input clauses used at earlier steps.

The length of an SLD-derivation δ, denoted by $len(\delta)$, is the number of SLD-derivation steps in δ. We denote by $Sel(\delta)$ the set of all the selected atom instances, one for each derivation step, of δ. If P is clear from the context, we speak of an SLD-derivation of Q_0. SLD-derivations can be finite or infinite. Consider a finite SLD-derivation $\delta := Q_0 \stackrel{\theta_1}{\Longrightarrow}_{P,c_1} Q_1 \cdots \stackrel{\theta_n}{\Longrightarrow}_{P,c_n} Q_n$ of a query $Q := Q_0$, also denoted by $\delta := Q_0 \stackrel{\theta}{\longmapsto}_{P,c_1,\ldots,c_n} Q_n$ (or simply $\delta := Q_0 \stackrel{\theta}{\longmapsto} Q_n$) with $\theta = \theta_1 \cdots \theta_n$. If $Q_n = \Box$ then δ is called *successful*. The restriction of θ to the variables of Q, denoted by $\theta_{|Q}$, is called a *computed answer substitution* (*c.a.s.*, in short) of Q and $Q\theta$ is called a *computed instance* of Q. If Q_n is non-empty and there is no input clause whose head unifies with its selected atom, then the SLD-derivation δ is called *failed*.

2.2 Interpretations

By the *extended Herbrand base* $\mathcal{B}^{\mathcal{E}}$ we mean the quotient set of all the atoms with respect to $\approx$. The ordering induced by $\leq$ on $\mathcal{B}^{\mathcal{E}}$ will still be denoted by $\leq$. For the sake of simplicity, we will represent the equivalence class of an atom A by A itself. An *interpretation* I is any subset of $\mathcal{B}^{\mathcal{E}}$.
We recall from [14] some definitions of useful operators on interpretations.

Definition 1. (Operators on Interpretations) *Let I be an interpretation. The* upward closure *of I is the set*

$$\lceil I \rceil = \{A \in \mathcal{B}^{\mathcal{E}} \mid \exists A' \in I, A' \leq A\}.$$

The set of ground atoms *of I is the set*

$$\lfloor I \rfloor = \{A \in I \mid A \textit{ is ground}\}.$$

The set of minimal elements *of I is the set*

$$Min(I) = \{A \in I \mid \forall A' \in I \textit{ if } A' \leq A \textit{ then } A = A'\}.$$

Example 1. Let I be the set $\{\textbf{append}(u, v, z) \mid u, v$ are terms and z is a list of at most n elements$\}$. Then

$$\begin{aligned} Min(I) = \{&\textbf{append}\,(X_s, Y_s, [\,]), \\ &\textbf{append}\,(X_s, Y_s, [Z_1]), \\ &\textbf{append}\,(X_s, Y_s, [Z_1, Z_2]), \\ &\ldots \\ &\textbf{append}\,(X_s, Y_s, [Z_1, Z_2, \ldots, Z_n])\} \end{aligned}$$

where $X_s, Y_s, Z_1, Z_2, \ldots, Z_n$ are distinct variables.

Let us introduce the notation $[I]$ as a shorthand for $\lfloor \lceil I \rceil \rfloor$. Note that $[I]$ is the set of all ground instances of atoms in I. Moreover (see [14]), $\lceil I \rceil = \lceil Min(I) \rceil$ and $Min(\lceil I \rceil) = Min(I)$.

The notion of truth extends the classical one to account for non-ground formulas in the interpretations.

Definition 2. ($\models$) *Let I be an interpretation and A be an atom . Then*

$$I \models A \textit{ iff } A \in \lceil I \rceil.$$

Moreover, if $Q := A_1, \ldots, A_n$ is a query then

$$I \models Q \textit{ iff } A_i \in \lceil I \rceil \textit{ for all } i \in \{1, \ldots, n\}.$$

The following properties hold [14]: $I \models A$ iff there exists $A' \in I$ such that $A' \leq A$; moreover, if $I \models A$ then for all A' such that $A \leq A'$, $I \models A'$.

Definition 3. (Minimal Instances of an Atom Satisfying I) *Let I be an interpretation and A be an atom. The* set of minimal instances of A satisfying I *is*

$$Min_I(A) = Min(\{A' \in \lceil A \rceil \mid I \models A'\}).$$

Example 2. Consider the interpretation I of the Example 1. Then

$$\begin{aligned} Min_I(\textbf{append}\,([\,], Y_s, Z_s)) = \{&\textbf{append}\,([\,], Y_s, [\,]), \\ &\textbf{append}\,([\,], Y_s, [Z_1]), \\ &\textbf{append}\,([\,], Y_s, [Z_1, Z_2]), \\ &\ldots \\ &\textbf{append}\,([\,], Y_s, [Z_1, Z_2, \ldots, Z_n])\} \end{aligned}$$

where $Y_s, Z_1, Z_2, \ldots, Z_n$ are distinct variables. Note that although I is infinite, in this case both $Min(I)$ and $Min_I(\textbf{append}\,([\,], Y_s, Z_s))$ are finite sets of atoms.

The notion of specialised unifier is introduced. It is the basic concept upon which specialised derivations are defined.

Definition 4. (Specialised Unifiers) *Let I be an interpretation and A_1 and A_2 be atoms. A* I-unifier *of A_1 and A_2 is a substitution θ such that $A_1\theta = A_2\theta$ and $I \models A_1\theta$. A* most general I-unifier *of A_1 and A_2, denoted by*

$$mgu_I(A_1, A_2),$$

is any idempotent I-unifier θ such that for any other I-unifier θ', either $\theta \leq \theta'$ or θ and θ' are not comparable.

For the sake of simplicity, we will write $\theta = mgu_I(A_1, A_2)$ even if $mgu_I(A_1, A_2)$ is not uniquely determined and can even denote an infinite set of substitutions.

Example 3. Consider again the interpretation I of the Example 1. Then

$$mgu_I(\textbf{append}\ (U, V, W), \textbf{append}\ ([\,], X_s, X_s))$$

denotes the following substitutions

$$\begin{aligned} \theta_0 &= \{U/[\,], V/X_s, W/X_s, X_s/[\,]\} \\ \theta_1 &= \{U/[\,], V/X_s, W/X_s, X_s/[Z_1]\} \\ \theta_2 &= \{U/[\,], V/X_s, W/X_s, X_s/[Z_1, Z_2]\} \\ &\dots \\ \theta_n &= \{U/[\,], V/X_s, W/X_s, X_s/[Z_1, Z_2, \dots, Z_n]\}. \end{aligned}$$

Note that the substitutions $\theta_0, \theta_1, \dots, \theta_n$ are pairwise not comparable. Moreover, they are idempotent but not relevant with respect to the variables occurring in the two unifying atoms. In fact, they contain new variables, $\{Z_1, \dots, Z_n\}$, which are introduced in order to satisfy I. We call these variables *place holders*. Note that the definition of specialised *most* general unifier imposes that they are pairwise disjoint and distinct from the variables occurring in the unifying atoms.

It is well known that set inclusion does not adequately reflect the property of non-ground atoms of being representatives of all their ground instances. So, in this paper, we refer to the partial ordering $\sqsubseteq$ on interpretations defined by Falaschi *et al.* in [14] as below.

Definition 5. *Let I_1 and I_2 be interpretation.*

- $I_1 \leq I_2$ *iff* $\forall A_1 \in I_1, \exists A_2 \in I_2$ *such that* $A_2 \leq A_1$.
- $I_1 \sqsubseteq I_2$ *iff* $(I_1 \leq I_2)$ *and* $(I_2 \leq I_1$ *implies* $I_1 \subseteq I_2)$.

Intuitively, $I_1 \leq I_2$ means that every atom verified by I_1 is also verified by I_2 (I_2 contains more positive information). Note that $\leq$ has different meanings for atoms and interpretations. $I_1 \sqsubseteq I_2$ means either that I_2 strictly contains more positive information than I_1 or that the amount of positive information is the same and I_1 expresses it by fewer elements than I_2. The relation $\leq$ is a preorder, whereas the relation $\sqsubseteq$ is an ordering. Moreover, if $I_1 \subseteq I_2$, then $I_1 \sqsubseteq I_2$.

Example 4. Consider the interpretation I of the Example 1. Then $I \leq Min(I)$, but also $Min(I) \sqsubseteq I$. Moreover, $Min_I(\mathbf{append}\ ([\,], Y_s, Z_s)) \sqsubseteq Min(I)$.

The set of all the interpretations $\mathcal{I}$ under the relation $\sqsubseteq$ is a complete lattice.

Proposition 1. *[14] The set of interpretations $\mathcal{I}$ with the ordering $\sqsubseteq$ is a complete lattice, noted by $\langle \mathcal{I}, \sqsubseteq \rangle$. $\mathcal{B}^{\mathcal{E}}$ is the top element and $\emptyset$ is the bottom element.*

3 Specialised Derivations and their Semantics

In this section we recall from [7] the notion of specialised derivation and show some properties. Top-down and a fixpoint semantics are presented.

3.1 Specialised Derivations

Given an interpretation I, a specialised derivation is an SLD-derivation where all the selected atoms are instantiated in order to satisfy the call-condition I. Specialised derivations are defined as SLD-derivations except that at each derivation step specialised most general unifiers are computed instead of usual mgus. In the following we assume given a program P.

Definition 6. *Let I be an interpretation. Let $\mathbf{A}, B, \mathbf{C}$ be a non empty query, c be a clause, $H \leftarrow \mathbf{B}$ be a variant of c variable disjoint with $\mathbf{A}, B, \mathbf{C}$. Let B and H unify and $\theta = mgu_I(B, H)$ where the place holders of θ are disjoint from $\mathbf{A}, \mathbf{B}, \mathbf{C}$. The query $(\mathbf{A}, \mathbf{B}, \mathbf{C})\theta$ is called an I-*resolvent of $\mathbf{A}, B, \mathbf{C}$ and c w.r.t. B, with *specialised mgu θ. The atoms B and $B\theta$ are called the I-*selected atom *and I-*selected atom instance, *respectively, of $\mathbf{A}, B, \mathbf{C}$. We write then*

$$\mathbf{A}, B, \mathbf{C} \stackrel{\theta}{\Longrightarrow}_{P,c,I} (\mathbf{A}, \mathbf{B}, \mathbf{C})\theta$$

*and call it I-*derivation step. *$H \leftarrow \mathbf{B}$ is its I-*input clause. *A maximal sequence*

$$\delta := Q_0 \stackrel{\theta_1}{\Longrightarrow}_{P,c_1,I} Q_1 \stackrel{\theta_2}{\Longrightarrow}_{P,c_2,I} \cdots Q_n \stackrel{\theta_{n+1}}{\Longrightarrow}_{P,c_{n+1},I} Q_{n+1} \cdots$$

*of I-derivation steps is called an I-*derivation of *$P \cup \{Q_0\}$ where for every step the I-standardization apart condition holds, i.e., the I-input clause c_i employed and the place holders of unifier θ_i are variable disjoint from the initial query Q_0 and from the substitutions and the input clauses used at earlier steps.*
We denote by $Sel(\delta)$ the set of all the I-selected atom instances of δ.
Consider a finite I-derivation $\delta := Q_0 \stackrel{\theta_1}{\Longrightarrow}_{P,c_1,I} Q_1 \cdots \stackrel{\theta_n}{\Longrightarrow}_{P,c_n,I} Q_n$ of a query $Q := Q_0$, also denoted by $\delta := Q_0 \stackrel{\theta}{\longmapsto}_{P,c_1,\ldots,c_n,I} Q_n$ (or simply $\delta := Q_0 \stackrel{\theta}{\longmapsto}_I Q_n$) with $\theta = \theta_1 \cdots \theta_n$. If $Q_n = \square$ then δ is called successful. *The restriction of θ to the variables of Q is called a I-*computed answer substitution *(I-c.a.s., in short) of Q and $Q\theta$ is called a I-*computed instance *of Q. If Q_n is non-empty and there is no I-input clause $H \leftarrow \mathbf{B}$ such that H unifies with the I-selected atom B of Q_n with $\theta = mgu_I(B, H)$, then δ is called* failed.

Whenever I is omitted, we assume that $I = \mathcal{B}^{\mathcal{E}}$. It is easy to see that if I is the extended Herbrand base $\mathcal{B}^{\mathcal{E}}$, then I-derivations (resp. I-derivation steps) are indeed SLD-derivations (resp. SLD-derivation steps).

Example 5. Consider the interpretation I of Example 1 and the program APPEND:

append $([\,], X_s, X_s) \leftarrow .$
append $([X|X_s], Y_s, [X|Z_s]) \leftarrow$ **append** (X_s, Y_s, Z_s).

Let $\theta_0, \theta_1, \ldots, \theta_n$ be the substitutions defined in the Example 3. Then

$$\mathbf{append}\,(U, V, W) \xrightarrow{\theta_0}_I \Box$$
$$\mathbf{append}\,(U, V, W) \xrightarrow{\theta_1}_I \Box$$
$$\ldots$$
$$\mathbf{append}\,(U, V, W) \xrightarrow{\theta_n}_I \Box$$

are successful I-derivations of the query **append** (U, V, W). Note that any I-derivation of the query **append** $([\,], \mathtt{foo}, \mathtt{foo})$ fails.

Observe that, for any I-derivation δ, $Sel(\delta) \leq I$, i.e., for all $A \in Sel(\delta)$, $I \models A$. Moreover, any SLD-derivation δ satisfying $Sel(\delta) \leq I$ is an I-derivation.

The following relation between successful I and SLD-derivations holds.

Lemma 1. *[7] Let I be an interpretation and $\delta := Q \xrightarrow{\theta}_{c_1,\ldots,c_n,I} \Box$ be a successful I-derivation of a query Q. Then, there exists a successful SLD-derivation $\delta' := Q\theta \xrightarrow{\gamma}_{c_1,\ldots,c_n} \Box$ of $Q\theta$ with $Q\theta\gamma = Q\theta$ and $Sel(\delta') \leq Sel(\delta)$.*

The next result is useful to reason on I-derivations.

Lemma 2. *Let I be an interpretation and $\delta := Q \xrightarrow{\theta}_I \Box$ be a successful I-derivation of a query $Q := A_1, \ldots, A_n$. Then, for all $j \in \{1, \ldots, n\}$, there exists a successful I-derivation $\delta_j := A_j\theta \xrightarrow{\gamma_j}_I \Box$ where $A_j\theta\gamma_j = A_j\theta$.*

Proof. Let $\delta := Q \xrightarrow{\theta}_I \Box$. By Lemma 1, there exists a successful SLD-derivation $\delta' := Q\theta \xrightarrow{\gamma} \Box$ with $Q\theta\gamma = Q\theta$ and $Sel(\delta') \leq Sel(\delta)$. By properties of SLD-derivations (see [1, 8, 15]), for all $j \in \{1, \ldots, n\}$, there exists a successful SLD-derivation $\delta_j := A_j\theta \xrightarrow{\gamma_j} \Box$ such that $A_j\theta\gamma_j = A_j\theta$ and $Sel(\delta_j) \leq Sel(\delta')$. Then, for all $j \in \{1, \ldots, n\}$, $Sel(\delta_j) \leq Sel(\delta)$. Moreover, since δ is an I-derivation, $Sel(\delta) \leq I$. Hence, for all $j \in \{1, \ldots, n\}$, $Sel(\delta_j) \leq I$ and then, by Definition 6, δ_j is a successful I-derivation $A_j\theta \xrightarrow{\gamma_j}_I \Box$.

We show that any I-computed instance is true in I.

Lemma 3. *Let I be an interpretation and $\delta := Q \xrightarrow{\theta}_I \Box$ be a successful I-derivation of a query Q. Then $I \models Q\theta$.*

Proof. Let $Q := A_1, \ldots, A_n$. We prove that for all $j \in \{1, \ldots, n\}$, $I \models A_j\theta$. By Lemma 2, for all $j \in \{1, \ldots, n\}$, there exists $\delta_j := A_j\theta \overset{\gamma_j}{\longmapsto}_I \Box$ where $A_j\theta\gamma_j = A_j\theta$. Let H_j be the head of the I-input clause used in the first I-derivation step of δ_j. Let also $\gamma_j^1 = mgu_I(A_j\theta, H_j)$. By Definition 4, $I \models A_j\theta\gamma_j^1$ and by Definition 6, $A_j\theta\gamma_j^1 \leq A_j\theta\gamma_j$. Hence, by Definition 2, $I \models A_j\theta\gamma_j$.

The Lifting Lemma for SLD-derivations [15, 1] can be generalized to specialised derivations as follows.

Lemma 4. (Specialised Lifting Lemma) *Let I be an interpretation and $\delta := Q\theta \overset{\sigma}{\longmapsto}_I \Box$ be a successful I-derivation of a query $Q\theta$. Then, there exists a successful I-derivation $\delta' := Q \overset{\sigma'}{\longmapsto}_I \Box$ where $\sigma' \leq \theta\sigma$.*

Proof. By induction on $len(\delta)$.
Basis. Let $len(\delta) = 1$. In this case Q consists of only one atom B and

$$\delta := B\theta \overset{\sigma}{\Longrightarrow}_I \Box$$

where $H \leftarrow$ is the I-input clause and $\sigma = mgu_I(B\theta, H)$. Because of standardization apart, we can assume that $\theta_{|H} = \epsilon$. Then, $\theta\sigma$ is a I-unifier of B and H. Hence, there exists $\sigma' = mgu_I(B, H)$ such that $\sigma' \leq \theta\sigma$ and

$$\delta' := B \overset{\sigma'}{\Longrightarrow}_I \Box$$

is a successful I-derivation.
Induction step. Let $len(\delta) > 1$. Then $Q := \mathbf{A}, B, \mathbf{C}$ and

$$\delta := (\mathbf{A}, B, \mathbf{C})\theta \overset{\sigma_1}{\Longrightarrow}_I (\mathbf{A}, \mathbf{B}, \mathbf{C})\theta\sigma_1 \overset{\sigma_2}{\longmapsto}_I \Box$$

where B is the I-selected atom of Q, $c := H \leftarrow \mathbf{B}$ is the first I-input clause, $\sigma_1 = mgu_I(B\theta, H)$ and $\sigma = \sigma_1\sigma_2$. Because of standardization apart, we can assume that $\theta_{|c} = \epsilon$. Then, $\theta\sigma_1$ is a I-unifier of B and H. Hence, there exists $\sigma_1' = mgu_I(B, H)$ such that $\sigma_1' \leq \theta\sigma_1$ and

$$(\mathbf{A}, B, \mathbf{C}) \overset{\sigma_1'}{\Longrightarrow}_I (\mathbf{A}, \mathbf{B}, \mathbf{C})\sigma_1'$$

is an I-derivation step. Let γ be a substitution such that $\sigma_1'\gamma = \theta\sigma_1$. By the inductive hypothesis, there exists a successful I-derivation

$$(\mathbf{A}, \mathbf{B}, \mathbf{C})\sigma_1' \overset{\sigma_2'}{\longmapsto}_I \Box$$

where $\sigma_2' \leq \gamma\sigma_2$. Therefore,

$$\delta' := (\mathbf{A}, B, \mathbf{C}) \overset{\sigma_1'}{\Longrightarrow}_I (\mathbf{A}, \mathbf{B}, \mathbf{C})\sigma_1' \overset{\sigma_2'}{\longmapsto}_I \Box$$

is a successful I-derivation. Let $\sigma' = \sigma_1'\sigma_2'$. Then,

$$\begin{aligned} \sigma' &= \sigma_1'\sigma_2' && \text{(by definition of } \sigma'\text{)} \\ &\leq \sigma_1'\gamma\sigma_2 && \text{(since } \sigma_2' \leq \gamma\sigma_2\text{)} \\ &= \theta\sigma_1\sigma_2 && \text{(since } \sigma_1'\gamma = \theta\sigma_1\text{)} \\ &= \theta\sigma && \text{(by definition of } \sigma\text{).} \end{aligned}$$

3.2 Specialised Top-down Semantics

We present below a top-down construction which computes the specialised semantics of logic programs. It models the computed answer substitutions of the specialised derivations.

Definition 7. (Specialised Computed Answer Substitution Semantics) *Let P be a program and I be an interpretation. The I*-computed answer substitution semantics of *P is*

$$\begin{aligned}\mathcal{O}_I(P) = \{A \in \mathcal{B}^{\mathcal{E}} \mid\ & \exists p \in \mathcal{P}, \exists X_1,\dots,X_n \textit{ distinct variables in } \mathcal{V},\ \exists\theta, \\ & p(X_1,\dots,X_n) \overset{\theta}{\longmapsto}_{P,I} \Box, \\ & A = p(X_1,\dots,X_n)\theta\}.\end{aligned}$$

Observe that if I is the extended Herbrand base $\mathcal{B}^{\mathcal{E}}$, then $\mathcal{O}_{\mathcal{B}^{\mathcal{E}}}(P)$ is the original s-semantics defined by Falaschi *et al.* in [13].

Example 6. Consider the interpretation I of Example 1. Then

$$\begin{aligned}\mathcal{O}_I(\texttt{APPEND}) = \{&\textbf{append}\ ([\,],[\,],[\,]), \\ &\textbf{append}\ ([\,],[X_1],[X_1]), \\ &\textbf{append}\ ([\,],[X_1,X_2],[X_1,X_2]), \\ &\dots \\ &\textbf{append}\ ([\,],[X_1,X_2,\dots,X_n],[X_1,X_2,\dots,X_n]), \\ &\textbf{append}\ ([X_1],[\,],[X_1]), \\ &\textbf{append}\ ([X_1],[X_2],[X_1,X_2]), \\ &\dots \\ &\textbf{append}\ ([X_1],[X_2,\dots,X_n],[X_1,X_2,\dots,X_n]), \\ &\textbf{append}\ ([X_1,X_2],[\,],[X_1,X_2]), \\ &\dots \\ \}&.\end{aligned}$$

Let us consider now the *success set* and the *non-ground success set* semantics formally defined in [13]. The corresponding specialised versions are defined below.

Definition 8. (Specialised Success Set Semantics) *Let P be a program and I be an interpretation. The I*-success set semantics of *P is defined by*

$$\mathcal{O}_{I,1}(P) = \{A \in \mathcal{B}^{\mathcal{E}} \mid A \textit{ is ground and } A \overset{\gamma}{\longmapsto}_I \Box \textit{ where } A\gamma = A\}.$$

Note that if I is the extended Herbrand base $\mathcal{B}^{\mathcal{E}}$, then $\mathcal{O}_{\mathcal{B}^{\mathcal{E}},1}(P)$ is the standard semantics, which is equivalent to the least Herbrand model [22].

Definition 9. (Specialised Non-ground Success Set Semantics) *Let P be a program and I be an interpretation. The I*-non-ground success set semantics of *P is defined by*

$$\mathcal{O}_{I,2}(P) = \{A \in \mathcal{B}^{\mathcal{E}} \mid A \overset{\gamma}{\longmapsto}_I \Box \textit{ where } A\gamma = A\}.$$

If I is equal to $\mathcal{B}^{\mathcal{E}}$, then $\mathcal{O}_{\mathcal{B}^{\mathcal{E}},2}(P)$ is the *set of atomic logical consequences* [8] of P.
It is easy to prove that the following relations hold: $\mathcal{O}_{I,1}(P) = \lfloor \mathcal{O}_I(P) \rfloor$ and $\mathcal{O}_{I,2}(P) = \lceil \mathcal{O}_I(P) \rceil$.

3.3 Specialised Fixpoint Semantics

We define an immediate consequence operator $T_{P,I}$ on the set of interpretations $\mathcal{I}$. Its least fixpoint has been shown to be equivalent to the specialised computed answer substitutions semantics $\mathcal{O}_I(P)$.

Definition 10. ($T_{P,I}$ Transformation) *Let P be a program and I and J be two interpretations.*

$$\begin{aligned} T_{P,I}(J) = \{A \in \mathcal{B}^{\mathcal{E}} \mid\ & \exists H \leftarrow B_1, \ldots, B_n \in P, \\ & \exists B'_1, \ldots, B'_n \text{ variant of atoms in } J \text{ and renamed apart}, \\ & \exists \theta = mgu_I((B_1, \ldots, B_n), (B'_1, \ldots, B'_n)), \\ & A \in Min_I(H\theta)\}. \end{aligned}$$

Note that if I is the extended Herbrand base $\mathcal{B}^{\mathcal{E}}$, then $T_{P,\mathcal{B}^{\mathcal{E}}}$ coincides with the S-transformation T_S defined in [13].

Proposition 2. (Monotonicity and Continuity of $T_{P,I}$) *For any interpretation I, transformation $T_{P,I}$ is monotonic and continuous in the complete lattice $\langle \mathcal{I}, \subseteq \rangle$.*

Definition 11. (Powers of $T_{P,I}$) *As usual, we define powers of transformation $T_{P,I}$ as follows:*

$$\begin{aligned} T_{P,I} \uparrow 0 &= \emptyset, \\ T_{P,I} \uparrow n+1 &= T_{P,I}(T_{P,I} \uparrow n), \\ T_{P,I} \uparrow \omega &= \textstyle\bigcup_{n \geq 0}(T_{P,I} \uparrow n). \end{aligned}$$

Proposition 3. *For any interpretation I, $T_{P,I} \uparrow \omega$ is the least fixpoint of $T_{P,I}$ in the complete lattice $\langle \mathcal{I}, \sqsubseteq \rangle$.*

Proof. By Proposition 2, $T_{P,I} \uparrow \omega$ is the least fixpoint of $T_{P,I}$ with respect to set inclusion. Moreover, for any fixpoint J of $T_{P,I}$, $T_{P,I} \uparrow \omega \subseteq J$. Hence, by Definition 5, $T_{P,I} \uparrow \omega \sqsubseteq J$.

The specialised fixpoint semantics is formally defined as follows.

Definition 12. (Specialised Fixpoint Semantics) *Let P be a program and I be an interpretation. The* I-fixpoint semantics of P *is defined as*

$$\mathcal{F}_I(P) = T_{P,I} \uparrow \omega.$$

4 Specialising Programs wrt Call/Post Specification

In this section we define a simple program transformation which given a call/post specification transforms a program into a weakly call-correct one satisfying the post-condition. The notion of weak call-correctness is formally defined as follows.

Definition 13. (Weak Call-correctness) *Let P be a program and I be an interpretation. We say that P is* weakly call-correct *with respect to the call-condition I iff for any query Q and SLD-derivation δ of $P \cup \{Q\}$, $Sel(\delta) \leq I$.*

Our specialisation is applied to so-called *specialised partially correct* programs which are introduced below.

4.1 Specialised Partially Correct Programs

In this section we introduce the concept of specialised partially correct program with respect to a given call/post specification. It provides a weaker notion of *partial correctness* where specialised derivations only are observed. In Section 6, a simple method for verifying specialised partial correctness will be presented.

Definition 14. *Let P be a program and Call and Post be interpretations. We say that P is* specialised partially correct *(*s.p.c.*, in short) with respect to the call-condition Call and the post-condition Post, noted*

$$\{Call\}P\{Post\}_{spec},$$

if and only if for any query Q,

$$Q \stackrel{\theta}{\longmapsto}_{P,Call} \Box \ \textit{implies}\ Post \models Q\theta.$$

Observe that, if $Call = \mathcal{B}^{\mathcal{E}}$ then P is correct with respect to the post-condition *Post* according to the standard correctness definition. In this case, P is s.p.c. with respect to any call-condition *Call* and the post-condition *Post*.

Example 7. Consider the program **APPEND** and the interpretations

$Call = \{\textbf{append}\ (u, v, z) \mid u, v$ are terms and z is a list of at most n elements$\}$
$Post = \{\textbf{append}\ (u, v, z) \mid u, v, z$ are lists, z has at most n elements and $z = u * v\}$

where $*$ is the list concatenation operator. The program **APPEND** is s.p.c. with respect to the specification *Call* and *Post*, i.e., the following assertion holds:

$$\{Call\}\ \textbf{APPEND}\ \{Post\}_{spec}.$$

We define the strongest post-condition of a program P with respect to a given call-condition as follows.

Definition 15. (Strongest Post-condition) *Let P be a program. The* strongest post-condition *of P with respect to a call-condition I, noted $sp(P, I)$, is the smallest interpretation J with respect to $\sqsubseteq$ such that $\{I\}P\{J\}_{spec}$.*

The next Proposition characterizes the strongest post-condition of a program P wrt a call-condition I in terms of the I-c.a.s. semantics of P.

Proposition 4. *Let P be a program and I be an interpretation. Then, $Min(\mathcal{O}_I(P)) = sp(P, I)$.*

Proof. We prove that $\{I\}P\{Min(\mathcal{O}_I(P))\}_{spec}$ holds, i.e., if $\delta := Q \stackrel{\theta}{\longmapsto}_I \Box$ is a successful I-derivation of a query Q then $Min(\mathcal{O}_I(P)) \models Q\theta$.
Let $Q := A_1, \ldots, A_n$. By Lemma 2, for all $j \in \{1, \ldots, n\}$ there exists a successful I-derivation $\delta_j := A_j\theta \stackrel{\gamma_j}{\longmapsto}_I \Box$ where $A_j\theta\gamma_j = A_j\theta$. For all $j \in \{1, \ldots, n\}$, let $p_j \in \mathcal{P}$ and $X_1, \ldots, X_n$ be distinct variables in $\mathcal{V}$ such that $p_j(X_1, \ldots, X_n) \leq$

$A_j\theta$. By Lemma 4, there exists a successful I-derivation $p_j(X_1,\ldots,X_n) \stackrel{\theta_j}{\longmapsto}_I \Box$ where $p_j(X_1,\ldots,X_n)\theta_j \leq A_j\theta$. By Definition 7, $p_j(X_1,\ldots,X_n)\theta_j \in \mathcal{O}_I(P)$. This proves that for all j, $Min(\mathcal{O}_I(P)) \models A_j\theta$ and then $Min(\mathcal{O}_I(P)) \models Q\theta$.

Further, for any interpretation J such that $\{I\}P\{J\}_{spec}$, $Min(\mathcal{O}_I(P)) \sqsubseteq J$. We first prove that $Min(\mathcal{O}_I(P)) \leq J$, i.e., for all $A \in Min(\mathcal{O}_I(P))$ there exists $A' \in J$ such that $A' \leq A$. Let $A \in Min(\mathcal{O}_I(P))$. By Definition 7, there exist $p \in \mathcal{P}$, $X_1,\ldots,X_n$ distinct variables in $\mathcal{V}$ and a substitution θ such that $p(X_1,\ldots,X_n) \stackrel{\theta}{\longmapsto}_I \Box$ is a successful I-derivation and $A = p(X_1,\ldots,X_n)\theta$. By the hypothesis $\{I\}P\{J\}_{spec}$, $J \models A$. So, there exists $A' \in J$ such that $A' \leq A$. Suppose now that $J \leq Min(\mathcal{O}_I(P))$. Then $Min(\mathcal{O}_I(P)) \subseteq J$. Indeed, from the fact that both $Min(\mathcal{O}_I(P)) \leq J$ and $J \leq Min(\mathcal{O}_I(P))$, for all $A \in Min(\mathcal{O}_I(P))$ there exists $A' \in J$ and $A'' \in Min(\mathcal{O}_I(P))$ such that $A'' \leq A' \leq A$. By Definition 1 of operator Min, $A'' = A$ and then $A \in J$.

4.2 Specialised Programs

Any s.p.c. program P with respect to a given call/post specification I and J, i.e., such that $\{I\}P\{J\}_{spec}$ holds, can be transformed into a specialised program P_I which is weakly call-correct with respect to the call-condition I and satisfies the property $\{\mathcal{B}^{\mathcal{E}}\}P_I\{J\}_{spec}$. This means that for any query Q and SLD-derivation δ of $P_I \cup \{Q\}$ with computed answer substitution θ, $Sel(\delta) \leq I$ and $J \models Q\theta$.

Specialised programs are obtained from the following program transformation.

Definition 16. (Specialised Program) *Let P be a program and I be an interpretation. The I*-program *corresponding to P, denoted by P_I, is defined as:*

$$P_I = \{(H \leftarrow \mathbf{B})\gamma \mid H \leftarrow \mathbf{B} \in P \textit{ and } H\gamma \in Min_I(H) \\ \textit{where } \gamma \textit{ is idempotent and} \\ Var(\gamma) \cap Var(H \leftarrow \mathbf{B}) \subseteq Dom(\gamma) = Var(H)\}.$$

The condition $Var(\gamma) \cap Var(H \leftarrow \mathbf{B}) \subseteq Dom(\gamma) = Var(H)$ allows us to avoid undesired bindings on the variables in the bodies.
Note that P_I may be an infinite program but it will be finite whenever $Min(I)$ is finite.

Example 8. Consider the program **APPEND** and the interpretations *Call* and *Post* given in the Example 7. The specialised program $\mathbf{APPEND}_{Call}$ is defined by:

append $([\,],[\,],[\,])$.
append $([\,],[X_1],[X_1])$.
append $([\,],[X_1,X_2],[X_1,X_2])$.
...
append $([\,],[X_1,X_2,\ldots,X_n],[X_1,X_2,\ldots,X_n])$.
append $([X_1|X_s],Y_s,[X_1]) \leftarrow$ **append** $(X_s,Y_s,[\,])$.
append $([X_1|X_s],Y_s,[X_1,X_2]) \leftarrow$ **append** $(X_s,Y_s,[X_2])$.
...
append $([X_1|X_s],Y_s,[X_1,X_2,\ldots,X_n]) \leftarrow$ **append** $(X_s,Y_s,[X_2,\ldots,X_n])$.

It is easy to see that the assertion $\{\mathcal{B}^{\mathcal{E}}\}$ $\mathtt{APPEND}_{Call}$ $\{Post\}_{spec}$ holds, meaning that for any query Q and successful SLD-derivation δ of $\mathtt{APPEND}_{Call} \cup \{Q\}$ with computed answer substitution θ, $Post \models Q\theta$. Moreover, for any selected atom instance $A \in Sel(\delta)$, $Call \models A$. Hence, $Sel(\delta) \leq Call$.

Proposition 5. *Let P be a program and I be an interpretation with $\{I\}P\{J\}_{spec}$. Then, P_I is weakly call-correct with respect to I.*

Proof. Let δ be an SLD-derivation of P_I. We prove that for all $A \in Sel(\delta)$, $I \models A$. Indeed, for all $A \in Sel(\delta)$ there exists and SLD-derivation step

$$\mathbf{A}, B, \mathbf{C} \stackrel{\theta}{\Longrightarrow}_{P_I,\mathcal{B}^{\mathcal{E}}} (\mathbf{A}, \mathbf{B}\gamma, \mathbf{C})\theta$$

of δ where B is the selected atom, $(H \leftarrow \mathbf{B})\gamma$ is the input clause, $\theta = mgu(B, H\gamma)$ and $A = B\theta$. By Definition 16, $H \leftarrow \mathbf{B}$ is a variant of a clause of P such that $H\gamma \in Min_I(H)$. Hence, $I \models H\gamma\theta = B\theta = A$.

Proposition 6. *Let P be a program and I be an interpretation. Then, $\{I\}P\{J\}_{spec}$ implies $\{\mathcal{B}^{\mathcal{E}}\}P_I\{J\}_{spec}$.*

Proof. We need the following result.

Claim. [7] Let P be a program, $Q := \mathbf{A}, B, \mathbf{C}$ and I be an interpretation. If

$$\mathbf{A}, B, \mathbf{C} \stackrel{\theta}{\Longrightarrow}_{P_I,\mathcal{B}^{\mathcal{E}}} (\mathbf{A}, \mathbf{B}, \mathbf{C})\theta$$

is an SLD-derivation step then there exists a substitution γ such that

$$\mathbf{A}, B, \mathbf{C} \stackrel{\gamma\theta}{\Longrightarrow}_{P,I} (\mathbf{A}, \mathbf{B}', \mathbf{C})\gamma\theta$$

is an I-derivation step where $\mathbf{B} = \mathbf{B}'\gamma$, $(\mathbf{A}, \mathbf{B}, \mathbf{C})\theta = (\mathbf{A}, \mathbf{B}', \mathbf{C})\gamma\theta$ and $\gamma_{|Q} = \epsilon$.

Suppose that $\{I\}P\{J\}_{spec}$ holds. We prove that for any query Q and successful SLD-derivation $\delta := Q \stackrel{\theta}{\longmapsto}_{P_I,\mathcal{B}^{\mathcal{E}}} \Box$, $J \models Q\theta$. In order to obtain this result, we prove that for any such δ, there exists a successful I-derivation $\delta' := Q\theta \stackrel{\sigma}{\longmapsto}_{P,I} \Box$ where $Q\theta\sigma = Q\theta$. The fact that $J \models Q\theta$ follows by the hypothesis $\{I\}P\{J\}_{spec}$. This is done by induction on $len(\delta)$.
Basis. Let $len(\delta) = 1$. In this case, Q consists of only one atom B and

$$\delta := B \stackrel{\theta}{\Longrightarrow}_{P_I,\mathcal{B}^{\mathcal{E}}} \Box.$$

By Claim 4.2, there exists a substitution γ such that

$$B \stackrel{\gamma\theta}{\Longrightarrow}_{P,I} \Box$$

is an I-derivation step and $\gamma_{|B} = \epsilon$. By Lemma 1, it follows that

$$\delta' := B\theta = B\gamma\theta \stackrel{\sigma}{\Longrightarrow}_{P,I} \Box$$

is a successful I-derivation of $B\theta$ where $B\theta\sigma = B\theta$.
Induction step. Let $len(\delta) > 1$. In this case $Q := \mathbf{A}, B, \mathbf{C}$ and

$$\delta := \mathbf{A}, B, \mathbf{C} \stackrel{\theta_1}{\Longrightarrow}_{P_I, \mathcal{B}^{\mathcal{E}}} (\mathbf{A}, \mathbf{B}, \mathbf{C})\theta_1 \stackrel{\theta_2}{\longmapsto}_{P_I, \mathcal{B}^{\mathcal{E}}} \Box$$

with $\theta = \theta_1\theta_2$. By Claim 4.2 there exists a substitution γ such that

$$\mathbf{A}, B, \mathbf{C} \stackrel{\gamma\theta_1}{\Longrightarrow}_{P,I} (\mathbf{A}, \mathbf{B}', \mathbf{C})\gamma\theta_1$$

is an I-derivation step where $\mathbf{B} = \mathbf{B}'\gamma$, $(\mathbf{A}, \mathbf{B}, \mathbf{C})\theta_1 = (\mathbf{A}, \mathbf{B}', \mathbf{C})\gamma\theta_1$ and $\gamma_{|Q} = \epsilon$. Let $H \leftarrow \mathbf{B}'$ be the input clause and $\gamma\theta_1 = mgu(B, H)$. Then, by properties of substitutions [1] there exists a substitution σ_1 such that $\sigma_{1|Q\theta} = \epsilon$, $\sigma_{1|H\leftarrow\mathbf{B}'} = \gamma\theta$ and $\sigma_1 = mgu_I(B\theta, H)$. So,

$$(\mathbf{A}, B, \mathbf{C})\gamma\theta \stackrel{\sigma_1}{\Longrightarrow}_{P,I} (\mathbf{A}, \mathbf{B}', \mathbf{C})\gamma\theta\sigma_1$$

is an I-derivation step. Since $\gamma_{|Q} = \epsilon$ and $(\mathbf{A}, \mathbf{B}, \mathbf{C})\theta_1 = (\mathbf{A}, \mathbf{B}', \mathbf{C})\gamma\theta_1$, also

$$(\mathbf{A}, B, \mathbf{C})\theta \stackrel{\sigma_1}{\Longrightarrow}_{P,I} (\mathbf{A}, \mathbf{B}, \mathbf{C})\theta\sigma_1$$

is an I-derivation step. By the inductive hypothesis,

$$(\mathbf{A}, \mathbf{B}, \mathbf{C})\theta \stackrel{\sigma_2}{\longmapsto}_{P,I} \Box$$

is a successful I-derivation where $(\mathbf{A}, \mathbf{B}, \mathbf{C})\theta\sigma_2 = (\mathbf{A}, \mathbf{B}, \mathbf{C})\theta$. Moreover,

$$\begin{aligned}
(\mathbf{A}, \mathbf{B}, \mathbf{C})\theta &= (\mathbf{A}, \mathbf{B}', \mathbf{C})\gamma\theta && \text{(since } (\mathbf{A}, \mathbf{B}, \mathbf{C})\theta_1 = (\mathbf{A}, \mathbf{B}', \mathbf{C})\gamma\theta_1\text{)} \\
&= \mathbf{A}\theta, \mathbf{B}'\gamma\theta, \mathbf{C}\theta && \text{(since } \gamma_{|Q} = \epsilon\text{)} \\
&= \mathbf{A}\theta, \mathbf{B}'\gamma\theta\sigma_1, \mathbf{C}\theta && \text{(since } \gamma\theta_{|H\leftarrow\mathbf{B}'} = \sigma_1 \text{ and } \sigma_1 \text{ is idempotent)} \\
&= \mathbf{A}\theta, \mathbf{B}\theta\sigma_1, \mathbf{C}\theta && \text{(since } \mathbf{B} = \mathbf{B}'\gamma\text{)} \\
&= (\mathbf{A}, \mathbf{B}, \mathbf{C})\theta\sigma_1 && \text{(since } \sigma_{1|Q\theta} = \epsilon\text{).}
\end{aligned}$$

Then,

$$\delta' := (\mathbf{A}, B, \mathbf{C})\theta \stackrel{\sigma_1}{\Longrightarrow}_{P,I} (\mathbf{A}, \mathbf{B}, \mathbf{C})\theta\sigma_1 \stackrel{\sigma_2}{\longmapsto}_{P,I} \Box$$

is a successful I-derivation. Let $\sigma = \sigma_1\sigma_2$. Then

$$\begin{aligned}
Q\theta\sigma &= (\mathbf{A}, B, \mathbf{C})\theta\sigma_1\sigma_2 && \text{(by definition of } Q \text{ and of } \sigma\text{)} \\
&= \mathbf{A}\theta\sigma_2, B\theta\sigma_2, \mathbf{C}\theta\sigma_2 && \text{(since } \sigma_{1|Q\theta} = \epsilon\text{)} \\
&= \mathbf{A}\theta, B\theta\sigma_2, \mathbf{C}\theta && \text{(by inductive hypothesis)} \\
&= \mathbf{A}\theta, B\theta, \mathbf{C}\theta && \text{(because of standardization apart)} \\
&= Q\theta && \text{(by definition of } Q\text{).}
\end{aligned}$$

5 Equivalence of the Top-down and Fixpoint Semantics

In this section we discuss the equivalence between the specialised top-down semantics $\mathcal{O}_I(P)$ and the fixpoint semantics $\mathcal{F}_I(P)$. The reader is referred to [7] for more details. The proof follows from the fact that for any program P and interpretation I, both $\mathcal{O}_I(P) = \mathcal{O}(P_I)$ and $\mathcal{F}_I(P) = \mathcal{F}(P_I)$ hold.

The equivalence between $\mathcal{O}_I(P)$ and $\mathcal{O}(P_I)$ follows from the following result.

Proposition 7. *[7] Let P be a program and I be an interpretation. Then, there exists a successful SLD-derivation $\delta := Q \overset{\theta}{\longmapsto}_{P_I,\mathcal{BE}} \Box$ of a query Q iff there exists a successful I-derivation $\delta' := Q \overset{\theta'}{\longmapsto}_{P,I} \Box$ where $Q\theta = Q\theta'$.*

Theorem 1. *For any program P and interpretation I, $\mathcal{O}(P_I) = \mathcal{O}_I(P)$.*

Proof. Recall that $\mathcal{O}(P_I) = \mathcal{O}_{\mathcal{BE}}(P_I)$. The result follows from Proposition 7.

The next Proposition relates powers of transformations $T_{P_I,\mathcal{BE}}$ and $T_{P,I}$. It allows us to prove the equivalence between $\mathcal{F}_I(P)$ and $\mathcal{F}(P_I)$.

Proposition 8. *[7] Let P be a program, I be an interpretation and A be an atom. Then for all $n > 0$, $A \in T_{P_I,\mathcal{BE}} \uparrow n$ iff $A \in T_{P,I} \uparrow n$.*

Theorem 2. *For any program P and interpretation I, $\mathcal{F}(P_I) = \mathcal{F}_I(P)$.*

Proof. Recall that $\mathcal{F}(P_I) = \mathcal{F}_{\mathcal{BE}}(P_I)$. The result follows from Proposition 8.

We are now in position to prove the equivalence between the specialised top-down and fixpoint semantics.

Theorem 3. (Equivalence of Specialised Top-Down and Fixpoint Semantics) *For any program P and interpretation I, $\mathcal{O}_I(P) = \mathcal{F}_I(P)$.*

Proof. By [13], $\mathcal{O}(P_I) = \mathcal{F}(P_I)$. The result follows from Theorems 1 and 2.

6 Verifying Specialised Partial Correctness

In this section, we show that the specialised partial correctness of a program with respect to a given call/post specification can be verified just by one application of the specialised immediate consequence operator $T_{P,I}$ to the given post-condition.

Let us first prove the following sufficient condition.

Lemma 5. *Let P be a program and I and J be two interpretations such that $sp(P, I) \sqsubseteq J$. Then, $\{I\}P\{J\}_{spec}$ holds.*

Proof. We prove that for any query Q and successful I-derivation $\delta := Q \overset{\theta}{\longmapsto}_I \Box$, $J \models Q\theta$. Let $Q := A_1, \ldots, A_n$. We show that for all $j \in \{1, \ldots, n\}$, $J \models A_j\theta$. By Lemma 2, for all $j \in \{1, \ldots, n\}$, there exists a successful I-derivation $\delta_j := A_j\theta \overset{\gamma_j}{\longmapsto}_I \Box$ where $A_j\theta\gamma_j = A_j\theta$. Let $p_j \in \mathcal{P}$ and $X_1, \ldots, X_n$ be distinct variables in $\mathcal{V}$ such that $p_j(X_1, \ldots, X_n) \leq A_j\theta$. By Lemma 4, for all j, there exists a successful I-derivation $p_j(X_1, \ldots, X_n) \overset{\theta_j}{\longmapsto}_I \Box$ where $p_j(X_1, \ldots, X_n)\theta_j \leq A_j\theta$. By Definition 7, $p_j(X_1, \ldots, X_n)\theta_j \in \mathcal{O}_I(P)$. Hence, by Proposition 4, $sp(P, I) \models A_j\theta$. The fact that $J \models A_j\theta$ follows from the hypothesis that $sp(P, I) \sqsubseteq J$.

The next Proposition provides a method for verifying specialised partial correctness with respect to a given call/post specification.

Proposition 9. *Let P be a program and I and J be interpretations. Then, $T_{P,I}(J) \sqsubseteq J$ implies $\{I\}P\{J\}_{spec}$.*

Proof. We first establish the following Claims. The proofs are given in [7].

Claim. Let P be a program and I and J be two interpretations.
Then $Min(T_{P,I}(J)) = Min(T_{P,I}(Min(J)))$.

Claim. For any interpretation I, the transformation $Min \circ T_{P,I}$ is monotonic in the complete lattice $\langle \mathcal{I}, \sqsubseteq \rangle$.

By Lemma 5, it is sufficient to prove that $T_{P,I}(J) \sqsubseteq J$ implies $sp(P, I) \sqsubseteq J$.
We first prove that for all $n \geq 0$, $Min(T_{P,I} \uparrow n) \sqsubseteq J$.
By induction on n
Basis. Let $n = 0$. Straightforward, since by Definition 11, $Min(T_{P,I} \uparrow 0) = \emptyset$.
Induction step. Let $n > 0$. In this case,

$$\begin{aligned}
Min(T_{P,I} \uparrow n) &= Min(T_{P,I}(T_{P,I} \uparrow n-1)) && \text{(by Definition 11)} \\
&= Min(T_{P,I}(Min(T_{P,I} \uparrow n-1))) && \text{(by Claim 6)} \\
&\sqsubseteq Min(T_{P,I}(J)) && \text{(by induction hypothesis and Claim 6)} \\
&\sqsubseteq T_{P,I}(J) && \text{(by Definiton 1)} \\
&\sqsubseteq J && \text{(by hypothesis).}
\end{aligned}$$

It follows that $Min(\bigcup_{n\geq 0}(T_{P,I} \uparrow n)) \sqsubseteq J$.
In fact, $Min(\bigcup_{n\geq 0}(T_{P,I} \uparrow n)) \leq J$, i.e., for all $A \in Min(\bigcup_{n\geq 0}(T_{P,I} \uparrow n))$ there exists $A' \in J$ such that $A' \leq A$. This property follows from the fact that for all $A \in Min(\bigcup_{n\geq 0}(T_{P,I} \uparrow n))$ there exists $n > 0$ such that $A \in Min(T_{P,I} \uparrow n)$. As proved above, $Min(T_{P,I} \uparrow n) \sqsubseteq J$. Hence, by Definition 5, $Min(T_{P,I} \uparrow n) \leq J$, i.e., there exists $A' \in J$ such that $A' \leq A$.
Moreover, if $J \leq Min(\bigcup_{n\geq 0}(T_{P,I} \uparrow n))$ then $Min(\bigcup_{n\geq 0}(T_{P,I} \uparrow n)) \subseteq J$. In fact, since both $Min(\bigcup_{n\geq 0}(T_{P,I} \uparrow n)) \leq J$ and $J \leq Min(\bigcup_{n\geq 0}(T_{P,I} \uparrow n))$, for all $A \in Min(\bigcup_{n\geq 0}(T_{P,I} \uparrow n))$ there exists $A' \in J$ and $A'' \in Min(\bigcup_{n\geq 0}(T_{P,I} \uparrow n))$ such that $A'' \leq A' \leq A$. By Definition 1 of operator Min, $A'' = A$ and then $A \in J$. Therefore,

$$\begin{aligned}
sp(P, I) &= Min(\mathcal{O}_I(P)) && \text{(by Proposition 4)} \\
&= Min(\mathcal{F}_I(P)) && \text{(by Theorem 3)} \\
&= Min(T_{P,I} \uparrow \omega) && \text{(by Definition 12)} \\
&= Min(\bigcup_{n\geq 0}(T_{P,I} \uparrow n)) && \text{(by Definition 11)} \\
&\sqsubseteq J && \text{(as proved above).}
\end{aligned}$$

7 An Example

In this section we illustrate by means of an example the specialisation method defined in Section 4.2. Consider the program **FRONT** [3] defined below,

$$\begin{array}{l}
\quad\texttt{front}\ (\texttt{void}, [\,]).\\
\quad\texttt{front}\ (\texttt{tree}\ (X, \texttt{void}, \texttt{void}), [X]).\\
\texttt{front}\ (\texttt{tree}\ (X, L, R), X_s) \leftarrow \texttt{nel_tree}\ (\texttt{tree}\ (X, L, R)),\\
\qquad\qquad\qquad\qquad\qquad\quad \texttt{front}\ (L, L_s),\\
\qquad\qquad\qquad\qquad\qquad\quad \texttt{front}\ (R, R_s),\\
\qquad\qquad\qquad\qquad\qquad\quad \texttt{append}\ (L_s, R_s, X_s).\\
\texttt{nel_tree}\ (\texttt{tree}\ (_, \texttt{tree}\ (_, _, _), _)).\\
\texttt{nel_tree}\ (\texttt{tree}\ (_, _, \texttt{tree}\ (_, _, _))).
\end{array}$$

augmented by the program **APPEND**. It computes the frontier of a binary tree, i.e., it is correct with respect to the post-condition

$$\begin{array}{rl}
\mathit{Post} = & \{\texttt{front}\ (t, l) \mid l \text{ is the frontier of the binary tree } t\} \cup \{\texttt{nel_list}\ (t) \mid t \text{ is}\\
& \text{a term}\} \cup \{\texttt{append}\ (u, v, z) \mid u, v, z \text{ are lists and } z = u * v\}
\end{array}$$

where $*$ is the list concatenation operator.

The auxiliary relation **nel_tree** is used to enforce that a tree is a non-empty, non-leaf tree, i.e., that it is a term of the form **tree (x, left, right)** where either **left** or **right** does not equal **void**.

Observe that the simpler program that is obtained by removing the first atom **nel_tree** (**tree**(X, L, R)) in the body of the third clause and by discarding the relation **nel_tree** is indeed incorrect. In fact, as shown in [3], the query **front**(**tree**$(X$, **void**, **void**$), X_s)$ would yield two different answers: $\{X_s/[X]\}$ by means of the second clause and $\{X_s/[\,]\}$ by means of the third clause.
Suppose that our application domain consists of the set of binary trees whose left subtrees are all leaves. This information can be expressed by means of the following call-condition:

$$\begin{array}{rl}
\mathit{Call} = & \{\texttt{front}\ (t, l) \mid t \text{ is either the empty tree or a leaf or a term of the form}\\
& \texttt{tree}(u, r, s) \text{ where } r \text{ is a leaf and } u, s \text{ and } l \text{ are terms}\} \cup\\
& \{\texttt{nel_list}\ (t) \mid t \text{ is a term}\} \cup \{\texttt{append}\ (u, v, z) \mid u, v, z \text{ are terms}\}
\end{array}$$

Note that, since the program is correct with respect to *Post*, then it is also s.p.c. with respect to the call/post specification *Call* and *Post*, i.e.,

$$\{\mathit{Call}\}\texttt{FRONT}\{\mathit{Post}\}_{spec}.$$

That can be also proven by computing $T_{\texttt{FRONT}, \mathit{Call}}(\mathit{Post})$. We obtain

$$\begin{array}{rl}
T_{\texttt{FRONT}, \mathit{Call}}(\mathit{Post}) = & \{\texttt{front}\ (\texttt{void}, [\,]),\ \texttt{front}\ (\texttt{tree}\ (X, \texttt{void}, \texttt{void}), [X])\} \cup\\
& \{\texttt{front}\ (t, l) \mid t \text{ is a binary tree whose left subtree is a}\\
& \text{leaf and } l \text{ is the frontier of } t\} \cup\\
& \{\texttt{nel_list}\ (t) \mid t \text{ is a non-empty, non-leaf tree }\} \cup\\
& \{\texttt{append}\ (u, v, z) \mid u, v, z \text{ are lists and } z = u * v\}.
\end{array}$$

Then the program can be specialised into a weakly call-correct program $\mathbf{FRONT}_{Call}$. Consider the Definition 16. Observe that for all head H, different from the third clause head, $Min_{Call}(H) = H$, whereas, $Min_{Call}(\mathtt{front}(\mathtt{tree}\ (X, L, R), X_s)) = \{\mathtt{front}(\mathtt{tree}(X, \mathtt{void}, \mathtt{void}), X_s), \mathtt{front}(\mathtt{tree}(X, \mathtt{tree}(L, \mathtt{void}, \mathtt{void}), R), X_s)\}$. The specialisation results in the program $\mathbf{FRONT}_{Call}$ defined by:

```
front (void, [ ]).
front (tree (X, void, void), [X]).
front (tree (X, void, void), Xs) ← nel_tree (tree (X, void, void)),
                                    front (void, Ls),
                                    front (void, Rs),
                                    append (Ls, Rs, Xs).
front (tree (X, tree (L, void, void), R), Xs) ←
            nel_tree (tree (X, tree (L, void, void), R)),
            front (tree (L, void, void), Ls),
            front (R, Rs),
            append (Ls, Rs, Xs).
```

augmented by definitions of the relations **nel_tree** and **append**.
Now by unfolding we obtain

```
front (void, [ ]).
front (tree (X, void, void), [X]).
front (tree (_, tree (L, void, void), R), [L|Rs]) ←  front (R, Rs).
```

where both the relation **nel_tree** and the relation **append** are not used.

Acknowledgements This work was partly supported by the Italian MURST with the National Research Project 9701248444-004 on "Tecniche formali per la specifica, l'analisi, la verifica, la sintesi e la trasformazione di sistemi software".

References

1. K. R. Apt. Introduction to Logic Programming. In J. van Leeuwen, editor, *Handbook of Theoretical Computer Science*, volume B: Formal Models and Semantics. Elsevier, Amsterdam and The MIT Press, Cambridge, 1990.
2. K. R. Apt. Program verification and prolog. In E. Börger, editor, *Specification and Validation Methods for Programming Languages and Systems*, pages 55–95. Oxford University Press, Oxford, 1995.
3. K. R. Apt. *From Logic Programming to Prolog*. Prentice Hall, 1997.
4. A. Bossi and N. Cocco. Verifying Correctness of Logic Programs. In G. Levi and M. Martelli, editors, *Proc. Sixth Int'l Conf. on Logic Programming*, pages 96–110. Springer-Verlag, Berlin, 1989.
5. A. Bossi, N. Cocco, and S. Dulli. A Method for Specializing Logic Programs. *ACM Transactions on Programming Languages and Systems*, 12(2):253–302, 1990.
6. A. Bossi, M. Martelli, M. Gabrielli, and G. Levi. The *s*-semantics approach: theory and applications. *Journal of Logic Programming*, 19-20:149–197, 1994.

7. A. Bossi and S. Rossi. Specialised semantics of logic programs. Technical Report CS-98-11, Dipartimento di Matematica e Informatica, Università di Venezia, 1998.
8. K. L. Clark. Predicate logic as a computational formalism. Research Report DOC 79/59, Imperial College, Department of Computing, London, 1979.
9. L. Colussi and E. Marchiori. Proving correctness of logic programs using axiomatic semantics. In *Proc. Eighth Int'l Conf. on Logic Programming*, pages 629–644. The MIT Press, Cambridge, Mass., 1991.
10. P. Deransart. Proof methods of declarative properties of definite programs. *Theoretical Computer Science*, 118:99–166, 1993.
11. W. Drabent and J. Maluszynski. Inductive Assertion Method for Logic Programs. *Theoretical Computer Science*, 59(1):133–155, 1988.
12. M. Falaschi, G. Levi, M. Martelli, and C. Palamidessi. A new Declarative Semantics for Logic Languages. In R. A. Kowalski and K. A. Bowen, editors, *Proc. Fifth Int'l Conf. on Logic Programming*, pages 993–1005. The MIT Press, Cambridge, Mass., 1988.
13. M. Falaschi, G. Levi, M. Martelli, and C. Palamidessi. Declarative Modeling of the Operational Behavior of Logic Languages. *Theoretical Computer Science*, 69(3):289–318, 1989.
14. M. Falaschi, G. Levi, M. Martelli, and C. Palamidessi. A model-theoretic reconstruction of the operational semantics of logic programs. *Theoretical Computer Science*, 103(1):86–113, 1993.
15. J. W. Lloyd. *Foundations of Logic Programming*. Springer-Verlag, Berlin, 1987. Second edition.
16. J. W. Lloyd and J. C. Shepherdson. Partial Evaluation in Logic Programming. *Journal of Logic Programming*, 11:217–242, 1991.
17. Lee Naish. Types and the intended meaning of logic programs. In Frank Pfenning, editor, *Types in logic programming*, pages 189–216. MIT Press, Cambridge, Massachusetts, 1992.
18. Lee Naish. Verification of logic programs and imperative programs. In Jean-Marie Jacquet, editor, *Constructing logic programs*, pages 143–164. Wiley, Chichester, England, 1993.
19. Lee Naish. A three-valued semantics for horn clause programs. Technical Report 98/4, Department of Computer Science, University of Melbourne, Melbourne, Australia, March 1998.
20. A. Pettorossi and M. Proietti. A theory of logic program specialization and generalization for dealing with input data properties. In *Proceedings of Partial Evaluation, International Seminar*, volume 1110 of *Lecture Notes in Computer Science*. Springer-Verlag, 1996.
21. A. Takeuchi and K. Furukawa. Partial evaluation of Prolog programs and its application to metaprogramming. In *Information Processing 86*, pages 415–420, 1986.
22. M. H. van Emden and R. A. Kowalski. The semantics of predicate logic as a programming language. *Journal of the ACM*, 23(4):733–742, 1976.

Generalization in Hierarchies of Online Program Specialization Systems

Robert Glück[1], John Hatcliff[2], and Jesper Jørgensen[3]

[1] University of Copenhagen, Dept. of Computer Science, Universitetsparken 1, DK-2100 Copenhagen, Denmark. Email: glueck@diku.dk

[2] Kansas State University, Dept. of Computing and Information Sciences, 234 Nichols Hall, Manhattan, KS 66506, USA. hatcliff@cis.ksu.edu

[3] Royal Veterinary and Agricultural University, Dept. of Mathematics and Physics, Thorvaldsensvej 50, DK-1871 Frederiksberg, Denmark. jesper@dina.kvl.dk

Abstract. In recent work, we proposed a simple functional language S-graph-n to study metaprogramming aspects of self-applicable online program specialization. The primitives of the language provide support for multiple encodings of programs. An important component of online program specialization is the termination strategy. In this paper we show that such a representation has the great advantage of simplifying generalization of multiply encoded data. After developing and formalizing the basic metaprogramming concepts, we extend two basic methods to multiply encoded data: most specific generalization and the homeomorphic embedding relation. Examples and experiments with the initial design of an online specializer illustrate their use in hierarchies of online program specializers.

1 Introduction

Multiple levels of metaprograms have become an issue for several reasons, on the one hand they are a natural extension of metaprogramming approaches, on the other hand they have been used to great advantage for program generation. Multi-level metaprogramming languages that support this style of metaprogramming have been advocated, *e.g.* [4, 11, 24]. Representing and reasoning about object level theories is an important field in logic and artificial intelligence and has led to the development of logic languages that facilitate metaprogramming (*e.g.* the logic languages Gödel [15], Reflective Prolog [6], λ-Prolog [20]).

Our goal is to lay the foundations for a *multi-level metaprogramming environment* that fully addresses the unique requirements of multi-level program hierarchies and to develop techniques for efficient computation on all levels of a metasystem hierarchy. The present work addresses these open issues in the context of S-graph-n — a simple functional language which provides primitives for manipulating metacode and metavariables.

Writing meta-interpreters is a well-known technique to enhance the expressive power of logic programs [23, 3]. The approach of applying a program transformer to another program transformer—not just to an ordinary program—has

P. Flener (Ed.): LOPSTR'98, LNCS 1559, pp. 179–198, 1999.

level 0 : p_0 : ______________________
level 1 : p_1 : ____________________
⋮ ⋮
level $n-1$: p_{n-1} : ______________
level n : p_n : _____________

Fig. 1. MST Scheme of a metasystem hierarchy

been put to good use in the area of program specialization [16, 7] (a notable example are the Futamura projections). Common to these approaches is the construction and manipulation of two or more program levels.

A *metasystem hierarchy* is any situation where a program p_0 is manipulating (*e.g.*, interpreting, transforming) another program p_1. Program p_1 may be manipulating another program p_2, and so on. A metasystem hierarchy can be illustrated using a metasystem transition scheme as in Figure 1 [26]. Metaprogramming requires facilities for encoding programs as data objects. In a metasystem hierarchy, such as displayed in Figure 1, programs may be metacoded many times. For example, program p_n of Figure 1 must be metacoded (directly or indirectly) n times, since n systems lie above it in the hierarchy. The representation of programs and data has been studied especially in the context of logic programming [3] (mostly two-level metasystem hierarchies).

Among others, exponential space consumption, time inefficiencies, and lack of representation invariance of meta-level operations are problems to be tackled. We now shortly illustrate some of these problems.

Example 1. To illustrate the **space consumption problem** in metasystem hierarchies, consider a straightforward strategy for encoding S-expressions (as known from Lisp) where μ is the metacoding function.

$$\mu\{(\texttt{CONS}\ exp_1\ exp_2)\} = (\texttt{CONS}\ (\texttt{ATOM}\ \texttt{CONS})\ (\texttt{CONS}\ \mu\{exp_1\}\ \mu\{exp_2\}))$$
$$\mu\{(\texttt{ATOM}\ atom)\} = (\texttt{CONS}\ (\texttt{ATOM}\ \texttt{ATOM})\ (\texttt{ATOM}\ atom))$$

Using this strategy, the expression `(CONS (ATOM a) (ATOM b))` metacoded twice is

```
μ{μ{(CONS (ATOM a) (ATOM b))}} = (CONS (ATOM CONS) (CONS (CONS (ATOM ATOM) (ATOM CONS)) (CONS
                                 (ATOM CONS) (CONS (CONS (ATOM CONS) (CONS (CONS (ATOM ATOM)
                                 (ATOM ATOM)) (CONS (ATOM ATOM) (ATOM a)))) (CONS (ATOM CONS)
                                 (CONS (CONS (ATOM ATOM) (ATOM ATOM)) (CONS (ATOM ATOM) (ATOM
                                 b))))))))
```

The naive encoding is straightforward, but leads to an exponential growth of expressions, and yields terms that are harder to reason about. In addition, various specialization procedures (*e.g.*, generalization algorithms) that repeatedly traverse metacode will suffer from a significant computational degrading effect as can be seen from this example.

The area of online program transformation (e.g., partial deduction, supercompilation) has seen a recent flurry of activity, e.g. [2, 5, 19, 21, 22, 26, 27]. Recently well-quasi orders in general, and homeomorphic embedding in particular, have gained popularity to ensure termination of program analysis, specialization and other program transformation techniques because well-quasi orders are strictly more powerful [18] than a large class of approaches based on well-founded orders. Despite the progress that has occurred during the last years, metasystem hierarchies still pose an challenge to online transformation and metaprogramming.

Example 2. To illustrate the **invariance problem**, consider the influence encoding has on the termination behavior of online transformer relying on the homeomorphic embedding relation $\trianglelefteq$ defined for S-expressions:

$$
\begin{array}{lll}
(\mathtt{ATOM}\, a) \trianglelefteq (\mathtt{ATOM}\, b) & \Leftarrow a = b \\
(\mathtt{CONS}\, s_1\, s_2) \trianglelefteq (\mathtt{CONS}\, t_1\, t_2) & \Leftarrow s_i \trianglelefteq t_i \text{ for all } i \in \{1,2\} \\
s \trianglelefteq (\mathtt{CONS}\, t_1\, t_2) & \Leftarrow s \trianglelefteq t_i \text{ for some } i \in \{1,2\}
\end{array}
$$

Consider the following two terms which may occur during direct transformation of a program (e.g., as arguments of a function or predicate). The embedding relation signals the transformer that it can continue:

$$(\mathtt{ATOM\ ATOM}) \not\trianglelefteq (\mathtt{CONS}\,(\mathtt{ATOM\ a})\,(\mathtt{ATOM\ a}))$$

Assume that we insert an interpreter (or another metaprogram) that works on encoded terms. Now the embedding relation signals the transformer that it should stop immediately:

$$\mu\{(\mathtt{ATOM\ ATOM})\} \trianglelefteq \mu\{(\mathtt{CONS}\,(\mathtt{ATOM\ a})\,(\mathtt{ATOM\ a}))\}$$

In short, encoding the terms leads to premature termination. Ideally, a termination condition is invariant under encoding, so that termination patterns are detected reliably regardless of the encoding of terms. Similar problems occur with other operations popular with online transformers. Existing transformers are only geared toward the direct transformation of programs. They often fail to perform well on an extra metasystem level, so that several refinements have been suggested, e.g. [29]. For a discussion of the invariance problem see also [17].

Higher-order terms provide a suitable data structure for representing programs in a higher-order abstract syntax. Higher-order logic programming utilizes higher-order logic as the basis for computation, e.g. [20]. The primary advantage of higher-order abstract syntax is that it simplifies substitution and reasoning about terms up to alpha-conversion. However, we believe that there are a number of theoretical difficulties that one would encounter when using high-order logic as the basis for multi-level metaprogramming. For instance, the question of whether or not a unifier exists for an arbitrary disagreement set is known to be undecidable. Moreover, extending online program transformers, e.g. partial deducers, to higher-order logic programming languages even for single-level transformation seems very challenging and has not yet been attempted. Finally, it is unclear how much higher-order abstract syntax would help the exponential explosion due to multiple encodings in self-application situations since its strength is the encoding of variable bindings – not the encoding of arbitrary syntax constructors.

Programs:

$prog ::= def^*$
$def ::=$ (DEFINE ($fname\ name_1 \ldots name_n$) $tree$)

Trees:

$tree ::=$ (IF $cntr\ tree\ tree$) | (CALL ($fname\ arg^*$)) | (LET $name\ exp\ tree$) | exp
$cntr ::=$ (EQA? $arg\ arg$) | (CONS? $arg\ name\ name$) | ($\mathtt{MV?}^n$ $arg^n\ name\ name$)
$exp ::=$ ($\mathtt{CONS}^n$ $exp\ exp$) | arg
$arg ::=$ ($\mathtt{ATOM}^n$ $atom$) | (PV $name$) | ($\mathtt{MV}^n$ $h\ name$)   for any $n, h \geq 0$

Fig. 2. Syntax of S-Graph-n (excerpts)

```
(define (rev x a)
  (if (cons? x hd tl)
      (call (rev tl (cons hd a)))
      a))
```

Fig. 3. Tail-recursive list reverse

In recent work [13], we proposed a simple language S-graph-n to study metaprogramming aspects of self-applicable online program specialization from a new angle. The primitives of the language provide support for multiple encodings of programs and the use of metavariables to track unknown values. They were motivated by the need for space and time efficient representation and manipulation of programs and data in *multi-level metaprogramming*. Previous work on generalization focuses only on single-level and has not addressed the unique features of metasystem hierarchies. In particular, we are not aware of another line of work that has approached foundational and practical issues involved in hierarchies of online specialization systems based on a multi-level metaprogramming environment.

Organization After presenting the subset of S-Graph-n needed for our investigation in Section 2, we develop and formalize the basic metaprogramming concepts in Section 3. Generalization of configuration values is addressed in Section 4 and a well-quasi order for ensuring termination is given in Section 5. In Section 6 we report on the initial design and first experiments with an online specializer for S-Graph-n to substantiate the claims. The papers concludes with a discussion of related work in Section 7 and future work in Section 8.

2 S-Graph-n

The choice of the subject language is important for studying foundational problems associated with hierarchies of online transformation systems. On the one hand the language must be simple enough, so that it can become the object of theoretical analysis is and program transformation, and, on the other hand, it must be rich enough to serve as a language for writing meta-programs which can substantiate theoretical claims by computer experiments.

In this section we present the language S-Graph-n and its meta-programming concepts. The full language is given in [13]; here we only need to consider a language fragment. The language seems well-suited for our purposes. Among others, a subset of the language was successfully used for clarifying basic concepts of supercompilation, e.g. [1, 12].

2.1 Syntax

Figure 2 presents excerpts of S-Graph-n — a first-order, functional programming language restricted to tail-recursion. A program is a list of function definitions where each function body is built from a few elements: conditionals **IF**, local bindings **LET**, function calls **CALL**, program variables (**PV** *name*), and data constructed from the indexed components $\texttt{CONS}^n$, $\texttt{ATOM}^n$, and $\texttt{MV}^n$. The components $\texttt{CONS}^n$ and $\texttt{ATOM}^n$ are the usual constructors for S-expressions, $\texttt{MV}^n$ is a constructor for metavariables (their use will be explained later). The full language [13] includes indexed components for each construct of the language (*e.g.*, $\texttt{IF}^n$, $\texttt{LET}^n$, *etc.*).

2.2 Semantics

The operational semantics of the language is given elsewhere [13]. Here we describe it only informally. Evaluation of a S-Graph-n program yields a *value* — a closed (*i.e.*, ground) term in the set described by the grammar shown in Figure 4. Values are either metavariables, atoms, or **CONS**-cells indexed by n. As syntactic sugar, metavariables ($\texttt{MV}^n$ h *name*) are written as $name^n_h$. Intuitively, constructs indexed by $n \geq 1$ represent encoded values from higher levels.

$$val \in Values$$

$$val ::= X^n_h \mid (\texttt{ATOM}^n\ atom) \mid (\texttt{CONS}^n\ val\ val) \qquad \textit{for any } n, h \geq 0$$

Fig. 4. S-Graph-n values (excerpts)

The test *cntr* in a conditional may update the environment. We excerpt three illustrative contractions [25] from the full language. They test and deconstruct values.

- (**EQA**? arg_1 arg_2) — tests the equality of two atoms arg_1, arg_2 of degree 0. If either argument is non-atomic or has a degree other than 0, then the test is undefined.
- (**CONS**? *arg h t*) — if the value of *arg* is a pair ($\texttt{CONS}^0$ val_1 val_2), then the test succeeds and variable h is bound to val_1 and variable t to val_2; otherwise it fails.

- (MV? *exp h x*) — if the value of *exp* is a metavariable ($\mathtt{MV}^0$ val_1 val_2), then the test succeeds and variable h is bound to elevation val_1 and variable x to name val_2; otherwise it fails.

When programming in S-Graph-n, one usually takes 0 as the reference level. In the programming examples, components where indices are omitted are at level 0. Figure 3 shows a tail-recursive version of list reverse at level 0. As shorthand, program variables ($\mathtt{PV}^0$ *name*) are written as *name*.

3 Meta-Programming Concepts

In this section we show how the primitives of the language provide support for multiple encodings of programs and then develop the basic meta-programming concepts [28] for S-Graph-n. We formalize the concepts and illustrate them with several examples.

3.1 Metacoding

The *indexed constructs* of S-Graph-n provide a concise and natural representation of programs as data. A program component is encoded by simply increasing its numerical index. This is formalized by the metacoding function μ given below (we show only the cases for data constructors). The injectivity of μ ensures that metacoded programs can be uniquely *demetacoded.*

$$\begin{aligned} \mu\{X_h^n\} &= X_h^{n+1} \\ \mu\{(\mathtt{ATOM}^n\ atom)\} &= (\mathtt{ATOM}^{n+1}\ atom) \\ \mu\{(\mathtt{CONS}^n\ sgn_1\ sgn_2)\} &= (\mathtt{CONS}^{n+1}\ \mu\{sgn_1\}\ \mu\{sgn_2\}) \end{aligned}$$

Fig. 5. S-Graph-n metacoding

Repeated metacoding given by iterated application of μ (denoted μ^i for some $i \geq 0$) avoids the exponential space explosion characteristic of naive metacoding strategies (cf. Example 1). Thereby, the degrading effect such encoding strategies have on operations traversing metacode is avoided (e.g., generalization, homeomorphic embedding).

Example 3. The following example illustrate the representation of encoded data in S-Graph-n.

$$\begin{aligned} \mu^1\{(\mathtt{CONS}\ (\mathtt{ATOM}\ \mathtt{a})\ (\mathtt{ATOM}\ \mathtt{b}))\} &= (\mathtt{CONS}^1\ (\mathtt{ATOM}^1\ \mathtt{a})\ (\mathtt{ATOM}^1\ \mathtt{b})) \\ \mu^2\{(\mathtt{CONS}\ (\mathtt{ATOM}\ \mathtt{a})\ (\mathtt{ATOM}\ \mathtt{b}))\} &= (\mathtt{CONS}^2\ (\mathtt{ATOM}^2\ \mathtt{a})\ (\mathtt{ATOM}^2\ \mathtt{b})) \\ \mu^3\{(\mathtt{CONS}\ (\mathtt{ATOM}\ \mathtt{a})\ (\mathtt{ATOM}\ \mathtt{b}))\} &= (\mathtt{CONS}^3\ (\mathtt{ATOM}^3\ \mathtt{a})\ (\mathtt{ATOM}^3\ \mathtt{b})) \\ \ldots &= \ldots \end{aligned}$$

One often needs to embed data with a lower indices as components of constructs with higher indices. The *degree* of an S-Graph-n term is the smallest index occurring in a term. As motivated in Section 1, the degree indicates to which level of a hierarchy a component belongs. Intuitively, if a component has degree n, then it has been metacoded n times (though some parts of the component may have been metacoded more times).

Example 4. Consider the following S-Graph-n values.

$$(\texttt{CONS}^2\ (\texttt{ATOM}^1\ \texttt{a})\ (\texttt{ATOM}^3\ \texttt{b})) \tag{1}$$
$$(\texttt{CONS}^2\ (\texttt{ATOM}^2\ \texttt{a})\ (\texttt{ATOM}^3\ \texttt{b})) \tag{2}$$
$$(\texttt{CONS}^3\ (\texttt{ATOM}^2\ \texttt{a})\ (\texttt{ATOM}^1\ \texttt{b})) \tag{3}$$

The components (1) and (3) have degree 1 and (2) has degree 2. They have been encoded at most once and twice, respectively.

3.2 Hierarchy of Metacoded Values

Repeated metacoding of values induces an important property: it creates a hierarchy of sets of metacoded values.

$$\mu^0\{\mathit{Values}\} \supset \mu^1\{\mathit{Values}\} \supset \mu^2\{\mathit{Values}\} \ldots$$

where for any S, $\mu\{S\}$ denotes the set obtained by element-wise application of μ. Each set of metacoded values is described by the grammar in Figure 6 (*i.e.*, $\mu^n\{\mathit{Values}\} = \mathit{Values}[n]$).

$$\mathit{val}^n \in \mathit{Values}[n]$$
$$\mathit{val}^n ::= X_h^{n+r} \mid (\texttt{ATOM}^{n+r}\ \mathit{atom}) \mid (\texttt{CONS}^{n+r}\ \mathit{val}^n\ \mathit{val}^n) \qquad \text{for any } r, h \geq 0$$

Fig. 6. Sets of metacoded values

The following property formalizes the characteristic of μ.

Property 1 (Hierarchical embedding).
$\forall n \geq 0 .\ \ \mathit{Values}[n] \supset \mathit{Values}[n+1]$

In situations where one has a hierarchy of metasystems as in Figure 1, *Values*[n] describes the set of values being manipulated by the program p_n. This observation plays an important role when we abstract from metacoded values in a hierarchy of metasystems.

Example 5. The values encoded in Example 3 belong to the following value sets.

$$\mu^1\{(\texttt{CONS}\ (\texttt{ATOM a})\ (\texttt{ATOM b}))\} \in \mathit{Values}[1]$$
$$\mu^2\{(\texttt{CONS}\ (\texttt{ATOM a})\ (\texttt{ATOM b}))\} \in \mathit{Values}[2]$$
$$\mu^3\{(\texttt{CONS}\ (\texttt{ATOM a})\ (\texttt{ATOM b}))\} \in \mathit{Values}[3]$$
$$\ldots$$

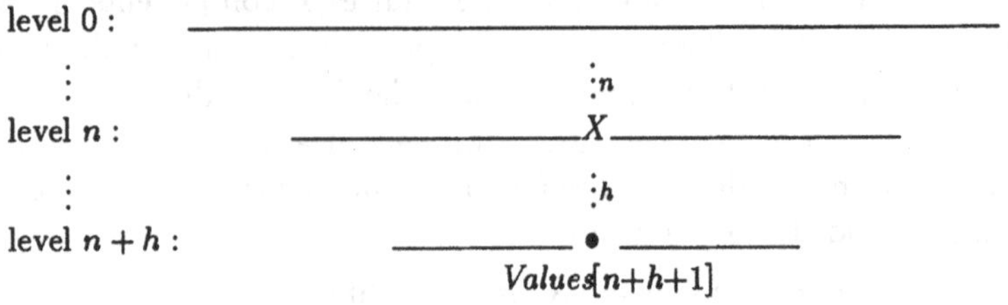

Fig. 7. Positioning of metavariable X_h^n in an MST Scheme

3.3 Metavariables and their Domain

The description of *sets of values* can be further refined by the use of *metavariables*. A metavariable is an abstraction that represents a set of values. A metavariable X_h^n has three attributes which determine its semantics: *degree*, *domain*, *elevation*.

$$\begin{aligned} degree(X_h^n) &= n \\ domain(X_h^n) &= Values[n+h+1] \\ elevation(X_h^n) &= h \end{aligned}$$

Degree n, as we have seen before, indicates the number of times that a metavariable has been metacoded. *Domain* is the set of values over which a metavariable ranges. *Elevation* h restricts the domain of the metavariable to a particular set of metacoded values. For instance, metavariable X_1^3 ranges over $Values[3+1+1]$ (the set of values metacoded five or more times). Although both, degree and elevation, are numerical attributes, degree is an absolute characteristics whereas elevation is a relative characteristic (it adjusts to the domain relative to degree). Thus, elevation is unchanged by metacoding and demetacoding (cf. Figure 5).

The positioning of a metavariable X_h^n can be illustrated using a metasystem transition scheme as in Figure 7.

3.4 Configuration Values

The set of S-Graph-n values is refined to form *configuration values* where, except for metavariables, all values are encoded at least once ($m \geq 1$). This reflects the situation that a metaprogram p_n manipulates pieces of metacode (*e.g.*, program fragments) that are encoded at least $n+1$ times (*i.e.*, the object level is at least one level lower). Intuitively, one can think of configuration values $cval^n$ as a description language for characterizing metacoded data patterns occurring in a metasystem hierarchy at level n.[1] The importance of correctly abstracting from metacoded values, e.g. when generalizing across several levels of metacode, has

[1] Logic variables in queries play a similar role as metavariables in configuration values in that both are placeholders that specify unknown entities (note that the latter

$$cval^{n} \in Cvalues[n]$$
$$cval^{n} ::= X_h^{n+r} \mid (\mathtt{ATOM}^{n+m}\ atom) \mid (\mathtt{CONS}^{n+m}\ cval^{n}\ cval^{n}) \qquad \textit{for any } r, h \geq 0,\ m \geq 1$$

Fig. 8. Configuration values

been explained elsewhere [28, 10]. Here we give a formal semantics that justifies the generalization and embedding operations defined in the following sections.

Formally, each configuration value $cval^{n} \in Cvalues[n]$ denotes a set $[\![cval^{n}]\!]^{n} \subseteq Values[n+1]$. Note that only X_h^{n} are considered as metavariables on level n; metavariables with degree $n+m$, where $m \geq 1$, are treated as encoded constructors.

$$\begin{aligned}
[\![\cdot]\!]^{n} &: Cvalues[n] \to \wp(Values[n+1]) \\
[\![X_h^{n}]\!]^{n} &= domain(X_h^{n}) \\
[\![X_h^{n+m}]\!]^{n} &= \{X_h^{n+m}\} \\
[\![(\mathtt{ATOM}^{n+m}\ atom)]\!]^{n} &= \{(\mathtt{ATOM}^{n+m}\ atom)\} \\
[\![(\mathtt{CONS}^{n+m}\ val_1\ val_2)]\!]^{n} &= \{(\mathtt{CONS}^{n+m}\ cval_1\ cval_2) \mid val_1 \in [\![cval_1]\!], val_2 \in [\![cval_2]\!]\}
\end{aligned}$$

Fig. 9. The value sets denoted by configuration values ($m \geq 1$)

Example 6. Consider the configuration value $(\mathtt{CONS}^1\ (\mathtt{ATOM}^1\ \mathtt{a})\ Y_0^0)$ which, at reference level 0, represents a set $[\![(\mathtt{CONS}^1\ (\mathtt{ATOM}^1\ \mathtt{a})\ Y_0^0)]\!]^0 \in Values[1]$ of metacoded values:

$$\begin{aligned}
[\![(\mathtt{CONS}^1\ (\mathtt{ATOM}^1\ \mathtt{a})\ Y_0^0)]\!]^0 = \{&(\mathtt{CONS}^1\ (\mathtt{ATOM}^1\ \mathtt{a})\ (\mathtt{ATOM}^1\ \mathtt{a})), (\mathtt{CONS}^1\ (\mathtt{ATOM}^1\ \mathtt{a})\ (\mathtt{ATOM}^1\ \mathtt{b})), \ldots, \\
&(\mathtt{CONS}^1\ (\mathtt{ATOM}^1\ \mathtt{a})\ (\mathtt{ATOM}^2\ \mathtt{a})), (\mathtt{CONS}^1\ (\mathtt{ATOM}^1\ \mathtt{a})\ (\mathtt{ATOM}^2\ \mathtt{b})), \ldots, \\
&(\mathtt{CONS}^1\ (\mathtt{ATOM}^1\ \mathtt{a})\ (\mathtt{ATOM}^3\ \mathtt{a})), (\mathtt{CONS}^1\ (\mathtt{ATOM}^1\ \mathtt{a})\ (\mathtt{ATOM}^3\ \mathtt{b})), \ldots\}
\end{aligned}$$

Consider the configuration value again, but metacode it once. Now $(\mathtt{CONS}^2\ (\mathtt{ATOM}^2\ \mathtt{a})\ Y_0^1)$ represents a singleton set at reference level 0. This is justified because the metacoded value contains no longer metavariables that belong to reference level 0. The metavariable originally contained in the configuration value has been 'pushed down' one level due to metacoding.

$$[\![(\mathtt{CONS}^2\ (\mathtt{ATOM}^2\ \mathtt{a})\ Y_0^1)]\!]^0 = \{(\mathtt{CONS}^2\ (\mathtt{ATOM}^2\ \mathtt{a})\ Y_0^1)\}$$

are designed for multi-level metasystem hierarchies and that different metaprograms may perform different operations on configuration values, e.g. program specialization, inverse computation).

4 Generalization of Configuration Values

The explicit identification of the hierarchical position of values given by configuration values is a *key* component of the strategy for successful self-application of online specializers given in *e.g.*, [28, 13]. This work describes how configuration values and metavariables are used to propagate information during specialization.

An equally important component is the *termination strategy*: avoiding an infinite sequence of specialization states by folding back to some previously encountered specialization state. This may require identifying the information common to two specialization states. Since two specialization states must now be described by one, precision may be lost. Thus, one desires the generalization to be as specific as possible.

In our setting, specialization states are described by configuration values that represent sets of values. Information belonging to $cval_1^n$ or $cval_2^n$ is given by $[\![cval_1^n]\!]^n \cup [\![cval_2^n]\!]^n$. Using configuration values as a description language, the goal of generalization is to find a description $cval_g^n$ such that $[\![cval_1^n]\!]^n \cup [\![cval_2^n]\!]^n \subseteq [\![cval_g^n]\!]^n$. Moreover, the $[\![cval_g^n]\!]^n$ should be as small (precise) as possible. In other words, $cval_g^n$ should be general enough to describe (contain) the sets $[\![cval_1^n]\!]^n$ and $[\![cval_2^n]\!]^n$, but it should be as specific as possible (to minimize the loss of information).

These concepts can be formalized by extending familiar concepts of *most-specific generalization*, as applied previously to program specialization in *e.g.*, [22], to level-index constructors and elevated metavariables.

4.1 Elevation and Generalization

Not only the positioning of metavariables by their degree is important in a hierarchy of metasystems (cf. Example 6), but also the domain specified by the elevation index is crucial. Elevation can be seen as (dynamic) typing of variables positioned in a metasystem hierarchy. One might imagine enforcing well-formedness with a type-system. We have not pursued this option, since typed languages are notoriously hard to work with in self-applicable program specialization.

Example 7. Suppose we want to generalize component $(\texttt{ATOM}^2\ \texttt{a}) \in \mathit{Values}[2]$ in

$$(\texttt{CONS}^2\ (\texttt{ATOM}^2\ \texttt{a})\ Y_0^1) \in \mathit{Values}[2]$$

such that at reference level 0 the resulting configuration value $cval^0$ describes a set $[\![cval^0]\!]^0 \subseteq \mathit{Values}[2]$. Introducing a metavariable X_0^0 leads to configuration value

$$[\![(\texttt{CONS}^2\ X_0^0\ Y_0^1)]\!]^0 \not\subseteq \mathit{Values}[2]$$

In other words, the configuration value does not satisfy our condition because it admits values such as

$$(\texttt{CONS}^2\ (\texttt{ATOM}^1\ \texttt{a})\ Y_0^1) \notin \mathit{Values}[2]$$

Without the use of elevation, a subset of *Values*[2] cannot be described by $cval^0$. Adjusting the domain of the metavariable relative to the degree, X_1^0, gives the desired generalization.

$$[\![(\texttt{CONS}^2\ X_1^0\ Y_0^1)]\!]^0 \subseteq Values[2]$$

4.2 Most Specific Domain Index

The most specific domain index will help us to determine the domain of metavariables upon generalization. Clearly, for every $cval^n$ there exists an i such that $[\![cval^n]\!]^n \subseteq domain(X_i^n)$ (one can always take $i = 0$). However, since domains $Values[\cdot]$ form a hierarchy, there exists a maximal k such that $[\![cval^n]\!]^n \subseteq domain(X_k^n)$ and $[\![cval^n]\!]^n \not\subseteq domain(X_{k+1}^n)$. Intuitively, $domain(X_k^n)$ describes the most specific value domain containing $[\![cval^n]\!]^n$. Therefore, we refer to k as the *most specific domain index of* $cval^n$ *at level* n (denoted $msdi^n(cval^n)$).

$$\begin{aligned}
msdi^n(\cdot)\ &:\ Cvalues[n] \to Number\\
msdi^n(X_h^n) &= h\\
msdi^n(X_h^{n+m}) &= m-1\\
msdi^n((\texttt{ATOM}^{n+m}\ atom)) &= m-1\\
msdi^n((\texttt{CONS}^{n+m}\ cval_1\ cval_2)) &= \min(m-1, msdi^n(cval_1), msdi^n(cval_2))
\end{aligned}$$

Fig. 10. Most specific domain index ($m \geq 1$)

Example 8. Consider the following examples of most specific domain indices.

$$msdi^0((\texttt{CONS}^2\ (\texttt{ATOM}^3\ \texttt{a})\ X_1^0)) = 1 \quad (4)$$
$$msdi^0((\texttt{CONS}^5\ (\texttt{ATOM}^3\ \texttt{a})\ X_1^3)) = 2 \quad (5)$$
$$msdi^3((\texttt{CONS}^5\ (\texttt{ATOM}^6\ \texttt{a})\ (\texttt{ATOM}^4\ \texttt{b}))) = 0 \quad (6)$$

4.3 Most Specific Generalization

We are now in the position to define most specific generalization. First we introduce elevation-compatible substitution and related operations.

A *binding* $X_h^n := cval$ is a metavariable/configuration value pair. A binding is *elevation-compatible* when $h \leq msdi^n(cval)$. Note that this ensures $[\![cval]\!]^n \subseteq domain(X_h^n)$. A *substitution at level* n, $\theta^n = \{X_{1\,h_1}^{\,n} := cval_1^n, \ldots, X_{t\,h_t}^{\,n} := cval_t^n\}$, is a finite set of bindings such that the metavariables $X_{i\,h_i}^{\,n}$ are pairwise distinct. A substitution is *elevation-compatible* when all of its bindings are elevation-compatible. An *instance* of $cval^n$ is a value of the form $cval^n\theta^n$ where θ^n is a substitution at level n.

$$\begin{pmatrix} \tau \\ \{X_h^n := X_i^{n+m}\} \cup \theta \\ \{X_h^n := X_i^{n+m}\} \cup \theta' \end{pmatrix} \rightarrow \begin{pmatrix} \tau\{X_h^n := X_i^{n+m}\} \\ \theta \\ \theta' \end{pmatrix}$$

$$\begin{pmatrix} \tau \\ \{X_h^n := (\texttt{ATOM}^{n+m}\ atom)\} \cup \theta \\ \{X_h^n := (\texttt{ATOM}^{n+m}\ atom)\} \cup \theta' \end{pmatrix} \rightarrow \begin{pmatrix} \tau\{X_h^n := (\texttt{ATOM}^{n+m}\ atom)\} \\ \theta \\ \theta' \end{pmatrix}$$

$$\begin{pmatrix} \tau \\ \{X_h^n := (\texttt{CONS}^{n+m}\ v\ w)\} \cup \theta \\ \{X_h^n := (\texttt{CONS}^{n+m}\ v'\ w')\} \cup \theta' \end{pmatrix} \rightarrow \begin{pmatrix} \tau\{X_h^n := (\texttt{CONS}^{n+m}\ Y_i^n\ Z_j^n)\} \\ \{Y_i^n := v, Z_j^n := w\} \cup \theta \\ \{Y_i^n := v', Z_j^n := w'\} \cup \theta' \end{pmatrix}$$

$$\textit{where } Y, Z \textit{ are fresh and } i = \min(msdi^n(v), msdi^n(v')) \quad j = \min(msdi^n(w), msdi^n(w'))$$

$$\begin{pmatrix} \tau \\ \{X_h^n := v, Y_h^n := v\} \cup \theta \\ \{X_h^n := v', Y_h^n := v'\} \cup \theta' \end{pmatrix} \rightarrow \begin{pmatrix} \tau\{X_h^n := Y_h^n\} \\ \{Y_h^n := v\} \cup \theta \\ \{Y_h^n := v'\} \cup \theta' \end{pmatrix}$$

Fig. 11. Computation of most specific generalization on level n ($m \geq 1$)

Definition 1 (renaming, generalization, msg).

1. *A* renaming substitution *for* $cval^n$ *is a substitution* $\{X_{1h_1}^n := Y_{1h_1}^n, \ldots, X_{th_t}^n := Y_{th_t}^n\}$ *such that there is a binding for every metavariable occurring in* $cval^n$ *and* $Y_{ih_i}^n$ *are pairwise distinct.*
2. *A* generalization *of* $cval_1^n, cval_2^n$ *at level n is a triple* $(cval_{gen}^n, \theta_1^n, \theta_2^n)$ *where* θ_1^n *and* θ_2^n *are elevation-compatible substitutions,* $cval_1^n \equiv cval_{gen}^n\theta_1^n$ *and* $cval_2^n \equiv cval_{gen}^n\theta_2^n$.
3. *A generalization* $(cval_{gen}^n, \theta_1^n, \theta_2^n)$ *of* $cval_1^n$ *and* $cval_2^n$ *at level n is* most specific *(msg) if for every generalization* $(cval'^n_{gen}, \theta'^n_1, \theta'^n_2)$ *of* $cval_1^n$ *and* $cval_2^n$, $cval_{gen}^n$ *is an instance of* $cval'^n_{gen}$.

Definition 2 (Algorithm of msg). *For any* $cval_1^n, cval_2^n \in Cvalues[n]$, *the most specific generalization* $msg^n(cval_1^n, cval_2^n)$ *is computed by exhaustively applying the rewrite rules of Figure 11 to the initial triple*

$$(X_h^n, \{X_h^n := cval_1^n\}, \{X_h^n := cval_2^n\}) \qquad h = \min(msdi^n(cval_1^n), msdi^n(cval_2^n))$$

where X_h^n *is a variable not occurring in* $cval_1^n$ *and* $cval_2^n$.

Theorem 1 (most specific generalization). *For any* $cval_1^n, cval_2^n \in Cvalues[n]$, *the procedure (Def. 2) is indeed an algorithm, i.e. it terminates and the result* $msg^n(cval_1^n, cval_2^n)$ *is the most specific generalization at level n.*

Proof. 1. *Termination of the algorithm.* In every rewrite rule the size of the substitutions Θ, Θ' or the size of the values in their bindings decreases. Since values are well-founded, the rewrite rules can only be applied finitely many times.

2. *Soundness of algorithm.* We prove by induction over the length of the reduction that the algorithm always computes a generalization.
   The initial triple is clearly a generalization. We will show one case; the rest is similar. Consider the third reduction rule. We will prove that the right hand side is a generalization of $cval_1^n$ and $cval_2^n$. Let θ'' be $\{ Y_i^n := v, Z_j^n := w\} \cup \theta$. We have:
$$\begin{aligned}
&\tau\{X_h^n := (\texttt{CONS}^{n+m}\ Y_i^n\ Z_j^n)\}\theta'' &&= \\
&\tau\{X_h^n := (\texttt{CONS}^{n+m}\ Y_i^n\ Z_j^n)\theta''\}\theta'' &&= \\
&\tau\{X_h^n := (\texttt{CONS}^{n+m}\ v\ w)\}\theta'' &&= \\
&\tau\{X_h^n := (\texttt{CONS}^{n+m}\ v\ w)\}\theta &&=_{\text{induction}} \\
&cval_1^n
\end{aligned}$$
   The second last equality holds because Y, Z are fresh variables. Analogously we can prove that:
$$\tau\{X_h^n := (\texttt{CONS}^{n+m}\ Y_i^n\ Z_j^n)\}\{ Y_i^n := v', Z_j^n := w'\} \cup \theta' = cval_2^n$$
   The condition on the rule ensures that the new substitutions are elevation-compatible, thus we have proved the case.
3. *Computation of msg.* We prove by contradiction that the generalization computed by the algorithm is an msg. Assume that the generalization $(cval_{gen}^n, \theta_1, \theta_2)$ computed by the algorithm is not an msg, then there exists an msg $(cval_{msg}^n, \theta_1', \theta_2')$ such that $cval_{msg}^n = cval_{gen}^n \theta^n$ where θ^n is not a renaming substitution. Therefore it must hold that $\theta^n \theta_1' = \theta_1$ and $\theta^n \theta_2' = \theta_2$. Since θ^n is not a renaming substitution it must have one of the two forms:
$$\begin{aligned}
&\{X_h^n := (\texttt{ATOM}^{n+m}\ atom)\} \cup \theta'^n \\
&\{X_h^n := (\texttt{CONS}^{n+m}\ v\ w)\} \cup \theta'^n
\end{aligned}$$
   for some substitution θ'^n. But if θ^n has one of these forms also θ_1 and θ_2 will have that form and either the second or the third rule of Figure 11 would apply and $(cval_{gen}^n, \theta_1, \theta_2)$ would not be in normal form. So we have arrived at a contradiction and the generalization computed by the algorithm must therefore be most specific.

Property 2 (metacode invariance of msg). For any $cval_1^n, cval_2^n \in Cvalues[n]$, the most specific generalization at level n is *invariant wrt. repeated metacoding* $\mu^m, m \geq 0$. Let
$$(cval^n, \theta_1^n, \theta_2^n) = msg^n(cval_1^n, cval_2^n)$$
for some $cval^n$, θ_1^n and θ_2^n then there exists $cval^{n+m}$, θ_3^n and θ_4^n such that
$$(cval^{n+m}, \theta_3^n, \theta_4^n) = msg^{n+m}(\mu^m\{cval_1^n\}, \mu^m\{cval_2^n\})$$
and $\mu^m\{cval^n\} = cval^{n+m}$ (modulo renaming of variables).

Example 9. Following are three examples of most specific generalization at level 2 and level 3. The first and the last illustrate the invariance property of msg:
$$\begin{aligned}
msg^2((\texttt{CONS}^3\ X_2^2\ (\texttt{ATOM}^4\ \texttt{a})), (\texttt{CONS}^3\ Y_1^2\ (\texttt{ATOM}^3\ \texttt{a}))) = ((&\texttt{CONS}^3\ Z_1^2\ R_0^2), \\
&\{Z_1^2 := X_2^2, R_0^2 := (\texttt{ATOM}^4\ \texttt{a})\}, \\
&\{Z_1^2 := Y_1^2, R_0^2 := (\texttt{ATOM}^3\ \texttt{a})\})
\end{aligned}$$

$$msg^2((\texttt{CONS}^3\ Y_2^2\ Y_2^2),(\texttt{CONS}^3\ Z_2^3\ Z_2^3)) = ((\texttt{CONS}^3\ X_0^2\ X_0^2),\{X_0^2 := Y_2^2\},\{X_0^2 := Z_2^3\})$$

$$\begin{aligned} msg^3((\texttt{CONS}^4\ X_2^3\ (\texttt{ATOM}^5\ \texttt{a})),(\texttt{CONS}^4\ Y_1^3\ (\texttt{ATOM}^4\ \texttt{a}))) = ((\texttt{CONS}^4\ Z_1^3\ R_0^3),& \\ \{Z_1^3 := X_2^3, R_0^3 := (\texttt{ATOM}^5\ \texttt{a})\},& \\ \{Z_1^3 := Y_1^3, R_0^3 := (\texttt{ATOM}^4\ \texttt{a})\})& \end{aligned}$$

5 Embedding of Configuration Values

The homeomorphic embedding relation known from term algebra [8] can be used to ensure that unfolding during a specialization process does not proceed infinitely. If $cval_1^n \trianglelefteq^n cval_2^n$ then this suggests that $cval_2^n$ might arise from $cval_1^n$ and may lead to some infinitely continuing process and that the transformation should be stopped. Variants of this relation are used in termination proofs for term rewriting systems and for ensuring termination of partial deduction and supercompilation, *e.g.* in [19,22,26].

In our setting, the embedding relation works on specialization states described by configuration values.

Definition 3 (Homeomorphic embedding). *The homeomorphic embedding relation $\trianglelefteq^n \subseteq Cvalues[n] \times Cvalues[n]$ is the smallest relation satisfying the rules in Figure 12.*

Since there is only a finite number of elevations in a given problem, we strengthen the embedding relation for variables on level n (rule *VAR*) with the condition that the elevation indices are identical. Because there may be infinitely many variables we have to be conservative and let all encoded variables embed all other encoded variables (as long as these have the same index and elevation). The rules *ATOM* and *CONS* require that the degree of the constructors is identical. Rule *DIVE-L* and *DIVE-R* detect a configuration value embedded as subterm in another larger configuration value; the other rules match components by components. It is not difficult to give an algorithm deciding whether $cval_1^n \trianglelefteq^n cval_2^n$.

The homeomorphic embedding relation as it is defined is, however, not a well quasi-ordering (WQO) on *Cvalues*[n], since the index and the elevation of of elements in *Cvalues*[n] is not limited, but since we assume that we always work with a finite number of elevations and therefore also maximum encoding we have the following theorem which is sufficient for ensuring termination for MST schemes:

Theorem 2 (WQO $\trianglelefteq^n$). *The relation $\trianglelefteq^n$ is a well-quasi order on $Cvalues[n] \backslash (Cvalues[n+m] \cup \{X_h^n \mid h \geq m\})$.*

Proof. Proven by a simple adaption of the proof in the literature [8], since there are only finitely many constructors in $Cvalues[n] \backslash (Cvalues[n+m] \cup \{X_h^n \mid h \geq m\})$[2]

[2] Without the limitation on the domain *Cvalues*[n] we could have infinitely many constructors, e.g. $(\texttt{ATOM}^{n+m}\ \texttt{a}), m \geq 1$.

$$X_h^{n+r} \trianglelefteq^n Y_h^{n+r} \qquad [VAR]$$

$$(\texttt{ATOM}^{n+m}\ atom) \trianglelefteq^n (\texttt{ATOM}^{n+m}\ atom) \qquad [ATOM]$$

$$\frac{cval_1 \trianglelefteq^n cval_1' \qquad cval_2 \trianglelefteq^n cval_2'}{(\texttt{CONS}^{n+m}\ cval_1\ cval_2) \trianglelefteq^n (\texttt{CONS}^{n+m}\ cval_1'\ cval_2')} \qquad [CONS]$$

$$\frac{cval \trianglelefteq^n cval_1}{cval \trianglelefteq^n (\texttt{CONS}^{n+m}\ cval_1\ cval_2)} \qquad [DIVE\text{-}L]$$

$$\frac{cval \trianglelefteq^n cval_2}{cval \trianglelefteq^n (\texttt{CONS}^{n+m}\ cval_1\ cval_2)} \qquad [DIVE\text{-}R]$$

Fig. 12. Homeomorphic embedding on level n ($m \geq 1,\ r \geq 0$)

Property 3 (metacode invariance $\trianglelefteq^n$). For any $cval_1^n, cval_2^n \in Cvalues[n]$, relation $\trianglelefteq^n$ is *invariant wrt. repeated metacoding* $\mu^m, m \geq 0,\ k \geq 0$:

$$cval_1^n \trianglelefteq^n cval_2^n \Longleftrightarrow \mu^m\{cval_1^n\} \trianglelefteq^{n+k} \mu^m\{cval_2^n\}$$

In other words, the invariance of $\trianglelefteq^n$ wrt. repeated metacoding avoids the problems described in Example 2.

Example 10. Here are a few examples with the homeomorphic embedding relation:

$$(\texttt{ATOM}^3\ \texttt{a}) \trianglelefteq^2 (\texttt{CONS}^3\ (\texttt{ATOM}^3\ \texttt{a})\ X_1^2)$$
$$(\texttt{ATOM}^3\ \texttt{a}) \ntrianglelefteq^2 (\texttt{CONS}^3\ (\texttt{ATOM}^4\ \texttt{a})\ X_1^2)$$
$$Y_0^2 \trianglelefteq^2 (\texttt{CONS}^3\ (\texttt{ATOM}^4\ \texttt{a})\ X_0^2)$$
$$Y_1^2 \ntrianglelefteq^1 (\texttt{CONS}^3\ (\texttt{ATOM}^4\ \texttt{a})\ X_0^2)$$

6 Self-Applicable Specialization

The previous sections were concerned with the development of the foundations and methods for dealing with multiply encoded data; this one is concerned with a practical study in a self-applicable specializer. This specializer performs constant propagation (no propagation of information as in supercompilation). First we give an example that introduces the notation, then we illustrate a case of self-application. The specializer has two arguments: **tree** and **def** where **tree** is the initial expression (metacoded once) and **def** contains the definitions of the program to be specialized. Figure 13 shows how the specialization is setup for the reverse program (Figure 3) when the first argument is known (the list [1, 2]) and the accumulator (a) is unknown (a metavariable on level 0 with elevation 0).

Initial call to the (self-applicable) specializer:

```
(let tree (call-1 (rev (cons-1 (atom-1 1)
                               (cons-1 (atom-1 2) (atom-1 nil)))
                       (mv 0 a)))
  (let defs (cons (cons (atom rev) (atom nil))
                  (cons <rev metacoded once> (atom nil)))
    (call (spec-start tree defs)))))
```

Result of specialization:

```
(cons-1 (atom-1 2) (cons-1 (atom-1 1) (pv-1 a)))
```

Fig. 13. Specialization example

A multi-level example We now turn to a multi-level example. The program we consider is again the reverse program, but this time we apply a second version of the specializer (self-application) to the specialization of the program, and the first list (**x**) is replaced by a meta-variable at level 0 with elevation 1 and the accumulator (**a**) by a meta-variable at level 1 with elevation 0. This means that **x** is a variable of the outer specializer and **a** is a variable of the inner specializer. This can be illustrated by the following MST scheme:

level 0 : $\mathbf{spec}_0$ ———— $\mathbf{x}_1^0$ ——
level 1 : $\mathbf{spec}_1$ —— | — $\mathbf{a}_0^1$
level 2 : **rev**(• , •)

We now examine some essential steps in the development of the computation. The initial call of metasystem hierarchy is shown in Figure 14. After some computation steps this leads to the configuration `(1)` which the outer specializer will memorize such that it can check whether later configurations embed this. We assume that a specializer does this for all calls, since unfolding of function calls is the only situation that can cause infinite specialization. Since our language is tail-recursive all memorized configuration will consists of a call to a function from the specializer and we will simply write `spec-*` to denote some function from the specializer. After memorizing the configuration the inner specializer (interpreted by the outer) unfolds the call to `rev`. This leads to a configuration:

```
(call (spec-*
  (call-1 (spec-* (if-2 (cons?-2 (mv 1 x) (pv-2 hd) (pv-2 tl))
                        (call-2 (rev (pv-2 tl)
                                     (cons-2 (pv-2 hd) (mv-1 0 a))))
                        (mv-1 0 a)) ...)) ...))
```

in which the inner specializer cannot continue, because to decide the outcome of the test it has to know the value of `(mv 1 x)` and this metavariable belongs to

Initial call to the self-applicable specializer:

```
(let tree
  (let-1 tree (call-2 (rev (mv 1 x) (pv-1 0 a)))
    (let-1 defs (cons-1 (cons-1 (atom-1 rev) (atom-1 nil))
                        (cons-1 <rev metacoded twice> (atom-1 nil)))
      (call-1 (spec-start (pv-1 tree) (pv-1 defs)))))
  (let defs <spec metacoded once>
    (call (spec-start tree env defs))))
```

Initial configuration after evaluation (unfolding) of the let-expressions:

```
(call (spec-* (call-1 (spec-* (call-2 (rev (mv 1 x) (mv-1 0 a))))     (1)
              ...)
      ...))
```

Configuration after some steps of computation (embedding (1)*):*

```
(call
  (spec-*
    (call-1
      (spec-* (call-2 (rev (mv 1 tl) (cons-2 (mv 1 hd) (mv-1 0 a)))) (2)
      ...))
  ...))
```

Generalized configuration (msg of (1) *and* (2)*):*

```
(call (spec-* (call-1 (spec-* (call-2 (rev (mv 1 x) (mv 1 z))))
              ...)
      ...))
```

Fig. 14. Specialization example showing embedding and generalization

the outer specializer. This means that the outer specializer takes over and drives the configuration by splitting it into two configurations: one for each branch of the conditional. The second of these configurations is (2) shown in Figure 14. We have reached a point where configuration (2) embeds (1).

The fragments represented by ... in configuration (1) and (2) are identical and, thus, trivially embed each other. Similarly, the functions `spec-*` are the same in both configurations. So we only have to consider whether the following holds:

`(rev (mv 1 x) (mv-1 0 a))` $\trianglelefteq^0$ `(rev (mv 1 tl) (cons-2 (mv 1 hd) (mv-1 0 a)))`

Since both trees have the same outer constructor we use the *CONS*-rule from Figure 12, which means that we consider:

`(mv 1 x)` $\trianglelefteq^0$ `(mv 1 tl)` and `(mv-1 0 a)` $\trianglelefteq^0$ `(cons-2 (mv 1 hd) (mv-1 0 a))` instead. The first of these two clearly holds because of the *VAR*-rule in Figure 12. The second holds because the *DIVE-R* rule and the *VAR*-rule (`(mv-1 0 a)` $\trianglelefteq$ `(mv-1 0 a)`). Configuration `(2)` embeds `(1)`.

Usually, when a late configuration embeds an early configuration during specialization this means that there is a risk that specialization will not terminate. So therefore we assume that our specializer in the example replaces the early configuration by the most specific generalization of the two configurations. For our example Figure 14 shows the msg of `(1)` and `(2)` that is obtained by the the method shown in Figure 11.

7 Related Work

The ideas presented in this paper have been heavily influenced by three concepts present in Turchin's work [25]: metacoding, metavariables, and metasystem transition. Subsequently, these concepts have been formalized [10] and studied in different contexts, *e.g.* [13,26].

Representing and reasoning about object level theories is an important field in logic and artificial intelligence (e.g. different encodings have been discussed in [14]) and has led to the development of logic languages that support declarative metaprogramming (*e.g.* the programming language Gödel [15]). Logic variables and unification as provided by their underlying logic system, lack, among others, the notion of elevation and the direct support for multiply encoded data. In recent work [13], we therefore proposed a simple language S-graph-*n* to study meta-programming aspects of self-applicable online program specialization. It will be interesting to study and possibly incorporate some of the notions developed here in a logic programming context (e.g. by extending an existing system).

MetaML, a statically typed multi-level language for hand-writing multi-level generating extensions was introduced in [24]. Another multi-level programming language is *Alloy* [4], a logic language which provides facilities for deductions at different meta-levels and a proof system for interleaving computations at different metalevels. A program generator for multi-level specialization [11] uses a functional language extended with multiple-binding times as representation of multi-level generating extensions. They allow the design and implementation of generative software [9].

Most specific generalization and the homeomorphic embedding relation are known from term algebra [8]. Variants of this relation are used in termination proofs for term rewrite systems and for ensuring local termination of partial deduction [5]. After it was taken up in [22], it has inspired more recent work [2, 19,27,26].

8 Conclusion

Our goal was to clarify foundational issues of generalization and termination in hierarchies of programs with multiple encoded data. We examined two popular methods, most specific generalization and the homeomorphic embedding relation, proved their properties and illustrated their working with simple examples. It is clear that several challenging problems lie ahead: the implementation of a full system based on the approach advocated in this paper and formalization of other termination and generalization strategies for multi-level hierarchies of programs.

On the theoretical side a thorough comparison of the approach taken in this contribution with higher-order logic programming concepts is on the agenda. Another challenging question is whether such approaches can be combined and used for metaprogramming in general.

To conclude, we believe the work presented in this paper is a solid basis for future work on multi-level program hierarchies and their efficient implementation on the computer.

Acknowledgments

We would like to thank Michael Leuschel and Bern Martens for stimulating discussions on topics related to this work. Anonymous referees as well as participants of LOPSTR'98 provided very useful feedback on this paper.

References

1. S.M. Abramov. Metacomputation and program testing. In *1st International Workshop on Automated and Algorithmic Debugging*, pages 121–135, Linköping University, Sweden, 1993.
2. M. Alpuente, M. Falaschi, and G. Vidal. Narrowing-driven partial evaluation of functional logic programs. In H.R. Nielson, editor, *European Symposium on Programming*, Lecture Notes in Computer Science, pages 46–61. Springer-Verlag, 1996.
3. K. Apt and F. Turini *Meta-Logics and Logic Programming*, MIT Press, 1995.
4. J. Barklund. A basis for a multilevel metalogic programming language. Technical Report 81, Uppsala University, Dept. of Computing Science, 1994.
5. R. Bol. Loop checking in partial deduction. *J of Logic Programming*, 16(1&2):25–46, 1993.
6. S. Costantini and G. Lanzarone. A metalogic programming language. In G. Levi and M. Martelli, editors, *Proceedings Sixth International Conference on Logic Programming*, pages 218–233. MIT Press, 1989.
7. O. Danvy, R. Glück, and P. Thiemann, editors. *Partial Evaluation*, volume 1110 of *Lecture Notes in Computer Science*. Springer-Verlag, 1996.
8. N. Dershowitz and J.-P. Jouannaud. Rewrite systems. In J. van Leeuwen, editor, *Handbook of Theoretical Computer Science*, pages 244–320. Elsevier, 1992.
9. U. Eisenecker. Generative programming with C++. In H. Mössenböck, editor, *Modular Programming Languages*, volume 1204 of *Lecture Notes in Computer Science*, pages 351–365. Springer-Verlag, 1997.
10. R. Glück. On the mechanics of metasystem hierarchies in program transformation. In M. Proietti, editor, *Logic Program Synthesis and Transformation (LOPSTR'95)*, volume 1048 of *Lecture Notes in Computer Science*, pages 234–251. Springer-Verlag, 1996.

11. R. Glück and J. Jørgensen. An automatic program generator for multi-level specialization. *Lisp and Symbolic Computation*, 10(2):113–158, 1997.
12. R. Glück and A.V. Klimov. Occam's razor in metacomputation: the notion of a perfect process tree. In P. Cousot, et al., editors, *Static Analysis. Proceedings.* Lecture Notes in Computer Science, Vol. 724, pages 112–123. Springer-Verlag, 1993.
13. J. Hatcliff and R. Glück. Reasoning about hierarchies of online specialization systems. In Danvy et al. [7].
14. P. Hill and J. Gallagher. Meta-programming in logic programming. Technical Report 94.22, School of Computer Studies, University of Leeds, 1994.
15. P. Hill and J.W. Lloyd. *The Gödel Programming Language.* MIT Press, 1994.
16. Neil D. Jones, Carsten K. Gomard, and Peter Sestoft. *Partial Evaluation and Automatic Program Generation.* Prentice-Hall, 1993.
17. M. Leuschel. Homeomorphic embedding for online termination. Technical Report DSSE-TR-98-11, University of Southampton, Dept. of Electronics and Computer Science, 1998.
18. M. Leuschel. On the power of homeomorphic embedding for online termination. G. Levi, editor, *Static Analysis. Proceedings.* Lecture Notes in Computer Science, Vol. 1503, pages 230–245, Springer-Verlag 1998.
19. M. Leuschel and B. Martens. Global control for partial deduction through characteristic atoms and global trees. In Danvy et al. [7], pages 263–283.
20. G. Nadathur and D. Miller. Higher-Order Logic Programming. In Handbook of Logic in AI and Logic Programming, Vol. 5, pages 499–590, Oxford University Press, 1998.
21. A. Pettorossi, M. Proietti. Transformation of logic programs: Foundations and techniques. *Journal of Logic Programming*, 19 & 20:261–320, 1994.
22. M.H. Sørensen and R. Glück. An algorithm of generalization in positive supercompilation. In J.W. Lloyd, editor, *Logic Programming: Proceedings of the 1995 International Symposium*, pages 465–479. MIT Press, 1995.
23. L. Sterling and E. Shapiro. *The Art of Prolog.* MIT Press, 1986.
24. W. Taha and T. Sheard. Multi-stage programming with explicit annotations. In *Symposium on Partial Evaluation and Semantics-Based Program Manipulation*, pages 203–217, 1997.
25. V.F. Turchin. The concept of a supercompiler. *Transactions on Programming Languages and Systems*, 8(3):292–325, 1986.
26. V.F. Turchin. Metacomputation: metasystem transitions plus supercompilation. In Danvy et al. [7].
27. V.F. Turchin. On generalization of lists and strings in supercompilation. Technical Report CSc. TR 96-002, City College of the City University of New York, 1996.
28. V.F. Turchin and A.P. Nemytykh. Metavariables: their implementation and use in program transformation. CSc. TR 95-012, City College of the City University of New York, 1995.
29. W. Vanhoof and B. Martens. To parse or not to parse. In N. Fuchs (ed.), *Logic Program Synthesis and Transformation (LOPSTR'97)*, Lecture Notes in Computer Science, Vol. 1463, pages 314–333, Springer-Verlag 1998.

Improving Homeomorphic Embedding for Online Termination

Michael Leuschel*

Department of Electronics and Computer Science, University of Southampton, UK
Department of Computer Science, K.U. Leuven, Belgium
DIKU, University of Copenhagen, Denmark
mal@ecs.soton.ac.uk
www: http://www.ecs.soton.ac.uk/~mal

Abstract. Well-quasi orders in general, and homeomorphic embedding in particular, have gained popularity to ensure online termination of program analysis, specialisation and transformation techniques. It has been recently shown that the homeomorphic embedding relation is strictly more powerful than a large class of involved well-founded approaches. In this paper we provide some additional investigations on the power of homeomorphic embedding. We, however, also illustrate that the homeomorphic embedding relation suffers from several inadequacies in contexts where logical variables arise. We therefore present new, extended homeomorphic embedding relations to remedy this problem.
Keywords: Termination, Well-quasi orders, Program Analysis, Specialisation and Transformation, Logic Programming, Functional & Logic Programming.

1 Introduction

The problem of ensuring termination arises in many areas of computer science and a lot of work has been devoted to proving termination of term rewriting systems (e.g. [9–11,40] and references therein) or of logic programs (e.g. [7,41] and references therein). It is also an important issue within all areas of program analysis, specialisation and transformation: one usually strives for methods which are guaranteed to terminate. One can basically distinguish between two kinds of techniques for ensuring termination:

- *offline* (or *static*) techniques, which prove or ensure termination of a program or process *beforehand* without any kind of execution, and
- *online* (or *dynamic*) techniques, which ensure termination of a process *during* its execution.

Offline approaches have less information at their disposal but do not require runtime intervention (which might be impossible). Which of the two approaches is taken depends entirely on the application area. For instance, static termination analysis of logic programs [7,41] falls within the former context, while termination of program specialisation, transformation or analysis is often ensured in an online manner.

* Part of the work was done while the author was Post-doctoral Fellow of the Fund for Scientific Research - Flanders Belgium (FWO).

P. Flener (Ed.): LOPSTR'98, LNCS 1559, pp. 199–218, 1999.

This paper is primarily aimed at studying and improving online termination techniques. Let us examine the case of partial deduction [34, 12, 26] — an automatic technique for specialising logic programs. Henceforth we suppose some familiarity with basic notions in logic programming [4, 33].

Partial deduction based upon the Lloyd and Shepherdson framework [34] generates (possibly incomplete) SLDNF-trees for a set $\mathcal{A}$ of atoms. The specialised program is extracted from these trees by producing one clause (called a resultant) for every non-failing branch. The resolution steps within the SLDNF-trees — often referred to as *unfolding* steps — are those that have been performed beforehand, justifying the hope that the specialised program is more efficient.

Now, to ensure termination of partial deduction two issues arise [12, 39]. One is called the *local termination* problem, corresponding to the fact that each generated SLDNF-tree should be finite. The other is called the *global termination* problem, meaning that the set $\mathcal{A}$ should contain only a finite number of atoms. A similar classification can be done for most other program specialisation techniques (cf., e.g., [31]).

Below we mainly use local termination to illustrate our concepts. (As shown in [39] the atoms in $\mathcal{A}$ can be structured into a global tree and methods similar to the one for local termination can be used to ensure global termination. See also [45] for a very general, language independent, framework for termination.)

However, the discussions and contributions of the present paper are also (immediately) applicable in the context of analysis, specialisation and transformation techniques in general, especially when applied to computational paradigms, such as logic programming, constrained logic programming, conditional term rewriting, functional programming and functional & logic programming. We also believe that our discussions are relevant for other areas, such as infinite *model checking* or *theorem proving*, where termination has to be insured in non-trivial ways.

One, albeit ad-hoc, way to solve the local termination problem is to simply impose an arbitrary *depth bound*. Such a depth bound is of course not motivated by any property, structural or otherwise, of the program or goal under consideration. In the context of local termination, the depth bound will therefore typically lead either to too little or too much unfolding.

Another approach, often used in partial evaluation of functional programs [19], is to (only) expand a tree while it is *determinate* (i.e. it only has one non-failing branch). However, this approach can be very restrictive and in itself does not guarantee termination, as there can be infinitely failing determinate computations at specialisation time.

Well-founded Orders Luckily, more refined approaches to ensure local termination exist. The first non-ad-hoc methods [6, 38, 37, 36] in logic and [43, 52] functional programming were based on *well-founded orders*, inspired by their usefulness in the context of static termination analysis. These techniques ensure termination, while at the same time allowing unfolding related to the structural aspect of the program and goal to be specialised, e.g., permitting the consumption of static input within the atoms of $\mathcal{A}$.

Definition 1. (wfo) *A* (strict) partial order $>_S$ *on a set* S *is an anti-reflexive, anti-symmetric and transitive binary relation on* $S \times S$. *A sequence of elements* $s_1, s_2, \ldots$ *in* S *is called* admissible wrt $>_S$ *iff* $s_i > s_{i+1}$, *for all* $i \geq 1$.
We call $>_S$ *a* well-founded order (wfo) *iff there are no infinite admissible sequences wrt* $>_S$.

Now, to ensure local termination for instance, one has to find a sensible well-founded order on atoms and then only allow SLDNF-trees in which the sequence of selected atoms is admissible wrt the well-founded order. If an atom that we want to select is not strictly smaller than its ancestors, we either have to select another atom or stop unfolding altogether.

Example 1. Let P be the *reverse* program using an accumulator:
$rev([\,], Acc, Acc) \leftarrow$
$rev([H|T], Acc, Res) \leftarrow rev(T, [H|Acc], Res)$
A simple well-founded order on atoms of the form $rev(t_1, t_2, t_3)$ might be based on comparing the termsize (i.e., the number of function and constant symbols) of the first argument. We then define the wfo on atoms by:
$$rev(t_1, t_2, t_3) > rev(s_1, s_2, s_3) \text{ iff } term\_size(t_2) > term\_size(s_2).$$
Based on that wfo, the goal $\leftarrow rev([a, b|T], [\,], R)$ can be unfolded into the goal $\leftarrow rev([b|T], [a], R)$ and further into $\leftarrow rev(T, [b, a], R)$ because the termsize of the first argument strictly decreases at each step (even though the overall termsize does not decrease). However, $\leftarrow rev(T, [b, a], R)$ cannot be further unfolded into $\leftarrow rev(T', [H', b, a], R)$ because there is no such strict decrease.

Much more elaborate techniques exist [6, 38, 37, 36], which, e.g., split the expressions into classes, use lexicographical ordering on subsequences of the arguments and even continuously refine the orders during the unfolding process. These works also present some further refinements on *how to apply* wfo's, especially in the context of partial deduction. For instance, instead of requiring a decrease wrt every ancestor, one can only request a decrease wrt the *covering ancestors*, i.e. one only compares with the ancestor atoms from which the current atom descends (via resolution). (Most of these refinements can also be applied to other approaches, notably the one we will present in the next section.)

However, it has been felt by several researchers that well-founded orders are sometimes too rigid or (conceptually) too complex in an online setting. Recently, *well-quasi orders* have therefore gained popularity to ensure online termination of program manipulation techniques [5, 44, 46, 30, 31, 14, 20, 2, 22, 50, 1, 8]. In [28] the reasons behind this move to well-quasi orders have been formally investigated. Notably, [28] shows that a rather simple well-quasi approach—the *homeomorphic embedding* relation— is strictly more powerful than a large class of involved well-founded approaches. Nonetheless, despite its power, we will show that the homeomorphic embedding is still unsatisfactory when it comes to variables. This paper aims at improving this situation by developing more adequate refinements of the homeomorphic embedding relation.

This paper is structured as follows. In Sections 2 and 3 we provide a gentle introduction to well-quasi orders and summarise the main results of [28]. In Section 4 we provide some additional investigation, discussing the concept of "near-foundedness" [36]. In Section 5 we show that, despite its power, the homeomorphic embedding is still unsatisfactory when it comes to variables. We provide a first solution, which we then improve in Section 6, notably to be able to cope with infinite alphabets.

2 Well-quasi orders and homeomorphic embedding

Formally, well-quasi orders can be defined as follows.

Definition 2. **(quasi order)** *A* quasi order $\geq_S$ *on a set* S *is a reflexive and transitive binary relation on* $S \times S$.

Henceforth, we will use symbols like $<$, $>$ (possibly annotated by some subscript) to refer to strict partial orders and $\leq$, $\geq$ to refer to quasi orders and binary relations. We will use either "directionality" as is convenient in the context. We also define an *expression* to be either a *term* (built-up from variables and function symbols of arity ≥ 0) or an *atom* (a predicate symbol applied to a, possibly empty, sequence of terms), and then treat predicate symbols as function symbols, but suppose that no confusion between function and predicate symbols can arise (i.e., predicate and function symbols are distinct).

Definition 3. **(wbr,wqo)** *Let* $\leq_S$ *be a binary relation on* $S \times S$. *A sequence of elements* $s_1, s_2, \ldots$ *in* S *is called* admissible wrt $\leq_S$ *iff there are no* $i < j$ *such that* $s_i \leq_S s_j$. *We say that* $\leq_S$ *is a* well-binary relation (wbr) *on* S *iff there are no infinite admissible sequences wrt* $\leq_S$. *If* $\leq_S$ *is a quasi order on* S *then we also say that* $\leq_S$ *is a* well-quasi order (wqo) *on* S.

Observe that, in contrast to wfo's, non-comparable elements are allowed within admissible sequences. An admissible sequence is sometimes called *bad* while a non-admissible one is called *good*. A well-binary relation is then such that all infinite sequences are good. There are several other equivalent definitions of well-binary relations and well-quasi orders. Higman [17] used an alternate definition of well-quasi orders in terms of the "finite basis property" (or "finite generating set" in [21]). Both definitions are equivalent by Theorem 2.1 in [17]. A different (but also equivalent) definition of a wqo is(e.g., [23,51]): A quasi-order $\leq_V$ is a wqo iff for all quasi-orders $\preceq_V$ which contain $\leq_V$ (i.e. $v \leq_V v' \Rightarrow v \preceq_V v'$) the corresponding strict partial order $\prec_V$ is a wfo. This property has been exploited in the context of *static* termination analysis to dynamically construct well-founded orders from well-quasi ones and led to the initial use of wqo's in the offline setting [9,10]. The use of well-quasi orders in an *online* setting has only emerged recently (it is mentioned, e.g., in [5] but also [44]) and [28] provides the first formal comparison.[1] Furthermore, in the online setting, transitivity of

[1] There has been some comparison between wfo's and wqo's in the offline setting, e.g., in [40] it is argued that (for "simply terminating" rewrite systems) approaches based upon quasi-orders are less interesting than ones based upon a partial orders.

a wqo is not really interesting (because one does not have to generate wfo's) and one can therefore drop this requirement, leading to the use of wbr's. Later on in Sections 5 and 6 we will actually develop wbr's which are not wqo's.

An interesting wqo is the *homeomorphic embedding* relation $\trianglelefteq$, which derives from results by Higman [17] and Kruskal [21]. It has been used in the context of term rewriting systems in [9, 10], and adapted for use in supercompilation [49] in [46]. Its usefulness as a stop criterion for partial evaluation is also discussed and advocated in [35]. Some complexity results can be found in [48] and [16] (also summarised in [35]).

The following is the definition from [46], which adapts the pure homeomorphic embedding from [10] by adding a rudimentary treatment of variables.

Definition 4. *The* (pure) homeomorphic embedding *relation* $\trianglelefteq$ *on expressions is inductively defined as follows (i.e.* $\trianglelefteq$ *is the least relation satisfying the rules):*

1. $X \trianglelefteq Y$ *for all variables* X, Y
2. $s \trianglelefteq f(t_1, \ldots, t_n)$ *if* $s \trianglelefteq t_i$ *for some* i
3. $f(s_1, \ldots, s_n) \trianglelefteq f(t_1, \ldots, t_n)$ *if* $\forall i \in \{1, \ldots, n\} : s_i \trianglelefteq t_i$.

The second rule is sometimes called the *diving* rule, and the third rule is sometimes called the *coupling* rule (notice that n is allowed to be 0). When $s \trianglelefteq t$ we also say that s is *embedded in* t or t is *embedding* s. By $s \triangleleft t$ we denote that $s \trianglelefteq t$ and $t \not\trianglelefteq s$.

The intuition behind the above definition is that $A \trianglelefteq B$ iff A can be obtained from B by "striking out" certain parts, or said another way, the structure of A reappears within B. Indeed, just applying the coupling rule 3 we get syntactic identity for ground expressions, rule 1 just confounds all variables, and the diving rule 2 allows to ignore a part (namely $f(t_1, \ldots, t_{i-1}, t_{i+1}, \ldots, t_n)$) of the right-hand term.

Example 2. We have $p(a) \trianglelefteq p(f(a))$ and indeed $p(a)$ can be obtained from $p(f(a))$ by "striking out" the f; see Fig. 1. Observe that the "striking out" corresponds to the application of the diving rule 2 and that we even have $p(a) \triangleleft p(f(a))$. We also have, e.g., that: $X \trianglelefteq X$, $p(X) \triangleleft p(f(Y))$, $p(X, X) \trianglelefteq p(X, Y)$ and $p(X, Y) \trianglelefteq p(X, X)$.

Proposition 1. $\trianglelefteq$ *is a wqo on the set of expressions over a finite alphabet.*

To ensure, e.g., local termination of partial deduction, we have to ensure that the constructed SLDNF-trees are such that the selected atoms do *not embed* any of their ancestors (when using a well-founded order as in Example 1, we had to require a *strict decrease* at every step). If an atom that we want to select embeds one of its ancestors, we either have to select another atom or stop unfolding altogether. For example, based on $\trianglelefteq$, the goal $\leftarrow rev([a, b|T], [\,], R)$ of Example 1 can be unfolded into $\leftarrow rev([b|T], [a], R)$ and further into $\leftarrow rev(T, [b, a], R)$ as $rev([a, b|T], [\,], R) \not\trianglelefteq rev([b|T], [a], R)$, $rev([a, b|T], [\,], R) \not\trianglelefteq rev(T, [b, a], R)$ and $rev([b|T], [a], R) \not\trianglelefteq rev(T, [b, a], R)$. However, $\leftarrow rev(T, [b, a], R)$ cannot be further unfolded into $\leftarrow rev(T', [H', b, a], R)$ as $rev(T, [b, a], R) \trianglelefteq rev(T', [H', b, a], R)$.

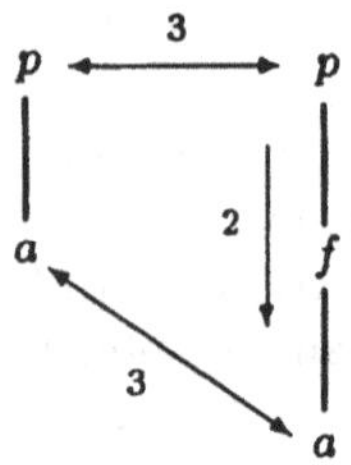

Fig. 1. Illustrating Example 2

Observe that, in contrast to Example 1, we did not have to choose how to measure which arguments. We further elaborate on the inherent flexibility of $\trianglelefteq$ in the next section.

The homeomorphic embedding relation is also useful for handling structures other than expressions. It has, e.g., been successfully applied in [30,26,31] to detect (potentially) non-terminating sequences of characteristic trees. Also, $\trianglelefteq$ seems to have the desired property that very often only "real" loops are detected and that they are detected at the earliest possible moment (see [35]).

3 Comparing wbr's and wfo's

In this section we summarise the main results of [28].

It follows from Definitions 1 and 3 that if $\leq_V$ is a wqo then $<_V$ (defined by $v_1 <_V v_2$ iff $v_1 \leq_V v_2 \wedge v_1 \not\geq_V v_2$) is a wfo, but not vice versa. The following shows how to obtain a wbr from a wfo.

Lemma 1. *Let $<_V$ be a well-founded order on V. Then $\preceq_V$, defined by $v_1 \preceq_V v_2$ iff $v_1 \not>_V v_2$, is a wbr on V. Furthermore, $<_V$ and $\preceq_V$ have the same set of admissible sequences.*

This means that, in an online setting, the approach based upon wbr's is in theory at least as powerful as the one based upon wfo's. Further below we will actually show that wbr's are strictly more powerful.

Observe that $\preceq_V$ is not necessarily a wqo: transitivity is not ensured as $t_1 \not> t_2$ and $t_2 \not> t_3$ do not imply $t_1 \not> t_3$. Let, e.g., $s < t$ denote that s is strictly more general than t. Then $<$ is a wfo [18] but $p(X,X,a) \not> p(X,Z,b)$ and $p(X,Z,b) \not> p(X,Y,a)$ even though $p(X,X,a) > p(X,Y,a)$.

Let us now examine the power of one particular wqo, the earlier defined $\trianglelefteq$.

The homeomorphic embedding $\trianglelefteq$ relation is very flexible. It will for example, when applied to the sequence of covering ancestors, permit the full unfolding of most terminating Datalog programs, the quicksort or even the mergesort program when the list to be sorted is known (the latter poses problems to some static termination analysis methods [41,32]; for some experiments see [28]). Also, the *produce-consume* example from [36] requires rather involved techniques (considering the context) to be solved by wfo's. Again, this particular example poses no problem to $\trianglelefteq$ (cf. [28]).

The homeomorphic embedding $\trianglelefteq$ is also very powerful in the context of metaprogramming. Notably, it has the ability to "penetrate" layers of (non-ground) meta-encodings (cf. [27] and [13] for further discussions on that matter; cf. also the appendix of [28] for some computer experiments). For instance, $\trianglelefteq$ will admit the following sequences (where, among others, Example 1 is progressively wrapped into "vanilla" metainterpreters counting resolution steps and keeping track of the selected predicates respectively):

Sequence
$rev([a,b\|T],[\,],R) \leadsto rev([b\|T],[a],R)$
$solve(rev([a,b\|T],[\,],R),0) \leadsto solve(rev([b\|T],[a],R),s(0))$
$solve'(solve(rev([a,b\|T],[\,],R),0),[\,]) \leadsto solve'(solve(rev([b\|T],[a],R),s(0)),[rev])$
$path(a,b,[\,]) \leadsto path(b,a,[a])$
$solve'(solve(path(a,b,[\,]),0),[\,]) \leadsto solve'(solve(path(b,a,[a]),s(0)),[rev])$

Again, this is very difficult for wfo's and requires refined and involved techniques (of which to our knowledge no implementation in the online setting exists). For example, to admit the third sequence we have to measure something like the "termsize of the first argument of the first argument of the first argument." For the fifth sequence this gets even more difficult.

We have intuitively demonstrated the usefulness of $\trianglelefteq$ and that it is often more flexible than wfo's. But can we prove some "hard" results? It turns out that we can and [28] establishes that — in the online setting — $\trianglelefteq$ is strictly more generous than a large class of refined wfo's containing the following:

Definition 5. *A well-founded order $\prec$ on expressions is said to be* monotonic *iff the following rules hold:*

1. *$X \not\succ Y$ for all variables X, Y,*
2. *$s \not\succ f(t_1,\ldots,t_n)$ whenever f is a function symbol and $s \not\succ t_i$ for some i and*
3. *$f(s_1,\ldots,s_n) \not\succ f(t_1,\ldots,t_n)$ whenever $\forall i \in \{1,\ldots,n\} : s_i \not\succ f_i$.*

Observe that point 2 need not hold for predicate symbols and that point 3 implies that $c \not\succ c$ for all constant and proposition symbols c. There is also a subtle difference between monotonic wfo's as of Definition 5 and wfo's which possess the replacement property (such orders are called rewrite orders in [40] and monotonic in [9]). More on that below.

[28] shows that most of the wfo's used in online practice are actually monotonic:

- Definitions 3.4 of [6], 3.2 of [38] and 2.14 of [37] all sum up the number of function symbols (i.e. termsize) of a subset of the argument positions of atoms. The algorithms only differ in the way of choosing the positions to measure. The early algorithms measure the input positions, while the later ones dynamically refine the argument positions to be measured. All these wfo's are monotonic.

- Definitions 3.2 of [37] as well as 8.2.2 of [36] use the lexicographical order on the termsizes of some selected argument positions. These wfo's are also monotonic, as proven in [28].

The only non-monotonic wfo in that collection of articles is the one defined specifically for metainterpreters in Definition 3.4 of [6] (also in Section 8.6 of [36]) which uses selector functions to focus on subterms to be measured.

We now adapt the class of simplification orderings from term rewriting systems. The power of this class of wfo's is also subsumed by $\trianglelefteq$.

Definition 6. *A* simplification ordering *is a wfo $\prec$ on expressions which satisfies*

1. $s \prec t \Rightarrow f(t_1, \ldots, s, \ldots, t_n) \prec f(t_1, \ldots, t, \ldots, t_n)$ (replacement property),
2. $t \prec f(t_1, \ldots, t, \ldots, t_n)$ (subterm property) *and*
3. $s \prec t \Rightarrow s\sigma \prec t\gamma$ *for all variable only substitutions σ and γ* (invariance under variable replacement).

The third rule of the above definition is new wrt term-rewriting systems and implies that all variables must be treated like a unique new constant. It turns out that a lot of powerful wfo's are simplification orderings [9, 40]: recursive path ordering, Knuth-Bendix ordering or lexicographic path ordering, to name just a few. However, not all monotonic wfo's are simplification orderings and there are wfo's which are simplification orderings but are not monotonic..

Proposition 2. *Let $\prec$ be a wfo on expressions. Then any admissible sequence wrt $\prec$ is also an admissible sequence wrt $\trianglelefteq$ if $\prec$ is* **a)** *monotonic or if it is* **b)** *a simplification ordering.*

This means that the admissible sequences wrt $\trianglelefteq$ are a superset of the union of all admissible sequences wrt simplification orderings and monotonic wfo's. In other words, no matter how much refinement we put into an approach based upon monotonic wfo's or upon simplification orderings we can only expect to approach $\trianglelefteq$ in the limit. But by a simple example we can even dispel that hope.

Example 3. Take the sequence $\delta = f(a), f(b), b, a$. This sequence is admissible wrt $\trianglelefteq$ as $f(a) \not\trianglelefteq f(b)$, $f(a) \not\trianglelefteq b$, $f(a) \not\trianglelefteq a$, $f(b) \not\trianglelefteq b$, $f(b) \not\trianglelefteq a$ and $a \not\trianglelefteq b$. However, there is no monotonic wfo $\prec$ which admits this sequence. More precisely, to admit δ we must have $f(a) \succ f(b)$ as well as $b \succ a$, i.e. $a \not\succ b$. But this violates rule 3 of Definition 5 and $\prec$ cannot be monotonic. This also violates rule 1 of Definition 6 and $\prec$ cannot be a simplification ordering.

These new results relating $\trianglelefteq$ to monotonic wfo's shed light on $\trianglelefteq$'s usefulness in the context of ensuring online termination.

But of course the admissible sequences wrt $\trianglelefteq$ are *not* a superset of the union of all admissible sequences wrt *any* wfo.[2] For instance the list-length norm $\|.\|_{llen}$ is not monotonic, and indeed we have for $t_1 = [1, 2, 3]$ and $t_2 = [[1, 2, 3], 4]$ that

[2] Otherwise $\trianglelefteq$ could not be a wqo, as *all* finite sequences without repetitions are admissible wrt some wfo (map last element to 1, second last element to 2, ...).

$||t_1||_{llen} = 3 > ||t_2||_{llen} = 2$ although $t_1 \trianglelefteq t_2$. So there are sequences admissible wrt list-length but not wrt $\trianglelefteq$. The reason is that $||.||_{llen}$ in particular and non-monotonic wfo's in general can completely ignore certain parts of the term, while $\trianglelefteq$ will always inspect that part. E.g., if we have $s \succ f(\ldots t \ldots)$ and $\succ$ ignores the subterm t then it will also be true that $s \succ f(\ldots s \ldots)$ while $s \trianglelefteq f(\ldots s \ldots)$,[3] i.e. the sequence $s, f(\ldots s \ldots)$ is admissible wrt $\succ$ but not wrt $\trianglelefteq$.

Of course, for any wfo (monotonic or not) one can devise a wbr (cf. Lemma 1) which has the same admissible sequences. Still there are some feats that are easily attained, even by using $\trianglelefteq$, but which *cannot* be achieved by a wfo approach (monotonic or not). Take the sequences $S_1 = p([\,],[a]), p([a],[\,])$ and $S_2 = p([a],[\,]), p([\,],[a])$. Both of these sequences are admissible wrt $\trianglelefteq$. This illustrates the flexibility of using well-quasi orders compared to well-founded ones in an online setting, as there exists *no* wfo (monotonic or not) which will admit *both* these sequences. It, however, also illustrates why, when using a wqo in that way, one has to compare with every predecessor state of a process. Otherwise one can get infinite derivations of the form $p([a],[\,]) \rightarrow p([\,],[a]) \rightarrow p([a],[\,]) \rightarrow \ldots$.[4] In other words, for wqo's, the composition $s_1, \ldots, s_m$ of two admissible sequences $s_1, \ldots, s_n$ and $s_n, s_{n+1}, \ldots, s_m$ is not necessarily admissible. This is in contrast to wfo's.

Finally, one could argue that it is possible to extend the power of the wfo-approach by defining wfo's over histories (i.e., sequences) instead of the individual elements. This is, however, not the way that wfo's are used in practice and one is faced with the difficulty of defining a sensible order on sequences. Of course, one could always use a wqo $\preceq$ to define such an order: $s_1, \ldots, s_n > s_1, \ldots, s_n, s_{n+1}$ iff $\forall i \in \{1, \ldots, n\} : s_i \not\preceq s_{n+1}$. One would thus get an approach with *exactly* the same power and complexity as the wqo-approach.

4 Nearly-Foundedness and Over-Eagerness

In [37], as well as in Section 8.2.4 of [36], a technique for wfo's is formally introduced, based upon *nearly-foundedness*. As already mentioned earlier, some of the techniques in [6, 38, 37, 36] start out with a very coarse wfo $<_1$ which is then continuously refined, enabling a clever choice of weights for predicates and their respective arguments (deciding beforehand upon appropriate weights can be extremely difficult or impossible; see examples in Section 3). For example we might have that $<_1$ is based upon measuring the sum of the termsize of all arguments and the process of refining consists in dropping one or more arguments. For example, suppose that we have some sequence $s_1, s_2, \ldots, s_i$ which is

[3] Observe that if f is a predicate symbols then $f(\ldots s \ldots)$ is not a valid expression, which enabled us to ignore arguments to predicates.

[4] When using a wfo one has to compare only to the closest predecessor [37], because of the transitivity of the order and the strict decrease enforced at each step. However, wfo's are usually extended to incorporate variant checking and then require inspecting every predecessor anyway (though only when there is no strict weight decrease, see, e.g., [36, 37]).

admissible wrt the initial wfo $<_1$ but where $s_{i+1} \not<_1 s_i$ with $s_{i+1} = p(a, s(s(b)))$ and $s_i = p(s(a), b)$. In that case we can move to a refinement $<_2$ of $<_1$ in which only the termsize of the first argument is measured, enabling the move from s_i to s_{i+1} (as $s_{i+1} <_2 s_i$). This, however, does not guarantee that the *whole* sequence $s_1, s_2, \ldots, s_i, s_{i+1}$ is admissible wrt $<_2$. E.g., for the sequence $p(s(a), s(s(s(c)))), p(s(a), b), p(a, s(s(b)))$ with $i = 2$ we have $s_2 \not<_2 s_1$ even though $s_2 <_1 s_1$.

To solve this problem, the earlier algorithms verified that a refinement keeps the whole sequence admissible (otherwise it was disallowed). The problem with this approach is that re-checking the entire sequence can be expensive. [37, 36] therefore advocates another solution: not re-checking the entire sequence on the grounds that it does not threaten termination (provided that the refinements themselves are well-founded). This leads to sequences $s_1, s_2, \ldots$ which are not well-founded but *nearly-founded* [37, 36] meaning that $s_i \not< s_j$ only for a finite number of pairs (i, j) with $i > j$.

In summary, the motivation for nearly-foundedness lies in speeding up the construction of admissible sequences (not re-scanning the initial sequence upon refinement). As a side-effect, this approach will admit more sequences and, e.g., solve some of our earlier examples (as a suitably large depth bound would as well). However, from a theoretical point of view, we argue below that nearly-foundedness is difficult to justify and somewhat unsatisfactory.

First, we call a technique *over-eager* if it admits sequences which are not admitted by the variant test (i.e., it admits sequences containing variants). We call such a technique *strictly over-eager* if it admits sequences which contain more than 1 occurrence of the same syntactic term.

A depth bound based technique is strictly over-eager, which is obviously a very undesirable property indicating some ad-hoc behaviour. The same can (almost always)[5] also be said for over-eagerness. For instance, in the context of partial deduction or unfold/fold program transformation, over-eager unfolding will "hide" possibilities for perfect folding (namely the variants) and also lead to too large specialised programs. An approach based upon homeomorphic embedding is not over-eager nor is any other wfo/wqo based approach which does not distinguish between variants. However, as we show below, using nearly-foundedness leads to *strict* over-eagerness.

Let us first describe the way nearly-founded sequences are constructed in [37, 36]. First, we define a well-founded order $\prec_{\mathcal{W}}$ acting on a set $\mathcal{W}$ of well-founded orders on expressions. To construct admissible sequences of expressions wrt $\prec_{\mathcal{W}}$ we start by using one wfo $<_1 \in \mathcal{W}$ until the sequence can no longer be extended. Once this is the case we can use another wfo $<_2 \in \mathcal{W}$ which admits the offending step, provided that $<_2 \prec_{\mathcal{W}} <_1$. It is *not* required that the whole initial sequence is admissible wrt $<_2$, just the last step (not admitted by $<_1$). We can now continue expanding the sequence until we again reach an offending step, where we can then try to refine $<_2$ into some $<_3$ with $<_3 \prec_{\mathcal{W}} <_2$, and so on, until no further expansion is possible.

[5] See discussion in Section 5 concerning the variant test *on covering ancestors*.

Example 4. Take the following program.

$p([a,a|T],[a|Y]) \leftarrow p(T,Y)$
$p([b,b,b|T],Y) \leftarrow p(T,[b,b|Y])$
$p(T,[b,b|Y]) \leftarrow p([a,a,b,b,b|T],[a|Y])$

Let us now define the following well-founded orders, where $||t||_{ts}$ denotes the termsize of t:

$<_{\{1,2\}}$: $p(s_1,s_2) < p(t_1,t_2)$ iff $||s_1||_{ts} + ||s_2||_{ts} < ||t_1||_{ts} + ||t_2||_{ts}$
$<_{\{1\}}$: $p(s_1,s_2) < p(t_1,t_2)$ iff $||s_1||_{ts} < ||t_1||_{ts}$
$<_{\{2\}}$: $p(s_1,s_2) < p(t_1,t_2)$ iff $||s_2||_{ts} < ||t_2||_{ts}$

We also define the wfo $\prec_W$ on the above well-founded orders: $<_{\{1\}} \prec_W <_{\{1,2\}}$ and $<_{\{2\}} \prec_W <_{\{1,2\}}$. In other words we can refine $<_{\{1,2\}}$ into $<_{\{1\}}$ or $<_{\{2\}}$, which in turn cannot be further refined.

We can now construct the following admissible sequence in which two terms ($p([a,a,b,b,b],[a])$ and $p([b,b,b],[])$) appear twice:

$p([a,a,b,b,b],[a])$
$\quad\downarrow <_{\{1,2\}}$
$p([b,b,b],[])$
$\quad\downarrow <_{\{1,2\}}$
$p([],[b,b])$
$\quad\downarrow <_{\{2\}}$ (refinement)
$\underline{p([a,a,b,b,b],[a])}$
$\quad\downarrow <_{\{2\}}$
$\underline{p([b,b,b],[])}$

Example 4 thus proves that nearly-foundedness may result in strict over-eagerness. (As a side-effect, the example also shows that the nearly-foundedness approach cannot be mapped to a wfo-approach, however involved it might be.) Although it is unclear how often such situations will actually arise in practice, we believe that the strict over-eagerness is just one of the (mathematically) unsatisfactory aspects of nearly-foundedness.

5 A more refined treatment of variables

While $\trianglelefteq$ has a lot of desirable properties it still suffers from some drawbacks. Indeed, as can be observed in Example 2, the homeomorphic embedding relation $\trianglelefteq$ as defined in Definition 4 is rather crude wrt variables. In fact, all variables are treated as if they were the same variable, a practice which is clearly undesirable in a logic programming context. Intuitively, in the above example, $p(X,Y) \trianglelefteq p(X,X)$ can be justified (see, however, Definition 8 below), while $p(X,X) \trianglelefteq p(X,Y)$ is not. Indeed $p(X,X)$ can be seen as standing for something like $and(eq(X,Y),p(X,Y))$, which embeds $p(X,Y)$, but the reverse does not hold.

Secondly, $\trianglelefteq$ behaves in quite unexpected ways in the context of generalisation, posing some subtle problems wrt the termination of a generalisation process.

Example 5. Take for instance the following generalisation algorithm, which appears (in disguise) in a lot of partial deduction algorithms (e.g., [30, 26, 31]). (In that context $\mathcal{A}$ is the set of atoms for which SLDNF-trees have already been constructed while $\mathcal{B}$ are the atoms in the leaves of these trees. The goal of the algorithm is then to extend $\mathcal{A}$ such that all leaf atoms are covered.)

Input: two finite sets $\mathcal{A}, \mathcal{B}$ of atoms
Output: a finite set $\mathcal{A}' \supseteq \mathcal{A}$ s.t. every atom in $\mathcal{B}$ is an instance of an atom in $\mathcal{A}'$
Initialisation: $\mathcal{A}' := \mathcal{A}$, $\mathcal{B}' := \mathcal{B}$
while $\mathcal{B}' \neq \emptyset$ **do**
  remove an element B from $\mathcal{B}'$
  if B is not an instance of an element in $\mathcal{A}'$ **then**
    if $\exists A \in \mathcal{A}'$ such that $A \trianglelefteq B$ **then**
      add $msg(A, B)$ to $\mathcal{B}'$
    else add B to $\mathcal{A}'$

The basic idea of the algorithm is to use $\trianglelefteq$ to keep the set $\mathcal{A}'$ finite in the limit. However, although the above algorithm will indeed keep $\mathcal{A}'$ finite, it still does not terminate. Take for example $\mathcal{A} = \{p(X, X)\}$ and $\mathcal{B} = \{p(X, Y)\}$. We will remove $B = p(X, Y)$ from $\mathcal{B}' = \{p(X, Y)\}$ in the first iteration of the algorithm and we have that B is not an instance of $p(X, X)$ and also that $p(X, X) \trianglelefteq p(X, Y)$. We therefore calculate the $msg(\{p(X, X), p(X, Y)\}) = p(X, Y)$ and we have a loop (we get $\mathcal{B}' = \{p(X, Y)\}$).

To remedy these problems, [30, 26, 31] introduced the so called strict homeomorphic embedding as follows:

Definition 7. *Let A, B be expressions. Then B* (strictly homeomorphically) *embeds A, written as $A \trianglelefteq^+ B$, iff $A \trianglelefteq B$ and A is not a strict instance of B.*[6]

Example 6. We now still have that $p(X, Y) \trianglelefteq^+ p(X, X)$ but not $p(X, X) \trianglelefteq^+ p(X, Y)$. Note that still $X \trianglelefteq^+ Y$ and $X \trianglelefteq^+ X$.

A small experiment, specialising a query `rotate(X,X)` (using the ECCE system [25] with $\trianglelefteq$ and $\trianglelefteq^+$ respectively on conjunctions for global control; the `rotate` program, rotating a binary tree, can be found in [25]) demonstrates the interest of $\trianglelefteq$: when using $\trianglelefteq^+$ we obtain an overall speedup of 2.5 compared to "only" 2.0 using $\trianglelefteq$.

Notice that, if we replace $\trianglelefteq$ of Example 5 by $\trianglelefteq^+$ we no longer have a problem with termination (see [31, 26] for a termination proof of an Algorithm containing the one of Example 5).

The following is proven in [26, 31].

Theorem 1. *The relation $\trianglelefteq^+$ is a wbr on the set of expressions over a finite alphabet.*

---

6 A is a strict instance of B iff there exists a substitution γ such that $A = B\gamma$ and there exists no substitution σ such that $B = A\sigma$.

Observe that $\trianglelefteq^+$ is not a wqo as it is not transitive: we have for example $p(X,X,Y,Y) \trianglelefteq^+ p(X,Z,Z,X)$ as well as $p(X,Z,Z,X) \trianglelefteq^+ p(X,X,Y,Z)$ but $p(X,X,Y,Y) \not\trianglelefteq^+ p(X,X,Y,Z)$. One might still feel dissatisfied with that definition for another reason. Indeed, although going from $p(X)$ to the instance $p(f(X))$ (and on to $p(f(f(X))),\ldots$) looks very dangerous, a transition from $p(X,Y)$ to $p(X,X)$ is often not dangerous, especially in a database setting. Take for example a simple Datalog program just consisting of the clause $p(a,b) \leftarrow p(X,X)$. Obviously P will terminate (i.e., fail finitely) for all queries but $\trianglelefteq^+$ will not allow the selection of $p(X,X)$ in the following derivation $\leftarrow \underline{p(X,Y)} \rightsquigarrow \leftarrow \underline{p(X,X)} \rightsquigarrow \leftarrow fail$ of $P \cup \{\leftarrow p(X,Y)\}$, hence preventing full unfolding and the detection of finite failure. On the practical side this means that neither $\trianglelefteq^+$ nor $\trianglelefteq$ will allow full unfolding of all terminating queries to Datalog programs (although they will allow full unfolding of terminating ground queries to range-restricted Datalog programs). To remedy this, we can develop the following refinement of $\trianglelefteq^+$.

Definition 8. *We define $s \trianglelefteq_{var} t$ iff $s \triangleleft t$ or s is a variant of t.*

We have $p(X) \trianglelefteq_{var} p(f(X))$ and $p(X,Y) \trianglelefteq_{var} p(Z,X)$ but $p(X,X) \not\trianglelefteq_{var} p(X,Y)$ and $p(X,Y) \not\trianglelefteq_{var} p(X,X)$.

It is obvious that $\trianglelefteq_{var}$ is strictly more powerful than $\trianglelefteq^+$ (if t is strictly more general than s, then it is not a variant of s and it is also not possible to have $s \triangleleft t$). It thus also solves the generalisation problems of $\trianglelefteq$ (i.e., if we produce a strict generalisation g of some expression t, then $t \not\trianglelefteq_{var} g$). In addition $\trianglelefteq_{var}$ has the following property: if we have a query $\leftarrow Q$ to a Datalog program which left-terminates then the LD-tree for $\leftarrow Q$ is admissible in the sense that, for every selected literal L, we have $L \not\trianglelefteq_{var} A$ for all covering ancestors A of L. Indeed, whenever we have that $L \trianglelefteq A$ for two Datalog atoms L and A then we must also have $A \trianglelefteq L$ (as the diving rule of $\trianglelefteq$ cannot be applied). Thus, for Datalog, $\trianglelefteq_{var}$ is equivalent to the variant test. Now, if a derivation from $\leftarrow A$ leads to a goal $\leftarrow L_1, \ldots, L_n$ where L_1 is a variant of a covering ancestor A, then it is possible to repeat this left-to-right derivation again and again and we have a real loop.

Theorem 2. *The relation $\trianglelefteq_{var}$ is a wqo on the set of expression over a finite alphabet.*

The proof can be found in [27]. Observe that $\trianglelefteq_{var}$ is, like $\trianglelefteq$ and $\trianglelefteq^+$, not a wqo over an infinite alphabet. More on that in Section 6.

Discussion

Observe that the variant test is (surprisingly) not complete for Datalog in general (under arbitrary computation rules). Take the program just consisting of $p(b,a) \leftarrow p(X,Z), p(Z,Y)$. Then the query $\leftarrow p(X,Y)$ is finitely failed as the following derivation shows:

$$\underline{p(X,Y)} \rightsquigarrow \underline{p(X',Z')}, p(Z',Y') \rightsquigarrow p(X'',Z''), p(Z'',Y''), \underline{p(a,Y')} \rightsquigarrow fail.$$

However, at the second step (no matter what we do) we have to select a variant of the covering ancestor $p(X,Y)$ and the variant test will prevent full unfolding.

An alternate approach to Definitions 7 and 8 — at least for the aspect of treating variables in a more refined way — might be based on numbering variables using some mapping $\#(.)$ and then stipulating that $X \trianglelefteq^{\#} Y$ iff $\#(X) \leq \#(Y)$. For instance in [35] a de Bruijn numbering of the variables is proposed. Such an approach, however, has a somewhat ad hoc flavour to it. Take for instance the terms $p(X,Y,X)$ and $p(X,Y,Y)$. Neither term is an instance of the other and we thus have $p(X,Y,X) \trianglelefteq^{+} p(X,Y,Y)$ and $p(X,Y,Y) \trianglelefteq^{+} p(X,Y,X)$. Depending on the particular numbering we will either have that $p(X,Y,X) \not\trianglelefteq^{\#} p(X,Y,Y)$ or that $p(X,Y,Y) \not\trianglelefteq^{\#} p(X,Y,X)$, while there is no apparent reason why one expression should be considered smaller than the other.[7]

6 Extended homeomorphic embedding

Although $\trianglelefteq^{+}$ from Definition 7 has a more refined treatment of variables and has a much better behaviour wrt generalisation than $\trianglelefteq$ of Definition 4, it is still somewhat unsatisfactory.

One point is the restriction to a finite alphabet. Indeed, for a lot of practical logic programs, using, e.g., arithmetic built-ins or even $=../2$, a finite alphabet is no longer sufficient. Luckily, the fully general definition of homeomorphic embedding as in [21, 10] remedies this aspect. It even allows function symbols with variable arity.[8] We will show below how this definition can be adapted to a logic programming context.

However, there is another unsatisfactory aspect of $\trianglelefteq^{+}$ (and $\trianglelefteq_{var}$). Indeed, it will ensure that $p(X,X) \not\trianglelefteq^{+} p(X,Y)$ while $p(X,X) \trianglelefteq p(X,Y)$ but we still have that, e.g., $f(a,p(X,X)) \trianglelefteq^{+} f(f(a),p(X,Y))$. In other words, the more refined treatment of variables is only performed at the top, but not recursively within the structure of the expressions. For instance, this means that $\trianglelefteq^{+}$ will handle `rotate(X,X)` much better than $\trianglelefteq$ but this improvement will often vanish when we add a layer of metainterpretation.

The following, new and more refined embedding relation remedies this somewhat ad hoc aspect of $\trianglelefteq^{+}$.

Definition 9. *Given a wbr $\preceq_F$ on the function symbols and a wbr $\preceq_S$ on sequences of expressions, we define the* extended homeomorphic embedding *on expressions by the following rules:*

1. $X \trianglelefteq^{*} Y$ *if X and Y are variables*
2. $s \trianglelefteq^{*} f(t_1,\ldots,t_n)$ *if* $s \trianglelefteq^{*} t_i$ *for some i*
3. $f(s_1,\ldots,s_m) \trianglelefteq^{*} g(t_1,\ldots,t_n)$ *if* $f \preceq_F g$ *and* $\exists 1 \leq i_1 < \ldots < i_m \leq n$ *such that* $\forall j \in \{1,\ldots,m\} : s_j \trianglelefteq^{*} t_{i_j}$ *and* $\langle s_1,\ldots,s_m\rangle \preceq_S \langle t_1,\ldots,t_n\rangle$

---

[7] [35] also proposes to consider all possible numberings (but leading to $n!$ complexity, where n is the number of variables in the terms to be compared). It is unclear how such a relation compares to $\trianglelefteq^{+}$ and $\trianglelefteq_{var}$.

[8] Which can also be seen as associative operators.

Observe that for rule 3 both n and m are allowed to be 0, but we must have $m \leq n$. In contrast to Definition 4 for $\trianglelefteq$, the left- and right-hand terms in rule 3 do not have to be of the same arity. The above rule therefore allows to ignore $n - m$ arguments form the right-hand term (by selecting the m indices $i_1 < \ldots < i_m$).

Furthermore, the left- and right-hand terms in rule 3 do not have to use the same function symbol: the function symbols are therefore compared using the wbr $\preceq_F$. If we have a finite alphabet, then equality is a wqo on the function symbols (one can thus obtain the pure homeomorphic embedding as a special case). In the context of, e.g., program specialisation or analysis, we know that the function symbols occurring within the program (text) and call to be analysed are of finite number. One might call these symbols *static* and all others *dynamic*. A wqo can the be obtained by defining $f \preceq g$ if either f and g are dynamic or if $f = g$. For particular types of symbols a natural wqo or wbr exists (e.g., for numbers) which can be used instead. Also, for associative symbols (such as $\wedge$) one can represent $c_1 \wedge \ldots \wedge c_n$ by $\wedge(c_1, \ldots, c_n)$ and then use equality up to arities (e.g., $\wedge/2 = \wedge/3$) for $\preceq_F$.

Example 7. If we take $\preceq_F$ to be equality up to arities and ignore $\preceq_S$ (i.e., define $\preceq_S$ to be always true) we get all the embeddings of $\trianglelefteq$, e.g., $p(a) \trianglelefteq^* p(f(a))$. But we also get $p(a) \trianglelefteq^* p(b, f(a), c)$ (while $p(a) \trianglelefteq p(b, f(a), c)$ does not hold), $\wedge(p(a), q(b)) \trianglelefteq^* \wedge(s, p(f(a)), r, q(b))$ and $\wedge(a, b, c) \trianglelefteq^* \wedge(a, b, c, d)$. One can see that $\trianglelefteq^*$ provides a convenient way to handle associative operators such as the conjunction $\wedge$. (Such a treatment of $\wedge$ has been used in [14,20,8] to ensure termination of conjunctive partial deduction. It might prove equally beneficial for constrained partial deduction [29].) Indeed, in the context of $\trianglelefteq$ one cannot use $\wedge$ with all possible arities and one has to use, e.g., a binary representation. But then whether $\wedge(a, b, c)$ is embedded in $\wedge(a, b, c, d)$ (which, given associativity, it is) depends on the particular representation: $\wedge(a, \wedge(b, c)) \trianglelefteq \wedge(a, \wedge(\wedge(b, c), d))$ but $\wedge(a, \wedge(b, c)) \not\trianglelefteq \wedge(\wedge(a, b), \wedge(c, d))$.

In the above definition we can now instantiate $\preceq_S$ such that it performs a more refined treatment of variables, as discussed in Section 5. For example we can define: $\langle s_1, \ldots, s_m \rangle \preceq_S \langle t_1, \ldots, t_n \rangle$ iff $\langle t_1, \ldots, t_n \rangle$ is not strictly more general than $\langle s_1, \ldots, s_m \rangle$. (Observe that this means that if $m \neq n$ then $\preceq_S$ will hold.) This relation is a wbr (by Lemma 1, as the strictly more general relation is a wfo [18]). Then, in contrast to $\trianglelefteq^+$ and $\trianglelefteq_{var}$, this refinement will be applied *recursively* within $\trianglelefteq^*$. For example we now not only have $p(X, X) \not\trianglelefteq^* p(X, Y)$ but also $f(a, p(X, X)) \not\trianglelefteq^* f(f(a), p(X, Y))$ while $f(a, p(X, X)) \trianglelefteq^+ f(f(a), p(X, Y))$.

The reason why a recursive use of, e.g., the "not strict instance" test was not incorporated in [30,26,31] which use $\trianglelefteq^+$ was that the authors were not sure that this would remain a wbr (no proof was found yet). In fact, recursively applying the "not strict instance" looks very dangerous. Take, e.g., the following two atoms $A_0 = p(X, X)$ and $A_1 = q(p(X, Y), p(Y, X))$. In fact, although $A_0 \trianglelefteq^+ A_1$ we do not have $A_0 \trianglelefteq^* A_1$ (when, e.g., considering both q and p as static function symbols) and one wonders whether it might be possible to create an infinite sequence of atoms by, e.g., producing $A_2 = p(q(p(X,Y), p(Y,Z)), q(p(Z,V), p(V,X)))$. We indeed have $A_1 \not\trianglelefteq^* A_2$, but luckily $A_0 \trianglelefteq^* A_2$ and $\trianglelefteq^*$ satisfies the wqo requirement of Definition 3. But can we construct some sequence for which $\trianglelefteq^*$ does not conform to Definition 3?

The following Theorem 3 shows that such a sequence *cannot* be constructed. However, if we slightly strengthen point 3 of Definition 9 by requiring that $\langle s_1, \ldots, s_m \rangle$ is not a strict instance of the selected subsequence $\langle t_{i_1}, \ldots, t_{i_m} \rangle$, we actually no longer have a wqo, as the following sequence of expression shows: $A_0 = f(p(X,X))$, $A_1 = f(p(X,Y), p(Y,X))$, $A_2 = f(p(X,Y), p(Y,Z), p(Z,X))$, ... Using the slightly strengthened embedding relation no A_i would be embedded in any A_j with $j \neq i$, while using Definition 9 unmodified we have, e.g., $A_1 \trianglelefteq^* A_2$ (but not $A_0 \trianglelefteq^* A_1$ or $A_0 \trianglelefteq^* A_2$).

Theorem 3. *$\trianglelefteq^*$ is a wbr on expressions. Additionally, if $\preceq_F$ and $\preceq_S$ are wqo's then so is $\trianglelefteq^*$.*

The proof can be found in [27].

7 Discussion and Conclusion

Of course $\trianglelefteq^*$ is not the ultimate relation for ensuring online termination. Although it has proven to be extremely useful superimposed, e.g., on determinate unfolding, on its own in the context of local control of partial deduction, $\trianglelefteq^*$ (as well as $\trianglelefteq^+$ and $\trianglelefteq$) will sometimes allow too much unfolding than desirable for efficiency concerns: more unfolding does not always imply a better specialised program. We refer to the solutions developed in, e.g., [31, 20]. Similar problems can arise in the setting of global control and we again refer to [31, 20] for discussions and experiments. Also, the issue of an efficient implementation of the homeomorphic embedding relation still remains open. (However, in Section 4 we have shown that the efficient way to use wfo's, which avoids re-scanning the entire sequence upon refinement, has very undesirable properties.)

For some applications, $\trianglelefteq$ as well as $\trianglelefteq^+$ and $\trianglelefteq^*$ remain too restrictive. In particular, they do not always deal satisfactorily with fluctuating structure (arising, e.g., for certain metainterpretation tasks) [50]. The use of characteristic trees [26, 31] remedies this problem to some extent, but not totally. A further step towards a solution is presented in [50]. In that light, it might be of interest to study whether the extensions of the homeomorphic embedding relation proposed in [42] and [24] (in the context of static termination analysis of term rewrite systems) can be useful in an online setting.

In summary, we have discussed the relation between wqo's and wfo's. We have illustrated that $\trianglelefteq$, despite its simplicity, is strictly more generous than the class of monotonic wfo's and simplification orderings combined. As all the wfo's used for automatic online termination (so far) are actually monotonic, this formally establishes the interest of $\trianglelefteq$ in that context. We have also compared to techniques based upon nearly-foundedness, and have shown that such techniques—contrary to $\trianglelefteq$— can lead to the undesirable property of strict over-eagerness.

We have also presented new embedding relations $\trianglelefteq^+$, $\trianglelefteq_{var}$ and $\trianglelefteq^*$, which inherit all the good properties of $\trianglelefteq$ while providing a refined treatment of (logical) variables. We believe that these refinements can be of value in other contexts and for other languages (such as in the context of partial evaluation of functional-logic programs [3, 2, 22, 1] or of supercompilation [49, 15, 47] of functional programming languages, where — at specialisation time – variables also appear). For instance, one can simply plug $\trianglelefteq^*$ into the language-independent framework of [45].

We also believe that $\trianglelefteq^*$ provides both a theoretically and practically more satisfactory basis than $\trianglelefteq^+$ or $\trianglelefteq$. We also believe that $\trianglelefteq^*$ can play a contributing role in other areas, such as controlling abstraction and ensuring termination of infinite model checking.

Acknowledgements

I would like to thank Danny De Schreye, Robert Glück, Jesper Jørgensen, Bern Martens, Maurizio Proietti, Jacques Riche and Morten Heine Sørensen for all the discussions and joint research which led to this paper. Anonymous referees, Patrick Cousot, Renaud Marlet, and Bern Martens provided extremely useful feedback on this paper.

References

1. E. Albert, M. Alpuente, M. Falaschi, P. Julián, and G. Vidal. Improving control in functional logic program specialization. In G. Levi, editor, Static Analysis. *Proceedings of SAS'98*, LNCS 1503, pages 262–277, Pisa, Italy, September 1998. Springer-Verlag.
2. M. Alpuente, M. Falaschi, P. Julián, and G. Vidal. Spezialisation of lazy functional logic programs. In *Proceedings of PEPM'97, the ACM Sigplan Symposium on Partial Evaluation and Semantics-Based Program Manipulation*, pages 151–162, Amsterdam, The Netherlands, 1997. ACM Press.
3. M. Alpuente, M. Falaschi, and G. Vidal. Narrowing-driven partial evaluation of functional logic programs. In H. Riis Nielson, editor, *Proceedings of the 6th European Symposium on Programming, ESOP'96*, LNCS 1058, pages 45–61. Springer-Verlag, 1996.
4. K. R. Apt. Introduction to logic programming. In J. van Leeuwen, editor, *Handbook of Theoretical Computer Science*, chapter 10, pages 495–574. North-Holland Amsterdam, 1990.
5. R. Bol. Loop checking in partial deduction. *The Journal of Logic Programming*, 16(1&2):25–46, 1993.
6. M. Bruynooghe, D. De Schreye, and B. Martens. A general criterion for avoiding infinite unfolding during partial deduction. *New Generation Computing*, 11(1):47–79, 1992.
7. D. De Schreye and S. Decorte. Termination of logic programs: The never ending story. *The Journal of Logic Programming*, 19 & 20:199–260, May 1994.
8. D. De Schreye, R. Glück, J. Jørgensen, M. Leuschel, B. Martens, and M. H. Sørensen. Conjunctive partial deduction: Foundations, control, algorithms and experiments. To appear in *The Journal of Logic Programming*, 1999.

9. N. Dershowitz. Termination of rewriting. *Journal of Symbolic Computation*, 3:69–116, 1987.
10. N. Dershowitz and J.-P. Jouannaud. Rewrite systems. In J. van Leeuwen, editor, *Handbook of Theoretical Computer Science, Vol. B*, pages 243–320. Elsevier, MIT Press, 1990.
11. N. Dershowitz and Z. Manna. Proving termination with multiset orderings. *Communications of the ACM*, 22(8):465–476, 1979.
12. J. Gallagher. Tutorial on specialisation of logic programs. In *Proceedings of PEPM'93, the ACM Sigplan Symposium on Partial Evaluation and Semantics-Based Program Manipulation*, pages 88–98. ACM Press, 1993.
13. R. Glück and J. Hatcliff, John Jørgensen. Generalization in hierarchies of online program specialization systems. In *this volume*.
14. R. Glück, J. Jørgensen, B. Martens, and M. H. Sørensen. Controlling conjunctive partial deduction of definite logic programs. In H. Kuchen and S. Swierstra, editors, *Proceedings of the International Symposium on Programming Languages, Implementations, Logics and Programs (PLILP'96)*, LNCS 1140, pages 152–166, Aachen, Germany, September 1996. Springer-Verlag.
15. R. Glück and M. H. Sørensen. A roadmap to supercompilation. In O. Danvy, R. Glück, and P. Thiemann, editors, *Proceedings of the 1996 Dagstuhl Seminar on Partial Evaluation*, LNCS 1110, pages 137–160, Schloß Dagstuhl, 1996. Springer-Verlag.
16. J. Gustedt. *Algorithmic Aspects of Ordered Structures*. PhD thesis, Technische Universität Berlin, 1992.
17. G. Higman. Ordering by divisibility in abstract algebras. *Proceedings of the London Mathematical Society*, 2:326–336, 1952.
18. G. Huet. Confluent reductions: Abstract properties and applications to term rewriting systems. *Journal of the ACM*, 27(4):797–821, 1980.
19. N. D. Jones, C. K. Gomard, and P. Sestoft. *Partial Evaluation and Automatic Program Generation*. Prentice Hall, 1993.
20. J. Jørgensen, M. Leuschel, and B. Martens. Conjunctive partial deduction in practice. In J. Gallagher, editor, *Proceedings of the International Workshop on Logic Program Synthesis and Transformation (LOPSTR'96)*, LNCS 1207, pages 59–82, Stockholm, Sweden, August 1996. Springer-Verlag.
21. J. B. Kruskal. Well-quasi ordering, the tree theorem, and Vazsonyi's conjecture. *Transactions of the American Mathematical Society*, 95:210–225, 1960.
22. L. Lafave and J. Gallagher. Constraint-based partial evaluation of rewriting-based functional logic programs. In N. Fuchs, editor, *Proceedings of the International Workshop on Logic Program Synthesis and Transformation (LOPSTR'97)*, LNCS 1463, pages 168–188, Leuven, Belgium, July 1998.
23. P. Lescanne. Rewrite orderings and termination of rewrite systems. In A. Tarlecki, editor, *Mathematical Foundations of Computer Science 1991*, LNCS 520, pages 17–27, Kazimierz Dolny, Poland, September 1991. Springer-Verlag.
24. P. Lescanne. Well rewrite orderings and well quasi-orderings. Technical Report N° 1385, INRIA-Lorraine, France, January 1991.
25. M. Leuschel. The ECCE partial deduction system and the DPPD library of benchmarks. Obtainable via `http://www.cs.kuleuven.ac.be/~dtai`, 1996.
26. M. Leuschel. *Advanced Techniques for Logic Program Specialisation*. PhD thesis, K.U. Leuven, May 1997. Accessible via `http://www.ecs.soton.ac.uk/~mal`.
27. M. Leuschel. Homeomorphic embedding for online termination. Technical Report DSSE-TR-98-11, Department of Electronics and Computer Science, University of Southampton, UK, October 1998.

28. M. Leuschel. On the power of homeomorphic embedding for online termination. In G. Levi, editor, Static Analysis. *Proceedings of SAS'98*, LNCS 1503, pages 230–245, Pisa, Italy, September 1998. Springer-Verlag.
29. M. Leuschel and D. De Schreye. Constrained partial deduction and the preservation of characteristic trees. *New Generation Computing*, 16(3):283–342, 1998.
30. M. Leuschel and B. Martens. Global control for partial deduction through characteristic atoms and global trees. In O. Danvy, R. Glück, and P. Thiemann, editors, *Proceedings of the 1996 Dagstuhl Seminar on Partial Evaluation*, LNCS 1110, pages 263–283, Schloß Dagstuhl, 1996. Springer-Verlag.
31. M. Leuschel, B. Martens, and D. De Schreye. Controlling generalisation and polyvariance in partial deduction of normal logic programs. *ACM Transactions on Programming Languages and Systems*, 20(1):208–258, January 1998.
32. N. Lindenstrauss, Y. Sagiv, and A. Serebrenik. Unfolding the mystery of mergesort. In N. Fuchs, editor, *Proceedings of the International Workshop on Logic Program Synthesis and Transformation (LOPSTR'97)*, LNCS 1463, pages 206–225, Leuven, Belgium, July 1998.
33. J. W. Lloyd. *Foundations of Logic Programming.* Springer-Verlag, 1987.
34. J. W. Lloyd and J. C. Shepherdson. Partial evaluation in logic programming. *The Journal of Logic Programming*, 11(3& 4):217–242, 1991.
35. R. Marlet. *Vers une Formalisation de l'Évaluation Partielle.* PhD thesis, Université de Nice - Sophia Antipolis, December 1994.
36. B. Martens. *On the Semantics of Meta-Programming and the Control of Partial Deduction in Logic Programming.* PhD thesis, K.U. Leuven, February 1994.
37. B. Martens and D. De Schreye. Automatic finite unfolding using well-founded measures. *The Journal of Logic Programming*, 28(2):89–146, August 1996.
38. B. Martens, D. De Schreye, and T. Horváth. Sound and complete partial deduction with unfolding based on well-founded measures. *Theoretical Computer Science*, 122(1–2):97–117, 1994.
39. B. Martens and J. Gallagher. Ensuring global termination of partial deduction while allowing flexible polyvariance. In L. Sterling, editor, *Proceedings ICLP'95*, pages 597–613, Kanagawa, Japan, June 1995. MIT Press.
40. A. Middeldorp and H. Zantema. Simple termination of rewrite systems. *Theoretical Computer Science*, 175(1):127–158, 1997.
41. L. Plümer. *Termination Proofs for Logic Programs.* LNCS 446. Springer-Verlag, 1990.
42. L. Puel. Using unavoidable set of trees to generalize Kruskal's theorem. *Journal of Symbolic Computation*, 8:335–382, 1989.
43. E. Ruf. *Topics in Online Partial Evaluation.* PhD thesis, Stanford University, March 1993.
44. D. Sahlin. Mixtus: An automatic partial evaluator for full Prolog. *New Generation Computing*, 12(1):7–51, 1993.
45. M. H. Sørensen. Convergence of program transformers in the metric space of trees. In *Mathematics of Program Construction, Proceedings of MPC'98*, LNCS 1422, pages 315–337. Springer-Verlag, 1998.
46. M. H. Sørensen and R. Glück. An algorithm of generalization in positive supercompilation. In J. W. Lloyd, editor, *Proceedings of ILPS'95, the International Logic Programming Symposium*, pages 465–479, Portland, USA, December 1995. MIT Press.
47. M. H. Sørensen, R. Glück, and N. D. Jones. A positive supercompiler. *Journal of Functional Programming*, 6(6):811–838, 1996.

48. J. Stillman. *Computational Problems in Equational Theorem Proving*. PhD thesis, State University of New York at Albany, 1988.
49. V. F. Turchin. The concept of a supercompiler. *ACM Transactions on Programming Languages and Systems*, 8(3):292–325, 1986.
50. W. Vanhoof and B. Martens. To parse or not to parse. In N. Fuchs, editor, *Proceedings of the International Workshop on Logic Program Synthesis and Transformation (LOPSTR'97)*, LNCS 1463, pages 322–342, Leuven, Belgium, July 1997.
51. A. Weiermann. Complexity bounds for some finite forms of Kruskal's theorem. *Journal of Symbolic Computation*, 18(5):463–488, November 1994.
52. D. Weise, R. Conybeare, E. Ruf, and S. Seligman. Automatic online partial evaluation. In *Proceedings of the Conference on Functional Programming Languages and Computer Architectures*, LNCS 523, pages 165–191, Harvard University, 1991. Springer-Verlag.

Successes in Logic Programs

Annalisa Bossi and Nicoletta Cocco

Dip. di Matematica Applicata e Informatica
Università di Venezia-Ca' Foscari - Italy
{bossi, cocco}@dsi.unive.it

Abstract. In this paper we study how to verify that a pure Prolog program has solutions for a given query. The detailed analysis of the failure/success behaviour of a program is necessary when dealing with transformation and verification of pure Prolog programs. In a previous work [10] we defined the class of noFD programs and queries which are characterized statically. We proved that a noFD query cannot have finitely failing derivations in a noFD program. Now, by introducing the concept of a set of exhaustive tests, we define the larger class of successful predicates. We prove that a noFD terminating query for successful predicates have at least one successful derivation. Moreover we propose some techniques based on program transformations for simplifying the verification of the successful condition.
Keywords and Phrases: pure Prolog programs, failure/success analysis, program transformations

1 Introduction

When developing a logic program we, more or less explicitly, have to analyze it with respect to correctness, termination properties and the existence of successful computations. On correctness and termination verification there have been rather many proposals such as [21, 8, 3, 12, 7, 24]. While for distinguishing failing and successful computations or for ensuring the presence of successes in a computation, very little is available, both in terms of methodology and tools. We can illustrate the kind of information on derivations we would like to infer through a few simple examples.

Example 1. Let us consider

```
reverse([], []).
reverse([X |Xs], Zs) ← reverse(Xs, Ys), append(Ys, [X], Zs).
app([], Ys, Ys).
app([X |Xs], Ys, [X |Zs]) ← app(Xs, Ys, Zs).
```

with the following modes and types: $reverse(+ : List, - : List)$ and $app(+ : List, + : List, - : List)$, where $+ : List$ means input term typed as a list and $- : List$ means output term typed as a list.
This well-known program shows the simplest case: a program which does not produce finitely failing derivations (FDs) when correctly queried. □

P. Flener (Ed.): LOPSTR'98, LNCS 1559, pp. 219–239, 1999.

In a previous work [10] we have given a sufficient condition for ensuring that a given program and query are without failures, namely they cannot have finitely failing derivations (noFD). Basically we formalize the following two observations. Let us consider *reverse* (or *app*), it is defined for any input in the specified mode and type, hence *any correct query cannot cause a failure in input.* Furthermore output terms in the body of its clauses are "new" variables, not appearing to the left, hence *reverse cannot cause a failure in output* since when the LD-resolution will reach the output terms, they will be still variables and then instantiable. As a consequence a well-typed query with "new" variables in output will not have FDs. The condition we give in [10] is very restrictive, since we want it to be simple and verifiable from the text of the program.

The requirement of not having FDs is useful in program transformations when we assume a Prolog interpreter, (this was our main motivation in [10]) and when reasoning on efficiency, but it is too strong in general. In fact in many cases we cannot expect the program not to have FDs, we would be satisfied to know that the program has at least one successful derivation for a given query.

Example 2. Let us consider

```
delete([], X, []).
delete([X |Xs], X, Ys) ← delete(Xs, X, Ys).
delete([X |Xs], Z, [X |Ys]) ← X ≠ Z, delete(Xs, Z, Ys).
```

with mode and type $delete(+ : List, + : Any, - : List)$.
This program can produce FDs since it contains *unification tests*, namely $X \neq Z$, which can fail. But, by examining also the heads of the clauses, we could observe that all possible cases are defined, namely they are *exhaustive on the input types.* Hence, since the mode and type guarantee termination, *delete* can be queried with at least one successful derivation. □

Example 3. Now let us consider:

```
posPivot(L, Pos) ← oddLength(L, Length),
   Pos is Length div 2 +1.
posPivot(L, 0) ← evenLength(L, Length).
oddLength(L, N) ← length(L, N), odd(N).
evenLength(L, N) ← length(L, N), even(N).
```

with modes and types: $posPivot(+ : List, - : Nat)$, $evenLength(+ : List, - : Nat)$, $oddLength(+ : List, - : Nat)$, $length(+ : List, - : Nat)$ and $even(+ : Nat)$, $odd(+ : Nat)$.
In this program the predicates $evenLength(L, N)$ and $oddLength(L, N)$ are used as tests and they can cause FDs. But also in this program we could show that the tests are exhaustive on the input types. Since the modes and types ensure termination, we can also show that *posPivot* can be queried with at least one successful derivation. □

From these few examples it should be evident that the failure/success analysis of a logic program is not such a simple task. The simple condition we define in [10], for ensuring that a program has no FDs, applies only to a rather small class of programs. Many programs have FDs since they use tests, which by definition are assumed to fail for some inputs. On the other hand, programs with tests generally use them to define a different behaviour for each possible input, namely they generally use a set of exhaustive tests. Hence in order to recognize that a program has at least one solution for a given query, we have to be able to recognize a set of exhaustive tests. Tests are not easy to characterize, they can be predefined and with input only, as in Example 2, or defined by the user and supplying also an output, as in Example 3. In this paper we intend to explore all these cases and to give a general methodology for failure/success analysis.

In Section 2 we set some notation and recall the definitions of noFD program and query. In Section 3 we give a general definition for *a set of exhaustive tests for a predicate* and we use it to define the *class of successful predicates*. We prove that *a noFD query, defined by successful predicates, has at least one successful LD-derivation, if it universally terminates*. In section 4 we propose some techniques, based on program transformations, for simplifying the verification of the successful property and describe a methodology for verifying that a predicate is successful. Conclusions follows in section 5.

2 Basic Notions

Given a substitution η and a set of variables X, we denote by $\eta_{|X}$ the substitution obtained from η by restricting its domain to X. Given an expression (term, atom, query,...) E, we denote the set of variables occurring in it by $Var(E)$. We often write $\eta_{|E}$ to denote $\eta_{|\,Var(E)}$. *A renaming* is a substitution which is a permutation of its domain. We write $E \sim E'$ to denote that E and E' are *variant expressions*, that is there exists a renaming ρ such that $E = E'\rho$. When a renaming of E maps $Var(E)$ in "new" variables we call it a *new renaming of* E and we speak of $E\rho$ as a *new variant of* E.

We consider definite logic programs executed by means of *LD-resolution*, which consists of the usual *SLD*-resolution combined with the leftmost selection rule as Prolog interpreters do. Throughout the paper we use queries instead of goals. A *query* is a sequence of atoms or **fail**. **fail** stands for the query associated to a failure and □ for the *empty query*. An *LD*-derivation ending with □ is a *successful LD-derivation*, one ending with **fail** is a *failing one (FD)*.

We consider the property of universal termination for a query **Q** in a program P, which means that the LD-tree of **Q** in P is finite. This termination property has been widely studied [7, 12, 24] and it ensures termination with a Prolog interpreter.

We denote sequences by bold characters and we call $p(\mathbf{X})$ a *general atom* when its terms are all distinct variables. We use identifiers to label clauses and derivations. Then $l : \mathbf{Q} \overset{*\sigma}{\longmapsto}_P \mathbf{R}$ stands for "an *LD*-derivation, l, of the query **Q** in P, which ends in the query **R** and σ is the composition of the relevant and idempotent *mgu's* applied during the derivation". Similarly $\mathbf{Q} \overset{*\sigma}{\longmapsto}_P$ □ denotes a successful LD-derivation of $\mathbf{Q}$ in P with c.a.s. $\sigma_{|\mathbf{Q}}$. $\mathbf{Q} \longmapsto^{\vartheta}_{P} \mathbf{R}$ denotes one derivation step, we say that it is *non-trivial* if $\mathbf{R}$ is not **fail**. The *length* of an LD-derivation l is denoted by $| \, l \, |$. The rest of the notation is more or less standard and essentially follows [23, 1].

We make use of the notion of modes and types introduced in [14, 5, 2]. We consider a combination of modes and types and adopt the following assumption: *every considered relation has a fixed mode and a fixed type associated with it.* This assumption allows us to talk about types of *input positions* and of *output positions of an atom.* For example, $app(+ : List, + : List, - : List)$ denotes a ternary relation *app* with the first two positions moded as input and typed as *List* and the third position moded as output and typed as *List*. A similar denotation is called *a directional type* in [13]. ¿From [5, 2] we take also the notion of *well-typed query and program,* which guarantees that mode and type properties are preserved through LD-resolution, and from [4] the notion of *simply moded clause and query.* Here we recall only the main definition of well-typed program. We need *type judgments,* namely statements of the form $\mathbf{s} : \mathbf{S} \Rightarrow \mathbf{t} : \mathbf{T}$. *A type judgment is true,* $\models \mathbf{s} : \mathbf{S} \Rightarrow \mathbf{t} : \mathbf{T}$, iff for all substitutions θ, $\mathbf{s}\theta \in \mathbf{S}$ implies $\mathbf{t}\theta \in \mathbf{T}$. To simplify the notation, when writing an atom as $p(\mathbf{u} : \mathbf{S}, \mathbf{v} : \mathbf{T})$, we assume that $\mathbf{u} : \mathbf{S}$ is a sequence of typed terms filling in the input positions of p and $\mathbf{v} : \mathbf{T}$ is a sequence of typed terms filling in the output positions of p.

Definition 1 (well-typed query, clause, program [2]).

- *A query* $p_1(\mathbf{i_1} : \mathbf{I_1}, \mathbf{o_1} : \mathbf{O_1}), \ldots, p_n(\mathbf{i_n} : \mathbf{I_n}, \mathbf{o_n} : \mathbf{O_n})$ *is* well-typed *iff for* $j \in [1, n]$
$$\models \mathbf{o_1} : \mathbf{O_1}, \ldots, \mathbf{o_{j-1}} : \mathbf{O_{j-1}} \Rightarrow \mathbf{i_j} : \mathbf{I_j}.$$
- *A clause* $p_0(\mathbf{o_0} : \mathbf{O_0}, \mathbf{i_{n+1}} : \mathbf{I_{n+1}}) \leftarrow p_1(\mathbf{i_1} : \mathbf{I_1}, \mathbf{o_1} : \mathbf{O_1}), \ldots, p_n(\mathbf{i_n} : \mathbf{I_n}, \mathbf{o_n} : \mathbf{O_n})$. *is* well-typed *iff for* $j \in [1, n+1]$
$$\models \mathbf{o_0} : \mathbf{O_0}, \ldots, \mathbf{o_{j-1}} : \mathbf{O_{j-1}} \Rightarrow \mathbf{i_j} : \mathbf{I_j}.$$
- *A program is* well-typed *iff every clause of it is.* □

Note that a query with only one atom is well-typed iff this atom is correctly typed in its input positions. Note also that being correctly typed in input does not necessarily implies groundness in input. For example $p([X_1, \ldots, X_n], N)$ is a well-typed query wrt the directional type $p(+ : List, - : Nat)$.

Besides we need the following definitions.

Definition 2 (simply moded sequence). *Let P be a well-typed program and $\mathbf{Q} = B_1, \ldots, B_m$ a well-typed query in P.* The input (output) terms of $\mathbf{Q}$, *denoted by $In(\mathbf{Q})(Out(\mathbf{Q}))$, are the terms in input (output) positions in $\mathbf{Q}$.*
$\mathbf{Q}$ *is simply moded iff* output positions are filled in with distinct variables which do not appear to the left, *namely* $\forall j \in [1, m]$, $Out(B_j) = Var(Out(B_j))$; *if $X_1, \ldots, X_k$ are the output terms in B_j, then $X_i \neq X_h$, for $i \neq h$, $i, h \in [1, k]$; and* $Out(B_j) \cap (Var(B_1, \ldots, B_{j-1}) \cup Var(In(B_j))) = \emptyset$. □

A simply moded sequence is exactly what is called simply moded query in [4].

Definition 3 (input-correct and simply moded instance). *Let A be an simply moded atom and α a substitution. We say that $A\alpha$ is an input-correct and simply moded instance of A iff $A\alpha$ is correctly typed in input and $Out(A\alpha)$ is a new variant of $Out(A)$.* □

Intuitively in an LD-derivation, FDs may happen when some term is instantiated in an "incorrect" way, namely this means that for avoiding FDs, inputs must be correctly given, while outputs should be correctly instantiated by the evaluation.

In [10] we define an interesting class of programs: *programs without failures (noFD programs)*. These programs have a clear functionality from input to output but they can be non-deterministic. They satisfy the strong property that, in an LD-derivation, for any selected atom correctly typed in input positions and with uninstantiated variables in output positions, there exists a unifying clause in P.

Definition 4 (noFD program). *Let P be a well-typed program.*
A clause $c : H \leftarrow A_1, \ldots, A_n.$ in P is without failures (noFD clause) *iff*

1. *c is simply moded (namely the sequence of atoms in the body, $A_1, \ldots, A_n$, is simply moded and $Var(In(H)) \cap Var(Out(A_1, \ldots, A_n)) = \emptyset$);*
2. *for all $i \in [1, n]$ and for any input-correct and simply moded instance $A_i\alpha$ of A_i, there exists a clause in P whose head unifies with $A_i\alpha$.*

A predicate p in P is without failures (noFD predicate) *iff all the clauses in (the deductive closure of) its definition in P are noFD ones. The program defining p is then* a program without failures (noFD program). □

The condition for being noFD is local, namely each clause can be considered separately. Only atoms in the clause bodies and in the queries have to satisfy the restrictions, on the head atoms no restriction is required. Hence *a well-typed program containing only facts is trivially noFD.*

We need also a similar condition on queries in order to guarantee that they do not introduce FDs.

Definition 5 (noFD query). *Let $\mathbf{Q} = B_1, \ldots, B_m$ be a well-typed query.*
$\mathbf{Q}$ is without failures (noFD query) in a program P *iff*

1. *the query $\mathbf{Q}$ is simply moded;*
2. *for $j \in [1, m]$ and for any input-correct and simply moded instance $B_j\alpha$ of B_j, there exists a clause in P whose head unifies with $B_j\alpha$.* □

Note that the first conditions in Definitions 4 and 5 are syntactic ones and then very simple to verify. The second conditions are more complex but, if a type definition is available, they can be statically verified since they just require unification. Hence the noFd-condition is decidable. For example given the definition of *list*, we can easily verify that *reverse* and *app* in Example 1 are noFD programs.

Let us consider the two queries $\mathbf{Q_1} = app([X], [2], [X|Xs])$ and $\mathbf{Q_2} = app([1], [2], [X|Xs])$ with the *app* program in Example 1. These queries are well-typed but they are not simply moded. Hence they are not noFD queries; they have no FDs though. This shows us that *the noFD property is a sufficient condition, but not necessary for the absence of FDs.*

noFD programs and queries form a rather restricted class since output terms in the query and in body atoms must always be uninstantiated variables. Moreover tests are not allowed. Let us consider the programs in Examples 2, 3. They are not noFD. The presence of test predicates in the bodies makes impossible to the second condition in the noFD definition to be satisfied for all clauses.

In [10] we also prove the "persistency" of the noFD property through LD-derivation and the main result, namely that a noFD query in a noFD program cannot have FDs.

Lemma 1. *Let P be a noFD program and* $\mathbf{Q}$ *a noFD query in P. Let us consider one non-trivial LD-derivation step* $\mathbf{Q} \longmapsto^{\vartheta}_{P} \mathbf{Q}'$. *The query* $\mathbf{Q}'$ *is also noFD.* □

Theorem 1. *Let P be a noFD program and* $\mathbf{Q}$ *a noFD query in P. Then* $\mathbf{Q}$ *cannot have finitely failing derivations.* □

In [10] we also discuss the use of noFD condition both in the field of verification of program properties and in the field of program transformations. We give some examples showing how the noFD property can greatly simplify the applicability conditions of transformation operations, such as decreasing unfolding, replacement and switch, in transformation systems which take into account termination properties.

3 Successful Predicates

As we saw the first condition in Definition 4 is simple but restrictive since it forbids compound terms in output. This could be either bypassed by program transformation or weakened by allowing also restricted compound terms in output.

The second solution could be obtained by considering *nicely moded clauses and queries* [16] instead of simply moded ones in Definitions 4 and 5. This would allow also compound terms in output, but they must contain only "new" variables. Nicely moded programs have been studied in connection with unification freedom properties. This enlargement would rather complicate the verification of the noFD property since we should check also the type structure in the compound terms.

The first solution can be illustrated by means of a simple example.

Example 4. Let us consider

```
last(L, E) ← reverse(L, [E| Xs]).
```

with directional type $last(+ : List, - : Any)$ and $reverse(+ : List, - : List)$. This program is not noFD since the atom $reverse(L, [E|Xs])$ is not simply moded. But we could transform it into the equivalent program

```
last(L, E) ← reverse(L, Zs), selFirst(Zs, E).
selFirst([X| Xs], X).
```

with directional type $last(+ : List, - : Any)$, $reverse(+ : List, - : List)$ and $selFirst(+ : List, - : Any)$.
This program is noFD. □

Hence *by explicitly introducing subterm selectors and constructors it is possible to transform a non-noFD program into a noFD one.*

Let us consider now the second, more serious, restriction given by our noFD definition: using tests in a program prevents it to be noFD. In this section we define a class which is wider than the one of noFD programs and which characterizes a weaker property: the programs in the class can have FDs but, when the query universally terminates, it has at least one successful derivation. We call it *the class of successful programs.* In order to give a simple definition of such a class of programs, we need to define the property of a set of tests of considering all possible cases in input.

First of all we need to identify tests. We do not give a definition of what a test is, for us it is just a predicate which can fail. Hence it cannot be noFD. The noFD property does not characterize non-failure (it is not a necessary condition), then also its negation, the non-noFD property, does not characterize the failure property (it is not sufficient). On the other hand the simplest heuristics for identifying tests among body atoms is to choose both non-noFD atoms (queries) and atoms which are noFD but their definition is not. In the following we assume that, given a program, we can partition the atoms in the clause bodies into tests and non-tests.

Definition 6 (exhaustive tests). *Let P be a well-typed program wrt the directional type T and let p be a predicate defined in P by the clauses* $p(\mathbf{t_i}) \leftarrow \mathbf{T_i}, \mathbf{B_i}.$, *with* $i \in [1, m]$.
$\{\mathbf{T_1}, \ldots, \mathbf{T_m}\}$ are exhaustive tests for p wrt input types in T *iff for any A, input-correct and simply moded instance of the general atom* $p(\mathbf{X})$, *there exists* i, $i \in [1, m]$, *such that* $\sigma = mgu(A, p(\mathbf{t_i}))$ *and* $\mathbf{T_i}\sigma$ *has at least one successful LD-derivation.* □

Example 5. Let us consider the following trivial program

```
p(X, Y, Z) ← X = Y, r(1, Z).
p(a, B, Z) ← some(B), r(2, Z).
p(b, a, Z) ← r(3, Z).
p(b, c, Z) ← r(4, Z).
some(b).
some(c).
r(X, Y) ← ...
```

with directional type:
$T = p(+ : \{a, b\}, + : \{a, b, c\}, - : R), = (+ : Any, + : Any), some(+ : \{a, b, c\}),$ $r(+ : \{1, 2, 3, 4\}, - : R)$.

We identify $X = Y$ and $some(B)$ as tests since they are not noFD (condition 2 in Definition 5 is not satisfied).
$\{X = Y, some(B), true, true\}$ are exhaustive tests for p wrt input types in T. In fact input-correct and simply moded instances A of $p(X1, X2, X3)$ are such that the first term of A is in $\{a, b\}$ and the second in $\{a, b, c\}$.
Let us consider all possible cases.
1) $A = p(a, a, T)$ or $A = p(b, b, T)$, then the first definition of p can be chosen and $\sigma = mgu(A, p(X, Y, Z))$, with $\sigma = \{X/a, Y/a, T/Z\}$ or $\sigma = \{X/b, Y/b, T/Z\}$. In both cases the test $(X = Y)\sigma$ is successful.
2) $A = p(a, b, T)$ or $A = p(a, c, T)$, then the second definition of p can be chosen and $\sigma = mgu(A, p(a, B, Z))$, with $\sigma = \{B/b, T/Z\}$ or $\sigma = \{B/c, T/Z\}$. In both cases the test $some(B)\sigma$ is successful.
3) $A = p(b, a, T)$, then the third definition of p can be chosen and $\sigma = mgu(A, p(b, a, Z))$, with $\sigma = \{T/Z\}$. The test $(true)\sigma$ is successful.
4) $A = p(b, c, T)$, then the forth definition of p can be chosen and $\sigma = mgu(A, p(b, c, Z))$, with $\sigma = \{T/Z\}$. The test $(true)\sigma$ is successful.
Since the condition in Definition 6 is satisfied, the tests are exhaustive. □

The previous example shows that *we can always introduce a dummy test "true" in a clause* in order to complete the set of exhaustive tests associated to a predicate p with types in T. When p is defined also by facts, the introduction of the dummy test "true" is necessary for satisfying Definition 6.

Verifying exhaustiveness of tests for a given predicate and input types is not easy, it is a semantic condition and not decidable in general, as shown in [18]. In the following Section we will discuss this issue by showing cases in which the verification is simple and we will propose simplifications which can help in the verification. For the moment we assume to be able to verify the exhaustive property when necessary.

Since we assume that we can partition the body atoms into tests and non-tests, we can restrict the deductive dependency relation to non-test predicates.

Definition 7 (s-dependency). *Let P be a well-typed program and p a predicate defined in P by the clauses $p(\mathbf{t_i}) \leftarrow \mathbf{T_i}, \mathbf{B_i}.$, with $i \in [1, m]$, and $\mathbf{T_i}$ tests.*
p s-depends on q *iff q is a predicate symbol in $\mathbf{B_i}$ with $i \in [1, m]$.*
$\prec_P$ denotes the transitive closure of s-dependency in P.
$sDep(p)$ is the set of predicates from which p s-depends also indirectly: $sDep(p) = \{q \mid p \prec_P q\}$. □

Now we can give the main definition.

Definition 8 (successful predicate). *Let P be a well-typed program wrt the directional type T.*
A predicate p in P is successful *wrt the input types in T iff*

for all the predicates q in $sDep(p) \cup \{p\}$ the following two conditions are verified:

let $q(\mathbf{t_i}) \leftarrow \mathbf{T_i}, \mathbf{B_i}.$, with $i \in [1, m]$, be the clauses defining q in P,

1. *$\mathbf{T_1}, \ldots, \mathbf{T_m}$ are exhaustive tests for q wrt input types in T;*

2. (noFD conditions) *for* $i \in [1, m]$
- *the sequence* $\mathbf{B_i}$ *is simply moded;*
- $Var(Out(\mathbf{B_i}) \cap (Var(In(q(\mathbf{t_i}))) \cup Var(\mathbf{T_i})) = \emptyset$;
- *for all* $D \in \mathbf{B_i}$ *and for any input-correct and simply moded instance* $D\alpha$ *of* D, *there exists a clause in* P *whose head unifies with* $D\alpha$. □

The intuitive idea is that if p is a successful predicate, for any input-correct and simply moded query $p(\mathbf{t})$, there is at least a clause in the definition of p which is applicable, whose tests are successful and which produces a non-finitely failing derivation (noFD conditions on the atoms in the body which follow the tests). Examples 2, 3 are successful predicates.

Note that we require that tests are leftmost in the clause bodies. This is clearly a restriction, since tests can appear also in other positions. For example let us consider a non-tail recursive definition of the maximum element in a list of integers. On the other hand this requirement could be dropped and we could give a more general (yet more complex) definition and proof.

Note also that *a noFD predicate which is defined for any well-typed input is a successful predicate.* In fact we can always introduce the dummy test *true* in all the clauses, thus having tests which are trivially exhaustive. For this reason also *reverse* and *app* in Example 1 are successful predicates.

For successful predicates we can prove that any noFD query which universally terminates has at least one successful derivation. We need two simple Lemmata first.

Lemma 2. *Let* $\mathbf{Q}$ *be simply moded and* σ *be a substitution such that* $Var(\sigma) \cap Var(\mathbf{Q}) \subseteq (Var(In(\mathbf{Q})) - Var(Out(\mathbf{Q})))$. *Then* $\mathbf{Q}\sigma$ *is simply moded.*

Proof. Immediate from the definition of simply moded sequence and the condition on the substitution σ. □

Lemma 3. *Let* $\mathbf{Q_1}$ *and* $\mathbf{Q_2}$ *be simply moded and such that* $Var(\mathbf{Q_1}) \cap Var(Out(\mathbf{Q_2})) = \emptyset$. *Then* $\mathbf{Q_1Q_2}$ *is simply moded.*

Proof. Immediate from the definition of simply moded sequence. □

Theorem 2. *Let* $\mathbf{Q}$ *be a noFD query in* P. *If* $\mathbf{Q}$ *is universally terminating in* P *and all the predicates in* $\mathbf{Q}$ *are successful in* P *wrt the input types, then* $\mathbf{Q}$ *has at least one successful LD-derivation in* P.

Proof. See the Appendix. □

4 How to Verify that a Program is Successful

The conditions in Definition 8 are not so easy to verify. Problems are in condition 1, namely how to single out tests and to prove that they are exhaustive. In this section we propose some techniques for simplifying such task and a strategy for the failure/success analysis.

4.1 Accepted input types

In Definitions 6 and 8 we state that a noFD predicate is successful only if it is defined for any correct input wrt to its directional type. A simple example will show the point.

Example 6. Let us consider the following simple program

```
last([X],X).
last([X, Y| Xs], E) ← last([Y| Xs], E).
```

with directional type $last(+ : List, - : Any)$.
last is noFD but not successful. In fact by introducing the dummy test true we get the program

```
last([X],X) ← true.
last([X, Y| Xs], E) ← true, last([Y| Xs], E).
```

where $\{true, true\}$ are not exhaustive tests for *last* wrt the input types since *last* is not defined for empty lists.
But we can restrict the directional type associated to *last* to $last(+ : List^+, - : Any)$, where $List^+ = List - \{[]\}$.
Now the program is both noFD and successful. □

Often the directional type associated to a predicate is actually larger than the types for which the predicate is defined. We can weaken the requirements in Definition 6 by introducing the notion of *input types accepted by a predicate.*

Definition 9 (accepted input types). *Let P be a well-typed program and p a predicate defined in P by the clauses* $p(t_{i1}, \ldots, t_{in}, s_{i1}, \ldots, s_{ir}) \leftarrow \mathbf{B_i}.$, *with* $i \in [1, m]$, *where* t_{ik}, $k \in [1, n]$, *are input terms and* s_{ih}, $h \in [1, r]$, *output terms. Let* T_k, *for* $k \in [1, n]$, *be the types associated to the input positions in the directional type of p.*
The input types accepted by p, AT_k, for $k \in [1, n]$, *shortly* accepted input types, *are given by the sets of all the instances of terms in the k-th input positions of the heads of the definitions of p which belongs to* T_k*:*
$AT_k = (\cup_\beta \{t_{1k}\beta, \ldots, t_{mk}\beta\}) \cap T_k$. □

In a well-typed program the accepted input types can be subsets of the input types declared in the directional type. They are the sets of terms which can be effectively used as inputs when querying the predicate.

Abstract Interpretation techniques can be used for inferring type information for a program [15, 19, 17], with these techniques accepted input types are inferred. In order to automatize the verification of the successful property, we could then exploit tools for Abstract Interpretation.

The definitions of exhaustive tests and successful predicate can be restricted to accepted input types. In this case the condition on exhaustive tests in Definition 6 is simplified since there always exists a clause $i \in [1, m]$ and an mgu σ for any input-correct and simply moded instance of the predicate.

Note that the property of being well-typed wrt a directional type is not preserved in general when we restrict the input types to the accepted ones.

Example 7. Let us consider the following program

```
last([X], X).
last([X| Xs], E) ← last(Xs, E).
```

this predicate is well-typed wrt the directional type $last(+ : List, - : Any)$ but it is not well-typed wrt $last(+ : List^{+}, - : Any)$ which is the directional type we obtain when we restrict it to accepted input types. □

The mismatch between the declared directional type and the accepted input types always causes problems wrt failure/success analysis: wrt the first directional type *last* is not noFD, in fact the second condition in Definition 4 is not satisfied since Xs in the body can be an empty list.

In the following we assume that the directional type associated to a predicate are already restricted wrt accepted input types.

4.2 Exhaustiveness of tests

A major difficulty in using Definition 8 is the identification of exhaustive tests. We need to be able to single out some body atoms in a predicate definition and to prove that they are a set of exhaustive tests for that predicate. Atoms which are eligible as tests are the ones which do not satisfy noFD conditions (condition 2 in Definition 8). Proving that they are exhaustive is not trivial. It is a semantic condition and not decidable in general, as shown in [18], but in most practical cases the conditions in Definition 8 can be verified.

Let us consider Example 3. *odd* and *even* are non-noFD predicates, hence also *oddLength* and *evenLength* which depend on them are non-noFD. In the definition of *posPivot* we choose them as tests. We should prove that $\{oddLength(L, Length), evenLength(L, Length)\}$ are exhaustive for *posPivot* wrt input types. This means to prove that $\forall L \in List, \mid L \mid = n \in Nat$ and then $\forall n \in Nat, even(n) \vee odd(n)$. In these very general cases, specifications could give us the knowledge we need for our proofs.

We could also study a priori a set of predicates and prove that for any input value at least one of them is successful. This would give us "a tool" for verifying the condition in Definition 6. An appropriate set of such "tools" could capture most sets of exhaustive tests.

Among the most common sets of tests are *arithmetic tests*. Let us consider the set $\{x < y, x \geq y\}$. We can verify once for all that for any pair $x, y \in S$, where S is any subset of Int, at least one inequality is true and successful with a Prolog interpreter. Similarly for $\{x \leq y, x > y\}$ and $\{x \leq y, x \geq y\}$.

Example 8. Let us consider the program

```
gcd(X, 0, X).
gcd(X, Y, Gcd) ← mod(X, Y, Z), gcd(Y, Z, Gcd).
mod(X, Y, X) ← X<Y.
mod(X, Y, Z) ← X>=Y, X1 is X-Y, mod(X1, Y, Z).
```

with directional type $gcd(+ : Int^+, + : Int^+, - : Int^+)$ and $mod(+ : Int^+, + : Int^+, - : Int^+)$, where Int^+ is the set of non-negative integers.
mod contains $X < Y$ and $X >= Y$. Any correct application of the clauses defining *mod* will instantiate both X and Y to terms in Int^+. We can then use our previous result and easily prove that such tests are exhaustive on the input types and then both *gcd* and *mod* are successful predicates. □

Another common set of tests which we can easily study a priori is given by *unification tests*, namely $\{x = y, x \neq y\}$, with $x, y \in T$ and T any type. Unification is decidable, then at least one of the two is true and successful.

If we allow negation in tests, we could consider also *user-defined ground tests* such as for all predicate symbol p $\{p(\mathbf{x}), not\ p(\mathbf{x})\}$, with $\mathbf{x} \in \mathbf{T}$ and $\mathbf{T}$ ground types. Since negation-as-failure for ground atoms corresponds to classical logic, we know that at least one of the two is true and successful with a Prolog interpreter.

Example 9. Let us consider

```
split([], Set2, [], []).
split(Set1, [], Set1, []).
split([X |Xs], Set2, [X |Complement], Intersection) ←
  not member(X, Set2), split(Xs,Set2,Complement,Intersection).
split([X |Xs], Set2, Complement, [X |Intersection]) ←
  member(X, Set2), split(Xs, Set2, Complement, Intersection).
member(X, [X |Xs]).
member(X, [Y |Ys]) ← member(X, Ys).
```

with directional type $split(+ : GroundList, + : GroundList, - : GroundList, - : GroundList)$ and $member(+ : Ground, + : GroundList)$.
This program contains tests predicates, namely $member(X, Set2)$ and $not\ member$ $(X, Set2)$, which for any correct use of *split* will become ground. By our previous observation we can easily prove that such tests are exhaustive on the input types. Then we can prove that *split* is successful. □

By knowing more on the interpreter we could enlarge our set of "tools".

Example 10. Let us consider $\{odd(x), even(x)\}$, with $x \in Nat$. Suppose we know that for each choice of x for the Prolog interpreter at least one of the two is successful. Then when considering the program

```
doubleEven([], []).
doubleEven([X |Xs], [X |Ys]) ← odd(X), doubleEven(Xs, Ys).
doubleEven([X |Xs], [Y |Ys]) ← even(X), Y is X*2,
   doubleEven(Xs, Ys).
```

with directional type $doubleEven(+ : NatList, - : NatList)$ and $even(+ : Nat)$, $odd(+ : Nat)$;
we could easily verify that $\{true, odd(X), even(X)\}$ are exhaustive for $doubleEven$, with $X \in Nat$. □

4.3 Input-normalization

In order to use the predefined knowledge in the "tools" we have to instantiate our set of tests with input types. But instantiation is often not enough in order to recognize a well-known case. Let us consider Example 2. There is only one explicit test, $X \neq Z$. Nevertheless we should recognize that *delete* is using unification tests, where the complementary test $X = Z$ is implicit in the head of the second clause. To make it easier (and more automatizable) we introduce a transformation for normalizing input arguments in a program.

Definition 10 (input-normalized definition). *Let P be a well-typed program and* $p(i_1, \ldots, i_n, o_1, \ldots, o_r)$ *a predicate defined in P, where* i_k*, with* $k \in [1, n]$*, are the input positions and* o_h*, with* $h \in [1, r]$ *the output positions in p. Let* $V = \{X_1, \ldots, X_n\}$ *be a set of new variables wrt p, namely variables which do not appear in the definition of p.*
The input-normalized definition of p, p^N, *is the program obtained by substituting each clause in the definition of p:* $p(t_1, \ldots, t_n, s_1, \ldots, s_r) \leftarrow \mathbf{D}$.
with the corresponding input-normalized clause*:* $p(X_1, \ldots, X_n, s_1, \ldots, s_r) \leftarrow X_1 = t_1, \ldots, X_n = t_n, \mathbf{D}$.
The program thus obtained is input-normalized wrt p. V *is* the set of normalized input variables for p^N.
$X_k = t_k$*, for* $k \in [1, n]$*, are* the input equalities in each clause in the definition of p^N, *with directional type* $= (+ : T_k, - : T_k)$*, where* T_k *is the type associated to the k-th input position.* □

Input-normalization is similar to a transformation, used both in program transformation techniques and in Abstract Interpretation, which we could call "head-normalization". In such transformation the resulting clauses heads must have only distinct variables as arguments and this is obtained by introducing appropriate equalities in the clauses bodies.

Let us now briefly discuss the properties of input-normalization.

Lemma 4. *Let P be a well-typed program and p a predicate defined in P. Let us associate in* p^N*, to each input equality* $X_k = t_k$*, the directional type* $= (+ : T_k, - : T_k)$*, where* T_k *is the type associated to the k-th input position in the directional type of p. Then* p^N *is well-typed.*

Proof. Trivial, by Definition of well-typed clause. □

Lemma 5. *Let P be a well-typed program and p a predicate defined in P.* p^N *is clause-wise equivalent to p.*

Proof. By unfolding the input equalities in each clause in p^N, we obtain the clauses of p again. On the other hand we already proved [9] that unfolding preserves both c.a.s. and universal termination. □

Note that *the property of being noFD is not preserved through input-normalization.* In fact even if the original predicate p is noFD, p^N can be non-noFD since in general input equalities do not satisfy the simply modedness condition in Definition 4.

Example 11. Let us define app^N wrt the directional type $app(+ : List, + : List, - : List)$.

```
app(X1, X2, Ys) ← X1 = [], X2 = Ys.
app(X1, X2, [X |Zs]) ← X1 = [X |Xs], X2 = Ys, app(Xs, Ys, Zs).
```

app^N is not noFD. It does not satisfy the first syntactic condition in Definition 4 since compound terms are in output in the input equalities in the bodies. □

We assume that *input-normalized programs always refer to the accepted input types of the original program.* Let us consider again Example 2.

Example 12. After input-normalization we obtain:

```
delete(X1,X2, []) ← X1 = [], X2 = X.
delete(X1,X2, Ys) ← X1 = [X |Xs], X2 = X,
    delete(Xs, X, Ys).
delete(X1,X2,[X |Ys]) ← X1 = [X |Xs], X2 = Z, X ≠ Z,
    delete(Xs, Z, Ys).
```

We can determine tests predicates by composing the input equalities introduced by input-normalization with atoms in the clause bodies for which noFD conditions are not satisfied. Namely we consider the tests:

$\mathbf{T_1} = (X_1 = [], X_2 = X)$,
$\mathbf{T_2} = (X_1 = [X \mid Xs], X_2 = X)$,
$\mathbf{T_3} = (X_1 = [X \mid Xs], X_2 = Z, X \neq Z)$.

Note that both the input equality $X_2 = X$ in the second clause and the built-in predicate $X \neq Z$ in the third clause have a directional type $(+ : Any, + : Any)$ which is induced by the well-typing condition.

Let us consider an input-correct and simply moded instance of delete. Either X_1 is an empty list and the first test $\mathbf{T_1}$ is successful, or X_1 is a non-empty list. In this second case $X \in Any$ and we have an alternative between $(X_2 = X)$ and $(X_2 = Z, X \neq Z)$. By unfolding $X_2 = Z$ in the second test we get to the two tests $(X_2 = X)$ and $(X \neq X_2)$, which have directional type $(+ : Any, + : Any)$. Since we know that they are an exhaustive set of tests (unification tests), also $\{\mathbf{T_1}, \mathbf{T_2}, \mathbf{T_3}\}$ are exhaustive for $delete^N$.

The other two (noFD) conditions are easy to verify on the recursive atoms. □

4.4 Input-subsumption

In order to make easier to prove the property of being exhaustive tests for a predicate, it is often useful to "simplify" the set of clauses we consider. To this purpose we introduce the following definition.

Definition 11 (Clause input-subsumed by a fact or a clause). *Let P be a well-typed program. Let $c_1 : A.$ be a fact, $c_2 : H \leftarrow \mathbf{B}.$ and $c_3 : K \leftarrow \mathbf{A}.$ be clauses in P which define the same predicate, namely $A = p(\mathbf{t_1})$, $H = p(\mathbf{t_2})$ and $K = p(\mathbf{t_3})$.*

Clause c_2 is input-subsumed by the fact c_1 *iff there exists an input substitution*

θ such that $A\theta = H$.
Clause c_3 is input-subsumed by clause c_2 *iff there exists an input substitution θ such that $H\theta = K$.* □

Example 13. Let us consider the trivial program

```
1: p(X, Y).
2: p(a, Y) ← r(a), s(Y).
3: p(X, b) ← r(X).
4: p(a, b) ← r(a), p(a, Y).
5: r(b).
6: s(b).
```

well-typed wrt the directional type $p(+ : Const, - : Const), r(+ : Const), s(- : Const)$.
Clause 2 is input-subsumed by fact 1.
Clause 4 is input-subsumed by clause 3. □

We have extended the usual concept of subsumption to fit the verification of the successful property. We are not interested in c.a.s. but in characterizing the presence of at least one successful derivation for each well-typed input substitution. A fact always produces a successful derivation, then it can input-subsume a clause independently from its body. Similarly for two clauses, if the one accepting a more general input produces a successful derivation, then the other one becomes irrelevant. Input-subsumption can be used to prune the program. If we can prove that a pruned definition of a predicate is successful, then also the original definition is successful. This means that we may simplify the verification of Definition 8 by first pruning the program of some input-subsumed clauses. The simplification phase must be applied before input-normalization; after input-normalization input-subsumption becomes trivial and useless.

Example 14. let us consider:

```
choose(Low, High, Low).
choose(Low, High, X) ← Low < High, L is Low +1,
    choose(L, High, Low).
```

with directional type $choose(+ : Int, + : Int, - : Int)$.
This program is non-deterministic and the second clause is input-subsumed by the first one which is a fact and then noFD. Hence we can conclude that also *choose* is successful. □

By pruning input-subsumed clauses we often succeed in reducing the non-trivial problem of verifying that a predicate is successful, to the much simpler problem of verifying that the pruned predicate is noFD.

4.5 Analysis strategy

We now propose a strategy for the failure/success analysis which allows us to exploit the simplifications already presented.

Given a predicate p in P the analysis could proceed as follows:

1. check that we are referring to *accepted input types* for p (for instance by Abstract Interpretation);
2. *check if the predicate* p *is noFD*;
3. otherwise *prune* p *by eliminating some input-subsumed clauses* and check if it is now noFD; in this case we can state that the predicate is successful;
4. If not, for all predicates q in $sDep(p) \cup \{p\}$:
   - *input-normalize*;
   - *single out the tests in the bodies of the definition clauses* (the input equalities plus the body atoms which do not satisfy the noFD conditions);
   - *prove that they are exhaustive* (with some predefined knowledge);
   - *prove that the noFD conditions in Definition 8 are verified*;

   in this case we can state that the predicate is successful.

With this strategy the verification of the successful condition is done only when the noFD property is not sufficient.

Step (1) is optional, but it can help to verify the next conditions.

The pruning step (3) can be performed in many ways in general, namely, given a predicate definition, it may be possible to identify many subsets of clauses with the property that each clause in the predicate definition is input-subsumed by at least one clause in the subset. We might need to explore this nondeterminism in order to find a solution to the failure/success analysis. The simplest case is when we succeed in reducing our initial problem of verifying that a predicate is successful to the much simpler one of verifying that it is noFD.

4.6 Applications

The property of being successful can be useful in the field of *program verification*. Let us assume to have a program which is partially correct wrt a specification and a query which is both universally terminating and partially correct wrt the specification. Then, if we prove that the query is noFD and the predicates in the query are successful, Theorem 2 guarantees the existence of at least one correct c.a.s. This corresponds to give a proof of completeness with respect to both the Herbrand semantics and the S-semantics (the c.a.s. semantics). In fact for a ground query we are exactly proving completeness, and in general we are proving that the model of the program is not empty wrt the query.

Also in the field of *program transformations* being successful can be useful in particular for switching atoms in the clause bodies. In [11] we consider left-terminating programs [6] and we define a sufficient condition for switching atoms while preserving left-termination. This condition for switching the atom A with B in a clause $c : H \leftarrow \mathbf{J}, A, B, \mathbf{K}$. depends on the property of A of being "non-failing", namely *for each grounding substitution* θ, *such that* $Dom(\theta) = Var(In(H), \mathbf{J}, In(A))$ *and* $\mathbf{J}\theta \in M_P$, *there exists* γ *such that* $A\theta\gamma \in M_P$, where M_P is the least Herbrand model of P. This intuitively means that if A is the selected atom in an LD-derivation, because c was used as input clause in a previous derivation step, then the computation of A will eventually succeed. This is a "semantic" condition which is not easy to verify in general. But *if we prove that the query A is universally terminating and noFD and the predicate in A is successful, then the non-failing condition is guaranteed.*

Example 15. Let us consider an example of transformation given in [11]. The following program defines the predicate $goodpath(X, Xs)$ which relates a node X with a list Xs of "good" nodes which are connected to X.

```
1: path(X, [X]).
2: path(X, [X |Xs]) ← arc(X, Y), path(Y, Xs).
3: goodlist([]).
4: goodlist([X |Xs]) ← good(X), goodlist(Xs).
d: goodpath(X, Xs) ← path(X, Xs), goodlist(Xs).
```

The directional type is $path(+ : Const, - : List), goodlist(+ : List), goodpath(+ : Const, - : List), arc(+ : Const, - : Const), good(+ : Const)$.
The predicates *good* and *arc* are test predicates defined in the program.
In [11] we consider a transformation which repeatedly unfold the body atoms in d until we get to:

```
d1:goodpath(X, [X]) ← good(X).
d2:goodpath(X, [X |Xs]) ← arc(X, Y),path(Y, Xs), good(X),
      goodlist(Xs).
```

In order to optimize the program by folding with d, we need to switch $path(Y, Xs)$ and $good(X)$ in $d2$.
Hence we need to prove that $path(Y, Xs)$ is non-failing in d2, namely that
a) for each grounding substitution θ, such that $Dom(\theta) = \{X, Y\}$ and $Y\theta \in Const$, $path(Y, Xs)\theta$ is a noFD query and
b) *path* is a successful predicate.
(a) is trivial. For (b) let us consider the definition of *path* given by clauses 1 and 2. We can prune 2, since it is input-subsumed by the fact 1. Hence we obtain a noFD program given by a single fact, which implies that *path* is successful. □

5 Conclusion

In program verification and transformation it is important to identify both the queries which have successful LD-derivations and those which have also finitely failing LD-derivations.

In a previous work we have defined the class of noFD programs and queries [10] which have the property of not having finitely failing derivations. In this paper we extend our previous work by defining the wider class of successful predicates which includes also programs using tests. We prove that noFD queries for successful predicates have the property of having at least one successful derivation, if they are universally terminating. This property is more complex to verify than the noFD one, hence we suggest some techniques, based on program transformations, for simplifying the failure/success analysis.

Our work is clearly related to those on cardinality analysis, for example in [20, 17]. In these works an approximation of the number of c.a.s. for a query is estimated by means of Abstract Interpretation.

Success analysis is interesting also for parallel execution optimization. In [18] a technique is proposed for detecting programs and queries which produce at least one solution or do not terminate. The technique deals with programs containing tests and it is based on a different notion of mode and type information from ours. An algorithm is given for unification and arithmetic tests. The algorithm can decide if they "cover" a type by using Abstract Interpretation. The technique is implemented and a report on its implementation is also given. The technique proposed in [18] is applicable to some of our examples: 8 and, after input-normalization, 2. Since they do not consider the simple case when there are noFD, their rather sophisticated algorithm is applied also to noFD programs such as 1.

In the Mercury language [22] a nondeterminism analysis is implemented which is related with our work. Given a predicate p with mode m, there are six *determinism categories* for describing the result of any query for p and m. The six categories are: *det* (exactly one success), *multi* (at least one success), *semidet* (fail or exactly one success), *nondet* (fail or at least one success), *failure* (fail) and *erroneous* (run-time error). Mercury can infer a category for p and m which is an approximation of the real one and can use such information for optimizing programs. The category *multi* corresponds to our successful class, while there is no Mercury category corresponding to our noFD class. It is not so easy to give a comparison with Mercury since no formal semantics is given, but we can make a few observations. The determinism analysis in Mercury is richer than our failure/success analysis, but it gives no information on the presence/absence of FDs in a non-finitely failing *LD*-tree. It infers an approximation of the real determinism category and it could then be not precise. The inference of *multi* cannot be simplified by first pruning the program and then verifying the noFD property as we propose, nevertheless also in Mercury there are explicit ways to eliminate nondeterminism and to prune a program. In Mercury well-moding, and then well-typing, are not wrt a leftmost selection rule (Prolog rule). For Mercury it is sufficient that there exists an order of body atoms for which clauses are well-typed.

Anyway the major difference between our work and related ones, is in purpose. The techniques based on Abstract Interpretation are generally meant for optimization in compilers, hence the emphasis is on automatizability and approximation. We are more interested in program verification and transformation, hence generality and precision is our concern.

Acknowledgments
This work was supported partly by Italian MURST with the National Research Project 9701248444-004 on "Tecniche formali per la specifica, l'analisi, la verifica, la sintesi e la trasformazione di sistemi software" and partly by Italian C.N.R. with the "Progetto Coordinato - Programmazione Logica: Strumenti per Analisi

e Trasformazione di Programmi; Tecniche di Ingegneria del Software; Estensioni con Vincoli, Concorrenza, Oggetti".

References

1. Apt, K. R.: Introduction to Logic Programming. In van Leeuwen, J. (ed.): Handbook of Theoretical Computer Science, volume B: Formal Models and Semantics. Elsevier, Amsterdam and The MIT Press, Cambridge (1990)
2. Apt, K. R.: Declarative Programming in Prolog. In Miller, D. (ed.): Proceedings of the 1993 International Symposium on Logic Programming, The MIT Press (1993) 12–35
3. Apt, K. R.: From Logic Programming to Prolog. Prentice Hall International Series in Computer Science (1997)
4. Apt, K. R., Etalle, S.: On the Unification Free Prolog Programs. In Borzyszkowski, A., Sokolowski, S. (eds.): Proceedings of the Conference on Mathematical Foundations of Computer Science (MFCS 93). Lecture Notes in Computer Science, vol.711, Springer-Verlag, Berlin (1993) 1–19
5. Apt, K. R., Marchiori, E.: Reasoning about Prolog Programs: from Modes through Types to Assertions. Formal Aspects of Computing, 6(6A) (1994) 743–765
6. Apt, K. R., Pedreschi, D.: Studies in Pure Prolog: Termination. In Lloyd J.W. (ed.): Proceedings of the Simposium in Computational Logic, Springer-Verlag, Berlin (1990) 150–176
7. Apt, K.R., Pedreschi, D.: Reasoning about Termination of Pure Prolog Programs. Information and Computation, 106(1) (1993) 109–157
8. Bossi, A., Cocco, N.: Verifying Correctness of Logic Programs. In Diaz, J., Orejas, F. (eds.): Proceedings of TAPSOFT '89, Lecture Notes in Computer Science, vol. 352, Springer-Verlag, Berlin (1989) 96–110
9. Bossi, A., Cocco, N.: Preserving Universal Termination through Unfold/Fold. In Levi, G., Rodriguez-Artalejo, M. (eds.): Algebraic and Logic Programming - Proceedings ALP'94, Lecture Notes in Computer Science, vol. 850, Springer-Verlag, Berlin (1994) 269–286
10. Bossi, A., Cocco, N.: Programs without Failures. In Fuchs, N. (ed.): Proceedings LOPSTR'97, Lecture Notes in Computer Science, vol. 1463, Springer-Verlag, Berlin (1997) 28–48
11. Bossi, A., Cocco, N., Etalle, S.: Transformation of Left Terminating Programs: The Reordering Problem. In Proietti, M. (ed.): Proceedings LOPSTR'95, Lecture Notes in Computer Science, vol. 1048, Springer-Verlag, Berlin (1996) 33–45
12. Bossi, A., Cocco, N., Fabris, M.: Norms on Terms and their Use in Proving Universal Termination of a Logic Program. Theoretical Computer Science, 124 (1994) 297–328
13. Boye, J., Maluszynski, J.: Two Aspects of Directional Types. In Sterling L. (ed.): Proc. Int'l Conf. on Logic Programming, The MIT Press (1995) 747–761
14. Bronsard, F., Lakshman, T. K., Reddy, U. S.: A Framework of Directionalities for Proving Termination of Logic Programs. In Apt, K. R. (ed.) Proceedings of the Joint International Conference and Symposium on Logic Programming, The MIT Press (1992) 321–335
15. Bruynooghe, M., Janssens, G.: An Instance of Abstract Interpretation: Integrating Type and Mode Inferencing. In Proceedings of the International Conference on Logic Programming, The MIT Press (1988) 669–683

16. Chadha, R., Plaisted, D.A.: Correctness of Unification Without Occur Check in Prolog. Journal of Logic Programming, 18(2) (1994) 99–122
17. Le Charlier, B., Leclere, C., Rossi, S., Cortesi, A.: Automated Verification of Behavioural Properties of Prolog Programs. In Advances in Computing Science - ASIAN'97, Lecture Notes in Computer Science, vol.1345 (1997) 225–237
18. Debray, S., Lopez-Garcia, P., Hermenegildo, M.: Non-Failure Analysis for Logic Programs. In Naish, L. (ed.): Proceedings of the International Symposium on Logic Programming, The MIT Press (1997) 48–62
19. Debray, S.K.: Static Inference of Modes and Data Dependencies in Logic Programs. ACM Transactions on Programming Languages and Systems, 11(3) (1989) 419–450
20. Debray, S.K., Lin, N.: Cost Analysis of Logic Programs. ACM Transactions on Programming Languages and Systems, 15(5) (1993) 826–875
21. Drabent, W., Maluszynski, J.: Inductive Assertion Method for Logic Programs. Theoretical Computer Science, 59 (1988) 133–155
22. Henderson, F., Conway, T., Somogyi, Z., Jeffery, D.: The Mercury Language Reference Manual. Technical Report TR 96/10, Dep. of Computer Science, University of Melbourne (1996)
23. Lloyd, J.W.: Foundations of Logic Programming. Springer-Verlag, Berlin (1987) Second edition.
24. De Schreye, D., Decorte, S.: Termination of Logic Programs: the Never-Ending Story. Journal of Logic Programming, 19-20 (1994) 199–260

6 Appendix

Theorem. *Let* $\mathbf{Q}$ *be a noFD query in* P. *If* $\mathbf{Q}$ *is universally terminating in* P *and all the predicates in* $\mathbf{Q}$ *are successful in* P *wrt the input types, then* $\mathbf{Q}$ *has at least one successful LD-derivation in* P.

Proof. Let us assume that $\mathbf{Q}$ is universally terminating in P, then it has a finite LD-tree in P.
The proof can be given by induction on the depth n of the LD-tree for a universally terminating, noFD query $\mathbf{Q}$ whose predicates are all successful.
$n = 1$. By contradiction let us assume that all the derivations have the form $\mathbf{Q} \longmapsto_P$ **fail**. Hence the first atom of $\mathbf{Q}$ can unify with no clause in P. But $\mathbf{Q}$ is noFD, hence well-typed, and its first atom is then input-correct and simply moded. By the second property in Definition 4, we have a contradiction for $\alpha = \epsilon$, the empty substitution.
$n > 1$. Let $\mathbf{Q} = B_1, \ldots, B_n$. $\mathbf{Q}$ is noFD, hence well-typed, and its first atom, B_1, is then input-correct and simply moded. Since the predicates in $\mathbf{Q}$ are successful there exists a clause $c_i : p(\mathbf{t_i}) \leftarrow \mathbf{T_i}, \mathbf{C_i}.$ in P, $i \in [1, m]$, standardized apart wrt $\mathbf{Q}$, and a substitution σ such that: $\sigma = mgu(B_1, p(\mathbf{t_i}))$ and $\mathbf{T_i}\sigma$ has at least one successful LD-derivation. Then, there exists the derivation $\mathbf{Q} \overset{\sigma}{\longmapsto}_P \mathbf{R}$, where $\mathbf{R} = (\mathbf{T_i}, \mathbf{C_i}, B_2, \ldots, B_n)\sigma$ and $\mathbf{R}$ is not empty. Let α be a computed answer substitution for $\mathbf{T_i}\sigma$, we have the LD-derivation:
$\mathbf{Q} \overset{\sigma}{\longmapsto}_P \mathbf{R} \overset{*\alpha}{\longmapsto}_P \mathbf{Q'}$, with $\mathbf{Q'} = (\mathbf{C_i}, B_2, \ldots, B_n)\sigma\alpha$.
$\mathbf{Q'}$ is still universally terminating and its predicates are successful since the predicates in $\mathbf{C_i}$ are in $sDep(p)$ and p is successful.

We prove that $\mathbf{Q}'$ is noFD. Then, by inductive hypothesis applied to $\mathbf{Q}'$, we have the thesis.

- Since p is successful and $\mathbf{Q}$ a noFD query, $\mathbf{C_i}$ and $B_2, \ldots, B_n$ are simply moded sequences.

We assume standardization apart and α is a c.a.s. for $\mathbf{T_i}\sigma$, then

- $Var(\sigma\alpha) \cap Var(B_2, \ldots, B_m) \subseteq Var(B_1)$.
  But $\mathbf{Q}$ is simply moded, then $Var(Out(B_2, \ldots, B_m)) \cap Var(B_1) = \emptyset$, hence $Var(\sigma\alpha) \cap Var(B_2, \ldots, B_m) \subseteq (Var(In(B_2, \ldots, B_m)) - Var(Out(B_2, \ldots, B_m)))$ and, by Lemma 2,
  (i) $(B_2, \ldots, B_n)\sigma\alpha$ is simply moded and
  (ii) $Out(B_2, \ldots, B_m)\sigma\alpha = Out(B_2, \ldots, B_m)$.
- $Var(\sigma\alpha) \cap Var(\mathbf{C_i}) \subseteq Var(p(\mathbf{t_i}), \mathbf{T_i})$.
  Moreover $Var(c_i) \cap Var(\mathbf{Q}) = \emptyset$ and $\sigma = \sigma_{|c_i} \cdot \sigma_{|\mathbf{Q}}$.
  Since $\sigma = mgu(B_1, p(\mathbf{t_i}))$ and B_1 is in the query and it is simply moded, we have that $Var(\sigma_{|c_i}) \cap (Var(Out(p(\mathbf{t_i}))) - Var(In(p(\mathbf{t_i})))) = \emptyset$.
  Then $Var(\sigma_{|c_i}) \cap Var(\mathbf{C_i}) \subseteq Var(In(p(\mathbf{t_i})))$ and $Var(\sigma_{|c_i}\alpha) \cap Var(\mathbf{C_i}) \subseteq Var(In(p(\mathbf{t_i})), \mathbf{T_i})$.
  Hence, since p is successful, $Var(\sigma_{|c_i}\alpha) \cap Var(\mathbf{C_i}) \subseteq (Var(In(\mathbf{C_i})) - Var(Out(\mathbf{C_i})))$ and, by Lemma 2,
  (iii) $\mathbf{C_i}\sigma_{|c_i}\alpha = \mathbf{C_i}\sigma\alpha$ is simply moded.
- $Var(\mathbf{C_i}\sigma\alpha) \cap Var(\mathbf{Q}\sigma\alpha)) \subseteq Var(B_1\sigma\alpha)$.
  Because of (ii) we have also that $Var(B_1\sigma\alpha) \cap Var(Out((B_2, \ldots, B_m)\sigma\alpha)) = \emptyset$. Then,
  (iv) $Var(\mathbf{C_i}\sigma\alpha) \cap Var(Out((B_2, \ldots, B_m)\sigma\alpha)) = \emptyset$.

Then, by (i), (iii), (iv) and Lemma 3, $\mathbf{Q}'$ is simply moded.
Let us now prove that $\mathbf{Q}'$ satisfies also the second condition for noFD queries. $(\mathbf{C_i}, B_2, \ldots, B_m)\sigma\alpha$ is simply moded, then for any atom D in $(\mathbf{C_i}, B_2, \ldots, B_m)\sigma\alpha$ and for any input-correct and simply moded instance $D\beta$ there exist D' in $\mathbf{C_i}, B_2, \ldots, B_m$ and a substitution β' such that $D\beta = D'\beta'$, and hence $D'\beta'$ is a input-correct and simply moded instance of D'. Hence the second condition for noFD queries immediately follows from the fact that p is successful and $\mathbf{Q}$ is noFD. □

Inferring and Compiling Termination for Constraint Logic Programs

Sébastien Hoarau and Fred Mesnard

IREMIA, Université de La Réunion
BP 7151 - 97715 Saint-Denis Messag. Cedex 9, FRANCE
{seb, fred}@univ-reunion.fr
URL: http://www.univ-reunion.fr/~gcc

Abstract. This paper presents an automated method that deals with termination of constraint logic programs in two steps. First, from the text of a program, the method *infers* a set of *potentially* terminating classes using abstract interpretation and boolean mu-calculus. By "potentially", we roughly mean that for each of these classes, one can find a static order over the literals of the clauses of the program to ensure termination. Then, given a terminating class among those computed at the first step, the second step consists of a "compilation" (or transformation) of the original program to another one by *reordering literals*. For this new program, the universal left-termination of any query of the considered class is guaranteed. The method has been implemented.

1 Introduction

Many research works have been devoted to termination analysis of (constraint) logic programs in recent years, as shown by the survey [5]. For most researchers, the main problem is universal left-termination of a given class of queries. This is a somehow restricted view of logic programming. In [9], we addressed a broader question: given a CLP(χ) program find the classes of queries for which universal left-termination is guaranteed. Here we go one step further: infer (automatically) larger classes of queries such that there exists a static reordering of the bodies of the clauses which insures universal left-termination.

Example 1. Let us consider the following CLP($\mathcal{N}$) program, called POWER-4:

rule r_1 : $\mathtt{p(X,Y)\ :-\ s(X,Z), s(Z,Y).}$

rule r_2 : $\mathtt{s(0,0).}$
rule r_3 : $\mathtt{s(X+1, Y+2X+1)\ :-\ s(X,Y).}$

The method described in [9] can infer that "$\leftarrow x$ *bounded*, $p(x,y)$" is a left-terminating query. Nethertheless, the resolution of the query $\leftarrow y \leq 16,\ p(x,y)$ could terminate if in the clause defining the predicate p we prove $s(z,y)$ before $s(x,z)$. We would like to conclude that there are two terminating classes of queries: $\leftarrow x$ *bounded*, $p(x,y)$ and $\leftarrow y$ *bounded*, $p(x,y)$. The new method we present in the following of this paper does this job.

P. Flener (Ed.): LOPSTR'98, LNCS 1559, pp. 240–254, 1999.

The rest of the paper is organized as follows: section 2 recalls some basic notions about CLP(χ) and approximations between two CLP systems. Section 3 summarizes our first results for the inference of left-termination conditions [9]. Then, sections 4 and 5 present the two points of the new method: the inference of larger classes of queries and the reordering of the literals inside clauses. Implementation issues are briefly discussed in section 6.

2 Preliminaries

2.1 CLP(χ)

Let us remind some notations and conventions about CLP introduced in [7]. For concision, we simplify the notations when we consider there is no ambiguity. Moreover, in concrete program examples we use the Edinburgh syntax.

In the following, we consider ideal[1] CLP systems without limit element. $\tilde{t}$ (resp. $\tilde{x}$) represents a sequence of terms (resp. distinct variables). Let o be a CLP(χ) object (a constraint, an atom, a goal or a clause). $var(o)$ denotes the set of variables of o and $o(\tilde{x})$ means o *where* $var(o) = \tilde{x}$. If o_1 and o_2 are two objects, $o_1 \equiv o_2$ means that o_1 and o_2 are *syntactically equal.* The χ-constraint c is χ-*solvable* and θ is a χ-*solution* of c if θ is a χ- *valuation* s.t. $\chi \models c\theta$. Otherwise c is χ- *unsolvable.* Let c_1 and c_2 be two χ-constraints. We write $c_1 \rightarrow_\chi c_2$ (resp. $c_1 \leftrightarrow_\chi c_2$) as a shorthand for $\chi \models \forall[c_1 \rightarrow c_2]$ (resp. $\chi \models \forall[c_1 \leftrightarrow c_2]$).

We use the following structures (where the symbols have their usual interpretation):

- $\mathcal{B} = \langle\{true, false\}; \{0, 1, \neg, \wedge, \vee, \Rightarrow, \Leftrightarrow\}; \{\Rightarrow, =\}\rangle$,
- $\mathcal{N} = \langle \mathbb{N}; \{0, 1, +\}; \{\geq, =\}\rangle$ where $\mathbb{N}$ is the set of natural numbers.

In $\mathcal{N}$, for $n \in \mathbb{N}$, $n \geq 1$, we write n (resp. nx) as an abbreviation for $1+\ldots+1$ (resp. $x + \ldots + x$), where 1 (resp. x) appears n times. Let $c(\tilde{x})$ a $\mathcal{N}$-constraint, $y \in \tilde{x}$ and $m \in \mathbb{N}$. We say that y is *bounded* (resp. *bounded by* m) in $c(\tilde{x})$ if there exists $n \in \mathbb{N}$ such that $c(\tilde{x}) \rightarrow_\mathcal{N} n \geq y$ (resp. $c(\tilde{x}) \rightarrow_\mathcal{N} m \geq y$).

On the set Π of predicate symbols defined by a program P, we define the binary relation $p \rightarrow q$ if P contains a rule of the form $p(\tilde{t_1}) \leftarrow \ldots, q(\tilde{t_2}), \ldots$. Let $\rightarrow^*$ denote the reflexive transitive closure of $\rightarrow$. The relation $p \sim q$ if $p \rightarrow^* q \wedge q \rightarrow^* p$ is an equivalence relation. We denote by $\bar{p}$ the equivalence class including p.

A rule $p(\tilde{x}) \leftarrow c, \tilde{B}$ is *recursive* if there is a predicate symbol $q \in \bar{p}$ s.t. $\tilde{B} = \ldots, q(\tilde{y}), \ldots$. A predicate symbol p is *directly recursive* if $\bar{p} = \{p\} \wedge (p \rightarrow p)$. The predicate symbols $\{p_1, \ldots, p_n\}$ $(n \geq 2)$ are *mutually recursive* if $\bar{p_1} = \ldots = \bar{p_n} = \{p_1, \ldots, p_n\}$. A predicate p is *recursive* if it is either directly recursive or mutually recursive. Otherwise p is *non-recursive.*

[1] i.e. systems which provide a decision procedure for the problem: $\models \exists\, c$ (where c is any constraint).

2.2 From CLP(χ) to CLP($\mathcal{B}ool$)

An *approximation*[2] $\mathcal{A}_\chi^\psi$ from χ to ψ consists in a pair of functions $\langle \mathcal{A}_{sx}, \mathcal{A}_{sm}\rangle$ with some properties ($\mathcal{A}_{sx}$ deals with syntax and $\mathcal{A}_{sm}$ with semantics; see [9] for details). The main approximation we use is $\mathcal{A}_\chi^\mathcal{B}$ which turns CLP(χ) objects into boolean objects and which is the composition of two approximations:

1. $\mathcal{A}_\chi^\mathcal{N}$: which, informally, replaces all data structures by their *sizes* (for example lists by their length, trees by the number of nodes, ...),
2. $\mathcal{A}_\mathcal{N}^\mathcal{B}$: $\mathcal{A}_{sx}(0) = 1$, $\mathcal{A}_{sx}(1) = 1$, $\mathcal{A}_{sx}(+) = \wedge$, $\mathcal{A}_{sx}(\geq) = \Rightarrow$, $\mathcal{A}_{sm}(n) = true$.

Intuitively, $\mathcal{A}_\mathcal{N}^\mathcal{B}$ is used to detect bounded variables. For instance, $\mathcal{A}_\mathcal{N}^\mathcal{B}(4 \geq X + Y) \equiv 1 \Rightarrow X \wedge Y$ which is equivalent to $X = 1 \wedge Y = 1$. Hence, from the properties of $\mathcal{A}_\mathcal{N}^\mathcal{B}$, we conclude that X and Y are bounded in $(4 \geq X + Y)$.

Example 2. Let $\mathcal{L}(\chi) = \langle D_\chi^*; \{[\,], [\_|\_]\}; \{=\}\rangle$ be the lists structure over χ, where as usual, the constant $[\,]$ denotes the empty list and the operator $[\_|\_]$ denotes the list constructor. We define the approximation $\mathcal{A}_{\mathcal{L}(\chi)}^\mathcal{N}$ from $\mathcal{L}(\chi)$ to $\mathcal{N}$: $\mathcal{A}_{sx}([\,]) = 0$, $\mathcal{A}_{sx}([x|y]) = 1 + \mathcal{A}_{sx}(y)$ and $\mathcal{A}_{sm}([e_1, \ldots, e_n]) = n$. Let us approximate the well-known APPEND CLP($\mathcal{L}(\chi)$) program:

CLP($\mathcal{L}(\chi)$) version	CLP($\mathcal{N}$) version	CLP($\mathcal{B}$) version
app([ ], Ys, Ys).	app(0, Ys, Ys).	app(1, Ys, Ys).
app([X|Xs], Ys, [X|Zs]) :− app(Xs, Ys, Zs).	app(1 + Xs, Ys, 1 + Zs) :− app(Xs, Ys, Zs).	app(1 ∧ Xs, Ys, 1 ∧ Zs) :− app(Xs, Ys, Zs).

Now, we give some results related to approximations. Let $\mathcal{A}_\chi^\psi$ be an approximation, P be a CLP(χ) program and S_P^χ its semantics [6]. Then, the image of the semantics of P is included in the semantics of the image of P:

Theorem 1. *[9]* $\mathcal{A}_\chi^\psi(S_P^\chi) \subseteq S^\psi_{\mathcal{A}_\chi^\psi(P)}$

Here is a useful property about the boolean approximation $\mathcal{A}_\mathcal{N}^\mathcal{B}$:

Proposition 1. *(see [9] for details and examples) Let c_1 be an $\mathcal{N}$-constraint and $t \equiv \vee_{j\in J}(\wedge_{i\in I_j} x_i)$ a boolean term. If $\mathcal{A}_\mathcal{N}^\mathcal{B}(c_1) \to_\mathcal{B} t$ then $\exists j \in J, \forall i \in I_j, x_i$ is bounded in c_1.*

Moreover, we can compute the *boolean model* of a CLP(χ) program and:

Remark 1. Let P be a CLP(χ) program. We can always assume that $S^\mathcal{B}_{\mathcal{A}_\chi^\mathcal{B}(P)}$, the model of $\mathcal{A}_\chi^\mathcal{B}(P)$, contains exactly one formula $p(\tilde{x}) \leftrightarrow_\mathcal{B} Post_p(\tilde{x})$ for each predicate symbol p of P.

We note $Post_p$ the boolean model of a predicate p because of the obvious link with the post condition of De Schreye and Decorte [5].

[2] An approximation is a simple way to present the abstract interpretation application in logic programs [4]

Example 3. If we consider one more time the APPEND program, then we have:

$$Post_{app}(x, y, z) = x \wedge (y \Leftrightarrow z).$$

Informally, it means that when a proof of a goal $\leftarrow app(x, y, z)$ terminates in CLP($\mathcal{L}(\chi)$), on one hand the length of x is bounded and, on the other hand, the length of y is bounded if and only if the length of z is bounded.

Remark 2. ¿From now on, in the following sections, we consider only CLP($\mathcal{N}$) programs and we denote by Π the set of predicate symbols of a program. For any other structure, we switch to CLP($\mathcal{N}$) by an appropriated approximation. For any numerical constraint c, we write $c^{\mathcal{B}}$ its boolean version.

3 Inferring left-termination conditions: The previous approach

In [9] for each predicate symbol p of a program P, a boolean term Pre_p is computed. This boolean term is a condition of left-termination such that for any query $\leftarrow c,\ p(\tilde{x})$ if $c^{\mathcal{B}} \rightarrow_{\mathcal{B}} Pre_p(\tilde{x})$ then the derivation of the query universally left-terminates. Let us summarize this result.

Definition 1. *A linear measure μ_p for a predicate symbol $p \in \bar{p}$ of arity n is a mapping defined by:*

$$\begin{array}{rccc} \mu_p : & \mathbb{N}^n & \rightarrow & \mathbb{N} \\ & (x_1, \ldots, x_n) & \mapsto & \sum_{i=1}^{n} a_i x_i \end{array}$$

s.t. a_i's are integers (we note I_{μ_p} the non empty set s.t. $i \in I_{\mu_p}$ implies $a_i \neq 0$) and for each rule $p(\tilde{x}) \leftarrow c, \tilde{B}$ defining p, for each solution θ of c, for each atom $q(\tilde{y})$ appearing in $\tilde{B}$ with $q \in \bar{p}$ we have: $\mu_p(\tilde{x}\theta) \geq 1 + \mu_q(\tilde{y}\theta)$.

Example 4. If we consider the CLP($\mathcal{N}$) version of APPEND program then:

$$\mu^1(x, y, z) = x \quad \text{and} \quad \mu^2(x, y, z) = z$$

are two linear measures.

The work of K. Sohn and A. Van Gelder [10] shows that there exists a complete polynomial procedure for deciding the existence of a linear measure. This procedure can be adapted to compute the coefficients of μ.

Definition 2. *Let P be a CLP($\mathcal{N}$) program. Let $p \in \bar{p}$ be a recursive predicate. Its set of maximal measures is always finite (see [9]). We write q_p the number of maximal measures for a predicate p and $\Gamma_{\bar{p}} = \{\mu_p^j \mid p \in \bar{p}, 1 \leq j \leq q_p\}$ the set of associated maximal linear measures for $\bar{p}$. For each $p \in \bar{p}$, we compute a boolean term called its boolean measure defined by:*

$$\gamma_p(\tilde{x}) = \bigvee_{1 \leq j \leq q_p} \left(\bigwedge_{i \in I_{\mu_p^j}} x_i \right)$$

If p is a non-recursive predicate, we set $\gamma_p(\tilde{x}) = 1$.

The informal use of the term γ is to give some information about potential decreasing of linear combinations of arguments of recursive predicates.

Example 5. If we continue our example 4, we have $\bar{p} = \{app\}$, $q_{app} = 2$ and $\Gamma_{\overline{app}} = \{\mu^1, \mu^2\}$ and the boolean measure is $\gamma_{app}(x, y, z) = x \vee z$.

Definition 3. *A boolean term $Pre_p(\tilde{x})$ is a left-termination condition for $p(\tilde{x})$ if, for every constraint c, $c^{\mathcal{B}} \rightarrow_{\mathcal{B}} Pre_p(\tilde{x})$ implies $\leftarrow c, p(\tilde{x})$ left-terminates.*

Let P be a CLP($\mathcal{N}$) program, p a predicate symbol of P defined by m_p rules. Let $P^{\mathcal{B}}$ be the boolean version of P and the kth-rule r_k defining p in $P^{\mathcal{B}}$ be:

$$p(\tilde{x}) \leftarrow c^{\mathcal{B}}_{k,0}, p_{k,1}(\tilde{x}_{k,1}), \ldots, p_{k,j_k}(\tilde{x}_{k,j_k})$$

Theorem 2. *Assume that for each predicate $q \notin \bar{p}$ appearing in the rules defining $\bar{p}$ we have a left-termination condition $Pre_q(\tilde{y})$. If $\{Pre_p(\tilde{x})\}_{p\in\bar{p}}$ verifies:*

$$\forall p \in \bar{p} \quad \begin{cases} Pre_p(\tilde{x}) \rightarrow_{\mathcal{B}} \gamma_p(\tilde{x}), \\ \forall 1 \le k \le m_p, \forall 1 \le j \le j_k, \\ \qquad \left(Pre_p(\tilde{x}) \wedge c^{\mathcal{B}}_{k,0} \bigwedge_{i=1}^{j-1} Post_{p_{k,i}}(\tilde{x}_{k,i})\right) \rightarrow_{\mathcal{B}} Pre_{p_{k,j}}(\tilde{x}_{k,j}) \end{cases}$$

then $\{Pre_p(\tilde{x})\}_{p\in\bar{p}}$ is a left-termination condition for $\bar{p}$.

Note that the above system of boolean formulae can be used not only to check that some relations Pre_p's are correct left-termination conditions but also to compute the Pre_p's by means of boolean μ-calculus[3] [3].

Let us explain the meaning of the formulae in the above theorem. The implication between Pre_p and γ_p, forces the pre-condition to verify a minimal condition: entities that appear in the pre-condition have to be among the decreasing ones. The second part says that when a rule such r_k is used to prove an atom $p(\tilde{x})$, for each atom $p_{k,j}$ appearing in the body, its calling context has to be sufficient to ensure its pre-condition. This calling context is the conjunction of the initial constraint of the rule and of course the post-conditions of all atoms placed (and thus proved) before $p_{k,j}$.

Example 6. Let us consider the CLP($\mathcal{N}$) program, POWER-4, of the introduction. We compute: $\gamma_s(x, y) = x \vee y$, $Post_s(x, y) = x \wedge y$, $\gamma_p(x, y) = 1$ and $Post_p(x, y) = x \wedge y$. For left-termination we find by the above method: $Pre_s(x, y) = x \vee y$ and $Pre_p(x, y) = x$. Informally, these relations give us the following informations:

- for predicate s: for any query $\leftarrow c, s(x, y)$, if x or y is bounded in c, then the considered query left-terminates (Pre_s) and after the proof x and y are bounded ($Post_s$).
- for predicate p: $\leftarrow c, p(x, y)$, if x is bounded in c, then the considered query left-terminates and after the proof x and y are bounded.

But as we said in the introduction, a query $\leftarrow c, p(x, y)$ s.t. y is bounded in c terminates if we prove $s(z, y)$ before $s(x, z)$ and then, for the predicate p, we would like to infer $Pre_p(x, y) = x \vee y$.

---

[3] A boolean μ-calculus module for SICStus Prolog is available at our URL address.

4 Inferring extended left-termination conditions

This section presents an important improvement of the previous method in order to infer larger termination conditions. The main idea consists in the introduction of the notion of order inside clauses.

Definition 4. *Let P be a CLP($\mathcal{N}$) program and p be a predicate symbol of P. A boolean term $Pre_p(\tilde{x})$ is an extended left-termination condition for $p(\tilde{x})$ if, for every constraint c, $c^{\mathcal{B}} \rightarrow_{\mathcal{B}} Pre_p(\tilde{x})$ implies that there exists a transformation of P and $\leftarrow c, p(\tilde{x})$, based on a renaming*[4] *of predicate symbols and a reordering of literals, such that the renamed goal $\leftarrow c, p'(\tilde{x})$ universally left-terminates with respect to the transformed program P'.*

The following definition presents the idea that allows us to deal with the notion of order inside clauses.

Definition 5. *Let P be a program. For each rule of P: $p(\tilde{x}) \leftarrow c, \tilde{B}$ where the body $\tilde{B}$ contains the literals: $p_1, \ldots, p_n$ (but we do not know the order of them), we can associate a sequence of $n(n-1)/2$ boolean variables $(b_{i,j})_{1 \leq i < j \leq n}$, called order variables, with the following constraints (which express transitivity of the order relation):*

$$\forall 1 \leq i < j < k \leq n, \left\{ \begin{array}{llll} b_{i,j} \wedge \ \ b_{j,k} \rightarrow_{\mathcal{B}} b_{i,k}, & & b_{j,k} \wedge \neg b_{i,k} \rightarrow_{\mathcal{B}} \neg b_{i,j}, \\ b_{i,k} \wedge \neg b_{j,k} \rightarrow_{\mathcal{B}} b_{i,j}, & & \neg b_{i,k} \wedge \ \ b_{i,j} \rightarrow_{\mathcal{B}} \neg b_{j,k}, \\ \neg b_{i,j} \wedge \ \ b_{i,k} \rightarrow_{\mathcal{B}} b_{j,k}, & & \neg b_{j,k} \wedge \neg b_{i,j} \rightarrow_{\mathcal{B}} \neg b_{i,k} \end{array} \right.$$

The semantics of these variables is:

$$\forall\ 1 \leq i < j \leq n, \left\{ \begin{array}{l} b_{i,j} = 1 \text{ if } p_i \text{ appears before } p_j, \\ \phantom{b_{i,j}} = 0 \text{ if } p_j \text{ appears before } p_i \end{array} \right.$$

Property 1. Let $(b_{i,j})_{1 \leq i < j \leq n}$ be a sequence of order variables associated to a set of predicate symbols $p_1, \ldots, p_n$. This sequence defines a partial order over the predicate symbols and can be extended to a total order. We can represent this order by a permutation σ over $\{1, \ldots, n\}$.

Example 7. Let p_1, p_2 and p_3 be three predicate symbols and $b_{1,2}, b_{1,3}, b_{2,3}$ be a sequence of order variables such that $b_{1,2} = 1$ and $b_{2,3} = 0$. Then we have the partial order: p_1 before p_2, p_3 before p_2, which leads to two possible total orders:

- p_1, p_3, p_2 which corresponds to $b_{1,3} = 1$ and the permutation σ defined by $\sigma_1 = 1$, $\sigma_2 = 3$ and $\sigma_3 = 2$,
- p_3, p_1, p_2 which corresponds to $b_{1,3} = 0$ and the permutation σ defined by $\sigma_1 = 3$, $\sigma_2 = 1$ and $\sigma_3 = 2$.

---

[4] Roughly speaking, the renaming specializes the logic definition of a predicate symbol p when p is used in different calling modes.

And now we give the main result of the section. Let P be a CLP($\mathcal{N}$) program, p a predicate symbol of P defined by m_p rules. Let $P^{\mathcal{B}}$ be the boolean version of P and the kth-rule r_k defining p in $P^{\mathcal{B}}$ be:

$$p(\tilde{x}) \leftarrow c^{\mathcal{B}}_{k,0}, p_{k,1}(\tilde{x}_{k,1}), \ldots, p_{k,j_k}(\tilde{x}_{k,j_k})$$

Theorem 3. *Assume that for each $q \notin \bar{p}$ and appearing in the rules defining $\bar{p}$, an extended left-termination condition Pre_q has been computed. If the set of terms $\{Pre_p\}_{p \in \bar{p}}$ verifies:*

$$\forall p \in \bar{p} \begin{cases} Pre_p(\tilde{x}) \rightarrow_{\mathcal{B}} \gamma_p(\tilde{x}), \\ \forall 1 \leq k \leq m_p \; \exists (b^k_{e,h})_{1 \leq e < h \leq j_k} \; \forall 1 \leq j \leq j_k \\ \Big(Pre_p(\tilde{x}) \wedge c^{\mathcal{B}}_{k,0} \wedge \bigwedge_{i=1}^{j-1} (\neg b^k_{i,j} \vee Post_{p_{k,i}}(\tilde{x}_{k,i})) \wedge \\ \qquad \bigwedge_{i=j+1}^{j_k} (b^k_{j,i} \vee Post_{p_{k,i}}(\tilde{x}_{k,i})) \Big) \rightarrow_{\mathcal{B}} Pre_{p_{k,j}}(\tilde{x}_{k,j}) \end{cases}$$

then $\{Pre_p\}_{p \in \bar{p}}$ is an extended left-termination condition for $\bar{p}$.

Proof. This proof will be given conjointly with the proof of theorem 4.

Like theorem 2, the system of boolean formulae of theorem 3 is actually used in our implementation to compute the terms Pre_p (here again by a fixpoint calculus using boolean μ-calculus; some results are presented in a table in section 6). The informal meaning is similar to the intuitive meaning of theorem 2. The only difference is in the second part. When we consider an atom $p_{k,j}$ of the body, we do not know the atoms $p_{k,i}$ that appear before $p_{k,j}$ and thus for each $p_{k,i}$:

- either $p_{k,j}$ appears before $p_{k,i}$ (i.e $b^k_{i,j} = 0$ or $b^k_{j,i} = 1$, it depends whether $i < j$ or $i > j$),
- or $p_{k,i}$ is proved before $p_{k,j}$ and in this case we add $Post_{p_{k,i}}$.

In the rest of the paper we choose a convenient way to write pre-conditions:

Definition 6. *An extended left-termination condition can be written as a disjunction of conjunctions of variables and in the following, we call class of queries such a conjunction (i.e. an extended left-termination condition is a disjunction of classes of queries).*

Example 8. Let us consider the following CLP($\mathcal{N}$) program. The meaning of these relations is: $s(x, y)$ iff $y = x^2$, $p(x, y)$ iff $y = x^2$ or $x = y^2$ and $q(x, y)$ iff $x = y$ or $x = y^4$ or $y = x^4$.

rule r_1 :	`s(0,0).`
rule r_2 :	`s(X+1,Y+2*X+1) :- s(X,Y).`
rule r_3 :	`p(X,Y) :- s(X,Y).`
rule r_4 :	`p(X,Y) :- s(Y,X).`
rule r_5 :	`q(X,Y) :- p(X,Z), p(Z,Y).`

The only rule where an order can appear is rule r_5. We assume that post/pre-conditions have been computed for predicate s and p: $Pre_s(x,y) = x \vee y$, $Post_s(x,y) = x \wedge y$, $Pre_p(x,y) = x \vee y$ and $Post_p(x,y) = x \wedge y$. Let us remind what these informations mean: Pre_s says that any proof of a goal $\leftarrow c,\ s(x,y)$ left-terminates if either x or y is bounded in c and $Post_s$ adds that at the end of such a proof x and y are bounded (idem for p). To compute the Pre_q condition, we solve the formula (since there is only one order variable in the formula, we write it b instead of $b_{1,2}$):

$$\exists b, \left\{ \begin{array}{l} (Pre_q(x,y) \wedge (b \vee Post_p(z,y))) \rightarrow_{\mathcal{B}} Pre_p(x,y) \\ \bigwedge \\ (Pre_q(x,y) \wedge (\neg b \vee Post_p(x,z))) \rightarrow_{\mathcal{B}} Pre_p(y,z) \end{array} \right.$$

The condition found is: $Pre_q(x,y) = x \vee y$. And finally, for each predicate we can summarize its classes of queries; for s: $C_s^1(x,y) = x$ and $C_s^2(x,y) = y$, for p: $C_p^1(x,y) = x$ and $C_p^2(x,y) = y$ and for q: $C_q^1(x,y) = x$ and $C_q^2(x,y) = y$.

5 Reordering to left-terminate

We did the first part of the work: compute for each predicate its extended left-termination condition. Now, if the user gives a query or a class of queries that entails the extended left-termination condition of the corresponding predicate, we must compile the program to another one by reordering the literals to ensure left-termination of the proof of the query. Let us define a formalism that allows us to capture the information we have on the program.

Definition 7. *Let $\{1,\ldots,n\}$ be a set of natural numbers. A permutation σ over $\{1,\ldots,n\}$ is a bijection from $\{1,\ldots,n\}$ to $\{1,\ldots,n\}$. We note σ_i the image of i by the permutation σ.*

Definition 8. *We define an environment as a tuple $\langle P, \{Pre_p \mid p \in \Pi\}, \phi\rangle$ where:*

- *P is a CLP($\mathcal{N}$) program with Π as the set of its predicate symbols,*
- *$Pre_p = \bigvee C_p^i$ is the extended left-termination condition of the predicate p,*
- *ϕ is a function that maps a rule $r_k : p \leftarrow c, p_{k,1}, \ldots, p_{k,j_k}$ and a class C_p^i to a permutation over $\{1,\ldots,j_k\}$.*

Concretely, an environment is computed as follows: after inferring the pre-conditions Pre_p for each predicate p (theorem 3), our implementation generates a permutation for each class C_p^l of Pre_p and for each rule r_k defining p. To this aim, it computes using a boolean solver a sequence $(b_{e,h}^k)_{1 \le e < h \le j_k}$ of booleans s.t. the following formula is true:

$$\bigwedge_{j \le j_k} \Big[\Big(C_p^l(\tilde{x}) \wedge c_{k,0}^{\mathcal{B}} \wedge \bigwedge_{i=1}^{j-1} (\neg b_{i,j}^k \vee Post_{p_{k,i}}(\tilde{x}_{k,i})) \wedge \\ \bigwedge_{i=j+1}^{j_k} (b_{j,i}^k \vee Post_{p_{k,i}}(\tilde{x}_{k,i})) \Big) \rightarrow_{\mathcal{B}} Pre_{p_{k,j}}(\tilde{x}_{k,j}) \Big]$$

We get a (partial) instantiation of order variables $b^k_{i,j}$'s that we turn into a total instantiation corresponding to a permutation σ. We define $\phi(C^l_p, r_k) = \sigma$. At this point, we have an environment for the program P. The rest of the section presents a top-down method to compile the initial CLP($\mathcal{N}$) program.

Before we give formal definitions and algorithms, we present the reordering on the example 8 to help the intuition.

Example 9. We consider the program of example 8 and the computed results: for each predicate we have its associated classes of queries. Suppose the user wants to prove the goal: $\leftarrow \{y < 10\},\ q(x, y)$. First we must create the permutations associated with each pair $\langle classe, rule\rangle$. Here only one rule is concerned: r_5. Applying the method described above, we find a boolean b such that the following formula is true:

$$\begin{cases} (C^1_q(x,y) \wedge (b \vee Post_p(y,z))) \rightarrow_B Pre_p(x,z) \\ \wedge \\ (C^1_q(x,y) \wedge (\neg b \vee Post_p(x,z))) \rightarrow_B Pre_p(y,z) \end{cases}$$

and a boolean b' s.t.:

$$\begin{cases} (C^2_q(x,y) \wedge (b' \vee Post_p(y,z))) \rightarrow_B Pre_p(x,z) \\ \wedge \\ (C^2_q(x,y) \wedge (\neg b' \vee Post_p(x,z))) \rightarrow_B Pre_p(y,z) \end{cases}$$

The values we find are: $b = 1$ (hence, in the body of r_5, $p(x, z)$ has to appear before $p(z, y)$ for the class $C^1_q(x, y)$) and $b' = 0$ (i.e. $p(z, y)$ has to appear before $p(x, z)$ for the class $C^2_q(x, y)$). Then the function ϕ is generated: $\phi(C^1_q, r_5) = \sigma$ and $\phi(C^2_q, r_5) = \tau$ where σ and τ are the two permutations over $\{1,2\}$ defined by $\sigma_1 = 1$, $\sigma_2 = 2$, $\tau_1 = 2$ and $\tau_2 = 1$.

Now we can begin to construct the new program (the reordered version of the original one). The user's goal belongs to the class C^2_q of the predicate q and thus we apply the permutation $\phi(C^2_q, r_5)$ to reorder the body of the clause. At the same time we rename the head and finally we obtain a preliminary version of the first rule of the new program:

```
rule r'5 :    q²(X, Y)  :- p(Z, Y), p(X, Z).
```

Then we must deal with the predicates appearing in the body of r'_5: the calling context of $p(z, y)$ is y *bounded* and thus belongs to the class C^2_p. Then, we perform the following operations:

- rename $p(Z, Y)$ by $p^2(Z, Y)$,
- recall recursively the method with the class of queries "y *bounded*, $p(z, y)$".

After these operations the new program is:

```
rule r'1 :    s¹(0,0).
rule r'2 :    s¹(X + 1, Y + 2 * X + 1)  :- s¹(X, Y).

rule r'3 :    p²(X, Y)  :- s¹(X, Y).
rule r'4 :    p²(X, Y)  :- s¹(Y, X).

rule r'5 :    q²(X, Y)  :- p²(Z, Y), p(X, Z).
```

The literal $p(x,z)$ remains to be processed. The calling context of $p(x,z)$ is again z *bounded* since at the end of the proof of $p(z,y)$ we have z and y *bounded* (information from $Post_p$). The final version of the program is:

rule r_1' : $\mathtt{s}^1(0,0)$.
rule r_2' : $\mathtt{s}^1(X+1, Y+2*X+1) \ :- \ \mathtt{s}^1(X,Y)$.

rule r_3' : $\mathtt{p}^2(X,Y) \ :- \ \mathtt{s}^1(X,Y)$.
rule r_4' : $\mathtt{p}^2(X,Y) \ :- \ \mathtt{s}^1(Y,X)$.

rule r_5' : $\mathtt{q}^2(X,Y) \ :- \ \mathtt{p}^2(Z,Y),\ \mathtt{p}^2(X,Z)$.$\triangleleft$

In the following, we present more precisely the method to rename and reorder a program. The renaming is realized by a table:

Definition 9. *Let $\langle P, \{Pre_p \mid p \in \Pi\}, \phi\rangle$ be an environment. We define a renaming table T as a mapping that associates an unique new symbol of predicate p^l to a pair $\langle p, C_p^l\rangle$ where $p \in \Pi$ and C_p^l is a class of the extended left-termination condition of p.*

Hypothesis - Let us give the hypothesis for the reordering algorithm (unformally presented in the example 9) and the two properties 2 and 4. We have a program P, $\langle P, \{Pre_p \mid p \in \Pi\}, \phi\rangle$ its computed environment, T the associated renaming table and $\leftarrow c, p(\tilde{x})$ a user query related to P s.t. $c^{\mathcal{B}}$ (the boolean version of c) verifies: $\exists C_p \in Pre_p, c^{\mathcal{B}} \rightarrow_{\mathcal{B}} C_p$.

The three points below summarizes the method described by the algorithm given in the appendix at the end of this paper:

1. we have a current goal $\leftarrow c, q(\tilde{x})$ (at the beginning, it is the user's goal); we compute C the class of queries corresponding to the current predicate q with its current calling context c,
2. we copy each rule r defining q in P, we rename q by the new symbol q', where $q' = T(C,q)$ and we use the permutation $\phi(r,C)$ to reorder literals of the bodies of the copied rules. Then we add these new rules in program P',
3. for each rule of P', for each predicate p appearing in this rule but not defined in P', we compute its calling context d. So we have a new current goal: $\leftarrow d, p(\tilde{y})$ and we apply the points 1 and 2 seen above. And so on. The procedure ends when all predicates appearing in P' are defined in P'.

The new program P' verifies the two properties:

Proposition 2. *For all $p' \in \Pi'$ there exists $p \in \Pi$ and $C \in Pre_p$ s.t. $\langle p, C, p'\rangle \in T$. If we rename each symbol p' by its corresponding symbol p then we have: $S_{P'}^{\mathcal{N}} = S_P^{\mathcal{N}}$.*

Proof. The following actions do not affect the semantic of a program: duplicating a clause, reordering literals inside the body of a clause.

Theorem 4. *The proof of the query $\leftarrow c, p'(\tilde{x})$ universally left-terminates with respect to P'.*

Proof. We can prove that each predicate p' of the new program P' and the corresponding term $Pre_{p'}$ (the renamed version of Pre_p) verify the hypothesis of theorem 2. Then we use this result to conclude.

Let p' be a predicate symbol of P' and r' one of the rules defining p' in its boolean version:

$$p'(\tilde{x}) \leftarrow c^{\mathcal{B}}, p'_1(\tilde{x}_1), \ldots, p'_n(\tilde{x}_n)$$

By construction we know that:

1. p' is a renaming of a predicate symbol p of P,
2. the rule r' has been constructed from a rule r (from the boolean version of P):
$$p(\tilde{x}) \leftarrow c^{\mathcal{B}}, p_1(\tilde{x}_1), \ldots, p_n(\tilde{x}_n)$$
defining p in P, a class of queries C_p^l of p and the corresponding permutation $\sigma = \phi(r, C_p^l)$,
3. each predicate symbol $p'_{j'}$ in the body of r' is a renaming of a predicate symbol p_j in the body of r: $\forall j' \in \{1, \ldots, n\}$, $\exists! j \in \{1, \ldots, n\}$ s.t. $p'_{j'}$ is a renaming of p_j.

To apply the result of theorem 2, we must verify that the following system of implications holds:

$$(\mathrm{SI}) \quad \begin{cases} Pre_{p'}(\tilde{x}) \rightarrow_{\mathcal{B}} \gamma_{p'}(\tilde{x}), \\ \forall 1 \leq j' \leq n \ \left(Pre_{p'}(\tilde{x}) \wedge c^{\mathcal{B}} \wedge \bigwedge_{i'=1}^{j'-1} (Post_{p'_{i'}}(\tilde{x}_{i'}))\right) \\ \qquad\qquad\qquad\qquad\qquad\qquad \rightarrow_{\mathcal{B}} Pre_{p'_{j'}}(\tilde{x}_{j'}) \end{cases}$$

Let $j' \in \{1, \ldots, n\}$ and j be the unique index in $\{1, \ldots, n\}$ such that $p'_{j'}$ is a renaming of p_j. By hypothesis of theorem 3, we know that there exists $(b_{e,h})_{1 \leq e < h \leq n}$ a sequence of order variables s.t.:

$$(\mathrm{H}) \quad \begin{cases} Pre_p(\tilde{x}) \rightarrow_{\mathcal{B}} \gamma_p(\tilde{x}), \\ \left(Pre_p(\tilde{x}) \wedge c^{\mathcal{B}} \wedge \bigwedge_{i=1}^{j-1} (\neg b_{i,j} \vee Post_{p_i}(\tilde{x}_i)) \wedge \right. \\ \qquad\qquad \left. \bigwedge_{i=j+1}^{n} (b_{j,i} \vee Post_{p_i}(\tilde{x}_i))\right) \rightarrow_{\mathcal{B}} Pre_{p_j}(\tilde{x}_j) \end{cases}$$

Since we have (modulo the renaming): $Pre_p \equiv Pre_{p'}$ and $\gamma_p \equiv \gamma_{p'}$, the first implication of (SI) holds. Since $Pre_{p_j}(\tilde{x}_j) \equiv Pre_{p'_{j'}}(\tilde{x}_{j'})$ (modulo the renaming), to achieve the proof we must show that:

$$Pre_{p'}(\tilde{x}) \wedge c^{\mathcal{B}} \wedge \bigwedge_{i'=1}^{j'-1} (Post_{p'_{i'}}(\tilde{x}_{i'}))$$

implies

$$Pre_p(\tilde{x}) \wedge c^{\mathcal{B}} \wedge \bigwedge_{i=1}^{j-1} (\neg b_{i,j} \vee Post_{p_i}(\tilde{x}_i)) \wedge \bigwedge_{i=j+1}^{n} (b_{j,i} \vee Post_{p_i}(\tilde{x}_i))$$

Let $i < j$ and i' the unique index in $\{1, \ldots, n\}$ such that $p'_{i'}$ is a renaming of p_i. We have two cases:

1. $i' < j'$: $p'_{i'}$ is a renaming of p_i thus $\bigwedge_{i'=1}^{j'-1}(Post_{p'_{i'}}(\tilde{x}_{i'}))$ implies $Post_{p_i}(\tilde{x}_i)$ and thus implies the conjunction $\bigwedge_{i=1}^{j-1}(\neg b_{i,j} \vee Post_{p_i}(\tilde{x}_i))$,
2. $i' > j'$: it means that the transformation from r to r' has changed the order between p_i and p_j. Inside r', $p'_{i'}$ appears after $p'_{j'}$ i.e. $b_{i,j} = 0$ thus $\neg b_{i,j} = 1$. Here again, $\bigwedge_{i'=1}^{j'-1}(Post_{p'_{i'}}(\tilde{x}_{i'}))$ implies $\bigwedge_{i=1}^{j-1}(\neg b_{i,j} \vee Post_{p_i}(\tilde{x}_i))$.

We deal with the second part of the conjunction $(\bigwedge_{i=j+1}^{n}(b_{j,i} \vee Post_{p_i}(\tilde{x}_i)))$ in a similar way. So, we know that (SI) is true and can conclude that $Pre_{p'}$ is a left-termination condition for p' and thus the proof of the considered goal universally left-terminates. □

Proof (of the Theorem 3). Let us remind that to prove this theorem, we had to exhibit a transformation of P based on renaming and reordering operations such that the new program ensures the universal left-termination property. The previous proof has just shown that the transformation performed by our method verifies this condition. □

We end this paper by the example of the introduction.

Example 10. When we apply our method on the program POWER-4 (examples 1 and 6). We find: $Pre_s(x,y) = x \vee y$, $Pre_p(x,y) = x \vee y$, $\phi(r_3, x) = \omega$ (defined by $\omega_1 = 1, \omega_2 = 2$), $\phi(r_3, y) = \omega'$ $(\omega'_1 = 2, \omega'_2 = 1)$.

Now let us consider the query of the introduction: $\leftarrow y \leq 16,\ p(x,y)$. It corresponds to the class "*y bounded*" i.e. $y = 1$ in the boolean version. The new program P' is:

```
rule r'1 :   p'(X,Y) :- s'(Z,Y), s'(X,Z).
rule r'2 :   s'(0,0).
rule r'3 :   s'(X+1,Y+2X+1) :- s'(X,Y).
```

The call $\leftarrow y \leq 16, p'(x,y)$ left-terminates with answers: $\{x = 0\}, \{x = 1\}, \{x = 2\}$.

6 Conclusion

Let us first summarize our approach. From our previous work on the inference of left-terminating classes of queries, we are able to get rid of any particular order of literals to compute the set of terminating classes of queries. The main idea is to encode all the orderings by introducing sequences of new boolean variables. Then, for any terminating class, we can statically compile the control into Prolog. In other words, we can produce a Prolog program such that for any query of this class, universal left-termination is guaranteed.

The approach described in [9] is now completely implemented. For the work presented here, we have implemented the computation of extended pre-conditions $\{Pre_p\}_{p \in \bar{P}}$ as defined in section 4. In the Table 1, we present some results on program tests found in N. Lindenstrauss et Y. Sagiv's works[5] (times are given

[5] in the full version of [8] available at: http://www.cs.huji.ac.il/~naomil.

Table 1. comparison with Linderstrauss & Sagiv method

Name of program	main predicate	Hoarau/Mesnard inferred classes	time
append	$append(x, y, z)$	$\{x \vee z\}$	0,47
reverse	$reverse(x, y, z)$	$\{(x \wedge y) \vee (x \wedge z) \vee (y \wedge z)\}$	0,89
permute	$permute(x, y)$	$\{x \vee y\}$	1,31
hanoiapp	$hanoi(w, x, y, z, t)$	$\{(w \wedge x \wedge y \wedge z) \vee t\}$	53,2
fib_t	$fib(x, y)$	$\{x\}$	7,3
occur	$occurall(x, y, z)$	$\{x \wedge y\}$	4,2
money	$money(a, b, c, d, e, f, g, h)$	$\{1\}$	3,65
zebra	$zebra(a, b, c, d, e, f, g)$	$\{1\}$	3,26
Machine: Ultra 1 SUN Station, 128MB			

Name of program	main predicate	Lindenstrauss/Sagiv checked classes	time
append	$append(x, y, z)$	$\{x \vee z\}$	0,51
reverse	$reverse(x, y, z)$	$\{x \wedge z\}$	0,17
permute	$permute(x, y)$	$\{x\}$	0,69
hanoiapp	$hanoi(w, x, y, z, t)$	$\{w \wedge x \wedge y \wedge z\}$	62,5
fib_t	$fib(x, y)$	$\{x\}$	0,79
occur	$occurall(x, y, z)$	$\{x \wedge y\}$	2,45
money	$money(a, b, c, d, e, f, g, h)$	$\{1\}$	27,5
zebra	$zebra(a, b, c, d, e, f, g)$	$\{1\}$	0,58
Machine: Super SPARC 51, 128MB			

in seconds). Concerning the reordering, a beta version of the implementation accepts only CLP($\mathcal{N}$) programs (with a time complexity insignificant with respect to the total time complexity).

Let us point out that in all cases the set of classes of queries that we *infer* is at least as large as the set of classes *checked* by Lindenstrauss et Sagiv (see also [2]). We cannot expect the timings given by [8] or [11] but we address a much more general problem. Note also that there is room for trying to optimize the control for a given logic: in the construction of an environment (section 5), among the orderings which ensure termination, we may choose an ordering which leads to a "small" search tree. This is work in progress.

Acknowledgments

Thanks to Antoine Rauzy for sharing with us his knowledge about the boolean mu-calculus and to anonymous referees who help to clarify the paper.

References

1. K.R. APT and D. PEDRESCHI. Reasoning about termination of pure Prolog programs. In Information and Computation, 106:1, pages 109–157, 1993.
2. M. CODISH and C. TABOCH. A semantic basis for termination analysis of logic programs and its realization using symbolic norm constraints. Proc. of the 6th ICALP, LNCS 1298, 1997.
3. S. COLIN, F. MESNARD, and A. RAUZY. Constraint logic programming and mu-calculus. ERCIM/COMPULOG Workshop on Constraints, 1997. URL : http://www.univ-reunion.fr/~gcc
4. P. COUSOT and R. COUSOT. Abstract interpretation and application to logic programs. Journal of Logic Programming, 13:103–179, 1992.
5. D. DE SCHREYE and S. DECORTE. Termination of logic programs: the never-ending story. Journal of Logic Programming, 12:1–66, 1994.
6. M. GABBRIELLI and G. LEVI. Modelling answer constraints in constraint logic programs. In MIT Press, Proc. of ICLP'91, pages 238–252, 1991.
7. J. JAFFAR and M.J. MAHER. Constraint logic programming: a survey. Journal of Logic Programming, 19:503–581, 1994.
8. N. LINDENSTRAUSS and Y. SAGIV. Automatic termination analysis of logic programs. In MIT Press, Proc. of the 14th ICLP, pages 63–77, 1997.
9. F. MESNARD. Inferring left-terminating classes of queries for constraint logic programs by means of approximations. In MIT Press, Proc. of JICSLP'96, pages 7–21, 1996.
10. K. SOHN and A. VAN GELDER. Termination detection in logic programs using argument sizes. In ACM Press, Proc. of PODS'91, pages 216–226, 1991.
11. C. SPEIRS, Z. SOMOGYI, and H. SØNDERGAARD. Termination analysis for Mercury. Proc. of SAS'97, LNCS 1302, 1997.

Appendix - The reordering algorithm

Procedure: reorder

Input: a program P, its environment $E = \langle P, \{Pre_p \mid p \in \Pi\}, \phi \rangle$, a renaming table T, a pair $\langle p, C_p^l \rangle$, s.t. $p \in \Pi$, C_p^l a class of queries of Pre_p.

Output: a new program P' and Π' its set of predicate symbols.

Function: reorder_aux(p: a predicate, C a class of queries of p): R a set of rules

Begin
- $R \leftarrow \emptyset$;
- let p' be s.t. $\langle p, C, p' \rangle \in T$;
- $\Pi' \leftarrow \Pi' \cup \{p'\}$;
- **for all** rule $r : p(\tilde{x}) \leftarrow c, p_1(\tilde{x}_1), \ldots, p_n(\tilde{x}_n) \in P$ **do**
  - $\sigma \leftarrow \phi(r, C)$;
  - $R \leftarrow R \cup \{p(\tilde{x}) \leftarrow c, p_{\sigma_1}(\tilde{x}_{\sigma_1}), \ldots, p_{\sigma_n}(\tilde{x}_{\sigma_n})\}$;
- **end for**
- **return** R;

End

Main:
Begin
- $\Pi' \leftarrow \emptyset$; $P' \leftarrow$ reorder_aux(p, C_p^l);
- **while** $\exists$ a rule r_k in P' s.t. a predicate in the body does not appear in Π' **do**
  - let $r_k : q^\alpha(\tilde{y}) \leftarrow c_{\alpha,0}, q_{\alpha,1}(\tilde{y}_{\alpha,1}), \ldots, q_{\alpha,j_\alpha}(\tilde{y}_{\alpha,j_\alpha}) \in P'$;
  - let C_q^α be the class of queries s.t. $\langle q, C_q^\alpha, q^\alpha \rangle \in T$;
  - **for** $i = 1$ **to** j_α **do**
    - **if** $q_{\alpha,i} \in \Pi$ **then**
      - let C^β be a class of queries of $Pre_{q_{\alpha,i}}$ s.t.
      - $C_q^\alpha(\tilde{y}) \wedge c_{\alpha,0} \bigwedge_{j=1}^{i-1} Post_{q_{\alpha,j}}(\tilde{y}_{\alpha,j}) \rightarrow_B C^\beta(\tilde{y}_{\alpha,i})$;
      - let $q_{\alpha,i}^\beta$ s.t.$\langle q_{\alpha,i}, C^\beta, q_{\alpha,i}^\beta \rangle \in T$;
      - $P' \leftarrow P' \setminus \{r_k\}$;
      - $P' \leftarrow P' \cup \{q^\alpha(\tilde{y}) \leftarrow c_{\alpha,0}, q_{\alpha,1}(\tilde{y}_{\alpha,1}), \ldots, q_{\alpha,i}^\beta(\tilde{y}_{\alpha,i}), \ldots, q_{\alpha,j_\alpha}(\tilde{y}_{\alpha,j_\alpha})\}$;
      - **if** $q_{\alpha,i}^\beta \notin \Pi'$ **then**
        - $P' \leftarrow P' \cup$ reorder_aux($q_{\alpha,i}, C^\beta$);
      - **end if**
    - **end if**
  - **end for**
- **end while**
- **return** $\langle P', \Pi' \rangle$;

End

Strictness Analysis as Finite-Domain Constraint Solving

Tihomir Gabrić, Kevin Glynn, and Harald Søndergaard

Dept. of Computer Science, The University of Melbourne, Parkville 3052, Australia

Abstract. It has become popular to express dataflow analyses in logical form. In this paper we investigate a new approach to the analysis of functional programs, based on synthesis of constraint logic programs. We sketch how the language Toupie, originally designed with logic program analysis as one objective, lends itself also to sophisticated strictness analysis. Strictness analysis is straightforward in the simplest case, that of analysing a first-order functional language using just two strictness values, namely divergence and "don't know". Mycroft's classical translation immediately yields perfectly valid Boolean constraint logic programs, which, when run, provide the desired strictness information. However, more sophisticated analysis requires more complex domains of strictness values. We recast Wadler's classical analysis over a $2n$-point domain as finite-domain constraint solving. This approach has several advantages. First, the translation is relatively simple. We translate a recursive function definition into one or two constraint program clauses, in a manner which naturally extends Mycroft's translation for the 2-point case, where the classical approach translate the definition of an n-place function over lists into 4^n mutually recursive equations. Second, the resulting program produces *relational* information, allowing for example to ask which combinations of properties of input will produce a given output. Third, the approach allows us to leverage from established technology, for solving finite-domain constraints, as well as for finding fixed points. Finally, the use of (disjunctive) constraints can yield a higher precision in the analysis of some programs.

1 Introduction

Strictness is an important concept in the efficient implementation of lazy functional programming languages. To improve generated code, compilers for such languages usually perform some sort of strictness analysis, trying to establish cases where relatively expensive call-by-name evaluation can be replaced by simpler call-by-value evaluation, without changing the program's behaviour. A seminal study of strictness analysis was done by Mycroft [6], who suggested that analysis can be viewed as abstract interpretation. Mycroft considered first-order programs and gave an appealing translation method for such programs; his strictness analysis consists of translating the given program into a functional program that manipulates only Boolean values. Running the resulting program yields strictness information about the original program.

P. Flener (Ed.): LOPSTR'98, LNCS 1559, pp. 255–270, 1999.

Strictness analysis was subsequently extended in two directions, to handle higher-order programs, and to deal with more complex strictness information. More complex strictness information is usually needed in the context of lists and user-defined data types. For example, the termination properties of a list-processing function may depend on the "shape" of the argument only, as is the case with the function **length**, which terminates if and only if the input list is finite, independently of the termination properties of the list's elements. Semantically, the more complex information can be modelled by "non-flat" domains. Considerable progress was made when Wadler [10] proposed a precise strictness analysis based on case analysis over a domain of four (or in fact a family of domains with $2n, n \geq 1$) strictness values. The four-element domain is[1]:

$\top_\in$ Any list
|
$\bot_\in$ Any infinite list, and any finite list, some member of which is $\bot$
|
∞ Any infinite list, and any list whose tail is $\bot$
|
$\bot$ The undefined list

There is no simple equivalent of Mycroft's translation in the non-flat case. This is not only due to the fact that strictness properties no longer form a two-valued Boolean domain. As Wadler points out, reasoning by enumeration of cases seems necessary in the non-flat case and this would not be captured in a Mycroft-style translation where functions are approximated by functions. For example, we generally have that $(head\ \bot_\in) = \top$, where $\top$ is the top element of the usual two-valued strictness domain, **2**, that is, $\top$ stands for any value, defined or not. We also have that $(tail\ \bot_\in) = \top_\in$, since $\bot_\in$ may represent, say, the list $[\bot, 2]$. However, these simple mappings do not tell the full story. For example, if $(head\ \bot_\in)$ is known to be defined, that is, not to be $\bot$, then $(tail\ \bot_\in)$ must be $\bot_\in$. Such interrelations among dependent sub-expressions are lost in a naive translation.

We are interested in the use of constraint programming languages for program analysis, and one contribution of this paper is to show that a translation scheme for strictness analysis over a non-flat domain is not only possible, but also natural, if we work in a finite-domain constraint programming language. Dependent sub-expressions can then be handled via the introduction of "linking variables" (logic variables) and their subsequent removal can be performed via existential quantification. This translation has advantages:

- It is easy to understand and quite general.
- The need to tabulate abstract functions exhaustively disappears.

[1] Wadler's original paper [10] describes the meaning of the four elements slightly differently; we consider each element a subset of any element above it, as is common in the literature, see for example Plasmeijer and van Eekelen [7], Section 7.6.

- The generated program can be run "forwards" or "backwards", so as to answer questions about what output results from what input, with either (or none) constrained to particular values.
- Sophisticated fixed point and constraint solving technology promises to make analysis fast.
- The use of constraints allows for more precise analysis.

We have implemented a strictness analysis method for a simple functional programming language with lists and pattern matching. The constraint language we use is Toupie [1]. Toupie can be considered a finite-domain μ-calculus interpreter which allows fixed point problems to be stated succinctly and solved efficiently. It was originally designed for the abstract interpretation of logic programs. However, it would seem that finite-domain constraint solvers would be of great help for a variety of static analyses used in the compilation and transformation of functional programs, and a uniform approach to several such analyses, for example usage analysis and binding-time analysis, seems perfectly possible.

We shall assume that the reader has some familiarity with functional programming and strictness analysis. Plasmeijer and van Eekelen [7] offer introductions to both, as well as a discussion of Wadler's method.

In Section 2 we outline classical strictness analysis via abstract interpretation and sketch the approach that uses constraint logic programming. Section 3 shows how we translate a functional program to a Toupie program that performs the strictness analysis. Section 4 briefly discusses the handling of other data types, and Section 5 concludes.

2 Strictness Analysis

Consider the functional program

```
power x n = if n=0 then 1 else x * (power x (n-1));
```

Following Mycroft [6] we can analyse this program for strictness by translating it to a recursively defined Boolean function:

$$power^{\#}(x,n) = n \wedge true \wedge (true \vee (x \wedge power^{\#}(x, n \wedge true))).$$

The idea is to translate termination behaviour into propositional logic, associating *truth* with lack of information and *falsehood* with inevitable non-termination. Thus a constant such as `0` translates to *true*, since it would be wrong to claim that evaluation of `0` fails to terminate, while the comparison `n=0` translates to $n \wedge true$ because '=' is strict in both positions. So evaluation of the expression `n=0` will terminate if and only if evaluation of `n` terminates.

The conditional translates to a formula of the form $c \wedge (t \vee e)$ where c is the translation of the condition and t and e are the translations of the 'then' and 'else' branches, respectively. Namely, evaluation of the conditional is guaranteed to diverge if the evaluation of the condition diverges *or* both of the branches diverge.

It is easy to see that we can simplify the right-hand side of the equation for *power* to get

$$power^{\#}(x,n) = n.$$

Clearly then the evaluation of **power** fails to terminate if evaluation of its second argument does. So **power** is strict in position 2.

In general, when solving recursive equations, we cannot rely on algebraic simplifications to make recursion "go away", as happened above. We then resort to Kleene iteration. Consider the program

```
gcd x y = if x=y then x
          else if x>y then gcd (x-y) y
          else gcd x (y-x);
```

The corresponding strictness equation is

$$gcd^{\#}(x,y) = x \wedge y \wedge (x \vee (x \wedge y \wedge (gcd^{\#}(x \wedge y, y) \vee gcd^{\#}(x, x \wedge y))))$$

To find a closed form, we iterate from the initial guess $gcd^{\#}(x,y) = false$, eventually reaching the fixed point $gcd^{\#}(x,y) = x \wedge y$.

2.1 Wadler's Method for Lists

In the case of list-manipulating programs, we need more than two strictness values to get useful information. A list may be (partially) divergent, or some of its elements may diverge. The advantage of Wadler's domain is that it allows us to identify cases where list-processing functions can safely evaluate their arguments using special evaluation mechanisms, such as element reduction, spine reduction, or reduction to head normal form [5, 7].

Consider the program

```
sum []     =  0;
sum (x:xs) =  x + sum xs;
```

To translate the program into strictness equations, Wadler first determines that the best approximation to the list constructor (:) is as follows. For the possible values of x and xs, the value of $(x : xs)$ is:

$x \backslash xs$	$\bot$	∞	$\bot_\in$	$\top_\in$
$\top$	∞	∞	$\bot_\in$	$\top_\in$
$\bot$	∞	∞	$\bot_\in$	$\bot_\in$

This makes it possible to set up (and subsequently solve) four equations describing the best approximation to *sum*, by a tedious but mechanical case analysis:

$$\begin{aligned}
sum^{\#}\ \top_\in &= \top \sqcup (\top \sqcap (sum^{\#}\ \top_\in))\\
sum^{\#}\ \bot_\in &= (\bot \sqcap (sum^{\#}\ \top_\in)) \sqcup (\top \sqcap (sum^{\#}\ \bot_\in))\\
sum^{\#}\ \infty &= \top \sqcap (sum^{\#}\ \infty)\\
sum^{\#}\ \bot &= \bot
\end{aligned}$$

For example, the equation for $sum^{\#}\ \top_{\in}$ is generated by observing that the (list) argument $\top_{\in}$ would either have been `[]` or it would have been a composite list. In the former case, the right-hand side translates to '$\top$'. In the latter case, the table for `(:)` shows that the list would have to be composed from prepending $\top$ to $\top_{\in}$, so the translation of '`x + sum xs`' should be $\top \sqcap (sum^{\#}\ \top_{\in})$. The result is finally obtained by taking the join (maximum) of the two possible results.

Solving the four recursive equations, we arrive at the solution

$$sum^{\#}\ xs = \begin{cases} \top \text{ if } xs = \top_{\in} \\ \bot \text{ otherwise.} \end{cases}$$

So the sum of a list is defined only if the list is finite and all of its elements are non-$\bot$, that is, they do not diverge.

Note that with this method, the analysis of an n-place function requires the solution of up to 4^n mutually recursive equations.

2.2 A Constraint-Based Method

We now sketch a solution which uses constraints and generates only one (albeit complex) recursive equation. First, it is convenient to use domains of integers to represent the strictness values (such as $\mathbf{2} = \{1, 2\}$ and $\mathbf{4} = \{1, 2, 3, 4\}$), since then the constraint solver (Toupie) knows about the intended ordering of these values. Thus, instead of using $\bot_{\in}$ we use 3 ($\in \mathbf{4}$), and so on. Note that it is not necessary to treat strictness properties as integers in Toupie—indeed the language makes it easy to capture partially ordered sets of properties—but in our case integers and their linear ordering are convenient. For example, a join operation is simply taking the maximum of its operands.

Here is how **sum** gets translated into a recursive constraint equation (the precise rules appear in Section 3):

$$\begin{aligned} sum^{\#}(xs, res) \quad += \quad & (xs = 1 \wedge res = 1) \\ & \vee (xs = 4 \wedge res = 2) \\ & \vee \exists\ hd, tl, res' : \\ & \quad res = min(hd, res') \wedge sum^{\#}(tl, res') \wedge cons^{\#}(hd, tl, xs) \end{aligned}$$

$$cons^{\#}(x, xs, res) \quad = \quad res = max(2, min(x + 2, xs))$$

The '$+=$' indicates that we want the *least* solution to the recursive equation. (Toupie also allows '$-=$' to specify that a greatest fixed point is wanted.)

The $cons^{\#}$ rule captures the effect of list construction `(:)`. This clause is used every time a program involves list construction or list patterns. It expresses exactly the information present in the table in Section 2.1. To rephrase the rule, the result $(x : xs)$ in general is the least defined (the minimum) of the lists $[x]$ and xs. For example, if x is $\bot$ (1) and xs is $\top_{\in}$ (4) then $[x]$ is $\bot_{\in}$ (3), and hence $(x : xs)$ is $\bot_{\in}$ (3). In general, if $x \in \mathbf{2}$ approximates some element h then $x + 2 \in \mathbf{4}$ approximates $[h]$. However, $(x : xs)$ does not diverge, even if x or xs

do. This explains the application of max which ensures that the result is at least ∞ (2).

As we shall later see, the domains of variables may be other than **2** and **4**, as nested lists may be described more precisely using higher domains **n**. The body of the $cons^\#$ rule remains the same, but $cons^\#$ may have different types of the form $\mathbf{n} \times (\mathbf{n}+\mathbf{2}) \times (\mathbf{n}+\mathbf{2}) \to \mathbf{Bool}$, for even **n**. Toupie needs to know the domains of variables, so a (simple) type analysis is necessary to establish these. In the rest of the paper we assume that programs have been decorated with type information. This is a reasonable assumption since the programming language is assumed to be typed and the analysis is only correct for well-typed programs.

The example clearly shows how dependencies of sub-expressions can be captured while the mechanics can be hidden through the use of existential quantification. The existentially quantified variables capture the dependencies. Their elimination is handled by Toupie. Their use render the kind of enumeration seen in Section 2.1 unnecessary and allows us to express all variable dependencies in a single clause. In this sense the use of constraints generalises Mycroft's method to non-flat domains in a natural way.

The solution to the recursive equation for $sum^\#$ is also left to the constraint programming language. Notice that it is perfectly possible to obtain a closed form for $sum^\#$, by Kleene iteration and constraint solving. After the first iteration step (setting $sum^\#(tl, res) = false$) we get

$$sum^\#(xs, res) = (xs = 1 \land res = 1) \lor (xs = 4 \land res = 2)$$

Using this approximation, the second iteration step adds

$$\exists\ hd : (res = 1 \land cons^\#(hd, 1, xs)) \lor (res = min(hd, 2) \land cons^\#(hd, 4, xs))$$

which simplifies to

$$(res = 1 \land xs = 2) \lor (res = 1 \land xs = 3) \lor (res = 2 \land xs = 4)$$

After this step, no more solutions are added. Indeed the Toupie solution comes out as

```
{Xs=1, Res=1}
{Xs=2, Res=1}
{Xs=3, Res=1}
{Xs=4, Res=2}
```

in agreement with Wadler's analysis. In Section 5 we argue that the constraint approach occasionally offers greater precision than Wadler's approach. Another advantage of the constraint-based approach is that the analyser can be queried in different ways—for example, it makes sense for a compiler to ask, for a given function call, which input combinations make the call diverge.

The programs that we generate are slightly more verbose than indicated by the example. Consider the following program:

```
fn_append(X0,X1,Result) +=
    exist V0,V1,V2,V3
    ( ( cr_nil(X0)
      & (Result = X1)
      )
    | ( exist E0
          ( cr_cons(V1,E0,Result)
          & fn_append(V2,X1,E0)
          )
      & cr_cons(V1,V2,X0)
      )
    | ( dm_bot(Result)
      & dm_bot(X0)
      )
    )
```

Fig. 1. The Toupie code generated for analysis of **append**

```
append []     ys = ys;
append (x:xs) ys = x : append xs ys;
```

The Toupie translation of **append** is given in Figure 1. (Again notice that we produce *one* recursive equation to solve, rather than the 16 equations suggested by the traditional case analysis.) Some of the auxiliary predicates are domain dependent. In the current example, `cr_nil(X0)` translates to `(X0 = 4)` because the domain is **4**. The answers produced for the query `fn_append(X,Y,Res)?` are:

```
{X=1, Y in 1..4, Res=1}
{X=2, Y in 1..4, Res=2}
{X=3, Y=1, Res=2}
{X=3, Y=2, Res=2}
{X=3, Y=3, Res=3}
{X=3, Y=4, Res=3}
{X=4, Y=1, Res=1}
{X=4, Y=1, Res=2}
{X=4, Y=2, Res=2}
{X=4, Y=3, Res=3}
{X=4, Y=4, Res=4}

2p -> 11 displayed solutions
2p -> 0s00
```

In the last line of output, Toupie indicates the time spent on finding the solution, in this case negligible time.

```
    Prog ::= {Def}*

     Def ::= Fname {Pat}* "=" Exp ";"

     Pat ::= Integer
           | Var
           | "[]"
           | "(" PatList ")"

 PatList ::= Pat
           | Pat ":" PatList

     Exp ::= Exp Op Exp
           | Integer
           | Fname {Exp}*
           | "[]"
           | "(" Exp ")"
           | "if" Exp "then" Exp "else" Exp
           | Var

      Op ::= "+" | "-" | ...
```

Fig. 2. A simple functional language

3 The Translation

We now give the details of the functional language analysed, and the rules for translating programs into Toupie programs. The syntax of our language is given in Figure 2. It is a simple first order functional language with pattern matching on lists and integer constants.

A natural approach when analysing a set of functions is to first divide them into so-called strongly connected components (SCCs), based on the program's call graph. As a non-trivial example, Figure 3 shows the call graph of the `revall` program used in Section 4. For example, `revall` calls both `maprev` and `rev` who in turn call other functions, possibly themselves. An SCC has the property that all functions within the SCC directly or indirectly call every other function in that SCC, but there is no mutual access between two functions in separate SCCs. In the example, each of the four functions forms its own SCC. The SCCs determine a stratification of the program, which is the natural order of analysis. In the example, we would analyse `append` first, then `rev`, then `maprev`, and finally `revall`.

Figure 4 gives the algorithm used to translate functional programs into Toupie, and Figure 5 shows how expressions and patterns are translated. Note that patterns are translated using the same techniques as expressions. The result returned by a function is represented by a `Result` variable in a logic program-

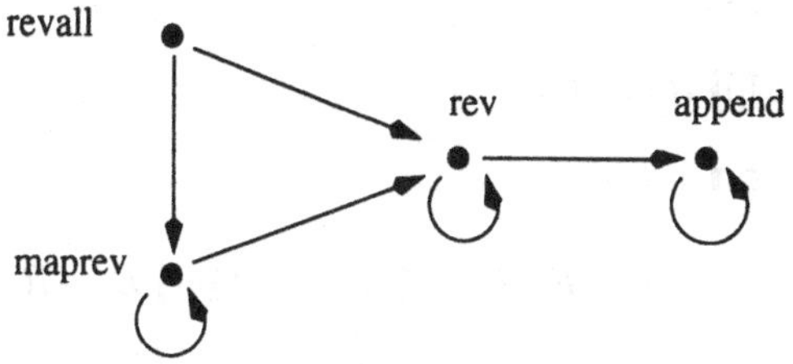

Fig. 3. A call graph

For each SCC S of the input program:

For each function f defined in S do:

Let k be the arity of f;
Let $D_1, \ldots, D_n$ be the n equations defining f, renamed apart so that $vars(D_i) \cap vars(D_j) = \emptyset$ whenever $i \neq j$;

For each $i \in \{1, \ldots, n\}$ do:
Let $[\![f\ p_{i1}\ \ldots p_{ik} = e_i]\!] = D_i$
Let $V = vars\{p_{qr} : q \in \{1 \ldots n\}, r \in \{1 \ldots k\}\}$

Emit the two clauses:

$$f^{\#}(X_1, \ldots, X_k, R) \mathrel{+}= f^{\#\#}(X_1, \ldots, X_k, R, true)$$

$$f^{\#\#}(X_1, \ldots, X_k, R, T) \mathrel{+}= \exists\, V : (T = true \wedge (e'_1 \vee \ldots \vee e'_n \vee (R = \bot \wedge somepat(f)))) \vee (T = false \wedge R = \bot \wedge allpat(f))$$

where
$e'_i = \mathcal{E}[\![e_i]\!]\ R\ \wedge\ \mathcal{E}[\![p_{i1}]\!]\ X_1 \wedge\ \ldots\ \wedge\ \mathcal{E}[\![p_{ik}]\!]\ X_k$
$somepat(f) = \bigvee\{X_q = \bot \mid \exists i : p_{iq} \text{ is not a variable}\}$
$allpat(f) = \bigwedge\{X_q = \bot \mid \exists i : p_{iq} \text{ is not a variable}\}$

Fig. 4. Translating function definitions

$$\mathcal{E}[\![n]\!]\ R = (R = \top)$$

$$\mathcal{E}[\![[]]\!]\ R = (R = \top_{\in})$$

$$\mathcal{E}[\![v]\!]\ R = (R = v)$$

$$\mathcal{E}[\![e_0\ \langle op \rangle\ e_1]\!]\ R = \exists\ E_0, E_1 : \mathcal{E}[\![e_0]\!]\ E_0 \wedge \mathcal{E}[\![e_1]\!]\ E_1 \wedge R = min(E_0, E_1)$$

$$\mathcal{E}[\![e_0 : e_1]\!]\ R = \exists\ E_0, E_1 : \mathcal{E}[\![e_0]\!]\ E_0 \wedge \mathcal{E}[\![e_1]\!]\ E_1 \wedge cons(E_0, E_1, R)$$

$$\begin{aligned}\mathcal{E}[\![f\ e_1 \ldots e_k]\!]\ R = {} & \exists\ E_1, \ldots, E_k, E_t\ f^{\#\#}(E_1, \ldots, E_k, R, E_t) \\ & \wedge\ \mathcal{E}[\![e_1]\!]\ E_1 \wedge\ \ldots\ \wedge\ \mathcal{E}[\![e_k]\!]\ E_k, \\ & \qquad\qquad \text{if } f \text{ is in the current SCC}\end{aligned}$$

$$\begin{aligned}\mathcal{E}[\![f\ e_1 \ldots e_k]\!]\ R = {} & \exists\ E_1, \ldots, E_k : f^{\#}(E_1, \ldots, E_k, R) \\ & \wedge\ \mathcal{E}[\![e_1]\!]\ E_1 \wedge\ \ldots\ \wedge\ \mathcal{E}[\![e_k]\!]\ E_k, \qquad \text{otherwise}\end{aligned}$$

$$\begin{aligned}\mathcal{E}[\![\text{if } e_1 \text{ then } e_2 \text{ else } e_3]\!]\ R = {} & \exists\ E_1, E_2, E_3 : \\ & (\mathcal{E}[\![e_1]\!]\ E_1) \wedge (\mathcal{E}[\![e_2]\!]\ E_2) \wedge (\mathcal{E}[\![e_3]\!]\ E_3) \wedge \\ & (((R = E_2 \vee R = E_3) \wedge (E_1 = \top)) \\ & \vee((R = \bot) \wedge (E_1 = \bot)))\end{aligned}$$

Fig. 5. Translating expressions into constraints

ming style. The function $\mathcal{E}$ takes an expression and a result variable name, and constructs a Toupie expression to constrain the result. For simplicity the rules assume that analysis of lists uses the 4-point domain, but this is easily generalised. In the next section we look at the handling of nested lists.

There are two complications in the translation, and we address these in turn. First, the translation in Figure 4 must account for the use of (eager) pattern matching. During execution, if a function needs to compare some input value against a pattern, it must first reduce the value to weak head normal form [7]. Only then is it able to make a meaningful comparison. However, if the input argument is $\bot$, this comparison does not terminate. The function *somepat* takes all the input patterns for a given function f, and for each argument position q, for which some clause has a proper pattern p_{iq} (not a variable), it generates the equation $X_q = \bot$. It then forms the disjunction *somepat(f)* of all such equations. The aim is to allow any solution

$$X_q = \bot \wedge R = \bot$$

since a pattern-matched argument in position q may fail to terminate, and then the function which is being defined by pattern matching also fails to terminate.

The other complication is that an analysis *must* return a result, that is, a Toupie clause should not be allowed to fail. The natural translation of a function definition

$$f\ p_{i1}\ \ldots p_{ik} = e_i$$

is the clause

$$f^{\#}(X_1,\ldots,X_k,R) \mathrel{+}= \exists\, V : e'_1 \vee \ldots \vee e'_n \vee (R = \bot \wedge \mathit{somepat}(f))$$

where $e'_i = \mathcal{E}[\![e_i]\!]\ R\ \wedge\ \mathcal{E}[\![p_{i1}]\!]\ X_1 \wedge\ \ldots \wedge\ \mathcal{E}[\![p_{ik}]\!]\ X_k$. However, this will not be correct when a recursively defined function f has no base case and does not use pattern matching (so *somepat(f)* is *false*).

Consider the function `inf` defined by

```
inf x = x : inf x;
```

The translation

```
fn_inf(X0,Result) +=
    exist E0
    (  cr_cons(X0,E0,Result)
    &  fn_inf(X0,E0)
    )
```

is not correct, since queries to `fn_inf` will fail.

The solution is to use an auxiliary function $f\#\#$ which ensures that fixed point iteration is started off at a point higher than *false*. The starting point for fixed point iteration is a constraint *allpat(f)* which is satisfiable and will not exclude any of the solutions that are due to pattern matching. Functions are given an additional parameter T. This is a tag which indicates whether a solution is a bona fide solution ($T = \mathit{true}$) or whether its purpose is to start fixed point iteration. For the vast majority of functions, the use of this is unnecessary, and in most cases the Toupie clauses can be simplified considerably. However, the more complex definition is needed for every function that may call itself recursively and does not have a non-recursive base case.

For the function `inf`, the correct translation is:

```
fn_inf(X0,Result) +=
    fn_inf1(X0,Result,2)

fn_inf1(X0,Result,Tag) +=
    ( (  exist E0,E1
         (  cr_cons(X0,E0,Result)
         &  fn_inf1(X0,E0,E1)
         )
      &  (Tag = 2)
      )
    | (  (Tag = 1)
```

Let k = the arity of f;
Let $D_1, \ldots, D_n$ be the n equations defining f, renamed apart so that $vars(D_i) \cap vars(D_j) = \emptyset$ whenever $i \neq j$;

For each $i \in \{1, \ldots, n\}$ do:
Let $[\![f\ p_{i1}\ \ldots p_{ik} = e_i]\!] = D_i$
Let $V = vars\{p_{qr} : q \in \{1 \ldots n\}, r \in \{1 \ldots k\}\}$

Emit the clause:

$$f^{\#}(X_1, \ldots, X_k, R) \mathrel{+}= \exists\ V : e'_1 \vee \ldots \vee e'_n \vee (R = \bot \wedge somepat(f))$$

where
$e'_i = \mathcal{E}[\![e_i]\!]\ R\ \wedge\ \mathcal{E}[\![p_{i1}]\!]\ X_1 \wedge\ \ldots \wedge\ \mathcal{E}[\![p_{ik}]\!]\ X_k$

Fig. 6. Simpler translation of function definitions

```
        & (Result = 1)
        )
    )
```

The result of querying the resulting Toupie program `fn_inf(X,Res)?` yields

```
{X=1, Res=2}
{X=2, Res=2}

2p -> 2 displayed solutions
2p -> 0s00
```

That is, every x is mapped to the result ∞, an infinite list.

There are several ways the generated Toupie programs can be simplified. Many of the generated existentially quantified variables can be removed in a post-processing step. The pattern $\exists V : \ldots \wedge V = X \wedge \ldots$ is common in the automatically generated programs, and V is easily eliminated by replacing every occurrence of V by X.

As discussed, if the definition of a function f has a base case, then $R = \bot \wedge somepat(f)$ is already a valid result, and there is no need to ensure that Toupie cannot fail. In this case the simpler translation given in Figure 6 suffices.

4 Other Data Types

The translation extends easily to handle cases with nested lists, using ideas from Wadler [10]. For example, lists of lists are approximated by the six-element domain **6**:

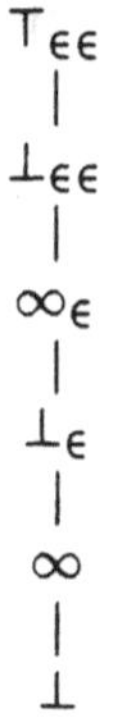

Here $\perp$ and ∞ have the same meaning as before, while an element of the form $d_{\in} \in \mathbf{6}$ corresponds to a list, some member of which is described by $d \in \mathbf{4}$. For example, $[[1, \perp, 3]]$ is approximated by $\perp_{\in\in}$ but not by $\infty_{\in}$.

An initial type analysis determines the domains for the various variables. Consider the following program which uses **append** from before:

```
revall xss = rev (maprev xss);

maprev [] = [];
maprev (x:xs) = rev x : maprev xs;

rev [] = [];
rev (x:xs) = append (rev xs) (x:[]);
```

The generated Toupie clauses are shown in Figure 7. In this case the list variables are in **6**. Notice that *cons* need not be redefined—it was defined in such a way that it extends gracefully. The output from asking the most general query `revall(X,Res)?` is shown below, both as output from Toupie and in tabular form.

```
{X=1, Res=1}
{X=2, Res=1}
{X=3, Res=3}
{X=4, Res=3}
{X=5, Res=5}
{X=6, Res=6}

2p ->  6 displayed solutions
2p ->  0s08
```

input	output
$\top_{\in\in}$	$\top_{\in\in}$
$\perp_{\in\in}$	$\perp_{\in\in}$
$\infty_{\in}$	$\perp_{\in}$
$\perp_{\in}$	$\perp_{\in}$
∞	$\perp$
$\perp$	$\perp$

Handling other free data types is not hard. In general we will not obtain a linearly ordered domain of abstractions, but the ordering relation can be programmed explicitly in the constraint programming language.

Alternatively, the components of a user-defined data structure can be represented by separate logic variables. For functions of several variables we have

```
fn_revall(X0,Result) +=
    ( exist E0
        ( fn_rev(E0,Result)
        & fn_maprev(X0,E0)
        )
    )

fn_maprev(X0,Result) +=
    exist V0,V1
    ( ( cr_nil(Result)
      & cr_nil(X0)
      )
    | ( exist E0,E1
        ( cr_cons(E0,E1,Result)
        & fn_rev(V0,E0)
        & fn_maprev(V1,E1)
        )
      & cr_cons(V0,V1,X0)
      )
    | ( dm_bot(Result)
      & dm_bot(X0)
      )
    )
```

```
fn_rev(X0,Result) +=
    exist V0,V1
    ( ( cr_nil(Result)
      & cr_nil(X0)
      )
    | ( exist E0,E1,E2
        ( fn_append(E0,E1,Result)
        & fn_rev(V1,E0)
        & ( cr_cons(V0,E2,E1)
          & cr_nil(E2)
          )
        )
      & cr_cons(V0,V1,X0)
      )
    | ( dm_bot(Result)
      & dm_bot(X0)
      )
    )
```

Fig. 7. Toupie clauses generated for the `revall` program

seen how detailed information can be maintained about their interrelation. This principle can be extended to include the components of results that are composite.

5 Conclusion

It has become popular to cast analyses for functional programs analysis in logical form. Examples are Jensen's "strictness logic" (for example [4]), and "usage logic" as developed by Wadler and by Wright and Baker-Finch—for an attempt to provide a unifying framework for these, see Wright [11]. Another trend is the formulation of analyses as "constraint" problems, as in the case of binding-time analysis [3] which uses a combination of Boolean and Herbrand constraints. In strictness analysis, Sekar and Ramakrishnan [8] have also embraced constraint solving techniques. These analysis methods have included the invention of some constraint system and its solver. It is natural to ask what constraint (logic) programming can offer, and whether some uniform approach can be developed.

Much research on constraint-based analysis views the problem as one of inference of "constrained types" in some sense. A good candidate for a basis for this is Sulzmann, Odersky and Wehr's *HM(X)* [9], which is a Hindley-Milner type system extended with additional constraint reasoning capabilities. The 'X'

refers to the constraint domain applied, so $HM(X)$ is parametric with respect to constraint domains.

As an alternative, we have here explored an approach based on abstract interpretation, in which we exploit available constraint programming technology for program analysis. We have developed a method for strictness analysis over non-flat domains, using a constraint programming language to express strictness properties of the program under analysis. This method reconciles Mycroft's classical two-valued approach with Wadler's technique for the non-flat case, translating a function definition into a single constraint program clause. This is preferable to the classical method of generating up to 4^n recursive equations for an n-place function. Exhaustive tabulation of abstract functions is replaced by more compact constraints. Moreover, the generated program can be run "forwards" or "backwards", so as to answer questions about what output results from what input, with either (or none) constrained to particular values.

We have found that Toupie offers easy expression of the analysis problem *and* supports high-precision analysis. Toupie has a fixed point operator and uses an efficient algorithm for finding fixed points over finite domains. Corsini et al. [1] applied Toupie to the analysis of logic programs, notably for groundness dependency analysis. In that application, constraint variables belong to a two-element domain, and it has been an interesting exercise to apply the same technology to a strictness analysis which uses domains of size greater than 2.

The constraint programming approach gives much flexibility with respect to the granularity of information, partly because it naturally leads to *disjunctive* analysis, and partly because the components of composite data structures can be represented by separate logic variables. Usually, in the analysis of functions defined by cases, or using if-then-else, one takes the join, or least upper bound, of the results obtained for the individual cases or branches of computation. It is recognised that it would be more precise to tabulate all possible (combinations of) outcomes, but usually this is not feasible because of the large number of possible computation paths and the consequent efficiency penalty. However, (symbolic) constraints allow for a more compact representation of information. Note that we do not apply a least upper bound operation in the analysis given in this paper.

Consider the program

```
f x = if B then (x,17) else (17,x);
g x = add (f x);
```

Jensen [4] uses this example to show how disjunctive information translates into greater precision, even when the result of an analysis is not disjunctive. Assume the value of the Boolean expression `B` cannot be determined at analysis time. If we were to take the join of the two contributions from the branches of the conditional, we would end up with $(x, \mathit{true}) \sqcup (\mathit{true}, x) = (\mathit{true}, \mathit{true})$ as the result of analysing `f`. Based on this, the result for `g` would be *true*, that is, we would fail to recognise that `g` is strict.

There have been other approaches to non-flat strictness analysis, such as projection analysis and PER analysis, see for example Cousot and Cousot [2].

It would be interesting to compare with these approaches. With constraints, complex interactions amongst both input and output components are naturally captured by the introduction of local "linking" variables that are subsequently eliminated through existential quantification. We feel that a method which uses these ideas, but also incorporates type inference, would be well worth developing and testing.

References

1. M.-M. Corsini, K. Musumbu, A. Rauzy, and B. Le Charlier. Efficient bottom-up abstract interpretation of Prolog by means of constraint solving over symbolic finite domains. In M. Bruynooghe and J. Penjam, editors, *Programming Language Implementation and Logic Programming*, LNCS 714, pages 75–91. Springer-Verlag, 1993.
2. P. Cousot and R. Cousot. Higher-order abstract interpretation (and application to comportment analysis generalizing strictness, termination, projection and PER analysis of functional languages. In *Proc. 1994 Int. Conf. Computer Languages*, pages 95–112. IEEE Computer Society, 1994.
3. F. Henglein. Efficient type inference for higher-order binding-time analysis. In J. Hughes, editor, *Functional Programming Languages and Computer Architecture*, LNCS 523, pages 448–472. Springer-Verlag, 1991.
4. T. P. Jensen. Disjunctive strictness analysis. In *Proc. Seventh Ann. IEEE Symp. Logic in Computer Science*, pages 174–185, 1992.
5. J. M. Kewley and K. Glynn. Evaluation annotations for Hope+. *Functional Programming: Proc. 1989 Glasgow Workshop*, pages 329-337. Springer-Verlag, 1990.
6. A. Mycroft. *Abstract Interpretation and Optimising Transformations for Applicative Programs*. PhD thesis, University of Edinburgh, Scotland, 1981.
7. R. Plasmeijer and M. van Eekelen. *Functional Programming and Parallel Graph Rewriting*. Addison-Wesley, 1993.
8. R. Sekar and I. V. Ramakrishnan. Fast strictness analysis based on demand propagation. *ACM Trans. Programming Languages and Systems*, 17(6):896–937, 1995.
9. Martin Sulzmann, Martin Odersky, and Martin Wehr. Type inference with constrained types (extended abstract). In B. Pierce, editor, *Proc. Fourth Int. Workshop Foundations of Object-Oriented Languages*, 1997. http://www.cs.indiana.edu/hyplan/pierce/fool.
10. P. Wadler. Strictness analysis on non-flat domains (by abstract interpretation over finite domains). In S. Abramsky and C. Hankin, editors, *Abstract Interpretation of Declarative Languages*, pages 266–275. Ellis Horwood, 1987.
11. D. A. Wright. Linear, strictness and usage logics. In M. Houle and P. Eades, editors, *Proc. CATS'96*, Australian Computer Science Communications **18** (3), pages 73–80, 1996.

Invariant Discovery via Failed Proof Attempts*

Jamie Stark and Andrew Ireland

Department of Computing & Electrical Engineering,
Heriot-Watt University, Riccarton
Edinburgh EH14 4AS, Scotland, UK
{jamie,air}@cee.hw.ac.uk
http://www.cee.ac.uk/~dsg

Abstract. We present a framework for automating the discovery of loop invariants based upon failed proof attempts. The discovery of suitable loop invariants represents a bottleneck for automatic verification of imperative programs. Using the proof planning framework we reconstruct standard heuristics for developing invariants. We relate these heuristics to the analysis of failed proof attempts allowing us to discover invariants through a process of refinement.

1 Introduction

Loop invariants are a well understood technique for specifying the behaviour of programs involving loops. The discovery of suitable invariants, however, is a major bottleneck for automatic verification of imperative programs. Early research in this area [18, 24] exploited both theorem proving techniques as well as domain specific heuristics. However, the potential for interaction between these components was not fully exploited. The proof planning framework, in which we reconstruct the standard heuristics, couples the heuristic and theorem proving components tightly, allowing us to focus on both of these components together. In particular this enables us to exploit the relationship between failed proof attempts and invariant discovery. The framework described here builds upon previous work [16] and shows how successive approximations are used to find a suitable invariant by a system automatically. This work was motivated by previous work on discovering generalisations for inductive proofs. We exploit the relationship between while loops and tail recursive functions, but rather than transform our loop programs into tail recursive functions and discover a generalisation we choose instead to transfer heuristics across domains. This enables us to communicate proof attempts, and specifications in the same language. Ultimately this will have significant benefits when integrating our approach within an interactive environment.

The paper is structured as follows. In §2 we introduce background material where we focus upon proof planning and the rippling heuristic. §3 gives a proof

* The contribution of the first author is supported by an EPSRC student ship award 96307451, and the contribution of the second author is supported by EPSRC grant GR/L11724

P. Flener (Ed.): LOPSTR'98, LNCS 1559, pp. 271–288, 1999.

plan for verification of loops. In §4 we show how the analysis of failed proof attempts can be used to guide the discovery of loop invariants. A detailed example, showing the refinement style of our approach, is presented in §5. §6 discusses results and implementation details. §7 discusses related work while future work is outlined in §8. Finally we draw our conclusions in §9.

2 Background

Hoare [12] first introduced his axiomatic proof rules for imperative programs involving loops in 1969. The aim was to assist the understanding of programs using rigorous logical techniques. The proof rules allow the transformation of a program, with suitable assertions, into a set of purely logical implications called verification conditions. These assertions are relationships between the program variables and program constants[1]. Program constants are important since they are used to capture initial inputs to a program and are used in the post condition to relate a desired property in terms of these initial values.

The verification of simple imperative programs involving loops falls short of full automation since Hoare's rule for while loops involves synthesising an assertion known as the invariant. The while rule for partial correctness takes the form:

$$\frac{P \rightarrow I, \quad \{I \wedge B\}S\{I\}, \quad (I \wedge \neg B) \rightarrow Q}{\{P\}\textbf{while}\ \ B\ \textbf{begin}\ S\ \textbf{end}\ \{Q\}}$$

The second premise is used to generate a verification condition using Hoare's other proof rules. It is this verification condition which establishes I to be an invariant of the loop body S and is the focus of our work.

The literature [1, 8, 10, 17] contains many heuristics for constructing invariants in a systematic way. These heuristics may weaken an initial guess, *e.g.* replacing a constant by a variable or term, or strengthen an guess, *e.g.* by introducing more conjuncts to the invariant. Previously, in [16], we showed how proof planing was able to successfully discover tail invariants. Here this work is extended by adding heuristics to replace program constants and strengthen invariants. A general strategy is presented that enables the successive approximation of invariants using these heuristics.

2.1 Proof Planning

Proof planning [3] consists of tactics, methods and critics. Tactics are rules of inference, either primitive or derived. Methods are partial specifications of tactics and allow the use of heuristics to focus their applicability. A method has preconditions and effects. Proof planning involves the search for a plan at the meta-level by using the methods and critics. A tactic is extracted from a plan and then run to ensure soundness. Critics [13] are used to handle the failure of

[1] Program constants are denoted as calligraphic letters throughout *e.g.* $\mathcal{X}$.

a proof attempt. They patch the failed proof attempt and provide a powerful mechanism for dealing with failure.

The CLAM proof planner [6] has been used, amongst other applications, for inductive proof [5]. The success of the proof plan for induction is due to the ripple heuristic which is explained more fully below.

Middle-out reasoning is a technique where meta terms are used to delay choice when planning a proof. The motivation is that the middle of a proof is typically more constrained than the start. Planning a proof from the *middle-out* therefore provides greater constraints than the conventional forwards or backwards style of proof construction. The implementation makes use of the higher-order features of λ-prolog [22]. Middle-out techniques have been used for generalisation [11, 14], logic program synthesis [19], lemma discovery and induction revision [15].

2.2 The Ripple Heuristic

Rewriting often involves the manipulation of a goal formula so that a target formula can be applied. We are interested in proving theorems of the form:

$$Hypothesis \rightarrow Conclusion$$

where *Hypothesis* is the target formula and *Conclusion* is the goal formula we want to manipulate. Rippling is a difference reduction technique which exploits syntactic similarities between the goal and target in guiding the selective application of rewrite rules. In particular it identifies term structure within the goal which prevents a match with the target. For example consider the following implication:

$$(x + (y + z) = (x + y) + z) \rightarrow (s(x) + (y + z) = (s(x) + y) + z) \quad (1)$$

The conclusion differs syntactically from the hypothesis in two places *i.e.* in the application of the successor function s around the two occurrences of x. We identify these differences with shading. Such term structures are called *wave-fronts*. Conversely any term structure within the goal which corresponds to the target is called *skeleton*. The parts of the skeleton inside a wave-front are called *wave-holes*. Wave-fronts, wave-holes and skeletons are meta-level notions. For the example above the conclusion is given the following meta-level annotation:

$$(x + (y + z) = (x + y) + z) \rightarrow \left(\boxed{s(\underline{x})} + (y + z) = (\boxed{s(\underline{x})} + y) + z \right)$$

Note that the wave-fronts are shaded. The skeleton of the conclusion is all the unshaded terms *i.e.* this corresponds to the hypothesis. An arrow is often used to indicate the direction in which a wave-front can be moved with respect to the skeleton term structure. Directed wave-fronts enable the termination of rippling to be guaranteed [2]. For ease of presentation we have dropped the directions attached to the wave fronts since in this paper we will only be concerned with outward ($\uparrow$) directed wave-fronts. The movement of wave-fronts is performed by *wave-rules*, a syntactic class of rewrite rule which preserves skeleton while making progress to eliminating wave-fronts. An algorithm exists which automatically generates wave-rules from all definitions and properties loaded into the system [2]. For any equation there are usually a number of corresponding wave-rules.

Consider the following recursive definition of plus[2] :

$$A + 0 = 0$$
$$s(A) + B = s(A + B) \tag{2}$$

An example wave-rule derived from (2) is[3]:

$$\boxed{s(A)} + B \Rightarrow \boxed{s(A + B)} \tag{3}$$

Notice that the skeleton on both sides of the wave-rules are the same, *i.e.* $A+B$. To use a wave-rule all the object-level and meta-level structure on the left hand side of the wave-rule must match with a sub-term of the goal formula. This sub-term is then replaced with right hand side of the wave-rule, taking into account any matching. We are able to reduce the differences between the hypothesis and conclusion in (1), by successive applications of wave-rule (3):

$$(x + (y + z) = (x + y) + z) \rightarrow \left(\boxed{s(x)} + (y + z) = (\boxed{s(x)} + y) + z\right)$$
$$(x + (y + z) = (x + y) + z) \rightarrow \left(\boxed{s(x + (y + z))} = (\boxed{s(x)} + y) + z\right)$$
$$(x + (y + z) = (x + y) + z) \rightarrow \left(\boxed{s(x + (y + z))} = (\boxed{s(x + y)}) + z\right)$$
$$(x + (y + z) = (x + y) + z) \rightarrow \left(\boxed{s(x + (y + z))} = \boxed{s((x + y) + z)}\right)$$

Notice how the wave-fronts move to the top of the term structure. This meta-level structure helps to guide the search for a proof. Now we have a copy of part of our hypothesis in the wave-hole. Since our hypothesis is an equality we can use it to rewrite the goal. This we call (weak) fertilization and gives us the trivial goal:

$$(x + (y + z) = (x + y) + z) \rightarrow (s((x + y) + z) = s((x + y) + z))$$

A stronger version of fertilization is applicable when a complete copy of the hypothesis appears within a wave-hole.

2.3 Summary

Rippling is a heuristic which supports the selective application of rewrite rules. This is achieved by firstly identifying the differences between two formulas. Secondly, only using those rewrite rules which guarantee that the identical parts stay

---

[2] We use the Prolog notation of denoting first order variables with capital letters throughout.

[3] Where $\Rightarrow$ denotes rewriting.

the same and thirdly, making sure that the differences are moved in a particular direction. Proofs guided by rippling can be classified in terms of the direction in which wave-fronts are moved with respect to the skeleton term structure. For a full account of rippling see [2, 5]. The annotation described here can also be seen as embedding the target formula within the goal formula [23].

Identifying differences and constructing wave-rules is automatic. The real advantage of rippling over conventional rewriting techniques becomes apparent when rewriting in the presence of meta variables, as will be illustrated below.

3 A Proof Plan for Verification

```
exp1:  {x = 𝒳 ∧ y = 𝒴}
       r := 1;
       while (y > 0) do
       begin
              r := r * x;
              y := y - 1
       end
       {r = exp(𝒳, 𝒴)}
```

Fig. 1. Algorithm for computing exponentiation

Consider the program in figure 1. To verify this program we need a loop invariant. A suitable invariant is not immediately obvious and finding one is often referred to as a *eureka* step. One such invariant for this loop is:

$$r = exp(\mathcal{X}, \mathcal{Y} - y) \wedge x = \mathcal{X}$$

In order to verify that this property is indeed invariant involves proving the following verification condition generated by the loop body:

$$(r = exp(\mathcal{X}, \mathcal{Y} - y) \wedge x = \mathcal{X} \wedge y \neq 0) \\ \rightarrow (r * x = exp(\mathcal{X}, \mathcal{Y} - (y - 1)) \wedge x = \mathcal{X}) \quad (4)$$

The differences between the hypothesis and conclusion arise from the assignment statements in the loop body. To show that this is invariant we must rewrite the conclusion and move these differences up through the term structure until we are able to appeal to our hypothesis. Rippling provides us with the power to do this if we are able to annotate the conclusion with respect to the hypothesis. This suggests the following proof plan:

> **Either** *a goal can be simplified* **or** *we annotate the conclusion with respect to the hypothesis* **then** *apply the wave method* **until** *we can fertilize with the hypothesis.*

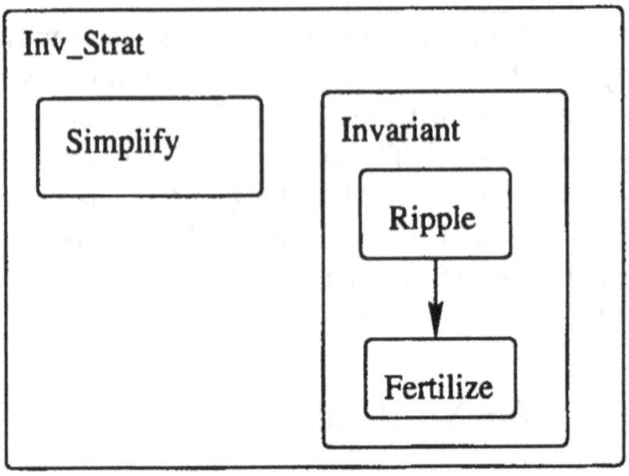

Fig. 2. Proof Plan for Verification

The power of the proof plan is not that it can do the verification, but that it can be used to encode the heuristics we need to use in order to discover a suitable invariant from an initial guess. Figure 2 shows `Inv_Strat`, the proof plan we have developed for invariant verification. The component methods are shown in more detail in figures 3, 4, 5 and 6. Note that rippling consists of the repeated application of the the wave method, which is presented in figure 5.

A Verification Proof

Consider the following wave-rules:

$$A - (B - C) \Rightarrow (A - B) + C \tag{5}$$

$$exp(A, B + 1) \Rightarrow exp(A, B) * A \tag{6}$$

$$A * C = B * D \Rightarrow A = B \wedge C = D \tag{7}$$

Note that wave-rule (7) is valid because we are reasoning in a goal directed style. Consider also the verification condition (4) above. In the proof of (4) we are given

$$r = exp(\mathcal{X}, \mathcal{Y} - y) \wedge x = \mathcal{X} \wedge y \neq 0$$

from which we must show the conclusion

$$r * x = exp(\mathcal{X}, \mathcal{Y} - (y - 1)) \wedge x = \mathcal{X}$$

Input sequent:

$$H \vdash G_1 \wedge \ldots \wedge G_i \wedge \ldots \wedge G_n$$

Method preconditions:

1. There exists a G_i such that G_i is unannotated $(1 \leq i \leq n)$.
2. And G_i follows from H trivially *i.e.* it is a tautology *e.g.* $r = r$ or it follows from some simply data type property *e.g.* $0 \neq s(0)$.

Output sequent:

$$H \vdash G_1 \wedge \ldots \wedge G_n$$

Fig. 3. The Simplify Method

Input sequent:

$$H \vdash G_1[f_1(\ldots)] \wedge \ldots \wedge G_n[f_n(\ldots)]$$

Method preconditions:

1. $G_1[f_1(\ldots)] \wedge \ldots \wedge G_n[f_n(\ldots)]$ is unannotated.
2. for all $G_i[f_i(\ldots)]$ there exists a member H_j of H such that $G_i[f_i(\ldots)]$ can be annotated with respect to H_j, *e.g.*

$$G_1[\boxed{f_1(\underline{\ldots})}] \wedge \ldots \wedge G_n[\boxed{f_n(\underline{\ldots})}]$$

Output sequent:

$$H \vdash G_1[\boxed{f_1(\underline{\ldots})}] \wedge \ldots \wedge G_n[\boxed{f_n(\underline{\ldots})}]$$

Sub Methods:
Repeat wave then fertilize.

Fig. 4. The Invariant Method

Input sequent:

$$H \vdash G[f_1(\boxed{c_1(\underline{\ldots})})]$$

Method preconditions:

1. there exists a sub-term T of G which contains wave-front(s), *e.g.*

$$f_1(\boxed{c_1(\underline{\ldots})})$$

2. there exists a wave-rule which matches T, *e.g.*

$$C \rightarrow f_1(\boxed{c_1(\underline{X})}) \Rightarrow \boxed{c_2(\underline{f_1(X)})}$$

3. any condition C follows from the context, *e.g.*

$$H \vdash C$$

Output sequent:

$$H \vdash G[\boxed{c_2(\underline{f_1(\ldots)})}]$$

Input sequent:

$$H[exp_1] \vdash \boxed{G_1 \wedge \ldots \wedge \boxed{exp_1} \wedge \ldots \wedge G_n}$$

Method preconditions:

1. There exists a hypothesis that matches with a conjunct in a wave hole in the conclusion, *e.g.*

$$exp_1$$

Output sequent:

$$H[exp_1] \vdash G_1 \wedge \ldots \wedge G_n$$

Fig. 6. The Fertilize Method

by the application of the `Inv_Strat` proof plan. The proof found by the proof planner is as presented below:

$$r * x = exp(\mathcal{X}, \mathcal{Y} - (y - 1)) \wedge x = \mathcal{X} \qquad \text{Conclusion}$$

$$r * x = exp(\mathcal{X}, \mathcal{Y} - (y - 1)) \qquad \text{By Simplify}$$

$$\boxed{\boxed{r} * x} = exp(\mathcal{X}, \mathcal{Y} - \boxed{(\boxed{y} - 1)}\ ) \qquad \text{By Invariant}$$

$$\boxed{\boxed{r} * x} = exp(\mathcal{X}, \boxed{(\boxed{\mathcal{Y} - y}) + 1}\ ) \qquad \text{By Wave using (5)}$$

$$\boxed{\boxed{r} * x} = \boxed{\boxed{exp(\mathcal{X}, \mathcal{Y} - y)} * \mathcal{X}} \qquad \text{By Wave using (6)}$$

$$\boxed{\boxed{r = exp(\mathcal{X}, \mathcal{Y} - y)} \wedge x = \mathcal{X}} \qquad \text{By Wave using (7)}$$

$$x = \mathcal{X} \qquad \text{By Fertilize}$$

$$true \qquad \text{By Simplify}$$

4 Analysis of Failure

In this section first we review two standard heuristics for discovering loop invariants from the literature [1, 8, 10, 17], namely replacing constants by terms and strengthening invariants. We formalise these heuristics within the proof planning framework as critics.

The full benefits of the rippling heuristic become apparent when the proof attempt fails. By relating this failure to a standard heuristic for developing loop invariants, we are able to suggest a patch which will give a new candidate invariant.

4.1 Replacement of Constants

A standard heuristic for developing loop invariants is replacing constants by terms containing program variables. The idea is that by replacing a constant with a term structure containing a program variable we increase the state space. Often it is only in this increased state space that the invariant relation can be established. To formalise this heuristic as a critic we need to relate it to the partial success of a proof method, namely the wave method. The wave method can fail because it fails to match the left hand side of a wave-rule with part of the goal. Wave-rule matching is defined as:

Wave-rule Match: Given a goal T and the left hand side of a wave-rule L, then T and L match iff:

- The object level term structures of L and T match.
- For all wave-fronts in L there exists a matching wave-front in T.

Constants can block a ripple because they can prevent a match between the left hand side of a wave-rule and a sub-term of the goal. This happens when at least one wave-front within a wave-rule is aligned with a term containing a constant in the goal. However, we can define a potential match which suggests we have the opportunity to match if we could introduce some difference *i.e.* wave-front, by replacing constants:

Potential Match: Given a goal T and the left hand side of a wave-rule L, then T and L potentially match iff:

- For all wave-fronts in L there exists either a matching wave-front in T or a term containing a constant.
- The object level term structures of L and T match every where expect at the positions where a wave-front in L matches a term containing a constant.

For example, attempting to match $\boxed{\boxed{r} * x} = exp(\mathcal{X}, \mathcal{Y})$ and the left hand side of the wave-rule (7):

$$\boxed{\boxed{A} * C} = \boxed{\boxed{B} * D}$$

would be a potential match because there is a term containing a constant on the right hand side of the equality in the sub-term, *e.g.* $exp(\mathcal{X}, \mathcal{Y})$, where the wave-rule has a wave, *e.g.* $\boxed{\boxed{B} * D}$. Note that all other meta-level and object-level term structures match.

Having a potential match tells us that we need a wave-front where we have a term containing a constant. The replacement of constants heuristic tells us to replace a constant with a term containing a variable which has been assigned within the loop body. To coerce this wave-rule match we need to do two things. Firstly we need to decide which constant to replace, if there is more than one. Secondly we need to discover the replacement term. The first step is achieved by taking the mismatched wave-front in the wave-rule and pushing them back towards the constants within the goal. This is achieved by applying the wave-rules backwards, with a schematic wave-front. For the potential match above we want to coerce $exp(\mathcal{X}, \mathcal{Y})$ to be the wave $\boxed{B * D}$. Since we are only replacing constants we know the skeleton must be $exp(T_1, T_2)$, where T_1 and T_2 are either new terms or the constants in those positions. We start with the wave $\boxed{exp(T_1, T_2) * D}$ and use wave-rule (6) backwards to get the term:

$$exp(D, \boxed{B + 1})$$

We now have identified that the required wave-front needed can be generated by replacing the second argument of *exp* with a term containing a wave-front of the form $\boxed{\ldots + 1}$. We could continue backwards to find the term we are looking for. However the search space is less controlled in this direction. We continue in a forwards direction by replacing the constant identified with a higher order meta-term. The arguments to the meta-term are the program variables assigned to in the body of the loop and the constant we have replaced.

The constant replaced and all the variables assigned to in the body are used as arguments for the meta-term. This then gives rise to a new candidate invariant which we use with the expectation that rippling will instantiate the meta-term. The replacing constants by terms patch is given in more detail in figure 7.

Blockage:

$$H \vdash G[g(\boxed{f_1(\ldots)}, f_2(\mathcal{X}, \ldots))]$$

Critic preconditions:

- precondition 1 of the wave method succeeds.
- precondition 2 of wave method has the potential to succeed, *i.e.*
  1. There exists a sub-term T of G that contains wave-front(s).

$$g(\boxed{f_1(\ldots)}, f_2(\mathcal{X}, \ldots))$$

  2. There exists a wave-rule which has the potential to match with T

$$g(\boxed{f_1(\ldots)}, \boxed{f_3(\ldots)}) \Rightarrow \ldots$$

Patch specification:
Coerce precondition 2 by replacing the blocking constant with a meta-variable *e.g.*

$$f_2(\mathcal{X}, \ldots) \text{ becomes } f_2(M(\ldots), \ldots)$$

Where M is a second-order meta-variable.

Fig. 7. Patch: Replacing Constants by Terms

4.2 Strengthening invariants

Gries [9] explains a simple, but powerful, heuristic for dealing with blocked proof obligations. The idea is to assume the very thing that we are trying to prove. This has the effect of instantly making the proof obligation trivial. However now we have to show that this proof obligation is itself invariant. To formalise this heuristic as a critic we observe that at the end of a ripple proof we are sometimes left with some proof residue. This is a sub-term that requires some further proof. This residue can sometimes be proved using the simplify method, but when it cannot, we have to start the invariant proof process again. The invariant method tries to annotate a subgoal. If we are unable to annotate it then we are blocked since we will not be able to ripple.

Using this failure to annotate the differences between a subgoal and the hypotheses we can refine our candidate invariant using the heuristic above. *i.e.* the conclusion we are unable to annotate is added to our candidate invariant and we start the proof again. For example suppose a proof attempt fails on the goal:

$$(r = exp(\mathcal{X}, \mathcal{Y} - y) \wedge y \neq 0) \rightarrow x = \mathcal{X}$$

The failure is due to the proof residue $x = \mathcal{X}$ which we can neither derive from the hypotheses nor annotate with respect to any particular hypothesis. The patch is to add $x = \mathcal{X}$ to the invariant candidate. Thus the new candidate invariant becomes:

$$r = exp(\mathcal{X}, \mathcal{Y} - y) \wedge x = \mathcal{X}$$

The strengthening invariant critic is given in more detail in figure 8.

Blockage:

$$H \vdash G$$

Critic preconditions:

- precondition 2 of invariant method fails, *i.e.*
  1. The conclusion is unannotated.
  2. We cannot annotate G with respect to a member of H.

Patch specification:
Coerce precondition 2 by introducing those parts of G that we are unable to annotate in our candidate invariant.

Fig. 8. Patch: Strengthening invariants

---

5 Refining Invariants

In this section we briefly explain the overall strategy used to find invariants and thus construct proofs of loop programs. We then show this in action using an example.

The above methods and critics have been encoded within the CLAM proof planning system. CLAM is allowed to exhaustively search before attempting to fire any critics.

The replacement of constants and strengthening invariants critics together allow us to successively refine approximation to our invariant. The idea is to use the post condition as our initial guess and successively refine our invariant candidate. If we have proved that our new property is invariant we then have to show that it actually implies the post condition *i.e.* it is not too weak. For example, suppose we have shown I to be invariant over successive refinements of our post condition Q we have to show that $(I \wedge \neg B) \rightarrow Q$ where B is the loop guard.

Example

For example, consider the program in figure (1), and the wave-rules (5), (6) and (7) introduced above.

First Approximation (Post-condition): We take the post-condition:

$$r = exp(\mathcal{X}, \mathcal{Y})$$

as our first approximation to the invariant. This gives the verification condition:

$$(r = exp(\mathcal{X}, \mathcal{Y}) \wedge y \neq 0) \rightarrow r * x = exp(\mathcal{X}, \mathcal{Y})$$

This goal cannot be simplified so we apply the invariant method giving:

$$(r = exp(\mathcal{X}, \mathcal{Y}) \wedge y \neq 0) \rightarrow \boxed{r * x} = exp(\mathcal{X}, \mathcal{Y})$$

Now we are stuck. We are unable to apply any of the wave-rules. We are left resorting to using the critics to try and patch our goal. Firstly we notice that we have a potential match between the goal:

$$\boxed{r * x} = exp(\mathcal{X}, \mathcal{Y})$$

and the left hand side of the wave-rule (7):

$$\boxed{A * C} = \boxed{B * D}$$

Secondly we decide which constant to replace. The right hand side of the wave-rule (6):

$$\boxed{exp(A, B) * A} \quad \text{matches with} \quad \boxed{exp(\mathcal{X}, \mathcal{Y}) * D}$$

the result of our potential match. Looking at the left hand side of this wave-rule we are able to determine that the difference came from the second argument of *exp*, so we replace the $\mathcal{Y}$ with the meta term $M_1(r, y, \mathcal{Y})$ giving the new candidate invariant:

$$r = exp(\mathcal{X}, M_1(r, y, \mathcal{Y}))$$

Second Approximation (Result of replacement of constants critic): This new candidate invariant is used to set up a verification condition:

$$(r = exp(\mathcal{X}, M_1(r, y, \mathcal{Y})) \wedge y \neq 0) \rightarrow r * x = exp(\mathcal{X}, M_1(r * x, y - 1, \mathcal{Y}))$$

The proof attempt continues:

$$r * x = exp(\mathcal{X}, M_1(r, y, \mathcal{Y})) \qquad \text{Conclusion}$$

$$\boxed{r * x} = exp(\mathcal{X}, M_1(\boxed{r * x}, \boxed{y - 1}, \mathcal{Y})) \qquad \text{By Invariant}$$

$$\boxed{r * x} = exp(\mathcal{X}, \boxed{(M_2(\boxed{r * x}, \boxed{y - 1}, \mathcal{Y}) - y) + 1}) \qquad \text{By Wave using (5)}$$

$$\boxed{r * x} = \boxed{exp(\mathcal{X}, M_2(\boxed{r * x}, \boxed{y - 1}, \mathcal{Y}) - y) * \mathcal{X}} \qquad \text{By Wave using (6)}$$

$$\boxed{r = exp(\mathcal{X}, M_2(\boxed{r * x}, \boxed{y - 1}, \mathcal{Y}) - y) \wedge x = \mathcal{X}} \qquad \text{By Wave using (7)}$$

$$x = \mathcal{X} \qquad \text{By Fertilize}$$

The first application of wave has the effect of finding an instantiation for M_1 to be $\lambda X.\lambda Y.\lambda Z.\ M_2(X, Y, Z) - Y$. The fertilization step instantiates the meta-variable M_2 to be a projection onto it's third argument *i.e.* M_2 is instantiated to $\lambda X.\lambda Y.\lambda Z.\ Z$, so M_1 becomes $\lambda X.\lambda Y.\lambda Z.(Z - Y)$.

Now we are stuck again, this proof obligation is not trivial and we are unable to annotate it. The strengthening critic now fires and generates a new candidate by including the proof residues, giving the next approximation:

$$r = exp(\mathcal{X}, \mathcal{Y} - y) \wedge x = \mathcal{X}$$

Third Approximation (Result of strengthening critic): Again we set up a verification condition:

$$(r = exp(\mathcal{X}, \mathcal{Y} - y) \wedge x = \mathcal{X} \wedge y \neq 0) \rightarrow (r * x = exp(\mathcal{X}, \mathcal{Y} - (y - 1)) \wedge x = \mathcal{X})$$

The proof now follows:

$$r * x = exp(\mathcal{X}, \mathcal{Y} - (y - 1)) \wedge x = \mathcal{X} \qquad \text{Conclusion}$$

$$r * x = exp(\mathcal{X}, \mathcal{Y} - (y - 1)) \qquad \text{By Simplify}$$

$$\boxed{r * x} = exp(\mathcal{X}, \mathcal{Y} - \boxed{(y - 1)}\,) \qquad \text{By Invariant}$$

$$\boxed{r * x} = exp(\mathcal{X}, \boxed{(\mathcal{Y} - y) + 1}\,) \qquad \text{By Wave using (5)}$$

$$\boxed{r * x} = \boxed{exp(\mathcal{X}, \mathcal{Y} - y) * \mathcal{X}} \qquad \text{By Wave using (6)}$$

$$\boxed{r = exp(\mathcal{X}, \mathcal{Y} - y) \wedge x = \mathcal{X}} \qquad \text{By Wave using (7)}$$

By Fertilize

$$true \qquad \text{By Simplify}$$

So we have shown that $r = exp(\mathcal{X}, \mathcal{Y} - y) \wedge x = \mathcal{X}$ is an invariant to the loop body. To finish the proof we check that our invariant satisfies the first and third premises of the while rule.

6 Results and Implementation

Our work on invariant discovery has been implemented within the CLAM proof planner [6]. It describes a systematic framework for refining initial approximations to a loop invariant automatically in a principled way. Initial results using examples from the literature are promising, and are summarised in table (1). We draw the readers attention to the more complex problems involving arrays, notably Gries' minimum sum segment problem [9]. Our approach is syntactically driven and requires defining equations and properties needed to complete the proof. There is no restriction that these defining equations are recursive or the specification is immediately executable. In the **exp** example (see figure 1), note that the definition of *exp* is constructive, while the imperative algorithm is destructive.

7 Related Work

Early research into Automatic Programming investigated heuristic based methods for discovering loop invariants. Wegbreit [24] developed an approach in which a candidate invariant was incrementally refined using both domain-independent and domain-specific heuristics. The choice of refinement was guided by the satisfiability and validity of the current candidate invariant. The theorem proving

Program	Post Condition	Invariant Discovered
exp	$r = exp(\mathcal{X}, \mathcal{Y})$	$r = exp(\mathcal{X}, \mathcal{Y} - y) \land x = \mathcal{X}$
sum	$r = sum(\mathcal{X})$	$r = sum(x)$
times	$r = \mathcal{X} * \mathcal{Y}$	$r = (\mathcal{X} - x) * \mathcal{Y} \land y = \mathcal{Y}$
factorial	$r = fac(\mathcal{X})$	$r = fac(x)$
min-array	$m = min(0 \leq i < \mathcal{N} : a[i])$	$m = min(0 \leq i < n : a[i])$
sum-array	$s = \sum_{i=0}^{i<\mathcal{N}} a[i]$	$s = \sum_{i=0}^{i<n} a[i]$
min-sum-seg	$s = min\,(0 \leq i < j \leq \mathcal{N}$ $\sum_i^j a[i])$	$s = min(0 \leq i < j \leq n : \sum_i^j a[i])$ $\land c = min(0 \leq i < n : \sum_i^n a[i])$

Program exp is given in figure (1). Programs sum and factorial compute the sum and factorial of the first $\mathcal{X}$ natural numbers respectively. The program times multiplies two natural numbers by successive addition. Programs min-array, sum-array and min-sum-seg find the least element of an array, the sum of an array and the minimum sum segment of an array respectively.

Table 1. Invariant Discovery Results

and heuristic components were only loosely coupled. This was reflected in other heuristic approaches at the time [18]. Wegbreit hinted, however, that a closer relationship between the heuristic guidance and the theorem prover would be desirable. The proof planning framework in which our heuristics are expressed enables this close relationship to be achieved.

Our approach, like all heuristic based techniques, is not complete. A complete approach has been designed [7] based upon a novel unskolemization technique for deriving logical consequences of first-order formulae. Completeness, however, comes with a price. In practice this means that any inductive lemmas required for a particular verification task must be provided by hand.

Our technique is very tightly coupled to the syntactic structure of the initial invariant. A more semantic approach to verification is described by Mili [21], where program semantics are found independently of their specifications and heuristics are given for discovering invariant properties. One way of discovering these invariant properties is to use the strongest invariant function of a loop body [20]. However it is unclear how we would be able to automate the discovery of such functions in general. In this work the programs are described by relations of input sets to output sets. Bundy and Lombart [4] have formalised the notion of relational rippling to reason with relations describing logic programs. The work on relational rippling may be relevant to Mili's approach.

Critics have been used in the context of inductive proof [13–15] to discover generalisations, revise induction rule selection, perform case splits and discover missing lemmas. Previously in [16] we showed how the work on generalisation for induction transfers to the domain of loop invariant verification. The critics reported here, however, have been developed directly from standard heuristics. So how do these critics relate to the inductive proof plan?

Program	Critic used
`exp`	RC and S
`sum`	RC
`times`	RC and S
`factorial`	RC
`min-array`	RC
`sum-array`	RC
`min-sum-seg`	RC and S

RC indicates the application of the replace constant critic and S indicates the application of the strengthening critic.

Table 2. Critic Usage

Firstly the replace constants by terms critic is very similar to the induction revision critic. This is not unsurprising as often we are replacing a constant by a local loop variable used to ensure termination *i.e.* an induction variable. This is reflected in the pattern of failure we observe in the ripple method. Both the replace constants by variables critic and the induction revision critic, achieve partial success with the second precondition of rippling, *i.e.* there is a wave-rule match.

Secondly the failure pattern for the strengthening invariants critic corresponds to a complete failure to annotate the conclusion with respect to a hypothesis. It has been observed that a similar failure pattern occurs when reasoning about mutually recursive functions.

8 Future Work

Extensions to the above framework build upon the premise that the post-condition is a good starting point for developing an invariant through successive refinements. The critic mechanism will be used to refine this initial invariant based upon the partial success of our proof methods. The nature of the planner's methods allows a systematic analysis of failure. Future work will involve extending the system to deal with more complex examples including nested loops, branching constructs within loop bodies and array assignment.

9 Conclusion

The discovery of loop invariants represents a bottleneck within the automatic verification of imperative programs. Building upon the proof planning framework and proof critics in particular, we have shown that by the productive use of failed proof attempts we are able to automate the synthesis of suitable invariants.

We believe that our success is due to the tight coupling between the heuristic and the theorem proving dimensions which proof planning facilitates.

Acknowledgments

The authors wish to thank Greg Michaelson for his helpful comments with regard to the presentation of our work. We would also like to thank the LOPSTR'98 anonymous reviewers for their helpful comments.

References

1. R.C. Backhouse. *Program Construction and Verification.* Prentice Hall, 1986.
2. David Basin and Toby Walsh. Annotated rewriting in inductive theorem proving. *Journal of Automated Reasoning*, 16(1–2):147–180, 1996.
3. A. Bundy. The use of explicit plans to guide inductive proofs. Research Paper 349, Dept. of Artificial Intelligence, University of Edinburgh, 1988. Short version published in the proceedings of CADE-9.
4. A. Bundy and V. Lombart. Relational rippling: a general approach. In C. Mellish, editor, *Proceedings of IJCAI-95*, pages 175–181. IJCAI, 1995. Longer version to appear as a DAI research paper.
5. A. Bundy, A. Stevens, F. van Harmelen, A. Ireland, and A. Smaill. Rippling: A heuristic for guiding inductive proofs. *Artificial Intelligence*, 62:185–253, 1993. Also available from Edinburgh as DAI Research Paper No. 567.
6. A. Bundy, F. van Harmelen, C. Horn, and A. Smaill. The Oyster-Clam system. Research Paper 507, Dept. of Artificial Intelligence, University of Edinburgh, 1990. Appeared in the proceedings of CADE-10.
7. Chadha and Plaisted. On the mechanical derivation of loop invariants. *JSL*, 15:705–744, 1993.
8. E. Dijkstra. *A Discipline of Programming.* Prentice-Hall, 1976.
9. D. Gries. A note on a standard strategy for developing loop invariants and loops. *Science of Computer Programming*, 2:207–214, 1982.
10. David Gries. *The Science of Programming.* Springer-Verlag, New York, 1981.
11. J.T. Hesketh. *Using Middle-Out Reasoning to Guide Inductive Theorem Proving.* PhD thesis, University of Edinburgh, 1991.
12. C.A.R. Hoare. An axiomatic basis for computer programming. *Communications of the ACM*, 12:576–583, 1969.
13. A. Ireland. The Use of Planning Critics in Mechanizing Inductive Proofs. In A. Voronkov, editor, *International Conference on Logic Programming and Automated Reasoning – LPAR 92, St. Petersburg*, Lecture Notes in Artificial Intelligence No. 624, pages 178–189. Springer-Verlag, 1992. Also available from Edinburgh as DAI Research Paper 592.
14. A. Ireland and A. Bundy. Extensions to a Generalization Critic for Inductive Proof. In M.A. McRobbie and J.K. Slaney, editors, *13th Conference on Automated Deduction*, pages 47–61. Springer-Verlag, 1996. Springer Lecture Notes in Artificial Intelligence No. 1104. Also available from Edinburgh as DAI Research Paper 786.
15. A. Ireland and A. Bundy. Productive use of failure in inductive proof. *Journal of Automated Reasoning*, 16(1–2):79–111, 1996. Also available as DAI Research Paper No 716, Dept. of Artificial Intelligence, Edinburgh.
16. A. Ireland and J. Stark. On the Automatic Discovery of Loop Invariants. In *Fourth NASA Langley Formal Methods Workshop*, number 3356 in NASA Conference Publications, 1997. Also available from Dept. of Computing and Electrical Engineering, Heriot-Watt University, Research Memo RM/97/1.

17. A. Kaldewaij. *Programming: The Derivation of Algorithms.* Prentice Hall, 1990.
18. S.M. Katz and Z. Manna. A heuristic approach to program verification. In *Proceedings of IJCAI-73.* International Joint Conference on Artificial Intelligence, 1973.
19. I. Kraan, D. Basin, and A. Bundy. Logic program synthesis via proof planning. In K.K. Lau and T. Clement, editors, *Logic Program Synthesis and Transformation*, pages 1–14. Springer-Verlag, 1993. Also available as Max-Planck-Institut für Informatik Report MPI-I-92-244 and Edinburgh DAI Research Report 603.
20. A. Mili, J. Desharhais, and J. Gagne. Strongest invariant functions: Their use in the systematic analysis of while statements. *Acta Informatica*, 22:47–66, 1985.
21. A. Mili, J. Desharhais, and F. Mili. *Computer Program Construction.* Oxford University Press, 1994.
22. D. Miller and G. Nadathur. An overview of λProlog. In R. Bowen, K. & Kowalski, editor, *Proceedings of the Fifth International Logic Programming Conference/ Fifth Symposium on Logic Programming.* MIT Press, 1988.
23. A. Smaill and I. Green. Higher-order annotated terms for proof search. Technical report, Dept. of Artificial Intelligence, University of Edinburgh, 1996. To appear in proceedings of TPHOLs'96.
24. Wegbreit. Heuristic methods for mechanically deriving inductive assertions. In *Proceedings of IJCAI-73.* International Joint Conference on Artificial Intelligence, 1973.

Preventing Instantiation Errors and Loops for Logic Programs with Multiple Modes Using `block` Declarations

Jan–Georg Smaus[1], Pat Hill[2], and Andy King[1]

[1] University of Kent at Canterbury, Canterbury, CT2 7NF, United Kingdom, {j.g.smaus, a.m.king}@ukc.ac.uk
[2] University of Leeds, Leeds, LS2 9JT, United Kingdom, hill@scs.leeds.ac.uk

Abstract. This paper presents several verification methods for logic programs with delay declarations. It is shown how type and instantiation errors related to built-ins can be prevented, and how termination can be ensured. Three features are distinctive of this work: it is assumed that predicates can be used in several modes; it is shown that `block` declarations, which are a very simple delay construct, are sufficient to ensure the desired properties; the selection rule is taken into account, assuming it to be the rule of most Prolog implementations. The methods can be used both to verify existing programs and to assist in writing new programs.

1 Introduction

Delay declarations are provided in logic programming languages to allow for more flexible control, as opposed to the left-to-right selection rule of Prolog. An atom in a query is selected for resolution only when its arguments are instantiated to a specified degree. This is essential to prevent run-time errors produced by built-in predicates (*built-ins*) and to ensure termination.

We assume that delay declarations may be used to enable programs to run in multiple modes. Although other authors [3, 15] have not explicitly assumed multiple modes, they mainly give examples where delay declarations are clearly used for that purpose. However, our results are also useful in the context of other applications of delay declarations, such as the test-and-generate paradigm [15] or parallel execution [3].

Our contributions are: showing how type and instantiation errors related to built-ins can be prevented; showing when delay declarations for built-ins can be omitted completely; and showing how termination can be ensured.

For all of the above, we demonstrate that under realistic assumptions, `block` declarations, which declare that certain arguments of an atom must be at least *non-variable* before that atom can be selected, are sufficient. As demonstrated in SICStus [8], `block` declarations can be efficiently implemented; the instantiation test has hardly any impact on performance. Thus, in practice, such constructs are the most frequently used delay declarations.

P. Flener (Ed.): LOPSTR'98, LNCS 1559, pp. 289–307, 1999.

For arithmetic built-ins, we exploit that for numbers, being non-variable implies being ground, and show how to prevent *instantiation* and *type* errors. Sometimes, it is not even necessary to have any delay declarations at all for built-ins.

Predicates which use their own output as input (*circular modes*) are a well-known source of loops which must be eliminated to ensure termination [15]. We generalise the idea of "well-behaved" modes to multi-moded predicates.

Another source of loops is *speculative output bindings*, that is bindings made before it is known that a solution exists [15]. We propose two methods for dealing with this problem and thus proving (or ensuring) termination. Which method must be applied depends on the program and on the mode being considered. The first method exploits that a program does not *use* any speculative bindings, by ensuring that no atom ever delays. The second method exploits that a program does not *make* any speculative bindings. We always reduce the problem to showing termination for programs without delay declarations, such that any method for programs without delay declarations [1,5] can be applied.

The approach to termination presented here is simple and formalises previous heuristics [14,15]. Although there are some clear limitations of the approach, it is not subsumed by any method we know of, in particular not by the method we presented in [16].

The rest of this paper is organised as follows. The next section gives some preliminaries. Section 3 defines some concepts of modes and types which are the basis of our verification methods. Section 4 is about errors related to built-ins. Section 5 is about termination. Section 6 investigates related work, and Section 7 concludes.

2 Preliminaries

We base the notation on [3,11]. For the examples we use SICStus notation [8]. We recall some important notions. The set of variables in a syntactic object o is denoted by $vars(o)$. A syntactic object is called **linear** if every variable occurs in it at most once. A **flat** term is a variable or a term of the form $f(x_1, \ldots, x_n)$, where $n \geq 0$ and the x_i are distinct variables. The **domain** of a substitution σ is $dom(\sigma) = \{x \mid x\sigma \neq x\}$.

For a predicate p/n, a **mode** is an atom $p(m_1, \ldots, m_n)$, where $m_i \in \{I, O\}$ for $i \in \{1, \ldots, n\}$. Positions with I are called **input positions**, and positions with O are called **output positions** of p. A **mode of a program** is a set containing one mode for each of its predicates.[1] A program can have several modes, so whenever we refer to the input and output positions, this is always with respect to the particular mode which is clear from the context. To simplify the notation, an atom written as $p(\mathbf{s}, \mathbf{t})$ means: $\mathbf{s}$ and $\mathbf{t}$ are the vectors of terms filling the input and output positions of p, respectively.

A **type** is a set of terms closed under instantiation. A **non-variable type** is a type that does not contain variables. *The* **variable type** is the type that

[1] This can easily be extended to allow for different *occurrences* of a predicate within a program to have different modes.

contains variables and hence, as it is instantiation closed, all terms. A **constant type** is a type that contains only (possibly infinitely many) constants. In the examples, we use the following types: *any* is the variable type, *list* the type of (nil-terminated) lists, *num* the type of numbers and *nl* the type of number lists.

We write $t : T$ for "t is in type T". We use $\mathbf{S}$, $\mathbf{T}$ to denote vectors of types, and write $\models \mathbf{s} : \mathbf{S} \Rightarrow \mathbf{t} : \mathbf{T}$ if for all substitutions σ, $\mathbf{s}\sigma : \mathbf{S}$ implies $\mathbf{t}\sigma : \mathbf{T}$. It is assumed that each argument position of each predicate p/n has a type associated with it. These types are indicated by writing the atom $p(T_1, \ldots, T_n)$ where $T_1, \ldots, T_n$ are types. The **type of a program** P is a set of such atoms, one for each predicate defined in P.

A **block** declaration [8] for a predicate p/n is a (possibly empty) set of atoms each of which has the form $p(b_1, \ldots, b_n)$ where $b_i \in \{?, -\}$ for $i \in \{1, \ldots, n\}$. A **program** consists of a set of clauses and a set of **block** declarations, one for each predicate defined by the clauses. If P is a program, an atom $p(t_1, \ldots, t_n)$ is **selectable in** P if for each atom $p(b_1, \ldots, b_n)$ in the **block** declaration for p, there is some $i \in \{1, \ldots, n\}$ such that t_i is non-variable and $b_i = -$.[2]

A **query** is a finite sequence of atoms. A **derivation step** for a program P is a pair $\langle Q, \theta \rangle; \langle R, \theta\sigma \rangle$, where $Q = Q_1, a, Q_2$ and $R = Q_1, B, Q_2$ are queries; θ is a substitution; a an atom; $h \leftarrow B$ a renamed variant of a clause in P and σ the most general unifier of $a\theta$ and h. We call a (or $a\theta$)[3] the **selected atom** and $R\theta\sigma$ the **resolvent** of $Q\theta$ and $h \leftarrow B$.

A **derivation** ξ **for** a program P is a sequence $\langle Q_0, \theta_0 \rangle; \langle Q_1, \theta_1 \rangle; \ldots$ where each pair $\langle Q_i, \theta_i \rangle; \langle Q_{i+1}, \theta_{i+1} \rangle$ in ξ is a derivation step. Alternatively, we also say that ξ is a **derivation of** $P \cup \{Q_0\theta_0\}$. We also denote ξ as $Q_0\theta_0; Q_1\theta_1; \ldots$.

An **LD-derivation** is a derivation where the selected atom is always the leftmost atom in a query. A **delay-respecting derivation** for a program P is a derivation where the selected atom is always selectable in P. A derivation is **left-based** if it is either an LD-derivation, or it contains at least one non-empty query where the leftmost atom is not selectable. To the best of our knowledge, derivations in most Prolog implementations are left-based.

3 Permutations and Modes

In [3], three correctness properties for programs are introduced: *nicely moded*, *well typed*, and *simply moded*. The idea of these concepts is that in a query, every piece of data is produced (output) before it is consumed (input), and every piece of data is produced only once. It is assumed that each predicate has a single mode. Nicely-modedness is used to show that the occur-check can safely be omitted. Well-typedness is used to show that derivations do not flounder. Finally, simply-modedness is a special case of nicely-modedness and is used to show that a program is free from errors related to built-ins. Other authors have

---

[2] Note that in the (pathological) case that p has a **block** declaration $p(?, \ldots, ?)$, an atom using p can never be selectable.

[3] Whether or not the substitution has been applied is always clear from the context.

also used these or similar concepts, for example to show that programs are unification free [2], successful [4], and terminating [6].

In a query (clause body), one can consider three different orderings among the atoms. First, there is the *textual* order. Secondly, there is a conceptual order given by the *producer-consumer relation* [10]. According to this order, the atom that produces a piece of data occurs before atoms that consume it. Thirdly, there is the execution order, which depends on the selection rule.

In the case of LD-derivations, all of these orders are identical. This assumption underlies the above concepts as used in [2,4,6].

In the case of arbitrary delay-respecting derivations, none of these orders is necessarily identical to another one. However, since the textual order is irrelevant for the selection of an atom and hence for the execution order, one might just as well assume, for the sake of notational convenience, that the textual order is identical to the producer-consumer order. Although not explicitly stated, this assumption underlies the above concepts as used in [3]. More precisely, any result stated there can be generalised trivially to programs where the atoms in the clause bodies are permuted in an arbitrary way.

In the case of left-based derivations, again none of these orders is necessarily identical to another one. However, the textual order is relevant for the execution order. Therefore it is not correct to make a simplifying assumption about the textual order as for arbitrary delay-respecting derivations. We need a formalism that makes both the textual order and the producer-consumer order explicit.

This is accomplished by associating, with each query and each clause in a program, a permutation π of the (body) atoms, which gives the producer-consumer order. For a different mode, the permutations would be different. Let π be a permutation on $\{1,\ldots,n\}$. For notational convenience we assume that $\pi(i) = i$ for $i \notin \{1,\ldots,n\}$. In examples, π is written as $\langle\pi(1),\ldots,\pi(n)\rangle$. Also, we write $\pi(o_1,\ldots,o_n)$ for the sequence obtained by applying π to the sequence $o_1,\ldots,o_n$, that is $o_{\pi^{-1}(1)},\ldots,o_{\pi^{-1}(n)}$.

Note that most results in this paper hold for arbitrary delay-respecting derivations, but the result in Subsec. 5.1 assumes left-based derivations. For the sake of consistency we use the permutations throughout.

3.1 Permutation Nicely Moded Programs

In a *nicely moded* query, a variable in an input position does not occur later in an output position, and each variable in an output position occurs only once. This has been generalised in [16].

Definition 3.1 (permutation nicely moded). Let $Q = p_1(\mathbf{s}_1,\mathbf{t}_1),\ldots,$ $p_n(\mathbf{s}_n,\mathbf{t}_n)$ be a query and π a permutation on $\{1,\ldots,n\}$. Then Q is **π-nicely moded** if $\mathbf{t}_1,\ldots,\mathbf{t}_n$ is a linear vector of terms and for all $i \in \{1,\ldots,n\}$

$$vars(\mathbf{s}_i) \cap \bigcup_{\pi(i)\leq\pi(j)\leq n} vars(\mathbf{t}_j) = \emptyset.$$

The query $\pi(Q)$ is a **nicely moded query corresponding to** Q.

The clause $C = p(\mathbf{t}_0, \mathbf{s}_{n+1}) \leftarrow Q$ is **π-nicely moded** if Q is π-nicely moded and $\mathbf{t}_0, \ldots, \mathbf{t}_n$ is a linear vector of terms. The clause $p(\mathbf{t}_0, \mathbf{s}_{n+1}) \leftarrow \pi(Q)$ is a **nicely moded clause corresponding to** C.

A query (clause) is **permutation nicely moded** if it is π-nicely moded for some π. A program P is **permutation nicely moded** if all of its clauses are. A **nicely moded program corresponding to** P is a program obtained from P by replacing every clause C with a nicely moded clause corresponding to C.

Example 3.1.

```
:- block permute(-,-).
permute([],[]).
permute([U|X],Y) :-
  permute(X,Z),
  delete(U,Y,Z).

:- block delete(?,-,-).
delete(X,[X|Z],Z).
delete(X,[U|Y],[U|Z]) :- delete(X,Y,Z).
```

In mode $\{$**permute**(I, O), **delete**$(I, O, I)\}$, this program is nicely moded. In mode $\{$**permute**(O, I), **delete**$(O, I, O)\}$, it is permutation nicely moded, since the second clause for **permute** is $\langle 2, 1\rangle$-nicely moded, and the other clauses are nicely moded.

Example 3.2.

```
:- block length(-,-).
length(L,N) :- len_aux(L,0,N).

:- block len_aux(?,-,?), len_aux(-,?,-).
len_aux([],N,N).
len_aux([_|Xs],M,N) :-
  less(M,N),
  M2 is M + 1,
  len_aux(Xs,M2,N).

:- block less(?,-), less(-,?).
less(A,B) :- A < B.
```

This program is permutation nicely moded in mode $\{$**length**(I, O), **len_aux**(I, I, O), **less**(I, I), **is**$(O, I)\}$ (the third clause is $\langle 3, 1, 2\rangle$-nicely moded). In mode $\{$**length**(O, I), **len_aux**(O, I, I), **less**(I, I), **is**$(O, I)\}$, it is *not* permutation nicely moded, since the input arguments of **len_aux([],N,N)** are not linear.

We now recall a persistence property of permutation nicely-modedness [16].

Lemma 3.1. Every resolvent of a permutation nicely moded query Q and a permutation nicely moded clause C, where $vars(C) \cap vars(Q) = \emptyset$, is permutation nicely moded.

For permutation nicely moded programs and queries, the occur-check can be omitted [3, 17].

3.2 Permutation Well Typed Programs

Well-typedness is a generalisation of a simpler concept called *well-modedness* [3]. The idea is that given a query Q, a, Q', when Q is resolved away, then the atom a becomes sufficiently instantiated to be selected. As with modes, we assume that the types are given. In the examples, they will be the obvious ones.

Definition 3.2 (permutation well typed [16]). Let $Q = p_1(\mathbf{s}_1, \mathbf{t}_1), \ldots, p_n(\mathbf{s}_n, \mathbf{t}_n)$ be a query, where $p_i(\mathbf{S}_i, \mathbf{T}_i)$ is the type of p_i for each $i \in \{1, \ldots, n\}$. Let π be a permutation on $\{1, \ldots, n\}$. Then Q is **π-well typed** if for all $i \in \{1, \ldots, n\}$ and $L = 1$

$$\models (\bigwedge_{L \leq \pi(j) < \pi(i)} \mathbf{t}_j : \mathbf{T}_j) \Rightarrow \mathbf{s}_i : \mathbf{S}_i. \tag{1}$$

The clause $(\mathbf{t}_0, \mathbf{s}_{n+1}) \leftarrow Q$, where $p(\mathbf{T}_0, \mathbf{S}_{n+1})$ is the type of p, is **π-well typed** if (1) holds for all $i \in \{1, \ldots, n+1\}$ and $L = 0$.

A **permutation well typed** query (clause, program) and a **well typed** query (clause, program) **corresponding to** a query (clause, program) are defined in analogy to Def. 3.1.

Example 3.3. Consider the program in Ex. 3.1 with type {`permute`(*list*, *list*), `delete`(*any*, *list*, *list*)}. It is well typed for mode {`permute`(I, O), `delete`(I, O, I)}, and permutation well typed for mode {`permute`(O, I), `delete`(O, I, O)}, with the same permutations as Ex. 3.1. The same holds assuming type {`permute`(*nl*, *nl*), `delete`(*num*, *nl*, *nl*)}.

The following lemma is analogous to Lemma 3.1 and has also been stated in [16].

Lemma 3.2. Every resolvent of a permutation well typed query Q and a permutation well typed clause C, where $vars(C) \cap vars(Q) = \emptyset$, is permutation well typed.

For permutation well typed programs and queries, no derivation flounders [17].

3.3 Permutation Simply Typed Programs

We now define *permutation simply-typedness*. The name *simply typed* is a combination of *simply moded* [3] and *well typed*. In a permutation simply typed query, the output positions are filled with variables, and therefore they can always be instantiated so that they are correctly typed.

Definition 3.3 (permutation simply typed). Let $Q = p_1(\mathbf{s}_1, \mathbf{t}_1), \ldots, p_n(\mathbf{s}_n, \mathbf{t}_n)$ be a query and π a permutation on $\{1, \ldots, n\}$. Then Q is **π-simply typed** if it is π-nicely moded and π-well typed, and $\mathbf{t}_1, \ldots, \mathbf{t}_n$ is a vector of *variables*.

The clause $p(\mathbf{t}_0, \mathbf{s}_{n+1}) \leftarrow Q$ is **π-simply typed** if it is π-nicely moded and π-well typed, $\mathbf{t}_1, \ldots, \mathbf{t}_n$ is a vector of *variables*, and $\mathbf{t}_0$ has a variable in each position of variable type and a flat term in each position of non-variable type.

A **permutation simply typed** query (clause, program) and a **simply typed** query (clause, program) **corresponding to** a query (clause, program) are defined in analogy to Def. 3.1.

Example 3.4. The following is a version of **quicksort**, where **leq** and **grt** are defined in analogy to **less** in Ex. 3.2.

```
:- block qs(-,-).
qs([],[]).
qs([X|Xs],Ys) :-
  append(As2,[X|Bs2],Ys),
  part(Xs,X,As,Bs),
  qs(As,As2),
  qs(Bs,Bs2).

:- block part(?,-,?,?), part(-,?,-,?), part(-,?,?,-).
part([],_,[],[]).
part([X|Xs],C,[X|As],Bs):-
  leq(X,C),
  part(Xs,C,As,Bs).
part([X|Xs],C,As,[X|Bs]):-
  grt(X,C),
  part(Xs,C,As,Bs).

:- block append(-,?,-).
append([],Y,Y).
append([X|Xs],Ys,[X|Zs]) :-
  append(Xs,Ys,Zs).
```

The program is permutation simply typed with respect to the obvious types for mode $\{\mathtt{qs}(I,O), \mathtt{append}(I,I,O), \mathtt{leq}(I,I), \mathtt{grt}(I,I), \mathtt{part}(I,I,O,O)\}$. It is not permutation simply typed for mode $\{\mathtt{qs}(O,I), \mathtt{append}(O,O,I), \mathtt{leq}(I,I), \mathtt{grt}(I,I), \mathtt{part}(O,I,I,I)\}$, due to the non-variable term `[X|Bs2]` in an output position.

The persistence properties stated in Lemmas 3.1 and 3.2 are independent of the selectability of an atom in a query. We show a similar persistence property for permutation simply typed programs. However this property only holds if the selected atom is sufficiently instantiated in its input arguments, since otherwise output positions of the resolvent might become non-variable. This motivates the following definition.

Definition 3.4 (bound position). Let P be a permutation simply typed program. An input position of a predicate p in P is **bound** if there is some clause defining p whose head has a non-variable term in that position.

Note that by Def. 3.3, a bound position must be of non-variable type.

Lemma 3.3. Let $Q = p_1(\mathbf{s}_1,\mathbf{t}_1),\dots,p_n(\mathbf{s}_n,\mathbf{t}_n)$ be a permutation simply typed query and $C = p_k(\mathbf{v}_0,\mathbf{u}_{m+1}) \leftarrow q_1(\mathbf{u}_1,\mathbf{v}_1),\dots,q_m(\mathbf{u}_m,\mathbf{v}_m)$ a permutation simply typed clause where $vars(C) \cap vars(Q) = \emptyset$. Suppose that for some $k \in \{1,\dots,n\}$, $p_k(\mathbf{s}_k,\mathbf{t}_k)$ is non-variable in all bound input positions[4] and θ is the

[4] This is similar to "the delay declarations imply matching" [3].

mgu of $p_k(\mathbf{s}_k, \mathbf{t}_k)$ and $p_k(\mathbf{v}_0, \mathbf{u}_{m+1})$. Then the resolvent of Q and C with selected atom $p_k(\mathbf{s}_k, \mathbf{t}_k)$ is permutation simply typed. Moreover,

a. $dom(\theta) \subseteq vars(\mathbf{t}_k) \cup vars(\mathbf{v}_0)$, and
b. $(\mathbf{t}_1, \ldots, \mathbf{t}_{k-1}, \mathbf{v}_1, \ldots, \mathbf{v}_m, \mathbf{t}_{k+1}, \ldots, \mathbf{t}_n)\,\theta =$
$\mathbf{t}_1, \ldots, \mathbf{t}_{k-1}, \mathbf{v}_1, \ldots, \mathbf{v}_m, \mathbf{t}_{k+1}, \ldots, \mathbf{t}_n$

Proof. By assumption $\mathbf{s}_k$ is non-variable in all bound positions, and $\mathbf{v}_0$ is a linear vector having flat terms in all bound positions, and variables in all other positions. Furthermore $\mathbf{v}_0$ is linear. Thus there is a substitution θ_1 such that $\mathbf{v}_0\theta_1 = \mathbf{s}_k$ and $dom(\theta_1) \subseteq vars(\mathbf{v}_0)$.

Since $\mathbf{t}_k$ is a linear vector of variables, there is a substitution θ_2 such that $dom(\theta_2) \subseteq vars(\mathbf{t}_k)$ and $\mathbf{t}_k\theta_2 = \mathbf{u}_{m+1}\theta_1$.

Since Q is π-nicely moded, $vars(\mathbf{t}_k) \cap vars(\mathbf{s}_k) = \emptyset$, and therefore $vars(\mathbf{t}_k) \cap vars(\mathbf{v}_0\theta_1) = \emptyset$. Thus it follows by the previous paragraph that $\theta = \theta_1\theta_2$ is a unifier of $p_k(\mathbf{s}_k, \mathbf{t}_k)$ and $p_k(\mathbf{v}_0, \mathbf{u}_{m+1})$. (a) holds since $dom(\theta_1) \subseteq vars(\mathbf{v}_0)$ and $dom(\theta_2) \subseteq vars(\mathbf{t}_k)$. (b) follows from (a) because of linearity.

By Lemmas 3.1 and 3.2, the resolvent is permutation nicely moded and permutation well typed. By (b), the vector of the output arguments of the resolvent is a linear vector of variables, and hence the resolvent is permutation simply typed. □

The following corollary of Lemma 3.3 holds since by Def. 3.2, the leftmost atom in a simply typed query is non-variable in its bound input positions.

Corollary 3.4. Every LD-resolvent of a simply typed query Q and a simply typed clause C, where $vars(C) \cap vars(Q) = \emptyset$, is simply typed.

The following definition gives a name to the condition that the selected atom must always be non-variable in bound input positions.

Definition 3.5 (input selectability). Let P be a permutation simply typed program. P has **input selectability** if, for every permutation simply typed query Q, an atom in Q is selectable in P if and only if and only it is non-variable in all bound input positions.

In a permutation simply typed query, the output positions of each atom are filled with variables. This gives us a way of checking input selectability: the `block` declarations must be such that an atom whose output positions are all variable is selectable if and only if all bound input positions are non-variable.

Note that for input selectability, it is sufficient that the selected atom is non-variable in the *bound* input positions. It is not necessary that *all* input positions, or even all input positions of non-variable type, are non-variable.

Example 3.5. Consider Ex. 3.1. In mode `delete`(I, O, I), the third position is the only bound input position. In mode `delete`(O, I, O), the second position is the only bound input position. The `block` declarations ensure input selectability. This is true assuming any type given in Ex. 3.3.

The next lemma says that in a derivation for a permutation simply typed program and query, it can be assumed without loss of generality that the output positions in each query are filled with variables that occur in the initial query or in some clause body used in the derivation.

Lemma 3.5. Let P be a permutation simply typed program with input selectability and Q_0 be a permutation simply typed query. Let $\theta_0 = \emptyset$ and $\xi = \langle Q_0, \theta_0\rangle; \langle Q_1, \theta_1\rangle; \ldots$ be a delay-respecting derivation of $P \cup \{Q_0\}$. Then for all $i \geq 0$, if x is a variable occurring in an output position in Q_i, then $x\theta_i = x$.

Proof. The proof is by induction on the position i in the derivation. The base case $i = 0$ is trivial since $\theta_0 = \emptyset$. Now suppose the result holds for some i and Q_{i+1} exists. By Lemma 3.3, $Q_i\theta_i$ is permutation simply typed. Thus the result follows for $i + 1$ by Lemma 3.3 (b). □

4 Errors Related to Built-ins

One problem with built-ins is that their implementation may not be written in Prolog. Thus, for the purposes of this paper, it is assumed that each built-in is conceptually defined by possibly infinitely many (fact) clauses. The ISO standard for Prolog [9] does not define the built-in predicates as conceptual clauses, but it is nevertheless so precise that it should generally be possible to verify whether such a definition is correct.

To prove that a program is free from errors related to built-ins, we require it to meet certain correctness conditions some of which have been introduced in the previous section (see Definitions 3.1, 3.2, 3.3). The correctness conditions have to be satisfied by the conceptual clauses for the built-ins as well as by the user-defined part of the program.

For instance, consider the atom `M2 is M + 1` in Ex. 3.2. Conceptually, we regard this as an atom with two arguments `M2` and `M`, and we assume that there are facts "`1 is 0+1.`", "`2 is 1+1.`", and so forth.

Some built-ins produce an error if certain arguments have a wrong type, and others produce an error if certain arguments are insufficiently instantiated. For example, `X is foo` results in a type error and `X is V` results in an instantiation error. In this section, we consider two approaches to ensure freedom from instantiation and type errors due to the presence of delay declarations. For different programs and built-ins, different approaches are applicable. Under certain conditions, we even show that no delay declarations are needed at all.

4.1 The Connection between Delay Declarations and Type Errors

At first sight, it seems that delay declarations do not affect the problem of type errors, be it positively or negatively. Delay declarations cannot enforce arguments to be correctly typed. Also, one would not expect that a selection rule that is not left-to-right could be the *cause* of wrongly typed arguments.

This is probably true in practice, but in theory, there is an aspect of type errors that is specifically related to delay declarations. Consider the program consisting of the fact clause '`two(2).`' and the built-in `is`, with type $\{\texttt{two}(num), \texttt{is}(num, num)\}$ and mode $\{\texttt{two}(O), \texttt{is}(O, I)\}$. The query

```
X is foo, two(foo)
```

is $\langle 2, 1\rangle$-well typed since trivially $\models \texttt{foo} : num \Rightarrow \texttt{foo} : num$. That is, since the output of `two` is wrongly typed, we can say that correctly typed output of `two` implies correctly typed input for `is`. The above query results in a type error.

For LD-derivations this problem does not arise. The well typed query corresponding to the above query is `two(foo), X is foo`. Since the type of `two` is *num* and the program is well typed, the atom `two(foo)` can never be resolved, and therefore the derivation fails without ever reaching `X is foo`.

4.2 Exploiting Constant Types

The approach described in this subsection aims at preventing instantiation and type errors for built-ins, for example arithmetic built-ins, that require arguments to be ground. It has been proposed in [3] that these predicates be equipped with delay declarations to ensure that they are only executed when the input is ground. This has the advantage that one can reason about arbitrary arithmetic expressions, say `quicksort([1+1,3-8],M)`. The disadvantage is that `block` declarations cannot be used. In contrast, we assume that the type of arithmetic built-ins is the constant type *num*, rather than arithmetic *expressions*. Then we show that `block` declarations are sufficient. The following lemma is similar to and based on [3, Lemma 27].

Lemma 4.1. Let $Q = p_1(\mathbf{s}_1, \mathbf{t}_1), \dots, p_n(\mathbf{s}_n, \mathbf{t}_n)$ be a π-well typed query, where $p_i(\mathbf{S}_i, \mathbf{T}_i)$ is the type of p_i for each $i \in \{1, \dots, n\}$. Suppose, for some $k \in \{1, \dots, n\}$, $\mathbf{S}_k$ is a vector of constant types, $\mathbf{s}_k$ is a vector of non-variable terms, and there is a substitution θ such that $\mathbf{t}_j\theta : \mathbf{T}_j$ for all j with $\pi(j) < \pi(k)$. Then $\mathbf{s}_k : \mathbf{S}_k$ (and thus $\mathbf{s}_k$ is ground).

Proof. By Def. 3.2, $\mathbf{s}_k\theta : \mathbf{S}_k$, and thus $\mathbf{s}_k\theta$ is a vector of constants. Since $\mathbf{s}_k$ is already a vector of non-variable terms, it follows that $\mathbf{s}_k$ is a vector of constants and thus $\mathbf{s}_k\theta = \mathbf{s}_k$. Therefore $\mathbf{s}_k : \mathbf{S}_k$. □

By Def. 3.3, for every permutation simply typed query Q, there is a θ such that $Q\theta$ is correctly typed in its output positions. Thus by Lemma 4.1 if the arithmetic built-ins have type *num* in all input positions, then it is enough to have `block` declarations such that these built-ins are only selected when the input positions are non-variable. This is stated in the following theorem which is a consequence of Lemma 4.1.

Theorem 4.2. Let P be a permutation simply typed program with input selectability and Q be a permutation simply typed query. Let p be a predicate whose input arguments are all of constant type. Then in any derivation of $P \cup \{Q\}$, an atom using p will be selected only when its input arguments are correctly typed.

Example 4.1. Consider the program in Ex. 3.4 in mode $\mathtt{qs}(I, O)$. No delay-respecting derivation for a permutation simply typed query and this program can result in an instantiation or type error related to the arithmetic built-ins.

4.3 Atomic Positions

Sometimes, when the above method does not work because a program is not permutation simply typed, it is still possible to show absence of instantiation errors for arithmetic built-ins. We observe that these built-ins have argument positions of the constant type *num*. Thus, the idea is to declare certain argument positions in a predicate, including the above argument positions of the built-ins, to be *atomic*. This means that they can only be ground or free but not partially instantiated. Then there needs to be a `block` declaration such that an atom delays until the arguments in these positions are non-variable, and hence ground. Just as with types and modes, we assume that the positions which are atomic are already known.

Definition 4.1 (respects atomic positions). A query (clause) **respects atomic positions** if each term in an atomic position is ground or a variable which *only* occurs in atomic positions. A program respects atomic positions if each of its clauses does.

A program need not be permutation nicely moded or permutation well typed in order to respect atomic positions.

Lemma 4.3. Let C be a clause and Q a query which respect atomic positions, where $vars(C) \cap vars(Q) = \emptyset$. Then every resolvent of C and Q also respects atomic positions.

Proof. Let $Q = a_1, \dots, a_n$ be the query and $C = h \leftarrow b_1, \dots, b_m$ be the clause. Let a_k be the selected atom and assume it is unifiable with h using mgu θ. We must show that

$$Q' = (a_1, \dots, a_{k-1}, b_1, \dots, b_m, a_{k+1}, \dots, a_n)\theta$$

respects atomic positions.

Let x be a variable which fills an atomic position in a_k or h. Since Q and C respect atomic positions, $x\theta$ is either a variable which only occurs in atomic positions in Q', or a ground term.

Consider a term s filling an atomic position in $a_1, \dots, a_{i-1}, a_{i+1}, \dots, a_n$ or $b_1, \dots, b_m$. If s is a ground term, then $s\theta$ is also a ground term. Suppose that s is a variable. If $s \notin dom(\theta)$, then $s\theta$ is also a variable. If $s \in dom(\theta)$ then s must fill an atomic position in a_k or h. By the previous paragraph, $s\theta$ is either a variable which only occurs in atomic positions in Q', or a ground term. □

Using Lemma 4.3 we can show freedom from instantiation errors for programs where the arguments of type *num* are variable-disjoint from any other arguments.

Example 4.2. Consider the program for `length` in Ex. 3.2. If the atomic positions are exactly those positions with arithmetic arguments, then the program respects atomic positions. The `block` declaration on the built-in `<` is realised with an auxiliary predicate `less`.

Note that in the second clause for `len_aux`, for each mode, the input for `is` is provided by the clause head. Therefore no `block` declaration and hence no auxiliary predicate is required for `is` — it is sufficient to have a `block` declaration for `len_aux`. This is formalised by the following definition and lemma.

Definition 4.2 ($\mathcal{B}$-ground). Let P be a program which respects atomic positions and $\mathcal{B}$ a set of predicates whose input positions are all atomic.

A query is **$\mathcal{B}$-ground** if it respects atomic positions and each atom using a predicate in $\mathcal{B}$ has ground terms in its input positions.

An argument position k of a predicate p in P is a **$\mathcal{B}$-position** if there is a clause $p(\mathbf{t}_0, \mathbf{s}_{n+1}) \leftarrow p_1(\mathbf{s}_1, \mathbf{t}_1), \ldots, p_n(\mathbf{s}_n, \mathbf{t}_n)$ in P such that for some i where $p_i \in \mathcal{B}$, some variable in $\mathbf{s}_i$ also occurs in position k in $p(\mathbf{t}_0, \mathbf{s}_{n+1})$.

The program P is **$\mathcal{B}$-ground** if every $\mathcal{B}$-position of every predicate in P is an atomic input position, and an atom $p(\mathbf{s}, \mathbf{t})$, where $p \notin \mathcal{B}$, is selectable only if it is non-variable in the $\mathcal{B}$-positions of p.

By the following theorem, for $\mathcal{B}$-ground programs and queries it is always guaranteed that the input of all atoms in $\mathcal{B}$ is ground, since that input originates either from the initial query or the clause head.

Theorem 4.4. Let P and Q be a $\mathcal{B}$-ground program and query, and ξ be a delay-respecting derivation of $P \cup \{Q\}$. Then each query in ξ is $\mathcal{B}$-ground.

Proof. The proof is by induction on the length of ξ. Let $Q_0 = Q$ and $Q_0; Q_1; \ldots$ be a delay-respecting derivation of $P \cup \{Q_0\}$. The base case holds by the assumption that Q_0 is $\mathcal{B}$-ground.

Now consider some Q_j where $j \geq 0$ and Q_{j+1} exists. By Lemma 4.3, Q_j and Q_{j+1} respect atomic positions.

Let $p(\mathbf{u}, \mathbf{v})$ be the selected atom, $C = p(\mathbf{t}_0, \mathbf{s}_{n+1}) \leftarrow p_1(\mathbf{s}_1, \mathbf{t}_1), \ldots, p_n(\mathbf{s}_n, \mathbf{t}_n)$ be the clause and θ the mgu used in the step $Q_j; Q_{j+1}$. Consider an arbitrary $i \in \{1, \ldots, n\}$ such that $p_i \in \mathcal{B}$. We have to distinguish two cases.

If $p \notin \mathcal{B}$, then by Def. 4.2, $\mathbf{u}$ is non-variable in the $\mathcal{B}$-positions of p, and hence, since Q_j respects atomic positions, $\mathbf{u}$ is *ground* in the $\mathcal{B}$-positions of p.

If $p \in \mathcal{B}$, then $\mathbf{u}$ is ground in the $\mathcal{B}$-positions of p by the induction hypothesis.

Thus it follows that in both cases, $\mathbf{s}_i\theta$ is ground. Since the choice of i was arbitrary, it follows that Q_{j+1} is $\mathcal{B}$-ground. □

Example 4.3. The program of Ex. 3.2 is $\{$`is`$\}$-ground, and the second position of `len_aux` is an $\{$`is`$\}$-position. By Thm. 4.4, it is justified that there is no `block` declarations for `is`.

5 Termination

We are interested in ensuring that *all* derivations of a query are finite. Therefore the clause order in a program is irrelevant. Furthermore, we do not prove termination as such, but rather reduce the problem of proving termination for a program *with* `block` declarations to the same problem for a corresponding program *without* `block` declarations. We always assume that termination for the latter program can be shown using an existing method for LD-derivations [1, 5]. We present two methods for showing termination, which are illustrated in the following example.

Example 5.1. The query `permute(V,[1])` (Ex. 3.1) loops because `delete` produces a *speculative output binding* [15]: The output variable `Y` is bound before it is known that this binding will never have to be undone. Assuming left-based derivations, termination in both modes can be ensured by replacing the second clause with

```
permute([U|X],Y) :-
  delete(U,Y,Z),
  permute(X,Z).
```

This technique has been described as *putting recursive calls last* [15].

To explain termination of this program, we have to apply a different reasoning for the different modes. In mode **permute**(O, I), the atom that produces the speculative output occurs *textually before* the atom that consumes it. This means that the consumer waits until the producer has completed (undone the speculative binding). The program does not *use* speculative bindings. In mode **permute**(I, O), **delete** is used in mode **delete**(I, O, I), and in this mode it does not *make* speculative bindings.

Note that termination for this example depends on derivations being left-based, and so any method which abstracts from the selection rule must fail.

Both methods described below formalise previous heuristics [14, 15] and rely on conditions that are easy to check. It can be shown using these methods that Ex. 5.1 will terminate. These methods are not adequate for Ex. 3.4. A more complex method suitable for Ex. 3.4 is described in [16]. However, we will also give two examples of programs for which termination can be shown using the methods described here, but not using the method of [16].

5.1 Termination by not Using Speculative Bindings

In LD-derivations, speculative bindings are never used [15]. A left-based derivation *is* an LD-derivation, provided the leftmost atom in each query in the derivation is always selectable. This implies the following proposition.

Proposition 5.1. Let Q be a well typed query and P a well typed program such that an atom is selectable in P whenever its input positions of non-variable type are non-variable. Then every left-based derivation of $P \cup \{Q\}$ is an LD-derivation.

We now give two examples of programs where by Prop. 5.1, we can use any method for LD-derivations to show termination for any well typed query.

Example 5.2. Consider **permute**(O, I) as defined in Ex. 5.1 with either of the types given in Ex. 3.3. This program is well-typed.

Example 5.3. Consider the following version of **delete**(O, I, O).

```
:- block delete(?,-,-).
delete(X,[X|Z],Z).
delete(X,[U|[H|T]],[U|Z]) :- delete(X,[H|T],Z).
```

Assuming either of the types given in Ex. 3.3, this program is well typed. Note that for this program, the method of [16] is not applicable.

5.2 Termination by not Making Speculative Bindings

Some programs have the nice property that there cannot be any failing derivations. In [4], such a class of programs called *noFD* was identified. *Non-speculative* programs are similar, but there are two differences: the definition of noFD programs allows only for *LD*-derivations, but on the other hand, the definition of non-speculative programs requires that the clause heads are input linear.

Definition 5.1 (non-speculative). A program P is **non-speculative** if it is permutation simply typed, has input selectability, and every simply typed atom[5] using a predicate in P is unifiable with some clause head in P.

Example 5.4. Both versions of the **permute** program (Examples 3.1 and 5.1), assuming either of the types given in Ex. 3.3, are non-speculative in mode {**permute**(I, O), **delete**(I, O, I)}. Every simply typed atom is unifiable with at least one clause head, and the **block** declarations ensure input selectability.

Both versions of the **permute** program are *not* non-speculative in mode {**permute**(O, I), **delete**(O, I, O)}, because **delete(A,[],B)** is not unifiable with any clause head.

A delay-respecting derivation for a non-speculative program P and a permutation simply typed query can neither flounder nor fail. However it could still be infinite. Theorem 5.2 says that this can only happen if the simply typed program corresponding to P also has an infinite (LD-)derivation for this query.

Theorem 5.2. Let P be a non-speculative program and P' a simply typed program corresponding to P. Let Q be a permutation simply typed query and Q' a simply typed query corresponding to Q. If there is an infinite delay-respecting derivation of $P \cup \{Q\}$, then there is an infinite LD-derivation of $P' \cup \{Q'\}$.

[5] We say "atom" for "query of length 1".

Proof. For simplicity assume that Q and each clause body do not contain two identical atoms. Let $Q_0 = Q$, $\theta_0 = \emptyset$ and $\xi = \langle Q_0, \theta_0\rangle; \langle Q_1, \theta_1\rangle; \ldots$ be a delay-respecting derivation of $P \cup \{Q\}$. The idea is to construct an LD-derivation ξ' of $P' \cup \{Q'\}$ such that whenever ξ uses a clause C, then ξ' uses the corresponding clause C' in P'. It will then turn out that if ξ' is finite, ξ must also be finite.

We call an atom a **resolved in** ξ **at** i if a occurs in Q_i but not in Q_{i+1}. We call a **resolved in** ξ if for some i, a is resolved in ξ at i. Let $Q'_0 = Q'$ and $\theta'_0 = \emptyset$. We construct an LD-derivation $\xi' = \langle Q'_0, \theta'_0\rangle; \langle Q'_1, \theta'_1\rangle; \ldots$ of $P' \cup \{Q'\}$ showing that for each $i \geq 0$ the following hold:

(1) If $q(\mathbf{u}, \mathbf{v})$ is an atom in Q'_i that is not resolved in ξ, then $vars(\mathbf{v}\theta'_i) \cap dom(\theta_j) = \emptyset$ for all $j \geq 0$.
(2) Let x be a variable such that, for some $j \geq 0$, $x\theta_j = f(\ldots)$. Then $x\theta'_i$ is either a variable or $x\theta'_i = f(\ldots)$.

We first show these properties for $i = 0$. Let $q(\mathbf{u}, \mathbf{v})$ be an atom in Q'_0 that is not resolved in ξ. Since $\theta'_0 = \emptyset$, $\mathbf{v}\theta'_0 = \mathbf{v}$. Furthermore, by Corollary 3.4 and Lemma 3.5 and since $q(\mathbf{u}, \mathbf{v})$ is not resolved in ξ, we have $\mathbf{v}\theta_j = \mathbf{v}$ for all j. Thus (1) holds. (2) holds because $\theta'_0 = \emptyset$.

Now assume that for some i, $\langle Q'_i, \theta'_i\rangle$ is defined, Q'_i is not empty, and (1) and (2) hold. Let $p(\mathbf{s}, \mathbf{t})$ be the leftmost atom of Q'_i. We define a derivation step $\langle Q'_i, \theta'_i\rangle; \langle Q'_{i+1}, \theta'_{i+1}\rangle$ with $p(\mathbf{s}, \mathbf{t})$ as the selected atom, and show that (1) and (2) hold for $\langle Q'_{i+1}, \theta'_{i+1}\rangle$.

Case 1: $p(\mathbf{s}, \mathbf{t})$ is resolved in ξ at l for some l. Consider the simply typed clause $C' = h \leftarrow B'$ corresponding to the *uniquely renamed* clause (using the same renaming) used in ξ to resolve $p(\mathbf{s}, \mathbf{t})$. Since $p(\mathbf{s}, \mathbf{t})$ is resolved in ξ at l, $p(\mathbf{s}, \mathbf{t})\theta_l$ is non-variable in all bound input positions. Thus each bound input position of $p(\mathbf{s}, \mathbf{t})$ must be filled by a non-variable term or a variable x such that $x\theta_l = f(\ldots)$ for some f. Moreover, $p(\mathbf{s}, \mathbf{t})\theta'_i$ must have non-variable terms in all bound input positions since $Q'_i\theta'_i$ is well typed. Thus it follows by (2) that in each bound input position, $p(\mathbf{s}, \mathbf{t})\theta'_i$ has the same top-level functor as $p(\mathbf{s}, \mathbf{t})\theta_l$, and since h has flat terms in the bound input positions, there is an mgu ϕ'_i of $p(\mathbf{s}, \mathbf{t})\theta'_i$ and h. We use C' for the step $\langle Q'_i, \theta'_i\rangle; \langle Q'_{i+1}, \theta'_{i+1}\rangle$.

We must show that (1) and (2) hold for $i + 1$. Consider an atom $q(\mathbf{u}, \mathbf{v})$ in Q'_i other than $p(\mathbf{s}, \mathbf{t})$. By Lemma 3.3 (b), $vars(\mathbf{v}\theta'_i) \cap dom(\phi'_i) = \emptyset$. Thus for the atoms in Q'_{i+1} that occur already in Q'_i, (1) is maintained. Now consider an atom $q(\mathbf{u}, \mathbf{v})$ in B' which is not resolved in ξ. By Lemma 3.5, $\mathbf{v}\theta'_{i+1} = \mathbf{v}$. Since $q(\mathbf{u}, \mathbf{v})$ is not resolved in ξ, for all $j > l$ we have that $q(\mathbf{u}, \mathbf{v})$ occurs in Q_j and thus by Lemma 3.5, $\mathbf{v}\theta_j = \mathbf{v}$. Thus (1) follows. (2) holds since it holds for i and $p(\mathbf{s}, \mathbf{t})$ is resolved using the same clause head as in ξ.

Case 2: $p(\mathbf{s}, \mathbf{t})$ is not resolved in ξ. Since P' is non-speculative, there is a (uniquely renamed) clause $C' = h \leftarrow B'$ in P' such that h and $p(\mathbf{s}, \mathbf{t})\theta'_i$ have an mgu ϕ'_i. We use C' for the step $\langle Q'_i, \theta'_i\rangle; \langle Q'_{i+1}, \theta'_{i+1}\rangle$.

We must show that (1) and (2) hold for $i + 1$. Consider an atom $q(\mathbf{u}, \mathbf{v})$ in Q'_i other than $p(\mathbf{s}, \mathbf{t})$. By Lemma 3.3 (b), $vars(\mathbf{v}\theta'_i) \cap dom(\phi'_i) = \emptyset$. Thus for the atoms in Q'_{i+1} that occur already in Q'_i, (1) is maintained. Now consider an atom $q(\mathbf{u}, \mathbf{v})$ in B'. Clearly $q(\mathbf{u}, \mathbf{v})$ is not resolved in ξ. Since $vars(C') \cap vars(Q_j\theta_j) = \emptyset$ for all j and since by Lemma 3.5, we have $\mathbf{v}\theta'_{i+1} = \mathbf{v}$, (1) holds for $i+1$.

By (1) for i, we have $vars(\mathbf{t}\theta'_i) \cap dom(\theta_j) = \emptyset$ for all j. By Lemma 3.3 (a), we have $dom(\phi'_i) \subseteq vars(\mathbf{t}\theta'_i) \cup vars(C')$. Thus we have $dom(\phi'_i) \cap dom(\theta_j) = \emptyset$ for all j. Moreover, (2) holds for i. Thus (2) holds for $i+1$.

Since this construction can only terminate when the query is empty, either Q'_n is empty for some n, or ξ' is infinite.

Thus we show that if ξ' is finite, then every atom resolved in ξ is also resolved in ξ'. So let ξ' be finite of length n. Assume for the sake of deriving a contradiction that j is the smallest number such that the atom a selected in $\langle Q_j, \theta_j\rangle; \langle Q_{j+1}, \theta_{j+1}\rangle$ is never selected in ξ'. Then $j \neq 0$ since Q_0 and Q'_0 are permutations of each other and all atoms in Q'_0 are eventually selected in ξ'. Thus there must be a $k < j$ such that a does not occur in Q_k but does occur in Q_{k+1}. Consider the atom b selected in $\langle Q_k, \theta_k\rangle; \langle Q_{k+1}, \theta_{k+1}\rangle$. Then by the assumption that j was minimal, b must be the selected atom in $\langle Q'_i, \theta'_i\rangle; \langle Q'_{i+1}, \theta'_{i+1}\rangle$ for some $i \leq n$. Hence a must occur in Q'_{i+1} since the clause used to resolve b in ξ' is a simply typed clause corresponding to the clause used to resolve b in ξ. Thus a must occur in Q'_n, contradicting that ξ' terminates with the empty query.

Thus ξ can only be infinite if ξ' is also infinite. □

Theorem 5.2 says that for non-speculative programs, atom order in clause bodies is irrelevant for termination. In other words, termination is independent of any particular selection rule, as long as derivations are delay-respecting.

We now give an example of a program for which termination can be shown using non-speculative programs but not using the method of [16].

Example 5.5. The following program has mode {`plus_one`(I), `minus_two`(I), `minus_one`(I), `two`(O), `one`(O), `zero`(O)}, and the type of all arguments is *nl*.

```
:- block plus_one(-).
plus_one(X) :- minus_two([1|X]).

:- block minus_two(-).
minus_two([A|X]) :- minus_one(X).
minus_two([]).

:- block minus_one(-).
minus_one([A|X]) :- plus_one(X).
minus_one([]).

two([2|X]) :- one(X).

one([1|X]) :- zero(X).

zero([]).
```

This program is non-speculative, and the query

$$Q = \texttt{plus\_one(X)},\ \texttt{two(X)}$$

is $\langle 2, 1\rangle$-simply typed. Moreover, it is easy to see that, for the corresponding simply typed query `two(X),plus_one(X)` , any *LD*-derivation is finite. Therefore by Thm. 5.2, all delay-respecting derivations of Q are finite.

6 Related Work

This work was inspired by **Apt** and **Luitjes** [3]. For arithmetic built-ins, they require declarations which delay an atom until the arguments are ground. Such declarations are usually implemented not as efficiently as `block` declarations. Little attention is given to termination, proposing a method limited to deterministic programs.

Naish [15] gives good intuitive explanations why programs loop, which directed our own search for further ideas and their formalisation. To ensure termination, he proposes some heuristics, without any formal proof.

Predicates are assumed to have a single mode. Alternative modes are achieved by multiple versions of a predicate. This approach is quite common [2, 3, 6] and is also taken in Mercury [18], where these versions are generated by the compiler. However, generating multiple versions implies code duplication and hence there is a loss of generality in assuming single-moded predicates.

Naish uses examples such as `permute` where under the above assumption, there is no reason for using delay declarations in the first place. Therefore, his discussion on delay declarations lacks motivation.

Lüttringhaus-Kappel [12] proposes a method to generate control automatically to ensure termination, giving practical evidence that control declarations were generated for many programs. The method assumes arbitrary delay-respecting derivations and hence does not work for programs where termination depends on derivations being left-based.

Marchiori and **Teusink** [13] base termination on norms and the *covering* relation between subqueries of a query. This is loosely related to well-typedness. However, their results are not comparable to ours because they assume a *local selection rule*, that is a rule which always selects an atom which was introduced in the most recent step. We are not aware of an existing language that uses a local selection rule. The authors state that programs that do not use *speculative bindings* deserve further investigation, and that they expect any method for proving termination with *full* coroutining either to be very complex, or very restrictive in its applications.

We have previously presented a method of proving termination which is based on identifying the so-called *robust* predicates, for which the textual position of an atom using this predicate is irrelevant [16]. That method is quite complex and not as intuitive as the methods described here. In practice, it is probably more widely applicable than the method of this paper, but we have seen in Examples 5.3 and 5.5 that there are programs for which the methods of this paper work and the method of [16] does not.

7 Conclusion and Future Work

We have shown methods of preventing instantiation and type errors related to built-ins and ensuring termination for logic programs with `block` declarations.

To prevent errors due to built-ins, we have provided two methods that show that `block` declarations, as opposed to more complicated delay constructs [3], are often sufficient. In addition, in many cases, particularly for the arithmetic predicates where the arguments must be atomic, we show that there is no need for any form of delay declarations. Whether one of these methods or even both are applicable depends on the program. Finding a more uniform approach to this problem could be a topic of future work.

For proving termination, we have presented two methods based on not *using* and not *making* speculative bindings, respectively. Proposition 5.1 states that for well typed programs meeting a simple condition on selectability, any left-based derivation of a well typed query is an LD-derivation. Theorem 5.2 states that for non-speculative programs, termination is independent of a particular selection rule. We have noted that in some cases such as Ex. 5.1, in one mode, the first method applies, and in the second mode, the other method applies. These methods are appealing because they are simple and formalise heuristics that have been known for some time [14, 15].

It is an ongoing discussion whether it is reasonable to assume predicates that run in several modes [7]. We believe that a formalism dealing with delay declarations should at least *allow* for multiple modes, while not excluding other applications such as the test-and-generate paradigm (coroutining). Our results are still applicable and relevant for programs with just a single mode. For example, our results about built-ins could be used to show absence of errors in a program for the n-queens problem, which is a well-known example for the test-and-generate paradigm [17]. Also, Thm. 5.2 is useful for single-moded programs. However, we admit that Prop. 5.1 lacks motivation without the assumption of multiple modes.

We envisage that an implementation of our work should take the form of a program development tool which would help a programmer to verify the various mode and type conditions introduced in this paper. It should also support transforming a program so that the conditions are met, which would mainly be limited to reordering atoms in clause bodies. Further research concerning the design and development of such a tool is ongoing work.

Acknowledgements

We thank the anonymous referees and all colleagues who commented on our work during the LOPSTR '98 workshop. Jan-Georg Smaus was supported by EPSRC Grant No. GR/K79635.

References

1. K. R. Apt. *From Logic Programming to Prolog.* Prentice Hall, 1997.
2. K. R. Apt and S. Etalle. On the unification free Prolog programs. In A. Borzyszkowski and S. Sokolowski, editors, *Proceedings of the Conference on Mathematical Foundations of Computer Science*, LNCS, pages 1–19, Berlin, 1993. Springer-Verlag.
3. K. R. Apt and I. Luitjes. Verification of logic programs with delay declarations. In *Proceedings of AMAST'95*, LNCS, Berlin, 1995. Springer-Verlag. Invited Lecture.
4. A. Bossi and N. Cocco. Successes in logic programs. In P. Flener, editor, *Proceedings of the 8th International Workshop on Logic Program Synthesis and Transformation*, LNCS. Springer-Verlag, 1999.
5. D. De Schreye and S. Decorte. Termination of logic programs: the never-ending story. *Journal of Logic Programming*, 19/20:199–260, 1994.
6. S. Etalle, A. Bossi, and N. Cocco. Well-terminating programs. *Journal of Logic Programming*, 1998. Accepted for publication.
7. P. M. Hill, editor. *ALP Newsletter*, `http://www-lp.doc.ic.ac.uk/alp/`, February 1998. Pages 17,18.
8. Intelligent Systems Laboratory, Swedish Institute of Computer Science, PO Box 1263, S-164 29 Kista, Sweden. *SICStus Prolog User's Manual*, 1997. `http://www.sics.se/isl/sicstus/sicstus_toc.html`.
9. International Organization for Standardization. *The ISO Prolog Standard*, 1995. `http://www.logic-programming.org/prolog_std.html`.
10. M. R. K. Krishna Rao, D. Kapur, and R. K. Shyamasundar. A transformational methodology for proving termination of logic programs. In *Proceedings of the 5th Conference for Computer Science Logic*, LNCS, pages 213–226. Springer-Verlag, 1991.
11. J. W. Lloyd. *Foundations of Logic Programming.* Springer-Verlag, 1987.
12. S. Lüttringhaus-Kappel. Control generation for logic programs. In D. S. Warren, editor, *Proceedings of the 10th International Conference on Logic Programming*, pages 478–495. MIT Press, 1993.
13. E. Marchiori and F. Teusink. Proving termination of logic programs with delay declarations. In J. W. Lloyd, editor, *Proceedings of the 12th International Logic Programming Symposium*, pages 447–461. MIT Press, 1995.
14. L. Naish. Automatic control of logic programs. *Journal of Logic Programming*, 2(3):167–183, 1985.
15. L. Naish. Coroutining and the construction of terminating logic programs. Technical Report 92/5, University of Melbourne, 1992.
16. J.-G. Smaus, P. M. Hill, and A. M. King. Termination of logic programs with `block` declarations running in several modes. In C. Palamidessi, editor, *Proceedings of the 10th Symposium on Programming Language Implementations and Logic Programming*, LNCS. Springer-Verlag, 1998.
17. J.-G. Smaus, P. M. Hill, and A. M. King. Verification of logic programs with `block` declarations running in several modes. Technical Report 7-98, University of Kent at Canterbury, Canterbury, CT2 7NF, United Kingdom, July 1998.
18. Z. Somogyi, F. Henderson, and T. Conway. The execution algorithm of Mercury, an efficient purely declarative logic programming language. *Journal of Logic Programming*, November 1996.

Algorithms for Synthesizing Reactive Systems: A Perspective

Pierre Wolper

Institut Montefiore
Université de Liège
B-4000 Liège, Belgium
pw@montefiore.ulg.ac.be

Abstract. Starting in the early 1980s, a number of algorithmic techniques have been proposed for synthesizing the synchronization kernel of reactive systems from high-level temporal logic specifications. These techniques are based on nontrivial results in logic and automata theory and appear to be quite powerful. Nevertheless, essentially none of this work has found its way to practical use. This paper reviews the main results from this area and tries to identify the main reasons that explain their nonexploitation.

P. Flener (Ed.): LOPSTR'98, LNCS 1559, pp. 308–308, 1999.

Schema-Guided Synthesis of CLP Programs *

Hamza Zidoum[1], Pierre Flener[2], and Brahim Hnich[3]

[1] UAE University, PO Box 15551, Al-Aïn, United Arab Emirates
[2] Dept of Info Science, Uppsala Univ., S-751 05 Uppsala, Sweden, pierref@csd.uu.se
[3] Dept of Info Technology, Tampere Univ. of Technology, SF-33101 Tampere, Finland

1 Introduction and Specifications

This work is inspired by D.R. Smith's research on synthesising global search (GS) programs (in the *Refine* language) from first-order logic specifications (also in *Refine*) [8–10]. We concentrate on synthesising constraint logic programs (CLP) [6] instead. We thus only have to synthesise code that (incrementally) *poses* the constraints, because the actual constraint propagation and pruning are performed by the CLP system. We here only tackle the family of decision assignment problems; the families of optimisation assignment problems, decision permutation problems, and optimisation permutation problems are covered in [4].

Specifications are the input to program synthesis. In *decision assignment problems*, a mapping M from a list V into the integer interval $1..W$ has to be found, satisfying certain constraints. Their formal specifications take the form

$$\begin{array}{c}\forall \langle V, W\rangle : list(term) \times int \,.\, \forall M : list(V \times 1..W)\,.\\ r(\langle V, W\rangle, M) \leftrightarrow \forall \langle I, J\rangle, \langle K, L\rangle \in M \,.\, \wedge_{i=1}^{m} P_i(I,J,K,L) \rightarrow Q_i(I,J,K,L)\end{array} \quad (1)$$

where the P_i and Q_i are formulas. This can be considered a *specification template*. This covers many problems, such as Hamiltonian path, n-Queens, and *graph colouring*, which problem consists of finding a mapping M from the list R of the regions of a map to a set of colours (numbered $1..C$) so that any two adjacent regions (as indicated in an adjacency list A) have different colours:

$$\begin{array}{c}\forall \langle R, C, A\rangle : list(term) \times int \times list(R \times R)\,.\, \forall M : list(R \times 1..C)\,.\\ col(\langle R, C, A\rangle, M) \leftrightarrow \forall \langle R_1, C_1\rangle, \langle R_2, C_2\rangle \in M \,.\, \langle R_1, R_2\rangle \in A \rightarrow C_1 \neq C_2\end{array} \quad (2)$$

2 A Global Search Program Schema for CLP

A *program schema* [3] for a programming methodology M (such as divide-and-conquer, generate-and-test, ...) is a couple $\langle T, A\rangle$, where *template* T is an open program showing the (problem-independent) data-flow and control-flow of programs constructed following M, and *axioms* A constrain the (problem-dependent) programs for the open relations in T such that the overall (closed) program will really be a program constructed following M.

* A full version of this extended abstract is published as [4].

P. Flener (Ed.): LOPSTR'98, LNCS 1559, pp. 309–312, 1999.

The basic idea of our GS schema for CLP is to start from an *initialised* descriptor of the search space, to incrementally *split* that space into subspaces, while declaring the domains of the involved variables and *constraining* them to achieve partial consistency, until no splits are possible and a variablised solution can be *extracted*. Then a correct solution is *generated*, by instantiation of the variables in the variablised solution. Our GS template is thus the open program:

$$\begin{aligned} r(X,Y) &\leftarrow initialise(X,D), \\ &\quad\; rgs(X,D,Y), \\ &\quad\; generate(Y,X) \\ rgs(X,D,Y) &\leftarrow extract(X,D,Y) \\ rgs(X,D,Y) &\leftarrow split(D,X,D',\delta), \\ &\quad\; constrain(\delta,D,X), \\ &\quad\; rgs(X,D',Y) \end{aligned} \qquad (GS)$$

where the open relations are informally specified as follows: $initialise(X, D)$ iff D is the descriptor of the initial space of candidate solutions to problem X; $extract(X, D, Y)$ iff the variablised solution Y to problem X is directly extracted from descriptor D; $split(D, X, D', \delta)$ iff descriptor D' describes a subspace of D wrt problem X, such that D' is obtained by adding δ to descriptor D; $constrain(\delta, D, X)$ iff adding δ to D leads to a descriptor defining a subspace of D that may contain correct solutions to problem X; $generate(Y, X)$ iff correct solution Y to problem X is enumerated from the constraint store, which is an implicit parameter representing X. Formalising this is the role of the axioms, as shown in [4]. There we also establish in what sense our GS schema is correct.

3 Schema Particularisations and the Synthesis Method

Using the GS schema like the divide-and-conquer schema was used in [7, 3] to guide synthesis puts heavy demands on automated theorem proving and turns out much more difficult [8]. Fortunately, a large percentage of GS programs falls into one of 7 families identified by Smith, each representing a particular case of the GS schema (in the sense that programs for *all* its open relations are adequately chosen in advance), here called a *particularisation*. In [4], we exhibit our particularisations for assignment and permutation problems, and show how to implement them as programs, called *closures*, because they "close" the open program *GS*. We also define the notion of *specification reduction*, expressing when it suffices to invoke a program P_g of specification S_g to implement a new specification S_r. The *synthesis method* is then as follows: Given a specification S_r, find (through a linear subcase of the decidable second-order semi-unification) a substitution θ under which S_r reduces to the specification template S_g attached to some particularisation P_g of the GS schema, and then obtain a (closed) program that correctly implements S_r by taking the *GS* template and $C_g\theta$.

Example Given specification (2), the fully automatically synthesisable program consists of the *GS* template and the following code:

$$
\begin{aligned}
P_{init} &: initialise(X, D) \leftarrow \\
&\quad D = \langle V, [\,]\rangle \\
P_{extr} &: extract(\_, D, Y) \leftarrow \\
&\quad D = \langle [\,], Y\rangle \\
P_{split} &: split(D, X, D', \delta) \leftarrow \\
&\quad D = \langle [I|T], M\rangle, \\
&\quad J \ in\ 1..W, \\
&\quad \delta = \langle I, J\rangle, \\
&\quad D' = \langle T, [\delta|M]\rangle \\
P_{constr} &: constrain(\_, D, \_) \leftarrow \\
&\quad D = \langle \_, [\,]\rangle \\
&\ \ constrain(\delta, D, \langle \_, \_, A\rangle) \leftarrow \\
&\quad \delta = \langle R_1, C_1\rangle, \\
&\quad D = \langle \_, [\langle R_2, C_2\rangle|M']\rangle, \\
&\quad \langle R_1, R_2\rangle \in A \rightarrow C_1 \neq C_2, \\
&\quad constrain(\delta, \langle \_, M'\rangle, \langle \_, \_, A\rangle) \\
P_{gen} &: generate(M, \_) \leftarrow \\
&\quad M = [\,] \\
&\ \ generate(M, \_) \leftarrow \\
&\quad M = [\langle \_, J\rangle|M'], \\
&\quad indomain(J), \\
&\quad generate(M', \_)
\end{aligned}
$$

4 Conclusion

At least one order of magnitude is gained in efficiency by switching from an ordinary symbolic language to a constraint one, and our automatically synthesisable CLP(FD) [2] programs are only 3 to 5 times slower than carefully hand-crafted ones [2], which is encouraging since none of the obvious problem-specific optimising transformations have been performed yet on our programs. Since our synthesis is fully automatable, starting from short and elegant formal specifications (which can even be generated from some form of controlled English [5]), our approach seems viable. Our formal specification language is equivalent in its expressiveness to CLP(Sets) programming languages, such as $CLPS$ [1]. We thus aim at new ways of compiling CLP(Sets) programs. Comparing execution times is still meaningless because of the prototypical nature of CLP(Sets) compilers.

The synthesised programs are not small (minimum 33 atoms, in a very expressive programming language), and making them steadfast reusable components for a programming-in-the-large approach by embedding their whole development in a framework-based approach [3] is straightforward.

Our results are more than a simple transcription of the KIDS approach from *Refine* to CLP, as they also reflect some new ideas.

First, we fully exploited CLP [as opposed to *Refine*, which is "only" an ordinary symbolic language], by significantly modifying the original GS schema, so that it reflects a *constrain-and-generate* programming methodology. Much of the constraint solving machinery that needs to be pushed into *Refine programs*, at synthesis time or at optimisation time, is already part of the CLP(FD) *language* and is implemented there once and for all in a particularly efficient way.

Second, we introduced the notion of specification template. This has nice effects on the KIDS approach, as shown in the next two items.

Third, the substitution under which a specification reduces to a specification template can be easily computed, so that there is no need of an automated theorem prover, at synthesis time, to compute it.

Fourth, the derivation of consistency-constraint-posing code can be calling-context-dependent, leading to rather effective (namely incremental) constraint-posing code [in contrast to Smith's calling-context-independent derivation of filters [8, 9] and cuts [10], which may be non-incremental]. Such code can even be pre-synthesised, for a given particularisation, so that there is no need of an automated theorem prover, at synthesis time, to derive its specification. [As opposed to filters and cuts] no forward constraints need to be posed, not even for efficiency reasons, due to the way CLP programs work [as opposed to *Refine* ones]: Solution construction (through *generate*) actually only starts in CLP once *all* constraints have been posed, and posing any forward constraints would thus be not only superfluous but also a way of slowing down the program, because the forward constraints of time t will become backward constraints at times larger than t and all constraints would thus have been posed twice. This does not prevent CLP from performing forward checks during solution generation.

All this means that synthesis can be fully automatic, without using any automated theorem prover, for some families of problems.

References

1. F. Ambert, B. Legeard, et E. Legros. Programmation en logique avec contraintes sur ensembles et multi-ensembles héréditairement finis. *TSI* 15(3):297–328, 1996.
2. D. Diaz and Ph. Codognet. A minimal extension of the WAM for clp(FD). In: D.S. Warren (ed), *Proc. of ICLP'93*, pp. 774–790. The MIT Press, 1993.
3. P. Flener, K.-K. Lau, and M. Ornaghi. Correct-schema-guided synthesis of steadfast programs. *Proc. of ASE'97*, pp. 153–160. IEEE Computer Society Press, 1997.
4. P. Flener, H. Zidoum, and B. Hnich. Schema-guided synthesis of constraint logic programs. *Proc. of ASE'98*. IEEE Computer Society Press, 1998.
5. N.E. Fuchs and U. Schwertel. Attempto Controlled English — Not just another logic specification language. This volume.
6. J. Jaffar and M.J. Maher. Constraint logic programming: A survey. *J. of Logic Programming* 19–20:503–582, 1994.
7. D.R. Smith. Top-down synthesis of divide-and-conquer algorithms. *Artificial Intelligence* 27(1):43–96, 1985.
8. D.R. Smith. The structure and design of global search algorithms. TR KES.U.87.12, Kestrel Institute, 1988.
9. D.R. Smith. KIDS: A semiautomatic program development system. *IEEE Trans. Software Engineering* 16(9):1024–1043, 1990.
10. D.R. Smith. Towards the synthesis of constraint propagation algorithms. In: Y. Deville (ed), *Proc. of LOPSTR'93*, pp. 1–9, Springer-Verlag, 1994.

Abstract: Proof Planning with Program Schemas

Julian Richardson*

Institute of Representation and Reasoning, Division of Informatics, Edinburgh University, 80 South Bridge, Edinburgh EH1 1HN, Scotland
julianr@dai.ed.ac.uk

1 Introduction

Schema-based program synthesis and transformation techniques tend to be either pragmatic, designed for carrying out real program transformation or synthesis operations but lacking the logical basis to ensure correctness of the programs they synthesise/transform, or rigorous, with strong theoretical foundations, but generating proof obligations which are difficult to satisfy.

What is needed is a framework which can address the rigorous logical foundations of schemas at a sufficient level of abstraction to make schema-based program synthesis and transformation practical while retaining correctness. We propose that *proof planning* offers a paradigm which combines logical rigour with usability, and, in addition, allows the employment of schemas to be integrated with the automatic satisfaction of any proof obligations which arise.

Further details of the work described in this abstract can be found in [4].

2 Proof Planning

Machine-assisted proofs are generally made up of many small steps. The depth and large branching rate mean that a large search space must be explored in order to generate them automatically, and they can be hard to understand. Proof planning addresses these issues by providing a more high-level view of the proof. This not only makes proofs easier to generate by reducing the size of the proof search space, but also aids the user by producing proofs which are made up of a small number of understandable steps. This is especially important when a proof attempt fails.

Proof plans are composed of building blocks called *methods*. A proof planning method (henceforth, we just write *method*) consists of a conjunction of heuristic conditions to determine when a proof operation should be applied and what its effects will be — the *meta-level* — and a tactic, which constructs the piece of proof which corresponds to the method — the *object-level*. A proof plan consists of a sequence of method applications which, at the meta-level, proves the initial conjecture. Since, however, the meta-level logic is informal and heuristic in nature, this does not in itself constitute a proof of the conjecture. Once a proof plan has been found, the tactics which correspond to the methods from which

* The author is supported by EPSRC Grant GR/L11724

P. Flener (Ed.): LOPSTR'98, LNCS 1559, pp. 313–315, 1999.

the proof plan is composed are combined to make a compound tactic, which can be executed to give an object-level proof.

Since proof planning allows us to carry out heuristic, and thus practical, reasoning, while guaranteeing correctness through the corresponding tactics, it provides us with an ideal paradigm for combining logical rigour with usability.

3 The Relationship of Schemas to Proof Planning

Each method has five slots: an *input pattern*, *preconditions*, *effects*, *output pattern* and a *tactic*. The method is applicable to a meta-level goal if the goal matches the input pattern and the preconditions and effects are satisfied. The resulting variable substitutions are used to instantiate the output pattern and the tactic.

By contrast, a schema has only three slots: an *input pattern*, *conditions*, and an *output pattern*. The schema applies to a goal if the goal matches the input pattern and the conditions are satisfied. The resulting variable substitutions are used to instantiate the output pattern.

The similarity between the two formalisms is clear. The main difference is that schemas have no tactic slot — this is crucial. The tactic part of a method provides us with a criterion for the correct application of the method. This in turn frees the preconditions and effects from this obligation, and allows much more flexible, human-oriented reasoning to occur in them. Since schemas lack this slot, it is either the responsibility of the schema conditions to ensure correctness, or the correctness issue is sidelined.

4 Augmenting Schemas with a Heuristic Component

In [3] a rigorous formulation of program synthesis schemas called *frameworks* is proposed. Application of such a schema involves choosing instantiations for its open symbols and proving that the required framework axioms are satisfied. Schema frameworks can be used to encode general program synthesis strategies, for example divide-and-conquer [3]. Schema frameworks do not contain heuristic information for deciding when they should be applied. Rather, they contain just the information needed to ensure correctness.

Drawing on the analogy of §3, we propose that schema frameworks should be implemented as methods. This entails carefully dividing each schema framework into object-level and meta-level parts. A good first approximation is to implement the technical proof conditions of the schema as a tactic. The corresponding method has *legal preconditions* which determine when the tactic will be applicable, but also has *heuristic preconditions/effects* which can decide when it is a good idea to apply the framework, and can suggest sensible instantiations for the framework's open symbols.

The development of proof planning has been partly driven by the need for techniques for automating program synthesis and verification. We therefore already have a catalogue of techniques which address the kinds of goals which arise during synthesis and verification. In particular *ripple analysis* and *rippling* [2] are techniques for selecting and applying induction schemes which are appropriate for proving a particular conjecture. Induction is vital for reasoning about recursive programs, and many algorithm design tactics (e.g. divide-and-conquer) correspond to induction schemas, suggesting that ripple analysis could also be useful in selecting algorithm design tactics. Middle-out reasoning [1] provides a way of finding appropriate values for unknown (open) symbols in a proof by progressively instantiating them as the proof proceeds. Proof planning can be applied to higher-order logic [5], which is important for reasoning about programs. These techniques (amongst others) should be useful not just in the selection and application of schema frameworks, but also in satisfying the proof obligations which arise. By implementing them as methods, schema frameworks can be integrated into and benefit from our existing proof plans for program synthesis, verification and transformation.

The adaptation of schema-based techniques to proof planning promises to offer advantages to proof planning. In particular, schema-based techniques offer a body of knowledge on program synthesis and transformation, and aspects of schema-based techniques, in particular the use of second-order patterns and constraints in their specification, could also be exploited in methods.

5 Conclusions

Schema frameworks are very similar to the methods used in proof planning. An integration of the two techniques would be beneficial for both. Proof planning provides a uniform mechanism both for deciding which frameworks to use during program synthesis (or transformation), and how to use them, and for satisfying proof obligations which then arise. Techniques developed for proof planning promise to be useful for automating schema application.

References

1. A. Bundy, A. Smaill, and J. Hesketh. Turning eureka steps into calculations in automatic program synthesis. In S. L.H. Clarke, editor, *Proceedings of UK IT 90*, pages 221–6. IEE, 1990. Also available from Edinburgh as DAI Research Paper 448.
2. A. Bundy, A. Stevens, F. van Harmelen, A. Ireland, and A. Smaill. Rippling: A heuristic for guiding inductive proofs. *Artificial Intelligence*, 62:185–253, 1993. Also available from Edinburgh as DAI Research Paper No. 567.
3. P. Flener, K.-K. Lau, and M. Ornaghi. On correct program schemas. In N. E. Fuchs, editor, *LOPSTR '97: Proceedings of the Seventh International Workshop on Logic Program Synthesis and Transformation, Leuven, Belgium, July 10-12 1997*, volume 1463 of *Lecture Notes in Computer Science*. Springer Verlag, 1998.
4. J.D.C. Richardson. Proof planning with program schemas. Research Paper, School of Artificial Intelligence, University of Edinburgh. Forthcoming.
5. J.D.C Richardson, A. Smaill, and I.M. Green. System description: proof planning in higher-order logic with lambdaclam. In C. Kirchner and H. Kirchner, editors, *Proceedings of CADE-15*, volume 1421 of *Lecture Notes in Computer Science*. Springer Verlag, 1998.

Logical Synthesis of Imperative O.O. Programs

Patrick Bellot and Bernard Robinet

ENST, 46 rue Barrault, F-75634 Paris, France
{Patrick.Bellot,Bernard.Robinet}@Email.enst.fr

The Ω logic, is designed to specify, to reason about and to synthesize imperative programs in an object oriented language, namely C++ . There exists a lot of systems where computing-by-proof is possible but there are based on more or less classical logics and produce λ-expressions. We make the distinction between programming and computing. Functional programs are obviously in the second category. Even if imperative programs can be modeled with functions, thanks to denotational semantics, this is not realistic. We are interested in the first category: we want to synthesize programs doing actions.

Handling actions requires a particular formal system. It has to be constructive, i.e. to support Disjunction Property and Existence Property. Then, it must be resources aware, for instance linear in the sense of J-Y. Girard. Finally, it has to at least express concurrency, sequentiality, causality and nondeterminacy. Sequentiality is obtained using non commutative versions of some usual linear connective. Causality is obtained by an *ad hoc* new connective.

The system is able to handle action formulae such as "to move the block x on the block y" and situation formulae such as "the block x is on the block y". We consider a situation A as the action "to do things in such a way that the situation A holds". Thus, everything is action. A mathematical formula is a modalized situation formula as in Linear Logic: the modality says that the formula is resource free, it can be duplicated or erased as we need.

Connectives will be used to describe and combine actions but they are still used to describe and combine situations and mathematical propositions. Therefore, our connectives have two meanings, one in term of actions and one in term of situations. For instance, the first linear conjunction $(A \otimes B)$ has its usual linear meaning when A and B are situations: both A and B are true and available at the same time. But if A and B are actions, then $(A \otimes B)$ is the action of executing concurrently A and B. However, there is only a single axiomatization for both meanings.

In order to use the system, we write down a set of extra-logical axioms describing the knowledge about the problem. For instance, in the World of Blocks, there are axioms to say that there is always a free place on the floor and there is one axiom describing a move of a single block. Secondly, we have a description of an action. E.g., $\forall x, y \cdot top(x) \otimes on(x, y) \Rightarrow top(x) \otimes on(x, floor) \otimes top(y)$ is a simple formula saying that we can move any top block x from its support y onto the floor. Then, we prove the action. And finally, we automatically extract from the proof a realization of the action formula.

The realization is an object in the sense of object-oriented programming. It has the method *prove*() which executes the proved action and returns an appropriate

P. Flener (Ed.): LOPSTR'98, LNCS 1559, pp. 316–318, 1999.

result. The logic is exposed as a sequent calculus. Theorems are **sequents** of the form:

$$R_1 : A_1, R_2 : A_2, \ldots, R_n : A_n \vdash S_1 : B_1, S_2 : B_2, \ldots, S_m : B_m$$

meaning that if R_i realizes A_i for $i \in [1, n]$ then S_j realizes B_j for $j \in [1, m]$. On both sides of the **entailment** sign $\vdash$, the realized formulae are implicitly linked by a **conjunction**. It means that all formulae and all realizations are available at the same time. The $R_i, i \in [1, n]$ are all different **realization variables**. The $S_j, j \in [1, m]$ are realizations built using the $R_i, i \in [1, n]$ and individual variables occurring in the formulae $B_1, \ldots, B_m$. We also assume that the $R_i, i \in [1, n]$ are **independent**, i.e. they can be executed in any order, sequentially or concurrently, without changing their semantics.

The axiomatization is difficult because an axiom or a rule must describe **everything** that has been done. Then comes the fact that realizations are imperative programs which do not have the **referential transparency** property: **when** and **where** executing them is crucial. We must be able to build the realizations of the conclusions from the realizations of the hypotheses in a sequent without any assumptions on them except their independence. The axiomatization is not classical because of the fully conjunctive nature of our sequents, it has an interesting impact on the proof structure. The three structural rules are given Fig. 1.

$$\mathcal{X} : \Gamma \vdash \mathcal{X}' : \Gamma' \qquad \text{(id), identity-exchange rule }^{(*)}$$

$$\frac{\mathcal{X} : \Gamma \vdash \mathcal{R} : \Delta \qquad \mathcal{Y} : \Delta \vdash \mathcal{S} : \Theta}{\mathcal{X} : \Gamma \vdash [\mathcal{R}/\mathcal{Y}]\mathcal{S} : \Theta} \qquad \text{(tr), transitivity rule}$$

$$\frac{\mathcal{X} : \Gamma \vdash \mathcal{R} : \Delta}{\mathcal{X} : \Gamma, \mathcal{Y} : \Theta \vdash \mathcal{R} : \Delta, \mathcal{Y} : \Theta} \qquad \text{(mn), monotony rule}$$

(*) $\mathcal{X}' : \Gamma'$ is a permutation of $\mathcal{X} : \Gamma$.

Fig. 1. Structural rules of Ω logic

Besides the classical tree structure of proofs, the transitivity axiom allows a **linear structure**. Using the rules above, we admit $\Theta_1, \Gamma, \Theta_2 \vdash \Theta_1, \Delta, \Theta_2$ as a **generalized instance** of an axiom $\Gamma \vdash \Delta$. Using linear proof and generalized instances of axioms, proofs are much simpler than classical tree-like proofs. E Zarpas showed that human and automatic search for proofs is less complex. Note that in this scheme, axioms are better than inference rules.

Besides these axioms and rules, we always have a method to build the realizations of the conclusion formulae from the realizations of the hypotheses. $A \otimes B$, A **times** B, is both the first linear conjunction and the concurrent execution of A and B. We detail Fig. 2 some of its axioms to show the problems encountered in a formal system about actions. Firstly, we remark the unusual axiom stating the commutativity of $\otimes$. This is due to the fact that a formula $A \otimes B$, concurrent execution of A and B, cannot be split into an execution of A and an execution of B to be recombined into $B \otimes A$. Secondly, we remark some redundancy of axioms. This is due to the fact that operational semantics of the conclusions (in term of realizations) are not the same.

$$A, B \vdash A \otimes B \qquad A \otimes B \vdash B \otimes A \qquad (A \otimes B) \otimes C \vdash A \otimes (B \otimes C)$$

$$\frac{A \vdash C}{A \otimes B \vdash C \otimes B} \qquad \frac{B \vdash D}{A \otimes B \vdash A \otimes D} \qquad A \otimes (B \otimes C) \vdash (A \otimes B) \otimes C$$

Fig. 2. Some axioms for $\otimes$

Here follows the unformal descriptions of some of the connectives. $A \gg B$, A then B, is the sequential execution of A and B. From a logical point of view, it is some non-commutative version of the $\otimes$ conjunction. $A > B$, A prefix B, has no logical meaning. In term of actions, it means doing B but beginning by doing A. That is: A is the first thing to do in order to do B. After, only consequences of B are valid. Following the corresponding linear conjunction, A & B, A and B, means that we have the choice of doing A or doing B but only one of them. $\oplus$ is roughly the same disjunction as in Linear Logic. In term of actions, doing $A \oplus B$, A plus B, means doing A or doing B without any way to know *a priori* which one. $A \Rightarrow B$, A implies B, has its usual linear logic meaning. In terms of actions, it means that we can do B if we know how to do A. $A \rightarrow B$, A causes B, means that doing A causes the execution of B. This connective could be useful for specifying event driven programs such as telecommunication protocols. $\forall x \cdot A$ has its usual linear logic meaning. In terms of actions, it means that we can do $[t/x]A$ for one chosen t. $\exists x \cdot A$ has its usual linear logic meaning. In terms of actions, it means that there exists a witness t such that we can do $[t/x]A$. Doing $!A$ is doing A but the modality "!" means that the formula can be duplicated or erased as we want. Typically, it is used for actions or states which do not need any resource to be done.

The axiomatization of these connectives is complete except for the causality connective and for the existence quantifier. The realization have been implemented in the C++ programming language. the system has been successfully applied to the World of Blocks problem. For instance, to move a stack of blocks one have to prove :

$$\forall s \cdot \forall c \cdot \forall d \cdot \begin{pmatrix} stack(s) & & stack(s) \\ \otimes & & \otimes \\ top(s) & & top(s) \\ \otimes & \Rightarrow & \otimes \\ on(s,c) & & on(s,d) \\ \otimes & & \otimes \\ top(d) & & top(c) \end{pmatrix}$$

From the proof, one builds a realization which realizes the move of the stacks of blocks. Of course, proving such theorems requires particular rules for iterating an operation. The system has been applied to the similar problem of the Towers of Hano. Finally, we are applying it to ordinary computer algorithms involving programming variables. A few documents about Ω logic are available by the WEB at the Internet adress: http://www.enst.fr/~bellot/DOCUMENTS/index.html.

Mathematical Foundations for Program Transformations

R. Ben Ayed[1], J. Desharnais[2], M. Frappier[3], and A. Mili[4]

[1] School of Engineering, University of Tunis II, Belvedere, 1002 Tunisia
[2] Laval University, Quebec City, PQ G1K 7P4, Canada
[3] University of Sherbrooke, Sherbrooke, PQ J1K 2R1 Canada
[4] The Institute for Software Research, Fairmont, WV 26554 USA

1 Program Transformations: An Emerging Paradigm

Traditional programming paradigms revolve around mapping a single requirements specification into a program. As less and less software is developed from scratch, and more and more is developed from existing software artifacts, this traditional paradigm is growing less and less predominant. Paradigms that are gaining ground include:

- *Program adaptation*, whereby a program is modified to satisfy a specification that it does not originally satisfy; this occurs in adaptive software maintenance and in white box software reuse.
- *Software Incrementation*, whereby a program is modified to have an additional functional feature, while preserving its current functional properties.
- *Software Merging*, whereby two (typically) similar software products are merged into a single product that cumulates the functional features of each; this arises typically when the two products are obtained by software incrementation from a common base version.
- *Software Composition*, whereby various existing reusable assets are composed together (by means of application-specific code) to produce a prespecified software application; this arises in component-based software development.

All these paradigms can be characterized by the following premise: they map a set of specifications (or programs) into a resulting program. It is possible to model these paradigms by a process of correctness-preserving stepwise transformations; unlike traditional programming calculi, these transformations joggle more than one specification (or program) at a time.

2 A Calculus of Programming by Parts

In [1] we discuss a refinement ordering between relational specifications (denoted by $\sqsubseteq$) and discuss its lattice properties; also, we recognize that complex specifications can naturally be structured as aggregates of simpler specifications by means of lattice operators (where the join is denoted by $\sqcup$). In [3] we use the lattice structure to derive a calculus of program construction by parts, whereby the solution to a complex specification is derived by focusing on the sub-specifications

P. Flener (Ed.): LOPSTR'98, LNCS 1559, pp. 319–321, 1999.

in turn then merging their solutions into a solution for the aggregate specification. To support this program derivation method, we provide the following tools: 1) A specification/programming notation that supports specification structuring (using lattice operators) as well as program structuring (using programming constructs). 2) A set of guidelines for deriving partially determined programs from component sub-specifications. 3) A set of rules for combining partially determined programs into (more) completely determined programs.

This programming calculus, dealing as it does with more than one specification simultaneously, serves as a basis for our foundation for program transformations. In the next four sections, we briefly review how it can be adapted to four distinct patterns of program transformation, namely: software incrementation; software merging; software adaptation; and software composition.

3 Software Incrementation

We consider a software system C and a feature F that we wish to add to C, and we are interested in how to augment C so that it has feature F. Our position is that this problem amounts to refining the specification $C \sqcup F$. Note that although C is a program, we can write it using our specification notation (we have rules for doing that, given in [3]). Our calculus of program construction by parts enables us to determine which part of C may be modified to accommodate the change imposed by F, and to ensure that the change in question does not alter the current functional properties of C.

4 Software Merging

We consider two versions, say V and W, of some software system, and we are interested in merging them into a single version that has all the features of V and all the features of W. We view this problem as that of refining the expression $V \sqcup W$. Because V and W stem presumably from a common original system by incrementation, it is reasonable to expect that large portions of V and W are common, and that their differences are localized. Our calculus allows us to match up homologous parts in V and W, to identify subsumpption relationships between homologous parts, and to guide modifications where necessary. Also, it produces verification conditions that ensure that the functional features of V and W are preserved and cumulated as V and W are merged.

5 Software Adaptation

We consider a software component C and a specification K; we assume that C does not satisfy specification K, but we have reasons to believe that it can easily be modified to satisfy it. This problem does look like the refinement of $K \sqcup C$, since it proceeds by considering information from two specifications/programs, but differs in two significant ways: First, whereas the refinement of $K \sqcup C$ seeks to satisfy both K and C, the modification of C to satisfy K really seeks to satisfy K only —but expects to use C towards this end. Second, whereas traditional refinement of $K \sqcup C$ proceeds by drawing semantic information from K and C interchangeably, the adaptation of C to satisfy K proceeds by drawing syntactic information from C (since we want to use the structure of C as a guide for our solution) and semantic information of K (since we must satisfy K, not C). To acknowledge the asymmetry between the roles played by K and C in the adaptation of C to satisfy K, we write the expression to refine as $K \triangleright C$, and we derive slightly different refinement rules for the $\triangleright$ operator than we had for the $\sqcup$ operator. Space limitations prohibit us from presenting these rules, and from giving an illustrative example.

6 Software Composition

We are given a software system S in which we must integrate a component C to fulfill some function F. Because C does not refine (subsume) F, the component cannot be integrated `verbatim`; on the other hand, we assume that C is a COTS product, so that we have no access to its code, but can only add code around it to satisfy F. We view this problem as that of refining the expression $(F' \sqcup C)$, where F' represents the weakest (least refined) specification that satisfies the condition: $F' \sqcup C \sqsupseteq F$. Intuitively, F' represents the weakest requirement that must be satisfied, in addition to C, in order to satisfy F. In [3] we discuss how F can be satisfied by inserting code to do preprocessing (upstream of C) or postprocessing (downstream of C) to satisfy F.

7 Conclusion

In this paper we briefly present a calculus of program construction, and we discuss its use for recent software development paradigms, such as software incrementation, software merging, software adaptation and software composition. Several authors have advocated using the join operator in the refinement of complex specifications [3,4,2]. Recent work of Hehner [4] includes laws of refinement for join-structured specifications. The work presented in this paper differs from other programming calculi by the fact that it deals with new software development paradigms rather than traditional *program construction*.

References

1. N. Boudriga, F. Elloumi, and A. Mili. The lattice of specifications: Applications to a specification methodology. *Formal Aspects of Computing*, 4:544–571, 1992.
2. C.A.R. Hoare et al. Laws of programming. *Communications of the ACM*, 30(8):672–686, 1987.
3. M. Frappier, J. Desharnais, and A. Mili. A calculus of program construction by parts. *Science of Computer Programming*, 6:237–254, 1996.
4. E.C.R. Hehner. *A Practical Theory of Programming.* Springer-Verlag, 1993.

An Exhaustive-Search Method Using Layered Streams Obtained Through a Meta-Interpreter for Chain Programs

David A. Rosenblueth

Instituto de Investigaciones en Matemáticas Aplicadas y en Sistemas
Universidad Nacional Autónoma de México
Apdo. 20-726, 01000 Mexico D.F.
drosenbl@servidor.unam.mx

1 Introduction

Okumura and Matsumoto have published [1] examples of logic programs using a data structure they call "layered stream," especially suited for completely traversing a search space in a deterministic manner [2,4]. A layered stream is a representation of a list of lists, in which common heads of adjacent sublists have been factored. This factorization allows the pruning of several branches of the search space in constant time and is also a source of parallelism [3, p. 147]. The published examples include the N-queen problem and "instant insanity" (a precursor of Rubik's cube). Each such deterministic, layered-stream program supposedly performs exhaustive search over the space generated by some nondeterministic, naive program. However, a method converting a nondeterministic program into a corresponding exhaustive-search, layered-stream version has not yet been proposed, as far as we know. Layered streams have thus remained difficult to use [3, p. 408], since the programmer must be concerned both about factorization of heads and exhaustive search. We build upon the work of Okumura and Matsumoto by showing how to translate nondeterministic programs into exhaustive-search, layered-stream form. Our method is restricted to generate-and-test programs fitting a certain schema.

2 Layered streams

We now give some basic definitions of layered streams.

Syntax. A layered stream is recursively defined as follows.

- *begin* and [] are *layered streams*.
- $[X*Xs|Ys]$ is a *layered stream* if $X*Xs$ is a $*$-pair and Ys is a layered stream.

Now we define $*$-pairs in terms of layered streams.

- $X*Xs$ is a *$*$-pair* if Xs is a layered stream.

P. Flener (Ed.): LOPSTR'98, LNCS 1559, pp. 322–324, 1999.

Semantics. Let $\overline{Xs}$ denote the list of lists represented by the layered stream or $*$-pair Xs. Then

$$\overline{begin} = [[\,]]$$
$$\overline{[\,]} = [\,]$$
$$\overline{[X*Xs|Ys]} = \overline{X*Xs} \bullet \overline{Ys}$$

where $\bullet$ denotes list concatenation. A $*$-pair $X*Xs$ represents the list obtained by inserting X in front of every list in $\overline{Xs}$.

$$\overline{X*Xs} = X \;\diamond\; \overline{Xs}$$

Note that a layered stream having only $*$-pairs that represent the empty list will also represent the empty list. This allows us to include "garbage" at any level. For instance the layered stream:

$$[\ 1*[3*[\,], 4*[2*[\,]]],\ 2*[4*[1*[3*begin]]],\ 3*[1*[4*[2*begin]]],\ 4*[1*[3*[\,]], 2*[\,]]\ ]$$

represents $[[2,4,1,3],\ [3,1,4,2]]$ and is also the answer to the four-queen program of [1] and the goal $\leftarrow fourQueen(begin, Z)$.

3 An exhaustive-search meta-interpreter for chain programs

3.1 Chain programs

We define a *chain program* as a definite program such that all its binary predicates are defined only by clauses of the form:

$$p(X_0, X_n) \leftarrow q_1(X_0, X_1),\ q_2(X_1, X_2),\ \ldots,\ q_n(X_{n-1}, X_n) \qquad (1)$$
$$\text{or}\ \ p(\langle t, Xs\rangle, [t'|Xs]) \leftarrow test(\langle u, Xs\rangle) \qquad (2)$$

where the X_i's are distinct variables, $\text{var}(u) \subseteq \text{var}(t)$, and $\text{var}(t') \subseteq \text{var}(t)$. We use angled brackets $\langle\ \rangle$ as a function symbol of a term grouping inputs and outputs.

3.2 An exhaustive-search meta-interpreter

Obtaining all answers for a chain program and a goal $\leftarrow p(\mathbf{x}_0, Z)$ translates to evaluating the expression $\{(\mathbf{x}_0, \mathbf{x}_0)\}\ ;\ P$, where ";" denotes relational composition and P is the relation denoted by p. We have to evaluate relational expressions of the form:

$$\{(\mathbf{x}_0, \mathbf{y}_1), \ldots, (\mathbf{x}_0, \mathbf{y}_k)\}\ ;\ (Q_1\ ;\ Q_2\ ;\ \ldots\ ;\ Q_m) \qquad (3)$$
$$\{(\mathbf{x}_0, \mathbf{y}_1), \ldots, (\mathbf{x}_0, \mathbf{y}_k)\}\ ;\ (P_1 \cup P_2 \cup \ldots \cup P_n) \qquad (4)$$

We wish to achieve as much factorization as possible of partial solutions. This suggests using a left-to-right evaluation of (3) and (4). (Using other strategies leads to meta-interpreters having essentially the same behavior as either the continuation-based [4] or the stream-based [2] exhaustive-search methods.) The top-level predicates would be:

$$comp([\,], Xs, Xs) \leftarrow$$
$$comp([Q|Qs], Xs, Zs) \leftarrow one\_component(Q, Xs, Ys),\ comp(Qs, Ys, Zs)$$
$$union([\,], Xs, [\,]) \leftarrow$$
$$union([Pj|Pjs], Xs, YsZs) \leftarrow one\_unend(Pj, Xs, Ys),\ union(Pjs, Xs, Zs),\ append(Ys, Zs, YsZs)$$
$$one\_component(Q, Xs, Zs) \leftarrow defn(Q, Pjs),\ union(Pjs, Xs, Zs)$$
$$one\_unend(Pj, Xs, Ys) \leftarrow is\_test(Pj),\ list\_cl\_test(Pj, Xs, Ys)$$
$$one\_unend(Pj, Xs, Zs) \leftarrow cl\_comp(Pj, Qs),\ comp(Qs, Xs, Zs)$$

Layered streams can be introduced in the definition of the *list_cl_test* predicate.

4 Beyond chain form

It is easy to handle programs having a slightly more general form, *quasi-chain form*, where we generalize (1) to:

$$p(\langle t_0, X_0\rangle, X_n) \leftarrow q_1(\langle t_1, X_0\rangle, X_1),\ q_2(\langle t_2, X_1\rangle, X_2),\ \ldots,\ q_n(\langle t_n, X_{n-1}\rangle, X_n)$$

where $\mathrm{var}(t_{i+1}) \subseteq \mathrm{var}(t_i)$.

If we fix the problem size, then all four layered-stream examples in [3] can readily be written in quasi-chain form: the N-queen problem [3, p. 117], instant insanity, [3, p. 241], the "turtle problem" [3, p. 266], and Waltz's polyhedra-scene labeling [3, p. 300]. Yet another generalization allows us to handle variable-size problems.

References

1. Akira Okumura and Yuji Matsumoto. Parallel programming with layered streams. In *Proceedings of the 1987 Symposium on Logic Programming*, pages 224–231, San Francisco, California, U.S.A., 1987. Lecture Notes in Computer Science 348.
2. H. Tamaki. Stream-based compilation of ground I/O Prolog into committed-choice languages. In *Proceedings of the Fourth International Conference on Logic Programming*, pages 376–393, Melbourne, Australia, 1987.
3. Evan Tick. *Parallel Logic Programming.* MIT Press, 1991.
4. Kazunori Ueda. Making exhaustive search programs deterministic. *New Generation Computing*, 5:29–44, 1987.

Bottom-Up Specialisation of Logic Programs

Wim Vanhoof, Danny De Schreye, and Bern Martens

Department of Computer Science, Katholieke Universiteit Leuven
Celestijnenlaan 200A, B-3001, Heverlee, Belgium
{wimvh,dannyd,bern}@cs.kuleuven.ac.be

1 Introduction and Motivation

Partial deduction is an important transformation technique for logic programs, capable of removing inefficiencies from programs [4,5]. As an on-line specialisation technique, it is based on an evaluation mechanism for logic programs. The input to a typical partial deducer is a program and a partially instantiated query. The instantiated part represents the information with respect to which one would like to specialise; the uninstantiated part represents the information not yet known. Therefore, all classical partial deduction techniques use *top-down* evaluation (or SLD-resolution) to evaluate the program parts that depend on the known input and generate a new program that computes its result using only the remainder of the input. Since the new program has less computations to perform, in general, it will be more efficient.

In this work, we argue the need for a complementary partial deduction technique that is based on *bottom-up* evaluation of a logic program: starting from the unit clauses, information is propagated upwards, and new facts and clauses are derived. The motivation for such a complementary technique is twofold:

- It enables specialisation that is hard to achieve using a top-down approach. When specialising programs in which control information flows bottom-up, a top-down specialiser is often not capable of obtaining this information in time, in order to decide whether or not to continue the specialisation.
- Sometimes, one wishes to specialise (or "concretise") a program with respect to a set of definitions, providing information that flows bottom-up into the program. Top-down, *goal-directed* specialisation often is not the most natural approach to achieve this kind of specialisation.

To illustrate the control problem, consider the following example:

$fill\_list(L,T,I,L) \leftarrow type(T,L).$
$fill\_list(L,T,I,R) \leftarrow fill\_list([I|L],T,I,R).$
$make\_list(T,I,R) \leftarrow fill\_list([],T,I,R).$

$type(list1,[X])$
$type(list3,[X_1,X_2,X_3]).$

The predicate $make\_list(T,I,R)$ can be used to create a list of a fixed length (type T), with each element initialised with I. The result is returned in R. This example represents a class of recursive predicates that build up some structure between calls before a base clause of the predicate (ending the recursion) is reached, depending on the structure built.

P. Flener (Ed.): LOPSTR'98, LNCS 1559, pp. 325–327, 1999.

Unfolding techniques, on which all top-down specialisers are based, are known to have problems with these. When unfolding e.g. $make\_list(list3, I, R)$ without the information provided by the *list*-predicate, it is impossible to detect whether the sequence

$$fill\_list([], \ldots) \rightarrow fill\_list([I], \ldots) \rightarrow fill\_list([I, I], \ldots) \rightarrow \ldots$$

will eventually terminate. If, on the other hand, this recursive predicate is handled in a bottom-up fashion, structure is shrinking between recursive calls, resulting in the facts
$make\_list(list1, I, [I]).$
$make\_list(list3, I, [I, I, I]).$

Apart from control, there are other reasons why a bottom-up approach might be preferred. Consider a program library M, in which n predicates are defined, all using the functionality provided by an abstract data type (ADT) to hide the concrete representation and manipulation of a data structure. Despite the advantages of abstracting information through several layers during program development and maintenance, every such layer of abstraction decreases efficiency. Therefore, it makes sense to propagate the concrete representation up into the program, to the places where it is really used, thus removing the overhead. This sort of information propagation can in principle be obtained by a top-down specialisation scheme. Achieving it in a *general* and *completely automatic* way, however, is far from trivial, precisely because of the bottom-up flow of control information. In particular, (Vanilla-like) meta-programs typically present difficulties of this kind. Moreover, a top-down specialiser needs a single goal to start specialisation from, which might not be available when specialising a library. Or the goal(s) will likely contain no information (all arguments free) since the latter flows bottom-up (further complicating top-down control).

So, in a number of cases, proceeding bottom-up is a more natural solution. Bottom-up transformation and specialisation has been considered occasionally before (see e.g. [3]). However, to the best of our knowledge, our ongoing effort is the first attempt to achieve these in a completely general and automatic way.

2 A Framework for Bottom-up Specialisation

The most important contribution of this work, the details of which can be found in [7], is the definition of a *formal framework*, capturing the notion of bottom-up partial deduction.

The transformation is based on a non ground T_P-operator, T_P^C, acting on sets of *clauses* instead of atoms, as in compositional semantics [2, 1]. In order to define a finitary transformation, the T_P^C-operator is combined with an *abstraction function*, mapping newly derived atoms (and clauses) onto more general clauses, capable of generating the former. This combination is denoted by an *abstract* T_P^C-operator, A_P^C. The resulting program can then be obtained from the least fixpoint of A_P^C, which can be ensured finitary through a suitable concrete control scheme. The transformation is proven sound and complete with respect to the S-semantics: transformation of a program P results in a program P' having the same minimal S-Herbrand model [1] as P.

The defined transformation can be used as a stand-alone specialisation technique, useful when a program needs to be specialised with respect to its internal structure instead of a goal (as in the library-example). On the other hand, the bottom-up transformation can be combined with a more traditional top-down partial deduction strategy. In [6], we describe a *concrete control scheme* for bottom-up partial deduction, derived from top-down control techniques. As an illustration, it is shown that the Vanilla meta-interpreter can excellently be specialised by alternating a bottom-up transformation and a classical top-down specialisation – both using straightforward and fully automatic control. The same result can be obtained using a top-down component alone, but only at the cost of using a very sophisticated unfolding strategy. It is therefore expected that more involved combinations of bottom-up and top-down strategies will in general lead to specialisation techniques that are powerful, yet conceptually cleaner than one overall approach.

Acknowledgments

Wim Vanhoof is supported by a specialisation grant of the Flemish Institute for the Promotion of Scientific-Technological Research in Industry (IWT), Belgium. Danny De Schreye is a Senior Research Associate of the Belgian National Fund for Scientific Research and Bern Martens is partially supported by Esprit project 25503, ARGo.

References

1. A. Bossi, M. Gabbrielli, G. Levi, and M. Martelli. The S-semantics approach: Theory and applications. *Journal of Logic Programming*, 19/20:149–197, 1994.
2. A. Bossi, M. Gabbrielli, G. Levi, and M. C. Meo. A compositional semantics for logic programs. *Theoretical Computer Science*, 122(1-2):3–47, 1994.
3. Y. Cosmadopoulos, M. Sergot, and R. W. Southwick. Data-driven transformation of meta-interpreters: A sketch. In H. Boley and M. M. Richter, editors, *Proceedings of the International Workshop on Processing Declarative Knowledge (PDK'91)*, volume 567 of *LNAI*, pages 301–308. Springer Verlag, 1991.
4. J. Gallagher. Specialisation of logic programs: A tutorial. In *Proceedings PEPM'93, ACM SIGPLAN Symposium on Partial Evaluation and Semantics-Based Program Manipulation*, pages 88–98, Copenhagen, June 1993. ACM Press.
5. J. W. Lloyd and J. C. Shepherdson. Partial evaluation in logic programming. *Journal of Logic Programming*, 11(3&4):217–242, 1991.
6. W. Vanhoof, B. Martens, D. De Schreye, and K. De Vlaminck. Specialising the other way around. In J. Jaffar, editor, *Proceedings of the Joint International Conference and Symposium on Logic Programming*, Manchester, United Kingdom, June 1998. MIT-Press.
7. W. Vanhoof, D. De Schreye, and B. Martens. A framework for bottom up specialisation of logic programs. In *Proceedings of the Joint International Symposia PLILP/ALP 1998*, volume 1490 of *Lecture Notes In Computer Science*, pages 54–72. Springer-Verlag, 1998.

Myrtle: A Set-Oriented Meta-Interpreter Driven by a "Relational" Trace for Deductive Databases Debugging

Sarah Mallet and Mireille Ducass

IRISA/INSA
Campus Universitaire de Beaulieu, CS 14315
F - 35042 Rennes Cedex, France
{smallet, ducasse}@irisa.fr

1 Introduction

Deductive databases manage large quantities of data and, in general, in a set-oriented way. The existing explanation systems for deductive databases [6, 4, 1] give information in the shape of forests of proof trees. Although proof trees are often useful, this representation is not sufficient. We propose a tracing technique which consists of integrating a "relational" trace and an instrumented meta-interpreter using substitution sets. The relational trace efficiently gives precise information about data extraction from the relational database. The meta-interpreter manages substitution sets and gives explanation on the deduction. The expensive aspects of meta-interpretation are reduced by the use of the trace which avoids many calculations. The flexibility of meta-interpretation is preserved. It allows different profiles of trace to be easily produced.

2 Debugging tools for deductive database systems

Debugging tools for deductive databases must be useful for their various kinds of users: implementors who develop the deductive part, knowledge engineers who maintain the data, and end-users who query the database. Implementors need to get rather low-level pictures of executions of the deductive databases in order to understand and fix errors in the kernel. Knowledge engineers do not necessarily know the details of the implementation of the kernel, but they need to understand how the data, they add or modify, fit with the existing ones ; they therefore need to get pictures of executions abstract enough for them not to be overwhelmed by implementation details. End-users, in general, do not have an in-depth knowledge of computers, but they nevertheless have to rely on the results of the system. They, therefore, need to get very high-level views of executions to understand how the answers to their queries was produced in order to accept these answers. A key feature of a debugging tool for deductive databases is therefore its **flexibility**. It must be able to provide information and explanations at various levels of abstraction.

P. Flener (Ed.): LOPSTR'98, LNCS 1559, pp. 328–330, 1999.

3 Driving a meta-interpreter with a trace

A well known flexible technique to produce explanations consists in instrumenting meta-interpreters (see for example [7]). This instrumentation can be easily adapted to users' needs. However, this technique is in general too inefficient. On the other hand, kernel developers usually instrument their compilers to produce some sort of low-level traces of executions. These traces are mostly intended at "private" usage and do not necessarily contain the information necessary to the explanations, but they are generated efficiently.

We propose a tracing technique which takes the best of the previous two techniques. In Myrtle, we integrate a low-level trace with an instrumented meta-interpreter. The trace efficiently gives precise and low-level information about the extraction of data from the relational database. The meta-interpreter gives explanations about the deduction and allows more abstract views to be built. The expensive aspects of meta-interpretation are reduced by the use of the trace which avoids many calculations. In particular, the accesses to the relational database are not repeated. When necessary, the meta-interpreter uses the transient information generated by the DB data extraction system, accessible via the relational trace. This feature is especially suited here as a deductive database program handles *a large quantity of data*. Avoiding to recalculate these data saves a significant amount of time. In addition, flexibility of meta-interpretation enables different traces to be easily produced, as illustrated at the end of the article.

Two specificities of deductive databases prevent usual Prolog meta-interpreters to be straightforwardly reused: *set-oriented management of data* and *termination*. Tuples of the relational databases are, in general, retrieved several at the same time, and not one at a time ; a possibly large number of tuples can be extracted from the base during a single access. Hence, in Myrtle substitutions are managed in a set-oriented way. Lastly, the restriction to Datalog and dedicated search strategies ensure that a request on a deductive database always terminates [3].

In Myrtle, we developed this technique for the Validity system based on EKS [5], which uses the SLD-AL technique to ensure termination, and the rule language DEL.

Abstractions can be easily integrated in the meta-interpreter by instrumentation. In Myrtle, as an illustration of flexibility, three possible abstractions of the execution are proposed. We cite them in a growing level order of abstraction starting from the level close to execution. The first one, a relatively low level, is a box-oriented representation of execution, which is interesting for developers. The second one reflects the operational semantics level, it is a representation of the multi-SLD-AL tree. The last one is closer to declarative semantics. The execution is abstracted by a forest of proof trees combined with substitution sets.

The meta-interpreter, the connexion with the "relational" trace of Validity and the three abstractions are described in details in [2].

4 Conclusion

The main contribution of this work is the integration of a relational trace and a meta-interpreter, which is, to our knowledge, original. The practical impact of such a technique is important. As already mentioned, users of deductive databases have many different profiles. The flexibility at reasonable cost offered by our technique enables the debugger to be adapted, in particular, to end users. They will better accept the results if they can understand how they were produced. One can conjecture that such a tool can help widen the acceptance of logic programming technologies.

The relational trace reduces the non determinism of meta-interpretation and avoids many calculations at debugging stage that have been already performed at execution. The meta-interpreter allows different abstract views of the execution to be constructed.

Acknowledgments

Alexandre Lefebvre, Laurent Vieille and Bernard Wappler from Next Century Media sacrificed part of their time to explain the operation of Validity. Moreover, Bernard Wappler has modified the relational trace of Validity in order to facilitate integration with the meta-interpreter.

References

1. T. Arora, R. Ramakrishnan, W.G. Roth, P. Seshadri, and D. Srivastava. Explaining program execution in deductive systems. In S. Ceri, K. Tanaka, and S. Tsur, editors, *Proceedings of the Deductive and Object-Oriented Databases Conference*, volume 760 of *LNCS*. Springer-Verlag, December 1993.
2. S. Mallet and M. Ducass. Myrtle : A set-oriented meta-interpreter driven by a "relational" trace for deductive databases debugging. Technical Report 1219, PI IRISA, 1998.
3. R. Ramakrishnan and J. D. Ullman. A survey of deductive database systems. *Journal of Logic Programming*, 23:125–149, 1995.
4. G. Specht. Generating explanation trees even for negations in deductive database systems. In M. Ducassé, B. Le Charlier, Y.-J. Lin, and U. Yalcinalp, editors, *Proceedings of ILPS'93 Workshop on Logic Programming Environments*, Vancouver, October 1993. LPE'93.
5. L. Vieille, P. Bayer, V. Küchenhoff, and A. Lefebvre. EKS-V1, a short overview. In *Workshop on Knowledge Base Management System*, Boston, USA, July 1990. AAAI-90.
6. C. Wieland. Two explanation facilities for the deductive database management system DeDex. In H. Kangassalo, editor, *Proceedings of the 9th Conference on Entity-Relationship Approach*, pages 189–203, 1990. ETH Zurich.
7. L.Ü. Yalcinalp. *Meta-programming for knowledge based systems in Prolog.* PhD thesis, Case Western Reserve University, Cleveland, Ohio 44106, August 1991. Technical Report TR 91-141.

Author Index

Lecture Notes in Computer Science

For information about Vols. 1–1490
please contact your bookseller or Springer-Verlag

Vol. 1491: W. Reisig, G. Rozenberg (Eds.), Lectures on Petri Nets I: Basic Models. XII, 683 pages. 1998.

Vol. 1492: W. Reisig, G. Rozenberg (Eds.), Lectures on Petri Nets II: Applications. XII, 479 pages. 1998.

Vol. 1493: J.P. Bowen, A. Fett, M.G. Hinchey (Eds.), ZUM '98: The Z Formal Specification Notation. Proceedings, 1998. XV, 417 pages. 1998.

Vol. 1494: G. Rozenberg, F. Vaandrager (Eds.), Lectures on Embedded Systems. Proceedings, 1996. VIII, 423 pages. 1998.

Vol. 1495: T. Andreasen, H. Christiansen, H.L. Larsen (Eds.), Flexible Query Answering Systems. IX, 393 pages. 1998. (Subseries LNAI).

Vol. 1496: W.M. Wells, A. Colchester, S. Delp (Eds.), Medical Image Computing and Computer-Assisted Intervention – MICCAI'98. Proceedings, 1998. XXII, 1256 pages. 1998.

Vol. 1497: V. Alexandrov, J. Dongarra (Eds.), Recent Advances in Parallel Virtual Machine and Message Passing Interface. Proceedings, 1998. XII, 412 pages. 1998.

Vol. 1498: A.E. Eiben, T. Bäck, M. Schoenauer, H.-P. Schwefel (Eds.), Parallel Problem Solving from Nature – PPSN V. Proceedings, 1998. XXIII, 1041 pages. 1998.

Vol. 1499: S. Kutten (Ed.), Distributed Computing. Proceedings, 1998. XII, 419 pages. 1998.

Vol. 1500: J.-C. Derniame, B.A. Kaba, D. Wastell (Eds.), Software Process: Principles, Methodology, and Technology. XIII, 307 pages. 1999.

Vol. 1501: M.M. Richter, C.H. Smith, R. Wiehagen, T. Zeugmann (Eds.), Algorithmic Learning Theory. Proceedings, 1998. XI, 439 pages. 1998. (Subseries LNAI).

Vol. 1502: G. Antoniou, J. Slaney (Eds.), Advanced Topics in Artificial Intelligence. Proceedings, 1998. XI, 333 pages. 1998. (Subseries LNAI).

Vol. 1503: G. Levi (Ed.), Static Analysis. Proceedings, 1998. IX, 383 pages. 1998.

Vol. 1504: O. Herzog, A. Günter (Eds.), KI-98: Advances in Artificial Intelligence. Proceedings, 1998. XI, 355 pages. 1998. (Subseries LNAI).

Vol. 1505: D. Caromel, R.R. Oldehoeft, M. Tholburn (Eds.), Computing in Object-Oriented Parallel Environments. Proceedings, 1998. XI, 243 pages. 1998.

Vol. 1506: R. Koch, L. Van Gool (Eds.), 3D Structure from Multiple Images of Large-Scale Environments. Proceedings, 1998. VIII, 347 pages. 1998.

Vol. 1507: T.W. Ling, S. Ram, M.L. Lee (Eds.), Conceptual Modeling – ER '98. Proceedings, 1998. XVI, 482 pages. 1998.

Vol. 1508: S. Jajodia, M.T. Özsu, A. Dogac (Eds.), Advances in Multimedia Information Systems. Proceedings, 1998. VIII, 207 pages. 1998.

Vol. 1510: J.M. Zytkow, M. Quafafou (Eds.), Principles of Data Mining and Knowledge Discovery. Proceedings, 1998. XI, 482 pages. 1998. (Subseries LNAI).

Vol. 1511: D. O'Hallaron (Ed.), Languages, Compilers, and Run-Time Systems for Scalable Computers. Proceedings, 1998. IX, 412 pages. 1998.

Vol. 1512: E. Giménez, C. Paulin-Mohring (Eds.), Types for Proofs and Programs. Proceedings, 1996. VIII, 373 pages. 1998.

Vol. 1513: C. Nikolaou, C. Stephanidis (Eds.), Research and Advanced Technology for Digital Libraries. Proceedings, 1998. XV, 912 pages. 1998.

Vol. 1514: K. Ohta, D. Pei (Eds.), Advances in Cryptology – ASIACRYPT'98. Proceedings, 1998. XII, 436 pages. 1998.

Vol. 1515: F. Moreira de Oliveira (Ed.), Advances in Artificial Intelligence. Proceedings, 1998. X, 259 pages. 1998. (Subseries LNAI).

Vol. 1516: W. Ehrenberger (Ed.), Computer Safety, Reliability and Security. Proceedings, 1998. XVI, 392 pages. 1998.

Vol. 1517: J. Hromkovič, O. Sýkora (Eds.), Graph-Theoretic Concepts in Computer Science. Proceedings, 1998. X, 385 pages. 1998.

Vol. 1518: M. Luby, J. Rolim, M. Serna (Eds.), Randomization and Approximation Techniques in Computer Science. Proceedings, 1998. IX, 385 pages. 1998.

1519: T. Ishida (Ed.), Community Computing and Support Systems. VIII, 393 pages. 1998.

Vol. 1520: M. Maher, J.-F. Puget (Eds.), Principles and Practice of Constraint Programming - CP98. Proceedings, 1998. XI, 482 pages. 1998.

Vol. 1521: B. Rovan (Ed.), SOFSEM'98: Theory and Practice of Informatics. Proceedings, 1998. XI, 453 pages. 1998.

Vol. 1522: G. Gopalakrishnan, P. Windley (Eds.), Formal Methods in Computer-Aided Design. Proceedings, 1998. IX, 529 pages. 1998.

Vol. 1524: G.B. Orr, K.-R. Müller (Eds.), Neural Networks: Tricks of the Trade. VI, 432 pages. 1998.

Vol. 1525: D. Aucsmith (Ed.), Information Hiding. Proceedings, 1998. IX, 369 pages. 1998.

Vol. 1526: M. Broy, B. Rumpe (Eds.), Requirements Targeting Software and Systems Engineering. Proceedings, 1997. VIII, 357 pages. 1998.

Vol. 1527: P. Baumgartner, Theory Reasoning in Connection Calculi. IX, 283. 1999. (Subseries LNAI).

Vol. 1528: B. Preneel, V. Rijmen (Eds.), State of the Art in Applied Cryptography. Revised Lectures, 1997. VIII, 395 pages. 1998.

Vol. 1529: D. Farwell, L. Gerber, E. Hovy (Eds.), Machine Translation and the Information Soup. Proceedings, 1998. XIX, 532 pages. 1998. (Subseries LNAI).

Vol. 1530: V. Arvind, R. Ramanujam (Eds.), Foundations of Software Technology and Theoretical Computer Science. XII, 369 pages. 1998.

Vol. 1531: H.-Y. Lee, H. Motoda (Eds.), PRICAI'98: Topics in Artificial Intelligence. XIX, 646 pages. 1998. (Subseries LNAI).

Vol. 1096: T. Schael, Workflow Management Systems for Process Organisations. Second Edition. XII, 229 pages. 1998.

Vol. 1532: S. Arikawa, H. Motoda (Eds.), Discovery Science. Proceedings, 1998. XI, 456 pages. 1998. (Subseries LNAI).

Vol. 1533: K.-Y. Chwa, O.H. Ibarra (Eds.), Algorithms and Computation. Proceedings, 1998. XIII, 478 pages. 1998.

Vol. 1534: J.S. Sichman, R. Conte, N. Gilbert (Eds.), Multi-Agent Systems and Agent-Based Simulation. Proceedings, 1998. VIII, 237 pages. 1998. (Subseries LNAI).

Vol. 1535: S. Ossowski, Co-ordination in Artificial Agent Societies. XV; 221 pages. 1999. (Subseries LNAI).

Vol. 1536: W.-P. de Roever, H. Langmaack, A. Pnueli (Eds.), Compositionality: The Significant Difference. Proceedings, 1997. VIII, 647 pages. 1998.

Vol. 1537: N. Magnenat-Thalmann, D. Thalmann (Eds.), Modelling and Motion Capture Techniques for Virtual Environments. Proceedings, 1998. IX, 273 pages. 1998. (Subseries LNAI).

Vol. 1538: J. Hsiang, A. Ohori (Eds.), Advances in Computing Science – ASIAN'98. Proceedings, 1998. X, 305 pages. 1998.

Vol. 1539: O. Rüthing, Interacting Code Motion Transformations: Their Impact and Their Complexity. XXI,225 pages. 1998.

Vol. 1540: C. Beeri, P. Buneman (Eds.), Database Theory – ICDT'99. Proceedings, 1999. XI, 489 pages. 1999.

Vol. 1541: B. Kågström, J. Dongarra, E. Elmroth, J. Waśniewski (Eds.), Applied Parallel Computing. Proceedings, 1998. XIV, 586 pages. 1998.

Vol. 1542: H.I. Christensen (Ed.), Computer Vision Systems. Proceedings, 1999. XI, 554 pages. 1999.

Vol. 1543: S. Demeyer, J. Bosch (Eds.), Object-Oriented Technology ECOOP'98 Workshop Reader. 1998. XXII, 573 pages. 1998.

Vol. 1544: C. Zhang, D. Lukose (Eds.), Multi-Agent Systems. Proceedings, 1998. VII, 195 pages. 1998. (Subseries LNAI).

Vol. 1545: A. Birk, J. Demiris (Eds.), Learning Robots. Proceedings, 1996. IX, 188 pages. 1998. (Subseries LNAI).

Vol. 1546: B. Möller, J.V. Tucker (Eds.), Prospects for Hardware Foundations. Survey Chapters, 1998. X, 468 pages. 1998.

Vol. 1547: S.H. Whitesides (Ed.), Graph Drawing. Proceedings 1998. XII, 468 pages. 1998.

Vol. 1548: A.M. Haeberer (Ed.), Algebraic Methodology and Software Technology. Proceedings, 1999. XI, 531 pages. 1999.

Vol. 1550: B. Christianson, B. Crispo, W.S. Harbison, M. Roe (Eds.), Security Protocols. Proceedings, 1998. VIII, 241 pages. 1999.

Vol. 1551: G. Gupta (Ed.), Practical Aspects of Declarative Languages. Proceedings, 1999. VIII, 367 pgages. 1999.

Vol. 1552: Y. Kambayashi, D.L. Lee, E.-P. Lim, M.K. Mohania, Y. Masunaga (Eds.), Advances in Database Technologies. Proceedings, 1998. XIX, 592 pages. 1999.

Vol. 1553: S.F. Andler, J. Hansson (Eds.), Active, Real-Time, and Temporal Database Systems. Proceedings, 1997. VIII, 245 pages. 1998.

Vol. 1555: J.P. Mueller, A. Rao, M.P. Singh (Eds.), Intelligent Agents V. Proceedings, 1998. XXIV, 455 pages. 1999. (Subseries LNAI).

Vol. 1557: P. Zinterhof, M. Vajteršic, A. Uhl (Eds.), Parallel Computation. Proceedings, 1999. XV, 604 pages. 1999.

Vol. 1558: H. J.v.d. Herik, H. Iida (Eds.), Computers and Games. Proceedings, 1998. XVIII, 337 pages. 1999.

Vol. 1559: P. Flener (Ed.), Logic-Based Program Synthesis and Transformation. Proceedings, 1998. X, 331 pages. 1999.

Vol. 1560: K. Imai, Y. Zheng (Eds.), Public Key Cryptography. Proceedings, 1999. IX, 327 pages. 1999.

Vol. 1561: I. Damgård (Ed.), Lectures on Data Security.VII, 250 pages. 1999.

Vol. 1563: Ch. Meinel, S. Tison (Eds.), STACS 99. Proceedings, 1999. XIV, 582 pages. 1999.

Vol. 1567: P. Antsaklis, W. Kohn, M. Lemmon, A. Nerode, S. Sastry (Eds.), Hybrid Systems V. X, 445 pages. 1999.

Vol. 1569: F.W. Vaandrager, J.H. van Schuppen (Eds.), Hybrid Systems: Computation and Control. Proceedings, 1999. X, 271 pages. 1999.

Vol. 1570: F. Puppe (Ed.), XPS-99: Knowledge-Based Systems. VIII, 227 pages. 1999. (Subseries LNAI).

Vol. 1572: P. Fischer, H.U. Simon (Eds.), Computational Learning Theory. Proceedings, 1999. X, 301 pages. 1999. (Subseries LNAI).

Vol. 1575: S. Jähnichen (Ed.), Compiler Construction. Proceedings, 1999. X, 301 pages. 1999.

Vol. 1576: S.D. Swierstra (Ed.), Programming Languages and Systems. Proceedings, 1999. X, 307 pages. 1999.

Vol. 1577: J.-P. Finance (Ed.), Fundamental Approaches to Software Engineering. Proceedings, 1999. X, 245 pages. 1999.

Vol. 1578: W. Thomas (Ed.), Foundations of Software Science and Computation Structures. Proceedings, 1999. X, 323 pages. 1999.

Vol. 1579: W.R. Cleaveland (Ed.), Tools and Algorithms for the Construction and Analysis of Systems. Proceedings, 1999. XI, 445 pages. 1999.

Vol. 1580: A. Včkovski, K.E. Brassel, H.-J. Schek (Eds.), Interoperating Geographic Information Systems. Proceedings, 1999. XI, 329 pages. 1999.